"Peering through the Lattices"

"Peering through the Lattices"

Mystical, Magical, and Pietistic Dimensions in the Tosafist Period

EPHRAIM KANARFOGEL

Wayne State University Press
Detroit

Manufactured in the United States of America.
04 03 02 01 00 5 4 3 2 1

Library of Congress Cataloging-in-Publication Data

Kanarfogel, Ephraim.
Peering through the lattices : mystical, magical, and pietistic dimensions in the Tosafist period / Ephraim Kanarfogel.
p. cm.
Includes bibliographical references and indexes.
ISBN 0-8143-2531-9 (alk. paper)
1. Tosafists. 2. Mysticism—Judaism—History—To 1500. 3. Magic, Jewish—History—To 1500. 4. Hasidism, Medieval. 5. Tosafot.
I. Title.
BM501.8.K36 2000
296.1'2''00902—dc21 99-14014

Published with the assistance of the Lucius N. Littauer Foundation and the Murray and Madeline Baumel Judaic Studies Faculty Incentive Award

[redacted]

For my parents

עוד ינובון בשיבה דשנים ורעננים יהיו

Contents

Preface *9*
Acknowledgments *13*
Abbreviations *17*
Introduction: Perceptions of Tosafist Spirituality *19*

1

Asceticism, Pietism, and *Perishut* *33*

2

Pietistic Tendencies in Prayer and Ritual *93*

3

Mysticism and Magic: Pre-Crusade Traditions and the Reaction of Early Tosafists *131*

4

Between Tosafists and German Pietists *189*

5

Integration and Expansion during the Thirteenth Century *221*

6

Conclusions and Implications *251*

Appendix: Ashkenazic Rabbinic Scholars *259*
Index of Manuscript References *261*
Index of Names and Subjects *265*

Preface

As often occurs in scholarship, findings and pathways that are chanced upon initially can ultimately yield significant results. After the completion of my *Jewish Education and Society in the High Middle Ages*, which focused primarily on the societal and curricular structures of education and rabbinic learning in medieval Ashkenaz, I began, mainly for a change of pace, to reread and to explore further kabbalistic and other mystical literature that appeared in Provence and Spain during the twelfth and thirteenth centuries. I was struck early on by the fact that a number of these texts mentioned or alluded to Ashkenazic rabbinic figures, including German Pietists and apparently some tosafists as well.

To be sure, these names were sometimes jumbled or misconstrued. Nonetheless, mindful of the illuminating studies by Israel Ta-Shma on the absorption and adoption of Ashkenazic customs and practices by the Zohar, and by a number of recent studies that successfully trace Provençal and Spanish kabbalistic themes directly back to *Ḥasidei Ashkenaz*, I set about trying to ascertain whether these Ashkenazic scholars were merely being co-opted by kabbalists in order to lend their kabbalistic material additional significance and context, or whether the Ashkenazic rabbinic figures mentioned were actually involved in some type of mystical studies, of which the kabbalists might have been aware.

The results of that initial inquiry were published under the title "Rabbinic Figures in Castilian Kabbalistic Pseudepigraphy: R. Yehudah *he-Ḥasid* and R. Elḥanan of Corbeil," as part of a special issue of the *Journal of Jewish Thought and Philosophy*.[1] In the documentation for that study, I pointed to evidence both

[1] *Journal of Jewish Thought and Philosophy* 3 [Studies in Jewish Mysticism, Esotericism, and Hasidism] (1993):77–109.

from manuscript sources and from published medieval rabbinic texts which suggests that tosafists such as R. Jacob of Corbeil, R. Isaac of Corbeil, and R. Meir of Rothenburg, among others, were indeed familiar with various types of mystical teachings. These results, in addition to other related findings, indicated that a larger study of additional manuscript texts and published works was worth undertaking, in order to evaluate properly the extent to which tosafists were involved in aspects of mysticism. The book now before you is a presentation and discussion of those findings.

The tosafists flourished in northern France and Germany (and, to a lesser extent, in Austria, Italy, and England) during the twelfth and thirteenth centuries. They revolutionized the study of the Talmud, following the pioneering efforts of their ancestor and teacher Rashi. The claim that a number of tosafists were familiar with mystical doctrines is rather new, and perhaps even startling. In previous studies, I have followed the dominant view in modern scholarship—which will be reviewed below in the introduction—that the tosafists were decidedly talmudocentric. This view assumes that despite the very full library of earlier Jewish literature which they had at their disposal, the tosafists concentrated their efforts and training on the mastery of the talmudic text and on the surrounding halakhic and rabbinic literature, with the possible exception of biblical studies. But even the study of the Bible was undertaken, for the most part, through the prism of the talmudic corpus.[2] There was no overt interest in or concern with extra-talmudic pietism, let alone with issues of theology and theosophy. Only *Ḥasidei Ashkenaz*—led by R. Judah *he-Ḥasid* and his devoted student, R. Eleazar of Worms, and reflecting interests of the pre-Crusade period—were involved in these disciplines and practices; at the same time, they critiqued aspects of tosafist dialectic and Ashkenazic religious life in general, including prevalent prayer customs and liturgical texts.

A few words about the structure of the presentation are in order. Chapters 1 and 2 will identify the varieties of ascetic and pietistic practices that can be found among northern French and German tosafists. There was certainly no formal pietistic movement among the tosafists, and a number of tosafists were categorically against ascetic practices that can be labeled as *perishut*. Nonetheless, forms of self-denial, *ḥasidut*, and even *tiqqunei teshuvah* (which have been associated heretofore only with the *Ḥasidei Ashkenaz*), can be traced in tosafist writings.[3] Possible connections between the tosafists who

[2]See my "On the Role of Biblical Studies in Medieval Ashkenaz," *The Frank Talmage Memorial Volume*, ed. Barry Walfish (Haifa, 1993), 1:151–66.

[3]Analogous material can be found in tosafist writings to all five sections on "religious issues" delineated by Yitzhak Baer in his classic study of *ḥasidut Ashkenaz*,

exhibited these tendencies and the German Pietists will be explored, as will the extent to which some tosafists appear to have adopted Pietist prayer practices, texts, and rituals. We shall see that many of those tosafists who were associated with *ḥasidut* and *perishut* were also involved with mystical teachings. The second chapter will conclude with a brief discussion about the relationship between pietism and mysticism in medieval Ashkenaz.

Chapters 3 through 5 will offer a detailed chronological survey and characterization of mystical studies within the rabbinic culture of Ashkenaz, from the pre-Crusade period through the end of the thirteenth century. Several distinct types of mystical and magical or theurgic teachings and practices, known to Ashkenazic scholars in the pre-Crusade period at the academy of Mainz in particular, can be identified. These include the interpretation of Divine Names and an awareness of their uses (e.g., for protection, for prophylactic techniques and procedures, or for oracular and quasi-prophetic prognostications, including various forms of *she᾿elat ḥalom*), and an understanding of the powers and roles of various angels and other heavenly beings.

These interests were not shared, however, by early tosafist leaders such as Rashbam, Rabbenu Tam, and Raban, despite their familiarity with some of them. Several explanations for this change in attitude will be suggested. It is clear that this posture affected many subsequent tosafists who displayed no inclination toward mystical teachings. This may also account, in part, for the prevailing perception of the tosafist period, and for the tendency in earlier scholarship to ignore or downplay interest in these areas during this period.

At the same time, however, in the second half of the twelfth century, several leading students of Rabbenu Tam do show signs of interest, which intensify throughout the remainder of the tosafist period. We shall see that the major areas of interest within the tosafist period correspond precisely to those of the pre-Crusade period. It is likely that a number of thirteenth-century tosafists and other rabbinic scholars, especially those hailing from Germany, were influenced by the German Pietists. But there is also evidence within northern France for mysticism and pietism of the type found amongst the *Ḥasidei Ashkenaz*, for which the question of influence is less easily resolved.

The presence within Ashkenazic rabbinic culture of elements of pietism and mysticism that had heretofore been associated only with the German

---

"Ha-Megammah ha-Datit/ha-Ḥevratit shel 'Sefer Ḥasidim,'" *Zion* 3 (1937):1–50 [sections three through seven: החסיד; היחס אל התלמוד; הלכות קידוש השם; נשמות המתים, "השד" וכו'; הלכות תשובה]. This is not the case, however, with regard to the social issues that Baer identifies.

Pietists requires a restatement, in narrower terms, of the extent of the Pietists' uniqueness within Ashkenaz itself and throughout the medieval Jewish world. Spanish kabbalists cited tosafists as well as German Pietists as repositories of *torat ha-sod* material, as I have indicated. Moreover, the interest in penances, pietistic prayer practices, and magic among Ashkenazic rabbinic scholars during the late medieval and early modern periods cannot be attributed solely to the impact of *Ḥasidei Ashkenaz*. The German Pietists remain, however, the only Ashkenazic figures who expressed a strong interest in theosophy and produced a substantial, if not systematic, corpus in this area.

I am not suggesting that the tosafists were outright mystics, nor that they attempted to invest their talmudic or halakhic interpretations with mystical significance. To be sure, the absence of esoteric teachings in medieval talmudic commentaries and halakhic works generally may be due primarily to the nature of these genres and the relationship between them.[4] There is hardly any reference to kabbalistic material in Naḥmanides' vast talmudic corpus, despite his prominent stature as an active kabbalistic thinker.[5] Nonetheless, a number of tosafists did acquire, perhaps from their ancestors as well as from the German Pietists, interest in areas that can certainly be termed mystical. Indeed, these tosafists must be added to the list of medieval rabbinic scholars who pursued spiritual disciplines outside the confines of pure legalism and talmudic studies. The inclusion of tosafists in this group constitutes a significant shift in our view of medieval Jewish intellectual history.

---

[4]See, e.g., Jacob Katz, "Halakhah ve-Kabbalah: Maggaʿim Rishonim," [reprinted in his] *Halakhah ve-Qabbalah* (Jerusalem, 1986), 28–33; idem, "Halakhah ve-Qabbalah ke-Nosʾei Limmud Mitḥarim," *Halakhah ve-Qabbalah*, 76–77; Isadore Twersky, *Rabad of Posquières* (Philadelphia, 1980^2), 299–300; Moshe Idel, "We have No Kabbalistic Tradition on This," in *Rabbi Moses Naḥmanides: Explorations in His Religious and Literary Virtuosity*, ed. Isadore Twersky (Cambridge, Mass., 1983), 52–63; idem, "R. Mosheh b. Naḥman—Qabbalah, Halakhah u-Manhigut Ruḥanit," *Tarbiz* 64 (1995):535–78. Cf. Israel Ta-Shma, *Ha-Nigleh shebe-Nistar* (Tel Aviv, 1995), 36–40.

[5]For possible kabbalistic references in Naḥmanides' talmudic commentaries, see *Ḥiddushei ha-Ramban*, *Shevuʿot* 29a, s.v. *ha di-tenan* (end), and Isak Unna, *R. Mosheh b. Naḥman, Ḥayyav u-Feʿulato* (Jerusalem, 1954), 23; *Bava Batra* 12a, s.v. *ha de-ʾamrinan*, and Shraga Abramson, "Navi, Roʾeh ve-Ḥozeh," *Sefer Yovel Muggash li-Khevod ha-Rav Mordekhai Kirschblum*, ed. David Telsner (Jerusalem, 1983), 118, n. 3; *Yevamot* 49b, s.v. *kol ha-neviʾim*, and Elliot Wolfson, *Through a Speculum That Shines* (Princeton, 1994), 344, n. 65, 351, n. 86; and Naḥmanides' *Milḥamot ha-Shem* to *Berakhot*, end. Cf. *Ḥiddushei ha-Ritva, Rosh ha-Shanah*, 35a (end); *Qiddushin* 39b–40; *Shevuʿot* 9a, s.v. *mai taʿama de-R. Yehudah*; my "On the Assessment of R. Moses b. Naḥman (Naḥmanides) and His Literary Oeuvre," *Jewish Book Annual* 51 (1993–94): 158–72 [reprinted in *Jewish Book Annual* 54 (1996–97):66–80]; and below, ch. 4, at n. 65.

Acknowledgments

The completion of a book represents an opportunity for appropriate recognition of those who contributed to its development and formulation, as well as to those who enhanced the author's intellectual, professional, and personal well-being. Unfortunately, I must begin by noting the untimely death of a lifelong mentor, Rabbi Hirsh Fishman *z"l*. I take some consolation in the fact that Rabbi Fishman had begun to replicate the *rebbe-talmid* relationship with one of my sons. It is our fervent hope that we can perpetuate his memory by continuing to espouse the Torah study and values for which he so firmly stood.

The steady encouragement and support of Professor Isadore Twersky *z"l* were always especially meaningful. His tragic passing leaves a great void in Jewish scholarship, and it deprives us of a singular teacher and role model. May his memory be for a blessing.

On a happier note, I am pleased to acknowledge my colleagues in administration at Stern College for Women, Deans Karen Bacon and Ethel Orlian. Ms. E. Billi Ivry, who endowed the Rebecca Ivry Department of Jewish Studies at Stern College that I am privileged to chair, is remarkable in her commitment to Jewish women's education and to other great Jewish causes. My family and I are deeply grateful to Ms. Ivry for her unflagging interest in my academic work as well. This interest has culminated in my recent appointment as E. Billi Ivry Professor of Jewish History, a milestone that I will always cherish.

Numerous colleagues, friends, and students have contributed both directly and indirectly to this book, and it is impossible to mention all of them by name. Three distinguished colleagues who reviewed a draft of the book, Moshe Idel, Israel Ta-Shma, and Elliot Wolfson, stand out for their willingness to discuss ideas and texts, and for their profound suggestions. Their impact on this work is greater than even the frequent citation of their writings suggests. In addition, Professor Idel was kind enough to invite me to an international conference on magic in Judaism that afforded me an excellent opportunity to present some of my findings; Professor Ta-Shma shared with me his immensely helpful note cards from a seminar that he and Professor Idel conducted a number of years ago at Hebrew University on *sod* in Ashkenaz; and Professor Wolfson edited and published an article of mine, which contains a number of first steps toward the present study, in a special issue of his *Journal of Jewish Thought and Philosophy.* Professors Charles Raffel and Moshe Sokolow, and my students Tzippy Russ and Yardaena Osband, have also read a draft of the book, offering a number of insightful comments and suggestions for which I am grateful.

I wish to thank the Lucius N. Littauer Foundation and its director, Pamela Ween Brumberg, for a significant publication grant. Yeshiva University has generously and consistently provided travel funds for academic conferences and meetings in Israel that were indispensable for my research there. In addition, President Norman Lamm has recognized my work by presenting me with the Murray and Madeline Baumel Faculty Incentive Award. I also wish to thank the Hebrew University of Jerusalem and the Blechner Chair of Jewish Studies at Ben-Gurion University of the Negev for their lecture invitations and hospitality, which facilitated two of my stays in Israel.

The majority of the published sources and works used in the course of this study were consulted at Yeshiva University's Benjamin Gottesman Library. Virtually all of the many manuscripts cited here were viewed at the Institute of Microfilmed Hebrew Manuscripts at the Jewish National and University Library in Jerusalem. My thanks to the staffs of both these institutions. Arthur Evans and Kathy Wildfong at the Wayne State University Press have once again done an excellent job in bringing this book to press. Their patience and trust are always appreciated.

The last and most heartfelt set of thanks goes to the members of my family. My parents, to whom this book is dedicated, made it clear to my sister Susan and to me, from the time that we were young, that nothing would give them greater pleasure than to see us develop into ethical, personable, and highly educated people who would share their knowledge with others. To this end, my parents have always taken an immense interest in my work, and it is my father who (only half-jokingly) continues to monitor my research and publication schedule.

My wife, Devorah, has expended herculean efforts to provide me with the time and the environment necessary for doing the work that she knows I so much enjoy. Words cannot fully express my gratitude; suffice it to say that I am still in complete agreement with the sentiments found at the end of the acknowledgments in my first book. Our children—Tova, Dovid, Moshe, Atara, Chaya, and Temima—do not always cooperate but, then again, they're not supposed to. I know, however, that they recognize and appreciate the importance of this endeavor to me, and that they also realize just how much a part of it they truly are.

Abbreviations

Journals

AHR	*American Historical Review*
AJS Review	*Association for Jewish Studies Review*
HUCA	*Hebrew Union College Annual*
JJS	*Journal of Jewish Studies*
JQR	*Jewish Quarterly Review*
JSQ	*Jewish Studies Quarterly*
MGWJ	*Monatsschrift für Geschichte und Wissenschaft des Judentums*
PAAJR	*Proceedings of the American Academy for Jewish Research*
REJ	*Revue des études juives*

Manuscript collections

B.M.	British Museum
Bodl.	Bodleian
Cambr.	Cambridge University
HUC	Hebrew Union College
JNUL	Jewish National and University Library
JTS	Jewish Theological Seminary of America
Mont.	Montefiore
Vat.	Vatican
SḤB	*Sefer Ḥasidim* (Bologna ms.), ed. Reuben Margoliot (Jerusalem, 1957)
SḤP	*Sefer Ḥasidim* (Parma ms.), ed. Jehuda Wistinetzki (Frankfurt, 1924)

Introduction: Perceptions of Tosafist Spirituality

The tosafists did not inherit a philosophical tradition, nor did they have access to or interest in the developments and changes regarding philosophy and religious thought that were occurring throughout contemporary Christian society.[1] Scholars who have studied the creativity and literature of the tosafists have assigned them a very limited role in mystical or esoteric studies as well. These researchers maintain that only the German Pietists, who were contemporaries of the tosafists, were involved in the study of *torat ha-sod*.[2]

Ephraim Urbach, the modern biographer of the tosafists, devotes nearly twenty-five pages of his 770-page work, *Ba^calei ha-Tosafot: Toledoteihem, Ḥibbureihem, Shitatam*, to the Pietist leader R. Eleazar of Worms. R. Eleazar composed not only a number of *tosafot* but also a halakhic work, *Sefer Roqeaḥ*,

---

[1]See my *Jewish Education and Society in the High Middle Ages* (Detroit, 1992), 60–73. Cf. Gad Freudenthal, "The Place of Science in Medieval Hebrew Communities," *Rashi, 1090–1990 [Hommage à Ephraim Urbach]*, ed. Gabrielle Sed-Rajna (Paris, 1993), 599–601; Bernard Septimus, *Hispano-Jewish Culture in Transition* (Cambridge, Mass., 1982), 50–51, 64–65; David Ruderman, *Jewish Thought and Scientific Discovery in Early Modern Europe* (New Haven, 1995), 45–47, 55–59; and below, ch. 3, n. 70, ch. 4, n. 40. On rationalism in medieval Ashkenaz, see below, ch. 3, nn. 67–69, 72, 75, 86.

[2]See, e.g., Heinrich Graetz, *Divrei Yemei Yisra'el*, vol. 4 (Warsaw, 1897), 270–78; Moritz Güdemann, *Ha-Torah veha-Ḥayyim be-Arẓot ha-Ma^carav Bimei ha-Benayim*, vol. 1 (Warsaw, 1897), 117–39; I. H. Weiss, *Dor Dor ve-Dorshav*, vol. 4 (New York, 1923), 298–312; Victor Aptowitzer, *Mavo le-Sefer Rabiah* (Jerusalem, 1938), 1–20; S. W. Baron, *A Social and Religious History of the Jewish People* (Philadelphia, 1957–58), 5:49–56, 6:42–45; *A History of the Jewish People*, ed. H. H. Ben-Sasson (Cambridge, Mass., 1976), 525–27, 545–53. Cf. my "The ^c*Aliyah* of 'Three Hundred Rabbis' in 1211: Tosafist Attitudes Toward Settling in the Land of Israel," *Jewish Quarterly Review* 76 (1986):210–11.

as well as related collections of halakhic rulings. To be sure, *Sefer Roqeaḥ* is more in the spirit of *sifrut de-Vei Rashi* than other tosafist halakhic works of the thirteenth century. Nonetheless, R. Eleazar's halakhic rulings and written opinions were accorded great authority by a number of German tosafists. At the outset of his treatment, however, Urbach writes that R. Eleazar of Worms's integration of exoteric and esoteric teachings had no followers among subsequent tosafists and Ashkenazic *posqim*, although R. Eleazar had some degree of influence on later scholars. This is apparently a reference to R. Eleazar's small group of students, especially R. Abraham b. Azriel of Bohemia, to whom Urbach refers several times in his discussion of R. Eleazar.[3]

Toward the end of this discussion, Urbach suggests that R. Eleazar's influence in promulgating Torah study that would lead to *ḥasidut* was not restricted to Eleazar's colleagues and students in Germany, but reached northern France and even Spain. As proof, Urbach cites Naḥmanides' well-known letter of 1232 to *rabbanei Ẓarefat* in conjunction with the Maimonidean controversy (טרם אענה אני שוגג) in which Naḥmanides asserts that one of Eleazar's treatises on *sod ha-yiḥud* had reached him in Spain and was also to be found in northern France. Urbach next notes the impact that R. Eleazar's *torat ha-sod* had on kabbalistic circles in Provence. He concludes that R. Eleazar's works "were available in northern France, as per Naḥmanides' testimony, although his name is not mentioned explicitly very often." Urbach goes on to suggest, without pointing to any specific examples, that R. Eleazar's halakhic writings contributed to the conception of piety in Ashkenaz that included "abiding devoutness, love of Torah study and the performance of its precepts while preserving the minute details of custom, and a desire to comprehend the inner meaning and secrets of the world and its existence."[4]

Urbach refers to R. Eleazar's Pietist teacher, R. Judah *he-Ḥasid*, only in passing, principally because R. Judah wrote next to nothing in the realm of *halakhah* or talmudic commentary. Indeed, Urbach notes that even the responsa of R. Judah that have survived deal almost exclusively with issues of

---

[3]See E. E. Urbach, *Baᶜalei ha-Tosafot* (Jerusalem, 1980[4]), 1:388–411. Urbach also published a three-volume critical edition of R. Abraham b. Azriel's massive liturgical and *piyyut* commentary, *ᶜArugat ha-Bosem*. In his introduction (vol. 4; Jerusalem, 1963), Urbach painstakingly locates *ᶜArugat ha-Bosem* within its genre in medieval Ashkenaz. In this work as well, Urbach conveys the impression (in a number of instances) that R. Eleazar of Worms and his student R. Abraham, who had an abiding interest in esoteric teachings and interpretations, were part of a relatively isolated circle that had little in common with recognized tosafists in these and related matters. Cf. below, n. 12.

[4]Urbach, *Baᶜalei ha-Tosafot*, 1:408–9.

custom and *ḥasidut*, rather than with talmudic interpretation or halakhic reasoning. Urbach also highlights the very different approaches to the same ritual question, as well as the differing methods of argumentation, taken by R. Judah and the tosafist R. Isaac *Or Zarua*ᶜ.[5]

The scattered references in Urbach's *Ba*ᶜ*alei ha-Tosafot* to *torat ha-sod* and *kabbalah* appear, for the most part, with regard to German Pietists and their associates or students.[6] Even in the few instances where Urbach acknowledges that *ḥasidut* or *torat ha-sod* considerations appear to have had an impact on a tosafist, he tends to portray them as uneventful.[7] The implication of Urbach's work is that tosafists had no abiding interest (or training) in *torat ha-sod*, or even in quasi-mystical areas such as magic.[8] This characterization accords fully with Urbach's views regarding the (small) extent to which rabbinic scholars of the talmudic period were involved in these disciplines, and especially with his

---

[5]*Ba*ᶜ*alei ha-Tosafot*, 1:390–92. This comparison is rendered even more significant by the fact, noted elsewhere by Urbach, that R. Isaac studied "issues of *ḥasidut* in particular" with R. Judah *he-Ḥasid* (and with R. Eleazar of Worms). See *Ba*ᶜ*alei ha-Tosafot*, 1:437–39, and below, ch. 1, n. 16. See also *Ba*ᶜ*alei ha-Tosafot*, 1:412–13, for R. Simḥah of Spires's response to a question asked of him by R. Judah. This incident is described by Urbach as "another example of the difference between the decisor who rules leniently based on halakhic grounds, and the *ḥasid* who is concerned and is stringent not for halakhic reasons but because of considerations of piety (*yir*ʾ*ah*)." Cf. below, ch. 2, n. 16. Urbach has a brief discussion of R. Judah's father, R. Samuel *he-Ḥasid* (1:192–95), in the context of the rabbinic leadership of Spires during the first half of the twelfth century.

[6]There are eleven entries for the terms *ḥasidut/ḥasidim* in the index (in addition to a separate listing for *Ḥasidei Ashkenaz*, which has seventeen entries). Many of these also refer, however, to the German Pietists, with no implication for the tosafists. The term *kabbalah* (the entry under *sod* says "see *kabbalah*") has only fourteen index entries, again several times in connection with the Pietists. Cf. *Ba*ᶜ*alei ha-Tosafot*, 2:586, n. 2. Urbach was, of course, fully aware of the esoteric teachings found in the prayer and *piyyut* commentaries of the German Pietists. See ᶜ*Arugat ha-Bosem*, ed. Urbach, 4:73–111.

[7]See, e.g., *Ba*ᶜ*alei ha-Tosafot*, 1:150–51, regarding R. Jacob of Corbeil; 1:161, regarding R. Eliezer of Metz; 1:387–88, regarding Rabiah; and 2:522, 547, 564, regarding R. Meir of Rothenburg. Urbach deals with Ri's extensive *sod* and *ḥasidut* proclivities in fewer than two pages (1:237–39). See also 1:199 (and cf. ᶜ*Arugat ha-Bosem*, 4:99–100, n. 75), regarding R. Isaac b. Mordekhai of Regensburg; and below, ch. 4, nn. 23, 29.

[8]One or two of the entries under *kabbalah* deal with magic. There is only one listing under *kishuf*, one listing under *mazzalot*, one under *Shem ha-Meforash* (which describes a magical usage), one on *shedim*, and three under *meḥashvei ha-qeẓ* (although one of these refers to a calculation that was arrived at through neither mystical nor magical means). Cf. *Teshuvot u-Fesaqim*, ed. Efraim Kupfer (Jerusalem, 1973), 310, n. 3; ᶜ*Arugat ha-Bosem*, 4:110, n. 30; and below, ch. 4, n. 38.

assertion that *Merkavah* mysticism emerged from a realm outside that of talmudic literature and thought.[9]

By the same token, those who have studied the *torat ha-sod* of *Ḥasidei Ashkenaz* make almost no mention of any tosafists.[10] Indeed, until relatively recently, even those who sought to characterize the exoteric teachings and pursuits of the German Pietists failed to notice any connection between Pietists and tosafists. Although Yizhak Baer makes reference, in his lengthy study of *Sefer Ḥasidim* and *ḥasidut Ashkenaz*, to Ashkenazic talmudism,[11] until the 1970s

---

In his review of Urbach's corpus, Yaacov Sussmann stresses the need to recognize and evaluate more accurately the overall impact of German Pietism on the intellectual history of medieval Ashkenaz. See Sussmann, "Mifᶜalo ha-Maddaᶜi shel Professor Ephraim Elimelekh Urbach," *E. E. Urbach, Bio-Bibliographyah Meḥqarit [Musaf Maddaᶜei ha-Yahadut]*, ed. David Assaf (Jerusalem, 1993), 61, n. 105. See also Sussmann, 34, n. 48, concerning the academy at Evreux; and cf. below, n. 22. (This observation is related to others made by Sussmann concerning the approach taken by Urbach in correlating the methods and writings of northern French tosafists with those of their German counterparts. See Sussmann, 39–40, 47–54; and cf. below, ch. 2, n. 27.) One has the sense, however, that Urbach was a bit more attuned to these issues in the revised (fourth) edition of *Baᶜalei ha-Tosafot*, which appeared in 1980, than he was in the first edition, which was published in 1955.

[9]See, e.g., Urbach, "Ha-Mesorot ᶜal Torat ha-Sod bi-Tequfat ha-Tannaʾim," *Studies in Mysticism and Religion Presented to Gershom G. Scholem*, ed. E. E. Urbach et al. (Jerusalem, 1967) [Hebrew section], 1–28; idem, *Ḥazal* (Jerusalem, 1983[5]), 81–114, 161–75; and cf. idem, "Asqezis ve-Yissurim be-Torat Ḥazal," *Sefer Yovel le-Yitzhak Baer*, ed. S. W. Baron et al. (Jerusalem, 1961), 48–68; *Ḥazal*, 384–96. See also the assessments of Sussmann, "Mifᶜalo ha-Maddaᶜi," 73–74, n. 148, 77–78, n. 151; Elliot Wolfson, *Through a Speculum That Shines* (Princeton, 1994), 78, 122; Yosef Dan, "Demuto shel Ḥakham Ḥe"n u-Maᶜamdo shel ha-Mequbbal be-Tarbut Yisraʾel," *Proceedings of the Eleventh World Congress of Jewish Studies* [Div. C, vol. 2] (Jerusalem, 1994) [Hebrew section], 7–8; idem, "Sheloshah Sefarim Ḥadashim be-Ḥeqer Sifrut ha-Hekhalot veha-Merkavah," *Tarbiz* 65 (1996):538.

[10]See, e.g., Y. Dan, *Torat ha-Sod shel Ḥasidut Ashkenaz* (Jerusalem, 1968). Dan refers to R. Isaac b. Moses Or Zaruaᶜ (66, 188), who preserved esoteric material from the German Pietists in his *Sefer Or Zaruaᶜ*, and to R. Jacob (b. Asher) *Baᶜal ha-Turim* (78), who mentions esoteric prayer interpretations of the Pietists. Gershom Scholem makes no mention of tosafists in his chapter on *Ḥasidei Ashkenaz* in *Major Trends in Jewish Mysticism* (New York, 1941). Note also the almost complete absence of references to tosafists in *Mysticism, Magic and Kabbalah in Ashkenazi Judaism*, ed. K. E. Grözinger and Joseph Dan (Berlin, 1995). Cf. Scholem, *Origins of the Kabbalah* (Princeton, 1987), 239–40, 249–51; Moshe Idel, *Kabbalah: New Perspectives* (New Haven, 1988), 91–92; and Wolfson, *Through a Speculum That Shines*, 111, 191.

[11]Yitzhak Baer, "Ha-Megammah ha-Datit/ha-Ḥevratit shel Sefer Ḥasidim," *Zion* 3 (1937):10–14; 18–19, at n. 38.

no discussion of the German Pietists referred in any meaningful way to the tosafist enterprise.

Studies which appeared in that decade maintained that significant aspects of a broad Pietist critique concerning talmudic and rabbinic studies, as well as prayer practices, were directed toward Ashkenazic talmudists—including tosafists—by implication if not by name. Among the Pietists' demands were an uncompromising insistence on certain textual variants and distinctive practices in prayer, the cultivation of liturgical poetry and its interpretation, the expansion of biblical studies, and the primacy of talmudic learning that would be geared more toward reaching practical halakhic conclusions and less toward unbridled dialectical exercises. Nonetheless, even in these studies, the Pietists remained fundamentally outside tosafist circles and vice versa, with both groups portrayed as somewhat at odds with each other.[12]

In addition, the interest expressed in the study of *sod* by certain Ashkenazic rabbinic scholars in the pre-Crusade period was believed to have bypassed the rabbinic legalists in twelfth-century northern France who changed the face of talmudic studies following the First Crusade. Scholars have assumed that this interest was retained only by the German Pietists, who were consciously driven to return to earlier patterns or models of spirituality. (Indeed, the influence of a number of pre-Crusade rabbinic values can also be seen in the Pietist critique, just described, with regard to exoteric areas of study.) Moreover, R. Judah *he-Ḥasid* was a direct descendant of the Qalonymides, a leading pre-Crusade family whose knowledge of *sod* has been documented. The sentiments expressed in the writings of *Ḥasidei Ashkenaz* concerning the importance of good lineage (*yiḥus*) in marriage and in other societal contexts undoubtedly stemmed from the fact that the Pietists were themselves German blue bloods.[13]

---

[12]H. H. Ben-Sasson, "Ḥasidei Ashkenaz ʿal Ḥaluqat Qinyanim Ḥomriyyim u-Nekhasim Ruḥaniyyim Bein Benei ha-Adam," *Zion* 35 (1970):77–79; Haym Soloveitchik, "Three Themes in the *Sefer Ḥasidim*," *AJS Review* 1 (1976):311–57; Israel Ta-Shma, "Miẓvat Talmud Torah ki-Veʿayah Ḥevratit-Datit be-Sefer Ḥasidim," *Sefer Bar Ilan* 14–15 (1977):98–113. See also idem, *Ha-Nigleh shebe-Nistar* (Tel Aviv, 1995), 104, n. 101; my *Jewish Education and Society*, 86-91; and cf. Ivan Marcus, *Piety and Society* (Leiden, 1981), 102–5.

[13]See Avraham Grossman, "Yiḥus Mishpaḥah u-Meqomo ba-Ḥevrah ha-Yehudit be-Ashkenaz ha-Qedumah," *Peraqim be-Toledot ha-Ḥevrah ha-Yehudit*, ed. E. Etkes and Y. Salmon (Jerusalem, 1980), 20–21; idem, *Ḥakhmei Ashkenaz ha-Rishonim* (Jerusalem, 1981), 29–48, 86–92, 408–9, 438–39; Soloveitchik, "Three Themes," 336–37, 345–54. The well-known responsum of R. Solomon Luria—in which he presents a listing and brief description of many of the leading tosafists, followed by a listing of the

The distance between tosafists and *Ḥasidei Ashkenaz* was presumed on the basis of a number of other factors as well. Identifying adherents of Pietist teachers such as R. Samuel *he-Ḥasid*, R. Judah *he-Ḥasid*, and R. Eleazar of Worms—who did not themselves represent a monolithic approach—is not an easy task. *Sefer Ḥasidim*, the main exoteric work of *ḥasidut Ashkenaz*, suggests that the number of *ḥasidim* in any particular locale was small.[14] Although the

---

Qalonymides and *Ḥasidei Ashkenaz* that highlights their involvement with *sod*—fosters the impression that these groups of scholars were fundamentally separate. It must be noted, however, that R. Solomon, by his own indication, reports his information from two distinct sources with different foci. The first (about which R. Solomon says אעתיק לך מה שמצאתי הועתק) is a late thirteenth- or early fourteenth-century treatise that is found also, with variants, in ms. Bodl. 847, fols. 36r–36v. [My thanks to Dr. Avraham David for providing me with a copy of his transcription of the ms. passage. Cf. Urbach, *Baʿalei ha-Tosafot*, 1:253, n. 4*; 321, n. 17. On the dating of this text, see Y. N. Epstein, "Liqqutim," *Ha-Qedem* 1 (1907–8):129–30, who attributes the version cited by Maharshal to a student of R. Meir of Rothenburg, arguably R. Asher b. Yeḥiʾel. The ms. Bodl. version (of which Epstein was unaware) does not contain the reference to Maharam noted by Epstein. See also Grossman, *Ḥakhmei Ashkenaz ha-Rishonim*, 46–47, n. 68.] This treatise compiles a list of medieval halakhists—beginning with R. Sherira, R. Hai, Rif, and R. Ḥananʾel—which then gives way to the naming of many tosafists. Included in this list are R. Eleazar of Worms, R. Judah *he-Ḥasid* (possibly of Regensburg, although the reference is unclear; these two names are found only in the version in *Teshuvot Maharshal*), and other tosafist figures whose pietistic affinities are noted, such as R. Elijah *he-Ḥasid* of Paris (see below, ch. 3, n. 95) and R. Ezra *ha-Navi* (of Moncontour; see below, ch. 5, n. 67). Cf. David Kaufmann, "Liste de Rabbins Dressée par Azriel Trabotto, *REJ* 4 (1882):208–25, and Eric Zimmer, "Seder ha-Posqim le-R. Azriel Trabot," *Sinai* 77 (1975):237–52.

R. Solomon Luria then adds a Qalonymide family chain of tradition, which he reports having found (שוב מצאתי). The bulk of this material—minus some embellishment; see, e.g., *Sefer Ḥasidim—Ms. Parma H3280*, ed. Ivan Marcus (Jerusalem, 1985), editor's introduction, 19–20, n. 45, and below, ch. 2, n. 85—is similar to passages in the esoteric prayer commentary of R. Eleazar of Worms. See *Perushei Siddur ha-Tefillah la-Roqeaḥ*, ed. Moshe Hershler (Jerusalem, 1992), 1:228–29; and cf. Grossman, *Ḥakhmei Ashkenaz ha-Rishonim*, 31–32, 44–47. Thus, the absence of any correlation between the names in the two listings copied by Maharshal in his responsum is a function of their separate origins, rather than a statement by Maharshal (or an earlier compiler) concerning the relationship (or lack of relationship) between the scholars in these texts.

[14]See, e.g., Jacob Katz, *Exclusiveness and Tolerance* (New York, 1962), 98–99; Gershom Scholem, "Three Types of Jewish Piety," *Eranos-Jahrbuch* 38 (1969):344; Soloveitchik, "Three Themes," 336–38; and cf. idem, "Le-Taʾarikh Ḥibburo shel 'Sefer Ḥasidim,'" *Tarbut ve-Ḥevrah be-Toledot Yisraʾel Bimei ha-Benayim*, ed. Reuven Bonfil et al. (Jerusalem, 1989), 383–88; and Tamar Alexander-Frizer, *The Pious Sinner* (Tübingen, 1991), 4–8.

tosafist R. Samson of Sens was aware of the distinctive *tallit* worn by *Ḥasidei Ashkenaz*,[15] no separate Pietist communities appear to have been established. Indeed, Ashkenazic rabbinic literature does not even allude to the struggles between Pietists and non-Pietists that are referred to explicitly in *Sefer Ḥasidim* and other Pietist texts.[16] R. Eleazar of Worms maintained there was no one to whom he could transmit Pietist esoteric lore (*torat ha-sod*); however, recent research indicates that he did have students in this realm, despite his statements to the contrary.[17]

In looking for disciples of *ḥasidut Ashkenaz*, a distinction should be made between those who followed certain Pietist teachings or doctrines and those who were full-fledged members of the Pietist movement. Another useful distinction that has already been drawn contrasts the sectarian approach favored by R. Judah *he-Ḥasid*, which entailed more radical forms of atonement and pietism, with the personalist program advocated by R. Eleazar of Worms (author not only of the oft-cited *Sefer Roqeaḥ* but also a signatory on *Taqqanot Shum*), which was more compatible with existing societal customs and institutions.[18] Ostensibly, R. Eleazar's pietistic and penitential regimens would have been easier to follow than those of R. Judah.

In any case, aspects of the foregoing analysis suggest that disciples and followers of the Pietists would be found primarily, if not exclusively, in Germany. Indeed, small circles of rabbinic scholars who followed aspects of the teachings of *Ḥasidei Ashkenaz* have been identified near where R. Judah

---

[15]See R. Samson's responsum, preserved in *She᾽elot u-Teshuvot Maharam mi-Rothenburg* (Prague, 1895), #287.

[16]See J. Dan, "Ashkenazi Hasidism, 1941–1991: Was There Really a Hasidic Movement in Medieval Germany?" *Gershom Scholem's Major Trends in Jewish Mysticism 50 Years After*, ed. Peter Schäfer and Joseph Dan (Tübingen, 1993), 87–101, and I. Marcus, "The Historical Meaning of *Ḥasidei Ashkenaz*: Fact, Fiction or Cultural Self-Image?" *Gershom Scholem's Major Trends*, 103–14.

[17]See, e.g., Daniel Abrams, "The Literary Emergence of Esotericism in German Pietism," *Shofar* 12 (1994):67–85, and Israel Ta-Shma, "Mashehu ᶜal Biqqoret ha-Miqra Bimei ha-Benayim," *Ha-Miqra bi-Re᾽i Mefarshav [Sefer Zikkaron le-Sarah Kamin]*, ed. Sarah Japhet (Jerusalem, 1994), 453–59.

[18]See, e.g., Marcus, *Piety and Society*, 54–74, 109–20, 127–29, and idem, "Judah the Pietist and Eleazar of Worms: From Charismatic to Conventional Leadership," *Conference Proceedings: Jewish Mystical Leadership, 1200–1270* (Jewish Theological Seminary, New York, 1989), 15–21. Cf. Soloveitchik, "Three Themes," 347–49, and my "On the Role of Bible Study in Medieval Ashkenaz," *The Frank Talmage Memorial Volume*, ed. Barry Walfish (Haifa, 1993), 1:166, n. 61.

he-Hasid resided, first in Spires and later in proximity to Regensburg. Some of these followers were themselves Qalonymide descendants.[19]

Yet specific teachings and more general goals of the German Pietists also appear to have had an impact on tosafists in northern France during the thirteenth century. Both Urbach and Jacob Katz suggested (approximately forty years ago) that R. Moses of Coucy was influenced by the German Pietists with regard to procedures for repentance and penance, as well as in his attitudes toward non-Jews. To be sure, R. Moses' unique role as a traveling preacher may have contributed to his interest in these areas, but this role also reflects the influence of *Ḥasidei Ashkenaz*.[20]

More recently, the tosafist academy at Evreux—headed by the brothers R. Moses, R. Samuel, and R. Isaac b. Shneʾur—has been identified as one that espoused several key doctrines and teachings of the German Pietists, even though there is scant evidence for any direct contact between them.[21] Some examples of affinity include the downplaying of tosafist dialectic, the study of those areas of the talmudic and rabbinic corpus that were often neglected in medieval Europe, the development of proper intention in prayer, and the production of liturgical commentaries and handbooks, as well as *piyyutim*.

---

[19]See Yaacov Sussmann, "Massoret Limmud u-Massoret Nosaḥ shel Talmud Yerushalmi," *Meḥqarim be-Sifrut ha-Talmudit le-Regel Melot Shemonim Shanah le-Shaʾul Lieberman* (Jerusalem, 1983), 14, n. 11, 34–35; idem, "Mifʿalo ha-Maddaʿi," 51–52, n. 87; Urbach, *Baʿalei ha-Tosafot*, 1:207, 222, 375–76, 420; Israel Ta-Shma, "Le-Toledot ha-Yehudim be-Polin ba-Meʾot ha-Yod Bet/ha-Yod Gimmel," *Zion* 53 (1988):347–69, and *Zion* 54 (1989):205–8; and my *Jewish Education and Society*, 75–76 [to 174, n. 62, add *Sefer Ḥasidim*, ed. Judah Wistinetzki, (Frankfurt, 1924), sec. 588]. Cf. my "On the Role of Bible Study," 1:157–58; and below, ch. 1, n. 76.

[20]See Urbach, *Baʿalei ha-Tosafot* (Jerusalem, 1955), 387, and Katz, *Exclusiveness and Tolerance*, 102–5. See also Shraga Abramson, "Inyanut be-Sefer Miẓvot Gadol," *Sinai* 80 (1976):210–16, and my "Rabbinic Attitudes Toward Nonobservance in the Medieval Period," *Jewish Tradition and the Nontraditional Jew*, ed. J. J. Schachter (Northvale, 1992), 24–26.

[21]The doctrines of the Pietists probably reached Evreux through literary channels. Nonetheless, a passage in Gedalyah ibn Yaḥya's *Shalshelet ha-Qabbalah* (sixteenth century) raises the possibility that a R. Samuel b. Judah—who studied with R. Eleazar of Worms and with Eleazar's teacher, R. Moses *ha-Kohen* of Mainz—also studied subsequently at Evreux. See Norman Golb, *Toledot ha-Yehudim be-ʿIr Rouen Bimei ha-Benayim* (Tel Aviv, 1976), 98–99; Aptowitzer, *Mavo le-Sefer Rabiah*, 199–200; Urbach, *Baʿalei ha-Tosafot*, 1:407; and cf. *Teshuvot u-Pesaqim*, ed. Kupfer, 312. [For evidence of a fourth brother, R. Ḥayyim, see *Tosafot Rabbenu Pereẓ ʿal Massekhet Eruvin*, ed. Chaim Dickman (Jerusalem, 1991), 215 (68b). Cf. *Tosafot ha-Rosh ʿal Massekhet Pesaḥim*, ed. Avraham Shoshana (Jerusalem, 1997), editor's introduction, 12–13.]

Moreover, significant parallels between several works of Rabbenu Yonah of Gerona (especially *Sefer ha-Yirʾah*) and *Sefer Ḥasidim*, noted by scholars at the beginning of the twentieth century but never sufficiently explained, can be easily accounted for by the fact that Rabbenu Yonah studied in his early years at the academy of Evreux.[22] Additional instances of pietistic practices and conceptions among tosafists, in forms similar to those of *Ḥasidei Ashkenaz*, are the subject of the first chapter.

In addition to considerations noted earlier in this introduction, the relative inability of modern scholarship to detect the presence of mysticism and magic in tosafist circles may be more fully understood by considering several of the approaches taken by Joshua Trachtenberg in his pioneering work, *Jewish Magic and Superstition* (subtitled *A Study in Folk Religion*), originally published sixty years ago.[23] Following the work of Lynn Thorndike in particular, Trachtenberg offered a thorough treatment of medieval Jewish magic, relying in large measure upon *Sefer Ḥasidim* and other published writings of the German Pietists, as well as the writings of Ashkenazic halakhists.

Nonetheless, Trachtenberg was unaware of several important developments, mostly because of circumstances beyond his control. He was not familiar with many manuscript passages involving both twelfth- and thirteenth-century tosafists, as well as German Pietists, that have an important bearing on the topics in which he was interested.[24] Nor did he know the full extent of the Pietists' rich theosophical literature (and the impact which that literature had on Spanish kabbalah). Finally, Trachtenberg was not sufficiently aware of the texts of *Hekhalot* literature, the significance of this literature for the German Pietists (and for other Ashkenazic rabbinic figures), or the role played by Ashkenazic Jews in preserving (and editing) this corpus.[25] It should be noted that in the first half of the ninth century, Agobard of Lyons learned from

---

[22]See my "Educational Theory and Practice in Ashkenaz during the High Middle Ages" (Ph.D. diss., Yeshiva University, 1987), 176–80; Israel Ta-Shma, "Ḥasidut Ashkenaz bi-Sefarad: Rabbenu Yonah Gerondi—Ha-Ish u-Foʿalo," *Galut Aḥar Golah*, ed. Aharon Mirsky, et al. (Jerusalem, 1988), 165–73, 181–88; and my *Jewish Education and Society*, 74–79, 172–80. Cf. Urbach, *Baʿalei ha-Tosafot*, 1:479–86; Shimon Shokek, *Jewish Ethics and Jewish Mysticism in Sefer ha-Yashar* (Lewiston, 1991), 18; J. N. Epstein, "Al ha-Kol," *Meḥqarim be-Sifrut ha-Talmud u-Vileshonot Shemiyyot* 2 (Jerusalem, 1988), 776–89; Binyamin Richler, "Al Kitvei Yad shel 'Sefer ha-Yirʾah' ha-Meyuḥas le-Rabbenu Yonah Gerondi," *ʿAlei Sefer* 8 (1981):51–57; and Sussmann, "Mifʿalo ha-Maddaʿi," 34, n. 48.

[23]New York, 1939. There have been numerous reprintings. Cf. Steven Wasserstrom in *AJS Review* 20 (1995):202.

[24]Cf. *Yosef Dan, Torat ha-Sod shel Ḥasidut Ashkenaz*, 37–38, n. 7; 184.

Jews in his realm about concepts and constructs such as the magical powers of the letters of the alphabet, the nature of the *kisse ha-kavod*, and *Shiʿur Qomah*-like descriptions of the Almighty, all of which reflect material found in the *Hekhalot* corpus. Whether or not the Jews who reported this material were fully aware of its esoteric dimensions, their report suggests that pieces of *Hekhalot* literature, if not entire sections, were known (and available) to Jews in central France well before the year 1000. The presence of this literature in southern Italy at that time, and in the Rhineland by at least the early eleventh century, has also been established.[26]

---

[25]See, e.g. Scholem, *Major Trends in Jewish Mysticism*, 84–110; Baron, *A Social and Religious History of the Jews*, 6:44; Dan, *Torat ha-Sod shel Ḥasidut Ashkenaz*, 13–14,19–20, 24–28, 205–8; idem, "Sheloshah Sefarim Ḥadashim" 540–42; Israel Ta-Shma, "Sifriyyatam shel Ḥakhmei Ashkenaz Benei ha-Meʾah ha-Yod Alef/ha-Yod Bet," *Qiryat Sefer* 60 (1985):307–9, and *Qiryat Sefer* 61 (1986–87):581; Moshe Idel, *Kabbalah: New Perspectives* (New Haven, 1988), 88–92, 191–97; idem, *Messianic Mystics* (New Haven, 1998), 47–51; Peter Schäfer, "The Ideal of Piety of the Ashkenazi Ḥasidim and Its Roots in Jewish Tradition," *Jewish History* 4 (1990):9–23; idem, *The Hidden and Manifest God: Some Major Themes in Early Jewish Mysticism* (Albany, 1992), 6, 64–65, 92–95, 157–62; Elliot Wolfson, "Demut Yaʿaqov Ḥaquqah be-Kisse ha-Kavod: ʿIyyun Nosaf be-Torat ha-Sod shel Ḥasidei Ashkenaz," *Massuʾot* [Studies in Kabbalistic Literature and Jewish Philosophy in Memory of Prof. Ephraim Gottleib], ed. M. Oron and A. Goldreich (Jerusalem, 1994), 131–85; idem, *Through a Speculum That Shines*, 80–81, 234–47; idem, "The Mystical Significance of Torah-Study in German Pietism," *Jewish Quarterly Review* 84 (1993):47–50; Ivan Marcus, "Qiddush ha-Shem be-Ashkenaz ve-Sippur R. Amnon mi-Magenẓa," *Qedushat ha-Ḥayyim ve-Ḥeruf ha-Nefesh*, ed. I. Gafni and A. Ravitzky (Jerusalem, 1993), 136–37; Annelies Kuyt, "Traces of a Mutual Influence of the Ḥaside Ashkenaz and the Hekhalot Literature," *From Narbonne to Regensburg: Studies in Medieval Hebrew Texts*, ed. N. A. van Uchelen and I. E. Zwiep (Amsterdam, 1993), 62–86; idem, "The Haside Ashkenaz and Their Mystical Sources: Continuity and Innovation," *Jewish Studies in a New Europe* (Copenhagen, 1998), 462–71; Michael Swartz, *Scholastic Magic* (Princeton, 1996), 219–20; *Siddur Rabbenu Shelomoh mi-Germaiza ve-Siddur Ḥasidei Ashkenaz*, ed. Moshe Hershler (Jerusalem, 1972), 82; and below, ch. 1, n. 40.

[26]See Moshe Idel, "'Ha-Maḥshavah ha-Raʿah' shel ha-E-l," *Tarbiz* 49 (1980):356–57; idem, "Tefisat ha-Torah be-Sifrut ha-Hekhalot ve-Gilgulehah ba-Qabbalah," *Meḥqerei Yerushalayim be-Maḥshevet Yisraʾel* 1 (1981):28, n. 21; Reuven Bonfil, "Eduto shel Agobard me-Liʾon ʿal ʿOlamam ha-Ruḥani shel Yehudei ʿIro ba-Meʾah ha-Teshiʿit," *Meḥqarim be-Qabbalah, be-Filosofyah Yehudit uve-Sifrut ha-Musar vehe-Hagut*, ed. J. Dan and J. Hacker (Jerusalem, 1986), 333–38, 347–48; Elliot Wolfson, "The Theosophy of Shabbetai Donnolo, with Special Emphasis on the Doctrine of *Sefirot* in His *Sefer Ḥakhmoni*," *The Frank Talmage Memorial Volume*, ed. Walfish, 2:281–316; Ta-Shma in the preceding note; and below, ch. 3, n. 1. See also Saul Lieberman, *Sheqiʿin* (Jerusalem, 1939), 11, for additional evidence from northern France; and cf. *ʿArugat ha-Bosem*, ed. Urbach, 4:78, n. 38*.

In addition—or perhaps as a result—as the subtitle of his book indicates, Trachtenberg viewed medieval Jewish magic as most closely related to superstition and folk religion rather than as an offshoot or an allied field of Jewish mysticism. Since the German Pietists recorded and were involved with many aspects of magic, and since their mystical teachings were (in Trachtenberg's view) markedly less sophisticated than those of their Spanish and Provençal counterparts, Trachtenberg was inclined to study this magic from the popular level up rather than from the mystical level down.[27] In fact, however, the nature of much of the magic itself—as well as the parallels to *Hekhalot* literature and the involvement of both the German Pietists and certain tosafists in studies that are decidedly mystical—suggests how Ashkenazic magic derived its status in the eyes of rabbinic scholars as a discipline related to mysticism rather than as a transformation of folk custom. We will find, for example, that within Ashkenazic rabbinic circles there was a greater interest in using Divine or angelic names for incantations and prayers than in using them in conjunction with amulets, talismans, or other kinds of objects and images.[28]

---

[27]Cf. Ithamar Gruenwald, "Ha-Mageyah veha-Mitos—Ha-Meḥqar veha-Meẓiʾut ha-Historit," *Eshel Beʾer Sheva* 4, ed. Haviva Pedaya (Jerusalem, 1996), 11–12, 23–24; Deena Stein's review of Daniel Sperber, *Magic and Folklore in Rabbinic Literature*, in *Meḥqerei Yerushalayim be-Folqlor Yehudi* 18 (1996):137–39; Jeffrey Russell, *Witchcraft in the Middle Ages* (Ithaca, 1984), 1–13; Richard Kieckhefer, "The Specific Rationality of Medieval Magic," *AHR* 99 (1984): 813–36; and idem, *Magic in the Middle Ages* (Cambridge, 1989), 151–75.

[28]See, e.g., Israel Ta-Shma, "Meqorah u-Meqomah shel Tefillat 'Aleynu le-Shabeaḥ' be-Siddur ha-Tefillah: Seder ha-Maʿamadot u-Sheʾelat Siyyum ha-Tefillah," *The Frank Talmage Memorial Volume*, ed. Walfish [Hebrew section], 1:88–90; and Y. Dan, *Torat ha-Sod shel Ḥasidut Ashkenaz* 28, 74–75, 88–94, 219–22. Cf. Baron, *A Social and Religious History of the Jews*, 6:46–47; Gerrit Bos, "Jewish Traditions on Strengthening Memory and Leone Modena's Evaluation," *Jewish Studies Quarterly* 2 (1995):41–45; Moshe Idel, *Hasidism: Between Ecstasy and Magic* (Albany, 1995), 68; Kieckhefer, *Magic in the Middle Ages*, 69–80; Ioan Couliano, *Eros and Magic in the Renaissance* (Chicago, 1997), 107–11, 130–43; Judah Goldin, "The Magic of Magic and Superstition," in his *Studies in Midrash and Related Literature*, ed. B. L. Eichler and J. H. Tigay (Philadelphia, 1988), 353–57; Norman Golb, "Aspects in the Historical Background of Jewish Life in Medieval Egypt," *Jewish Medieval and Renaissance Studies*, ed. Alexander Altmann (Cambridge, Mass., 1967), 13; Yuval Harari, "Im Biqqashta Laharog Adam: Kishfei Hezeq ve-Hitgonenut Mipneihem be-Mageyah ha-Yehudit ha-Qedumah," *Maddaʿei ha-Yahadut* 37 (1997): 127–34; and idem, *Ḥarba de-Mosheh* (Jerusalem, 1997), introduction, 70–76. A similar distinction can be made between *Hekhalot* literature itself and *Sefer ha-Razim*. See, e.g., Rebecca Lesses, "Speaking with Angels: Jewish and Greco-Egyptian Revelatory Adjurations," *Harvard Theological Review* 89 (1996):57–58. See below, ch. 3, n. 116; ch. 4, n. 42; and cf. Dov Schwartz, *Astrologiyyah u-Mageyah be-Hagut ha-Yehudit Bimei ha-Benayim* (Ramat Gan, 1999), 23, 265–66.

This suggestion leads us in a direction that is similar to what Immanuel Etkes has concluded with regard to increased reliance upon magic by Ashkenazic scholars in eastern Europe at the end of the seventeenth century. The heightened interest of talmudic scholars in kabbalah led to a strengthening of their belief in the efficacy of magic against demonic forces. The association of magic with kabbalah during a period in which kabbalah was prominent enhanced the status of magical practices for these rabbinic scholars.[29]

Evidence for the correlation between mysticism and magic held by rabbinic scholars in medieval Ashkenaz, primarily in manuscript passages, will be seen throughout the course of this study. For now, two brief statements about the overarching relationship between these two disciplines will suffice. Moshe Idel has argued that Jewish magic—which he defines as "a series of acts and beliefs that presume the possibility of achieving (beneficial) physical results through the use of techniques not subject to empirical explanation"—and Jewish mysticism ought to be studied and classified together, as forms of religious expression that are virtually intertwined. The soundness of this approach has already been demonstrated by the greater emphasis in recent scholarship on the interplay between mysticism and magic in *Hekhalot* literature, *ḥasidut Ashkenaz*, and Hasidism. To be sure, magic is a "lower" form of religious expression than mysticism, since magic seeks to effect a lower stratum of existence. Yet Jewish magic, no less than *torat ha-sod*, is based on reliable traditions and teachers.[30] Idel also compares and contrasts the mystical study or contemplation of Divine Names and their powers with the magical activation and use of these powers.[31]

---

[29] I. Etkes, "Meqomam shel ha-Mageyah u-Vaʿalei Shem ba-Ḥevrah ha-Ashkenazit be-Mifneh ha-Meʾot ha-Yod Zayin/ha-Yod Ḥet," *Zion* 60 (1995):69–104. See also Moshe Rosman, *Founder of Hasidism: A Quest for the Historical Baʿal Shem Tov* (Berkeley, 1996), 13–26; and Idel, "Jewish Magic from the Renaissance Period to Early Hasidism," *Religion, Science, and Magic*, ed. Jacob Neusner (New York, 1989), 108–10.

[30] See Idel, "Yahadut, Mistiqah Yehudit u-Mageyah," *Maddaʿei ha-Yahadut* 36 (1996):25–40 [= "On Judaism, Jewish Mysticism and Magic," *Envisioning Magic*, ed. Peter Schäfer and H. G. Kippenberg (Leiden, 1997), 195–214]; idem, *Hasidism*, 65–81; and cf. R. J. Z. Werblowsky, *Joseph Karo: Lawyer and Mystic* (Philadelphia, 1980), 38–83; and Scholem, *Origins of the Kabbalah*, 97–123. Note the classic distinction—formulated by Evelyn Underhill, *Mysticism* (London, 1910), 70—that magic signifies the wish to control reality for the magician's personal agenda, while mysticism promotes the unselfish goal of mystical union. On the relationship between secrecy and magic, see Richard Kieckhefer, *Magic in the Middle Ages*, 140–44.

[31] Cf. Idel, "Al Kavvanat Shemoneh ʿEsreh Eẓel R. Yiẓḥaq Sagi-Nahor," *Massuʾot*, ed. Oron and Goldreich, 25–42; idem, "Defining Kabbalah: The Kabbalah of the Divine Names," *Mystics of the Book*, ed. Robert Herrera (New York, 1993), 97–122.

Similarly, Elliot Wolfson has written recently that "in some cases it is extremely hard to draw the line between mysticism and magic within Jewish sources.... One may legitimately distinguish mysticism from magic on the basis of the stated goals of a given source, but one must at the same time recognize the conceptual underpinnings shared by both enterprises." Wolfson also notes the close relationship between magic and mysticism in the *Hekhalot* corpus. The mystical component utilizes magical techniques, while the magical component is often linked to mystical experiences.[32]

More precise definitions of magic and mysticism, as these two phenomena manifest themselves in medieval Ashkenazic rabbinic texts, will emerge from our treatment of those texts.[33] Before proceeding to that phase of our discussion, however, I shall turn to an analysis of pietism in medieval Ashkenaz. This analysis will ultimately show that the connection between pietism and mysticism found within *ḥasidut Ashkenaz* also holds true for those tosafists who were inclined toward mysticism and magic.

---

[32]See Elliot Wolfson, "Jewish Mysticism: A Philosophical Approach," in *History of Jewish Philosophy*, ed. D. H. Frank and Oliver Leaman (London, 1997), 454–55, 459. Cf. Alexander Altmann, *The Meaning of Jewish Existence*, ed. Alfred Ivry (Hannover 1991), 58–61; and L. H. Schiffman and M. D. Swartz, *Hebrew and Aramaic Incantation Texts from the Cairo Geniza* (Sheffield, 1991), 12–26.

[33]Michael Swartz, *Scholastic Magic*, 18–20, identifies three central elements in Jewish magical texts from late antiquity and the early Middle Ages: emphasis on the power of the name of God, intermediacy of the angels in negotiating between Divine providence and human needs, and application of Divine Names and ritual practices for the needs of specific individuals. In addition to the studies cited by Swartz as the basis of his formulation, see Michael Fishbane, "Aspects of Jewish Magic in the Ancient Rabbinic Period," *The Samuel Goldman Lectures* 2 (Chicago, 1979), 29–38; Peter Hayman, "Was God a Magician? Sefer Yesira and Jewish Magic," *Journal of Jewish Studies* 40 (1989):225–37; Claudia Rohrbacher-Sticker, "Magische Traditionen der New Yorker Hekhalot-Handscriften JTS 8128 im Kontext ihrer Gesamtredaktion," *Frankfurter Judaistische Beiträge* 17 (1989):101–49; Lesses, "Speaking with Angels," 41–60; Brigitte Kern-Ulmer, "The Depiction of Magic in Rabbinic Texts: The Rabbinic and the Greek Concept of Magic," *Journal for the Study of Judaism* 27 (1996):289–303; and below, ch. 3, n. 10. Cf. Dov Schwartz, "Mageyah, Madda Nisyoni u-Metodah Maddaᶜit be-Mishnat ha-Rambam," *Meḥqerei Yerushalayim be-Maḥshevet Yisraʾel* 14 (1998): 25–45.

1

Asceticism, Pietism, and *Perishut*

The Approach of *Ḥasidei Ashkenaz*

The German Pietists combined their interest in esoteric studies with an extensive program of pietistic behaviors and outlooks. These included manifestations of asceticism and *perishut* such as acts of self-denial (beyond those observances mandated by Jewish law), the professing of extreme humility bordering on self-humiliation, and sustained or pronounced stringency in ritual matters.[1] In order to identify and evaluate properly the presence of ascetic and pietistic practices within the larger rabbinic culture of medieval

---

[1] See, e.g., Yitzhak Baer, "Ha-Megammah ha-Datit/ha-Ḥevratit shel Sefer Ḥasidim," *Zion* 3 (1937):1–50, esp. 6–7; Gershom Scholem, *Major Trends in Jewish Mysticism* (Jerusalem, 1954^{3}), 92; Yosef Dan, *Sifrut ha-Musar veha-Derush* (Jerusalem, 1975), 62–65; Haym Soloveitchik, "Three Themes in the *Sefer Ḥasidim*," *AJS Review* 1 (1976):318–20, 329–37, 352–54; Ivan Marcus, *Piety and Society* (Leiden, 1981), 11, 34; Daniel Sperber, *Minhagei Yisraʾel* 1 (Jerusalem, 1989), 194–97, *Minhagei Yisraʾel* 2 (Jerusalem, 1991), 106–7; and Israel Ta-Shma, *Halakhah, Minhag u-Meẓiʾut* (Jerusalem, 1996), 160–63, 249–50. Scholem lists "ascetic renunciation of the things of this world" as one of the "three things above all others [that] go to make the true Hasid." Of course, the *tiqqunei teshuvah* (penances) of the German Pietists were also suffused with a large measure of asceticism. See Baer, 18–20; Scholem, 105–6; Asher Rubin, "The Concept of Repentance Among Ḥasidey Ashkenaz," *Journal of Jewish Studies* 16 (1965):161–76; Dan, 133; idem, "Le-Toledot Torat ha-Teshuvah shel Ḥasidut Ashkenaz," *Yovel Orot*, ed. B. Ish Shalom and S. Rosenberg (Jerusalem, 1985), 221–28; Marcus, 124–28; Sperber, 1:128–32; Shimon Shokek, *Ha-Teshuvah be-Sifrut ha-Musar ha-Ivrit, be-Filosofyah ha-Yehudit uva-Qabbalah* (Lewiston, 1995), 64–70; Talya Fishman, "The Penitential System of

Ashkenaz, it is worthwhile to assess briefly the scope and intent of these practices in the thought of *Ḥasidei Ashkenaz*.

Stringency, self-denial, and even self-affliction were cultivated and valued by the German Pietists not as ends unto themselves, but as means of fulfilling the hidden Will of God, securing atonement, or achieving future rewards: "for according to what one enjoys in this world, one loses reward in the world to come."[2] Passages in *Sefer Ḥasidim* recommend regular fasting and other forms of personal asceticism not only as part of the German Pietists' penitential system—i.e., as a response to sins that have already been committed—but also as a means of avoiding sin and enhancing an individual's devotion by recognizing his debt to his Creator.[3] R. Judah *he-Ḥasid* himself fasted regularly

---

Ḥasidei Ashkenaz and the Problem of Cultural Boundaries," *Journal of Jewish Thought and Philosophy* (forthcoming). Several of these studies discuss the impact of Christian penitential practices on the penances prescribed by the Pietists. See also M.-D. Chenu, *Nature, Man, and Society in the Twelfth Century*, ed. Jerome Taylor and Lester Little (Chicago, 1968), 204–13; and I. Ta-Shma, *Ha-Sifrut ha-Parshanit la-Talmud*, vol. 1 (Jerusalem, 1999), 95–96.

Paragraph 1661 (p. 400) in *Sefer Ḥasidim*, ed. Jehuda Wistinetzki (Frankfurt, 1924) [based on ms. Parma (De Rossi) 1131, referred to hereafter as *SḤP*]—which appears as part of a unit entitled **גם כאן ענייני שחיטה וטהרה ופרישות**—asserts that in cases where rabbinic opinions differ, it is best to follow the stringent position in situations where no economic loss is involved, even if the *halakhah* can be legitimately decided in favor of the more lenient position. See below, ch. 2, n. 59.

[2]*SḤP* para. 277 (p. 89), and cf. para. 15 (p. 15). See also *Sefer Ḥasidim*, ed. Reuven Margoliot (Jerusalem, 1957) [based on the edition published in Bologna (1538), referred to hereafter as *SḤB*], para. 89 (**פרישות מן העולם פנאי ללב ומנוחה לגוף, ואהבת עולם טרדת הלב ויגיעת הגוף**), 97 (=*SḤP* 280): **חכם אחד צוה לבנו שלא יהנה יותר מדי בעולם הזה שלא יעברו עליו ארבעים יום בלא תענית**. [Cf. the formulations of Rabbenu Yonah, below, n. 90.] On the nature and provenance of the penitential material in the first unit of *SḤB* (secs. 1–152), see Ivan Marcus, "The Recensions and Structure of Sefer Ḥasidim," *Proceedings of the American Academy for Jewish Research* 45 (1978): 137, 152–53, and cf. Yehudah Galinsky, "Rabbenu Mosheh mi-Coucy ke-Ḥasid, Darshan u-Folmosan: Hebbetim me-ʿOlamo ha-Maḥshavti u-Feʿiluto ha-Ẓibburit," (M.A. thesis, Yeshiva University, 1993), 74, n. 55, and below, n. 71. Although the strongly ascetic forms of penance are largely absent from this unit, the attitudes expressed regarding asceticism as a religious value are consistent with what is found in *SḤP*. See the next note, and below, ch. 4, n. 2.

[3]See, e.g., *SḤP* 281, 19, 41, 66–67 (cf. *SḤB* 527), 942 (*SḤB* 340), 1129, 1137, 1290, 1553, 1722 (*SḤB* 575), 1882, 1950, and cf. Gerald Blidstein, *Honor Thy Father and Mother* (New York, 1976), 196–97, n. 31, and E. E. Urbach, *Baʿalei ha-Tosafot* (Jerusalem, 1980[4]), 1:192. With regard to *perishut* and *Ḥasidei Ashkenaz*, I have suggested that the medieval educational blueprint entitled *Sefer Ḥuqqei ha-Torah*, which describes the establishment of academies that housed **פרושים**, reflects a German milieu

in general and a series of teachings of the German Pietists in particular. The *perishut* referred to in this document has specific parallels to material in *Sefer Ḥasidim*, and in other texts of the German Pietists. See my *Jewish Education and Society in the High Middle Ages* (Detroit, 1992), appendix A, 101–5.

Haggai Ben-Artzi, "Ha-Perishut be-Sefer Ḥasidim," *Daʿat* 11 (1983):39–45, has argued that despite espousing a philosophy that could lead to asceticism, an ascetic lifestyle was not considered "the good way" according to *Sefer Ḥasidim*. Although it is true that *Sefer Ḥasidim* advocates a full marital life, which is one of the proofs offered by Ben-Artzi (see also Soloveitchik, "Three Themes," 329, n. 51), his argument concerning ascetic practices is flawed in several respects. First, while asserting that *SḤP* presents a somewhat different view, Ben-Artzi restricts himself to an analysis of *SḤB*. Moreover, he misses a significant nuance within this text. He stresses that *SḤB* advises that one should not fast all the time (*tamid*) or that one whose services are needed by others should not weaken himself through fasting (52, 617; note also 527). But at the same time, unnoticed by Ben-Artzi, *SḤB* reports (97, 225; see also the end of 617, and the parallel passages in *SḤP*) that a number of *ḥasidim* instructed their children to fast at regular intervals, lest they become too immersed in worldly pleasures. Clearly, *SḤB* is advocating a level of asceticism that, at the same time, would not incapacitate a person and thereby defeat its purpose. [Cf. R. Eleazar of Worms, *Sefer Roqeaḥ*, sec. 209, regarding fasting on Mondays and Thursdays; *Arbaʿah Turim, Oraḥ Ḥayyim*, 134; and Gedalyahu Alon, "Le-Yishuvah shel Baraita Aḥat," *Tarbiẓ* 4 (1933): 285–91.]

Finally, Ben-Artzi seems to misinterpret *SḤB* 12. He reads this passage as suggesting that one may enjoy pleasurable foods (*maʿadanim*) that are not being consumed merely to sustain oneself, as long as one does not eat so much as to satiate himself completely. A reading of the full passage, which begins with the phrase שורש חסידות יראה כשאדם מתאוה לדבר הנאה ועוזב את יצרו מפני יראת ה׳, yields a different conclusion. *SḤB* maintains that a measure of *ḥasidut* is achieved when a person wishes to enjoy something but he refuses it as a sign of *yirʾat ha-Shem*—not because he is under any external pressure or even because of fear of sin, but simply as a means of demonstrating his complete love for and awe of the Almighty. Refusing certain foods is an excellent vehicle for reaching this state, since indulgence in culinary pleasures can lead to bad thoughts. If a person has the opportunity to eat fish or meat or other pleasant foods, he should resist eating them only because of his *yirʾat ha-Shem* (and not because of other considerations), and he should not allow himself to become satiated to the full extent of his desire. See also Reuven Margoliot's notes, ad loc., and cf. *SḤP* 1017. In this instance as well, *SḤB* is advocating controlled asceticism as a means of expressing genuine dedication and devotion. See also *Sefer Gematriʾot le-R. Yehudah he-Ḥasid* (Los Angeles, 1998), ed. Daniel Abrams and Israel Ta-Shma, 32 (fol. 4v): וחייב אדם להאכיל את עצמו כדי שיהיה בו כח לפרנס את אשתו ובניו. כת׳ [משלי 27:27] ודי חלב עזים ללחמך שלא תשחוט עזים אלא תתפרנס מן החלב תן חיים לנערותיך שלא ילמוד לבניו לאכל בשר בכל יום כדאמ׳ [השוה חולין פד:] לעולם יאכל אדם פחות ממה שיש לו ויתכסה אשתו ובניו במה שיש לו. See *SḤP* 1031 for a situation in which a demanding manifestation of personal *perishut* associated with the wearing of *tefillin* is discouraged, because the difficulty in sustaining the *persihut* might lead to neglect of the *miẓvah* itself (מאחר שצריכין כך פרישות לא נוכל לסבול). See also below, n. 34.

(and frequently), even on the Sabbath.[4] Moreover, R. Eleazar of Worms suggested that various modes of pietistic thought and behavior could prepare an individual for mystical study or experience.[5] Members of contemporary mystical conventicles in Provence were often referred to as *perushim*, *nezirim*, and *ḥasidim*, reflecting similar considerations on their part.[6]

We shall see over the course of this study that among tosafists as well there is a strong correlation between those who advocated or practiced forms of pronounced pietism and those who were involved with dimensions of magic and mysticism. Pietism in tosafist circles did not entail a search for the hidden Divine Will; that was unique to the German Pietists.[7] But it did include patterns of personal behavior subsumed under the headings of asceticism and *perishut* outlined above.[8] Although all tosafists demonstrated fealty to Jewish law and its observance, only some tended toward supererogatory behaviors. Before moving, however, to the identification of those tosafists and Ashkenazic rabbinic figures of the twelfth and thirteenth centuries who embraced aspects

---

[4]See *Haggahot Maimuniyyot, Hilkhot Taᶜanit*, 1:2[6]. Cf. Yaakov Gartner, *Gilgulei Minhag be-ᶜOlam ha-Halakhah* (Jerusalem, 1995), 99–100, and S. W. Baron, *A Social and Religious History of the Jews* (Philadelphia, 1958), 6:49.

[5]See Marcus, *Piety and Society*, 21–22, 36, 117–18. Cf. Elliot Wolfson, "The Mystical Significance of Torah-Study in German Pietism," *JQR* 84 (1993):44, n. 4; Soloveitchik, "Three Themes," 321, n. 27; Moshe Idel, *R. Menaḥem Reqanati ha-Mequbbal* (Jerusalem, 1998), 113–19; and below, ch. 2, n. 76, for further discussion. Note that *perishut* is included among the aphorisms of R. Pinḥas b. Yaʾir (*ᶜAvodah Zarah* 20b, and the parallel passage in some editions of *Mishnah Sotah* 9:15), as a stage in achieving spiritual perfection. Cf. *Sefer Roqeaḥ*, *Hilkhot Ḥasidut*, שורש טהרה פרישות וזהירות. Note also the stratification of *perishut* in *Sotah* 22b and *Yerushalmi Berakhot* 9:5.

[6]See Gershom Scholem, *Reshit ha-Qabbalah* (Tel Aviv, 1948), 84–91; idem, *Origins of the Kabbalah* (Princeton, 1987), 229–33; Isadore Twersky, *Rabad of Posquières* (Philadelphia, 1980[2]), 25–29; cf. Idel, "Kabbalah and Elites in Thirteenth-Century Spain," *Mediterranean Historical Review* 9 (1994):6–7, n. 2; and Gartner, *Giglulei Minhag*, 90. On asceticism and its role in promoting spirituality in the thought of Naḥmanides, see Ritva, *Sefer ha-Zikkaron*, ed. Kalman Kahana (Jerusalem,1982[2]), 91–92; Chaim Henoch, *Ha-Ramban ke-Ḥoqer ukhe-Mequbbal* (Jerusalem, 1978), 131–36; Bezalel Safran, "R. Azriel and Naḥmanides and the Fall of Man," *R. Moses Naḥmanides (Ramban): Explorations in His Religious and Literary Virtuosity*, ed. Isadore Twersky (Cambridge, Mass., 1983), 83–85; and my "Nezirut ve-Nidrei Issur be-Mishnatam shel ha-Rambam veha-Ramban," *Hadarom* 50 (1990):79–84.

[7]See Soloveitchik, "Three Themes," 311–25.

[8]See S. D. Fraade, "Ascetical Aspects of Ancient Judaism," *Jewish Spirituality from the Bible Through the Middle Ages*, ed. Arthur Green (New York, 1987), 253–88, for an excellent methodological overview of the categorization of asceticism in rabbinic literature.

of asceticism and pietism, it will be helpful to survey manifestations of these behaviors in pre-Crusade Ashkenaz.

Pre-Crusade Antecedents

As Avraham Grossman has noted, the liturgical poetry of R. Simeon b. Isaac *ha-Gadol* (c. 950–1030) refers to the cultivation of holiness and *perishut*,[9] and to related themes: the virtue of modesty; the importance of being able to feel embarrassment and humiliation and thus to recognize more generally the relative insignificance of man; and the goal of being satisfied with little in terms of physical needs and desires.[10] R. Jacob b. Yaqar, a student of R. Simeon *ha-Gadol* and Rabbenu Gershom, and Rashi's major teacher at Mainz in the second half of the eleventh century, was also known for being exceedingly humble and self-effacing in his Divine service and for his *perishut*.[11]

According to a tradition recorded in *Sefer Ḥasidim*, R. Jacob would stoop to clean the floor in front of the Holy Ark with his beard. Although the method of cleaning used by R. Jacob may have been exaggerated by *Sefer Ḥasidim*,[12] there is no reason to doubt the evidence that R. Jacob regularly performed menial tasks that were perhaps better left to others as an indication of his deeply felt piety. Moreover R. Jacob, who is described as being exceedingly

---

[9]Avraham Grossman, *Ḥakhmei Ashkenaz ha-Rishonim* (Jerusalem, 1981), 100–1, 415, n. 15. Note, e.g., the passage in A. M. Habermann, *Piyyutei R. Shimᶜon b. Yiẓḥaq* (Berlin-Jerusalem, 1938), 101: קדש עצמך בפרישות אדרת.

[10]See Habermann, *Piyyutei R. Shimᶜon b. Yiẓḥaq*, 103: יקר כספו וזהבו ונועם גדלו צאנו ואלפיו משקהו ומאכלו חברתו וכל מחמדי מכללו קרוץ מחומר מה מועילו וחומד ומתאוה את שאינו שלו ... יבין וישכיל בדעתו ושכלו ישמח ויעוז במתת גורלו.

[11]Grossman, *Ḥakhmei Ashkenaz ha-Rishonim*, 246–48. For R. Jacob's teachers, see ibid., 237. For the unusually deep modesty of R. Eliezer *ha-Gadol*, an older contemporary of R. Jacob's at Mainz (who was also a student of R. Simeon *ha-Gadol* and Rabbenu Gershom, [ibid., 216]), see ibid., 223.

[12]See *SḤP* 991, and David Berger's review of Grossman entitled "Ḥeqer Rabbanut Ashkenaz ha-Qedumah," *Tarbiz* 53 (1984):486–87. On the importance of growing a beard in Pietist thought, cf. ms. Parma 1033, fol. 26r, column 3 (in the name of R. Judah *he-Ḥasid*, who also commends there the loud and deliberate recitation of *pesuqei de-zimra* [שלמ"ש]; cf. *SḤP* 1620, and Soloveitchik, "Three Themes," 330–33). On the gravity of the prohibition in Pietist thought of shaving with a razor, see the Pietist sources cited in my "Rabbinic Attitudes Toward Nonobservance in the Medieval Period," *Jewish Tradition and the Nontraditional Jew*, ed. Jacob J. Schacter (Northvale, 1992), 26, n. 66; in Eric Zimmer, *ᶜOlam ke-Minhago Noheg* (Jerusalem, 1996), 49; in Israel Ta-Shma, "Od li-Veᶜayat ha-Meqorot ha-Ashkenaziyyim be-Sefer ha-Zohar," *Kabbalah* 3 (1998): 262; and in Israel Yuval, *Ḥakhamim be-Doram* (Jerusalem, 1989), 296–97, n. 54. Cf. below, n. 30, and ch. 4, n. 46.

careful with regard to the performance of ritual slaughter, also ruled that post-partum bleeding—which was considered by the Torah to be non-menstrual blood (*dam tohar*)—should in fact be treated as menstrual blood (*dam niddah*). Those (few) who ruled this way were characterized by Rashi's students as "*benei* ʾ*adam* . . . *perushim*" who were "exceedingly strict" in separating themselves. This ruling was also espoused by R. Jacob's student, R. Solomon b. Samson. R. Solomon issued a number of stringent rulings in critical ritual matters and argued consistently against the implementation of newly issued halakhic rulings that conflicted with established customs and practices.[13]

A second teacher of Rashi's in Mainz, R. Isaac b. Judah, is also described in the *sifrut de-Vei Rashi* as a *parush*. He earned this sobriquet by eating only a single egg for the final meal before the fast of *Tish*ʿ*ah be-Av*.[14] R. Isaac's intention was to eat as little before the fast as possible, thereby rendering the fast, which was viewed as a vehicle for repentance, more arduous.[15]

Rashi's teacher at Worms, R. Isaac *ha-Levi*, fasted two days in observance of *Yom ha-Kippurim*. Although R. Isaac adopted this position based on his understanding of the requirements of talmudic law, the motivation of personal piety is apparent, since he did not require others to do it. Moreover, the only German authorities who followed this practice in the tosafist period were

---

[13]Grossman, *Ḥakhmei Ashkenaz ha-Rishonim*, 334–38. Both these tendencies are broadly characteristic of the German Pietists as well. See Soloveitchik, "Three Themes," 353, n. 133. Zimmer maintains (229–31, esp. n. 45), against Grossman, that the stance of R. Jacob and R. Solomon in their *dam tohar* ruling may reflect purely halakhic considerations rather than a notion of *perishut*. But, as has been noted, the association of these rabbinic scholars with other rulings and characteristics of *perishut* and pietism suggests that *perishut*, as an extra-halakhic value, played a role in this instance as well. Indeed, the stringency which treated *dam tohar* as *dam niddah* was later espoused almost exclusively by members of *Ḥasidei Ashkenaz* and other rabbinic scholars connected with them. See Zimmer, 232–34, and below, ch. 2, n. 86.

[14]Grossman, *Ḥakhmei Ashkenaz ha-Rishonim*, 310. Cf. Israel Ta-Shma, "Al Kammah ʿInyanei Maḥzor Vitry," *ʿAlei Sefer* 11 (1984): 83, n. 5a, and below, n. 18.

[15]Cf. *Sefer Roqeaḥ*, sec. 310; *Arba*ʿ*ah Turim, Oraḥ Ḥayyim*, sec. 552. The attempt by *Ḥasidei Ashkenaz* to drastically limit the priestly blessing in the diaspora to the festivals only—because of concerns about ritual impurity (see Zimmer, 135–40, and cf. below, ch. 2, n. 51)—would undoubtedly have been aided, if not partially adumbrated, by R. Isaac b. Judah's ruling that a *kohen* who is a mourner may not participate in the priestly blessing, especially since this ruling was extended to include all unmarried *kohanim*. See, e.g., *She*ʾ*elot u-Teshuvot R. Meir b. Barukh [mi-Rothenburg*], ed. Prague, #345; *Shibbolei ha-Leqet*, ed. S. K. Mirsky (New York, 1966), 201; and *Shibbolei ha-Leqet*, ed. S. Buber (Vilna, 1887), *hilkhot semaḥot*, sec. 43.

R. Judah *he-Ḥasid* and R. Eliezer b. Joel *ha-Levi* (Rabiah). Even their mutual student, R. Isaac b. Moses *Or Zarua*ᶜ,[16] felt that this practice should be discontinued because it was dangerous—further evidence for the lack of general acceptance of this position.[17]

R. Isaac *ha-Levi* also did not eat meat for the entire three-week period between the seventeenth of Tammuz and the ninth of Av,[18] a practice that Rabiah attributed to *perushim*.[19] *Sefer Ma*ᶜ*aseh ha-Geonim* reports, at the beginning of a section entitled *minhag Tish*ᶜ*ah be-Av*, that R. Isaac b. Moses

---

[16]Israel Ta-Shma, *Ha-Nigleh shebe-Nistar* (Tel Aviv, 1995), 96, n. 56, suggests that a reference by R. Isaac *Or Zarua*ᶜ to an interpretation of his teacher, R. Judah *Ḥasid* (which appears to conflict with a passage in *Sefer Ḥasidim*), is to material from one of R. Isaac's main teachers, R. Judah b. Isaac Sir Leon of Paris, not from R. Judah *he-Ḥasid* of Spires and Regensburg, founder of the German Pietists. This resolution is, however, problematic. Although R. Judah Sir Leon is called R. Judah *he-Ḥasid* by some later rabbinic scholars, medieval halakhists do not usually refer to him in this way. Moreover, R. Isaac certainly received teachings, especially pietistic ones, from R. Judah *he-Ḥasid* of Regensburg—even if he was not one of R. Isaac's major teachers, as R. Judah Sir Leon and Rabiah were. See Urbach, *Ba*ᶜ*alei ha-Tosafot*, 1:323, 437–39 (and cf. above in the introduction, nn. 5, 10); the gloss from *Sefer Or Zarua*ᶜ, *hilkhot Shabbat*, 2:42, found at *SḤP* 427 (pp. 126–28); *Sefer Or Zarua*ᶜ (responsa), 1:114; and *Sefer Or Zarua*ᶜ, *pisqei* ᶜ*avodah zarah*, 4:200. Cf. *Sefer Or Zarua*ᶜ, 1:399; *hilkhot moẓa*ʾ*ei Shabbat*, 2:89, 95; *pisqei* ᶜ*avodah zarah*, 4:267; the introductory *Alfa Beta* to *Sefer Or Zarua*ᶜ, secs. 25, 30; and below, at the beginning of ch. 5, regarding the mystical doctrines in *Sefer Or Zarua*ᶜ. Finally, ms. Parma 1033 (fols. 123r–123v) records an interpretation similar to the one referred to by R. Isaac *Or Zarua*ᶜ, that is attributed (by a R. Moses) to ר' יהודה החסיד מר[גנ]שבורג. See also *Siddur Rabbenu Shelomoh mi-Germaiza ve-Siddur Ḥasidei Ashkenaz*, ed. Moshe Hershler (Jerusalem, 1972), 184.

[17]Grossman, *Ḥakhmei Ashkenaz ha-Rishonim*, 287. Cf. *Sefer Rabiah*, ed. Avigdor Aptowitzer, 3:658–59, for a clear indication that Rabiah as well did not demand this of others. See also below, n. 37; and cf. Y. N. Simḥoni, "Ha-Ḥasidut ha-Ashkenazit Bimei ha-Benayim," in *Dat ve-Ḥevrah be-Mishnatam shel Ḥasidei Ashkenaz*, ed. Ivan Marcus (Jerusalem, 1987), 68. In n. 117, Grossman demonstrates that although two texts attribute this practice to R. Isaac b. Judah of Mayence rather than to R. Isaac *ha-Levi* of Worms, it was in fact the latter's practice. Grossman further suggests, without firm proof, that R. Isaac *ha-Levi* had seen this done already by his major teacher, R. Eliezer *ha-Gadol* of Mainz, who was also a direct Qalonymide ancestor (and spiritual mentor) of R. Judah *he-Ḥasid* (see below, ch. 3, n. 11). See ms. Cambr. Or. 786, published in *Shitat ha-Qadmonim*, ed. M. Y. Blau (New York, 1992), 373. In this collection of *pesaqim* [see below, ch. 2, n. 18], mention is made of a R. Samuel b. Isaac (cf. Urbach, *Ba*ᶜ*alei ha-Tosafot*, 1:248) who also fasted for two days. R. Isaac of Dampierre (Ri) appears to have been the only major tosafist in northern France who observed the fast of Yom Kippur for two days. See below, n. 30.

[18]Grossman, *Ḥakhmei Ashkenaz ha-Rishonim*, 288.

(a pious scholar of Mainz who demonstrated great religious devotion as an "active" martyr in 1096, serving also as a role-model for others)[20] did not bathe from the seventeenth of Tammuz through the ninth of Av. R. Isaac b. Judah abstained from eating meat from *Rosh Ḥodesh* until after the fast, R. Meshullam b. Moses did not eat meat on the tenth of Av throughout his life, and other individuals (ועוד יש בני אדם) fasted on both the ninth and tenth of Av.[21]

It should be noted that all of the eleventh-century German rabbinic scholars who espoused the various pietistic and ascetic tendencies outlined above were associated with the academy of Mainz. Two of them taught at Worms (R. Isaac *ha-Levi* and R. Solomon b. Samson), but both had been students of pietists at Mainz.[22] As we shall see in chapter 3, when magical and mystical studies of the pre-Crusade period are surveyed, these disciplines as well were pursued only in Mainz, with barely an exception. An explanation for the concentration of these interests in Mainz, and away from Worms, will emerge from that discussion.

---

[19]*Sefer Rabiah*, 3:659–60. As in the case of the *Ashkenazim* who fasted two days for *Yom ha-Kippurim*, whom he characterized as חסידים ואנשי מעשה (*Arba*ᶜ*ah Turim, Oraḥ Ḥayyim*, sec. 624), R. Jacob b. Asher *Ba*ᶜ*al ha-Turim* referred to those who abstained from meat during the three weeks as פרושים and יחידים (*O. Ḥ.*, sec. 551). On the use of these terms in *Arba*ᶜ*ah Turim*, cf. below, n. 35.

[20]See Grossman, *Ḥakhmei Ashkenaz ha-Rishonim*, 393–94. To be sure, the entire phenomenon of medieval Ashkenazic martyrdom presumes a pietistic orientation, even though the degree to which martyrdom during the Crusades had a specific impact on the development of *Ḥasidei Ashkenaz* is a matter of contention. See, e.g., Jacob Katz, *Exclusiveness and Tolerance* (New York, 1961), 82–94; Yosef Dan, "Beᶜayat Qiddush ha-Shem be-Toratah ha-ᶜIyyunit shel Tenuᶜat Ḥasidut Ashkenaz," *Milḥemet Qodesh u-Martir*ᵓ*ologiyyah be-Toledot Yisra*ᵓ*el uve-Toledot ha-*ᶜ*Ammim* (Israel Historical Society: Jerusalem, 1968), 121–29; Robert Chazan, *European Jewry and the First Crusade* (Berkeley, 1987), 143–47, 206–7, 214–15, 325–26, n. 14; idem, "The Early Development of *Ḥasidut Ashkenaz*," *JQR* 75 (1985):199–211; Marcus, *Piety and Society*, 150–51, n. 57; idem, "Hierarchies, Religious Boundaries and Jewish Spirituality in Medieval Germany," *Jewish History* 1 (1986):7–26; Haym Soloveitchik, "Religious Law and Change: The Medieval Ashkenazic Example," *AJS Review* 12 (1987):205–21; and see below, n. 31, regarding Riba.

[21]*Sefer Ma*ᶜ*aseh ha-Geonim*, ed. Abraham Epstein (Berlin, 1910), 34. See also *Sefer Rabiah*, 3:657–60; *Arba*ᶜ*ah Turim, Oraḥ Ḥayyim*, sec. 558; *Shibbolei ha-Leqet*, ed. Buber, sec. 274 [יש מן היחידים שנוהגים שלא לאכול... וכן מצאתי שנהג ר' משולם זצ"ל כל ימיו...]; Sefer ha-Pardes, ed. H. L. Ehrenreich (Budapest, 1924), 260; *She*ᵓ*elot u-Teshuvot Maharil*, ed. Isaac Satz (Jerusalem, 1979), 220 (and the reference to *Sefer Ḥasidim* in n. 9). Cf. Zimmer, ᶜ*Olam ke-Minhago Noheg*, 188–89, and Gartner, *Gilgulei Minhag be-*ᶜ*Olam ha-Halakhah*, 9–21, for possible antecedents from the talmudic and geonic periods of some of these practices.

For now, one additional locus of rabbinic asceticism in this period, which also had a connection to Mainz, should be mentioned. R. Simeon *ha-Gadol* of Mainz was a member of the Abun family, which originated in Le Mans in northern France. Indeed, while it is possible that R. Simeon's grandfather, R. Abun (d.c.970), had already emigrated to the Rhineland, it is probable that R. Simeon was still in Le Mans for part of his student days. In any event, the rabbinic leaders of the Le Mans community in the generation after R. Abun were R. Menaḥem and his sons, R. Elijah and R. Isaac.[23]

At the time of his death, R. Menaḥem was characterized by his son, R. Elijah, as a holy and devout person who consecrated his body throughout his lifetime by afflicting it via fasting and denial.[24] The second son of R. Menaḥem, R. Isaac, is described as being one of those *perushim* who, like

---

[22]See Grossman, *Ḥakhmei Ashkenaz ha-Rishonim*, 177, 243–45 (regarding R. Jacob b. Yaqar), 326, and above, n. 13. Cf. Gartner, *Gilgulei Minhag*, 31–39. Although all three of Rashi's teachers were associated with ascetic or pietistic practices (see above at nn. 11, 14, 17), Rashi did not, for the most part, affect these behaviors. Thus, for example, he chided *perushim* (יש מן הפרושים) who fasted for *taᶜanit Esther* on both Thursday and Friday when Purim occurred on Sunday (see *Maḥzor Vitry*, see 245, ed. Simon Hurwitz [Nuremberg, 1923], 210; the variants in *Shibbolei ha-Leqet*, ed. Buber, sec. 194; and *Sefer ha-Pardes ha-Gadol*, sec. 204). He also criticized those who fasted two days for Yom Kippur (see Sperber, *Minhagei Yisraʾel*, 4 [Jerusalem, 1995], 207, n. 6). Nonetheless, Rashi's great humility, his stringent personal conduct in situations where he had granted latitude to others, his striking position on minimizing prayer during times of illness because of the difficulty in maintaining proper *kavvanah*, and even his concern about overeating with regard to *seᶜudah shelishit* may be the result of this training. See Grossman, *Ḥakhmei Ẓarefat ha-Rishonim* (Jerusalem, 1995), 136–38, 141–42; idem, *Ḥakhmei Ashkenaz ha-Rishonim*, 282, 371–72 (describing the humility of R. Isaac *ha-Levi* and the Makhirites); and cf. Soloveitchik, "Three Themes," 330–33. Note also Rashi's definition of *perishut* in his commentary to *ᶜAvodah Zarah* 20b, s.v. *perishut*: אף מדבר המותר פורש להחמיר על עצמו. On the noteworthy humility displayed by Rashbam, who grew up in the house of Rashi, see Urbach, *Baᶜalei ha-Tosafot*, 1:47–48, 73, 76.

[23]Grossman, *Ḥakhmei Ẓarefat ha-Rishonim*, 38–39, 95.

[24]See the passage reproduced in Grossman, ibid., 83: ר׳ מנחם רבי׳ הקדוש, גוף הקדש גוף המעונה גוף המסוגף כל ימיו בתענית. Note the reference in *Sefer Minhag Tov* (ed. Meir Weiss, *Ha-Ẓofeh le-Ḥokhmat Yisraʾel* 13 [1929]:200–221) to a R. Elijah *ha-Zaqen*, who was linked to the heavenly angels and is described as conducting himself as a *parush*. This passage probably refers to R. Elijah b. Menaḥem of Le Mans rather than to the early tosafist, R. Elijah b. Judah of Paris. Cf. Grossman, *Ḥakhmei Ẓarefat ha-Rishonim*, 85, 104–5; Hananel Mack, "Derashah shel R. Eliyahu ha-Zaqen be-Tokh Midrash Mimei ha-Benayim," *Zion* 61 (1996):213; and below, ch. 3, n. 95. [R. Judah *he-Ḥasid* appears to have been a direct descendant of R. Elijah of Le Mans; see now the addenda to the second edition of Grossman, *Ḥakhmei Ẓarefat ha-Rishonim* (Jerusalem, 1997), 610.]

R. Isaac b. Judah of Mainz, ate a minimal amount of food prior to the fast of the ninth of Av.[25]

The Evidence from Twelfth-Century Tosafist Texts and Related Literature

In the twelfth century there were groups of people as well as individuals who pursued forms of *perishut* or asceticism. Rabbenu Jacob Tam, the leading tosafist of the day, encountered this phenomenon but appears not to have supported it. He was asked to respond to a report that "many devout Jews who have embraced purity and *perishut* (כי רבו עובדי א-להים המתפרשים בטהרה ובפרישות בישראל) do not wish to feed their young children on Yom Kippur, even though these children have not yet reached the age when they are to be trained [to fast]. And those who do feed [their young children] are told that they have violated a commandment, since adults are required to prevent children from committing overt sins." Without offering an assessment of their motives or their ideological position, Rabbenu Tam ruled simply that feeding these children was completely permissible.[26] It should be noted that the tendency toward *perishut* in this case (as in a number of the other instances mentioned above) may have had its roots in earlier Palestinian custom. Although the precise age of the youngsters who were urged to fast is tied to variant readings in Palestinian rabbinic texts, the tendency itself, which finds no support in the Babylonian Talmud, was quite pronounced.[27]

---

[25]Grossman, *Ḥakhmei Ẓarefat ha-Rishonim*, 84. R. Isaac b. Menaḥem ate only salted bread and water, without any vegetable or relish. Cf. above, n. 14. On the nature and place of fasting and asceticism in the medieval Christian milieu, see Caroline Bynum, *Holy Fast and Holy Feast* (Berkeley, 1987), esp. 31–47, 107–10, 208–18, 294–96.

[26]*Sefer ha-Yashar le-Rabbenu Tam (Ḥeleq ha-Teshuvot)*, ed. Shraga Rosenthal (Berlin, 1898), 108, 111. Cf. Sperber, *Minhagei Yisra'el*, 2:130–32; and Giles Constable, *The Reformation of the Twelfth Century* (Cambridge, 1996), 150–53, 192–94. [In this instance, Rabbenu Tam did not allow young boys to perform the religious obligation of adults. Cf. Ivan Marcus, *Rituals of Childhood* (New Haven, 1996) 119–20, and Israel Ta-Shma, "Be-Koaḥ ha-Shem: Le-Toledotav shel Minhag Nishkaḥ," *Bar Ilan* 26–27 (1995):389–99.] In another context, Rabbenu Tam referred to *perushim* as those who exhibited a high level of moral conduct, a status which some sought to attain illegitimately. See Urbach, *Baᶜalei ha-Tosafot*, 1:91. The use of the term in this context, however, is based on a talmudic passage concerning the Pharisees (*Sotah* 22b), although it may also be indicative of Rabbenu Tam's understanding of this term in general. See also *Sefer ha-Yashar*, 85.

[27]See *Massekhet Soferim*, ed. Michael Higger (New York, 1937), 318–19. The variants range from the ages of one and two to eleven and twelve. Cf. Ivan Marcus, "The Dynamics of Ashkenaz and Its People Centered Authority," *Proceedings of the Rabbinical*

Rabbenu Tam also ruled, without additional comment, in the case of an individual who had vowed and then undertaken "many fasts" without accepting them through verbal declaration the day before, as is usually required for personal fasts. Rabbenu Tam argued that these fasts were effective in fulfilling the person's vow(s) because the individual had definitely intended to undertake them; formal verbal acceptance was preferred but was not an absolute requirement.[28]

At the end of the *Tosafot* texts that contain this ruling of Rabbenu Tam, R. Isaac b. Samuel of Dampierre (Ri) is noted as following the preferred practice of accepting a personal fast by inserting a formula of request at the conclusion of the *ᶜAmidah* of the afternoon service on the day before. The texts state further that it was Ri's standard practice [ור״י היה רגיל / רגיל ר׳] to do this even on Sabbath afternoon, when he wanted to fast on Sunday. The implication of this passage is that Ri undertook personal fasts with some frequency.[29]

Assembly 54 (1992):134; idem, *Rituals*, 39–41; and Y. D. Gilat, "Ben Shelosh-ᶜEsreh le-Mizvot," *Meḥqerei Talmud* 1, ed. Yaacov Sussmann and David Rosenthal (Jerusalem, 1990), 44–45. See also the parallel passage in *Orḥot Ḥayyim*, pt. 2 (1–2), sec. 24, and *Kol Bo*, sec. 74, which records the Ashkenazic initiation ceremony and describes it as a venerable custom practiced by the elders of Israel in Jerusalem (see Marcus, *Rituals of Childhood*, 33, and below ch. 3, n. 18) and still in vogue in some places. This is followed by another bona fide Jerusalem custom: instructing children from the ages of three, four, and five to complete their fasts on Yom Kippur. [For a discussion of the overall impact of *minhagei Erez̤ Yisraʾel* on Ashkenaz, see, e.g., Avraham Grossman, "Ziqqatah shel Yahadut Ashkenaz ha-Qedumah ʾel Erez̤ Yisraʾel," *Shalem* 3 (1981):57–92; Israel Ta-Shma in *Qiryat Sefer* 56 (1981):345–48; Grossman in *Zion* 47 (1982):192–97; and Ta-Shma, *Minhag Ashkenaz ha-Qadmon* (Jerusalem, 1992), 21, 61–69, 98–103.]

28 *Tosafot ᶜAvodah Zarah*, 34a, s.v. *mitᶜanin le-shaᶜot*. Cf. *Tosafot Rabbenu Elḥanan*, ed. David Frankel (Husiatyn, 1901), ad loc.; Urbach, *Baᶜalei ha-Tosafot*, 1:131. Rabbenu Tam had no difficulty, of course, in establishing a public fast day and day of mourning to commemorate the deaths of the Jews of Blois in 1171, as the result of a ritual murder charge. See Urbach, 1:112, and Robert Chazan, "The Blois Incident of 1171: A Study in Jewish Intercommunal Organization," *PAAJR* 36 (1968):13–31.

29 See also *Semaq*, sec. 97: ושמעתי כי הר״י היה אומר בא-להי נצור הריני לפניך בתענית יחיד למחר. In a responsum in which Ri nullified a vow undertaken by a young man to severely restrict his diet in the event that he continued to gamble (Urbach, *Baᶜalei ha-Tosafot*, 1:259–60; cf. my "Rabbinic Attitudes Toward Non-Observance," 27–29), Ri observed that the young man in question, who may have been a Torah scholar, was not, however, חסיד ופרוש כל כך שיכוף את יצרו [לקיים את נדרו] כל ימי צבאו. This phrasing further speaks Ri's own familiarity with a regimen of *perishut*. Ri was in contact with well-know Provençal *perushim* such as R. Asher b. Meshullam of Lunel, who, according to R. Benjamin of Tudela, "removed himself from [the pleasures of] this world, studied day and night, and fasted and did not eat meat," although the direction of influence is uncertain. See Urbach, 1:237–38, and below, ch. 4, n. 10.

A passage in *Pisqei ha-Tosafot* concludes that since a stringent position must be taken with regard to a doubt that concerns a law of biblical origin, it would be appropriate to fast two days for Yom Kippur in the Diaspora, where each *yom tov* segment of the biblical festivals was observed for two days because of doubts concerning the appearance of the new moon. Since, however, a decree that cannot be upheld by the general public ought not be promulgated, this practice could not actually be required. According to this text, Ri did, however, fast for two days.[30]

R. Isaac b. Asher *ha-Levi* (Riba) of Spires was an older tosafist contemporary of Rabbenu Tam. He had studied in Mainz prior to the First Crusade and with Rashi in Troyes. An account recorded in a fourteenth-century work, *Pisqei Reqanati*, details the circumstances under which Riba died c. 1133. He was seriously ill prior to Yom Kippur. His doctors advised him that if he fasted on Yom Kippur he would surely die, but that even if he ate, he might still die. Riba decided that the possibility of his dying did not outweigh his obligation to fast. He did not eat that day and subsequently passed away.[31]

---

[30] *Pisqei ha-Tosafot li-Menaḥot* #201, cited by Urbach, *Baᶜalei ha-Tosafot*, 1:238. [On the compiler of the *Pisqei ha-Tosafot*, see Urbach, 2:734–38.] Cf. above, n. 17, for the similar practice of R. Judah *he-Ḥasid* and Rabiah. According to a passage in ms. Cambr. Or. 786, fols. 181v–182r, Ri also permitted fasting on *Rosh ha-Shanah*, as R. Judah *he-Ḥasid* did. Ri's reasoning was that a fast for repentance on *Rosh ha-Shanah* would not be any worse than a *taᶜanit ḥalom*, which is permitted on *Rosh ha-Shanah*. See also Ri in *Tosafot Berakhot*, 49b, s.v. אי בעי אכיל, and below, ch. 2, n. 46, for additional references and discussion; and cf. *Sefer Mordekhai ᶜal Massekhet ᶜEruvin*, sec. 494. [Rabiah was aware from his teachers that some fasted on *Rosh ha-Shanah*, but he ruled against it; see *Sefer Rabiah*, 3:634, and below, n. 37.] Ri also followed the same *ḥumra* as the German Pietists with regard to permissible means of shaving and hair-cutting—a situation characterized by *Sefer Ḥasidim* as one in which it was necessary to prohibit something that is technically permissible in order to prevent that which is definitely prohibited from being done—as opposed to Rabbenu Tam, who held the more prevalent, lenient view. See Zimmer, *ᶜOlam ke-Minhago Noheg*, 47–49. Urbach also notes that Ri was known for taking an inordinately long time to say his prayers, always finishing them after everyone else in his group. In addition, Ri's father was called a *ḥasid*; see Urbach, 1:228, n. 4.

[31] See Urbach, *Baᶜalei ha-Tosafot*, 1:173. On the implications of this source for a patient's right to refuse medical treatment, see Daniel Sinclair, "Patient Autonomy: The Right to Choose," *Leᶜela* (September, 1994): 15; idem, "Maᶜamadah shel ha-Refuʾah ve-Tippul Refuʾi Neged Reẓono shel ha-Ḥoleh," *Shenaton ha-Mishpat ha-ᶜIvri* 18–19 (1993–94):281–82; and Eliezer Ben-Shelomoh, "Himanᶜut me-Tippul Refuʾi mi-Tokh 'Ẓidqut,'" *Assia* 49–50 (1990):77–79. Note also the reference to a רבינו יב"א הלוי and *Hekhalot* literature in R. Moses Taku, *Ketav Tamim*, ms. Paris 711, fol. 19v.

Rabiah, Ri's younger contemporary in Germany, cites two Yom Kippur practices that he ascribes to *perushim*, and he suggests several rabbinic and midrashic sources on which they are based. By immersing themselves prior to Yom Kippur and remaining on their feet throughout the night (during the evening service, or perhaps literally the entire night) and day of Yom Kippur, these *perushim*, according to Rabiah, sought to imitate the behavior of the angels.[32]

The *perushim* to whom Rabiah refers may have been pious individuals who were not formally associated with each other or with any organized group or movement. But since Rabiah flourished in Germany at precisely the same time as R. Judah *he-Ḥasid* and his student, R. Eleazar of Worms, it is tempting to suggest that these *perushim* were connected in some way to *Ḥasidei Ashkenaz* and their leaders. Indeed, two late thirteenth-century Italian works that followed the teachings of the German Pietists also mention these (or related) customs. The author of *Sefer Tanya Rabbati* writes that he had heard of places where they did not leave the synagogue on the night of Yom Kippur but remained awake reciting penitential prayers (*seliḥot ve-taḥanunim u-vidduyim*).[33] *Sefer Minhag Tov* recommends that one stand the entire night on Yom Kippur in the synagogue, not sleeping at all, and reciting *Shir ha-Yiḥud* and other *yiḥudim* and *baqqashot* until daybreak, when the congregational prayers begin.[34] The practice of standing all night and all day on Yom Kippur

---

[32]See *Sefer Rabiah*, 2:185, 190; and see also above, n. 19.

[33]*Sefer Tanya Rabbati*, ed. Simon Hurwitz (Warsaw, 1879), 172, sec. 81. On the relationship of this work and its parallel, *Shibbolei ha-Leqet* (see Israel Ta-Shma, "Shibbolei ha-Leqet u-Khefelav," *Italia* 11 [1995]:39–51), to the pietism and teachings of *ḥasidut Ashkenaz*, see below, ch. 2, n. 34.

[34]*Sefer Minhag Tov*, ed. M. Z. Weiss, *Ha-Ẓofeh* 13 (1929):235. The author of *Sefer Minhag Tov*, who composed his treatise c. 1275, may have studied with northern French tosafists. He did study with R. Moses b. Meir of Ferarra and perhaps settled in Bari or Taranto, although it is unclear whether he was of Italian origin. See Eric Zimmer, "Tiqqunei ha-Guf bi-Sheᶜat Tefillah," *Sidra* 5 (1987):91, n. 10 [=ᶜ*Olam ke-Minhago Noheg*, 74, n. 10]; Israel Ta-Shma, "Le-Toledot ha-Yehudim be-Polin ba-Meᵓot ha-Yod Bet/ha-Yod Gimmel," *Zion* 53 (1988):365, n. 65; idem, "Havdalah ᶜal ha-Pat," *Sefer ha-Zikkaron leha-Rav Nissim* (Jerusalem, 1985), 1:145.

This work is full of ascetic practices in the spirit of *Ḥasidei Ashkenaz* and the academy at Evreux (below, nn. 82–83); see esp. 232, 237. (R. Judah *he-Ḥasid* is cited once by name, in sec. 69.) It recommends such practices as walking barefoot, enduring lengthy fasts, and the frequent recitation of *vidduyim* and *taḥanunim*. In the author's introductory remarks (218), he discourages indulging even in pleasures that are permitted and suggests the need to undertake many kinds of *perishut*. Like *Sefer*

(and spending the entire night reciting hymns and praises) is attributed by R. Jacob b. Asher in his *Arba^cah Turim* to *ʾanshei maʿaseh*, a term he employs with regard to *Ḥasidei Ashkenaz*.[35]

In supporting the position that on the Sabbath a Jew may warm himself over a fire that a non-Jew has kindled expressly for use by the Jew, R. Yom Tov of Joigny—a student of Rabbenu Tam who settled in York, England (c. 1180)—asserts that this was done by both his father and R. Meshullam (of Melun), "who were *perushim*." The term *perushim* in this context would appear to refer simply to individuals who observed Jewish law punctiliously and did not allow themselves to be overly lenient. The force of R. Yom Tov's claim is that if two pious and conservative decisors permitted this practice, it was certainly an acceptable position.

At the same time, all major rabbinic decisors in Germany (through the late thirteenth century) held the stringent view: that a Jew may not warm himself by a fire that has been kindled by a non-Jew on the Sabbath, even in cases where the non-Jew has done so without being asked by the Jew. In a

---

Ḥasidim, this work stresses complete decorum in the synagogue, with no talking whatsoever (224, sec. 3; cf. below, n. 151). For other liturgical practices and interpretations common to *Ḥasidei Ashkenaz* and *Sefer Minhag Tov*, see, e.g., B. S. Bamberger, *Shorashei Minhag Ashkenaz* (Bnei Brak, 1995), 188, 206–7. On the composition of *Shir ha-Yiḥud* by a member of the German Pietists, see below, n. 88.

35 *Arbaʿah Turim, Oraḥ Ḥayyim*, sec. 619. Cf., however, R. Eleazar of Worms, *Sefer Roqeaḥ*, sec. 217 (end), and below, n. 68. On the use of the terms *ḥasidim* and *ʾanshei maʿaseh* by *Arbaʿah Turim* to connote *Ḥasidei Ashkenaz*, see, e.g., *Oraḥ Ḥayyim*, secs. 98, 241, 249 (and cf. *Bayit Ḥadash*, s.v. *ve-yirʾeh*, and in sec. 686, s.v. *ukeshe-ḥal*), 460, 624; and cf. 46, 101, 113, 268, 529, 539, 551, 554, 557, 591, 602, 624, and *Yoreh Deʿah*, sec. 361; Moshe Hallamish, "Beʿayyot be-Ḥeqer Hashpaʿat ha-Qabbalah ʿal ha-Tefillah," *Massuʾot* [Studies in Kabbalistic Literature and Jewish Philosophy in Memory of Prof. Ephraim Gottlieb], ed. Michael Oron and Amos Goldreich (Jerusalem, 1994), 204; *Shitat ha-Qadmonim* (above, n. 17), 334 (וכן ראיתי אנשי מעשה תלמידיו של ר׳ יהודה החסיד); Yehudah Liebes, *Ḥetʾo shel Elisha* (Jerusalem, 1990), 106–7; and below, n. 93, ch. 2, n. 52, and ch. 5, n. 75. [Note Ramban's use of the phrase חסידים ואנשי מעשה to characterize those from whom he received a *seder ha-viddui* for a person near death. See *Kitvei ha-Ramban*, ed. C. D. Chavel (Jerusalem, 1964), 2:47, cited also in *Perush R. Asher b. Yeḥiʾel le-Massekhet Moʿed Qatan*, 3:76, and in *Arbaʿah Turim, Yoreh Deʿah*, sec. 338; and see also ms. Sassoon 408 [=B. M. Or. 14055], fol. 150. On Ramban's awareness of *Ḥasidei Ashkenaz*, see, e.g., my "On the Assessment of R. Moses b. Naḥman (Naḥmanides) and His Literary Oeuvre," *Jewish Book Annual* 51 (1993–94):170–71 (=*Jewish Book Annual* 54 [1996–97] 78–79). Cf. ms. Vat. Rossiana 356, fol. 2r; ms. Parma 1138, fol. 96v; and Elliot Horowitz, "The Jews of Europe and the Moment of Death in Medieval and Modern Times," *Judaism* 44 (1995):273–74.]

responsum, R. Meir of Rothenburg—whose close relationship with *ḥasidut Ashkenaz* will be discussed below—acknowledges the validity of the French position, held (also) by one of his French teachers and by R. Jacob of Orleans; this was predicated on the notion that people become somewhat ill sitting in an unheated home, a situation in which instructing a non-Jew to kindle the fire would be permissible according to the letter of the law. Nonetheless, Maharam concludes that this is prohibited "in our kingdom" for reasons of "חומרא ופרישות." Moreover, R. Judah *he-Ḥasid* had earlier prescribed harsh penances (*tiqqunei teshuvah*) consisting of fasts, lashes, and confessions over a six-month period for anyone who instructed a non-Jew or a maidservant to light a fire to warm their home on the Sabbath. Thus, in the German orbit, another practice rooted in and characterized as *perishut* was, in fact, associated with *Ḥasidei Ashkenaz*.[36]

Although Rabiah cannot be characterized as a committed follower of the German Pietists, he was familiar with a number of their teachings and pietistic

---

[36]See Israel Ta-Shma, *Halakhah, Minhag u-Meẓiʾut be-Ashkenaz* (Jerusalem, 1996), 160–67; Jacob Katz, *Goy shel Shabbat* (Jerusalem, 1984), 47–53; Urbach, *Baʿalei ha-Tosafot*, 1:144. Perhaps this development was also a factor in the use of the term *perushim* by R. Yom Tov of Joigny, although we cannot be absolutely certain that he was aware of the German position. Three of the most prominent supporters of the German position—R. Simḥah of Spires, R. Avigdor *Kohen Ẓedeq*, and R. Isaac b. Moses *Or Zaruaʿ*—were also closely connected to *Ḥasidei Ashkenaz*, as we shall see below. [Ta-Shma counters effectively Katz's contention that Rabiah held the lenient position. He also demonstrates that the stringent German position (once again) follows Palestinian *halakhah*—which was based on several passages in the Talmud Yerushalmi—while the lenient northern French position was based primarily on Rabbenu Tam's interpretation of the Bavli.]

Similar to R. Yom Tov of Joigny, R. Joseph of Orleans [*Bekhor Shor*], who was also a student of Rabbenu Tam, employs the term *perushim* to describe individuals who followed carefully an established Ashkenazic custom of splitting the second meal into two; this would ensure that a third, separate meal could be eaten on the Sabbath. In this particular case, however, R. Joseph considers the *perushim* to be foolhardy (מעשה נערות), since their observance of this custom may lead them to overeat (אכילה גסה), and this would undermine the legitimacy of the third meal. See Ta-Shma, *Minhag Ashkenaz Qadmon* (Jerusalem, 1992), 210–12. In all likelihood, the reference in *Sefer ha-Orah*, ed. Solomon Buber (repr. Jerusalem, 1967), 89, to *ḥasidim* who postponed baking *maẓot* until as close to Passover as possible connotes individuals who conducted themselves stringently (according to the German practice, instead of the more lenient French practice), rather than an organized group of *ḥasidim*. Indeed, R. Yehudah *he-Ḥasid* himself agreed with the French position in this instance. See Ta-Shma, *Minhag Ashkenaz ha-Qadmon*, 248; Zimmer, *ʿOlam ke-Minhago Noheg*, 281–83; and below, ch. 2, n. 44.

practices. Rabiah fasted two days for Yom Kippur as R. Judah *he-Ḥasid* did,[37] and he cites interpretations and legal decisions of R. Judah on a handful of occasions, referring to him in a responsum to R. Eleazar of Worms as "our teacher."[38] Rabiah also records a *gematria* interpretation that he heard in the name of R. Samuel *he-Ḥasid*: The numerical value of the opening words of the *Avinu Malkenu* prayer, אבינו מלכנו חטאנו לפניך, corresponds to that of the phrase "R. Aqiva who composed it."[39]

---

[37]See above, n. 17. Note that Rabiah (like R. Eleazar of Worms) did not, however, advocate fasting on *Rosh ha-Shanah*; see above, n. 30. See also *Haggahot Maimuniyyot, Hilkhot Shofar*, 1:1 [1]; a passage in *Sefer Assufot* (ms. Jews College 134/Montefiore 115), whose author appears to have been a student of both Rabiah and R. Eleazar of Worms (transcribed in *Zekhor le-Avraham*, ed. Avigdor Berger [Jerusalem, 1993], 25, and see also 19–20); and cf. *Sefer Or Zarua*ᶜ, 2:257, and below, ch. 2, n. 36; ch. 3, n. 62. Nor did Rabiah support undertaking a *ta*ᶜ*anit ḥalom* on the Sabbath. See *Sefer Rabiah*, 2:621–22, and cf. *Sefer Or Zarua*ᶜ, 2:407, and below, ch. 2, n. 46.

[38]See Aptowitzer, *Mavo la-Rabiah*, 22, 252, 343. See also E. E. Urbach, "Liqqutim mi-Sifrei de-Vei Rashi," *Sefer Rashi* (Jerusalem, 1956), 333, n. 6.

[39]ושמעתי בשם ר׳ שמואל החסיד אבינו מלכנו חטאנו לפניך עולה בגימטריא רבי עקיבא הוא יסדו. See *Sefer Rabiah*, 2:232 (and n. 6); and cf. *Ta*ᶜ*anit* 25b; and Urbach, *Ba*ᶜ*alei ha-Tosafot*, 1:195, n. 79. For other citations of this *gematria*, see ms. Hamburg 152, fol. 106v.; *Sefer Assufot* (above, n. 37), 27; *Sefer Or Zarua*ᶜ, 2:281; ms. Cambr. Add. 858, fols. 45r–45v (a commentary to *Avinu Malkenu* by R. Avigdor Katz; see below, ch. 2, n. 30); *Sefer Matteh Mosheh*, ed. Mordechai Knoblowicz (Jerusalem, 1978^2); ᶜ*Ammud ha-*ᶜ*Avodah*, pt. 5, para. 801 (p. 254). In this *gematria* (as Rabiah himself notes subsequently), the word חטאנו is counted as it is read, without the ᵓ*alef*. Cf. R. Moses Isserles' gloss to *O. Ḥ.*, sec. 583:2 (and his *Darkhei Mosheh*, ad loc.), and Sperber, *Minhagei Yisra*ᵓ*el*, 4:49. Also, in most of the texts that record the *gematria*, R. Aqiva is spelled with a *heh* at the end, rather than with an ᵓ*alef*—as in Palestinian texts from the talmudic period, and as this name was often spelled in texts of the German Pietists. Cf. below, ch. 4, n. 31.

In *Siddur Rabbenu Shelomoh mi-Germaiza ve-Siddur Ḥasidei Ashkenaz* (ed. Moshe Hershler, 222), R. Aqiva's authorship of *Avinu Malkenu* is derived, anonymously, by noting that the 247 words in *Avinu Malkenu* correspond in *gematria* to הנה עקיבה. (Cf. *Siddur*, 20, n. 14.) The number 247=רמז also confirms that this prayer should be recited with a slow cadence, as a זמר, and that adding any words or phrases to this prayer, as was advocated in non-Pietist circles, is inappropriate. A manuscript passage attributes this derivation and discussion to R. Samuel Bamberg; see now Simcha Emanuel, "Ha-Polmos ᶜal Nosaḥ ha-Tefillah shel Ḥasidei Ashkenaz," *Meḥqerei Talmud* 3 [in press], n. 135 (end); and below, ch. 2, n. 15.

On the other hand, while *Sefer Ḥasidim* advised that two weddings should not take place at the same time because of ᶜ*ayin ha-ra* considerations, Rabiah felt this consideration could be routinely ignored if there were economic exigencies, ושומר פתאים ה׳. See *Sefer Rabiah*, 3:504–5, and n. 1; and cf. ᶜ*Arugat ha-Bosem*, ed. E. E. Urbach, vol. 4 (Jerusalem, 1963), 110.

Rabiah endorsed the custom of menstruant women not entering the synagogue. This custom originated in the *Baraita de-Massekhet Niddah*, a text related to *Hekhalot* literature and preserved by the German Pietists, who also supported its stringencies.[40] In addition, Rabiah records two passages from *Hekhalot* literature itself, a corpus that the German Pietists played a role in shaping.[41] Rabiah was the first Ashkenazic rabbinic authority to cite a formulation in *Hekhalot Rabbati* that instructs the eyes should be raised heavenward during the recitation of the *Qedushah*. Rabiah asserts that when the Almighty sees and hears this demonstration, He responds by kissing three times the image of Jacob that is engraved on the *kisse ha-kavod*.[42]

The second *Hekhalot* passage, which Rabiah mentions as appearing in (mystical) *sefarim ḥiẓoniyyim*, was cited to justify the practice of bowing during the recitation of the *ʿAvodah* on Yom Kippur. According to this passage (which also is found in fuller form in *Hekhalot Rabbati*), R. Neḥunyah b. *ha-Qanah*

---

[40]*Sefer Rabiah*, 1:45, *Sefer Or Zaruaʿ*, 1:360. At the same time, Rabiah (*Sefer Or Zaruaʿ*, loc. cit.) relaxed some of the *Baraita*'s additional restrictions (*harḥaqot*) concerning a husband and wife eating together. On Rabiah's position—as well as the nature of the *Baraita*, its affinity with *Hekhalot* literature, and its adoption and dissemination by the German Pietists and other Ashkenazic rabbinic figures—see Yedidyah Dinari, "Minhagei Tumʾat ha-Niddah—Meqoram ve-Hishtalshelutam," *Tarbiz* 49 (1980):302–24; idem, "Ḥillul ha-Qodesh ʿal Yedei Niddah ve-Taqqanat Ezra," *Teʿudah* 3 (1983):17–38; Israel Ta-Shma, "'Miqdash Meʿat'—Ha-Semel veha-Mamashut," *Knesset Ezra [Sifrut ve-Ḥayyim be-Veit ha-Knesset]*, ed. Shulamit Elizur et al. (Jerusalem, 1994), 359–64; Sharon Koren, "Mysticism and Menstruation: The Significance of Female Impurity in Jewish Spirituality" (Ph.D. diss., Yale University, 1999), ch. 1; and below, ch. 2, nn. 81–82.

[41]See the extensive literature cited above in the introduction, n. 25. [Note that a passage found in *Sefer Orḥot Ḥayyim*, as part of R. Eleazar of Worms's *Sefer ha-Kapparot*, is cited in *liqqutim* on the *Semaq mi-Ẓurich* as *leshon Sefer Hekhalot*. See Israel Ta-Shma, "Issur Shetiyyat Mayyim ba-Tequfah u-Meqoro," *Meḥqerei Yerushalayim be-Folqlor Yehudi* 17 (1995):32.]

[42]See *Sefer Rabiah*, 1:70, and n. 19; Eric Zimmer, "Tiqqueni ha-Guf bi-Sheʿat ha-Tefillah," *Sidra* 5 (1989):94–95 [=Zimmer, *Olam ke-Minhago Noheg*, 77–78]. The *Hekhalot* characterization of the response of the Almighty during the *Qedushah* is alluded to already in an *ʾofan* by R. Ephraim of Bonn (1133–1197): **ינשק צור דמות היצור בכס עצור והוא נכבד**. See A. M. Habermann, *Piyyutei R. Ephraim b. Yaʿaqov mi-Bonn* (Jerusalem, 1969), 17, and below, ch. 2, n. 26. See also below, ch. 2, n. 25, for a reference to this *Hekhalot* notion in an *ʾofan* by R. Barukh b. Samuel of Mainz (d. 1221). See also *Sefer Rabiah*, 1:26, regarding movement of the head during the recitation of *Shema* as an indication of proper intention, a practice with roots in *Sefer Yeẓirah*; and cf. Zimmer, "Tenuḥot u-Tenuʿot ha-Guf bi-Sheʿat Qeriʾat Shema," *Assufot* 8 (1995):360–61.

instructed his students to bow and prostrate themselves when he taught them the pronunciation of the Tetragrammaton. Rabiah adds, on the basis of the Yom Kippur liturgy, that those who heard the *Kohen Gadol* pronounce the Tetragrammaton on Yom Kippur also prostrated themselves; he further remarks that this practice is not mentioned in the Talmud.[43] It should be noted, however, that Rabiah's citation of *Hekhalot* texts to explain (common) liturgical or synagogue practices does not mean that Rabiah was necessarily attuned to the mystical nature of these texts.[44]

Rabiah did record mystical material with regard to the protective powers of *mezuzot* and the structure and efficacy of the priestly benediction. Victor Aptowitzer, Rabiah's modern biographer, has argued cogently, however, that while Rabiah may have been a kind of *ḥasid*, these two texts should not be taken as evidence that he was a *ba*ᶜ*al sod*, since in both instances he cites the esoteric material from geonic or other earlier rabbinic scholars (*rabbotenu ha-darshanim*).[45]

To be sure, there are additional mystical texts or concepts—whose association with Rabiah will be evaluated later in this study—that might also serve to link him to *Ḥasidei Ashkenaz*. In these instances as well, however, the evidence does not suggest that Rabiah himself was mystically inclined.[46] At this

[43]*Sefer Rabiah*, 2:196, and n. 20. Cf. Zimmer, "Tiqqunei ha-Guf," 114–15 [=ᶜ*Olam Ke-Minhago Noheg*, 94–95.] On the term *ḥiẓoniyyim* as an indication of a work of *sod*, see *Sefer Rabiah*, n. 20; and cf. below, nn. 61–62, for a similar usage of the term *sefarim penimiyyim*.

[44]The *Hekhalot* passage concerning *Qedushah* is found in a printed version of *Seder Rav Amram Gaon*, although this version does not appear at all in Daniel Goldschmidt's critical edition of the *Seder*; see Elliot Wolfson, "Demut Yaᶜaqov Ḥaquqah be-Kisse ha-Kavod: ᶜIyyun Nosaf be-Torat ha-Sod shel Ḥasidut Ashkenaz," *Massu*ᵓ*ot* ed. Oron and Goldreich, 152, n. 110. For the citation of this passage in subsequent Ashkenazic rabbinic literature, see below, n. 60. Although Rabiah attributes this passage to *Sefer Hekhalot*, some of the subsequent citations refer to its source as *Ma*ᶜ*aseh Merkavah*; see below, ch. 3, n. 37.

[45]See Aptowitzer, *Mavo la-Rabiah*, 19–20, 481–82. Cf. Ta-Shma, *Ha-Nigleh shebe-Nistar*, 94, n. 33; Urbach, *Ba*ᶜ*alei ha-Tosafot*, 1:388; Jacob Elbaum, *Teshuvat ha-Lev ve-Qabbalat Yissurim* (Jerusalem, 1993), 19, n. 1; and Ruth Langer, *To Worship God Properly* (Cincinnati, 1998), 221–24. The *mezuzah* treatise (וזה מצאתי בתשובת הגאונים) was published with annotations by Avigdor Aptowitzer in "Mi-Sifrut ha-Geonim," *Sefer ha-Yovel li-Professor Shemu*ᵓ*el Krauss* (Jerusalem, 1937), 96–102. See also below, n. 156. The *birkat kohanim* passage was first published by Aptowitzer in *Ve-Zot li-Yehudah* [Festschrift for J. L. Landau] (Tel Aviv, 1936), and more recently in *Sefer Rabiah*, ed. David Deblitsky (Bnei Brak, 1976), 263–66.

[46]See below, ch. 4, nn. 56–57.

point, then, we cannot conclude with certainty that the *perushim* on *Yom ha-Kippurim* referred to by Rabiah should be identified mainly with the German Pietists, despite several suggestive points in common between the Pietists and Rabiah. Rabiah also refers to those who did not eat meat or drink during the three weeks prior to the ninth of Av and who undertook additional fasts during this period as *perushim*. But as we have seen with regard to standing on Yom Kippur, the notion that *Ḥasidei Ashkenaz* may have espoused these particular practices is found, or implied, only in later Ashkenazic sources.[47]

On the other hand, R. Abraham b. Nathan *ha-Yarḥi*, author of *Sefer ha-Manhig*, identifies those who had the custom of standing the entire day on Yom Kippur not as *perushim* but as **חסידי צרפת**, although like Rabiah he cites a passage from *Pirqei de-R. Eliezer* to support this custom.[48] R. Abraham, who hailed from Provence, was a wandering scholar who visited centers of Torah study throughout western Europe. He traveled first to the north, where he studied primarily with R. Isaac of Dampierre—whom he refers to several times as *Rabbenu ha-Qadosh* (and whose pietism was noted earlier).[49] R. Abraham also journeyed southward, reaching the Spanish city of Toledo around the beginning of the thirteenth century.[50]

R. Abraham mentions other tosafists by name and incorporates much material from northern France into his *Sefer ha-Manhig*, as well as some German material,[51] although it is uncertain whether he studied in or even

[47]See above, n. 19, and nn. 33–35. Cf. *SḤP* 548; Joseph b. Moses, *Leqet Yosher*, ed. Jacob Freimann (Berlin, 1903), pt. 1, 107; *Sefer Minhag Tov*, ed. M. Z. Weiss, *Ha-Ẓofeh* 13 (1929):237; Moritz Güdemann, *Ha-Torah veha-Ḥayyim*, vol. 1 (Warsaw, 1897), 219, regarding references to *perushim* in *Sefer Assufot* (cf. above, n. 37); Gartner, *Gilgulei Minhag be-ᶜOlam ha-Halakhah*, 32–34; and Zimmer, *ᶜOlam ke-Minago Noheg*, 229–39. Zimmer (233–34) seeks to identify (a practice of) *perushim* at the time of Rashi with *Ḥasidei Ashkenaz*. Note that with regard to ritual stringencies associated with *Ḥasidei Ashkenaz* having to do with various forms of impurity, Rabiah's views do not coincide with those of *Ḥasidei Ashkenaz* nearly as much as do those of his student, R. Isaac b. Moses *Or Zaruaᶜ*; see below, ch. 2, nn. 82, 86.

[48]*Sefer ha-Manhig*, ed. Yizhak Raphael (Jerusalem, 1978), 1:363.

[49]See *Sefer ha-Manhig*, 2:475, 478, 519, 526, and see above, n. 29.

[50]See Twersky, *Rabad of Posquières*, 240–43; *Sefer ha-Manhig*, editor's introduction, 11–18; Bernard Septimus, *Hispano-Jewish Culture in Transition* (Cambridge, Mass., 1982), 32–35, 48, 55; and Israel Ta-Shma, "Ḥasidut Ashkenaz bi-Sefarad: Rabbenu Yonah Gerondi—Ha-Ish u-Foᶜalo," *Galut Aḥar Golah*, ed. Aharon Mirsky et al. (Jerusalem, 1988), 171–73.

[51]*Sefer ha-Manhig*, editor's introduction, 38–39.

visited Germany. Two of three versions of the laws of *tefillin* in *Sefer ha-Manhig* record a *gematria* interpretation (concerning the two *shins* that are engraved on the *tefillin shel rosh*) which he "received in the name of the German Pietists" (קבלתי בשם חסידי אלמניא); this suggests that R. Abraham did not meet these Pietists personally.[52] Parenthetically, these formulations are highly significant, for they establish that in the late twelfth century, behaviors of *ḥasidut Ashkenaz* were already being practiced by a group of people. These manifestations did not result only from the impact of *Sefer Ḥasidim*, nor did they remain within a single family.[53]

Although this is the only context in *Sefer ha-Manhig* in which the term חסידי אלמניא appears, it is not the only instance in which R. Abraham included material that is associated with the German Pietists. *Sefer ha-Manhig* records a *rashei/sofei tevot* application derived from the final word of each book of the Pentateuch, which had been heard by an informant in the name of R. Isaac *ha-Lavan*. This application—which equates the word חרם with the 248 limbs of a person's body, thus suggesting that whoever violates a *ḥerem* causes harm to his entire being and is thereby subject to all the punitive oaths contained in the Pentateuch—is found almost verbatim in one version of *Sefer Ḥasidim*.[54]

---

[52]*Sefer ha-Manhig*, 2:607, 626. R. Abraham refers to three German tosafists—R. Efraim [of Regensburg] (1:201–2), R. Isaac b. Asher (Riba) [of Spires] (2:508, 627), and Ri *ha-Lavan* [of Prague] (1:33)—as being from the larger area of Allemagne, although R. Efraim is also referred to by *Sefer ha-Manhig* as R. Efraim of Regensburg (2:659), and Ri *ha-Lavan*'s name in the oldest manuscript of *Sefer ha-Manhig* (Bodl. 900) is replaced by that of R. Isaac of Spires. [Ri *ha-Lavan* cites Riba often, and toward the end of his life he served as a judge in Regensburg. See Urbach, *Ba*ᶜ*alei ha-Tosafot*, 1:216, 218.] There is no evidence that R. Abraham had personal contact with any of these scholars. He mentions a written formulation of their views or indicates that he heard their position. The material that R. Abraham cites from Ri *ha-Lavan* can be found in *Sefer Ḥasidim*; see below, n. 54.

In one instance, R. Abraham cites an interpretation he heard from the mouth of R. Ḥayyim (b. Ḥananʾel) *ha-Kohen* (*Sefer ha-Manhig*, 1:36). R. Ḥayyim studied with Rabbenu Tam in Troyes (or Ramerupt) and lived in Paris; see Urbach, 1:112, 124. In one of the later manuscripts of *Sefer ha-Manhig* (cited in the critical apparatus, loc. cit.), R. Ḥayyim is characterized as *ha-Qadosh R. Ḥayyim b. Ḥananʾel me-Allemagne*. Even if this reading is correct, however, the identification of *Ḥasidei Allemagne* in *Sefer ha-Manhig* with *Ḥasidei Ashkenaz* remains well-based.

[53]Cf. Marcus, *Piety and Society*, 131, 147, n. 3, and above, in the introduction.

[54]*Sefer ha-Manhig*, 1:33, and *SḤB* 106 (and cf. below, n. 71). See also Jacob Gellis, *Tosafot ha-Shalem*, 2:35; *Shibbolei ha-Leqet*, pt. 2, ed. Simcha Hasida (Jerusalem, 1988), 231 (sec. 49); and *Sefer Kol Bo*, sec. 139, fol. 98b. On Ri *ha-Lavan*'s possible connections to *Ḥasidei Ashkenaz* (through R. Judah b. Qalonymus of Spires), see Urbach, *Ba*ᶜ*alei*

R. Abraham also follows closely a formulation of R. Samuel *he-Ḥasid*, without mentioning his name, in outlining the content of the liturgy of the final paragraph of the *Shema* that leads into the *ʿAmidah*.[55]

Sefer ha-Manhig maintains that the custom in northern France and Provence of the prayer leader calling out *ḥazaq* to each person who received an *ʿaliyyah* to the Torah was based on a passage in *Bereshit Rabbah*. Modern scholarship has had difficulty locating this passage in extant versions of *Midrash Rabbah*. A recent suggestion points to a formulation in *Bereshit Rabbah*

---

ha-Tosafot, 1:222–23. See also *Perushei ha-Torah le-R. Yehudah he-Ḥasid*, ed. Y. S. Lange (Jerusalem, 1975), 8. [At least one of Ri *ha-Lavan*'s brothers, R. Petaḥyah of Regensburg, had contact with R. Judah *he-Ḥasid*; see Avraham David, "Sibbuv R. Petaḥyah me-Regensburg be-Nosaḥ Ḥadash," *Qoveẓ ʿal Yad* n. s. 13 (1996): 239–43; *ʿArugat ha-Bosem*, ed. Urbach, 4:125–26; and Israel Ta-Shma, "Le-Toledot ha-Yehudim be-Polin ba-Meʾot ha-Yod Bet/ha-Yod Gimmel," *Zion* 53 (1988):352, n. 16, 368–69.] In the *Kol Bo* text, this passage is part of an actual *ḥerem* pronouncement, and it is followed by a formulation in which both angelic and Divine Names are adjured in order to punish anyone who violates the *ḥerem*. This *ḥerem* form, which appears to have been in wide use although no location or area is specified, bears similarities to various magical and mystical adjurations discussed below; see ch. 3, n. 112. For the impact of these formulations in judicial and societal contexts, see Simha Goldin, "Tafqidei ha-'Ḥerem' veha-'Taqqanot' ba-Qehillah ha-Yehudit ha-Ashkenazit Bimei ha-Benayim," *Proceedings of the Eleventh World Congress of Jewish Studies* (Jerusalem, 1994) [Div. B, vol. 1], 107–8.

[55]See *Sefer ha-Manhig*, 1:77–78, and the editor's notes, ad loc. Cf. *ʿArugat ha-Bosem*, ed. Urbach, 4:86–87, and S. Emanuel, "Ha-Polmos ʿal Nosaḥ ha-Tefillah shel Ḥasidei Ashkenaz," nn. 85–86. The formulation of R. Samuel was an interpretation of a liturgical reading favored originally by R. Meir *Ḥazzan* (שליח ציבור) that was subsequently challenged by R. Judah *he-Ḥasid* and R. Eleazar of Worms (whose view was shared by Rabbenu Tam). On R. Meir, cf. below, ch. 2, n. 65, and ch. 3, n. 122. *Sefer ha-Manhig*, 2:402, describes the atonement associated with *Hoshana Rabbah* in terms similar to those found in sources linked to the German Pietists. These notions were conflated further by the Zohar. See Ta-Shma, *Ha-Nigleh shebe-Nistar*, 22–23, and below, ch. 2, n. 34, and ch. 5, n. 27. Note also the affinities between *Sefer ha-Manhig* (cited in one instance in the name of *ha-Qadosh* R. Yom Tov [of Joigny?]; see below, n. 67) and a Pietist prayer commentary, with regard to the number of times the word *barukh* appears in *Barukh she-Amar*. See *Sefer ha-Manhig*, 1:42, 51, and Moshe Hallamish, "Beʿayot be-Ḥeqer Hashpaʿat ha-Qabbalah ʿal ha-Tefillah," *Massuʾot*, ed. Oron and Goldreich, 214–15.

The author of *Sefer ha-Manhig* could easily have been a conduit for the asceticism of the German Pietists (and of Ri), which may have penetrated into southern France. See Marc Saperstein, "Christians and Christianity in the Sermons of Jacob Anatoli," *The Frank Talmage Memorial Volume*, ed. Bary Walfish (Haifa, 1993), 2:233–34; idem, *"Your Voice Like a Ram's Horn": Themes and Texts in the Tradition of Preaching* (Cincinnati, 1996), 69; and below, ch. 4, n. 10.

that conveys the essence of what is found in *Sefer ha-Manhig*, albeit in different terms.[56] Interestingly, two related medieval Ashkenazic texts also identify this passage from *Bereshit Rabbah* as the source of the custom, citing it from "the writing of R. Judah *he-Ḥasid*" (מכתיבת הר׳ יהודה החסיד).[57]

Sefer ha-Manhig displays additional affinities with the German Pietists with respect to magical and mystical phenomena that will be discussed later. One aspect of this material that relates directly to the passages in *Sefer ha-Manhig* under consideration here should be mentioned. In outlining the proper conduct or form a person must display during the *ᶜAmidah* prayer in particular, R. Abraham writes that he found a midrashic source that obligates a person to move himself or sway during prayer based on a verse in Psalms: "All my limbs should say, God who is like thee?" He further indicates that this was the practice of רבני צרפת וחסידיה.[58] The notion of swaying during prayer, together with its biblical source, is found in *Sefer Ḥasidim* as an imperative.[59] R. Zedekiah b. Abraham *ha-Rofe* Anav writes in his *Shibbolei ha-Leqet*—a mid-thirteenth century halakhic compendium that preserves Ashkenazic

---

[56]See *Sefer ha-Manhig*, 1:182, and Ta-Shma, *Minhag Ashkenaz ha-Qadmon*, 182–83. Ta-Shma also notes a similar approach in the commentary to *Bereshit Rabbah* composed in eleventh-century Mainz.

[57]See Moshe Hershler, "Minhagei Vermaiza u-Magenẓa, de-Vei Rashi ve-Rabbotav, u-Minhagei Ashkenaz shel ha-Roqeaḥ," *Genuzot* 2 (1985):19, sec. 34, and *Sefer Minhagim de-vei Maharam ben Barukh mi-Rothenburg*, ed. Israel Elfenbein (New York, 1938), 12. The reference to *Sefer Roqeaḥ* in the text published by Elfenbein refers only to the customs concerning the Torah reading for a groom before his wedding that are mentioned just prior to the *ḥazaq* custom, not to the *ḥazaq* custom itself. In Elfenbein's version, the custom of reciting *ḥazaq* was limited to the completion of each book of the Torah. See now Yaᶜakov Spiegel, "Amirat Ḥazaq ve-Yishar Koaḥ," *Bar Ilan* 26–27 (1995):343–57.

[58]*Sefer ha-Manhig*, 1:85. Cf. *Sefer ha-Manhig*, 1:191, and below, ch. 3, n. 56.

[59]*SḤB*, sec. 57. It is also found in R. Jonah of Gerona's *Sefer ha-Yirʾah*, ed. B. Y. Zilber (Bnei Brak, 1969), 33, sec. 78, which has marked affinities with *Sefer Ḥasidim*; see below at n. 84. R. Judah *ha-Levi*, *Kuzari*, 2:79, offered a simple logistical explanation for swaying (since many people read from the same volume), although it appears the *Kuzari* passage refers to several people reading from a biblical text rather than from a prayerbook. Another tradition in medieval rabbinic literature explains the appropriateness of swaying (or at least moving one's head) during Torah study, based directly on the verse which notes that the children of Israel trembled or moved when they got close to the Divine presence at Mount Sinai: וירא העם וינועו (Exodus 20:15). It is found in several versions of the Ashkenazic educational initiation ceremony [see my *Jewish Education and Society*, 116–17, 197], e.g., *Maḥzor Vitry*, 628, 630 (sec. 508), and R. Aaron *ha-Kohen* of Lunel, *Orḥot Ḥayyim*, pt. 2, ed. Moshe Schlesinger (Berlin, 1899), sec. 3, 24–25 (=*Kol Bo*, sec. 74, fol. 43a), which adduces additional biblical prooftexts. Cf.

customs and liturgical practices—that he found the source of this practice (based on the aforementioned verse in Psalms) in *Ma^caseh Merkavah*, which connotes a *Hekhalot* text.[60]

Sefer ha-Manhig continues by discussing another procedure, which appears in "internal [mystical] books" (*sefarim ha-penimiyyim*), concerning the intentions one should have while reciting blessings to the Almighty. This procedure is found in *Hekhalot* literature.[61] Moreover, Moshe Idel has argued recently that the particular aspects of *kavvanah* described in this passage reflect

---

Moshav Zeqenim ᶜal ha-Torah, ed. Solomon Sassoon (Jerusalem, 1982), 169; *Tosafot ha-Shalem*, ed. Jacob Gellis, vol. 8 (Jerusalem, 1990), 122; *Baᶜal ha-Turim ᶜal ha-Torah*, ed. Jacob Reinitz (Jerusalem, 1993), 1:207; and *Zohar*, 218b. See also Zimmer, "Tiqqunei ha-Guf bi-Sheᶜat ha-Tefillah," 118–20 [=*ᶜOlam ke-Minhago Noheg*, 99–101], and Marcus, *Rituals of Childhood*. 72–73.

[60]*Shibbolei ha-Leqet*, ed. S. K. Mirsky (New York, 1966), 183 (sec. 17). According to Zimmer, "Tiqqunei ha-Guf," 120, n. 164 [=*ᶜOlam ke-Minhago Noheg*, 100, n. 164], the source for this practice cannot be found in extant *Hekhalot* texts but is alluded to in *Midrash Tehillim* (which also reflects the editing of *Ḥasidei Ashkenaz*; see below, n. 63) and in a *piyyut* of R. Eleazar Qallir. *Shibbolei ha-Leqet*, 194 (sec. 20), also cites the practice of raising one's eyes (and heels) during *Qedushah* (found in *Hekhalot Rabbati*), from a text that he again calls *Maᶜaseh Merkavah*. Cf. Gershom Scholem, *Jewish Gnosticism, Merkabah Mysticism, and Talmudic Tradition* (New York, 1960), 101–2, and below, ch. 2, n. 34. [Raising one's eyes during *Qedushah* is also mentioned by (the Pietist) R. Abraham b. Azriel in his *ᶜArugat ha-Bosem* (based on "*Sefer Hekhalot*") and by *Sefer Minhag Tov*. Cf. *SḤB*, sec. 18, and *SḤP*, secs. 1582–87. Indeed, it appears from a passage in *Arbaᶜah Turim, O. Ḥ.* sec. 125 (also citing "*Sefer Hekhalot*"), that this was the custom throughout Ashkenaz (although the raising of the heels was omitted by a number of authorities, including R. Eleazar of Worms and Rabiah). See Zimmer, *Olam ke-Minhago Noheg*, 77–78, 109–110; Ivan Marcus, "Prayer Gestures in German Hasidism," *Mysticism, Magic and Kabbalah in Ashkenazi Judaism*, ed. K. E. Grözinger and Joseph Dan (Berlin, 1995) 49–53; and above, n. 42. *Sefer ha-Manhig*, 1:88, records these practices from *sefarim penimiyyim*, a term that connotes *Hekhalot* literature. See the next note, and cf. Zimmer, 109, n. 215.]

[61]See *Sefer ha-Manhig*, 1:85, editor's notes to line 21. As in the *Sefer ha-Manhig* passage cited in the previous note, the reference to *sefarim penimiyyim* is apparently to *Hekhalot Rabbati* in particular. In *Sefer ha-Manhig*, 2:622, the term connotes unspecified esoteric works that are cited together with *Alfa Beta de-R. Aqiva*. Cf. Twersky, *Rabad of Posquières*, 242–43. [The use of this term in *Maḥzor Vitry*, ed. Hurwitz, 112, sec. 144, is probably taken from *Sefer ha-Manhig*; see below, ch. 3, n. 56]. *Sefer ha-Manhig* also appears to have had access to *Otiyyot de-R. Aqiva* (1:14, 16, 90), and *Sefer Yeẓirah* is cited explicitly. See 1:12, 2:611, and 2:625: וקבלתי לפי טבע העולם וסוד היצירה בספר יצירה. Although *Sefer ha-Manhig* may have received some of this material from Provençal and Spanish kabbalists, (see editor's introduction, 19, 29), the parallels to Ashkenazic material with regard to the *Hekhalot* passages are quite clear. See also below, n. 63.

esoteric teachings of the German Pietists that were received by Provençal mystics such as R. Isaac *Sagi Nahor*.[62] *Sefer ha-Manhig* concludes this section by noting that this concept should be transmitted only to those who are appropriate (*ẓenuʿim*).[63]

The link between *Ḥasidei Ashkenaz* and *Hekhalot* literature is, as has already been noted, strong and well established.[64] As we shall see throughout this study, the impact of *Hekhalot* literature on Ashkenazic rabbinic literature as a whole, in both esoteric and exoteric contexts, was also substantial. Given that R. Abraham b. Nathan *ha-Yarḥi* was originally from Provence, and that there are several significant correlations in his work between practices of *Ḥasidei Ẓarefat* and *Ḥasidei Ashkenaz/Allemagne*, it is possible that R. Abraham viewed Ashkenazic *ḥasidut* as a larger single entity, with adherents in both northern France and Germany.[65]

---

[62]See Moshe Idel, "Al Kavvanat Shemoneh ʿEsreh Eẓel R. Yizhaq Sagi Nahor," *Massuʾot*, ed. Oron and Goldreich, 31–32; idem, "Ha-Tefillah be-Qabbalat Provence," *Tarbiz* 62 (1993): 265–72; and cf. idem, "Ha-Kavvanah ba-Tefillah be-Reshit ha-Qabbalah: Bein Ashkenaz u-Provence," *Porat Yosef* [Studies Presented to Rabbi Dr. Joseph Safran], ed. Bezalel Safran and Eliyahu Safran (New York, 1992), 5–14 [Hebrew section]; below, ch. 2, n. 14; and ch. 4, n. 10.

[63]See, e.g., *Qiddushin*, 71a, where the transmission of the forty-two-letter Divine name is restricted to *kohanim ẓenuʿim*, and cf. *Synopse zur Hekhalot-Literatur*, ed. Peter Schäfer (Tübingen, 1981), sec. 303, which concludes that the *Sar ha-Torah* formula was preserved for the generations, להשתמש בו צנועים. Just prior to the comment on swaying during prayer, *Sefer ha-Manhig* (1:84) cites *Midrash Tehillim* (ed. Buber, 122), for a discussion of the way God is referred to in the formulation of blessings. On the presence of Ashkenazic (esoteric) teachings, including those of the German Pietists, in versions of this midrash, see below, ch. 3, n. 13. Indeed, a very similar formulation is found in the prayer commentary of R. Eleazar of Worms. See *ʿArugat ha-Bosem*, ed. Urbach, 4:81–82, and Elliot Wolfson, *Through a Speculum That Shines* (Princeton, 1994), 203. The passage in *Sefer ha-Manhig* ends with the comment, *veha-mevin yavin*; cf. 1:153. For additional examples of Ashkenazic influence on *Sefer ha-Manhig* in matters of *sod* and *ḥasidut*, see, e.g., 1:56–57 (regarding the interpretation of *kaddish*), and cf. below, ch. 3, n. 55. See also 2:550, 1:300–303 (regarding fasting on *Rosh ha-Shanah*). Cf. Reuven Bonfil, "Bein Ereẓ Yisraʾel le-Vein Bavel," *Shalem* 5 (1987):18, n. 63, and below, ch. 2, n. 38.

[64]See above, n. 41.

[65]Even after he settled in Spain, R. Abraham *ha-Yarḥi* traveled back to northern France, serving as a kind of go-between in the earliest phase of the Maimonidean controversy. See Septimus, *Hispano-Jewish Culture in Transition*, 32–35, 48, 55. Note that the *Ḥug ha-Keruv ha-Meyuḥad* was a mystical circle whose members lived in northern France and England but whose ideas had much in common with *ḥasidut Ashkenaz*. See, e.g., Yosef Dan, "Ḥug ha-Keruv ha-Meyuḥad bi-Tenuʿat Ḥasidut Ashkenaz," *Tarbiz* 35 (1966):349–72; Moshe Idel, *Golem* (Albany, 1990), 81–82, 92–93; and Wolfson, "Demut Yaʿaqov," 140–41, 183–85.

At the same time, it is also plausible that the *Ḥasidei Ẓarefat* and the רבני צרפת וחסידיה referred to by R. Abraham included tosafists, or even consisted primarily of them. That all of the northern French tosafists whom R. Abraham calls *ha-Qadosh*—Ri, R. Elijah of Paris, and R. Jacob of Corbeil—were involved to some degree in pietistic practices or mystical teachings[66] cannot be mere coincidence.[67] To be sure, the possibility remains that *Ḥasidei Ẓarefat* who stood throughout Yom Kippur, like the *perushim* referred to by Rabiah, were unconnected individuals who exhibited similar forms of pietistic behavior.[68]

---

[66]For Ri, see *Sefer ha-Manhig*, 2:475, 478, 487, 519, 526; and see above, n. 29, and below, ch. 4, n. 10. For R. Elijah, see *Sefer ha-Manhig*, 1:49, 337, 2:649; and below, ch. 3, nn. 95–96 (although it would appear from these references that R. Abraham did not have personal contact with R. Elijah). R. Meshullam of Melun writes about R. Elijah: **שאין עזרה ננעלת בישראל על אדם כמותו בענוה וביראת חטא** (*Sefer ha-Yashar*, 92, cited in Urbach, *Baᶜalei ha-Tosafot*, 1:76). Rabbenu Tam refers to this description of R. Elijah by R. Meshullam (**והזכרת מעשה נסים של נעילת דלת עזרה על הרב ידעתי כי לא לכבודו אלא לשוחדו בדברים**), indicating his agreement with it, if not with R. Meshullam generally (Urbach, 1:79, and see also 1:122). For R. Jacob of Corbeil, see *Sefer ha-Manhig*, 2:649, and cf. below, ch. 4, nn. 22–23. In this instance, R. Abraham indicates he heard R. Jacob's view (on the question of invalidating the *ẓiẓit* at burial, which was the same as R. Elijah's) from R. Jacob's mouth. [This passage in *Sefer ha-Manhig* is the only medieval rabbinic text I have come across that provides the name of R. Jacob of Corbeil's father (Isaac); see my "Rabbinic Figures in Castilian Kabbalistic Pseudepigraphy: R. Yehudah *he-Ḥasid* and R. Ellḥanan of Corbeil" *Journal of Jewish Thought and Philosophy* 3 (1993):88.]

[67]The same manuscript of *Sefer ha-Manhig* (JTS) that refers to R. Ḥayyim *ha-Kohen* (*Sefer ha-Manhig*, 1:36)—about whom there is no evidence for pietistic practices (although cf. my "The ᶜ*Aliyah* of 'Three Hundred Rabbis' in 1211: Tosafist Attitudes Toward Settling in the Land of Israel," *JQR* 76 [1986]: 191–215)—as *ha-Qadosh* also refers to *ha-Qadosh* R. Yom Tov (1:51). If this is R. Yom Tov of Joigny, I have noted an element of *perishut* associated with him and a liturgical interpretation similar to one held by *Ḥasidei Ashkenaz*; see above, nn. 36, 55. Cf., however, the critical notes to *Sefer ha-Manhig*, loc. cit., and the editor's introduction, 36, where a different R. Yom Tov is indicated. At the same time, R. Ḥayyim *ha-Kohen* is identified in this manuscript as hailing from Allemagne. If the variants in the JTS manuscript are seen as possible scribal embellishments and ignored (as Raphael did in establishing the main text of *Sefer ha-Manhig*), what emerges is that all northern French tosafists called *ha-Qadosh* by *Sefer ha-Manhig* had a pietistic or mystical bent. Cf. Zimmer, ᶜ*Olam ke-Minhago Noheg*, 100, n. 165. On the use of the title *Qadosh* in medieval rabbinic texts to connote piety, saintliness, or ascetic tendencies (rather than martyrdom), see my "Rabbinic Figures in Castilian Kabbalistic Pseudepigraphy," 84–85, n. 30.

[68]R. Asher b. Yeḥiʾel writes simply that "many people in Ashkenaz" stood during Yom Kippur, based on a passage in *Pirqei de-R. Eliᶜezer*; see his commentary to *Yoma*, 8:24, and above, n. 48. The practice of immersing on the eve of Yom Kippur, which was

R. Abraham makes mention (once) of *Ḥasidei Provence*, who were particularly careful that from the time that the wheat for making *maẓot* was cut, no water come in contact with that wheat. In this context, *ḥasidut* merely connotes a special or added measure of observance.[69] Nonetheless, the uses of the term **חסידי צרפת** in *Sefer ha-Manhig* that we have encountered point to a loosely connected group of northern French pietists or scholars, if not an organized movement,[70] that may have had ideological connections with the German Pietists and perhaps tutorial links as well.

These findings lead us to consider several possibilities. Do examples of Pietist-like behavior in northern France and Germany at this time suggest that German Pietists had followers in tosafist circles—aside from those who resided in close geographic proximity—or was this pietism an aspect of the broader Ashkenazic rabbinic culture? To put it differently, thirteenth-century tosafists who displayed these types of behavior may have received them as traditions that originated in the pre-Crusade period, just as the German Pietists themselves did. Or they may have been introduced to them by the Pietists directly or through their works. The latter possibilities are viable even if the tosafists did not subscribe to the full range of Pietist teachings or to all of the embellishments and reworkings of the pre-Crusade concepts that the Pietists undertook.

---

also ascribed by Rabiah to **פרושים** (above, n. 32), is found in geonic sources; see *Seder R. ᶜAmram Gaon*, ed. Daniel Goldschmidt (Jerusalem, 1971), 160, and the literature cited there. Cf. R. Asher b. Yeḥiʾel, loc. cit.; *Arbaᶜah Turim, Oraḥ Ḥayyim*, 606; *Sefer Roqeaḥ*, sec. 218; and *Sefer Or Zaruaᶜ*, 2:277 (fol. 63a). The earliest record for the custom of standing all day on Yom Kippur may in fact be the passages in *Sefer ha-Manhig* and *Sefer Rabiah*. [The cryptic reference in *Maḥzor Vitry*, 389 (sec. 351), found in a pericope labeled **ת'** (=**תוספת**), may have originated with R. Abraham b. Nathan, who added material to this work. See *Sefer ha-Manhig*, editor's introduction, 35–37, and cf. *Maḥzor Vitry*, 382 (sec. 346).] Although R. Asher b. Yeḥiʾel writes that this practice was widespread in Ashkenaz, cf. *Sefer Or Zaruaᶜ* (above); *Tanya Rabbati* and *Sefer Minhag Tov* (above, nn. 33–34); and *Arbaᶜah Turim, O. Ḥ.*, 619, who notes explicitly that this was the custom only of *ʾanshei maᶜaseh be-Ashkenaz*. [R. David Abudarham, writing in Seville in 1340, indicates that only *yeḥidim* stood the entire day. See his *Abudarham ha-Shalem* (repr. Jerusalem, 1963), 291, and cf. *Beit Yosef*, loc. cit.]

[69] *Sefer ha-Manhig*, 2:460. A similar usage may be evident in a passage in which *Sefer ha-Manhig*, 1:59, delineates the portions of rabbinic texts that "*ḥakhamim ve-ḥasidim*" substituted for the *Qaddish, Barekhu*, and *Qedushah* prayers, when they prayed individually without a quorum.

[70] Cf. Zimmer, *ᶜOlam ke-Minhago Noheg*, 230, 233.

The Academy at Evreux, Rabbenu Yonah, and R. Moses of Coucy

Specific teachings and more general goals of the German Pietists do seem to have had an impact on tosafists in northern France during the thirteenth century.[71] As we have noted, a school of tosafists in northern France during the first half of the thirteenth century—the academy of the brothers R. Moses b. Shneʾur and R. Samuel b. Shneʾur of Evreux—appears to have internalized a number of Pietist teachings concerning talmudic study and interpretation.[72] It is helpful to summarize briefly some of the documentation for that phenomenon, in order to appreciate the extent to which Pietist doctrines and practices permeated tosafist circles.

Many of the *Tosafot* texts that emerged from this *beit midrash*—including the standard *Tosafot* to *Qiddushin, Nazir, ʿArakhin*, and *Temurah, Tosafot R. Samson of Sens* to *Sotah*, and the so-called *Tosafot Rashba* to *Menaḥot*—emphasize simple, straightforward interpretation of the talmudic text. These *Tosafot* also seek to clarify and explain Rashi's comments, often reproducing Rashi's comments in full, and they contain much less comparative dialectic than is normally found in *Tosafot* texts.[73] As Haym Soloveitchik and Israel Ta-Shma have demonstrated, the German Pietists were gravely concerned about the overuse of dialectic and the development of dialectical *ḥiddushim* by unqualified students. They wished to promote a talmudic studies that would direct the student more clearly in matters of *halakhah* and allow him to master the talmudic text at hand.[74] The unusual *Tosafot* just described would make a major contribution toward achieving this aim. It is therefore likely that the

---

[71]Many of the *leʿazim* in *SḤB* are French, and there is a (shortened) northern French version of *Sefer Ḥasidim* (called "*Sefer Ḥasidut*") in ms. Bodl. 875, which was copied in 1299 (=*SḤB* 1–152). See, e.g., Güdemann, *Ha-Torah veha-Ḥayyim*, 1:229–30; I. G. Marcus, "The Recensions and Structure of 'Sefer Ḥasidim,'" *PAAJR* 45 (1978):131–53; and Marcus's introduction to *Sefer Ḥasidim* [ms. Parma H 3280] (Jerusalem, 1985), 10. This development may indicate the presence of followers of *ḥasidut Ashkenaz* in northern France or it may simply reflect the diffusion and adaptation of *Sefer Ḥasidim* through western Europe. Cf. above, n. 2.

[72]See above, introduction, at n. 21.

[73]Urbach, *Baʿalei ha-Tosafot*, 1:455–56, 482–84, 2:632–33, 636, 655–57, 670–71. See also Avigdor Arieli's note in *ʿAlei Sefer* 16 (1989):149–50, and *ʿOlat Shelomoh* (Petah Tikva, 1989), 1:14–17.

[74]See Soloveitchik, "Three Themes," 339–52; Ta-Shma, "Mizvat Talmud Torah ki-Veʿayah Ḥevratit-Datit be-Sefer Ḥasidim," *Sefer Bar Ilan* 14–15 (1977):98–113. See also Marcus, *Piety and Society*, 102–5; my *Jewish Education and Society*, 86–91; and note, e.g., *SḤP* 801: ובזמן הזה שאין חכמה צריך לרב לפרש הכל. גם אם יכתוב פירושים יפרש הכל כדי שלא יהא יגיע לחשוב ויתבטל משאר דברי תורה.

brothers of Evreux composed these *Tosafot* under the influence of the educational critique of the German Pietists.[75]

This contention is buttressed by the fact that another interpretational strategy characteristic of the academy at Evreux also corresponds to a position of the German Pietists. The brothers of Evreux commented on virtually all the tractates in *Seder Qodashim* (as well as tractate *Sheqalim* in the Jerusalem Talmud), an area that many Ashkenazic talmudists understandably ignored. The German Pietists valued greatly the study of *Seder Qodashim* (as well as other "unpopular" tractates) precisely because it was being ignored in many circles.[76] Additionally, *Seder Qodashim* was the focus of a commentary compiled in eleventh-century Mainz.[77] The concern shown by the German Pietists for the study of *Seder Qodashim* may also be a reflection of their

---

[75]Urbach's suggestion, *Ba^calei ha-Tosafot*, 1:482–83, that these *Tosafot* were composed to compensate for the significant loss of talmudic texts following the Trial of the Talmud (by providing additional Rashi texts that included Rashi's citations from the Talmud, and by allowing students to grasp more easily the correct interpretation of the talmudic *sugya* at hand) is undercut by the fact that no tosafists in this period other than the brothers of Evreux reacted in this manner to the shortage of books. Cf. Baron, *A Social and Religious History of the Jews*, 9:65–71, who is skeptical about whether the shortage of volumes had a significant impact on talmudic study and, indeed, about the extent of the loss in western Europe.

[76]See *SḤP*, pars. 1 (p. 2), 1509, and cf. 765, 1495; and cf. R. Yonah's *Sefer ha-Yir[>]ah*, ed. Zilber, 64, sec. 248. Yaacov Sussmann, "Massoret Limmud u-Massoret Nosaḥ shel Talmud Yerushalmi," *Meḥqarim be-Sifrut Talmudit le-Regel Melot Shemonim Shanah le-Sha[>]ul Lieberman* (Jerusalem, 1983), 14, n. 11, maintains that a circle of thirteenth-century Spires scholars who were closely linked (and in most cases related) to the *Ḥasidei Ashkenaz* (e.g., R. Judah b. Qalonymus) attempted to stretch the scope of study from the "three orders" (*Mo^ced, Nashim, Neziqin*) to include *Qodashim, Talmud Yerushalmi*, and other relatively neglected areas of rabbinic literature, such as *[>]aggadah* and *tefillah*. Cf. Ta-Shma, "Miẓvat Talmud Torah," 105, n. 6. Sussmann also notes (34–35) that the German Pietists and their relatives and students were practically the only *rishonim* to produce commentaries on *Yerushalmi Sheqalim* (whose content is closely related to *Seder Qodashim*). There is a commentary to *Sheqalim* that Saul Lieberman attributed to a student of R. Samuel b. Shne[>]ur of Evreux; see *Sefer ha-Yovel li-Khevod Alexander Marx* (New York, 1950) [Hebrew section], 295. Both Urbach (*Ba^calei ha-Tosafot*, 1:405) and Sussmann (35) reject this identification and suggest that this commentary was authored by R. Eleazar of Worms or one of his circle. However, the relationship between the brothers of Evreux and the teachings of the German Pietists being reviewed here lends additional support to Lieberman's attribution. See also below, ch. 2, n. 61.

[77]See Grossman, *Ḥakhmei Ashskenaz ha-Rishonim*, 165–70.

deep-seated desire to return to or imitate the curriculum of the pre-Crusade period.[78]

R. Moses of Evreux issued a statement on achieving proper *kavvanah* in prayer that could have been composed by a German Pietist: "A person must remove all extraneous thoughts from his heart during prayer and direct his heart only to the source. He must consider every word before he expresses it. If he does this in every instance and does not sin, his prayers will be pure and acceptable before the Almighty."[79] This statement is almost identical to a formulation at the end of a text attributed to R. Moses that is recorded in both *Sefer Kol Bo* and *Sefer Orḥot Ḥayyim*. In *Sefer Kol Bo*, the text is entitled **דברים המביאים לידי יראת החטא אשר כתב הר"מ מאיור"א**.[80]

This text contains a number of additional parallels to passages in *Sefer Ḥasidim*. Included are the avoidance of haughty and other sinful behavior

---

[78]See also above, introduction, n. 12. On *ḥumra* at Evreux, see below, n. 175, and ch. 2, n. 65.

[79]*Haggahot Rabbenu Pereẓ* to R. Isaac of Corbeil, *Sefer Miẓvot Qatan*, precept 11, n. 3 (the precept is headed *le-hitpallel be-kavvanah*), and cf. below, n. 153; Urbach, *Ba*ʿ*alei ha-Tosafot*, 1:480–81; *SHP*, sec. 11 (**כשיתפלל האדם צריך שיעמוד ביראה... שלא ירוץ בתפלה כאלו שמח אם היה כבר מסיים אלא בכל תיבה ימשוך לתת בלבו כוונה בכל מה שמוציא מפיו**), 440–43, 1585, 1605; and Soloveitchik, "Three Themes," 333–34. The gloss of R. Pereẓ containing the statement of R. Moses of Evreux appears at a point where R. Eleazar of Worms is cited by *Sefer Miẓvot Qatan* on the importance of maintaining appropriate *kavvanah* throughout the blessings of the ʿ*Amidah* prayer: **מי שמתכוין בשאלתו ולא יכוין בשבחו של הקב"ה מחייב את עצמו** (cf. *SHP* 1577–79, 393, and R. Abraham Oppenheim, *Eshel Avraham* to *Shulḥan* ʿ*Arukh, Oraḥ Ḥayyim*, sec. 97); see below, n. 152. A statement by R. Samuel of Evreux on *kavvanah* is recorded by Rabbenu Perez in a gloss to *Semaq*, precept 97.

[80]See *Sefer Kol Bo*, sec. 66 (end), fol. 32a; R. Aharon *ha-Kohen of Lunel*, *Orḥot Ḥayyim* (Florence, 1750), vol. 1, 103a (at the end of a section entitled ʿ*inyanim aḥerim bi-teshuvah*); and cf. Tuvia Preschel, "Iggeret she-Yuhsah be-Taʿut la-Ramban," *Talpiyyot* 8 (1961):49–53. R. Samuel of Evreux was called *he-Ḥasid* by his student, R. Yedidyah b. Israel (who may have been a teacher of R. Judah *he-Ḥasid*'s son R. Zal[t]man). See *Shitah* ʿ*al Mo*ʿ*ed Qatan le-Talmido shel R. Yeḥiel mi-Paris*, ed. M. Zaks (Jerusalem, 1937), 2:113, and cf. Urbach, *Ba*ʿ*alei ha-Tosafot*, 2:569, n. 25. R. Samuel was also the teacher of R. Isaac of Corbeil, who bore the title *ḥasid* (see Urbach, 2:572–73) and had other affinities with the German Pietists, and of R. Meir of Rothenburg, who was strongly influenced by the Pietists; see below regarding both of these scholars. Moshe Hershler, in his edition of *Siddur R. Shelomoh mi-Germaiza ve-Siddur Ḥasidei Ashkenaz* (Jerusalem, 1972), 184, identified the R. Samuel who found a liturgical interpretation "written in the hand of R. Judah the Pious" as R. Samuel of Evreux. Cf. Hershler, 88. It is likely, however, that this scholar was R. Samuel Bamberg. Cf. Hershler, 119, 136, 223, 296; and below, ch. 2, n. 15.

through the cultivation of meekness toward others and by remembering the Divine Presence at all times, and the acquisition of knowledge about how to fulfill the law as the primary goal of Torah study.[81] Moreover, it is appended in *Sefer Kol Bo* to a treatise by R. Eleazar of Worms entitled *Sefer Moreh Ḥatta'im/ Sefer ha-Kapparot*.

Both R. Moses and R. Samuel of Evreux exhibited forms of ascetic behavior. *Orḥot Ḥayyim* and *Kol Bo* list the five prohibitions on the ninth of Av which are based, in part, on the restrictions that a mourner has during the *shivʿah* period. On *Tishʿah be-Av*, however, it was agreed that one need not "turn over the bed" and sleep on the floor. "But R. Samuel of Evreux was personally strict and slept on the floor."[82] R. Isaac b. Joseph (or R. Pereẓ b. Elijah) of Corbeil ruled that one should not enjoy the physical pleasures of the world during the week any more than he needs to sustain his body. He may do so in public, however, to avoid ridicule. "And R. Moses [of Evreux] would cut his meat into very fine pieces in order not to be able to savor the taste of the meat."[83]

The affinities between the academy at Evreux and *ḥasidut Ashkenaz* help to resolve a long-standing question of authorship. Several works by Rabbenu Yonah of Gerona bear the unmistakable influence of the German Pietists. Notable among these is *Sefer ha-Yir'ah*, a veritable program of pietistic behavior

---

[81]Cf., e.g., *SHP*, sec. 754; *SHB*, sec. 53; Rabbenu Yonah, *Sefer ha-Yir'ah*, 35, sec. 105; Soloveitchik, "Three Themes," 329, 344; Galinsky, "Rabbenu Mosheh mi-Coucy ke-Ḥasid, Darshan u-Folmosan," 40–43, 70–71.

[82]See *Sefer Orḥot Ḥayyim, Hilkhot Tishʿah be-Av*, sec. 13 (end), fol. 95a, *Kol Bo*, sec. 62, fol. 27a. Cf. Zimmer, *ʿOlam ke-Minhago Noheg*, 194. A colleague and associate of the brothers of Evreux, R. Netan'el *ha-Qadosh* of Chinon, fasted during the daytime when he sat *shivʿah*; see *Kol Bo*, sec. 114, fol. 88b, and below, ch. 3, n. 104.

[83]See S. Sha'anan, "Pisqei Rabbenu Pereẓ va-Aḥerim be-ʿInyanei Oraḥ Ḥayyim," *Moriah* 17:9–10 (1991):12, sec. 15, and cf. above, n. 3. These *pesaqim* were published by Sha'anan from ms. Paris 407, fols. 236c–237a. The first group of *pesaqim* in this manuscript match other *pesaqim* from R. Pereẓ. The notion of not enjoying the pleasures of this world and the description of R. Moses' practice are found, however, on fol. 236d, after the name of R. Isaac (of Corbeil) is mentioned. Moreover, these passages appear in ms. Cambr. Add. 3127 (fol. 165v), in a section of *pesaqim* attributed to R. Isaac of Corbeil, in which R. Isaac is referred to as *ha-qadosh* and in which other expressions of self-denial are found (fol. 166r). On these manuscripts, see Simcha Emanuel, "Sifrei Halakhah Avudim shel Baʿalei ha-Tosafot" (Ph.D. diss., Hebrew University, 1993), 238–40. Both R. Isaac of Corbeil and R. Pereẓ of Corbeil were students at Evreux. See Urbach, *Baʿalei ha-Tosafot*, 2:571, 576; *Tosafot Rabbenu Pereẓ ʿal Massekhet Sukkah*, ed. Shemayah Greenbaum (Jerusalem, 1972) [appended to his *Siʿata di-Shemaya*], editor's introduction, 195–96; and below, nn. 168, 177, and ch. 2, n. 69.

that has many parallels to passages in *Sefer Ḥasidim* but does not seem to reflect the Spanish milieu. Despite these parallels, a number of scholars have questioned and even rejected the attribution of this work to Rabbenu Yonah.[84] In fact, however, Rabbenu Yonah's authorship may be retained, for he studied at Evreux with both R. Moses and R. Samuel, and it was there that he came into contact with the teachings of *Ḥasidei Ashkenaz*. Indeed, the only medieval rabbinic scholar mentioned by name in *Sefer ha-Yir'ah* is R. Samuel b. Shne'ur, who is referred to as the author's teacher.[85]

---

[84]See Benjamin Richler, "Al Kitvei ha-Yad shel Sefer ha-Yir'ah ha-Meyuḥas le-Rabbenu Yonah Gerondi," *ʿAlei Sefer* 8 (1980):51–59, and the literature cited in nn. 1–2; Yehiel Zilber, "Sefer ha-Yir'ah le-Rabbenu Yonah Gerondi he-Ḥasid," *Moriah* 10:9–10 (1981):94–96; and cf. Galinsky, "Rabbenu Mosheh mi-Coucy ke-Ḥasid," 123, n. 21; and above, nn. 59, 76. On the prohibition of gazing at women in R. Yonah's writings and in *Sefer Ḥasidim*, cf. A. T. Shrock, *Rabbi Jonah b. Abraham of Gerona* (London, 1946), 161; Soloveitchik, "Three Themes," 329; and below, n. 178.

The work is attributed in some manuscripts to R. Yehudah *he-Ḥasid* and in others to a R. Yiẓḥaq *Ḥasid*. In three places in R. Aharon *ha-Kohen* of Lunel's *Orḥot Ḥayyim* (*hilkhot ẓiẓit*, sec. 23 [fol. 3b], *hilkhot qeri'at shema*, sec. 18 [fol. 12b], and *hilkhot tefillah*, sec. 16 [fol. 14a]), material from *Sefer ha-Yir'ah* is attributed to ר״י חסיד. Richler has suggested, on the basis of a copyist's mistaken assumption and the prologue to *Orḥot Ḥayyim*, that this refers not to R. Yehudah *he-Ḥasid* but to R. Yiẓḥaq (*Ḥasid*) of Corbeil, author of the *Semaq*. While I agree that R. Aharon *ha-Kohen* may not have considered Rabbenu Yonah to be ר״י חסיד, author of *Sefer ha-Yir'ah* [Rabbenu Yonah is cited in *Orḥot Ḥayyim* by name more than ten times, although *Orḥot Ḥayyim* attributes a passage from *Sefer ha-Yir'ah* to Rabbenu Yonah on one occasion (see the next note)], it is highly unlikely that he equated ר״י חסיד with R. Isaac of Corbeil. R. Isaac is cited with great frequency throughout *Orḥot Ḥayyim*, always as ר״י (מ)קורביל. Moreover, there are two sections in *Orḥot Ḥayyim* where ר״י חסיד and ר״י קורביל are both listed (separately) as espousing the same position [*hilkhot tefillah*, sec. 16 (fol. 14a) and sec. 33 (fol. 15b)], and another place in which ר״י חסיד and ר״י קורביל are mentioned in very close proximity (*hilkhot ẓiẓit*, secs. 21, 23–24). [R. Yehudah *he–Ḥasid* is mentioned once by name, in *hilkhot ʿerev Yom ha-Kippurim*, sec. 6 (fol. 103b).] For further discussion of this problem and its ramifications, see my "Rabbinic Figures in Castilian Kabbalistic Pseudepigraphy: R. Yehudah *he-Ḥasid* and R. Elḥanan of Corbeil," *Journal of Jewish Thought and Philosophy* 3 (1993): 90–95.

[85]*Sefer ha-Yir'ah*, 16, sec. 43: ומפי מורי הרב ר׳ שמואל ב״ר שניאור שמעתי דאין צריך לברך משום משמוש אלא כשהן [התפילין] נעקרין ממקומן והוא מחזירן למקומן. Richler notes that R. Samuel's name is included in only five non-Ashkenazic, relatively late manuscripts from among the more than forty extant manuscripts, suggesting a later addition to the text. *Sefer Orḥot Ḥayyim*, however, which predates virtually all the extant manuscripts, records this formulation in the name of Rabbenu Yonah (*hilkhot tefillin*, sec. 4 [fol. 7a], citing his teacher R. Samuel), thus confirming, somewhat ironically, Rabbenu Yonah's authorship of *Sefer ha-Yir'ah*. See also R. Yom Tov b. Abraham Ishvilli

Sefer ha-Yir'ah focuses largely on piety and prayer and on modesty in personal comportment—areas for which there is ample evidence that the brothers of Evreux took their cue from the German Pietists.[86] Close parallels in phrasing as well as content between *Sefer ha-Yir'ah* and R. Moses of Evreux's treatise, *Devarim ha-Mevi'im Lidei Yir'at ha-Ḥet*, referred to above, are found in passages that stress the need to eliminate haughtiness and replace this tendency with constant striving for modesty and humility. The demands of extreme personal humility common to both works include not walking at one's fullest height or stature, not looking directly into the face of another, and the need to always remember that every thought a person has and every act he performs is done before the Almighty and must be for the sake of Heaven.[87] Moreover, a significant number of manuscript copyists transcribed *Sefer ha-Yir'ah* (which

---

[Ritba, c. 1300, recorded by R. Yosef Ḥaviva, *Nimmuqei Yosef, Hilkhot Ẓiẓit*, in the standard editions of the Babylonian Talmud following tractate *Menaḥot*, fol. 12a], who cites this position as "a comment of R. Yonah in the name of R. Mosheh b. Shne'ur of Evreux." (The names of the brothers of Evreux are associated with R. Yonah interchangeably). As Ta-Shma notes in a postscript to his "Ḥasidut Ashkenaz bi-Sefarad," (above, n. 50), 193, *Ḥiddushei ha-Ritba* (*Rosh ha-Shanah*, 34a) cites a passage from "*Sefer ha-Yir'ah le-Rabbenu Yonah*," removing any doubt concerning R. Yonah's authorship.

[86]See above, nn. 78–80. A student of R. Moses of Evreux compiled *Sefer ᶜal ha-Kol*, an unusual handbook of legal decisions and customs regarding prayer, including discussions about the correct *nosaḥ ha-tefillah*. R. Moses' son (and perhaps R. Moses himself) composed a *siddur*, and R. Isaac, a lesser known brother of R. Moses, wrote *piyyutim*. See Urbach, *Baᶜalei ha-Tosafot*, 1:485; J. N. Epstein, "Al ha-Kol," *Sinai* 94 (1984):123–36 [=Epstein's *Meḥqarim be-Sifrut ha-Talmud u-Vileshonot Shemiyyot*, ed. E. Z. Melammed, vol. 2 (Jerusalem, 1988), 776–89]; and Henri Gross, *Gallia Judaica* (Paris, 1897), 40–41.

[87]See *Sefer ha-Yir'ah*, secs. 4–7, 14, 105–6, 128, 146. R. Moses' treatise is followed in *Sefer Kol Bo* (sec. 67) by a section entitled *Seder Darkhei Teshuvah* that is actually R. Yonah's *(Ye-)Sod ha-Teshuvah*. The lengthier treatment in *Sefer ha-Yir'ah* counsels that intense focus on these issues is to begin from the time one awakens and should continue throughout the day at every opportunity. Cf. the "*seder ha-yom*" description attributed by Israel Ta-Shma, "Quntresei 'Sodot ha-Tefillah' le-R. Yehudah he-Ḥasid," *Tarbiz* 65 (1996):75–76, to Rabbenu Yonah, and cf. Emanuel, "Ha-Polmos ᶜal Nosaḥ ha-Tefillah shel Ḥasidei Ashkenaz," n. 69. For a similarity between *Sefer Ḥasidim* and *Sefer ha-Yir'ah* with regard to the proper way for a scribe to copy Hebrew works and commentaries, see Malachi Beit-Arié, "Paleographic Identification of Hebrew Mss.: Methodology and Practice," *Jewish Art* 12–13 (1986–87): 17, n. 7, and idem, "Ideal Versus Reality: Scribal Prescriptions in *Sefer Ḥasidim* and Contemporary Scribal Practices in Franco-German Manuscripts," *Rashi, 1040–1990: Hommage à Ephraim Urbach*, ed. Gabrielle Sed-Rajna (Paris, 1993), 562–63.

was also entitled *Sefer Ḥayyei ʿOlam*) together with works of the German Pietists.[88] Similarly, Rabbenu Yonah's authorship of *Shaʿarei ʿAvodah*—which cites midrashim and *piyyutim* that appear to have been known only in Ashkenaz (and, in some cases, that were quoted almost exclusively in works by German Pietists)—may also be confirmed.[89]

---

[88]Bodl. 875 (completed in Ashkenaz in 1299) contains *ʿAmmudei Golah (Semaq)* followed by *Ḥayyei ʿOlam* and a version of *Sefer Ḥasidim* with predominantly French glosses. Bodl. 1098 (Ashkenaz, c. 1290) and Breslau [*Signatur*] 255 also juxtapose *Sefer Ḥasidut/Ḥasidim* and *Sefer Ḥayyei ʿOlam/Sod ha-Teshuvah*. [The Breslau ms., which is no longer extant—apparently having been lost in the Holocaust—is listed and described as no. 248 in *Catalogue of the Hebrew Manuscripts in the Library of the Juedisch-Theologisches Seminar in Breslau*, ed. D. S. Loewinger and B. D. Weinryb (Wiesbaden, 1965^2), 175–76; cf. the editors' foreword, vii–ix. In this ms., Rabbenu Yonah's works are followed by a later collection of *sifrut de-Vei Rashi* that cites R. Judah *he-Ḥasid* among others, and was possibly compiled by R. Isaiah di Trani. See E. E. Urbach, "Liqqutim mi-Sifrei de-Vei Rashi," *Sefer Rashi* (Jerusalem, 1956), 322–25, and cf. Israel Ta-Shma, "Sefer Shibbolei ha-Leqet u-Khefelav,'" *Italia* 11 (1995): 46–47]. Bodl. 2343 and 1114 (Ashkenaz, c. 1410) and Parma 3175 (De Rossi 166) group *Sefer ha-Yirʾah/Sefer Ḥayyei ʿOlam* with *Sod ha-Teshuvah* and (R. Judah *he-Ḥasid's*) *Shir ha-Yiḥud*. (These manuscripts attribute all three texts to R. Yiẓḥaq *ḥasid*. See above, n. 84.) [On the attribution of *Shir ha-Yiḥud* to R. Judah *he-Ḥasid*, or another of the *Ḥasidei Ashkenaz*, see Joseph Dan's introduction to the Jewish National and University Library's edition of *Shirei Yiḥud* (Jerusalem, 1981), 7–15. Cf. below, ch. 3, n. 110. Note that the version of *Sod ha-Teshuvah* found in the margins of ms. Cambr. Add. 377, fols. 105v–107r, is attributed to R. Eliezer (*sic.*) of Worms.] Bodl. 884 (Ashkenaz 1384) contains *Semaq*, the testament (*ẓavaʾah*) of R. Judah *he-Ḥasid*, and a brief section of *tiqqun shetarot*, followed by *Sefer Ḥayyei ʿOlam* and *Sod ha-Teshuvah*, which was also written by Rabbenu Yonah; see Shrock, *Rabbi Jonah b. Abraham of Gerona*, 69–79. The first part of Bodl. 2274 (Ashkenaz, c.1390) contains *Ḥayyei ʿOlam*, R. Eleazar of Worms's *Hilkhot Teshuvah*, a prayer commentary attributed to Naḥmanides but in fact similar to tracts of *ḥasidut Ashkenaz*, citing R. Judah *he-Ḥasid*, R. Saʿadyah Gaon, and R. Samuel of Bamberg; a brief eschatological text and one on Holy Names; and *Sheʾelot u-Teshuvot le-R. Yaʿaqov of Marvège*, attributed here to Rabbenu Jacob Tam instead. Ms. Casanatense 117 (fourteenth century) juxtaposes R. Jacob of Marvège's *Teshuvot min ha-Shamayim, Sefer Ḥayyei ʿOlam*, and R. Eleazar of Worms's *Moreh Ḥattaʾim*. (*Semaq* precedes this group of texts in fairly close proximity). Cambr. Add. 2580 (1397) contains *Semaq, Sefer ha-Yirʾah*, and R. Eleazar of Worms's *Moreh Ḥattaʾim*. See also Cambr. Add. 3127, which contains *Sefer Ḥayyei ʿOlam* followed by *Semaq* and several Pietist works, including *sodot ha-tefillah* (see the next note) and *Ẓavaʾat R. Yehudah he-Ḥasid*.

[89]See Norman Bronznick, "Baʿaluto shel R. Yonah Gerondi ʿal Sefer Shaʿarei ha-ʿAvodah ha-Nidpas," *Ha-Darom* 28 (1969):238–42. Cf. Y. S. Zachter, "Kavvanat Qeriʾat Shema," *Yeshurun* 2 (1996):32, n. 19, and M. M. Kasher, *Shema Yisraʾel* (Jerusalem, 1980), 253–55. Israel Ta-Shma has raised the possibility that R. Yonah was the editor of a collection of *sodot ha-tefillah* of *Ḥasidei Ashkenaz* (with some additional

Rabbenu Yonah's approach and attitudes toward asceticism, especially as expressed in his *Sefer ha-Yir'ah* and *Sod ha-Teshuvah*, are strikingly similar to those of *Sefer Ḥasidim*. He recommends a regular regimen of fasting and encourages, as a form of asceticism, the diminution of pleasures associated with eating.[90] To be sure, a passage in *Shaʿarei Teshuvah* condemns excessive fasting as an ascetic impulse and especially as a means of grieving.[91] But *Sefer Ḥasidim*, no less than Rabbenu Yonah, expresses concern about excess and abuses or over zealousness in fasting.[92] Moreover, other passages in *Shaʿarei*

Provençal material) that are characterized (inaccurately) in several manuscripts as the *sodot* of Ramban. See Ta-Shma, "Quntresei 'Sodot ha-Tefillah' le-R. Yehudah he-Ḥasid," *Tarbiz* 65 (1996)73–77 (and idem, *Ha-Nigleh shebe-Nistar*, 50–52); but cf. Emanuel, "Ha-Polmos ʿal Nosaḥ ha-Tefillah shel Ḥasidei Ashkenaz," (above, n. 39), nn. 68–71; below, ch. 3, nn. 110, 118; and ch. 5, nn. 47, 74.

[90]See *Sefer ha-Yir'ah le-Rabbenu Yonah*, ed. Zilber, 73, sec. 328: One day a month or more, a person should undertake a fast or at least eat only bread and water. That day should be a day of weeping and introspection about specific sins or about how the person has incurred great liability before the Master of the Universe. See also *Sefer ha-Yir'ah*, 2–3, secs. 4–10; the ms. version of *Sefer Ḥayyei ʿOlam* cited by Margoliot in his notes to *SHB* 12 (*Meqor Ḥesed*, n. 1); and cf. Shokek, *Ha-Teshuvah be-Sifrut ha-Musar ha-ʿIvrit*, 77–88. This formulation is similar to a passage in Rabbenu Yonah's *(Ye-)Sod ha-Teshuvah*: A person should continue to afflict himself over prior sins that he has already overcome. If a person is not strong enough to withstand harsh afflictions and fasts, he should at least resist his desires. He should not allow his desires to be fulfilled regarding food and drink. As Rabad said, a significant means of restraint concerns the withholding of food. This does not mean a person should give up meat and wine entirely. Rather, when a person eats and still has the desire to eat more, he should abstain in honor of the Creator and not satiate fully his desires. This behavior will keep a person from sin and remind him of the precept to love the Creator more effectively than fasting once a week. Each day, as he eats and drinks, he should deny his desires in honor of his Creator. [On Rabad and asceticism, see above, n. 6.]

[91]See *Shaʿarei Teshuvah*, 3:82, and cf. Saperstein, "Christians and Christianity in the Sermons of Jacob Anatoli," (above, n. 55). Rabbenu Pereẓ, in a gloss to *Sefer Miẓvot Qatan*, sec. 175, cites a version of this formulation in the name of Rabbenu Yonah: While it is inappropriate to tear one's clothing more than is required or destroy one's property as a sign of mourning over a death, and while it is also inappropriate to abuse or weaken one's body, e.g., by fasting, as a reaction to one's troubles or to mourn a loss, one who grieves and fasts for his sins is considered commendable. It should also be noted that *Shaʿarei Teshuvah* appears to represent the Spanish phase of R. Yonah's ethical writings. See Ta-Shma, "Ḥasidut Ashkenaz bi-Sefarad," 181–88; and Shokek in the preceding note.

[92]On *Sefer Ḥasidim* and asceticism, see above, at the beginning of this chapter, esp. nn. 2–3. For a parallel between *Sefer ha-Yir'ah* and a pietistic practice of R. Eleazar of Worms, see *Sefer ha-Yir'ah*, 72, sec. 309, and cf. Elliot Ginsburg, *The Sabbath in the Classical Kabbalah* (Albany, 1989), 246, n. 21.

Teshuvah stress the importance of refraining from pleasure and obliterating lustful desires.[93]

The process by which Pietist teachings were transmitted to these talmudists in northern France remains unclear. There was no direct contact between the brothers of Evreux and R. Judah *he-Ḥasid* or R. Eleazar of Worms. Nor is there evidence that the academy of Evreux received personal instruction from any other associates of *Ḥasidei Ashkenaz*.[94] Indeed, there is the possibility of parallel development rather than influence, although the number and nature of the affinities certainly point to influence. The doctrines of the Pietists probably reached Evreux through literary channels. It is possible that the brothers of Evreux became aware of and adopted some of the basic values and formulations of the Pietists from the exoteric literary sources that may have been available to them. Perhaps they shared the concerns of R. Judah *he-Ḥasid* and R. Eleazar of Worms concerning the disappearance of the religious values

---

[93]In several passages in *Shaᶜarei Teshuvah*, R. Jonah recommends **הצער במעשה**, **שבירת התאוה**, and **מניעת נפשו מן התענוגים**. See H. J. Zimmels, *Ashkenazim and Sephardim* (London, 1958), 241, nn. 4–5 [the final reference to *Shaᶜarei Teshuvah* in n. 5 should be to 4:12], and cf. 242, at n. 5. Similarly, R. Jonah discusses the virtues of forgoing permitted pleasures (*perishut*) in his Commentary to *Avot*. See *Perushei Rabbenu Yonah me-Gerondi ᶜal Massekhet Avot*, ed. M. S. Kasher (Jerusalem, 1969), 7 (1:5), 34–35 (2:16), 48–49 (3:17), 53 (3:21). See also the commentary of *Talmidei Rabbenu Yonah* to *Berakhot* at the beginning of ch. 5 (30b–31a). This passage, citing Rabbenu Yonah, describes the intense *kavvanah* necessary during prayer, which will lead to a total separation of the pure spirit from all physical desires and pleasures. Note the similar notion found in *Tur, O. Ḥ.*, sec. 98 (referring to the German Pietists; see above, n. 35): **וכן היו עושין חסידים ואנשי מעשה שהיו מתבודדים ומכוונין בתפלתם עד שהיו מגיעין להתפשטות הגשמיות ולהתגברות רוח השכלית עד שהיו מגיעים קרוב למעלת הנבואה**. As a result, if an extraneous thought entered the mind of the *ḥasid* during prayer, he would be silent until it passed. See also *SḤP* 451, and *SḤB* 773; *Semaq*, sec. 11, and below, nn. 150, 153; *Beit Yosef* and *Darkhei Moshe* to *Tur*, loc. cit. (ר"י in the *Darkhei Mosheh* passage is ר' יונה); A. J. Heschel, "ᶜAl Ruaḥ ha-Qodesh Bimei ha-Benayim," *Sefer ha-Yovel li-Khevod Alexander Marx* (New York, 1950) [Hebrew section], 186–87; Daniel Abrams, "From Germany to Spain: Numerology as a Mystical Technique," *JJS* 47 (1996):93; and Elliot Wolfson, "Sacred Space and Mental Iconography," *Ki Barukh Hu*, ed. Robert Chazan et al. (Winona Lake, 1999), 602–5.

[94]Small esoteric circles connected to the main branch of the German Pietists, such as the *Ḥug ha-Keruv ha-Meyuḥad*, flourished in northern France (see above, n. 65). But there is no evidence that the brothers of Evreux were involved in the esoteric studies pursued by *Ḥasidei Ashkenaz*, nor is there any specific evidence that members of the *Ḥug ha-Keruv ha-Meyuḥad* practiced exoteric forms of pietism. For a possible conduit between R. Eleazar of Worms' circle and Evreux (a R. Samuel b. Judah), suggested only on the basis of a later medieval Jewish chronicle, see the introduction, n. 21.

of old Ashkenaz in the face of the domination of their northern French tosafist colleagues. But it must also be noted that the academy of Evreux was also characterized by a fair degree of openness. The brothers of Evreux produced *Tosafot* texts that adhered to the classic style of tosafist dialectic,[95] and they allowed younger students to decide matters of religious law and open their own study halls in ways that would seem antithetical to the teachings of *ḥasidut Ashkenaz*.[96] Although the voice of German Pietism, or at least its spirit, appears to have called out to the study hall at Evreux, Pietist teachings were not followed blindly or even completely.

Similar problems of classification and transmission arise with respect to R. Moses b. Jacob of Coucy, a slightly older contemporary of the brothers of Evreux.[97] As a devoted student of R. Judah Sir Leon, R. Moses was a direct heir of the leading tosafists of the twelfth century—Rabbenu Tam and Ri—and some of his *Tosafot* have survived.[98] But R. Moses is best known for two related activities that were not undertaken by these earlier tosafists. He composed a full-fledged halakhic code, *Sefer Mizvot Gadol* (*Semag*). And he preached in Ashkenazic locales, but especially in Spain, about precepts that were being neglected out of confusion, ignorance, or lack of interest.[99] Indeed, R. Moses indicates that his preaching experiences led him, in part, to compose *Semag*.[100]

The image of *Ḥasidei Ashkenaz* can be seen in both these enterprises. As Israel Ta-Shma has noted, the spate of halakhic works spawned by tosafists in the last part of the twelfth century and throughout the first half of the thirteenth century—works such as R. Eleazar of Metz's *Sefer Yereʾim*; R. Barukh b. Isaac of Worms's *Sefer ha-Terumah; Sefer ha-Rabiah*; R. Eleazar of Worms's *Sefer Roqeaḥ*; the (lost) *Sefer ha-Ḥokhmah* of R. Barukh b. Samuel of Mainz;

---

[95]See Ta-Shma, "Ḥasidut Ashkenaz bi-Sefarad," 167–68; and see now *Tosafot Maharam ve-Rabbenu Perez ʿal Masskehet Yevamot*, ed. Hillel Porush (Jerusalem, 1991), 15; *Tosafot Yeshanim ha-Shalem ʿal Masseket Yevamot*, ed. A. Shoham (Jerusalem, 1992), 24–26.

[96]See my "Rabbinic Authority and the Right to Open an Academy in Medieval Ashkenaz," *Michael* 12 (1991): 233–50.

[97]See, e.g., *Pisqei R. Yeḥiel mi-Paris*, ed. E. D. Pines (Jerusalem, 1973), editor's introduction, 9–10.

[98]Urbach, *Baʿalei ha-Tosafot*, 1:477–78.

[99]On the geographic areas in which R. Moses preached, see my "Rabbinic Attitudes Toward Nonobservance in the Medieval Period," *Jewish Tradition and the Nontraditional Jew*, ed. Schachter, 9–10, n. 16, and 24–25, n. 62.

[100]See *Semaq*, introduction, and Judah Galinsky, "Qum ʿAseh Sefer Torah mi-Shenei Ḥalaqim, Le-Birur Kavvanat R. Mosheh mi-Coucy bi-Khetivat ha-Semag," *Ha-Maʿayan* 35 (1994):23–31.

R. Isaac b. Moses of Vienna's *Sefer Or Zaruaᶜ*; and R. Moses of Coucy's *Sefer Miẓvot Gadol*—all conform to the recommendation of *Sefer Ḥasidim* that practical *halakhah* and other ethical and religious dimensions of Torah study be given preference over the more intellectualized pursuit of dialectical *ḥiddushim.*[101] Even those authors who studied with northern French tosafists and focused on the dialectical initiatives of Rabbenu Tam and Ri[102] summarized and correlated this material in brief halakhic terms, thereby minimizing the dialectical extensions and nomenclature.

To be sure, there may have been other factors that led to the composition of these codes. The revolutionary scope and achievements of twelfth-century tosafist dialectic virtually demanded an effort at summation (especially in view of the worsening conditions for Jews in Christian Europe),[103] in addition to the influence of Sefardic codes and halakhic methodology on Ashkenaz—a process that was already underway by the second quarter of the thirteenth century.[104] Nonetheless, the fact that R. Moses of Coucy and others who had connections with *ḥasidut Ashkenaz*—such as R. Eliezer of Metz[105] and R. Isaac *Or Zaruaᶜ*[106]—composed these codes points to a degree of Pietist influence.

---

[101]See Ta-Shma, "Miẓvat Talmud Torah," 104–6, and my *Jewish Education and Society* (above, n. 74); and see also Ta-Shma, "Qavvim le-Ofiyyah shel Sifrut ha-Halakhah be-Ashkenaz ba-Meʾot ha-Yod Gimmel/Yod Daled," *ᶜAlei Sefer* 4 (1977):20–41.

[102]See Soloveitchik, "Three Themes," 348–49; idem, "Religious Law and Change: The Medieval Ashkenazic Example," *AJS Review* 12 (1987):216–17; idem, *Halakhah, Kalkalah ve-Dimmui ᶜAẓmi* (Jerusalem, 1985), 82–84. As noted by Soloveitchik, R. Eleazar of Worms's *Sefer Roqeaḥ* does not generally take into account new developments of the tosafist period. See also Urbach, *Baᶜalei ha-Tosafot*, 1:397–401, and below, ch. 2, n. 61.

[103]See the formulation of Arnold Toynbee, cited and applied to medieval halakhic literature by Isadore Twersky, *Introduction to the Code of Maimonides* (New Haven, 1980), 72; Soloveitchik, "Rabad of Posquières: A Programmatic Essay," *Peraqim be-Toledot ha-Ḥevrah ha-Yehudit*, ed. E. Etkes and Y. Salmon (Jerusalem, 1980) [English section], 16; idem, "Three Themes," 339.

[104]See, e.g., Avraham Grossman, "Ha-Qesharim Bein Yahadut Sefarad le-Yahadut Ashkenaz Bimei ha-Benayim," *Moreshet Sefarad*, ed. Haim Beinart (Jerusalem, 1992), 179–85, and Septimus, *Hispano-Jewish Culture in Transition*, 46–51, 59–60.

[105]See Urbach, *Baᶜalei ha-Tosafot*, 1:160–61. Cf. Galinsky, "R. Mosheh mi-Coucy ke-Hasid," (above, n. 2), 10–12. In addition to the connections discussed by Urbach, which include the fact that R. Eliezer was a teacher of R. Eleazar of Worms, the introduction to *Sefer Yereʾim* (whose very title bespeaks an inclination toward pietism) adumbrates, in briefer and somewhat milder fashion, the critique leveled by *Sefer Ḥasidim* against the unchecked use of dialectic (*pilpul ha-qushyot*), which can lead to the

Israel Ta-Shma has also emphasized the decidedly German provenance of this wave of codification, which extended the model established by R. Eliezer b. Nathan of Mainz (in his *Sefer Raban*). R Moses of Coucy, who hailed from northern France, would appear, at first blush, to be outside this schema. And yet, other affinities or connections between R. Moses of Coucy and *ḥasidut Ashkenaz* have been identified. Jacob Katz linked the approach taken by R. Moses of Coucy in preaching and writing about Jewish-Gentile relations to *ḥasidut Ashkenaz*. Like *Sefer Ḥasidim*, R. Moses employed moral considerations beyond the letter of talmudic law, ruling more stringently than other tosafists on certain forms of Jewish-Gentile contact and urging his fellow Jews to espouse a high standard of moral perfection in order to justify their redemption, even in the eyes of the Gentiles.[107]

There are also several significant similarities between R. Moses and R. Yonah of Gerona that lead back to *Ḥasidei Ashkenaz*. Unique among leading medieval talmudists, both men publicly preached *derashot* and offered admonition on similar issues, utilizing similar styles. Indeed, Ta-Shma has identified and published a fragmentary letter and public sermon that he concludes were composed by either R. Moses of Coucy or R. Yonah of

---

neglect of *mizvot* and the absence of *yir*ʾ*at ha-Shem*. Cf. Urbach, 1:26, and below, n. 171. See below, ch. 4, n. 19–21, for pronounced similarities between formulations in *Sefer Yere*ʾ*im* and *Sefer Ḥasidim* regarding the permissibility of communication with souls after they have departed, and other mystical issues. For additional pietistic affinities, see Zimmer, ʿ*Olam ke-Minhago Noheg*, 281, n. 2 (and above, n. 36); idem, "Tenuḥot u-Tenuʿot ha-Guf bi-Sheʿat Qeriʾat Shema," *Assufot* 8 (1994):348, n. 25; Elimelekh Horowitz, "Ẓedaqah, ʿAniyyim u-Fiquaḥ Ḥevrati bi-Qehillot Yehudei Eiropah bein Yemei ha-Benayim le-Reshit ha-ʿEt ha-Ḥadashah," *Dat ve-Kalkalah*, ed. Menahem Ben-Sasson (Jerusalem, 1995), 227–28; ms. Bodl. 659, fol. 27v; I. Ta-Shma, "Eliezer b. Samuel of Metz," *Encyclopaedia Judaica*, 6:628–29; and idem, *Halakhah, Minhag u-Meẓi*ʾ*ut be-Ashkenaz*, 249–50; and below, ch. 2, at nn. 46, 62. See also *Sefer Yere*ʾ*im*, secs. 404–7, on the nature of *yir*ʾ*at ha-Shem*, and cf. Soloveitchik, "Three Themes," 311–20, 327–28, n. 50. Note that ms. Livorno (Leghorn Talmud Torah) Cod. 2 [=ms. JNUL 4°621], fols. 22r-v, attributes a penitential program (*seder teshuvah*) of R. Eleazar of Worms to R. Eliezer of Metz. Cf. V. Aptowitzer, *Mavo la-Rabiah*, 314, and Ivan Marcus, "Ḥasidei Ashkenaz Private Penitentials," *Studies in Jewish Mysticism*, ed. J. Dan and F. Talmage (Cambridge, Mass., 1982), 69. R. Eleazar of Worms's Pietist student, R. Abraham b. Azriel of Bohemia (see below), makes extensive use of *Sefer Yere*ʾ*im*. See ʿ*Arugat ha-Bosem*, ed. Urbach, 4:164. For R. Eliezer's own commentaries on *piyyutim*, see E. E. Urbach, "Sefer ʿArugat ha-Bosem le-R. Avraham b. Azriel," *Tarbiz* 10 (1939):40.

[106]See, e.g., Urbach, *Ba*ʿ*alei ha-Tosafot*, 1:437–39; Marcus, *Piety and Society*, 112; and above, n. 16.

[107]Jacob Katz, *Exclusiveness and Tolerance* (New York, 1961), 102–5.

Gerona.[108] The firm impact of *ḥasidut Ashkenaz* on Rabbenu Yonah in these matters, possibly through the Evreux connection,[109] is beyond question.[110]

---

[108]Israel Ta-Shma, "Iggeret u-Derashat Hit^{c}orerut le-Eḥad mi-Rabbotenu ha-Rishonim [Ba^{c}al ha-Semag $^{\supset}$o Rabbenu Yonah Gerondi]," *Moriah* 19:5–6 (1994): 7–12. The texts were found in a Moscow ms. in a Sefardic hand, at the end of Rabbenu Yonah's *Iggeret ha-Teshuvah* (which was probably written in northern France, and certainly reflects Pietist influence). Ta-Shma is inclined to think the sermon was from R. Moses of Coucy, based on parallel passages in *Semag* and the feeling of closeness to the redemption that R. Moses affected—which also explains partially the great success he enjoyed (by his own account) in getting thousands of Spanish Jews to repent and return to fuller observances. The letter, which may have been from R. Moses to the people of his hometown or region in northern France, comes from a Torah scholar who traveled to a faraway land to preach and arrived in a particular city where he achieved great success, especially in the realm of communal Torah study. He decided to stay a little while longer there, to address certain difficulties that had arisen. While the overall thrust and circumstances of the letter accord more with the career of R. Moses, R. Jonah also traveled a great deal, stressing Torah study and ethical teachings in addition to establishing *yeshivot*. Indeed, the language of the letter and the details of its author's own scholarly writings accord more with Rabbenu Yonah. In any event, Ta-Shma's admitted inability to draw any definitive conclusions on the question of authorship demonstrates effectively the pronounced similarities between Rabbenu Yonah and R. Moses of Coucy in terms of career, religious orientation, and expression. Note also the significant parallel between *Semag, miẓvat ^{c}aseh* 3 and R. Yonah's *Sha^{c}arei ^{c}Avodah* (see above, n. 89) discussed by Galinsky, "Rabbenu Mosheh mi-Coucy ke-Ḥasid," 28. See also *Semag, lo ta^{c}aseh* 2; *Sefer ha-Yir$^{\supset}$ah*, sec. 139; and cf. below, n. 112.

[109]Urbach, *Ba^{c}alei ha-Tosafot* (Jerusalem, 1955), 387. See also Urbach, *Ba^{c}alei ha-Tosafot* (1980), 1:469–70; and cf. Yitzhak Baer, "Ha-Megammah ha-Datit/ha-Ḥevratit shel Sefer Ḥasidim," *Zion* 3 (1937):6–7. Urbach notes that Baer, *Toledot ha-Yehudim bi-Sefarad ha-Noẓerit* (Jerusalem, 1959), 148–54, posited Pietist influences on Rabbenu Yonah's preaching and pronounced interest in the dissemination of ethical teachings, while apparently unaware of R. Moses of Coucy, whose potential as a source of influence was better documented. On the other hand, Urbach was himself unaware of the connection between Rabbenu Yonah and the German Pietists, via Evreux. Cf. Ta-Shma, "Rabbenu Yonah Gerondi," 171, and Galinsky, "Rabbenu Mosheh mi-Coucy ke-Ḥasid," 16, 84.

[110]See also Abramson, below, n. 115, and my "Rabbinic Attitudes Toward Nonobservance in the Medieval Period," 24–26; and cf. R. Langer, *To Worship God Properly*, 228–30. Interestingly, *Sefer Ḥasidim* restricts the imperative of giving *tokhehah* (admonition) to these situations in which the one offering the rebuke believes there is at least a chance he will be heeded. This position is held also by *Semag* (and *Semaq*). Rabbenu Yonah's position appears to have been closer to that of R. Eliezer of Metz (codified also by Maimonides), who held that the imperative was operative in (virtually) all circumstances. See Soloveitchik, "Three Themes," 336, n. 82; Marcus, *Piety and Society*, 87–88; Eli Yassif, "Ha-Sippur ha-Eksemplari be-Sefer Ḥasidim," *Tarbiz* 57

Rabbenu Yonah copied a penitential supplication composed by R. Moses of Coucy, without attribution, into his [*Ye-*]*Sod ha-Teshuvah* (which was itself appended by Rabbenu Yonah to his *Sefer ha-Yir'ah*).[111] This supplication, and similar manuscript texts by R. Moses that have also been identified, reflect the spirit of the *tiqqunei teshuvah* of *Ḥasidei Ashkenaz* and contain parallels to penitential prayers authored by R. Eleazar of Worms and R. Judah *he-Ḥasid*. Indeed, an early manuscript version of one of R. Moses' supplications was copied immediately following a very similar prayer by R. Eleazar of Worms, תפלת השב בכל כחו.[112]

(1988):243–44, n. 53; Bernard Septimus, "Piety and Power in Thirteenth-Century Catalonia," *Studies in Medieval Jewish History and Literature*, ed. Isadore Twersky (Cambridge, Mass., 1979), 215–21; Norman Lamm, "Hokheaḥ Tokhiaḥ ʾet ʿAmitekha," *Gesher* 10 (1982): 170–76; and Galinsky, "Rabbenu Mosheh mi-Coucy ke-Ḥasid," 99–100.

[111]See Ta-Shma, "Rabbenu Yonah Gerondi," 170. On the (mistaken) attribution of *Sod ha-Teshuvah* to R. Eleazar of Worms, see above, n. 88.

[112]Versions of two supplications attributed to R. Moses were published by Y. D. Gilat, "Shetei Baqqashot le-R. Mosheh mi-Coucy," *Tarbiz* 28 (1959):54–58, from two Bodl. mss.: Oppenheim 759=Neubauer 1118 [France, late thirteenth century], fol. 134v, entitled בקשה מהרב ר׳ משה מקוצי and beginning אנא ה׳ א-להי אברהם יצחק וישראל בוראי שבראתני וגדלתני, and Michael 355=Neub. 554 [Italy, late fifteenth century], fol. 106v, entitled תפילה תקן הסמ״ג לאומרה בכריעה, and beginning אנא ה׳ א-להי ישראל חטאתי עויתי פשעתי. The version found in Opp. 156=Neub. 1114 [Ashkenaz, 1410, see above, n. 88], fol. 103v (column 3) [which follows *Shir ha-Yiḥud veha-Kavod* (attributed here to R. Judah *he-Ḥasid*), R. Jonah's *Ḥayyei ʿOlam/Sod ha-Teshuvah* (attributed here to R. Isaac *Ḥasid*), Maimonides' *Ḥayyei ʿOlam* (=a passage from *Moreh Nevukhim*), and a prayer for resurrection that included Maimonides' thirteen articles of faith] is similar to Opp. 759/Bodl. 1118, but adds a brief coda asking for the rebuilding of Jerusalem and the advent of the messiah. This version of R. Moses' prayer is also found, with variations (and entitled תפלה מאת ר׳ משה מקוצי . . . התחינה יסד ר׳ משה מקוצי), in ms. Cincinnati 436 (an Ashkenazic *siddur* copied in 1435) on fol 213v, immediately following R. Judah *he-Ḥasid*'s addenda for each day of the week (based on *Berakhot* 17b) that were inserted in *E-lohai Neẓor* at the conclusion of the *ʿAmidah* (fols. 212v–213a). [For an earlier manuscript version of these addenda, see ms. Paris 646, fol. 237r.]

This form of R. Moses' prayer also follows immediately after the prayer by R. Eleazar of Worms, entitled תפלת השב בכל כוחו, in ms. Opp. 758=Bodl. 1105 [Ashkenaz, 1326–27], fols. 435r–435v. R. Eleazar's prayer is preceded by several other texts associated with the German Pietists, including *shirei ya-Yiḥud veha-Kavod* (fols. 390r–420v); see below, ch. 3, n. 110. R. Moses' prayer is followed by two *Hekhalot*-style prayers and a text entitled *Birkat ha-Evarim*, which was composed by a member of *Ḥasidei Ashkenaz* (see below, n. 114). In ms. Parma 1220 (Spain, fifteenth/sixteenth centuries), fol. 106r, a shorter form of this version (which is identified by a different hand in the margin as a *teḥinnah* from the mouth of R. Moses of Coucy) follows a

R. Moses refers to one of these *baqqashot* in his *Sefer Mizvot Gadol*. Toward the end of his lengthy exposition of the laws of repentance, he writes: "One should bow on his knees (*yikhra ʿal birkav*) for one hour a day, with his hands outstretched heavenward, and confess (*ve-yitvaddeh*), and ask for mercy

---

penitential work by R. Eleazar of Worms known as *Moreh Ḥatta'im* or *Sefer ha-Kapparot* (fols. 103–5). This work, which is referred to simply as *hilkhot teshuvah*, opens with a Pietist chain of tradition. Cf. Ivan Marcus, "*Ḥasidei 'Ashkenaz* Private Penitentials: An Introduction and Descriptive Catalogue of Their Manuscripts and Early Editions," *Studies in Jewish Mysticism*, ed. Joseph Dan and Frank Talmage (Cambridge, Mass., 1982), esp. 70–71.

The earliest record of the second supplication published by Gilat is found in *Orḥot Ḥayyim, Hilkhot Rosh ha-Shanah*, sec. 26, which contains R. Jonah's *Sod ha-Teshuvah*. R. Jonah included the supplication in his work, without attribution; see Ta-Shma in the preceding note. With regard to this text as well, Urbach, *Baʿalei ha-Tosafot*, 1:470, n. 18, notes similar *viddui* supplications in *Sefer Roqeaḥ, Hilkhot Teshuvah*, esp. sec. 20, תפלת השב בכל כחו. The juxtaposition of R. Moses' and R. Eleazar's prayers in Bodl. 1105 supports Urbach's suggestion. [Ms. Vat. 331 (fourteenth century), fols. 240v–241r, copies this prayer as a *tefillah/teḥinnah* of R. Yonah *ha-Qadosh*. Ms. Parma 1354 (Italy, sixteenth century), fols. 152r–153r, entitles this supplication תפלה השב בכל כחו but does not attribute it to anyone.] Cf. *Sefer Roqeaḥ, Hilkhot Teshuvah*, sec. 21, and Marcus, "*Ḥasidei 'Ashkenaz* Private Penitentials," 57–61.

For a *viddui* attributed to R. Judah *he-Ḥasid*, see ms. Paris l'Alliance 482 (Ashkenaz, fourteenth century), fol. 33, and ms. Vat. Rossiana 356 (Italy, 1412), fol. 2v. For a *tefillah u-teḥinnah* attributed to R. Judah *he-Ḥasid* (beginning יוצרי ברוב רחמיך כבוש אפך מזעמך... תעביר את חטאתי סלח נא על כל פשעי כפר לעונותי חלצני מיסורין ומרוחות ומזיקין), see ms. Parma 1138, fol. 139v (Hebrew foliation), found also in ms. Brit. Mus., Add. 26883 (*Catalogue of the Hebrew and Samaritan Manuscripts in the British Museum*, ed. G. Margoliouth, vol. 2 [London, 1905], 255 [no. 640]). Cf. below, ch. 3, n. 99. [Note also the *seliḥah* for the morning service of Yom Kippur by R. Judah *he-Ḥasid*, א-להים בישראל גדול יחודיך, whose lines are structured according to a sequence of Divine Names. See *Maḥzor le-Yamim Nora'im*, ed. E. D. Goldschmidt, vol. 2 (Jerusalem, 1970), 237–38; Israel Ta-Shma, "Mashehu ʿal Biqqoret ha-Miqra Bimei ha-Benayim," *Ha-Miqra bi-Re'i Mefarshav* (*Sefer Zikkaron le-Sarah Kamin*), ed. Sarah Japhet (Jerusalem, 1994), 454, n. 13; ms. Montefiore 6 (Northern France, 1394), fol. 1r; ms. Bodl. 1812, fol. 145v; ms. Macerata 310 (see below, ch. 3, n. 110); ms. JTS Mic. 1640, fol. 179v; ms. Parma 1138, fol. 134 (in Hebrew foliation; 91r–91v in standard foliation); and ms. Paris 633, fol. 30 (in a section copied by R. Isaac b. Isaac; see Colette Sirat in *REJ* 119, pp. 10, 20–21, n. 6, and cf. below, ch. 3, n. 100). In some of the manuscript versions, the phrase ומי שאומרה מובטח שהוא בן עולם הבא appears. Among the penitential supplications in this prayer is the phrase אנא נורא קדוש תרבה מחילתך פשענו סלחה תגלגל מדותיך.] Cf. ms. Paris 835, fols. 119v–120r (in the name of Ramban); *Shirei ha-Yiḥud veha-Kavod*, ed. A. M. Habermann (Jerusalem, 1948), 12–13, 16; ms. Parma 1221 (Spain, fifteenth century), 189v (cf. below, ch. 5, n. 49); ms. Bodl. 1209 (Ashkenaz, 1329), 19r (אנא מורה חטאים); and below, n. 142.

that the Almighty should assist him in his repentance. I have composed a special supplication (*baqqashah*) for this [purpose] which is written [and available] for everyone."[113]

A passage in *Sefer Ḥasidim* explains and commends the practice of blessing the Almighty upon arising by comparing one who arises to one who is released from prison and is obligated to offer thanks. While a person is asleep, he is in effect shackled, since he has no control over his body. Upon awakening, he must therefore offer a blessing for each of his limbs "that had been bound, but has now been released, so that you may use them for your benefit (לעשות תקנתך בהם)." This passage further relates the actions of a *ḥasid* who blessed his various limbs and prayed that each of them would be faithful to their Creator and not be the cause of sin.[114] A passage in *Semag* has a

---

[113]*Semag*, ᶜ*aseh* 16 (fol. 69a). Galinsky, "Rabbenu Mosheh mi-Coucy ke-Ḥasid," 29–30, argues that *Semag* is referring here to the first supplication described in the preceding note (Bodl. 1118). While Galinsky notes some suggestive parallels between this first text and other passages in R. Moses' corpus, in his view the second text (Bodl. 554) appears to reflect concepts that were more central to *ḥasidut Ashkenaz*. One of the main distinctions between the two texts that Galinsky suggests, however—that of *baqqashah* versus *tefillah*—cannot be maintained throughout the manuscript variants. Thus, for example, the version of the first text found in Bodl. 1114 (see the preceding note) is entitled תפלת הר' משה מקוצי (rather than *baqqashah*). Moreover, the manuscript juxtaposition described in the preceding note indicates similarities between writings of the German Pietists and the first text as well. Finally, the requirement of bowing during the supplication expressed in *Semag* appears specifically in the second text. See also Y. D. Gilat, "Tiqqunei ha-Guf bi-Sheᶜat Tefillah (heᶜarah)," *Sidra* 7 (1991):159. Urbach, *Baᶜalei ha-Tosafot*, 1:469–70, describes this passage in ᶜ*aseh* 16—together with several that precede it and others found in nearby sections—as reflecting the intense penitential style of the German Pietists without the aspect of *teshuvat ha-mishqal* (in which the penitent must afflict himself physically in a manner judged to be commensurate or proportional to the pleasure he received from his sin). Cf. Jacob Elbaum, *Teshuvat ha-Lev ve-Qabbalat Yissurim* (Jerusalem, 1993), 20, n. 3, and 31, n. 31.

[114]*SḤP* 2 (p. 4)=*SḤB* 155. A passage in *Midrash Tehillim* (ed. Solomon Buber, 124a–b), whose Ashkenazic manuscript versions are replete with passages reflecting distinctly Ashkenazic customs and traditions (see below, ch. 3, n. 13), lists the names of the limbs and the precepts they are suited to perform. Both the *Midrash Tehillim* passage and the *SḤB* passage cite the verse that was also used by *Sefer Ḥasidim* to support the pietistic practice of swaying during prayer; see above, n. 59. Malachi Beit-Arie, "Birkat ha-Evarim," *Tarbiz* 56 (1987):265–72, cogently suggests that a series of actual blessings collected in a listing entitled "blessings of the limbs" (found in ms. Bodl. 1105, fols. 436v–438v) was composed by a member of the German Pietists as a reflection of the instruction in *Sefer Ḥasidim*. This text appears in a portion of the manuscript that contains other texts of the German Pietists, as well as one of R. Moses of Coucy's

lengthy listing of many of the limbs in the body and what each of them allows the human being to do. Although this passage is based almost verbatim on a formulation in R. Shabbetai Donnolo's *Sefer Ḥakhmoni* (or *Takhkemoni*),[115] its purpose in *Semag* is to impress on the individual the incredible favor the Almighty has bestowed upon him in providing all these limbs with all their functions. By recognizing this, the human being will serve the Almighty with great love and will strive to do as many *miẓvot* as possible, since he knows he cannot repay the Almighty's kindness in full. *Semag*'s approach to *ḥovat ha-ʾevarim* is consonant with the material in *Sefer Ḥasidim*. It should also be noted that *Ḥasidei Ashkenaz* were familiar with *Sefer Ḥakhmoni* and were influenced by it in a number of contexts.[116]

Judah Galinsky has recently sought to portray R. Moses of Coucy as a northern French *ḥasid*, a tosafist deeply interested in promoting the development of ethical behavior and proper character traits, rather than as someone under the direct influence of the German Pietists. Galinsky demonstrates that while R. Moses' formulations with regard to the primacy of truthfulness in all dealings and forums seem to draw both conceptually and linguistically upon *Sefer Ḥasidim*, his formulations with respect to humility and anger do not. To be sure, these two character traits are also discussed extensively in *Sefer Ḥasidim*, and the ideological positions found in *Sefer Ḥasidim* are close to those taken by *Semag*. Nonetheless, a pattern of direct influence is not evident with regard to these issues. Rather, it appears that R. Moses based his positions on those of Rashi.[117]

In addition, Galinsky notes that R. Moses was uninterested in some of the theological doctrines that were central to the German Pietists. He did not attempt to search for the larger or hidden Divine Will, nor did he stress particular resourcefulness regarding *yirʾah* in order to discover that Will.

---

supplications; see above, n. 112. On the concept of *ḥovat ha-ʾevarim* and its implications in the works of Rabbenu Yonah and R. Isaac of Corbeil, see Ta-Shma, "Ḥasidut Ashkenaz bi-Sefarad," 168, n. 8, and below, n. 171.

[115] See Shraga Abramson, "Inyanut be-Sefer Miẓvot Gadol," *Sinai* 80 (1977): 209–16.

[116] See Elliot Wolfson, "The Theosophy of Ṣhabbetai Donnolo, with Special Emphasis on the Doctrine of *Sefirot* in *Sefer Ḥakhmoni*," *The Frank Talmage Memorial Volume*, ed. Walfish, 2:281–316; and the literature cited in n. 55. Cf. Israel Ta-Shma in *Qiryat Sefer* 60 (1985):307.

[117] Galinsky, "R. Mosheh mi-Coucy ke-Ḥasid," 39–50. See now idem, "Ve-Lihiyot Lefanekha ʿEved Neʾeman Kol ha-Yamim—Pereq be-Haguto ha-Datit shel R. Mosheh mi-Coucy," *Daʿat* 42 (1999):13–31.

Moreover, R. Moses attached no importance to fasting or other forms of self-denial. R. Moses' *ḥasidut* expresses itself through dedicated Torah study, unquestioning service of the Creator, and especially through intereaction with others. By being particularly humble, slow to anger, and steadfastly honest, the *ḥasid* serves his Maker as well, and indeed, truly comes to know Him. Concerns expressed by R. Moses about the need to control one's impulses may have been derived as much from Maimonides' *Mishneh Torah*, upon which *Semag* was based, as from the writings of the German Pietists. In Galinsky's view, the (northern French) pietism represented by R. Moses of Coucy was interested neither in philosophical teachings nor in mystical studies or practices as means of perceiving the Divine realm. The northern French *ḥasid*, R. Moses of Coucy, was able to address certain issues in Jewish thought without recourse to the German Pietists and their esotericism.[118]

Galinsky also questions Ta-Shma's focus on the influence of *Ḥasidei Ashkenaz* in R. Moses' attempt at halakhic codification. He suggests there were a number of other motives that propelled R. Moses to write his work, including the requests of individuals and the importance of adjusting the *Mishneh Torah* from an Ashkenazic perspective. Moreover, R. Moses wished to provide a proper vehicle for Torah study. Had he merely wished to give practical halakhic guidance to the masses, he could have written a much more compact, basic work. In addition, R. Moses refers to the dream he had in which he was instructed to compose the work he did.[119]

As we have noted, however, R. Moses of Coucy had significant affinities with *Ḥasidei Ashkenaz*, many of which are acknowledged by Galinsky. Even R. Moses' concern with and treatment of humility and anger is similar to the approaches of the Pietists, as well as to those of R. Moses of Evreux and Rabbenu Yonah.[120] Moreover, the special supplications for one seeking penance, common to both *Ḥasidei Ashkenaz* and R. Moses of Coucy, represent a shared view[121]—even if R. Moses did not subscribe, in terms of concept and terminology, to every aspect of the Pietist program of *tiqqunei teshuvah*. R. Moses

---

[118]See Galinsky, "R. Mosheh mi-Coucy ke-Ḥasid," 65; and idem, "Da ᵓet E-lohei Avikha ve-ᶜAvdehu: Havvanato shel Baᶜal ha-Tosafot R. Mosheh mi-Coucy ᵓet ha-Horaᵓah Ladaᶜat ᵓet ha-Shem," *Mi-Safra le-Sayfa* 48 (1995):59–64.

[119]See Galinsky, "R. Mosheh mi-Coucy ke-Ḥasid," 24, n. 24, and above, n. 102.

[120]See ibid., 4–5, 16, 28, 67, n. 12, 71, nn. 29–30, 73–74, nn. 54–55; and see the next note. I have demonstrated that there are close parallels between *Sefer Ḥasidim* and formulations of R. Moses to which Galinsky refers in 71, n. 30; see above, nn. 79–81.

[121]See Galinsky, "R. Mosheh mi-Coucy ke-Ḥasid," 80–81, n. 108. On similarities regarding the parameters of *tokhehah* (Galinsky, 82–84), cf. above, n. 109.

of Coucy also appears to have been one of the only tosafists who was not a *pashtan* in the mold of Rashbam or R. Joseph *Bekhor Shor* to have authored a systematic commentary to the Pentateuch.[122] As I have demonstrated elsewhere, tosafists who were not *pashtanim* did not generally value biblical study as a separate discipline. They were thus content to offer scattered *Tosafot*-like comments on various verses, reflecting their talmudocentric approach to biblical literature. The German Pietists, however, recognized the importance of Bible study as a separate discipline in both the exoteric and esoteric realms, and their commentaries reflect this view. R. Moses' affinity with the German Pietists and his role as a *darshan*, which is also consistent with Pietist thought as we have seen, may explain his unique efforts at Torah commentary.[123]

Semag fits the profile of a halakhic work that is consonant with the approach of *ḥasidut Ashkenaz*, regardless of any other expressed motivations. Giving practical halakhic guidance was precisely the aim of the directives in *Sefer Ḥasidim*.[124] R. Moses' stated reliance on a dream that directed him to compose *Semag*,[125] and his acknowledgment of another dream that dictated the inclusion of לא תשכח את ה׳ אלקיך as a *mizvat lo taᶜaseh* despite the fact that

---

[122]Urbach, *Baᶜalei ha-Tosafot,* 1:478–79.

[123]See my *Jewish Education and Society*, 75–90, and my "The Role of Bible Study in Medieval Ashkenaz," *The Frank Talmage Memorial Volume*, ed. Walfish, 1:151–66. A biblical interpretation by R. Judah *he-Ḥasid* is cited in *Peshatei Ram mi-Coucy.* See *Perushei ha-Torah le-R. Yehudah he-Ḥasid*, ed. Y. S. Lange (Jerusalem, 1975), 159. As Galinsky notes ("R. Mosheh mi-Coucy ke-Ḥasid," 6, n. 6), considerations of Jewish-Christian polemic may have also played a role in R. Moses' commentary. Among tosafists, R. Isaiah di Trani also composed a systematic Torah commentary, a fuller version of which has been discovered only recently. He too had connections with the German Pietists, via his German tosafist teachers. See, e.g., ms. Moscow-Guenzberg 303, fols. 63r, 68v, 65r, 87v, 97r; Israel Ta-Shma, "Sefer 'Nimmuqei Ḥumash' le-R. Yishayahu di Trani," *Qiryat Sefer* 64 (1992–93):751–53; idem, "Sefer Shibbolei ha-Leqet u-Khefelav," *Italia* 11 (1995):47; C. B. Chavel, *Nimmuqei Ḥumash le-Rabbenu Yeshayah* (Jerusalem, 1972), editor's introduction, 5 (and cf. below, ch. 2, n. 23); Ta-Shma, "Ha-Rav Yeshayah di Trani ha-Zaqen u-Qesharav ᶜim Bizantiyyon ve-Ereẓ Yisraʾel," *Shalem* 4 (1984):409–16; idem, *Ha-Nigleh shebe-Nistar*, 55, and below, ch. 2, n. 60, and ch. 5, nn. 21–23.

[124]Note also R. Moses of Coucy's statement, in the introduction to the *mitẓvot ᶜaseh*, concerning the importance of understanding the *miẓvot* derived from the orders of *Qodashim, Zeraᶜim*, and *Taharot*. *Semag* is the only tosafist code to incorporate these areas. See above, n. 76, for parallels in the thought of the German Pietists, and cf. Galinsky, "R. Moses mi-Coucy ke-Ḥasid," 10–11, 17.

[125]*Semag, ᶜaseh* 3 (end), and cf. Galinsky, "Qum ᶜAseh Sefer Torah," (above, n. 100).

Maimonides did not do so[126] are examples of a phenomenon that was sometimes associated with magic or *sod* in Ashkenazic rabbinic traditions.[127] On the other hand, the very brief description of these dream experiences, and the fact that the dreams were related to R. Moses' planned literary endeavor, raise certain questions. Were they inspired through mystical means or conjured magically, or were they agitated by R. Moses' deep convictions and spirituality, without any form of magical or mystical manipulation?[128]

R. Moses refers to an unidentified heavenly reason (סיבה מן השמים) that impelled him to travel to various locales preaching the observance of the commandments.[129] While this term need not reflect an actual mystical experience on the part of R. Moses,[130] the messianism which he espoused—and which may have been part of his (heavenly) reason for wanting to bring others to a higher level of observance—was linked to forms of prophetic dreams and expressions that existed in Ashkenaz in his day.[131] As we shall see, R. Judah *he-Ḥasid* and his father, R. Samuel, were involved in prophetic messianism, as were other thirteenth-century tosafists engaged in mystical activities.[132] A manuscript passage contains R. Moses' presentation of an eschatological formulation of his older colleague, R. Isaac b. Abraham, which also reflects an esoteric approach.[133] As was the case with Rabiah, there is, on

---

[126]*Semag*, negative precept 64 (end).

[127]See Monford Harris, *Studies in Jewish Dream Interpretation* (Northvale, 1994), 15–38; and below, ch. 3, nn. 3, 77–80; ch. 4, n. 59; ch. 5, nn. 22–23.

[128]See Steven Kruger, *Dreaming in the Middle Ages* (Cambridge, 1992), 15–34, 43–46, 89–92, 151; Ḥida, *Shem ha-Gedolim*, s.v. *Rabbenu Mosheh mi-Coucy* (*maᶜarekhet ha-gedolim*, 100, sec. 178); and see now Judah Galinsky, "Rav Mosheh mi-Coucy veha-Polmus ha-Yehudi Noẓeri ba-Meʾah ha-13," (forthcoming), pt. 1.

[129]*Semag*, introduction to the negative precepts (end), and cf. Galinsky, "Qum ᶜAseh Sefer Torah," and idem, "R. Mosheh mi-Coucy ke-Ḥasid," 84–85.

[130]See, e.g., Twersky, *Rabad of Posquières*, 291–97; Gershom Scholem, *Origins of the Kabbalah* (Princeton, 1987), 206–7; A. J. Heschel, "Al Ruaḥ ha-Qodesh Bimei ha-Benayim," 193–201; *Sheʾelot u-Teshuvot min ha-Shamayim*, ed. Margoliot, editor's introduction, 6–13; and Moshe Idel's preface to A. J. Heschel, *Prophetic Inspiration After the Prophets*, ed. Moses Faierstein (Hoboken, 1996).

[131]See Galinsky, "R. Mosheh mi-Coucy ke-Ḥasid," 87–90; Katz, *Exclusiveness and Tolerance*, 80–81; Gilat, "Shetei Baqqashot le-R. Mosheh mi-Coucy," 54–55; and Israel Yuval, "Liqrat 1240: Tiqvot Yehudiyyot, Paḥadim Noẓriyyim," *Proceedings of the Eleventh World Congress of Jewish Studies* [Div. B, vol. 1], 113–20.

[132]See Alexander Marx, "Maʾamar ᶜal Shenat Geʾulah," *Ha-Ẓofeh le-Ḥokhmat Yisraʾel* 5 (1921):194–202; and below, ch. 4, nn. 8–9; ch. 5, n. 67.

[133]See ms. Darmstadt Cod. Or. 25, fols. 13v–17v; Yuval, above, n. 131; Urbach, *Baᶜalei ha-Tosafot*, 1:468–69; and below, ch. 4, n. 37.

balance, insufficient evidence to conclude that R. Moses of Coucy was among those (northern French) tosafists who were significantly involved with mystical studies. His strong manifestations of pietistic leanings are, however, without question.[134]

It is entirely possible, as Galinsky has proposed, that there was a northern French version of *ḥasidut*, with R. Moses of Coucy as one of its prime exemplars. Like the brothers of Evreux, R. Moses remained a dedicated tosafist and continued to pursue tosafist methods and intellectual values. It should not be expected that he would espouse a *ḥasidut* completely identical to that of the German Pietists.

The establishment of this phenomenon, however, begs several questions. Where and with whom did it originate, and how did R. Moses acquire pieces of material that are quite similar to Pietist teachings? In light of the affinities that have been noted, it is difficult to imagine that this branch of *ḥasidut* had a completely separate development from *ḥasidut Ashkenaz*. Indeed, even if Rashi were one of the sources for French Pietism, we shall see that he too was familiar with several aspects of pre-Crusade *torat ha-sod*.[135] Based on all the material I have presented thus far—including the pre-Crusade manifestations of piety and character development, and the practices attributed to *Ḥasidei Ẓarefat* by *Sefer ha-Manhig*—the most likely possibility is that both the northern French and German forms of *ḥasidut* emerged from common aspects of the rabbinic culture of early Ashkenaz. Thus, R. Moses of Coucy may have received certain pietistic teachings from sources within *Ḥasidei Ashkenaz*, and he may have derived others from either pre-Crusade traditions or twelfth-century northern French predecessors.[136]

---

[134]Cf. Galinsky, "R. Mosheh mi-Coucy ke-Ḥasid," 59–61, and idem, "Da ᵓet E-lohei Avikha ve-ᶜAvdehu," 59–64. Although I agree with Galinsky that R. Moses was not philosophically inclined (cf. above, introduction, at n. 1), his contention that R. Moses wished to suppress esotericism in the same manner as Rashbam (cf. below, ch. 3, nn. 67–69) has not been amply demonstrated. Cf. also below, n. 156.

[135]See below, ch. 3, sec. 2. Rashi was not inclined, however, toward asceticism or *perishut*; see above, n. 22.

[136]*Sefer Yereᵓim* by R. Eliezer of Metz (whose affinities with *Ḥasidei Ashkenaz* have been noted [above, n. 105]) had a significant influence on *Semag*. See, e.g., Urbach, *Baᶜalei ha-Tosafot*, 1:474, and Galinsky, "Rabbenu Mosheh mi-Coucy ke-Ḥasid," 11–12. In theory, the same two paths were open to Rabbenu Yonah at Evreux, although his relationship with German Pietism in particular appears to have been highly developed. [Regarding R. Yonah and mysticism, see Joseph Dan, *Jewish Mysticism and Jewish Ethics* (Seattle, 1986), 28–39, and Gershom Scholem, *Meḥqerei Qabbalah*, ed. Yosef ben Shelomoh and Moshe Idel, vol. 1 (Jerusalem, 1998), 35.] The links between German

An example of the latter path of transmission, which bypasses the German Pietists, can be seen in the following instance. A number of medieval rabbinic sources record customs concerning the positioning of the hands during the ʿ*Amidah*. No discussion of how to position the hands is found, however, in the writings of any German authorities, including *Ḥasidei Ashkenaz*. Indeed, the issue was hardly even mentioned in German rabbinic literature. Rabiah and *Sefer Or Zaruaʿ* cite a talmudic passage that sometimes served as the basis for one practice, but they offer no discussion or direction.[137] On the other hand, both *Sefer ha-Yirʾah* and *Semag* offer practical instructions. Rabbenu Yonah discusses how to hold one's hands while praying (the right above the left) and where to place them while sitting or standing during prayer.[138] R. Moses of Coucy notes that one ought to "stretch his hands heavenward" while reciting the confessional (*viddui*) to atone for one's sins.[139] Thus, two northern French *ḥasidim*, R. Jonah and R. Moses of Coucy, dealt with these forms of pietistic practice, while the German Pietists were completely silent about them.[140]

Pietism and the pre-Crusade period have been firmly established; see my *Jewish Education and Society*, 86–91, and above, introduction, n. 13.

[137]See Eric Zimmer, "Tiqqunei ha-Guf bi-Sheʿat ha-Tefillah," *Sidra* 5 (1989):101 [=ʿ*Olam ke-Minhago Noheg*, 84].

[138]See Zimmer, "Tiqqunei ha-Guf," 102. Zimmer regards R. Yonah as a Sefardic rabbinic scholar in this context, rather than as a student of northern France, despite the appearance of the passage in *Sefer ha-Yirʾah*; cf. above, at n. 84. Zimmer further suggests that material from R. Aharon *ha-Kohen* of Lunel's *Orḥot Ḥayyim* may have had an impact upon R. Jonah (מצא הדים). This suggested pattern of transmission is difficult to accept, however. *Orḥot Ḥayyim* was composed after R. Jonah's works and cites R. Jonah by name on a number of occasions, once specifically in conjunction with *Sefer ha-Yirʾah*; see my "Rabbinic Figures in Castilian Kabbalistic Pseudepigraphy," 92, n. 52, and above, n. 85. [Views similar to that of R. Jonah concerning the positioning of the hands during prayer are also found in the pietistic *Sefer Minhag Tov* (see above, n. 34) and later in the biblical commentary of the kabbalist Rabbenu Baḥya b. Asher. For the possible impact of Christian ritual on this aspect of Jewish prayer practice, cf. Daniel Sperber, *Minhagei Yisraʾel* 3 (Jerusalem, 1994), 88–91; 4:71–74; and H. Soloveitchik in *AJS Review* 23 (1998): 225.]

[139]See *Semag*, ʿ*aseh* 16, and Gilat (above, n. 113).

[140]This development is somewhat curious, in light of the fact that *Ḥasidei Ashkenaz* were generally quite interested in various kinds of movement during prayer, as we have seen. This practice is not mentioned in *Sefer ha-Manhig*, either. On the other hand, as noted by Zimmer ("Tiqqunei ha-Guf," 99–100), Ramban, the Zohar, and other mystically inclined sources of the period endorse it. Cf. Marcus, "Prayer Gestures in German Hasidism" (above, n. 60).

The small number of full-fledged students who have been associated with the Pietists (not to mention the absence of any Pietist communities or settlements) belies the extent to which certain of their values were broadly held—especially those values that were part of Ashkenazic rabbinic culture in the pre-Crusade period. Whether or not the German Pietists were the source, we have been able to discover various forms of *ḥasidut* and *perishut* within rabbinic circles in both northern France and Germany. As we shall now see, the presence of these phenomena continued and even intensified in the second half of the thirteenth century, perhaps under more direct Pietist influence.

The Case of R. Isaac of Corbeil

R. Isaac b. Joseph of Corbeil (d.c.1280) was a northern French tosafist. Like R. Moses of Coucy, he authored a halakhic code, known as *ʿAmmudei Golah* or *Sefer Miẓvot Qatan*. Indeed, R. Isaac's work owes much to R. Moses' *Sefer Miẓvot Gadol* in terms of content and approach, even as it employs a somewhat different style of presentation.[141] In addition, it appears that R. Isaac shared a number of more overtly pietistic affinities with R. Judah *he-Ḥasid* and with his student, R. Eleazar of Worms, reflecting a significant measure of influence.

R. Isaac recorded all four modes of penance that were the hallmarks of the penitential programs of both R. Judah and R. Eleazar. These include *teshuvat ha-mishqal* and *teshuvat ha-katuv*, which often required the penitent to undergo harsh physical afflictions.[142] This inclusion is rendered even more suggestive by the fact that R. Abraham b. Azriel—a devoted Pietist student of

[141]See Israel Ta-Shma, "Isaac ben Joseph of Corbeil," *Encyclopaedia Judaica* vol. 9, 21–22, and idem, "Ḥasidut Ashkenaz bi-Sefarad," 168, n. 8.

[142]*ʿAmmudei Golah* (=*Sefer Miẓvot Qatan* [*Semaq*], Kapust, 1820), sec. 53: ד׳ מיני תשובה הם: תשובת הגדר תשוב׳ הכתוב תשובת המשקל תשובת החרטה. Cf. *Sefer ha-Roqeaḥ ha-Gadol* (Jerusalem, 1967), 25, *Hilkhot Teshuvah*, sec. 1 (end): וד׳ עניני תשובה הם: תשובת הבאה תשובת הגדר תשובת המשקל תשובת הכתוב. On the four modes of penance in the writings of R. Judah *he-Ḥasid* and R. Eleazar of Worms, see Baer, "Ha-Megammah ha-Datit/ha-Ḥevratit," 18–20; Yosef Dan, *Sifrut ha-Musar veha-Derush* (Jerusalem, 1975), 128–33; and Marcus, *Piety and Society*, 39–52. The substitution of חרטה for תשובת הבאה in the *Semaq* passage is not a problematic discrepancy. The term תשובה חרטה appears as a substitute or definition for תשובת הבאה in *SḤP* 37 and in other related Pietist texts. See *Sefer Roqeaḥ*, *Hilkhot Teshuvah*, sec. 4; Israel al-Nakawa, *Menorat ha-Maʾor*, ed. H. G. Enelow, vol. 3 (New York, 1933), 114–15; and Marcus, 50.

Cambr. Add. 394 (Ashkenaz, fourteenth/fifteenth centuries), fols. 83v–84r, records a penitential *teḥinnah* by an Isaac b. Joseph (of Corbeil?) [See also Israel Davidson, *Oẓar ha-Shirah veha-Piyyut*, vol. 1 (New York, 1924), 73, #1594]:

R. Eleazar of Worms who cites formulations of R. Eleazar on the *teshuvah* process and its efficacy—makes no reference to *teshuvat ha-mishqal* or to the need for physical afflictions as part of the *teshuvah* process.[143]

R. Moses of Coucy, whose affinities with the *hilkhot teshuvah* of the German Pietists have been discussed, also stopped short of requiring forms of self-affliction as an aspect of repentance.[144] On the other hand, R. Simḥah of Spires, a contemporary of R. Moses who was also linked to R. Judah *he-Ḥasid*,[145] issued a ruling regarding repeated domestic abuse (requiring the husband to be physically punished according to the judgment of the court) that appears to allude to the concept of *teshuvat ha-mishqal* as its basis.[146] R. Meir of Rothenburg, a younger contemporary of R. Isaac of Corbeil who studied with R. Samuel of Evreux and was influenced by a number of teachings of *ḥasidut Ashkenaz*,[147] prescribed physical punishments and afflictions as penance in a number of responsa. In one instance, R. Meir referred specifically to *Sefer Roqeaḥ* as his source.[148] Nonetheless, R. Isaac of Corbeil remains the first northern French halakhist to refer to the full program of Pietist penances.[149]

אודה על חטאתי בעוד בי נשמתי ויראתי וחרדתי מפני פחד ה׳... ואיככה אתנפל מפני האדון ה׳... צרכי אני ספרתי ואת חטאתי זכרתי... כי חטאתי לה׳... נפשי על יצרך ואויה לי על שברך מה אשיב לה׳... חולי נא וגוחי... אולי יחנן ה׳... לבי דוה עלי כי קרוב יום ה׳ רגזו ואל תחטאו כי חטאתם לה׳... ישיב גוף לנשמה אם עושים מאומה לסלוח לי אשר לא יאבה ה׳... ואיככה אמרת נקי אני מה׳... הטיבה ה׳ קדוש ישמע לקוראיו כי א-ל רחום ה׳.

This passage is followed by liturgical and halakhic material from other thirteenth-century Ashkenazic rabbinic figures, such as R. Netanʾel of Chinon (see below, ch. 3, n. 104), R. Solomon b. Samuel (below, ch. 2, n. 4), and R. Azriʾel (see A. Havazalet, "Teshuvot R. Azriʾel b. Yeḥiʾel," *Ẓefunot* 1 [1989]:5–14, and Z. Leitner, "Seridim mi-Perush R. Azriʾel le-Massekhet Nazir," *Sefer ha-Zikkaron li-Khevod R. Shmuʾel Barukh Werner* [Jerusalem, 1996], 156–62), supporting the possibility that the Isaac b. Joseph in this passage is the author of *Semaq*. For similar *teḥinnot* or *vidduyim* attributed to R. Moses of Coucy, R. Judah *he-Ḥasid*, and R. Eleazar of Worms, see above, n. 112.

[143]See *ʿArugat ha-Bosem*, ed. Urbach, 4:179–80.

[144]See Urbach, *Baʿalei ha-Tosafot*, 1:469–70.

[145]See below, ch. 2, n. 16, and ch. 5, n. 12.

[146]See Avraham Grossman, "Yaḥasam shel Ḥakhmei Yisraʾel ʾel Hakkaʾat Nashim," *Proceedings of the Tenth World Congress for Jewish Studies* (Jerusalem, 1990) [Div. B, vol. 1], 121–23 [="Rabbinic Views on Wife Beating, 800–1300," *Jewish History* 5 (1991):59–61.] Cf. Marcus, *Piety and Society*, 126–27.

[147]See below, ch. 2, sec. 3.

[148]See Baer, "Ha-Megammah ha-Datit/ha-Ḥevratit," 19, n. 38; Jacob Elbaum, *Teshuvat ha-Lev ve-Qabbalat Yissurim* (Jerusalem, 1993), 19–22; H. J. Zimmels,

R. Isaac's striking formulation on synagogue decorum and comportment, found without attribution at the end of his lengthy discussion of the precept of prayer and its performance, owes much to the writings of the German Pietists:

> Woe to those who chatter idly or act frivolously in the synagogue during the prayer service. They prevent their children from meriting the world to come. We should draw an *a fortiori* argument for ourselves from the Christians. If they can stand silently [*ke-ʾilmim*] in their churches, we who stand before the King of kings, the Holy One blessed be He, can certainly do so. Our predecessors have told us, and we have seen with our own eyes, that several synagogues have been turned into churches because people acted foolishly in them.... Thus, everyone must feel the need to be in awe and tremble before Him and not talk, at least during the cantor's repetition of the *Shemoneh ʿEsreh.*[150]

Using almost identical phrases and terms, two passages in *Sefer Ḥasidim* address the three points that are the focus of the *Semaq* passage: the need to eliminate talking and frivolous behavior in the synagogue, the fact that the need for better behavior can be derived, a fortiori, from the behavior of the Christians (בבית תפילתם עומדים בתרבות), and the incidence of Jewish houses of worship that were destroyed or taken over by Christians because of the frivolous behavior that had occurred in them. In addition, the penitential literature of the Pietists prescribes very harsh penance regimens for those who talk during prayer services in the synagogue.[151]

Ashkenazim and Sephardim (London, 1958), 241–43. On Maharam and *Semaq*, see below, n. 169. For references to Pietist penances in the rabbinic literature of the fourteenth and fifteenth centuries, see Marcus, *Piety and Society*, 128–29; Yedidyah Dinari, *Ḥakhmei Ashkenaz be-Shilhei Yemei ha-Benayim* (Jerusalem, 1984), 85–93; Elbaum, *Teshuvat ha-Lev ve-Qabbalat Yissurim*, passim.

[149]Although *Semaq* lists the four Pietist modes of penance without providing any specific guidance regarding their application, R. Pereẓ of Corbeil offers a brief definition of each type, fully consonant with Pietist literature, in his gloss to the *Semaq* text. Cf. R. Pereẓ's gloss to *Semaq*, sec. 175, citing Rabbenu Yonah (above, n. 91); S. Shaʾanan, "Pisqei Rabbenu Pereẓ va-Aḥerim," *Moriah* 17/9–10 (1991):12, sec. 15 (above, n. 83); and below, ch. 2, nn. 69–70. See Eric Zimmer, *ʿOlam ke-Minhago Noheg*, 230–34 (esp. n. 54), for *Semaq*'s inclusion of a stringent practice regarding *yemei tohar* associated with both northern French *perushim* and German Pietists, and cf. below, ch. 2, n. 86.

[150]*Semaq*, sec. 11 (end). Cf. Ivan Marcus, "Jews and Christians Imagining the Other in Medieval Europe," *Prooftexts* 15 (1995):220–21.

[151]See *SHP* 1589, 224; Moshe Hallamish, "Siḥat Ḥullin be-Veit ha-Knesset: Meẓiʾut u-Maʾavaq," *Milet* 2 (1985):226–27, 243–44; Moritz Güdemann, *Ha-Torah veha-Ḥayyim*,

Sefer Mizvot Qatan, which does not mention many contemporary names—aside from R. Isaac's immediate teachers, the two major twelfth-century northern French tosafist masters, Rabbenu Tam and Ri, and the pillars of Sefardic *halakhah*, Rabbenu Ḥanan᾿el, Rif and Rambam—cites (from the *hilkhot ḥasidut* of) R. Eleazar of Worms at the beginning of its treatment of prayer. The material on prayer begins with a discussion of the need for proper *kavvanah*. *Semaq* defines *kavvanah* as thinking about the meaning of each word and making sure that not one word is skipped, taking the same care one uses when counting coins. German Pietists underscored the importance of not skipping or changing a word or even a single letter of prayer, since this would disturb the internal harmony and overall efficacy of the prayers. Indeed, they counted and analyzed the number of words and letters in many prayers, as a means of arriving at each prayer's inner meaning. They believed that reciting the liturgy slowly and accurately unlocks the esoteric meanings of the prayers and, at the same time, faithfully preserves ancient rabbinic formulae.[152]

R. Isaac writes that if one cannot have proper *kavvanah* throughout all the blessings of the *Shemoneh ᶜEsreh*, one should at least try to maintain *kavannah* during the first three blessings (the unit entitled *Avot*) and during the blessing of *Modim*:

> And R. Eleazar of Worms wrote in his book[153] that it is very good to have *kavvanah* at the conclusion of each of the blessings (of the

---

1:69. *SḤP* 1484 also employs the term תרבות in connection with proper decorum in the synagogue. On the importance of proper comportment during prayer in the thought of the German Pietists, see also *SḤP* 517, 1574; Soloveitchik, "Three Themes," 330–34; and below, n. 153. See also the pietistic *Sefer Minhag Tov*, ed. Weiss, *Ha-Ẓofeh* 13 (1929):224, sec. 3, and Urbach, *Baᶜalei ha-Tosafot*, 2:572–73. Despite the strictness of the German Pietists regarding Jewish-Gentile relations, they emulated those behaviors of non-Jews which they felt had merit. See Katz, *Exclusiveness and Tolerance*, 93–105; Baer, "Ha-Megammah ha-Datit/ha-Ḥevratit shel Sefer Ḥasidim," passim; Soloveitchik, 315–25; and cf. D. Berger, *The Jewish-Christian Debate in the High Middle Ages* (Philadelphia, 1979), 27. [Note R. Isaac of Corbeil's statement in *Semaq*, sec. 1, in which he repudiates sharply the view of the "philosophers," that the world is governed by the constellations.]

[152] See, e.g., *SḤP* 1575; *Arbaᶜah Turim, O. Ḥ.* 113; *ᶜArugat ha-Bosem*, ed. Urbach, 4:83–99; Sperber, *Minhagei Yisra᾿el*, 1:121–24, 2:95–98; and below, n. 162, and ch. 2, nn. 15, 26.

[153] See *Sefer Roqeaḥ, hilkhot ḥasidut, shoresh zekhirat ha-Shem veha-tefillah be-᾿ahavah uve-simḥah tamid kol ha-yom*. Cf. *Roqeaḥ*, sec. 322; *SḤP*, secs. 1577–79, 393; and R. Abraham Oppenheim's *Eshel Avraham* to *Shulḥan Arukh, Oraḥ Ḥayyim*, sec. 97. See also *Orḥot Ḥayyim, Hilkhot Tefillah*, sec. 37 (fol. 16a) and *Kol Bo*, sec. 11, fols. 5a–b, which include the formulations of *Semaq* and R. Eleazar of Worms (and R. Jonah as well) regarding *kavvanah*. Cf. *Mishneh Torah, Hilkhot Tefillah*, 4:15, and *Haggahot*

> *Shemoneh ʿEsreh)* since they [the conclusions] contain [all together] 113 words, equivalent to the 113 words in the prayer of Hannah. And it stands to reason that whoever has proper *kavvanah* during his requests, but not during [the blessings which are in] praise of the Holy One blessed be He, does himself harm. One should think that since if he were standing before a human king he would be very precise with his words, he certainly must do so before the King of kings, the Holy One blessed be He.[154]

R. Isaac cites R. Judah *he-Ḥasid* by name just once in *Sefer Miẓvot Qatan*, but the context and location give the citation prominence. In delineating the extent to which one must be prepared to give up his life to sanctify the Divine Name (*ʿal qiddush ha-Shem*), R. Isaac, like other medieval Ashkenazic halakhists, extends some of the basic parameters found in talmudic literature.[155] He notes that while, strictly speaking, a Jew whose life is threatened by a non-Jew may transgress all prohibitions (with the exceptions of adultery, murder or idolatry) in order to save himself, it is a *middat ḥasidut*—a commendable act of unusual piety—not to transgress any prohibition even under the penalty of death. R. Isaac includes this discussion at the very beginning of his work (in the third precept discussed), as part of the precept to demonstrate love for the Almighty (*ʾahavat ha-Shem*).

The second of two anecdotal proofs that R. Isaac presents in support of his position involves R. Judah *he-Ḥasid*. *Semaq* recounts an incident in which Rabbi Judah instructed his students not to travel to attend a wedding because armed robbers frequented the road they would have to take. The students went anyway, confident they could invoke a Divine Name to save themselves. When they returned, R. Judah informed them they stood to lose their share in the world to come unless they retraced their path without invoking the Name,

---

Maimuniyyot, ad loc. It is at this point, when *Semaq* cites R. Eleazar of Worms, that R. Pereẓ in his gloss cites R. Moses of Evreux on the importance of thinking about each word as it is being said. See above, n. 79. Cf. R. Pereẓ's gloss to *Semaq*, sec. 97, citing R. Samuel of Evreux on *kavvanah*; and below, ch. 2, n. 69.

[154]*Semaq*, sec. 11, beginning. Cf. *Arbaʿah Turim, O. Ḥ.*, sec. 98; *Beit Yosef*, ad loc., s.v. *ve-yaʾir*; and above, n. 93. See Mark Verman, *The History and Varieties of Jewish Meditation* (Northvale, 1996), 155–57, regarding the appropriate *kavvanot* during the recitation of the *Shema* as delineated in *Semaq* and in the writings of R. Ezra of Gerona.

[155]See, e.g., Katz, *Exclusiveness and Tolerance*, 82–85, and Haym Soloveitchik, "Religious Law and Change: The Medieval Ashkenazic Example," *AJS Review* 12 (1987):207–11.

even if doing so meant they would perish. They went back on the road and were killed.[156]

This episode does not appear in full narrative form in the literature of *Ḥasidei Ashkenaz*, but it is consonant with a passage in *Sefer Ḥasidim*: "A person who embarks on a journey should not say, 'I will adjure [the name of] angels to protect me,' but should instead pray to the Master of the universe. Several prophets were killed but they did not adjure the Holy Name (ולא השביעו בשם הקודש). Rather, they stood in prayer saying, 'If He does not hear our prayers, we are not worthy of being saved.' They did not undertake any tactic other than prayer."[157] Other passages in *Sefer Ḥasidim* associate the inappropriate or untutored magical adjuration of *Shemot* with extremely dire consequences and shed further light on the gravity of such acts.[158]

---

[156]See *Semaq*, sec. 3; Urbach, *Baᶜalei ha-Tosafot*, 2:572, and cf. 1:387–88; Soloveitchik, "Religious Law and Change," 210, n. 8; and cf. *Orḥot Ḥayyim*, pt. 2, sec. 4 (*Din Ahavat ha-Shem ve-Yirᵓato*), 26. On *qiddush ha-Shem* in the thought of *Ḥasidei Ashkenaz*, see Baer, "Ha-Megammah ha-Datit ha-Ḥevratit," 14–15; and above, n. 20.

Semaq, sec. 154, following *Semag*, *ᶜaseh* 23, instructs that the words כוזו במוכסז כוזו be written on the outside of the *mezuzah*. These fourteen letters represent the three Divine Names found in the verse of *Shema Yisraᵓel*, the name *E-lohenu* surrounded by two Tetragrammatons. (The letters of these Names are represented by the letter that follows it in the Hebrew alphabet). On the so-called fourteen-letter Name, see Trachtenberg, *Jewish Magic and Superstition*, 92, and below, ch. 5, n. 63. Cf. *Synopse zur Hekhalot-Literatur*, ed. Schäfer, sec. 513. Although R. Asher b. Yeḥiᵓel (*Hilkhot Mezuzah*, sec. 18) and *Tur* (*Y. D.*, sec. 288) identify this as an accepted Ashkenazic custom (in northern France as well as Germany), *Semag*, *Semaq*, and Sefer Assufot (see Moses Gaster, *Studies and Texts* [London, 1925–25], 3:230) are the only Ashkenazic rabbinic sources to mention it explicitly. [In the geonic treatise on *mezuzot* cited by Rabiah this practice is alluded to only in cryptic fashion; see Aptowitzer, "Mi-Sifrut ha-Geonim," 100–101; and above, n. 45. On *Sefer Assufot*'s involvement with *sod* interpretations and magical practices, see below, ch. 3, nn. 18, 59; ch. 4, n. 57.] On the use of this Name in Ashkenaz for protection, see Trachtenberg, 148–50. The Zohar also adopted this practice regarding *mezuzot*; see Ta-Shma, *Ha-Nigleh shebe-Nistar*, 23; and idem, "Od li-Veᶜayat ha-Meqorot ha-Ashkenaziyyim be-Sefer ha-Zohar," 263.

[157]*SḤP* 211=*SḤB* 205. See Margoliot's note to this passage (*Meqor Ḥesed*, n. 5) for citations (and embellishments) of the story in subsequent rabbinic and kabbalistic literature, and cf. *SḤP* 583, regarding the performance of circumcision in a dangerous situation. In one version, the story involving R. Judah is traced to the rabbis of northern France (=*Semaq*?), and in another R. Jonah *Ḥasid* is suggested as the teacher of the students; cf. above, n. 84, and below, n. 171. Note also the passage in *Hekhalot* literature, adduced by Margoliot, that is parallel to part of the narrative.

[158]See, e.g., *SḤP* 210, 212–13, 379, 797, 1452; *SḤB* 206, 1172, and Margoliot's appendix entitled *Ḥasidei ᶜOlam*, 586–89; Dan, *Torat ha-Sod shel Ḥasidut Ashkenaz*, 19, 28, 74–76, 218–22; Haviva Pedaya, "Pegam ve-Tiqqun shel ha-E-lohut be-Qabbalat

R. Isaac offers no further comment on the story involving R. Judah *he-Ḥasid* and his students. R. Judah's posture will be analyzed more fully below, when his views on the use of Divine Names for magical purposes are discussed. Nonetheless, it is clear that R. Isaac relied on R. Judah's response to suggest that there are situations in which one should voluntarily give up his life *ᶜal qiddush ha-Shem* (or in order not to desecrate God's Name), even if it is possible within the letter of the law to avoid this fate. R. Isaac defined such an act as one of pietistic devotion (*middat ḥasidut*). R. Eleazar of Worms's student, R. Abraham b. Azriel, enunciated the same concept in different terms: when it comes to *qiddush ha-Shem*, כל המחמיר תבוא עליו ברכה.[159] In addition, R. Isaac of Corbeil's inclusion of this episode demonstrates his awareness that Divine Names could be invoked magically in order to avoid danger. According to R. Judah *he-Ḥasid*, the use of *Shemot* had to be carefully controlled, but their potential efficacy was acknowledged by both R. Judah and R. Isaac.[160]

An account of the origin of the *ᶜAleynu* prayer and the reflection of this origin in the text of *ᶜAleynu*, attributed in other sources to R. Judah *he-Ḥasid*, is presented in *Sefer Orḥot Ḥayyim* as the explanation of R. Isaac of Corbeil. "R. Isaac of Corbeil (*Ha-Ri mi-Corbeil*) wrote: I heard that Joshua instituted it [*ᶜAleynu*] at the time that he conquered the land [of Israel] and he inscribed his name of humility [*shem qatnuto* (his original name), *Hosheaᶜ*] in reverse [ע= עלינו לשבח, ש= שלא שם חלקנו, ו= וא[נח]נו כורעים, ה= הוא אלקינו]. [Therefore,] One who says אבל אנחנו [כורעים] errs [since the *vav* of *Hosheaᶜ* would be supplanted by *ʾalef*, the first letter of אבל]."[161]

Two extant traditions from R. Judah *he-Ḥasid* concern Joshua's authorship of *ᶜAleynu*. One is that the prayer contains 152 words, which is the *gematria* (numerical) equivalent of his father's name, בן נון (*bin Nun*). The second is that Joshua composed this prayer when the Jewish people entered the land of Israel and began to capture various cities and regions. "Joshua saw the many man-made idols which were being destroyed and authored this hymn of praise to God. He inscribed his name in it backward, at the beginning of each verse, for reasons of modesty, so that not all would understand that he had composed it." The letters and their related phrases are then spelled out to form *Hosheaᶜ*, exactly as they are in the *Orḥot Ḥayyim* passage attributed to

---

R. Yizḥaq Sagi Nahor," *Meḥqerei Yerushalayim be-Maḥshevet Yisraʾel* 6/3–4 (1987):157, n. 1; and below, ch. 4, nn. 41–42.

[159]See *ᶜArugat ha-Bosem*, ed. Urbach, 4:167, n. 76.

[160]Cf. *Semaq*, sec.143, on sorcery, and cf. below, ch. 3, n. 87.

[161]*Orḥot Ḥayyim, Teḥinnah aḥarei shemoneh ᶜesreh*, sec. 8, fol. 21b; and cf. *Kol Bo*, ch. 16 (*Tefillah*), 9a.

R. Isaac of Corbeil. "Therefore, every God-fearing person should be careful not to add or subtract any word from what our forefathers have established because all depends on the measurement [amount] of the words."[162]

There are several other suggestive parallels between teachings of the German Pietists and formulations of R. Isaac of Corbeil. These include material on *neḥush* and *siman* (symbolic devination),[163] *tokekhah* (admonition and rebuke),[164] monetary compensation for the teaching or study of Torah,[165] and the extent of a woman's obligation to study Torah.[166] R. Isaac's relationship with *Ḥasidei Ashkenaz* also helps to account for a recurring pattern in manuscript collections. Copyists from the late thirteenth and early fourteenth centuries and beyond juxtaposed *Semaq* with works of *Ḥasidei Ashkenaz*, suggesting that a perception developed quickly that these works were related.

---

[162]Ms. Kaufmann A399, fol. 50r, cited in *ᶜArugat ha-Bosem*, ed. Urbach, 4:98. See also Elliot Wolfson, "Hai Gaon's Letter and Commentary on ᶜAleynu: Further Evidence of Moses De Leon's Pseudepigraphic Activity," *JQR* 81 (1991):380–81. Wolfson lists a series of manuscript texts and published works that contain this tradition, occasionally in the name of R. Judah *he-Ḥasid*. I have demonstrated that all these works and their authors or compilers were connected, in different ways, to the German Pietists; see my "Rabbinic Figures in Castilian Kabbalistic Pseudepigraphy," 97–98, n. 73. As the present study serves to indicate, R. Isaac of Corbeil also had a connection to R. Judah *he-Ḥasid* and his followers. [In *Orḥot Ḥayyim, ha-Ri mi-Corbeil* invariably refers to R. Isaac b. Joseph; see also my "Rabbinic Figures," 92–93, 98, n. 74.]

[163]*Semaq*, sec. 136; *SḤB* 59; *SḤP* 14, 377; *Sefer Roqeaḥ, hilkhot Yom ha-Kippurim*, 106; *Semag, lo taᶜaseh* 53; *Sefer ha-Yirʾah*, ed. Zilber, 53, sec. 228; Güdemann, *Ha-Torah veha-Ḥayyim*, 1:159; and Dinari, *Ḥakhmei Ashkenaz*, 157. Cf. ms. Parma 541, fol. 264v (end): ויהי ערב ויהי בקר יום רביעי באותה פרשה לא תמצא פ׳ כי אין לו פה מי שמתחיל ללמוד ביום ד׳ או מי שמסיים בו וזהו שאמרו חכמים אין מסיימין בד׳... כי לילית הולכת בליל רביעי ואין סימן ברכה באותו יום וביום שני כמו״כ על כן אין מתחילין ואין מסיימין כי טוב בפרשת יום שני; Ta-Shma, *Ha-Nigleh shebe-Nistar*, 98, n. 65 (end); Georges Vajda, "Liqqutim mi-Sefer Musar Bilti Yaduaᶜ le-Eḥad me-Rabbanei Ẓarefat," *Sefer Ḥayyim Schirmann*, ed. Shraga Abramson and Aaron Mirsky (Jerusalem, 1970), 103–6; idem, "Une Traite de Morale d'Origine Judeo-Française," *REJ* 125 (1966):267–85; and Richard Kieckhefer, *Magic in the Middle Ages* (Cambridge, 1989), 85–91.

[164]*Semaq*, sec. 112; *SḤP* 1338, 1972; *Semag, ᶜaseh* 11. Cf. Soloveitchik, "Three Themes," 336, n. 82; Marcus, *Piety and Society*, 87–88, n. 4; and above, n. 110.

[165]See my *Jewish Education and Society*, 43–46, 91–97.

[166]On the obligation to teach women the commandments for which they are responsible and their obligation to study that material, see *SḤP* 835 and the introduction to *Semaq* (which consists of written remarks from R. Isaac, preserved by his students). Cf. *Sefer ha-Agur*, sec. 2; *Beit Yosef* to *Oraḥ Ḥayyim*, sec. 47 (end); and Ḥida, *Yosef Omeẓ*, sec. 67. See also my review of S. P. Zolty, *"And All Your Children Shall Be Learned": Women and the Study of Torah in Jewish Law and History* (Jason Aronson, 1993), in *JQR* 87 (1996):192–95.

This relationship may also account for some unusual intertwinings of R. Judah *he-Ḥasid* and R. Isaac in subsequent medieval halakhic texts, such as R. Aharon *ha-Kohen* of Lunel's *Orḥot Ḥayyim*.[167]

There is no evidence of any personal contact between R. Isaac of Corbeil and the central figures of *Ḥasidei Ashkenaz*. Several of the parallels that have been noted suggest that R. Isaac may have read *Sefer Ḥasidim* and *Sefer Roqeaḥ*, and perhaps other Pietist works as well. In addition, R. Isaac studied at the academy of Evreux.[168] This could account not only for the similarities between R. Isaac and the German Pietists with respect to their approaches to prayer and penance, but also for various aspects of *Semaq* itself. With its unswerving dedication to the formulation of practical *halakhah* that could be studied by the masses, as demonstrated by its simplicity and accessibility, *Semaq* conforms fully to the specifications of the German Pietists concerning the goal of Torah study[169]—despite the fact that much of *Semaq* represents the fruits of twelfth-century tosafist dialectic.[170]

Moreover, sayings and exempla employed by *Semaq* to exhort the reader to higher levels of ethical and religious conduct—as well as the classification of the commandments in accordance with various parts of the body and the

---

[167]See my "German Pietism in Northern France: The Case of R. Isaac of Corbeil," in *Ḥazon Naḥum* [Studies in Jewish Law, Thought, and History Presented to Dr. Norman Lamm], ed. Jeffrey Gurock and Yaakov Elman (New York, 1997), 222–27.

[168]See, e.g., *Semaq*, sec. 151 (ורבותינו מאי״ברא היו נוהגין); sec. 153, in which both R. Samuel of Evreux (כך קבלתי ממורי השר [=ר׳ שמואל] מאי״ברא) and his brother Ri [=R. Isaac] b. Shneʾur are mentioned [R. Isaac is also cited at the end of sec. 281, regarding ספק סכנת נפשות בשבת.]; sec. 219 (ונהגו רבותינו מאוי״ורא); and cf. Urbach, *Baᶜalei ha-Tosafot*, 2:571. Note also the references to R. Isaac's teachers at Evreux in his *pesaqim*. See Moshe Hershler, "Pisqei Rabbenu Yiẓḥaq mi-Corbeil Baᶜal ha-Semaq mi-Tokh Ketav Yad," *Sinai* 67 (1970):244–49; Y. S. Lange, "Pisqei R. Yiẓḥaq mi-Corbeil," *Ha-Maᶜayan* 16:4 (1976):95–104; H. S. Shaʾanan, "Pisqei Rabbenu Ri mi-Corbeil," *Sefer Ner li-Shemaᶜayah* [*Sefer Zikkaron le-Zikhro shel ha-Rav Shemaᶜayah Shaʾanan*] (Bnei Brak, 1988), 5–32. Cf. Y. S. Lange, "Le-ᶜInyan ha-Semaq mi-Ẓurich," *Alei Sefer* 4 (1977): 178–79; Henri Gross, *Gallia Judaica* (Paris, 1897), 39; and Emanuel, "Sifrei Halakhah Avudim shel Baᶜalei ha-Tosafot," 231–45.

[169]See *Semaq*, introduction, for R. Isaac's own assessment of his purpose in authoring *Semaq*, as a means of insuring that all would know the essentials of those precepts which can still be performed. Note also the strong approbation of *Semaq* expressed by R. Meir of Rothenburg, whose own relationship with *Ḥasidei Ashkenaz* will be discussed below (ch. 2, sec. 3). See Urbach, *Baᶜalei ha-Tosafot*, 2:573, and cf. below, ch. 2, n. 62. Some editions of *Semaq* append a group of *liqqutim* from R. Meir to the end of sec. 81 (laws of oaths and vows).

[170]See above, n. 102.

division of the work into seven sections, one for each day of the week—are techniques that can be found in the writings of R. Isaac's fellow student at Evreux, Rabbenu Yonah.[171] *Semaq* includes a distinct precept for looking at the *ẓiẓit* during the recitation of *Shema*. Geonic sources had earlier rejected this interpretation of the phrase וראיתם אותו, arguing that the *ẓiẓit (tallit)* were already inspected when the initial blessing was made over them. In his *Sefer ha-Yirʾah*, Rabbenu Yonah also instructs one to hold the *ẓiẓit* and look at them during the recitation of *Shema*.[172]

In addition to all these conceptual and textual affinities with *Ḥassidei Ashkenaz*, R. Isaac was given to deep personal piety.[173] Both contemporaries and students refer to him as *ḥasid*,[174] just as one of R. Isaac's teachers in northern France, R. Samuel of Evreux, and R. Isaac's father-in-law, R. Yeḥiel of Paris, were also called *ḥasid*.[175] Moreover, a collection of R. Isaac's *pesaqim* and

---

[171]See Ta-Shma, "Ḥasidut Ashkenaz bi-Sefarad," 168, n. 8. Urbach, *Baʿalei ha-Tosafot*, 2:572, notes the influence of the proto-Pietist *Sefer Yereʾim* on the structure of *Semaq*. Cf. above, n. 105.

[172]See *Semaq*, sec. 29; *Sefer ha Yirʾah* (ed. Zilber), 22, sec. 73. See also *Beit Yosef, Oraḥ Ḥayyim*, sec. 24, s.v. *katav Baʿal ha-ʿIttur*; S. K. Mirsky, "Meqorot ha-Halakhah ba-Midrashim," *Talpiyyot* 1 (1944): 49–51, 54–55; and S. Kook, *ʿIyyunim u-Meḥqarim* (Jerusalem, 1963), 1:335–37. R. Yonah is cited in *Semaq*, sec. 281 (in *hilkhot Shabbat*, regarding אופה).

[173]See Urbach, *Baʿalei ha-tosafot*, 2:573.

[174]See the introduction to *Semaq*; Gross, *Gallia Judaica*, 563; and Urbach, *Baʿalei ha-Tosafot*, 2:572–75. R. Isaac of Corbeil is also described as *ḥasid* in the heading of the two versions of his *pesaqim*, Bodl. 781, fol. 68v, and Paris 390, fol. 251v. To be sure, these titles may have been included by copyists or others simply as a sign of general piety or spiritual greatness. Nonetheless, depending upon their dating and provenance, these manuscripts may reflect the impression that R. Isaac of Corbeil was connected with the German Pietists or another pietist group, such as the one at Evreux, on the basis of specific *pesaqim* that he issued. [Note also that R. Isaac was called *he-Ḥasid* in the colophon of the version of *Semaq* preserved in Bodl. 875, an Ashkenazic manuscript copied in 1299. See Richler, "Al Kitvei Yad shel Sefer ha-Yirʾah" (above, n. 84); above, n. 88; and my "German Pietism in Northern France" (above, n. 167), 222, 226, n. 69.]

[175]R. Samuel of Evreux is called *he-Ḥasid* by his student, R. Yedidyah b. Israel; see *Shitah ʿal Moʿed Qatan le-Talmido shel R. Yeḥiel mi-Paris*, ed. M. L. Zaks (Jerusalem, 1937), 2:113. [R. Yedidyah may have been the teacher of R. Judah *he-Ḥasid*'s son, R. Zal(t)man; see Urbach, *Baʾalei ha-Tosafot*, 2:569, n. 25.] R. Yeḥiel of Paris is referred to as *ḥasid* in *Orḥot Ḥayyim*, pt. 2, *Issurei Maʾakhalot*, sec. 12 (p. 286). In *Hilkhot Ẓiẓit*, sec. 15 (fol. 3b) he is called *ha-qadosh*. In Bodl. 2343 and Parma 3175 (De Rossi 166), R. Yeḥiel's *pesaqim* are called פסקי (הוראות מ)החסיד ר' יחיאל. Cf. above, n. 88; Israel Ta-Shma, "Li-Meqorotav ha-Sifrutiyyim shel ha-Zohar," *Tarbiz* 60 (1991):663–65; and see now idem, *Ha-Nigleh shebe-Nistar*, 95, n. 42. Note that the brothers of Evreux were

personal practices is replete with manifestations of asceticism and *perishut*.[176] These include stern warnings against gazing at women and their clothing, looking into the face of a *rasha*, cultivating frivolous behavior (*seḥoq*) and aimless activities (e.g., *letayyel be-ḥinnam*), and enjoying food and other pleasures on weekdays to a greater extent than is required for healthful subsistence (*derekh taᶜanug*). In addition, one should fast on a regular basis.[177] On these fast days, which ideally should occur every few weeks (in imitation of the *ʾanshei maᶜamad*), one must repent completely, confess his sins and specify his wrongdoings to a *rav*, and ask the Almighty for forgiveness. If one cannot fast, one should set aside charity funds for that day. Indeed, when any member of the household of *ha-qadosh R. Yiẓḥaq* was sick, or when he himself was suffering, he would give eighteen (*ḥai*) *peshitim* to charity.

Several of these practices bear unmistakable similarities to doctrines of the German Pietists.[178] It must be stressed, however, that, like the brothers of Evreux who continued to produce standard *Tosafot* texts that employed

---

involved in the compilation of certain versions of R. Yeḥiel's *pesaqim*; see Emanuel, "Sifrei Halakhah Avudim shel Baᶜalei ha-Tosafot," 231–36. *Pesaqim* of R. Yeḥiel are also found in ms. Cambr. 786, in a collection of rulings primarily from associates of *Ḥasidei Ashkenaz*; see below, ch. 2, nn. 18, 41.

R. Pereẓ of Corbeil cautioned that one should not speak during the quasi-repetition of the *ᶜAmidah* on Friday evenings (*berakhah ʾaḥat meᶜen sheva*), since a soul once told R. Yeḥiel of Paris that the angels threw him up and let him fall by himself because he talked during this prayer. See below, ch. 2, n. 70, and ch. 5, n. 43. A similar notion is found in *SHP* 1073 (and cf. below, ch. 2, n. 52). To be sure, even those northern French tosafists given to *ḥasidut* expressed their concern (and disagreement) with stringencies they believed were without halakhic basis (מנהג שטות); see below, ch. 2, n. 11.

[176] Ms. Cambr. Add. 3127, fols. 165v–166v. On this collection of rulings (and its parallels described in the next note) see Emanuel, "Sifrei Halakhah Avudim," 238–40. This manuscript also contains *pesaqim* from R. Yeḥiel of Paris and works by other students at the academy of Evreux. See now Stephan Reif, *Hebrew Manuscripts at Cambridge University Library* (Cambridge, 1997), 219–21.

[177] The text offers an example of this regimen through a description of R. Moses (of Evreux), who would slice his meat into very thin pieces in order not to experience its full flavor (שלא לטעום טעם בשר חשוב). Some of these notions (and the description of R. Moses) are also found in ms. Paris 407 (fol. 236d), published by S. Shaʾanan, "Pisqei Rabbenu Pereẓ va-Aḥerim," *Moriah* 17:9–10 (1991):12. There is some confusion as to which *pesaqim* in these manuscripts belong to R. Isaac of Corbeil and which to R. Pereẓ of Corbeil. See above, n. 83. In any case, both studied at Evreux and either could have recorded the practice of R. Moses. It is conceivable that the practices of *ha-qadosh R. Yiẓḥaq* recorded in these *pesaqim* associated with R. Isaac of Corbeil refer to R. Isaac b. Shneʾur, the third brother at Evreux, but it is more likely that they reflect the practices of R. Isaac of Corbeil, as recorded by one of his students. Cf. above, n. 34.

dialectic even as they produced others that curtailed its use, R. Isaac of Corbeil did not renounce his tosafist background in order to pursue pietistic ideals.

R. Isaac of Corbeil's German contemporary, R. Meir of Rothenburg, exhibited even greater affinities with *Ḥasidei Ashkenaz*, in both pietistic and esoteric contexts. The pietistic affinities can be seen not only in R. Meir's ritual practices, but also in his halakhic rulings and in his biblical and prayer interpretations. Before focusing on R. Meir, the next chapter will identify a group of lesser-known tosafists in thirteenth-century Germany and Austria who were clearly under the influence of the German Pietists in regard to these disciplines and areas as well.

Several of these figures impacted directly on R. Meir of Rothenburg, who appears to represent a kind of amalgamation of tosafist and Pietist teachings. A complete assessment, however, of the impact of these rabbinic scholars on R. Meir (and the extent of R. Meir's activities) must follow a discussion of their mystical proclivities, and can be found in chapter 5.

---

[178]On the strongly formulated prohibitions against gazing at women, and exhortations to minimize *seḥoq* and even idle strolls, see Soloveitchik, "Three Themes," 328–30, esp. n. 53, and *SḤP*, secs. 102–3, 432, 770. On confessing sins to a *ḥakham*, see Marcus's analysis of the sage-penitential found in *Sefer Ḥasidim* in his *Piety and Society*, 75–76, 142–43. Approbation for the notion of giving charity to memorialize the dead is found in *SḤP* 35, 273; in *Sefer Roqeaḥ*, sec. 217; and in the name of R. Shemaryah b. Mordekhai of Spires, a student of R. Eliezer Ḥazzan of Spires (who instructed R. Samuel Ḥasid in *torat ha-sod*). See Ta-Shma, *Minhag Ashkenaz ha-Qadmon*, 301, n. 9; *Maḥzor Vitry*, sec. 353; and cf. Louis Finkelstein, *Jewish Self-Government in the Middle Ages* (New York, 1964^2), 230; and below, ch. 2, n. 7. [Included in these *pesaqim* is the instruction to consciously train eight- or nine-year-old children not to mention a Divine Name in vain and not to speak profanity or *leshon ha-ra*. This is perhaps related to the concept found in *Sefer Ḥasidim*, that children can be held fully accountable for their actions even before the age of twelve or thirteen (see below, ch. 2, nn. 22–23), although the goal of the *pesaqim* may simply have been to ensure that children not do these things when they grow older. The great concern which Jews displayed in training young children in these behaviors is highlighted in polemical literature. See., e.g., R. Joseph Kimḥi, *Sefer ha-Berit*, ed. Frank Talmage (Jerusalem, 1974), 25–27, and Joel Rembaum, "A Re-evaluation of a Medieval Polemical Manuscript," *AJS Review* 5 (1980):86–88.]

2

Pietistic Tendencies in Prayer and Ritual

I

There were a number of rabbinic figures and tosafists in medieval Ashkenaz who subscribed to and worked with the exoteric biblical interpretations of the German Pietists, including the Pietists' particular usages of techniques such as *gematria* and *notariqon*, and their interpretation of patterns or anomalies within the masoretic text (*teᶜamim shel Torah/Ḥumash*).[1] Moreover, there were those who accepted and promulgated the Pietists' readings and variants of liturgical texts, setting aside even northern French prayer rites in favor of those of *Ḥasidei Ashkenaz*.[2] As we shall see, those tosafists who supported the Pietists' readings were more likely to refer to their correctness than to their mystical

---

[1]See, e.g., Ivan Marcus, "Exegesis for the Few and for the Many," *Meḥqerei Yerushalayim be-Maḥshevet Yisraʾel* 8 (1989):1*–24*; Joseph Dan, "The Ashkenazi Concept of Language," in *Hebrew in Ashkenaz*, ed. Lewis Glinert (New York, 1993), 11–25; my "On the Role of Bible Study in Medieval Ashkenaz," *The Frank Talmage Memorial Volume*, ed. Barry Walfish (Haifa, 1993), 1:151–66; Joseph Davis, "Philosophy, Dogma, and Exegesis in Medieval Ashkenazic Judaism: The Evidence of *Sefer Hadrat Qodesh*," *AJS Review* 18 (1993):216–18; *Perushei ha-Torah le-R. Ḥayyim Paltiʾel*, ed. Y. S. Lange (Jerusalem, 1981), editor's introduction, 10–11; *Perush Baᶜal ha-Turim ᶜal ha-Torah*, ed. Y. K. Reinitz (New York, 1993), editor's introduction, 12–16; and below, n. 52.

[2]See, e.g., Eric Zimmer, *ᶜOlam ke-Minhago Noheg* (Jerusalem, 1996), 114–18; Elliot Wolfson, "Hai Gaon's Letter and Commentary on ᶜAleynu: Further Evidence of Moses de Leon's Pseudepigraphic Activity," *JQR* 81 (1990–91):380–83; Moshe Hallamish, "Beᶜayot be-Ḥeqer Hashpaᶜat ha-Qabbalah ᶜal ha-Tefillah," *Massuʾot*, ed. Michal Oron and Amos Goldreich (Jerusalem, 1994), 213 (*Sefer ha-Maḥkim* follows a Franco-German rite; see my "Rabbinic Figures in Castilian Kabbalistic Pseudepigraphy," *Journal of Jewish Thought*

underpinnings. Nonetheless, this aspect of the discussion will begin to move us past pietistic prayer practices and postures toward mysticism, since the Pietists' liturgical readings do reflect, after all, deeply held considerations of *sodot ha-tefillah.*[3]

Israel Ta-Shma has published a brief article that presents and assesses all that is known about R. Solomon b. Samuel *ha-Ẓarefati.*[4] R. Solomon (c.1160–

---

and Philosophy 3 [1993], 97, n. 73); and below, ch. 3, n. 74. See also ms. Paris 633 (a northern French collection from the thirteenth century, described in Collete Sirat, "Un Rituel Juif de France: Le Manuscrit Hébreu 633 de la Bibliothèque Nationale de Paris," *REJ* 119 [1961]:7–39), fols. 30r, 48v (material from R. Judah *he-Ḥasid* and R. Eleazar of Worms.) See also ms. Uppsala 21 [a northern French *maḥzor* for the festivals with a German component, copied in the fourteenth or fifteenth century], fol. 146r, and David Wilhelm, "Le-Minhag Ẓarefat ha-Yashan," *Tarbiz* 24 [1955]:133; fol. 81r (*Shir ha-Yiḥud* by R. Judah *he-Ḥasid*); fol. 104 (prayers according to the *nusḥa*ʾ*ot* of *Ḥasidei Ashkenaz*); below, ch. 3, nn. 103, 110; and ms. B.M. 243 (Or. 2853; sixteenth-century Ashkenaz), described by A. Marmorstein in *REJ* 76 (1923):113–29. Marmorstein notes there is a general blending of Ashkenazic customs with *minhagei Ẓarefat*, including *tefillah*. A number of associates of R. Judah *he-Ḥasid* are referred to in this manuscript, such as R. Moses Fuller (see below, n. 41) and R. Jacob of Corbeil (see below, ch. 4, nn. 26–28). On problems in identifying the author or compiler of this manuscript, cf. Urbach, *Ba*ᶜ*alei ha-Tosafot*, 1:486, n. 32. The frequently mentioned ר״ץ is most likely R. Yiẓḥaq, but it could also be R. Ẓadoq or *rabbanei Ẓarefat*. See, e.g., Menahem Kahana, "Perushim la-Sifrei ha-Genuzim bi-Khetuvei Yad," *Sefer Zikkaron leha-Rav Yiẓḥaq Nissim* (Jerusalem, 1985), 2:100–105, esp. 102, n. 60; and Israel Ta-Shma, "Le-Toledot ha-Yehudim be-Polin ba-Meʾot ha-Yod Bet/ha-Yod Gimmel," *Zion* 53 (1988):358–59. On the use of ר״ץ to represent R. Isaac b. Samuel (Ri) in a number of northern French and German rabbinic texts—including R. Eleazar of Worms's *Sefer Roqeaḥ*—see Yaᶜakov Lisfhitz, "Hilkhot Hagᶜalah mi-Khetav Yad le-Rabbenu Avigdor Kohen Ẓedeq," *Sefer ha-Zikkaron li-Khevod R. Shmuʾel Barukh Werner*, ed. Yosef Buksboim (Jerusalem, 1996), 132, n. 15. On the composition of Brit. Mus. 243 and its parallels—including ms. Hamburg 45 (known as *Perushim u-Fesaqim* ᶜ*al ha-Torah le-R. Avigdor*), ms. Mantua 36, and the printed edition of *Moshav Zeqenim* ᶜ*al ha-Torah*, ed. Solomon Sassoon (Jerusalem, 1959)—see Simcha Emanuel, "Sifrei Halakhah Avudim shel Baᶜalei ha-Tosafot" (Ph.D. diss., Hebrew University, 1993), 226–30, and below, n. 9. Large parts of B. M. 243/ Hamburg 45 have recently been published by Makhon Harerei Qedem under the title *Sefer Perushim u-Fesaqim le-R. Avigdor Ẓarefati* (Jerusalem, 1996). See also below, n. 28.

[3]See, e.g., ᶜ*Arugat ha-Bosem*, ed. E. E. Urbach (Jerusalem, 1963), 4:73–111; Joseph Dan, "The Emergence of Mystical Prayer," *Studies in Jewish Mysticism*, ed. Joseph Dan and Frank Talmage (Cambridge, Mass., 1982), 85–120; and Shimon Shokek, *Ha-Teshuvah be-Sifrut ha-Musar ha-*ᶜ*Ivrit* (Lewiston, 1966), 65.

[4]Israel Ta-Shma, "Mashehu ᶜal Biqqoret ha-Miqra Bimei ha-Benayim," *Ha-Miqra bi-Re*ʾ*i Mefarshav* [*Sefer Zikkaron le-Sarah Kamin*], ed. Sarah Japhet (Jerusalem, 1994), 453–59.

1240) was born in northern France, but he studied in Spires with R. Samuel *he-Ḥasid* and with R. Samuel's sons, R. Judah *he-Ḥasid* and R. Abraham, and then in Regensburg with R. Judah *he-Ḥasid* and others. R. Solomon's commentary, *Teᶜamim shel Ḥumash*, contains *gematria*, as well as exoteric and *sod* interpretations that are similar in style to those associated with R. Judah *he-Ḥasid* and his students; both R. Judah and R. Samuel *he-Ḥasid* are among those cited.[5] After these *Teᶜamim*, R. Solomon offers interpretations of difficult portions within Ibn Ezra's biblical commentaries, especially those dealing with Divine Names. Among the *sodot* which R. Solomon explains is the notion, mentioned cryptically by Ibn Ezra, that Moses did not write all the biblical verses himself but that several phrases or expressions were added by others. This concept is also found in the biblical commentaries of R. Judah *he-Ḥasid* and other members of his circle.[6] Indeed, Ta-Shma has also identified another (anonymous) biblical exegete from northern France who was heavily

---

[5]See ms. Paris 353, fols. 68v–81v. The manuscript continues (through fol. 89) with additional formulations from R. Solomon that employ similar techniques, including *gematria* and the אתב"ש method. One passage contains an analysis of the Hebrew alphabet from the beginning and then backward from the end. On the mystical significance of the letters of the alphabet taken backward (as a Divine Name, according to R. Eleazar of Worms), which is also a component of the Ashkenazic educational initiation ceremony, see Ivan Marcus, *Rituals of Childhood* (New Haven, 1996), 109–10, 145, n. 29, and the studies of Moshe Idel that are cited. [For an earlier controversy about whether the author of *Teᶜamim shel Ḥumash* was from the pre-Crusade period or the twelfth century (predicated on the regular appearance of the name R. Leontin in the text), see Avraham Grossman, *Ḥakhmei Ashkenaz ha-Rishonim*, (Jerusalem, 1981), 86–87, n. 36. See also I. Levi in *REJ* 49 (1909): 231, and *ᶜArugat ha-Bosem*, ed. Urbach, 4:82–83, n. 62; these sources list the same incorrect ms. number, Paris 358. There is no longer any doubt that R. Solomon, who was familiar with pre-Crusade traditions through the German Pietists, is the actual author.] *Teᶜamim shel Ḥumash* is preceded in the manuscript by a *yiḥud* composition of R. Eleazar of Worms, among other *sod* and kabbalistic material.

[6]See H. J. Zimmels, "Ketav Yad Cod. hebr. Hamburg 45 ve-Yiḥuso le-R. Avigdor Katz," *Maʾamarim le-Zikhron R. Ẓevi Pereẓ Chajes*, ed. A. Aptowitzer and Z. Schwarz (Vienna, 1933), 248–61 (esp. 252, 259, n. 7). [Zimmels cogently suggests that the commentaries to the five *megillot* in this manuscript (Ashkenaz, fourteenth/fifteenth centuries) were composed by R. Avigdor himself. The Torah commentaries (and *pesaqim*) may also have been composed, in part, by R. Avigdor, although it appears that students or other members of his circle were also involved; cf. above, n. 2. As a result, biographical details that have been understood to apply to R. Avigdor (such as the references to R. Yom Tov of Joigny as his grandfather) may in fact apply to one of the other, unnamed composers. See also Zimmels, "Le-Toledot R. Avigdor b. Eliyyahu Kohen Ẓedeq me-Vienna," *Ha-Ẓofeh le-Ḥokhmat Yisraʾel* 11 (1931):110–26.]

influenced by exegetical methodologies and doctrines of *Ḥasidei Ashkenaz*, including their approach to biblical authorship.[7]

Ultimately, R. Solomon returned to northern France, where he was in contact with R. Yeḥiel of Paris.[8] Ta-Shma suggests that R. Solomon was the father of the tosafist, R. Samuel b. Solomon of Falaise, who was involved with R. Yeḥiel of Paris in the Trial of the Talmud. In his commentary to R. Yosef *Tov Elem*'s liturgical poem for *Shabbat ha-Gadol, E-lohei ha-ruḥot lekhol basar*, R. Samuel cites two *gematria* interpretations from his father. These are the only

---

The difficulties some have expressed regarding the notion of post-Mosaic authorship and the Pentateuch, noted by Israel Ta-Shma at the beginning of his article (above, n. 4), may be mitigated somewhat by the fact that the Ashkenazic scholars who espoused this notion were closely connected to *Ḥasidei Ashkenaz* (see also the next note), suggesting that it was not widely held among medieval rabbinic scholars. See now Ta-Shma, "Perush Anonimi Biqorti (bi-Khetav Yad) le-Sefer Tehillim," *Tarbiz* 66 (1997):417–23. On R. Avigdor Katz and *Ḥasidei Ashkenaz*, see below, at the end of this section. Cf. M. Shapiro in *The Torah u-Madda Journal* 4 (1993):202–3. Avraham Ibn Ezra, who expressed similar ideas, had a significant impact on the thought of *ḥasidut Ashkenaz*. See, e.g., Yosef Dan, *Torat ha-Sod shel Ḥasidut Ashkenaz* (Jerusalem, 1968), 29–31, 113–16, 138–45, and cf. below, n. 8, and ch. 3, n. 97; Avraham David, "Le-Toledotav shel R. Eleazar b. he-Ḥasid R. Matatyah me-Ḥakhmei Ereẓ Yisraʾel (?) ba-Meʾah ha-Yod Gimmel," *Qiryat Sefer* 63 (1991):996–98; and below, ch. 4, n. 68. [For the possible Byzantine roots of the notion of post-Mosaic authorship, see Richard Steiner, "The Byzantine Commentary to Ezekiel and Minor Prophets and Its Place in the History of Biblical Exegesis," unpublished paper read at the Twelfth World Congress of Jewish Studies (Jerusalem, 1997); and idem, "Beḥinot Lashon be-Ferush li-Yeḥezqel ule-Trei ʿAsar shebe-Megillot ha-Ivriyyot mi-Byzantion," *Leshonenu* 59 (1996):39–56. Cf. Dov Schwartz, *Astrologiyyah u-Mageyah* (Ramat Gan, 1999), 332–34, citing "R. Yeshayah *me-Ereẓ Trani*," and below, ch. 5, n. 21.]

[7]Israel Ta-Shma, "Perush Divrei ha-Yamim shebi-Ketav Yad Munich 5," *Me-Ginzei ha-Makhon le-Taẓlumei Kitvei ha-Yad ha-Ivriyyim*, ed. Avraham David (Jerusalem, 1996), 135–41. The teachers of the author's teacher were R. Eleazar (Eliezer) b. Meshullam *Ḥazzan* and the northern French *peshat* exegete R. Yosef Qara. (According to J. N. Epstein, the author's teacher was R. Samuel *he-Ḥasid*.) R. Eleazar received *sodot* from R. Qalonymus, the father of R. Samuel *he-Ḥasid*, and practiced customs, continued by the German Pietists, which had mystical or magical connotations. These include the elongation of the chanting of *Barekhu* on *moẓaʾei Shabbat* and the dropping of sixteen droplets of wine from the *Seder* cup. See Grossman, *Ḥakhmei Ashkenaz ha-Rishonim*, 230, 390 (the reference to *Sefer Or Zaruaʿ* in n. 136 should be to pt. 2, sec. 89 [end]); and below, ch. 3, nn. 12, 25.

[8]The recorded contact that R. Solomon had with R. Yeḥiel concerned the biblical teachings of R. Abraham Ibn Ezra. See ms. Paris 353, fol. 77r. Cf. Shraga Abramson, "Iggeret ha-Qodesh ha-Meyuḥeset la-Ramban," *Sinai* 90 (1982):244–49, and below, ch. 4, n. 39.

extant references by R. Samuel to his father, and there is no other evidence linking R. Solomon to tosafist teachings.[9] R. Samuel does refer, in his liturgical commentary, to his tosafist teachers, R. Solomon of b. Judah of Dreux (whom

---

[9]Ms. Bodl. 2273 contains a relatively short biblical commentary by a R. Avigdor (headed by the phrase נכתוב עדין בקוצר, כמלקט בשבלים, מפי החכם אביגדור) that was published recently by Avraham Goldmintz, "Perush ha-Torah le-Rabbenu Avigdor," *Sefer ha-Zikkaron li-Khevod R. Shmu'el Barukh Werner*, 166–97. This commentary is replete with exegetical methods employed by the German Pietists involving letters and words (such as *gematria, notariqon, millui, semukhin*, א"ת ב"ש; see above, n. 1), as Goldmintz's consistent noting of parallels to the so-called *Perush Roqeaḥ* and to the *Perush Ba'al ha-Turim* demonstrates. This commentary cites R. Eleazar (of Worms) by name in one instance, concerning the absence of the final form of the letter *peh* in the grace after meals; see Goldmintz, 196, n. 88; *Sefer Roqeaḥ*, sec. 337; and below, ch. 3, n. 59. It also cites R. Qalonymus and R. Joel (Goldmintz, 185) together with a R. Sa'ad'el, R. Aaron, and R. Amitai (the early Ashkenazic *payyetan*?) on the names and functions of various angelic *memunim*. R. Qalonymus and R. Joel are referred to as *ḥasidim* and are mentioned together with R. Judah *he-Ḥasid* in an Ashkenazic (*Shi'ur Qomah*) commentary to the forty-two-letter Name; see *Merkavah Shelemah*, fol. 30a, and Elliot Wolfson, *Through a Speculum That Shines* (Princeton, 1994), 232. A *gematria* interpretation that relates an angelic name to Creation, composed by R. Qalonymus and R. Joel *Ḥasidim*, is found in ms. Parma 541, fol. 264v. The sixteen-sided sword, referred to by R. Qalonymus b. Isaac (father of R. Samuel *he-Ḥasid*) and other Qalonymides, is mentioned twice in Bodl. 2273; see Goldmintz, 177, 179, and cf. below, ch. 3, nn. 13–14. On R. Joel *he-Ḥasid*, cf. *Sefer Gematri'ot le-R. Yehudah he-Ḥasid*, ed. Daniel Abrams and Israel Ta-Shema (Los Angeles, 1998), editors' introduction, 3.

The precise identity of this R. Avigdor is, nonetheless, unclear. He proposes the year 1212 for the redemption, in the name of another scholar (Goldmintz, 190). This would suggest he is definitely not the tosafist R. Avigdor b. Elijah Katz of Vienna, who was a student of R. Simḥah of Spires and died c.1275 (see below, at n. 28, and cf. Efraim Kupfer, "Li-Demutah ha-Tarbutit shel Yahadut Ashkenaz ve-Ḥakhamehah ba-Me'ah ha-Yod Daled/ha-Tet Vav," *Tarbiz* 42 [1972]:119, n. 27). Although there are a number of common methodologies and even some exact parallels between Bodl. 2273 and the biblical commentary from the school of R. Avigdor b. Elijah (see above, n. 6), these are neither sufficiently weighty nor numerous enough to overcome the large chronological disparity. (Perhaps R. Avigdor b. Elijah had the commentary of the other R. Avigdor in front of him.) For the similarities, see, e.g., *Perushim u-Fesaqim le-R. Avigdor*, editor's introduction, 15, n. 24; 82–83, 92, 131 (regarding שר הממונה על גיהנם ששמו סגי[נ]אל), 240, (סר צלם מעליהם בגימ׳ [ליל] הושענא רבה והוא סימן / רמז שבאותה לילה מסתכלין / לראות בצלו של אדם וכו׳; cf. below, n. 34), 269, 284–85, 323 (and 444), 434, 436; Goldmintz, 181–82 (2), 185, 189, 190, 191, 192, 195, 197; and cf. Goldmintz's introduction, 163. In any case, the R. Avigdor of Bodl. ms. 2273 (who appears to have been a slightly older contemporary of R. Judah *he-Ḥasid*) does have a connection to *Ḥasidei Ashkenaz* and represents another example of a scholar who utilized their biblical interpretations and methodology. Cf. Daniel Abrams, *Sexual Speculation and Merkavah*

he refers to as *ha-Qadosh mi-Dreux*) and R. Jacob of Provins (who had an awareness of mystical concepts), and also to an unidentified teacher named R. Menahem *Ḥasid*.[10] Aside from his hesitancy in ruling leniently against

---

Mysticism in Medieval Germany (Tübingen, 1997), 66–67. He may also be the R. Avigdor *Ẓarefati* who was involved in the transmission of certain *Ḥug ha-Keruv ha-Meyuḥad* texts; see Yosef Dan, "Ḥug ha-Keruv ha-Meyuhad bi-Tenuʿat Ḥasidut Ashkenaz," *Zion* 35 (1966):356–58, and esp. n. 33, and idem, *The 'Unique Cherub' Circle* (Tübingen, 1999), 51–52, 119–20. A northern French origin would give him one more point in common with R. Solomon b. Samuel. Unlike R. Solomon b. Samuel, however, the R. Avigdor of Bodl. 2273 is not linked to any tosafists. [A. R. Avigdor b. Isaac is mentioned in the northern French polemical tract, *Sefer Yosef ha-Meqanne*, ed. Judah Rosenthal (Jerusalem, 1970), 53, n. 1, but he appears to have been a contemporary of R.Yeḥiʾel of Paris (c.1240). See also Zadoc Kahn, "Le Livre de Joseph le Zelateur," *REJ* 3 (1881):3, and cf. *Perushim u-Fesaqim le-R. Avigdor*, 13.]

A treatise by yet another R. Avigdor is cited by a student of the German Pietists in the late thirteenth century, R. Asher of Osnabruck (see below, n. 21). See, e.g., *Siddur Rabbenu Shelomoh mi-Germaiza ve-Siddur Ḥasidei Ashkenaz*, ed. Moshe Hershler (Jerusalem, 1972), 71, 157, and cf. Jordan Penkower, *Nosaḥ ha-Torah be-Keter Aram-Ẓovah: Edut Ḥadashah* (Ramat Gan, 1992), 48, n. 118. This R. Avigdor appears to be the copyist of ms. Parma 655, R. Avigdor b. Menaḥem. See *ʿArugat ha-Bosem*, ed. Urbach, 4:55, 58, 69–70, and Emanuel, "Sifrei Halakhah Avudim shel Baʿalei ha-Tosafot," 248. [The author of *Sefer Matat* was a student of R. Avigdor b. Menaḥem, and R. Judah b. Yaqar was the teacher of this R. Avigdor; it is unlikely that R. Judah was also the teacher of R. Avigdor b. Elijah Katz. Cf. *Perushim u-Fesaqim le-R. Avigdor*, editor's introduction, 9–10.] See also ms. B. M. 752, fol. 72r [=B. M. 756, 116v–117r; Milan Cod. Ambrosiana 53/10 (P12 sup.), 140r; and cf. ms. Munich 92, 3r]: **אני אביגדור קבלתי מר׳ אלעזר מי כמכה באלים מי כמכה נאדר בקדש תרי כמכה רמז לי׳ ספירות וכו׳.**

[10]See Urbach, *Baʿalei ha-Tosafot*, 1:462–63; and cf. Norman Golb, *The Jews in Medieval Normandy* (Cambridge, 1998), 394–99. There is a reference to *ha-qadosh R. Yaʿaqov* (see *Sefer Or Zaruaʿ*, pt. 2, sec. 256, fol. 114) that may refer to R. Jacob of Provins. On R. Jacob's mystical proclivities, see below, ch. 4, n. 38. R. Solomon *ha-Qadosh* of Dreux is also referred to as **החסיד הגדול**; see *Tosafot ha-Shalem*, ed. Jacob Gellis, v. 1 (Jerusalem, 1982), 241–42. Cf. ms. Cambr. Or. 71 (Ashkenaz, 1398), fol. 166r:

> **זאת מצאתי בירושלמי. שלח הר״ר יעקב מגרמוזייה אח הקדוש מדרוייש חנוך**
> **ואליהו גיבורי א-ל מלך וחזק לא טעמו טעם מיתה הלכו ביום ובלילה ולא הוזקו.**
> **יה״ר מלפניך א-להי השמים כשם שלא הוזקו כך אני לא אזוק.**

(Cf. Urbach, *Baʿalei ha-Tosafot*, 2:519, n. 47, in regard to R. Jacob b. Judah of Dreux.) Prior to this passage are a number of pieces dealing with pietism and magic: the ethical will of R. Judah *he-Ḥasid* (fol. 139v–140); a series of angelic adjurations and *segullot* for protection in various situations, and to achieve love; and an amulet to be written on deerskin that would insure success in non-Jewish courts (fol. 162r). Fols. 165r–165v record prayer interpretations and versions of R. Judah *he-Ḥasid* [that the prayer *ha-Shem*

established customs (even when the halakhic reasoning behind the customs is somewhat questionable), R. Samuel of Falaise displays no overt tendencies toward *ḥasidut* or *perishut*.[11]

E-lohei Yisraʾel was composed by Hezekiah and the correct versions of *Or Ḥadash* and *Ẓur Yisraʾel*; see, e.g., *ʿArugat ha-Bosem*, ed. Urbach, 4:84–87, 92–93 (and above, ch. 1, n. 55), and Simcha Emanuel, "Ha-Polmos ʿal Nosaḥ ha-Tefillah shel Ḥasidei Ashkenaz," *Meḥqerei Talmud* 3 (in press), nn. 95, 97.] Just prior to the passage that mentions *ha-qadosh mi-Dreux*, on fol. 166r, is a תפלת הדרך בדוק ומנוסה from R. Eleazar of Worms (found in a number of manuscripts, e.g., ms. Parma 1033, fol. 26r, col. 2 [המהלך בדרך במקום סכנה וכו׳], and see below, ch. 4, n. 49), which details a magical procedure for traveling to a dangerous place that involves the use of three stones and the recitation of verses, and concludes with the phrase ולא יהא ניזוק. R. Eleazar's prayer is followed by another magical adjuration for protection from danger on the road:

> תפלה ותחנה בדרך-בקשה מכם מיכאל וגבריאל ורפאל ואכתריאל שתעמידו בבקשה לפני מלך מלכי המלכים הקב״ה שאצליח בכל דרכי שאלך, הן מליסטים שלא יזיקו אותי, הן משדים הן מלולין הן מאדם הן מאשה הן מכל פגע רע ומחרב... הן מכל מיני פורעניות המתרגשות לבוא לעולם ושלא ישלוט שטן... ולא ממונה... לא בגופי ולא בממוני. יהי רצון מלפניך שתשמע תחנתי ובבקשתי (ג׳ פעמים לישועתך) וכו׳... למי שהו ירא משום דבר בדרך או במקום אחר יאמר זה השם ג׳ פעמים לאהבה... זה השם נקרא חרבו של הקב״ה וטוב לאומרו כנגד שונאו.

For R. Menahem Ḥasid, see Urbach, *Baʿalei ha-Tosafot*, 1:149, 369–70, 2:620, n. 12. Cf. below, ch. 4, n. 33; Daniel Abrams, "Ketivat ha-Sod be-Ashkenaz veha-Maʿavar li-Sefarad," *Maḥanayim* 6 (1992):97–98; and idem, "The Literary Emergence of Esotericism in German Pietism," *Shofar* 12 (1994):73.

[11]Cf. below, ch. 3, n. 93. See Urbach, *Baʿalei ha-Tosafot*, 1:463–64 (regarding *qitniyyot*); and Ta-Shma, "Samuel ben Solomon of Falaise," *Encyclopaedia Judaica*, 14:814. Urbach sees R. Isaac *Or Zaruaʿ* as similar to R. Samuel in this regard, while R. Yeḥiʾel of Paris was much less hesitant in declaring invalid accepted stringencies that were, in his view, not well based. See *Haggahot R. Pereẓ* to *Semaq*, sec. 93:4, and Urbach, 1:459, concerning the use of *fenouil* (fennel) for *sekhakh*. Although R. Samuel of Evreux sided with R. Yeḥiel in this case and allowed the fennel, both R. Samuel and R. Isaac of Corbeil agreed with R. Samuel of Falaise and prohibited the use of *qitniyyot* on Passover. See *Mordekhai Pesaḥim*, sec. 588, and *Haggahot Maimuniyyot*, cited in *Beit Yosef, O. Ḥ.* 453, s.v. *ve-yesh ʾoserim*. See also *Sefer Or Zaruaʿ*, pt. 2, fol. 59a, and Israel Ta-Shma, *Minhag Ashkenaz ha-Qadmon* (Jerusalem, 1992), 248. R. Samuel of Falaise notes that the custom in Ashkenaz was to be strict and bake the *maẓot* on Passover eve, after all leaven had been removed or destroyed. In northern France, however, this was only done as a *hiddur miẓvah*. Nonetheless, R. Samuel writes that he insisted upon this stringency, despite the fact that the lenient ruling had been accepted widely in his region, and with ample justification: ואעפ״כ אני מחמיר לעצמי... ואף על פי שהדבר פשוט להיתר.

R. Samuel of Falaise (and his brother, R. Isaac b. Solomon) may have been the authors of a letter during the 1230s phase of the Maimonidean controversy that called

There is another aspect of R. Solomon b. Samuel's writings that points to other rabbinic scholars who had intellectual contacts with tosafists while being heavily involved with interpretations of the German Pietists. R. Solomon composed addenda to a standard twelfth-century Ashkenazic prayer commentary, composed or edited by R. Eliezer b. Nathan (Raban); these addenda appear in several manuscripts, mostly as marginal notes.[12] The notes cite *sodot ha-tefillah* from a R. Eleazar of Forcheim (Vorcheim)[13] and liturgical

---

for the literal acceptance of ʾ*aggadah* (regarding such issues as the nature of *gan* ʿ*eden*), while eschewing the need for either esotericism or philosophy: כי אין להעמיק כמה למעלה ולמטה. See Joseph Shatzmiller, "Li-Temunat ha-Maḥloqet ha-Rishonah ʿal Kitvei ha-Rambam," *Zion* 34 (1969):128, 139, and cf. Joseph Davis, "Philosophy, Dogma and Exegesis in Medieval Ashkenazic Judaism," *AJS Review* 18 (1993):216. [Note, on the other hand, ms. Vat. 266, which has a version of R. Samuel's *E-lohei ha-Ruḥot* commentary followed by the Ashkenazic paraphrase of *Emunot ve-De*ʿ*ot* utilized by *Ḥasidei Ashkenaz* and their associates (such as *Semag*, R. Elḥanan b. Yaqar, and R. Meir of Rothenburg; see Davis, 209, n. 57, and ʿ*Arugat ha-Bosem*, ed. Urbach, 1:176, n. 17), and R. Eleazar of Worms's *hilkhot ḥasidut*. See Urbach, *Ba*ʿ*alei ha-Tosafot*, 462, n. 4. Cf. below, nn. 50–52; and ch. 4, n. 68.]

12 See Ta-Shma, "Mashehu ʿal Biqqoret ha-Miqra," 454, nn. 7–8. See also Add. ms. Verona (Municipal Library) 101 (85.2), and Cambr. Add. 491/1 (which refers, on fol. 131r, to R. Solomon as שלמה בה"ר שמואל הצרפתי הקדוש); and Abrams, "The Emergence of Esotericism," 72–73. The relationship between R. Solomon's glosses and the base of *siddur Raban* is seen most clearly in ms. Vat. 274 (Ashkenaz, c.1430), fols. 186r–211v. (R. Solomon's comments are often marked by *taf* for *tosefet*.) Note that Raban himself does not include any *sod* material; see below, ch. 3, n. 72.

13 See *Siddur Rabbenu Shelomoh mi-Germaiza ve-Siddur Ḥasidei Ashkenaz*, ed. Hershler, 42, 115. The first comment attributed to R. Eleazar (בסודות של הרב אלעזר מוורכהם) is that the terms צנה וסחרה in Psalm 91 (יושב בסתר עליון) are the names of angels appointed over the demons (הממונים על השדים) that are alluded to in the psalm. The role of the angels is to prevent the demons from having their way with people in order to damage them (להזיקם). R. Solomon cites this passage from the liturgical commentary of R. Ephraim of Bonn; see below, n. 26. For the manuscript variants of this passage, see ms. Vat. 274, fol. 198v; Kaufmann A399, fol. 13v; and Munich 393, fol. 18v. For a similar type of interpretation cited by both R. Solomon and R. Eleazar of Worms in the name of R. Jacob *ha-Nazir*, see the next note.

The second of R. Eleazar of Vorcheim's interpretations cited by R. Solomon (פי' החסיד ר' אלעזר מוורכהים) suggests that King Hezekiah composed the prayer ה' א-להי ישראל, as evidenced by a mnemonic pattern that appears in the prayer. For additional manuscript references to this passage, see Bodl. 1102, fol. 26; Cambr. Add. 394, 17r; and Munich 393, 57v; and cf. ʿ*Arugat ha-Bosem*, ed. Urbach, 4:98, n. 64; and Moshe Hershler, "Perush Siddur ha-Tefillah veha-Maḥzor Meyuḥas le-R. Eliezer b. Nathan mi-Magenza," *Genuzot* 3 (1991):71. A statement on the authorship of this prayer by Hezekiah is attributed to R. Judah *he-Ḥasid* himself in ms. Cambr. Or. 71, fol. 165r, and interpretations from R. Samuel *he-Ḥasid*, R. Judah *he-Ḥasid*, and especially from the prayer commentaries and *sodot* of R. Eleazar of Worms. The influence of *Hekhalot* literature can also be detected.[14]

JTS Mic. 8122, fol. 100r; see above, n. 10. See also Hershler, *Siddur R. Shelomoh mi-Germaiza*, 116, n. 18; and *Perushei Siddur ha-Tefillah la-Roqeaḥ*, ed. Hershler (Jerusalem, 1992), 2:403, n. 1. On R. Eleazar of Vorcheim's contact with R. Judah *he-Ḥasid* (see *Perushei ha-Torah le-R. Yehudah he-Ḥasid*, ed. Y. S. Lange [Jerusalem, 1975], 143) and his awareness of R. Judah's prayer interpretations, see Simcha Emanuel, "Ha-Polmos ᶜal Nosaḥ ha-tefillah shel Ḥasidei Ashkenaz," n. 121. R. Solomon b. Samuel's teacher, R. Isaac *ha-Zaqen* b. Joseph, also preserved interpretations he heard from R. Judah.

[14]A sampling of the citations found in ms. Cambr. Add. 394 (Ashkenaz, fourteenth/fifteenth centuries) includes: (1) a *sod* commentary by R. Eleazar of Worms to the prayer *E-lohai Neshamah* (fol. 1v); see also *Perushei Siddur ha-Tefillah la-Roqeaḥ*, 1:6–8, ms. Vat. 274, fol. 194; Cambr. Add. 561 (fourteenth century), fols. 7v–8v (in the margin); (2) the number of words in total and the number of times the word ברוך appears in ברוך שאמר (fol. 3v) [cf. ms. Vat. 274, fol. 186r; *Siddur Rabbenu Shelomoh mi-Germaiza* (see nn. 14–15 for *Hekhalot* influence); Moshe Hallamish, "Beᶜayot be-Ḥeqer Hashpaᶜat ha-Qabbalah ᶜal ha-Tefillah," *Massuʾot*, ed. Michal Oron and Amos Goldreich (Jerusalem, 1994), 214]; (3) a *piyyuṭ* following *Barekhu*, authored by R. Judah *he-Ḥasid*, which outlines a similar pattern of angelic response to the one angel who calls out *Barekhu* and alludes to the inclusion of the Divine Name of twenty-two (or forty-two) letters in the angelic response (fols. 12v–13r; cf. *Siddur Rabbenu Shelomoh*, 82, n. 86, for a *Hekhalot* source.); (4) a passage in *sodot shel geonim*, attributed also to R. Eleazar of Worms, that the seventy-two words in the *Qedushah* (through the blessing *ha-E-l ha-qadosh*) correspond to the שם המפורש of seventy-two letters. This explains the custom of not speaking until the blessing is completed (fol. 15v; cf. *Siddur*, 107).

Among the citations in ms. Vat. 274 are: (1) R. Solomon's interpretation of the *plene* spelling of the word *E-lohai* (with a *vav*) toward the beginning of *Ashrei* as an allusion to the six characteristics of Messiah (listed in Isaiah 11) and also as a hint that Hezekiah, who had six lofty names (see Isaiah 9:5), would come from King David (fol. 190v, and see also ms. Cambr. 561, fol. 15r) [R. Shelomoh writes that he received this from פחד יצחק הזקן בן יוסף. Urbach (ed., *ᶜArugat ha-Bosem*, 4:82–83, n. 62) is unable to identify Isaac *ha-Zaqen*. Cf., however, S. Emanuel (in the above note), who identifies him as a teacher of Solomon; and below, ch. 3, n. 4]; (2) a סוד עמוק on כבוד (מלכותך) from R. Judah *he-Ḥasid* and from R. Eleazar of Worms, which R. Solomon stresses should not be revealed to everyone; (3) an explanation for the absence of the letter *nun* in *Ashrei* according to an interpretation of R. Eleazar of Worms citing R. Judah *he-Ḥasid*; (4) the claim that one who deletes the *vav* in the verse וחרב פיפיות בידם (Psalms 149:6) is considered כמחריב העולם, because the *gematria* equivalent of the word וחרב is אריה, as in the verse (Amos 3:8) referring to the call of the Almighty, אריה שאג מי לא ירא (fol. 191r; cf. *Siddur*, 65); (5) the number of words in the blessings *ᶜal netilat yadayim* and *ʾasher yaẓar* and the connotations, from the *sodot* of R. Eleazar of Worms (194r); (6) the need to preserve precisely the text of blessing *gomel ḥasadim tovim le-ᶜammo Yisraʾel* (and

Several of the manuscripts in which R. Solomon's comments appear also contain similar marginal notes and comments on the liturgy by R. Samuel b. Barukh of Bamberg. R. Samuel strongly supports the prayer interpretations, wordings, and numerical analyses of *Ḥasidei Ashkenaz* and earlier Qalonymides.[15] R. Samuel studied with R. Eliezer of Metz and R. Simḥah of Spires.[16]

---

not to add or delete even a single word), since the number of words is equivalent to the numerical value of the word חן (ביסודו של הר' אלעזר בן ריב"ק; fol. 194v).

On fols. 205v–206r, R. Solomon writes that he heard from מהר"י העזרי, in the name of R. Jacob *ha-Nazir*, that two of the descriptions in the prayer *E-l Adon* (*daʿat* and *tevunah*) are in fact the names of two angels who surround the *kisse ha-Kavod*, and, further, that *tifʾeret* and *gedulah* in that prayer are the *gematria* equivalents of the angels Mikhaʾel and Gavriʾel. See Scholem, *Reshit ha-Qabbalah*, 72, n. 4; idem, *Origins of the Qabbalah*, 207–9; and cf. Meir Bar-Ilan, *Sitrei Tefillah ve-Hekhalot* (Jerusalem, 1987), 115–20; *ʿArugat ha-Bosem*, ed. Urbach, 4:117–19; and below, ch. 4, n. 58. R. Eleazar of Worms presents this interpretation in his prayer commentary (ms. Bodl. 1204, fol. 152v, and cf. *Siddur Rabbenu Shelomoh*, 160) without mentioning R. Jacob *ha-Nazir*. Urbach suggests that both R. Eleazar and R. Jacob, who apparently visited northern France, received this teaching from R. Judah *he-Ḥasid*. See also *ʿArugat ha-Bosem*, 4:38, n. 82, and *Siddur*, 228. On the connections between R. Jacob *ha-Nazir* and the German Pietists, see also the studies of Moshe Idel cited above, ch. 1, n. 62, and below, ch. 4, n. 10.

R. Solomon also includes the interpretations of northern French exegetes: ואני שלמה ב"ר שמואל מצאתי בפירוש רבינו שמואל הצרפתי בן הח"ר מאיר לכך קורא אותה [ריש אשרי] תהלה לפי שמן תהלה לדוד עד סוף הספר לא תמצא בו אפי' תיבה אחת לשון בקשה אלא הכל לשון שבח הוא ותהלה. ת' [תוספת] (fol. 190v). There is an additional citation from Rashbam at the end of fol. 191r. These citations are possibly from the nonextant commentary of Rashbam to Psalms. Cf. *ʿArugat ha-Bosem*, 4:12, 153–54, for interpretations of Rashbam on verses in Psalms cited by R. Eleazar of Worms and his student R. Abraham b. Azriel, and see also *Rashbam ʿal ha-Torah*, ed. David Rosin (Breslau, 1882), xix. On fol. 198r, R. Solomon discusses Moses' authorship of several chapters in Psalms.

15 See, e.g., ms. Cambr. Add. 394, fols. 18v (cf. *Siddur R. Shelomoh*, 119), and 20v; Bodl. 1205, fol. 48v; Bodl. 2274, fol. 24v; and above, ch. 1, n. 39. See also *Perushei Siddur ha-Tefillah la-Roqeaḥ*, ed. Hershler, 1:359, 2:403, 442, 471–73, 543; ms. Cambr. 561, fol. 50r (margin); *Siddur R. Shelomoh*, 136 (based on a *piyyut* of R. Simeon *ha-Gadol*), and 184 (אבל הר"ר שמואל מצא מכתיבת ידו של רבינו יודא חסיד), 221–23; ms. B. M. 534, fols. 13r–15v; B. M. 754, fols. 130r–134v; Bodl. 1103, fols. 40, 54v, 75; Paris 646, fol. 6; and cf. C. Sirat in *REJ* 119 (1961):11. A number of these texts contain pieces of the "liturgical polemic" associated with *Ḥasidei Ashkenaz*. See *ʿArugat ha-Bosem*, ed. Urbach, 4:92–97; Israel Ta-Shma, "Quntresei 'Sodot ha-Tefillah' le-R. Yehudah he-Ḥasid," *Tarbiz* 65 (1996):65–77; and Emanuel, "Ha-Polmos ʿal Nosaḥ ha-Tefillah shel Ḥasidei Ashkenaz."

16 See Urbach, *Baʿalei ha-Tosafot*, 1:429. Note that both R. Eliezer of Metz and R. Simḥah of Spires had a relationship with *Ḥasidei Ashkenaz*. For R. Eliezer of Metz, see

He exchanged a series of letters on halakhic matters with R. Simḥah—who regarded R. Samuel as the worthy successor of his father, R. Barukh b. Samuel of Mainz—and he also sent queries to Rabiah. It is not known whether R. Samuel composed any halakhic monographs or *Tosafot*. A number of his responsa have survived, mostly in the collections of his student, R. Meir of Rothenburg.[17] Many of his *pesaqim* are found in a collection edited by one of his students, in which R. Samuel is referred to as "*mori ha-ro'eh*."[18]

R. Samuel appears to have composed a full-fledged prayer commentary of which remnants are extant, and it is possible that his marginal comments, similar to the kind made by R. Solomon b. Samuel, were part of this larger commentary.[19] A number of R. Samuel of Bamberg's comments were preserved by his student, R. Asher b. Jacob *ha-Levi* of Osnabruck, himself a copyist and editor of liturgical collections[20] with his own connections to *Ḥasidei*

---

above, ch. 1, n. 105. R. Simḥah studied with R. Eliezer of Metz, R. Abraham b. Samuel *he-Ḥasid*, R. Judah b. Qalonymus of Spires, and R. Moses *ha-Kohen* of Mainz (who was also a teacher of R. Eleazar of Worms). See Urbach, 1:411–20. Urbach notes that R. Simḥah was asked a halakhic question by R. Judah *he-Ḥasid*; cf. ms. Bodl. 659, fol. 82v. He also points to a midrashic interpretation offered by R. Simḥah that is very similar, in both form and content, to a comment made by R. Eleazar of Worms at the beginning of his pietistic introduction (*shoresh 'ahavat ha-Shem*) to *Sefer Roqeaḥ*. R. Simḥah authored a commentary to *Sifra* and is included in the "Spires circle" that was encouraged and influenced by *Ḥasidei Ashkenaz* to expand their studies beyond the traditional talmudic tractates and into other areas of rabbinic literature as well (see above, introduction, n. 14, and ch. 1, n. 76). For R. Simḥah's additional affinities with *ḥasidut Ashkenaz*, see Ta-Shma, *Halakhah, Minhag u-Meẓi'ut be-Ashkenaz*, 160–63; Elbaum, *Teshuvat ha-Lev ve-Qabbalat Yissurim*, 225–26; Emanuel, "Sifrei Halakhah Avudim shel Baʿalei ha-Tosafot," 213–14, n. 12; above, ch. 1, n. 146 (regarding *teshuvat ha-mishqal*); and below, ch. 5, n. 12. Note the pietistic formulation by R. Simḥah recorded in the introductory *Alfa Beta* to *Sefer Or Zaruaʿ* (cf. below, ch. 5, nn. 3–6), sec. 44.

17. Urbach, *Baʿalei ha-Tosafot*, 1:430–32. See also the halakhic decision issued by R. Samuel of Bamberg and R. Moses Taku in *Siddur Rabbenu Shelomoh mi-Germaiza*, 296.

18. This collection, found in ms. Cambr. Or. 786 (fols. 167d–186b), was published in *Shitat ha-Qadmonim*, ed. M. Y. Blau (New York, 1992), 319–95. On the editor of the collection, cf. Emanuel, "Sifrei Halakhah Avudim shel Baʿalei ha-Tosafot," 289–90, and 163, n. 4. The manuscript is dated 1282. On this collection, see also Ta-Shma, below, n. 41.

19. See Daniel Goldschmidt, *Meḥqerei Tefillah u-Piyyut* (Jerusalem, 1980), 61–62; Israel Ta-Shma, "Quntresei 'Sodot ha-Tefillah' le-R. Yehudah he-Ḥasid," 70–77; and S. Emanuel, "Ha-Polmos ʿal Nosaḥ ha-Tefillah shel Ḥasidei Ashkenaz," sec. 4.

20. See Israel Ta-Shma, "Al Kammah ʿInyanei Maḥzor Vitry," *ʿAlei Sefer* 11 (1984):81–89; Simcha Emanuel's response in *ʿAlei Sefer* 12 (1985):129–30; Ta-Shma's rejoinder, ibid., 131–32; and *ʿArugat ha-Bosem*, ed. Urbach, 4:70–72.

Ashkenaz.[21] The prayer comments of R. Samuel of Bamberg demonstrate his familiarity not only with the liturgical interpretations of the German Pietists, but also with their insistence that particular *nusḥaʾot* be preserved precisely, in order to retain their internal structure and harmony. Only in this way could the full effects of these prayers be realized, in both exoteric and esoteric realms.

Moreover, R. Samuel of Bamberg offered a scriptural derivation of a significant aspect of *ḥasidut Ashkenaz*, which was cited elsewhere in the name of R. Judah *he-Ḥasid*. Part of the German Pietists' search for the larger Divine Will entailed emphasizing the thoughts and feelings that lay behind an act, as well as the notion that the intellectual ability to discern, rather than the fixed age of legal adulthood alone, determined responsibility for one's deeds. This principle was derived, in two passages in *Sefer Ḥasidim*, from the case of Er and Onan (following the approach of one version of *Midrash Tanḥuma* that they were eight or nine years old), and from instances involving other biblical figures. The derivation is also cited in R. Judah *he-Ḥasid*'s biblical commentary [which was compiled by his son R. Moses Zal(t)man] and in R. Judah *he-Ḥasid*'s name in several collections of so-called tosafist biblical interpretations.[22]

---

[21]See Joseph Perles, "Die Berner Handschrift des Kleinen Arukh," *Jubelschrift zum siebzigten Geburstage des Prof. Dr. H. Graetz*," (Breslau, 1887), 2–3, 16–20. For R. Asher's citation of R. Judah *he-Ḥasid* and R. Eleazar of Worms using the title *mori*, see also Ta-Shma, "Al Kammah ʿInyanei Maḥzor Vitry," 85. For other examples of R. Asher's connection with *Ḥasidei Ashkenaz*, see, e.g., ms. Kaufmann A399, fols. 29r, 33v [=Bodl. 1102, fols. 17, 19]; and ms. Munich 423, 55a [=Bodl. 1102, fol. 21].

According to Ta-Shma, "Quntresei Sodot ha-Tefillah" (above, n. 15), which seeks to modify significantly the earlier conclusions of Joseph Dan concerning R. Judah *he-Ḥasid*'s disdain for the inaccuracy of northern French prayer texts in particular, R. Asher received material on the *sodot ha-tefillah* of *Ḥasidei Ashkenaz* in the form of a treatise compiled by the brother-in-law of R. Judah *he-Ḥasid*'s brother, R. Abraham. R. Asher edited, embellished, and distributed this treatise. Indeed, it was he (and not R. Judah *he-Ḥasid* or R. Eleazar of Worms) who incorporated the anti-French animus that has been associated with German Pietists. Emanuel, "Ha-Polmos ʿal Nosaḥ ha-Tefillah," construes the process of transmission somewhat differently, concluding that the treatise under discussion was composed by an unknown student of R. Samuel Bamberg (although like Ta-Shma, Emanuel also removes R. Judah *he-Ḥasid*, and probably R. Eleazar of Worms as well, from any passages which express a particular anti-French bias). Emanuel demonstrates conclusively that R. Judah and his immediate students were concerned about any version, be it French or German, that deviated from their own precisely formulated liturgical readings. Cf. *ʿArugat ha-Bosem*, ed. Urbach, 4:92, and Soloveitchik, "Three Themes," 351, n. 28.

[22]See Soloveitchik, "Three Themes," 324–25, and esp. n. 33; *Perushei ha-Torah le-R. Yehudah he-Ḥasid*, ed. Lange, 52–53; *Tosafot ha-Shalem*, ed. Gellis, vol. 4 (Jerusalem, 1985), 63–64; and cf. above, ch. 1, n. 80; ms. Moscow 348, fol. 245v.

One formulation, composed by R. Judah's son, reads: "My father asked: Why were Er and Onan punished since they had not yet reached the age of punishment? He answered that these are the Heavenly laws (*dinei shamayim*), that a person is punished according to [the level of] his intelligence. If a minor is as perspicacious as a twenty-year-old, then he is punished. And proof may be brought from Samuel [the prophet], whom Eli wanted to punish for issuing a halakhic ruling in his presence, even though he [Samuel] was only two years old." This passage is cited elsewhere, in shorter form but with exact linguistic parallels, in the name of R. Samuel of Bamberg.[23]

On the basis of parallel passages in *Yerushalmi Pe᾿ah* (8:8) and *Sheqalim* (5:4), *Sefer Ḥasidim* instructs that funds which an individual has available for charity are best given to righteous scholars involved in the study of Torah for its own sake (*le-yir᾿ei ha-Shem ha-ʿosqin be-Torah lishmah*), rather than toward the building of (additional) houses of worship. R. Samuel of Bamberg is cited as adducing one of these Yerushalmi passages to prove that it is preferable to give charity to teach young men (לל[י]מוד נערים), rather than to give charity to the synagogue.[24]

R. Samuel's affinities with the liturgical teachings and commentaries of the German Pietists may have come to him through his father, R. Barukh b. Samuel of Mainz. R. Barukh was a *payyetan* and tosafist halakhist who authored the voluminous and oft-cited, but no longer extant, *Sefer ha-Ḥokhmah*. According to E. E. Urbach, it was R. Barukh who asked

---

[23]Ms. B. M., Or. 9931 [=Gaster 730 (Ashkenaz, fourteenth century)], fol. 16r. (Cf. *Nimmuqei Ḥumash le-R. Yeshayah*, ed. C. B. Chavel, 28.) The formulation of R. Samuel of Bamberg was preserved by (a student of) R. Yedidyah b. Israel (of Nuremberg) as part of a collection of Ashkenazic biblical comments. This compilation contains numerous interpretations from the tosafists R. Jacob and Joseph of Orleans and R. Yom Tov of Joigny. It also cites R. Judah *he-Ḥasid* frequently, as well as other figures who were connected to his teachings, such as R. Yaqar *ha-Levi* of Cologne (26v–27r) and R. Isaac Fuller (fol. 121r); see below, n. 41, and ch. 5, n. 81. Another interpretation of R. Samuel Bamberg is cited on fol. 76r. On the connection between R. Yedidyah and the son of R. Judah *he-Ḥasid*, see above, ch. 1, n. 175. [A R. Nathan b. *he-Ḥaver* R. Moses of Bamberg appears in *Perushei ha-Torah le-R. Yehudah he-Ḥasid*, 154.]

[24]See *SḤP* 862, 1707, and R. Samson b. Ẓadoq, *Sefer Tashbeẓ* (Lemberg, 1858), sec. 536 (*dinei ḥasidut*). Cf. Soloveitchik, "Three Themes," 344, n. 109; my *Jewish Education and Society*, 17, n. 10; and *Shitat ha-Qadmonim*, ed. Blau (above, n. 18), 334, 367. The passage in *Sefer Tashbeẓ* appears as part of a section entitled *dinei ḥasidut* (secs. 532–65), which lists a number of pietistic practices of R. Meir of Rothenburg and mentions R. Judah *he-Ḥasid* three times. See below, nn. 49, 52. Regarding R. Samuel's pietistic affinities, see also below, n. 46.

R. Judah *he-Ḥasid* about how to deal with the obligation of reciting *Qeri'at Shema* in the morning, by the prescribed time, on those festivals and occasions where the length of the prayer service made reaching that deadline impossible. R. Judah, whose penchant for the slow recitation of the prayers in order to enhance *kavvanah* is well-documented, responded that he relied on the *Shema* that was recited at the very beginning of the morning service for this purpose. He then went on to discuss his recurring theme of retaining proper *piyyut* and other liturgical texts, and how local custom cannot be maintained if the texts conflict with certain principles. R. Judah demonstrated some of his points using *piyyutim* of R. Simeon *ha-Gadol* and R. Eleazar *ha-Qallir*. As a *payyetan* and interpreter of *piyyutim*, R. Barukh would have been most interested in R. Judah's guidance, and indeed, Urbach maintains, it is possible to see the influence of R. Judah in R. Barukh's work.[25]

This influence can also be found in the work of R. Barukh's senior colleague on the Mainz rabbinical court, R. Ephraim b. Jacob of Bonn.[26] Recent

---

[25]See *ʿArugat ha-Bosem*, ed. Urbach, 4:94–96. Cf. Soloveitchik, "Three Themes," 333, n. 70; and Israel Ta-Shma, "Barukh ben Samuel of Mainz," *Encyclopaedia Judaica* 4:280–81. On the importance of the slow recitation of prayer in the thought of *Ḥasidei Ashkenaz*, see above, ch. 1, n. 12. The very involvement of R. Barukh and his son R. Samuel in the writing and interpretation of *piyyutim* perhaps bespeaks the influence of the German Pietists; cf. Soloveitchik, 351–52, and below. See also A. M. Habermann, "Piyyutei R. Barukh b. Shmu'el mi-Magenza," *Yediʿot ha-Makhon le-Ḥeqer ha-Piyyut* 6 (1946):56, 60–61, 79–82, for examples of *Hekhalot* material included by R. Barukh in his *piyyutim*. Like R. Simḥah of Spires (above, n. 16), R. Barukh studied with R. Judah b. Qalonymus b. Meir in Spires, with R. Eliezer of Metz, and with R. Moses b. Solomon *ha-Kohen* of Mainz, whom he replaced on the rabbinical court of Mainz. On *Sefer ha-Ḥokhmah*, see Urbach, *Baʿalei Ha-Tosafot*, 1:425–29; and Emanuel, "Sifrei Halakhah Avudim shel Baʿalei ha-Tosafot," 122–55.

[26]R. Ephraim of Bonn, who may also have been a teacher of R. Barukh, was a prolific commentator on *piyyut* and liturgy, in addition to authoring responsa and *ḥiddushim* to a number of tractates. See *ʿArugat ha-Bosem*, ed. Urbach, 4:39–51. He was in contact with R. Judah *he-Ḥasid* (who appears to have been slightly younger than R. Ephraim), with R. Judah's brother R. Abraham, and with Rivaq of Spires, and he may have received material from R. Samuel *he-Ḥasid*. Like *Ḥasidei Ashkenaz*, he counted carefully the number of words in various prayers and offered interpretations based on those numbers. Cf. *Maḥzor Vitry*, 519, and *ʿArugat ha-Bosem*, 4:110, n. 30. R. Ephraim's comments on the themes of Divine Names and the *kisse ha-Kavod* are occasionally linked with those of R. Eleazar of Worms. See, e.g., *Siddur Rabbenu Shelomoh mi-Germaiza*, ed. Hershler, 60, 70–71, 98, 109, n. 38, 114, 154, and cf. Emanuel, "Ha-Polmos ʿal Nosaḥ ha-Tefillah shel Ḥasidei Ashkenaz," n. 2; Elliot Wolfson, "Demut Yaʿaqov Ḥaquqah be-Kisse ha-Kavod," *Massu'ot*, ed. M. Oron and A. Goldreich (Jerusalem, 1994), 140, n. 44; above, ch. 1, n. 42; and below, ch. 4, nn. 52–54.

scholarship has confirmed the impact of *Ḥasidei Ashkenaz* on the fixing and interpretation of prayer and *piyyut* texts in both Germany and northern France. If thirteenth-century Ashkenaz was dominated by northern France in terms of talmudic studies and interpretation, Germany was dominant in terms of prayer and liturgical poetry.[27]

Another student of R. Simḥah of Spires who had significant pietistic (and mystical) connections with *Ḥasidei Ashkenaz* was R. Avigdor b. Elijah *ha-Kohen* (d.c.1275), often referred to as R. Avigdor Katz (*Kohen Ẓedeq*). R. Avigdor was a native of Italy who studied in Spires and taught in Ferrara and Verona. Among those who corresponded with him were R. Zedekiah b. Abraham *ha-Rofe min ha-Anavim*, author of the *Shibbolei ha-Leqet*, and several of Zedekiah's relatives. R. Avigdor is mentioned in standard *Tosafot* texts. He succeeded R. Isaac *Or Zarua*ᶜ in Vienna, and was a teacher of R. Meir of Rothenburg. R. Avigdor authored a commentary on the *Megillot*, and he and members of his circle produced a lengthy multi faceted commentary to the Torah (which also includes legal practices and customs). These commentaries often reflect the exegetical methods of the German Pietists, and there are specific parallels in interpretation and doctrine.[28]

According to one manuscript passage, R. Solomon b. Samuel quoted the *sodot* of R. Eleazar of Vorcheim from a commentary by R. Ephraim of Bonn; see *Siddur*, 42, and above, n. 13, and cf. Ruth Langer, *To Worship God Properly* (Cincinnati, 1998), 215–18. R. Ephraim transmitted the story of R. Amnon and the bishop of Mainz, and he concludes by noting that R. Amnon appeared after his death to R. Qalonymus b. Meshullam in a dream (*be-mar*ʾ*ot ha-lailah*), at which time he transmitted the text of *U-Netaneh Toqef* to R. Qalonymus. See *Sefer Or Zarua*ᶜ, pt. 2, sec. 276, and below, ch. 3, n. 3. Ms. Parma 1274 (Morocco, 1449) records *piyyutim* of R. Ephraim of Bonn and R. Samuel Bamberg.

[27]See Sussmann, "Mifᶜalo ha-Maddaᶜi shel Professor E. E. Urbach," (above, introduction, n. 8), 61; and cf. Soloveitchik, "Three Themes," 349–50. [For *piyyutim* composed by northern French tosafists, see *Leqet Piyyutei Selihot*, ed. D. Goldschmidt (Jerusalem, 1993), 217–18 (R. Judah Sirleon); 263–73 (R. Joseph of Orleans); 357–61 (Ri); 191–202 (R. Tuvyah of Vienne); and cf. 662–91 (northern French manuscripts). See also Urbach, *Ba*ᶜ*alei ha-Tosafot*, 1:124 (R. Elijah of Paris); 140 (R. Joseph of Orleans); 146 (R. Yom Tov of Joigny); 260 (Ri); 270 (Rizba); 492 (R. Tuvia of Vienne); and cf. 2:528, 564.] On the impact of Germany with regard to prayer texts, see also above, nn. 2, 21.

[28]See I. A. Agus, "Avigdor b. Elijah *ha-Kohen*," *Encyclopaedia Judaica*, 2:963. Urbach has no focused discussion of R. Avigdor; see his *Ba*ᶜ*alei ha-Tosafot*, 2:607, 628 for references to R. Avigdor in the standard *Tosafot* to ᶜ*Eruvin* and *Ketubot*. Cf. H. J. Zimmels, "Le-Toledot R. Avigdor b. Eliyyahu Kohen Ẓedeq me-Vienna," *Ha-Ẓofeh me-Ereẓ Hagar* 15 (1931):110–26; *Shibbolei ha-Leqet ha-Shalem*, ed. Mirsky, editor's

R. Avigdor reported that R. Judah *he-Ḥasid* in his day (*be-doro*) fasted on *Rosh ha-Shanah*, while his own teacher, R. Simḥah of Spires, did not.[29] R. Avigdor authored a commentary to *Avinu malkenu*, which included the

---

introduction, 13–25; *Shibbolei ha-Leqet*, vol. 2, ed. M. Z. Hasida (Jerusalem, 1988²), editor's introduction, 23–26, 32–35; Israel Ta-Shma, "Sefer Shibbolei ha-Leqet u-Khfelav," *Italia* 11 (1996):46–47; Urbach, 2:565, n. 4; and above, nn. 2, 6, 9, regarding the Torah commentary. A number of individual sections from ms. Hamburg 45, primarily those labeled *pesaqim*, have been published in recent years. See, e.g., S. E. Stern, "Pisqei Rabbenu Avigdor Kohen Ẓedeq be-ᶜInyanei Shemittah ve-Yovel," *Moriah* 19:10–12 (1994):10–14; idem, *Seder Qiddush ve-Havdalah le-Rabboteinu ha-Rishonim* (Bnei Brak, 1991), 51–57. [For additional responsa and *pesaqim* of R. Avigdor, see, e.g., ms. Parma 918, fol. 26r; ms. Paris 1408, 56v–57r; Parma 425, fols. 31v–32r; Parma 1237, fols. 47v, 143v; Parma 929, fols. 96, 150, 223; and cf. Eliyahu Lichtenstein, "Beʾur bi-Yerushalmi le-R. Avigdor Kohen Ẓedeq," *Bi-Netivot Yam* 3 (Petach Tikva, 1972), 171–73.]

Although R. Avigdor refers to R. Judah *he-Ḥasid* and R. Eleazar of Worms by name in only a handful of instances (see *Perushim u-Fesaqim le-R. Avigdor* [above, n. 2], editor's introduction, 15–16), numerous parallels show that he was clearly aware of and attuned to their biblical comments and other writings. See, e.g., *Perushim u-Fesaqim*, 12, 13–14, 15, 21, 28, 32 (and esp. n. 8), 37, 52, 70, 82, 84, 90, 107, 111 (including the Pietist conception of the *Kavod*), 131, 166, 176, 208, 220, 230, 263, 265, 321, 324, 339, 344. A similar pattern can be seen in *Perush R. Avigdor Katz li-Megillat Esther*, ed. Zvi Leitner (Jerusalem, 1994), and *Perush R. Avigdor Katz le-Shir ha-Shirim*, ed. S. A. Wertheimer (Jerusalem, 1971; based on the edition of Y. Bamberger on *Shir ha-Shirim*, Frankfurt 1899]). See also Jacob Gellis, "Qetaᶜim mi-Baᶜalei ha-Tosafot ᶜal Megillat Esther," *Moriah* 21:5–6 (1997):3–4.

R. Avigdor, like R. Judah *he-Ḥasid* and R. Samuel Bamberg (above, n. 22), interpreted that ᶜEr and Onan were fully culpable for their actions, even at age eight or nine (*Perushim*, 13). R. Avigdor's position concerning the donning of *tefillin* on *Tishᶜah be-Av* (at *Minḥah*) and his explanation (*Perushim*, 30, 474) are in line with the Pietist approach to compromise, where possible, between conflicting ritual and halakhic views, a viewpoint that was championed by (his student) R. Meir of Rothenburg; see below, n. 59, 65. See also *Perushim*, 161, 434, and below, nn. 52, 62. R. Avigdor cites approvingly the view held also by R. Judah *he-Ḥasid* (in both *Sefer Ḥasidim* and in R. Judah's Torah commentary), that one who writes a Torah scroll must gather together a quorum and write the Divine Names in their presence; see *Perushim*, 109, and nn. 20–21. R. Avigdor also cites a passage from *Midrash Avkir* (*Perushim*, 123–24), a text associated with the German Pietists in particular (see below, ch. 3, n. 13). His discussions of giving charity on behalf of the sick and the departed (*Perushim*, 315, and cf. n. 18, as well as 462, from ms. Mantua 36; see also *Shibbolei ha-Leqet*, secs. 81, 239) and the recitation of חזק following the reading of the Torah (*Perushim*, 317) are also consonant with the unique views of *Ḥasidei Ashkenaz*. See also above, ch. 1, nn. 56–57, 178, and below, n. 34; and above, n. 6.

[29]See Urbach, *Baᶜalei ha-Tosafot*, 1:419. Cf. Ta-Shma, above, n. 16.

gematria by R. Samuel *he-Ḥasid* that demonstrates R. Aqiva's role in the dissemination of this prayer.[30] He also followed prayer *nusḥa'ot* favored by *Ḥasidei Ashkenaz*.[31]

Moreover, R. Avigdor authored a treatise of ethics and beliefs entitled *Sha'arei Musar*, which contains a number of similarities to material in *Sefer Ḥasidim*. R. Avigdor stresses the development of fear of Heaven and sin by remembering that all one's actions are done under the eye of the Creator. He writes about breaking the desire to sin (*le-shabber 'et libbo*) and considering always the proximity of one's death (*yom ha-mitah*). He also describes the powerful efficacy of *kavannah* in prayer even after one has sinned, the need to be extremely humble and self-effacing in dealing with others, and the paramount importance of doing *teshuvah*, which is to be preceded by shame (*bushah*) and weeping.[32]

A close parallel to *Sefer Ḥasidim* can be seen in a passage that recommends specific strategies and opportunities for engaging an unrelated child or adult in Torah study, even on a small scale, thereby preventing them from sitting idly by (כדי שלא ילכו בטלים).[33] In this treatise, R. Avigdor also cites the passage from *Hekhalot Rabbati* (referred to by R. Avigdor as "*Ma'aseh Merkavah*") that describes the lifting of the eyes and the body by those reciting *qedushah* and the response of the Almighty.[34] R. Avigdor's brother, Eliezer b. Elijah *ha-Kohen*, authored a rhymed treatise of rebuke (*tokheḥah*).[35]

---

[30]See ms. Cambr. Add. 858 (Ashkenaz, fifteenth century), fols. 45r–45v (פירוש אבינו מלכנו דקדוקי הרא"ך [=ר' איגדור כ"ץ]); above, ch. 1, n. 39; and below, ch. 5, n. 14.

[31]See Benyamin Hamberger, *Shorashei Minhag Ashkenaz* (Bnei Brak, 1995), 61–62, 67–69, 72–73. In this instance, retention of the *nosaḥ* in question (וישמחו בך ישראל אוהבי שמך) stemmed from similar perceptions between *Ḥasidei Ashkenaz* and R. Avigdor on the requirement to manifest *simḥah* on the Sabbath. See also Zimmer, *'Olam ke-Minhago Noheg*, 126–27; and Wieder, below, n. 65.

[32]See *Sha'arei Musar le-R. Avigdor Kohen Ẓedeq* in *Shitat ha-Qadmonim*, ed. M. Y. Blau (New York, 1989), 1–7, based on ms. Rome Casanatense 159 (Italy, 1454), fols. 21r–25r. Other manuscript versions are Paris 839 (Ashkenaz, fourteenth century), fol. 72 (which contains only the first page); Sasoon 405 (Italy, 1415), fols. 82–85; and Vat. 251 (Italy, fourteenth century), fols. 28r–32v. A text of *Sha'arei Musar* was also published separately in Jerusalem in 1993. See also *Shibbolei ha-Leqet*, pt. 2, ed. Simcha Hasida, 226–27 (sec. 48).

[33]See *SHP*, secs. 762–64.

[34]See also the parallel citation in *Perush R. Avigdor Katz le-Shir ha-Shirim*, ed. Wertheimer, 27. The earliest Ashkenazic rabbinic scholar to cite the *Hekhalot* passage itself (from "*Sefer Hekhalot*") was Rabiah; see above, ch. 1, nn. 42–44. R. Avigdor is the first to mention *Ma'aseh Merkavah* as the source of the passage. On the interpretation of

the *Ḥekhalot* passage, cf. Elliot Wolfson, "Demut Yaᶜaqov Ḥaquqah be-Kisse ha-Kavod," *Massuᵓot*, ed. Oron and Goldreich, 152–57. This passage is also cited by R. Zedekiah b. Abraham in his *Shibbolei ha-Leqet ha-Shalem*, sec. 20, and in R. Jacob b. Asher's *Arbaᶜah Turim, O. Ḥ.*, sec. 125. Like his teacher R. Avigdor, R. Zedekiah refers to the source (in *Shibbolei ha-Leqet*, sec. 17, as well; see above, ch. 1, n. 60) as *Maᶜaseh Merkavah*, while R. Jacob calls it *Sefer Hekhalot*. Cf. Wolfson, *Along the Path* (Albany, 1995), 142–43, n. 184, and Daniel Abrams, "Maᶜaseh Merkavah as a Literary Work: The Reception of Hekhalot Traditions by the German Pietists and Kabbalistic Reinterpretation," *Jewish Studies Quarterly* 5 (1998):339, nn. 46, 47. [Rashi is the earliest Ashkenazic rabbinic authority to refer to the work entitled *Maᶜaseh Merkavah*; see below, ch. 3, nn. 34–37.] For another reference to *Hekhalot* literature (along with the teachings of R. Eleazar of Worms) in R. Avigdor's commentary to *Shir ha-Shirim*, see *Perush R. Avigdor*, ed. Wertheimer, 11. Cf. *Perushim u-Fesaqim le-R. Avigdor*, 473, nn. 5–6; Wieder (below, n. 50); and I. Ta-Shma, "Od li-Veᶜayat ha-Meqorot ha-Ashkenaziyyim be-Sefer ha-Zohar," *Kabbalah* 3 (1998):259–60. For R. Avigdor's interest in mysticism, see below, ch. 5.

On the tendency toward *perishut* and (German) pietism in *Shibbolei ha-Leqet*, see, e.g., *Shibbolei ha-Leqet*, sec. 93 (R. Aqiva's crying on the Sabbath; cf. *Ginzei Schechter*, 2:54, and below, n. 45); Zimmer, *ᶜOlam ke-Minhago Noheg*, 49–50, 135–37, 139–40, 227–31; Yaakov Gartner, "Yehe Sheme Rabbah Mevorakh—Shitot u-Meqorot," *Sidra* 11 (1996):47, n. 40; M. Hallamish, "Beᶜayot be-Heqer Hashpaᶜat ha-Qabbalah ᶜal ha-Tefillah," *Massuᵓot*, ed. Oron and Goldreich, 211–13; I. Weinstock, *Be-Maᶜagalei ha-Nigleh veha-Nistar* (Jerusalem, 1969), 249–59; M. Fishbane, *The Exegetical Imagination* (Cambridge, Mass., 1998), 139–40; Ta-Shma, *Ha-Nigleh shebe-Nistar*, 22–23 [add to the Pietist sources regarding the practice for **הושענא רבה** as **ליל חיתום** (esp. looking at one's shadow in the moonlight): *Perushim u-Fesaqim le-R. Avigdor*, 240, and Goldmintz, "Perush ha-Torah le-Rabbenu R. Avigdor," (above, n. 9) 188]; and see also Moshe Idel, *R. Menaḥem Reqanati ha-Mequbbal*, vol. 1 (Tel Aviv, 1998), 113–15; idem, "Gazing at the Head in Ashkenazi Hasidism," *Journal of Jewish Thought and Philosophy* 6 (1997):276–79; *Sefer Gematriᵓot le-R. Yehudah he-Ḥasid*, ed. Abrams and Ta-Shma, introduction, 16, and 58 (fol. 17v); Moritz Güdemann, *Ha-Torah veha-Ḥayyim*, vol. 1 (Warsaw, 1897), 164, n. 6; above, n. 28; ch. 1, nn. 15, 21–22, 54, 60; and below, ch. 5, nn. 25–27.

R. Yeḥiᵓel b. Yequtiᵓel *Anav*, copyist of the *Yerushalmi* ms. Leiden and relative of R. Zedekiah b. Abraham *ha-Rofe*, was the author of *Sefer ha-Tanya*, a halakhic compendium parallel to *Shibbolei ha-Leqet*. He also wrote an ethical work entitled *Maᶜalat ha-Middot* that is comparable to *Sefer Ḥasidim* in a number of respects. See, e.g., Güdemann, *Ha-Torah veha-Ḥayyim*, vol. 2 (Warsaw, 1899), 171–80, 293–95; Ta-Shma, "Sefer Shibbolei ha-Leqet u-Khfelav," 47–48; and above, ch. 1, n. 33.

[35]See ms. Vat. Urb. 22 (Italy, fifteenth century), fols. 65r–66r (**הבה נתחכמה לתור לנשמה... יסד ר׳ אליעזר אחיו של ר׳ אביגדור כהן צדק**), and Emanuel, "Sifrei Halakhah Avudim shel Baᶜalei ha-Tosafot," 228; ms. Parma 147, fol. 145; ms. Bodl. 913, fols. 15r–16v; Bodl. 914, fols. 182r–183v; Bodl. 2287, fols. 19r–28r; Bodl. 2858, fols. 3r–14r.

II

Interactions between *Ḥasidei Ashkenaz*, tosafists, and other Ashkenazic rabbinic figures with regard to certain issues of observance and ritual may also reflect pietistic affinities among these groups. The problem of fasting on *Rosh ha-Shanah* serves as an illustration. Although it was not discussed explicitly in either the Babylonian or Palestinian Talmud, by the early geonic period a Palestinian custom had developed to fast on *Rosh ha-Shanah* as an additional measure of repentance. Leading Babylonian Geonim were aware of this custom and condemned it; *Rosh ha-Shanah* was a festival, and special meals were therefore required. Although R. Nissim Gaon of Kairwan offered some support for fasting, the medieval Sefardic orbit followed the position of the Babylonian Geonim. Moreover, Rabiah, Riẓba, R. Eleazar of Worms, R. Simḥah of Spires, and *Shibbolei ha-Leqet* all prohibited fasting, despite the awareness on the part of some that there were still individuals in Ashkenaz who did fast—and that this practice extended back to early Ashkenaz. Not surprisingly, among those who fasted was R. Judah *he-Ḥasid*.[36]

In the mid-thirteenth century, a new series of discussions on this matter was initiated by colleagues, students, and followers of R. Judah *he-Ḥasid*. Most significant about these discussions was not only the position taken by some to fast, but also their argumentation. All of the earlier rabbinic discussions revolved around halakhic constructs, such as the nature of *Rosh ha-Shanah* as a *yom tov* (should it be considered akin to the *shalosh regalim*) or the controversy between the Tannaim R. Joshua and R. Eliezer as to whether a *yom tov* should be celebrated primarily through festive meals or through Torah study (in which case fasting might be permissible).

In one of these newer exchanges, it was reported that R. Abraham Ḥaldiq of Bohemia, a halakhic decisor connected to *Ḥasidei Ashkenaz*,[37] fasted on *Rosh ha-Shanah*. His proof was a somewhat unusual *kal va-ḥomer* from a fast that was permitted on the Sabbath, the *taᶜanit ḥalom*, which was undertaken as the

---

36For a fully-documented discussion of this issue, see Yaakov Gartner, *Gilgulei Minhag be-ᶜOlam ha-Halakhah* (Jerusalem, 1995), 74–96. Cf. Y. D. Gilat, "Taᶜanit be-Shabbat," *Tarbiz* 52 (1982): 10–15.

37On R. Abraham Ḥaldiq, see *ᶜArugat ha-Bosem*, ed. Urbach, 123–25; Shlomo Spitzer, "Minhagei ha-R. Avraham Ḥaldiq," *Qoveẓ ᶜal Yad*, n.s. 9 (1980):153–215; and cf. Ta-Shma, below, n. 41. [Toward the end of R. Abraham's collection of customs (214), there is an adjuration to neutralize *Potah* and remove forgetfulness (to be recited before or after *Havdalah*) that contains the same *Shemot* as those found in *Maḥzor Vitry*, sec. 150, 115–16; see below, ch. 3, n. 58. To Spitzer's list of manuscript citations in 153 n. 2, add ms. Bodl. 682, fols. 163v, 278r; and ms. Budapest (National Museum) 2°1, fol. 153b.]

result of a troubling dream. R. Abraham reasoned that if a *taᶜanit ḥalom* was permitted on the Sabbath—even though it is unclear if the dream was brought on by an angel (in which case its contents are genuine) or by a demon (in which case the contents are contrived)—one may certainly fast on *Rosh ha-Shanah* when all are being judged by the Almighty (in order to avoid a harsh judgment).

R. Abraham b. Azriel, the well-known Pietist student of R. Eleazar of Worms, disagreed with this reasoning. In the case of a negative dream, if in fact it was transmitted by an angel, a person must fast, and it is for this reason (in order that he fast and repent) that Heaven revealed the dream to him. But as for *Rosh ha-Shanah*, it is possible that the person is due to receive a positive judgment, so there is no need for him to fast. And if a person knows that he has sinned, let him fast prior to *Rosh ha-Shanah*. A R. Yiẓḥaq, however, asserted in the name of ha-R. Abraham (Ḥaldiq?) that one must fast so that "your table shouldn't be full while the Almighty's is empty." The explanation given for this phrase is that while the number of bullocks offered on all other festivals is at least two, on *Rosh ha-Shanah* only one is offered, and the portion which the Almighty receives is therefore diminished. R. [Abraham b.] Azriel responded that if this is so, one would also have to fast on *Shemini ᶜAẓeret*, because only one bullock was offered then as well. Additional proofs to prohibit fasting on *Rosh ha-Shanah* were apparently offered, but they were not reproduced in this version of the exchange.[38]

E. E. Urbach thought originally that the R. Yiẓḥaq who cited R. Abraham Ḥaldiq was R. Yiẓḥaq *Or Zaruaᶜ*.[39] But in *Sefer Or Zaruaᶜ* itself the same discussion is recorded between scholars from Prague and Regensburg, one generation earlier. "My teacher R. Isaac b. Mordekhai [Ribam] of Prague fasted on *Rosh ha-Shanah*, applying a *kal va-ḥomer* from *taᶜanit ḥalom* . . . and R. Moses b. Ephraim [of Regensburg] said to fast on *Rosh ha-Shanah* so your table shouldn't be full. . . . R. Barukh b. Isaac of Regensburg retorted that if so, you must fast on *Shemini ᶜAẓeret* as well."[40] Clearly, this was a running controversy

[38]This version is found in *Maᶜaseh Roqeaḥ*, sec. 130 (Sanok, 1912), fol. 31. See also the responsum of R. Avigdor of Vienna (above, n. 29). Regarding dreams transmitted by angels or by *shedim*, cf. *Berakhot* 55b.

[39]See the first edition of Urbach, *Baᶜalei ha-Tosafot*, 333–34; cf. *ᶜArugat ha-Bosem*, ed. Urbach, 4:124, and the 1980 edition of *Baᶜalei ha-Tosafot*, 1:402.

[40]*Sefer Or Zaruaᶜ*, *Hilkhot Rosh ha-Shanah*, sec. 257. Cf. *Beit Yosef* and *Bayit Ḥadash* to *O. Ḥ.*, sec. 597, s.v. *ve-ʾokhlin*, and below, ch. 4, n. 30. R. Moses b. Ephraim's son Judah transmitted *sodot ha-tefillah* from the school of R. Eleazar of Worms. See ms. Moscow-Guenzberg 511, fol. 1r; Henri Gross in *MGWJ* 49 (1905):692–700; and Urbach, *Baᶜalei ha-Tosafot*, 1:207.

over two generations, with the later scholars deriving their positions from their predecessors. What is striking here is that all of the rabbinic scholars involved are from Regensburg, Austria, and Bohemia—locations which have recently been shown to have had a fairly high degree of fealty to R. Judah *he-Ḥasid*. Indeed, Israel Ta-Shma has explained that R. Judah *he-Ḥasid*'s move from Spires to Regensburg was an attempt to be closer to his students and followers in central and eastern Europe.[41]

In a related development, Eric Zimmer has demonstrated that *minhag Austreikh* (Österreich), which tended to follow the halakhic rulings and positions of R. Judah *he-Ḥasid*, is generally more stringent than *minhag Reinus* (Rhineland), where R. Judah's teachings were less accepted. In a number of cases (e.g., the status of *dam tohar* and the counting of *shivᶜah neqiyyim*), the more stringent position was also found in northern France in the pre-Crusade period or in the early twelfth century, suggesting that R. Judah favored older French customs over Rhineland practices.[42] Zimmer sees additional support for his claim in the finding of Y. M. Pelles, that the customs of R. Ḥayyim Palti'el and R. Abraham Ḥaldiq, which reflect *minhag Austreikh* on the whole as well as the customs of Magdeburg in particular, were based on *minhagim* of *sifrut de-Vei Rashi*.[43] This thesis yields two conclusions. One is that there was

---

[41]Israel Ta-Shma, "Le-Toledot ha-Yehudim be-Polin ba-Me'ot ha-Yod Bet/ha-Yod Gimmel," *Zion* 53 (1988):347–69, and idem, "Yediᶜot Ḥadashot le-Toledot ha-Yehudim be-Polin ba-Me'ot ha-Yod Bet/ha-Yod Gimmel," *Zion* 54 (1989):205–8. Ta-Shma has identified a number of central and eastern European rabbinic scholars who were committed followers (in terms of halakhic rulings) of R. Judah *he-Ḥasid*. His research is based in large measure on manuscripts, including three related ones that contain halakhic and other material from the German Pietists and from Regensburg (Cambr. Or. 786 [see above, n. 18], Bodl. 696 [Ashkenaz, fourteenth/fifteenth centuries], and Bodl. 1150 [Ashkenaz, fourteenth century]). Included in this group of scholars, aside from R. Abraham Ḥaldiq, are such names as R. Moses Fuller, R. Jacob b. Naḥman of Magdeburg, R. Jacob *ha-Kohen* of Cracow, and R. Moses Taku. On R. Jacob *ha-Kohen*, see also *Sefer Gematri'ot le-R. Yehudah he-Ḥasid*, introduction, 14, and cf. Haym Soloveitchik in *AJS Review* 23 (1998):230.

[42]Zimmer, *ᶜOlam ke-Minhago Noheg*, passim, and esp. 296–97. Cf. *Sefer Raban*, *massekhet ᶜAvodah Zarah*, sec. 299: **ואני שמעתי שחסידי רינשבורק מחמירין ... אבל חכמי ריינוס לא הקפידו כלל**.

[43]See *Minhagei Vermaiza le-R. Yuda Liva Kircheim*, ed. Y. M. Pelles (Jerusalem, 1987), 16, n. 6. R. Ḥayyim Palti'el was a student of R. Meir of Rothenburg. Both R. Ḥayyim and R. Abraham were in Magdeburg with R. Jacob b. Naḥman, whose link with R. Judah *he-Ḥasid* had been quite close; see above, n. 41. In support of this claim, it is also argued that R. Ḥayyim Palti'el spent time in northern France (which would explain references to him as R. Ḥayyim of Falaise; see *ᶜAlei Sefer* 8 [1980]:142, 145). Indeed, R. Ḥayyim appears to have married the daughter of R. Samuel of Falaise.

some tendency toward *ḥumra* and *perishut* in *sifrut de-Vei Rashi* (which comports with the findings in chapter 1). The second is that R. Judah *he-Ḥasid* had a fairly significant impact on Ashkenazic *minhagim*, at least in central and eastern Europe.[44] Thus, R. Judah's own proclivities toward fasting, even on *Rosh ha-Shanah* (and on the Sabbath as well), undoubtedly played a role in engendering the discussion about the appropriateness of fasting on *Rosh ha-Shanah*.[45]

Moreover, the mode of this discussion is almost meta-halakhic. Neither approach deals with the halakhic status of *Rosh ha-Shanah* as a festival. The first approach deals with the nature of dreams and the roles of angels and demons. The response to it does not question the existence of these aspects, but only their impact. The second approach works with a talmudic formulation (*Beẓah* 20b, *Ḥagigah* 7a), but applies it in a manner that the Talmud does not. The Talmud uses this concept (in both *sugyot*) to suggest that those aspects of the sacrificial service and the offerings on a festival that are directed primarily to the Almighty must be on a par with what is offered on the festival by an individual for his own consumption. In this case, however, the reasoning is extended and applied to suggest that God must be given more than a person receives and that one must deny his own needs in order to provide properly for God. The direction of the argumentation may be explained by the fact that this

---

[44]See also Zimmer, *ʿOlam ke-Minhago Noheg*, 271, 277. Indeed, Zimmer claims (281–83, 286) that R. Judah *he-Ḥasid* himself preferred the old *minhag Ẓarefat*, against Rhineland custom, in one instance (concerning the baking of *maẓot* only on *ʿerev Pesaḥ* after *haẓot* or on *Pesaḥ* itself when the festival began on Saturday night). It remains unclear, however, whether this is true for R. Eleazar of Worms as well, despite similarities between *Sefer Roqeaḥ* and the *sifrut de-Vei Rashi*. Cf. Ta-Shma, *Minhag Ashkenaz ha-Qadmon*, 245–48, and Soloveitchik, "Three Themes," 348–49. For another potential example regarding R. Judah *he-Ḥasid*, note that *minhag Austreikh* was to exempt *rashei yeshivah* from taxes, while *minhag Reinus* did not; see *Terumat ha-Deshen*, #342. *Sefer Ḥasidim* was more lenient than the rest of Ashkenaz when it came to tax exemptions; see my *Jewish Education and Society*, 45–46, 91–95. The difficulty here, however, is that the lenient position of *Sefer Ḥasidim*, which perhaps gave rise to *minhag Austreikh*, appears to have been *sui generis*. To this point, there is no evidence that the earlier French practice was similar. See also below, n. 86. On the interaction between R. Judah *he-Ḥasid* and students of Rabbenu Tam, see now Rami Reiner, "Rabbenu Tam: Rabbotav (Ha-Ẓarefatim), ve-Talmidav Benei Ashkenaz," (M.A. thesis, Hebrew University, 1997), 68–70; and cf. *ʿArugat ha-Bosem*, ed. Urbach, 4:113, 163; and Soloveitchik in *AJS Review* 23 (1998):231–32.

[45]For R. Judah's regular regimen of fasting, which could include the Sabbath, see above, ch. 1, n. 4. Cf. *Shibbolei ha-Leqet*, sec. 93, citing R. Aqiva; R. Moses Isserles' gloss and *Taz* to *O. Ḥ.* 288:2; and Gartner, *Gilgulei Minhag*, 99–100.

circle of rabbinic scholars was reacting to a pietistic practice that originated in Israel and made its way to pre-Crusade Europe, after which it was continued by R. Judah *he-Ḥasid* and others. Given their relationship with R. Judah, these rabbinic scholars responded in what was essentially a pietistic idiom.[46]

III

R. Meir (Maharam) of Rothenburg (d.1293), who studied in both northern France and Germany, exhibited numerous affinities with the German Pietists, and he followed many of their specific formulations. Several of R. Meir's teachers were either themselves students of *Ḥasidei Ashkenaz* or were otherwise involved in magical or mystical studies. These teachers include R. Isaac b. Moses *Or Zarua*ᶜ (with whom R. Meir studied in Würzburg), R. Avigdor *Kohen Ẓedeq* of Vienna, R. Judah b. Moses *ha-Kohen* of Mainz (whom R. Meir referred to as *mori ha-qadosh*, and whose father R. Moses was a teacher of R. Eleazar of Worms), R. Ezra *ha-Navi* of Moncontour, R. Yeḥiʾel of Paris, R. Samuel of Falaise (son of R. Solomon b. Samuel), and R. Samuel of Evreux.[47] R. Meir imposed an intense form of *teshuvat ha-mishqal*, including lashes, wandering, and "a year or two of fasting" on those who sought expiation for crimes of

---

[46]Since Ribam (a student of Riba *ha-Levi* and Rabbenu Tam) was the teacher of the one who transmitted the account recorded in *Sefer Or Zarua*ᶜ (above, n. 40), it is possible that R. Isaac *Or Zarua*ᶜ had an earlier literary source in front of him. Cf. Urbach, *Ba*ᶜ*alei ha-Tosafot*, 1:196, n. 8. Note that R. Judah *he-Ḥasid* asked Ribam a question concerning *torat ha-mal*ʾ*akhim*; see below, ch. 4, n. 29. Note also that R. Isaac *Or Zarua*ᶜ held, against R. Qalonymus and Rabiah, that it was still appropriate in their time to fast a *ta*ᶜ*anit ḥalom* on the Sabbath. See *Sefer Or Zarua*ᶜ, pt. 2, sec. 407. [Fasting on the Sabbath was also permitted by R. Eliezer of Metz and R. Samuel Bamberg; see *Mordekhai Shabbat*, sec. 229.] For other evidence of R. Isaac *Or Zarua*ᶜ's pietism, see, e.g., Zimmer, ᶜ*Olam ke-Minhago Noheg*, 94–95, 109; Elbaum, *Teshuvat ha-Lev ve-Qabbalat Yissurim*, 19, n. 1, and 225–26; Marcus, *Piety and Society*, 112, and 126–27 (regarding *tiqqunei teshuvah* of *Ḥasidei Ashkenaz*); *Sefer Or Zarua*ᶜ, *pisqei Bava Meẓi*ᶜ*a*, pt. 3, sec. 359 (and cf. Rabbenu Tam's formulation in *Tosafot Bava Batra* 5a, s.v. *arba*ᶜ*ah*, and Naḥmanides' commentary to Deuteronomy 6:18, s.v. *ve-*ᶜ*asita ha-yashar veha-tov*); and below, nn. 82–83, 86. (For R. Ephraim of Regensburg and R. Judah *he-Ḥasid*, see below, ch. 3, n. 78.)

In Cambr. Or. 786, fols. 181d–182a [=*Shitat ha-Qadmonim*, ed. M. Y. Blau, 377, sec. 284], and in *Mordekhai ha-Shalem* ᶜ*al Massekhet Rosh ha-Shanah*, ed. Y. Horowitz (Jerusalem, 1989), 24, ר׳ יצחק מדנפיר (Ri) is cited as espousing the first position (to fast on *Rosh ha-Shanah*), instead of Ribam. See the discussion of these texts in Emanuel, "Sifrei Halakhah Avudim shel Baᶜalei ha-Tosafot," 192–93. On Ri's propensity for fasting, similar in many respects to that of R. Judah *he-Ḥasid*, see above, ch. 1, n. 30.

[47]See Urbach, *Ba*ᶜ*alei ha-Tosafot*, 2:523–28, and below, ch. 5.

informing; he also imposed fasts and lashes on anyone who verbally denigrated a son of an important family.[48]

According to one of his students, R. Meir cautioned not to say [לך] אכול בשמחה לחמך after a *hatavat ḥalom*, because he had a tradition (*qabbalah*) from Rabbenu Yehudah *Ḥasid* not to say it, since the first letter of each of these words spells א׳ב׳ל׳ (mourner).[49] R. Meir derived and supported the wording of prayer texts using *gematria* and other methods similar to those used by *Ḥasidei Ashkenaz* for this purpose.[50] Following the lead of his father, R. Barukh, he interpreted earlier *piyyutim* in the style of *Ḥasidei Ashkenaz* as well.[51] R. Meir

---

[48]See R. Meir's *Responsa* (Cremona, 1507), 214; Y. Baer, "He-Megammah ha-Datit/ha-Ḥevratit shel Sefer Ḥasidim," *Zion* 3 (1937):19, n. 38; Urbach, *Baᶜalei ha-Tosafot*, 2:536; Elbaum, *Teshuvat ha-Lev ve-Qabbalat Yissurim*, 22, n. 9; Daniel Sperber, *Minhagei Yisrael*, 2 (Jerusalem, 1991), 129, n. 5; and above, ch. 1, nn. 147–48.

[49]R. Samson b. Ẓadoq, *Sefer Tashbeẓ (dinei ḥasidut)*, sec. 553. Cf. *Ẓavaʾat R. Yehudah he-Ḥasid* in *Sefer Ḥasidim*, ed. Margoliot, 33, sec. 12. On Maharam and R. Eleazar of Worms, see Elliot Ginsburg, *The Sabbath in the Classical Kabbalah* (Albany, 1989), 246, n. 21. A practice attributed to R. Eleazar of Worms (found also in Rabbenu Yonah's *Sefer ha-Yirʾah*; and cf. ms. Parma 1033, fol. 26r, col. 3) is found in *Minhagim de-Vei Maharam* (ed. Israel Elfenbein, p. 7).

[50]See Urbach, *Baᶜalei ha-Tosafot*, 2:547. See also Naftali Wieder, "Beᶜityah shel Gematria Anti-Noẓerit ve-Anti Islamit," *Sinai* 76 (1975):5–10; idem, "Tiqqunim be-Nosaḥ ha-Tefillah be-Hashpaᶜat Leshonot Loᶜaziyyot," *Sinai* 81 (1977):27–29, for R. Meir's citation of passages in *Hekhalot* literature to support liturgical readings favored by the German Pietists. See also above, n. 11. Cf. ms. Cambr. Add. 1022 (Byzantium, 1425), fol. 100v, which describes R. Meir as following a practice of *Ḥasidei Ashkenaz* that *Qeriʾat Shema* must be recited from a prayerbook and may not be said by heart: ולכן נוהגין חסידי אשכנז להתפלל ק״ש שמע מתוך הכתב ובפרט שליח ציבור מה״ר מאיר מרוטבורק ז״ל כ׳[תב] שאסור לקראתו שלא מן הכתב... ולכן בכל מקום שלוחי ציבור האשכנזי׳ קורין ק״ש בלחש. Cf. *Arbaᶜah Turim, O. Ḥ.*, 49 *Tosafot ha-Rosh ᶜal Massekhet Sotah*, ed. Y. Lifshitz (Jerusalem, 1969), 75 (406); and *Teshuvot Maharam*, ed. Prague, #313. Maharam also supported, at least partially, the sometimes criticized Pietist custom (see, e.g., *Sefer Roqeaḥ*, sec. 320, and *Sefer Minhag Tov* [above, ch. 1, n. 34], sec. 11) of standing during the recitation of the first portion of *Shema*. See Eric Zimmer, "Tenuḥot u-Tenuᶜot bi-Sheᶜat Qeriʾat Shema," *Assufot* 8 (1994):348. See also *Sefer Berakhot le-Maharam*, ed. Shlomo Spitzer (Jerusalem, 1988), 133; but cf. *Beit Yosef* to *O. Ḥ.* 98, s.v. *u-mah she-katav be-shem ha-Ram*, and *Haggahot Maimuniyyot, Hilkhot Tefillah*, 4:15[20]. Note also Güdemann, *Ha-Torah veha-Ḥayyim*, 1:131–36, who maintained that R. Judah *he-Ḥasid* and Maharam were at opposite ends of the spectrum with regard to esoteric teachings. Cf. below, ch. 5.

[51]See Urbach, *Baᶜalei ha-Tosafot*, 2:564, and *ᶜArugat ha-Bosem*, ed. Urbach, 4:59–60. Like *Sefer Ḥasidim*, Maharam restricted the priestly benediction to festivals, since he held that immersion was required (just as he preferred immersion in order for a *baᶜal qeri* to pray). See Zimmer, *ᶜOlam ke-Minhago Noheg*, 135–36, and cf. 22–24; *SḤB* 18, 53;

authored a treatise on *ta^camei ha-mesorah*, a subject dealt with extensively by R. Judah *he-Ḥasid* and R. Eleazar of Worms. Subsequent work in this discipline by R. Meir's students, R. Asher b. Yeḥiel and R. Jacob b. Asher *Ba^cal ha-Turim*, preserved and built upon the earlier material.[52]

---

and *Sefer ha-Yir^ɔah,* ed. Zilber, sec. 22. On the attitude(s) of *Ḥasidei Ashkenaz* and R. Meir toward the land of Israel, see my "The *^cAliyah* of 'Three Hundred Rabbis' in 1211: Tosafist Attitudes Toward Settling in the Land of Israel," *JQR* 76 (1986):205–9; Israel Ta-Shma, "Al Odot Yaḥasam shel Qadmonei Ashkenaz le-^cErekh ha-^cAliyah le-Ereẓ Yisra^ɔel," *Shalem* 6 (1992)315–17; and Avraham Grossman, "Ziqqato shel Maharam mi-Rothenburg le-Ereẓ Yisra^ɔel," *Cathedra* 84 (1997):63–84.

[52]See Y. S. Lange, *Ta^camei Mesoret ha-Miqra le-R. Yehudah he-Ḥasid* (Jerusalem, 1981), 11; idem, "Perush Ba^calei ha-Tosafot ^cal ha-Torah—Ketav Yad Paris 48," *Alei Sefer* 5 (1978):73; *Maharam mi-Rothenburg: Teshuvot, Pesaqim, u-Minhagim*, ed. I. Z. Kahana, vol. 1 (Jerusalem, 1957), editor's introduction, 14–15; *Perush Ba^cal ha-Turim ^cal ha-Torah*, ed. Y. K. Reinitz (Jerusalem, 1993), editor's introduction, 16. [Indeed, some manuscripts (e.g., Bodl. 271, and Moscow-Guenzberg 82) mixed or juxtaposed the comments of R. Judah *he-Ḥasid* and Maharam.] For the impact of R. Eleazar of Worms on R. Meir's work, see Jordan Penkower, "Ya^caqov ben Ḥayyim u-Ẓemiḥat Mahadurat ha-Miqra^ɔot ha-Gedolot" (Ph.D. diss., Hebrew University, 1982), 31–50. See also Penkower, *Nosaḥ ha-Torah be-Keter Aram-Ẓovah*, 38–39, for the interest shown by R. Judah *he-Ḥasid*'s nephew, R. Eleazar b. Moses *ha-Darshan*, in masoretic studies. R. Eleazar b. Moses was also involved in the transmission of Pietist teachings; see, e.g., Wolfson, *Through a Speculum That Shines*, 198, 232, and below, ch. 3, nn. 12–13. Note also the *Te^camim shel Ḥumash* of the Pietist R. Solomon b. Samuel (above, n. 5).

In his marginal notes to ms. Leipzig 1, Makhir b. Qershavya, a thirteenth-century copyist and *naqdan*, lists several early Ashkenazic talmudists and tosafists who composed masoretic treatises and were involved in masoretic studies: R. Gershom, R. Joseph Tov Elem, the tosafist R. Menaḥem of Joigny, R. Meir, and R. Pereẓ. Both Penkower, "Ba^cal ha-Tosafot R. Menaḥem mi-Joigny ve-Ḥibbur ha-Mesorah 'Okhlah ve-Okhlah,' Mahadurat Ketav Yad Halle," *^cIyyunei Miqra u-Farshanut* 3 (1993) [*Sefer Zikkaron le-Moshe Goshen-Gottstein*], 291, n. 26, and Avraham Grossman, "Haggahot R. Shemayah ve-Nosaḥ Perush Rashi," *Tarbiz* 60 (1991):91–92, are inclined to identify R. Pereẓ with R. Pereẓ b. Elijah of Corbeil (who studied with R. Yeḥiel of Paris, the brothers of Evreux, and R. Meir of Rothenburg). They are also inclined to identify R. Meir as R. Meir b. Qalonymus of Spires (although R. Meir ha-Levi Abulafia is also a possibility for Grossman). In light of R. Meir of Rothenburg's involvement in composing interpretations or *te^camim* of the *mesorah*, and because of the relationship between R. Meir and Rabbenu Pereẓ (see below, ch. 5, regarding *sod*), the possibility that R. Meir of Rothenburg is the intended reference should not be discarded. Cf. Abraham Epstein, *Mi-Qadmoniyyut ha-Yehudim* (Jerusalem, 1965), 266–69. In any event, it is significant that the three tosafist representatives (including either R. Meir of Rothenburg or R. Meir of Spires) had connections to *ḥasidut Ashkenaz* or to other forms of pietism. R. Meir of Spires was part of the Spires circle that included R. Samuel and his son R. Judah *he-Ḥasid*. See Sussmann, above, ch. 1, n. 76, and Urbach, *Ba^calei ha-Tosafot*, 1:363–65. For R. Pereẓ, see below, nn. 69–71.

An important aspect of Maharam *mi-Rothenburg*'s legal methodology also reflects a position found in *Sefer Ḥasidim*. In order to fully appreciate this comparison, a brief discussion of Maharam's legal methodology is necessary. Despite the hundreds of Maharam's legal decisions that are extant, it is impossible to categorically describe R. Meir's tendencies toward strictness (*ḥumra*) or leniency. For every programmatic statement that appears, one can find examples that contradict it. R. Meir writes, "In all matters that the great scholars (*gedolim*) disagree, I rule with the stricter view, unless there is an obvious leniency that has been transmitted and adopted (*heter pashut she-pashat hetero*) in the practices of the earlier [sages] who have preceded us."[53] Yet there are responsa in which R. Meir challenges his predecessors directly and rules leniently, against them.[54] Nonetheless, R. Meir's proclivities in deciding matters of Jewish law may be accurately described as conservative, especially when compared to the tendencies of many of his tosafist predecessors.[55]

On R. Asher b. Yeḥiel's familiarity with *sodot ha-tefillah* of *Ḥasidei Ashkenaz* and with their tendency to count every word, see his *Responsa*, 4:20, and cf. *Perushei Siddur ha-Tefillah la-Roqeaḥ*, 1:254–55, 342–46; M. Hallamish, "Beᶜayot be-Ḥeqer Hashpaᶜat ha-Qabbalah ᶜal ha-Tefillah," *Massuʾot*, ed. Oron and Goldreich, 204; and Emanuel, "Ha-Polmos ᶜal Nosaḥ ha-Tefillah shel Ḥasidei Ashkenaz," n. 2. See also Jacob b. Asher, *Arbaᶜah Turim, O. Ḥ.*, sec. 113, and cf. Elliot Wolfson, "The Mystical Significance of Torah Study in German Pietism," *JQR* 84 (1993):51, n. 29; D. Abrams, "From Germany to Spain: Numerology as a Mystical Technique," *JJS* 47 (1996):92–93, n. 39; Yoel Catane, "Sefer 'Hanhagat ha-Rosh' ha-Mekhuneh 'Orḥot Hayyim,'" *Ẓefunot* 9 (1991):13–24, and 10 (1991):15–19; Aharon Ahrend, "Ha-Perush ha-Qaẓar shel Baᶜal ha-Turim la-Torah," *Maḥanayim* 3 (1993):180–87; and below, ch. 5, nn. 70, 75. Note the citation from *SHP* 1073 in *Arbaᶜah Turim, O. Ḥ.*, sec. 268: **בספר חסידים מעשה בחסיד אחד שראה לחסיד אחר במותו ופניו מוריקות א״ל למה פניך מוריקות אמר לו מפני שהייתי מדבר בויכולו בשעה שהציבור אומרים אותו**. Cf. *Baḥ* and *Perishah*, loc. cit., and below, ch. 3, n. 46. For other references to pietistic practices associated with *ḥasidut Ashkenaz* in *Arbaᶜah Turim*, see above, ch. 1, n. 35; and see Jacob b. Asher's ethical will, published by Solomon Schechter in *Beit ha-Talmud* 4 (1885):377–79. See above, nn. 24, 49, for the section in *Sefer Tashbeẓ* (authored by Maharam's student, R. Samson b. Ẓadoq) entitled *Dinei Ḥasidut*. This section includes pietistic practices from R. Judah *he-Ḥasid*, R. Samuel of Bamberg, and R. Meir himself, among others. See also *Sefer Tashbeẓ*, secs. 248, 257–58, and below, ch. 5, n. 44.

[53]*Responsa* (Berlin, 1891), 294 (#356).

[54]See Urbach, *Baᶜalei ha-Tosafot*, 2:447–51; I. A. Agus, *Rabbi Meir of Rothenburg* (Philadelphia, 1947), 1:41–48; and Yedidya Dinari, *Ḥakhmei Ashkenaz be-Shilhei Yemei ha-Benayim* (Jerusalem, 1984), 94, n. 117.

[55]See *Terumat ha-Deshen*, #101, who cites the view of Maharam that a *ḥumra* against the Talmud itself is nonetheless appropriate. Cf. Yehudah Levi, "Ḥumrot

Rather than advocating one position or the other, R. Meir often concluded that both sides of a halakhic controversy should be represented by or even incorporated into his final ruling. Thus, Maharam ruled that a new fruit or garment should be procured to enable one to make the *she-heḥeyanu* blessing on the second day of *Rosh ha-Shanah*. This ruling skirted the unresolved dilemma, stemming from the days of Rashi and his teachers, of whether the two days of *Rosh ha-Shanah* are to be considered one elongated day or viewed as two separate festival days—in which case the *she-heḥeyanu* blessing for the festival itself would have to be repeated.[56] Similarly, R. Meir ruled that a non-Jew should dig the grave and fabricate the coffin and shrouds for a Jew who was to be buried on the second day of a festival (*yom tov sheni shel galuyyot*), while Jews should carry the coffin. This decision effectively bridged the opposing positions of R. Isaac *Or Zarua*ᶜ (who held with the *She*ʾ*iltot* that a Jew should not be involved at all in the burial of his dead on *yom tov sheni* unless no Gentiles were available) and Rabiah (who not only rejected the position of the *She*ʾ*iltot* vis-à-vis the second day of *yom tov*, but also required that Jews carry the coffin if the burial took place on the first day of the festival.)[57] In essence, R. Meir felt that the demands of both opposing halakhic positions must be satisfied.

Sefer Ḥasidim, aside from displaying a general tendency toward *ḥumra*,[58] offers the following guideline in a section entitled **עניני שחיטה טהרה ופרישות** (matters of ritual slaughter, purity, and asceticism): "In all situations where rabbinic scholars argue but there is no issue of monetary loss or damage to others, and one position is lenient and the other is strict, even if the law is according to the lenient view, it is better to follow the stricter view in a situation where the two positions do not contradict each other."[59] This pietistic notion appears to be behind Maharam's legal reasoning, although there were other Ashkenazic decisors who employed a similar strategy before him. A series of tosafists—including R. Barukh of Worms, R. Moses of Coucy, R. Samuel of Evreux, R. Isaac of Corbeil, and finally R. Meir of Rothenburg (and his students R. Asher b. Yeḥiel and R. Mordekhai b. Hillel)—recommended that in

---

Meshubaḥot, Hedyotot va-Appiqorsuyyot," *Ha-Ma*ᶜ*ayan* 18:2 (1975):19–33; above, n. 11; and see my "Preservation, Creativity and Courage: The Life and Works of R. Meir of Rothenburg," *Jewish Book Annual* 50 (1992–93):249–59.

56. See the sources in *Maharam: Teshuvot, Pesaqim u-Minhagim*, ed. Kahana,1:298–99 (#531–35).

57. See the sources cited in Katz, *Goy shel Shabbat*,169.

58. See Soloveitchik, "Three Themes," 318–19.

59. *SHP*, sec. 1661.

accordance with the talmudic concept of ירא שמים יוצא ידי שניהם / לצאת ידי שניהם, both the *tefillin* of Rashi and the *tefillin* of Rabbenu Tam should be worn.[60]

Although all these tosafists were associated to some extent with *Ḥasidei Ashkenaz*, except perhaps R. Barukh b. Isaac of Worms,[61] it is difficult to demonstrate that their solution necessarily reflects the thinking of the Pietists.

---

[60]See the sources cited in Yaakov Gartner, "Toledot Minhag Hanaḥat Shetei Zuggot Tefillin ʿad Zemanno shel R. Yosef Karo," *Sidra* 8 (1992):8–12 [=Gartner, *Gilgulei Minhag be-ʿOlam ha-Halakhah*, 147–52.] Gartner makes no mention of *Ḥasidei Ashkenaz* in his discussion. Cf. Ta-Shma, *Ha-Nigleh shebe-Nistar*, 96, n. 54, and Daniel Sperber, *Minhagei Yisraʾel*, 1 (Jerusalem, 1989), 41–42.

The talmudic principle is enunciated by R. Naḥman b. Yiẓḥaq in *Berakhot* 39b and *Shabbat* 61a. Note also the strategy employed by R. Pappa to combine two competing liturgical variants into one inclusive statement (הלכך נימרינהו לתרוייהו); see *Megillah* 21b, *Taʿanit* 6b–7a, and cf. *Ḥullin* 46a. See also Avraham Grossman, "Al Darko shel ha-Qallir ba-ʿAsiyyat Pesharah be-Divrei Aggadah," in Sperber, *Minhagei Yisraʾel*, 2:72–75; *Tosafot Berakhot* 39b, s.v. *ha-kol modim* (ופעמים מפיק הר"י נפשיה מפלוגתא) and 18a, s.v. *le-maḥar* (והריצב"א היה רגיל... לאפוקי נפשיה מפלוגתא); *Pisqei ha-Rid le-Massekhet Yoma*, ed. A. Y. Wertheimer (Jerusalem, 1966), 465–66; and *Teshuvot ha-Rid*, ed. Wertheimer (Jerusalem, 1967), 298 (responsum 61).

An additional aspect of the *tefillin* ritual should also be noted in this regard. An older Italian pre-Crusade tradition, preserved in *Sefer ha-Pardes* and ratified by R. Judah *he-Ḥasid* and R. Simḥah of Spires (as recorded in *Sefer Or Zaruaʿ*), and by R. Eleazar of Worms, R. Eliezer of Metz, and R. Judah b. Qalonymus, recommended making one blessing on the *tefillin shel yad* and a second on the *tefillin shel rosh*. In his talmudic commentary, Rashi takes the position, held by a number of Spanish authorities, that only one blessing should be made for both; Rabbenu Tam suggests that the one blessing be made only after both *tefillin* have been put on. R. Asher b. Yeḥiel, citing his brother, notes a ruling of R. Samuel of Evreux that since there is a controversy in this matter, it is preferable to make only one blessing and not make a second about which there is some doubt. R. Asher himself made only one blessing in his youth but was ultimately convinced that two blessings should be made, as was the widespread practice throughout northern France and Germany. In this case, the Evreux position, rather than the one espoused by *Ḥasidei Ashkenaz*, appears to reflect the more conservative view of halakhic decision-making. It should be noted, however, that the German Pietists were defending an older Ashkenazic (Italian) position against the incursion of a newer talmudic interpretation. Indeed, this battle was already under way in the eleventh century, as the passage in *Sefer Or Zaruaʿ* indicates. For all the relevant primary sources, see Ta-Shma, *Ha-Nigleh shebe-Nistar*, 53–58.

[61]Despite his association with Worms, R. Barukh was a devoted tosafist student of Ri, and his *Sefer ha-Terumah* reflects the dialectical enterprise in northern France; see above, ch. 1, n. 102; Urbach, *Baʿalei ha-Tosafot*, 1:349–50, and esp. n. 27; and my "The ʿ*Aliyah* of 'Three Hundred Rabbis' in 1211," 202–4, 211–12. But if R. Barukh is indeed

Several of these tosafists mention the underlying talmudic concept explicitly. Moreover, their application of this concept addresses a situation in which the opposing positions, held by two of the most important halakhists of the day were mutually exclusive.[62] Maharam, on the other hand, used this methodology on a number of occasions, in situations that fit the guidelines in *Sefer Ḥasidim* more closely. In addition to the two instances described above, he employed this methodology with regard to contested procedures for breaking bread (*beẓiᶜat ha-pat*)[63] and *seᶜudah shelishit*,[64] and to the problem of wearing

---

the author of the so-called פירוש למסכת תמיד המיוחס לראב"ד, as a number of scholars have suggested, he espoused a stringency usually associated with *Ḥasidei Ashkenaz*, that a *kohen* whose wife was a *niddah* should not participate in *birkat kohanim*, since he may have become contaminated with her *tum'at niddah* by touching objects that she touched. See Zimmer, *ᶜOlam ke-Minhago Noheg*, 135–37, esp. n. 25. Note also that *Sefer Roqeaḥ* cites *Sefer ha-Terumah* at least five times, referring to it once as *Sefer ha-Terumah she-yasad ha-R. Barukh b. Yiẓḥaq mi-Ẓarefat*; see Urbach, *Baᶜalei ha-Tosafot*, 1:348, n. 21, and 353, n. 51. Urbach (354–56) is skeptical about R. Barukh's authorship of the commentary to *Tamid*, precisely because it criticizes certain French *Tosafot* and because it cites R. Samuel *he-Ḥasid* and "the *Ḥasid*" (=R. Judah *he-Ḥasid*). The latter is described by the author of the commentary as his teacher; he is cited primarily about spiritual issues, such as the nature of miracles and the *Shekhinah*. Urbach observes that "R. Barukh, author of *Sefer ha-Terumah*, was not a student of 'the Ḥasid.'" Urbach is more inclined, however, to accept the possibility that R. Barukh authored the פירוש לתורת כהנים המיוחס לר"ש משאנץ (based on correlations to the standard *Tosafot Zevaḥim*, which were composed by R. Barukh). See *Baᶜalei ha-Tosafot*, 1:315. R. Barukh authored *Tosafot* to several other tractates in *Seder Qodashim* (as well as to *Nazir*; see Urbach, 1:354). These compositions place R. Barukh squarely in the camp of the brothers of Evreux and *Ḥasidei Ashkenaz*, who encouraged the study of these "neglected" areas in particular; see above, ch. 1, n. 76. See also ms. Sassoon 290, fol. 107, sec. 207, for an amulet that would cause its bearer to have no fear of any ruler (שלא תירא ממלך ושלטון). This amulet is attributed to a R. Menaḥem, who received it from his father-in-law, R. Barukh. R. Barukh of Worms had a son-in-law named Menaḥem; see below, ch. 4, n. 39, for further discussion.

[62]*Semaq*, sec. 154, also rules that the *mezuzah* should be placed diagonally on the doorpost as a compromise between the positions of Rashi and Rabbenu Tam. Here too, however, he employs the phrase לצאת ידי שניהם to explain his approach. See also *Sefer Yere'im*, sec. 400 (end), and Sperber, *Minhagei Yisra'el*, 1:50. *Sefer Yerei'im*, sec. 325, uses the phrase וירא שמים יצא ידי כולם to justify his ruling that a razor should not be used even to shave facial hair that is not technically considered to be *pe'ot*. See also *Semaq*, sec. 70; R. Jonah of Gerona, *Shaᶜarei Teshuvah*, 3:78; and cf. Zimmer, *ᶜOlam ke-Minhago Noheg*, 48.

[63]See *Haggahot Maimuniyyot, Hilkhot Berakhot*, 7:3[3]; the variant in *Teshuvot, Pesaqim u-Minahagim*, ed. Kahana, 1:158 (sec. 131); and Sperber, *Minhagei Yisra'el*, 1:39–40.

(or not wearing) *ẓiẓit* and *tefillin* on the ninth of *Av*, which he resolved by donning his *tallit* and *tefillin* only in the (late) afternoon.[65]

---

[64]*Teshuvot, Pesaqim u-Minahagim*, ed. Kahana, 1:221 (#257), 1:266 (#420); and Sperber, *Minhagei Yisra*ʾ*el*, 2:38–40. Cf. Kahana, ed. 1:288–89 (#496), for Maharam's approach to writing on the intermediate days of a festival, which represents something of a compromise between the differing views concerning the permissibility of writing an ʾ*iggeret shalom*. Cf. *Sefer Roqeaḥ*, sec. 308, and *Beit Yosef* to *Oraḥ Ḥayyim*, sec. 546. See also R. Jonah's view on the procedure for kindling the *Ḥannukah* lights, cited in R. Yeroham, *Toledot Adam ve-Ḥavvah*, 9:1, and in *Darkhei Mosheh* to *Oraḥ Ḥayyim*, 676:1, which would bridge the differing opinions of earlier authorities on the nature of the blessing *she*ʿ*asah nissim*. Cf. the analysis of R. Joseph Soloveitchik recorded in *Mesorah* 4 (1991):7–9.

[65]See *Haggahot Maimuniyyot, Hilkhot Ta*ʿ*anit*, 5:1[5]; Sperber, *Minhagei Yisra*ʾ*el*, 2:44–45, Zimmer, ʿ*Olam ke-Minhago Noheg*, 181–82; and above, n. 28. (The fact that R. Eleazar of Worms did not propose the same procedures does not detract from the intent of Maharam's methodology; see Zimmer, nn. 39, 42.) In several of the cases noted in this discussion, R. Meir's solution is characterized by the phrase **לאפוקי נפשי(ה) מפלוגתא** rather than by a version of the talmudic phrase, suggesting perhaps that R. Meir had extra-talmudic considerations. R. Moses of Evreux, or perhaps Maharam himself, also used this phrase (see *Sefer* ʿ*al ha-Kol*, ed. M. Z. Weiss, *Ha-Goren*, 7 [1908]:5–6, sec. 1) to explain the custom of beginning the blessing before *Shema* with two different (competing) phrases in *Shaḥarit* and in *Ma*ʿ*ariv*. See also Sperber, 2:33–35. This practice was already found, however in the geonic period. Indeed, *Sefer Or Zarua*ʿ writes: **והגאונים פסקו לקיים דברי שניהם**, although it is perhaps significant that this practice appears to have been followed only in Germany for the most part, not in northern France. See Israel Ta-Shma, "Ahavat ʿOlam ve-Ahavah Rabbah," *Sefer ha-Yovel le-Rav Mordekhai Breuer*, ed. Moshe Ahrend et al. (Jerusalem, 1992), 2:601–11, esp. 608. [Note also the "compromise" regarding the text of the ʿ*Amidah* on Sabbath eve proposed by R. Meir **שליח ציבור** (who was venerated by *Ḥasidei Ashkenaz* as **בקי ... בסודות ובמדרשים ובטעמים**; see ms. Kaufmann A399, fol. 34r, and Grossman, *Ḥakhmei Ashkenaz ha-Rishonim*, 294). Also see Naftali Wieder, "Yishmaḥ Mosheh," *Meḥqarim ba-Aggadah, Targumim u-Tefillot Yisra*ʾ*el le-Zekher Yiẓḥaq Heinemann*, ed. Ezra Fleisher (Jerusalem, 1981), 96–98.] and Zimmer, ʿ*Olam ke-Minhago Noheg*, 123–27.

Maharam's approach to the issue of rule by the majority, in which he amalgamates Rabbenu Tam's more "stringent" position (requiring unanimity) with the more commonly held view advocated by Rabiah (majority rule), may also be understood as an attempt by R. Meir to harmonize these positions, although this case does not conform in several respects to the guidelines in *Sefer Ḥasidim*. See my "Unanimity, Majority, and Communal Government in Ashkenaz During the High Middle Ages," *PAAJR* 58 (1992):79–106, and my "Preservation, Creativity and Courage," 252–55. See also *Arba*ʿ*ah Turim, O. Ḥ.*, sec. 128, for R. Meir's compromise position (between the views of Rambam and R. Gershom/Rashi) on whether repentance allows a *kohen* who has killed someone to resume pronouncing the priestly blessing. Such a *kohen* should not be told to ascend the *dukhan* (to offer the blessing) but, if he does so on his own, he should not be removed.

Two responsa of R. Meir regarding martyrdom also appear to reflect the influence of both *ḥasidut Ashkenaz* and *Hekhalot* literature. In the first, R. Meir was asked to respond concerning the tragic situation of an individual who slaughtered his family as Christian attackers neared, and who was then saved either before he could commit suicide or prior to his death as a result of the suicide attempt. The question put to Maharam was whether the individual required any form of penance (*kapparah*) for his actions. R. Meir ruled that he did not, because his actions were justifiable and conformed to Ashkenazic rabbinic precedent.[66] It appears from this text, however, that Maharam was completely comfortable with the notion of securing expiation through prescribed physical penances, a hallmark of Pietist thought, as we have seen.

In another responsum, R. Meir asserted that once someone had made the decision to undertake martyrdom, he felt none of the pain of death, regardless of the means of execution. R. Meir supported this contention with two textual proofs: a passage from *Sefer Hekhalot* and an explanation based on the structure of the biblical *mesorah*.[67] He saved his most striking proof, however, for last.

---

[66]*Teshuvot, Pesaqim u-Minhagim*, ed. Kahana, vol. 2 (Jerusalem, 1960), 54 (#59), and cf. Haym Soloveitchik, "Religious Law and Change: The Medieval Ashkenazic Example," *AJS Review* 12 (1987): 209–11, nn. 7–8.

[67]*Responsa* (Prague), #517: וכן אמר מהר"ם מאחר שגמר אדם בדעתו למסור את נפשו על קידוש השם, מכאן ואילך כל מיתה שעושים לו אינו מרגיש כלל. וראיה מן המסורה הכוני ב׳. הכוני בל חליתי וחד הכוני פצעוני. כלומר כשהכוני ופצעוני לא היה לי כאב הכוני בל חליתי. ומביא ראיה מספר היכלות שר׳ חנניה בן תרדיון היה במקום קיסר ששה חדשים והרג שיתא אלפין דוכסין והגמונים. לסוף ו׳ חדשים נלקח למעלה ושרפו רק אחד במקומו כדמותו. Cf. Maharam's *Taʿamei Mesoret ha-Miqra* (published by Kahana in his edition of Maharam's responsa, above, n. 52), 39; *Sefer Tashbeẓ*, sec. 415; *Orḥot Ḥayyim, hilkhot Rosh ha-Shanah*, sec. 24 (end). *Kol Bo*, sec. 67 (end); ms. Vat. 471, fol. 58r; and ms. Budapest/Kaufmann A266, fol. 410. In ms. Bodl. 378, fol. 22r–22v, and ms. Bodl. 1106, fol. 342v, the proof from *Sefer Hekhalot* is cited (incorrectly) in the name of Rabbenu Tam. Cf. *Teshuvot, Pesaqim u-Minhagim*, ed. Kahana, 2:231–32 (#136), and below, ch. 3, n. 87. For the mystical implications in the formulation of Maharam and its association with the *Hekhalot* corpus, see Michael Fishbane, *The Kiss of God: Spiritual and Mystical Death in Judaism* (Seattle, 1994), 51–55, and idem, "The Imagination of Death in Jewish Spirituality," *Death, Ecstasy and Other Worldly Journeys*, ed. John Collins and Michael Fishbane (New York, 1995), 191. Cf. R. J. Z. Werblowsky, *Joseph Karo, Lawyer and Mystic* (Philadelphia, 1977), 172–73. In ms. Kaufmann A266, fol. 411, Maharam is cited as mandating a blessing for those who were about to sanctify the Name through martyrdom. Cf. Soloveitchik, "Religious Law and Change," 208–9, and the literature cited in n. 6. For the possible roots of this blessing in *Hekhalot* literature, see Meir Bar-Ilan, *Sitrei Tefillah ve-Hekhalot* (Jerusalem, 1987), 141–52; and cf. Peter Schäfer and Shaul Shaked, *Magische Texte aus der Kairoer-Geniza*, vol. 2 (Tübingen, 1997), 105, 114, 155, 159.

"There is no one in the world who will not scream when he touches fire with even the smallest finger (or limb). Even if he tries to restrain himself, he will be unable to do so. But [we have seen] many [times] martyrs (*qedoshim moserim* ᶜ*aẓmam* ᶜ*al qiddush ha-Shem*) [who are burned or killed who] do not scream at all."[68]

R. Pereẓ b. Elijah of Corbeil, a younger colleague of Maharam who also studied with R. Yeḥiel of Paris and at the academy of Evreux, cited his teachers at Evreux regarding means for achieving *kavvanah* in prayer.[69] He also referred approvingly to a number of ascetic practices. These include fasting and limiting one's enjoyment of food, as well as an awareness of the full range of *tiqqunei teshuvah* and other stringencies endorsed by German Pietists.[70] R. Pereẓ, like Maharam, accepted the notion that a devoted martyr could withstand the challenge and feel no pain, if initially he had proper intentions regarding the Tetragrammaton (אם כוון שם המיוחד בתחלה).[71]

---

[68]Cf. David Tamar in *Qiryat Sefer* 33 (1948):376, and ms. Moscow 348, fol. 246v.

[69]When *Semaq* (at the beginning of section 11) cites R. Eleazar of Worms on the importance of maintaining appropriate *kavvanah* throughout the blessings of the ᶜ*Amidah* prayer (מי שמתכוין בשאלתו ולא יכוין בשבחו של הקב"ה מחייב את עצמו), R. Pereẓ in his gloss cites the Pietist-like formulation of R. Moses of Evreux on the importance of thinking about each word as it is being said. Cf. R. Pereẓ's gloss to *Semaq*, sec. 97, citing R. Samuel of Evreux on *kavvanah*. See above, ch. 1, n. 79.

[70]See above, ch. 1, n. 91, in the name of R. Jonah. In his *pesaqim*, R. Pereẓ appears to endorse the ascetic eating practices of R. Moses of Evreux; see above, ch. 1, nn. 83, 177. He also lists his own practices concerning *ta*ᶜ*anit ḥalom* for a dream experienced during the day (which he notes differed from that of R. Judah *he-Ḥasid*) and avoiding conversation with any woman in his home, including his mother-in-law, unless there was another male present. R. Pereẓ cautioned that one should not speak during the quasi-repetition of the ᶜ*Amidah* on Friday evenings (*berakhah* ᵓ*aḥat me*ᶜ*en sheva*), because a soul once told R. Yeḥiᵓel of Paris that the angels threw him up and let him fall by himself because he talked during this prayer. Cf. above, n. 52, for a similar notion in *Sefer Ḥasidim*. (R. Pereẓ also refused to take water to drink from even the youngest of his students.) See S. Shaᵓanan, "Pisqei Rabbenu Pereẓ va-Aḥerim," *Moriah* 17/9–10 (1991):10–14, secs. 7, 8, 15, 26; ms. Paris 407, fols. 236c–237a; and ms. JTS Rab. 1077, fol. 20r. Although R. Isaac of Corbeil (*Semaq*, sec. 53) lists the four Pietist modes of penance without providing any specific guidance regarding their application (see above, ch. 1, n. 142), R. Pereẓ of Corbeil in his gloss offers a brief definition of each type, fully consonant with Pietist literature. [On R. Isaac and R. Pereẓ of Corbeil, see also Getzel Ellinson, "Le-Ḥeqer Qavvei ha-Pesiqah shel ha-Rosh," *Sinai* 93 (1983):236–37.]

[71]See *Orḥot Ḥayyim*, *hilkhot Rosh ha-Shanah*, sec. 24 (end); *Sefer Kol Bo*, sec. 67 (end); and cf. above, n. 67. On R. Pereẓ and masoretic studies (similar to those undertaken by *Ḥasidei Ashkenaz* and R. Meir of Rothenburg), see above, n. 52. See also Samson b. Eliezer, *Barukh She*ᵓ*amar*, ed. M. M. Meshi-Zahav (Jerusalem, 1970), 19.

IV

Brief reference was made earlier to a correlation between rabbinic figures who espoused *perishut* or *ḥasidut* and were also involved in esoteric studies. A number of Provençal mystics were called by titles *parush*, *nazir*, or *ḥasid*, indicating that their mystical studies were coupled with ascetic practices and other forms of self-denial. These behavioral modes were thought to be part of the mystical experience, as they were in the kabbalistic schools of Gerona[72] and in the mystical circles of sixteenth-century Safed.[73]

Similarly, Moshe Rosman has argued recently that there was an existing "mystic-ascetic-hasidic tradition" in seventeenth- and eighteenth-century Germany and Poland that preceded the rise of Hasidism. Rabbinic scholars who pursued this outlook undertook additional fasts and other physical penances, prayed with intense devotion that included both crying and ecstatic movements, and studied kabbalistic literature, in addition to their regimen of regular Torah study. Rosman suggests that this tradition was generated in part by a renewed commitment to ideals and practices of *Ḥasidei Ashkenaz*, especially with regard to *teshuvah*.[74] The pietism and asceticism that underlie the magical and mystical rituals in *Hekhalot* literature represent further suggestive examples of this kind of correlation.[75]

Chapters 1 and 2 have identified a range of pietistic and ascetic behaviors and outlooks among tosafists and rabbinic figures in medieval Ashkenaz. Prior to a discussion of the involvement of these scholars in mysticism and magic, it

---

R. Abraham of Sensheim writes that "from the time that I left R. Meir of Rothenburg, I have not found anyone observing the precepts of fringes, phylacteries and *mezuzah* fully and punctiliously except for R. Pereẓ of Corbeil, and my teacher *ha-qadosh, ha-rav, he-ḥasid* R. Zuslein, and my teacher R. Malkiʾel of Hagenau." Cf. my "Rabbinic Attitudes Toward Nonobservance in the Medieval Period" (above, ch. 1, n. 99), 7–14. On R. Pereẓ and *sod*, see below, ch. 5 (end).

[72]See above, ch. 1, n. 6.

[73]See, e.g., Werblowsky, *Joseph Karo, Lawyer and Mystic*, 38–83, 149–51.

[74]M. Rosman, *Founder of Hasidism: A Quest for the Historical Ba'al Shem Tov* (Berkeley, 1996), 27–39. Cf. Gedalyah Nigal, "Qabbalah Maʿasit be-Frankfurt be-Meʾah ha-Shemonah ʿEsreh," *Sinai* 118 (1996):88–95.

[75]See, e.g., Peter Schäfer, *Hidden and Manifest God*, 89–95, and M. Swartz, *Scholastic Magic*, 153–66; cf. Elliot Wolfson, "Jewish Mysticism: A Philosophical Overview," in *History of Jewish Philosophy*, ed. Daniel Frank (London, 1997), 451–52. Cf. Robert Mathieson, "A Thirteenth-Century Ritual to Attain the Beatific Vision," *Conjuring Spirits*, ed. Claire Fanger (Phoenix Mill, 1998), 151–53; and Richard Kieckhefer, "The Devil's Contemplatives: The *Liber Iuratus*, the *Liber Visionum* and the Christian Appropriation of Jewish Occultism," ibid., 250–65.

is appropriate to review, in greater detail, evidence for the correlation just described within medieval Ashkenaz itself. Ivan Marcus, mindful of Gershom Scholem's characterization of *ḥasidut Ashkenaz* as "mystical moralism," has argued that the emphasis placed by R. Eleazar of Worms—in the *Hilkhot Ḥasidut* preamble to his *Sefer Roqeaḥ*—on the religious perfection of the individual through personal pietism had as its ultimate goal the preparation of the individual for mystical experiences in prayer. R. Eleazar's focus on the development of spiritual inwardness reaches its climax in the twelfth section of his *hilkhot ḥasidut* (called *shoresh qedushat ha-yiḥud u-Shemo u-Merkavah ve-sodotav*), which is, in essence, a mystical tract of contemplation and analysis concerning *yiḥud ha-Shem*.[76]

Peter Schäfer has established conceptual and even linguistic parallels between typical ascetic and pietistic practices of *hasidut Ashkenaz*, and instructions contained in *Hekhalot* literature for the one seeking to enter the Heavenly palaces (*yored Merkavah*). He suggests that this body of earlier Jewish literature (with which the German Pietists were very familiar, since they served as its transmitters and editors) was the source of these practices of *Ḥasidei Ashkenaz*—rather than Christian asceticism or other temporal stimuli, such as the trauma of the Crusades and other intense persecutions.[77]

---

[76]See above, ch. 1, n. 5, and cf. K. E. Grözinger, "Between Magic and Religion—Ashkenazi Hasidic Piety," *Mysticism, Magic and Kabbalah in Ashkenazi Judaism* (Berlin, 1995), 28–42. (Marcus also writes [*Piety and Society*, 85] that even as most followers of *ḥasidut Ashkenaz* were initiated into a life of pietism, they were not initiated "into the mysteries of the esoteric tradition about God." At the same time, "they received guidance and counsel from [Pietist] Sages who did have such knowledge.") See also Dan, *Torat ha-Sod shel Ḥasidut Ashkenaz*, 71–73, and idem, "Sifrut ha-Yiḥud shel Ḥasidei Ashkenaz," *Qiryat Sefer* 41 (1966):533–44. Although Dan maintains that the area of *sifrut ha-yiḥud* is one of the more exoteric within the thought of *Ḥasidei Ashkenaz* (cf. Urbach, *Baᶜalei ha-Tosafot*, 1:408–9), he notes that the twelfth section of R. Eleazar's ethical introduction to *Sefer Roqeaḥ* is a departure from what precedes it. It appears to be an opening into the world of *sod* for those who studied R. Eleazar's halakhic and pietistic material; see esp. 537 (sec. 7). There are intimations of mystical experience in the opening section of R. Eleazar's *hilkhot ḥasidut* and in his discussion of *kavvanah* in prayer. In the sections on pietism and the study of Torah, however, *sod* refers to the deep (exoteric) knowledge that Torah scholars acquire through their study of Torah and *musar*. These aspects of R. Eleazar's introduction are similar to the program propounded by *Midrash Mishlei*. Proper participation in a regular regimen of Torah study can lead ultimately to the study of *sod*. See *The Midrash on Proverbs*, ed. Burton Visotzky (New Haven, 1992), 56–57, and the editor's introduction, 4.

[77]Peter Schäfer, "The Ideal of Piety of the Ashkenazi Ḥasidim and Its Roots in Jewish Tradition," *Jewish History* 4 (1990):9–23. On the issue of asceticism and martyrdom, see also Israel Marcus, "Hierarchies, Religious Boundaries and Jewish

Schäfer does not discuss at any length the esoteric traditions of German Pietism and their relationship to the pietistic elements. Nonetheless, the following formulation suggests that he envisions the linkage between *ḥasidut Ashkenaz* and *Hekhalot* literature as reflecting a very similar, even commonly held, approach to the relationship between pietism and mysticism.

> Both traditions clearly assume that their adepts, the Hasid and the esoteric of early Jewish mysticism, are capable of wisdom and special cognition. Indeed, this confidence in the ability of their fellows to enjoy a special, deeper insight was perhaps the element which cemented the sense of group solidarity evidenced by the Pietists and the Yorede Merkavah.[78]

The tosafists based some of the examples of pietistic and ascetic practices described in chapters 1 and 2 on *Hekhalot* practices. In the following chapters, we shall encounter an even wider array of magical and mystical techniques and concepts (with many based on *Hekhalot* literature as well) expressed in most instances by the same tosafists. The correlation between pietism and mysticism in *Ḥasidei Ashkenaz* and, indeed, in *Hekhalot* literature itself, suggests that this correlation in the tosafist realm cannot be coincidental. As has been noted, tosafists did not pursue the study of theosophy as the Pietists did, and they cannot be properly classified as mystics. Nonetheless, the findings in chapters 1 and 2 regarding pietism, asceticism, stringency, and *perishut* serve as a kind of foundation for the magical and mystical dimensions which can be discerned among certain tosafists.

It is appropriate to close this chapter with an example of how pietism and *perishut* may directly reflect magical and mystical concerns as well. There are several types of restrictions designed to promote separation (*harḥaqot*) prescribed for a menstruant—having to do primarily with dining with her husband, modes of dress, reciting blessings, and entering the synagogue—which cannot be found, for the most part, in talmudic literature, but which are found in the so-called *Baraita de-Massekhet Niddah*.[79] This unusual text, which

---

Spirituality in Medieval Germany," *Jewish History* 1 (1986):25, n. 34. The evidence presented in ch. 1 and in this chapter for asceticism in tosafist circles, and its origins, offers strong proof for the role of internal religious stimuli. Cf. Y. N. Simḥoni, "Ha-Ḥasidut ha-Ashkenazit Bimei ha-Benayim," in *Dat ve-Ḥevrah be-Mishnatam shel Ḥasidei Ashkenaz*, ed. Ivan Marcus (Jerusalem, 1987), 68–78.

[78] Schäfer, "The Ideal of Piety," 17.

[79] Yedidyah Dinari, "Minhagei Tumʾat Ha-Niddah Meqoram ve-Hishtalshelutam," *Tarbiz* 49 (1980):302–5.

appears to have originated in *Ereẓ Yisra᾽el* during the early geonic period, is linked to *Hekhalot* literature.[80] From its earliest days, Ashkenazic Jewry accepted many of these stringencies; so did its rabbinic authorities. Early tosafists—such as Raban, whose goal was to harmonize accepted practice with the talmudic corpus—undertook to evaluate these stringencies in light of talmudic law. This effort produced a rationalistic or legalistic interpretation for these *harḥaqot* (as a function of ritual impurity) that contributed to their mitigation.[81]

R. Isaac b. Moses *Or Zarua*ᶜ, however, continued to support many of these *harḥaqot* (*kol mah she-yakhol ᾽adam le-haḥmir ba-niddah yaḥmir*), because of considerations of "danger" (*va᾽ani shamati mi-taᶜam sakkanah*). In doing so, R. Isaac b. Moses of Vienna was perhaps following R. Eleazar of Worms, who located their presence in the eleventh-century *Ma᾽aseh ha-Geonim*, as a means of stressing the authentic (and binding) nature of the stringencies. The danger associated with the menstruant by R. Isaac—noted also by Naḥmanides in his Torah commentary (הבלן מזיק, גם מבטן מוליד גנאי ועושה רושם רע)—derives from the *Baraita de-Massekhet Niddah*, in which the menstruant is described as possessing the ability not only to transmit impurity but also to (magically) impart certain diseases or afflictions, such as boils, leprosy, and physical disabilities. Both R. Isaac *Or Zarua*ᶜ and Ramban mention the *Baraita* in their formulations.[82]

---

[80]See Lieberman, *Sheqiᶜin*, 22; Zimmer, *ᶜOlam ke-Minhago Noheg*, 222, and the literature cited in n. 7; Swartz, *Scholastic Magic*, 164–65, 214–15; Israel Ta-Shma, "'Miqdash Meᶜat'—Ha-Semel veha-Mamashut," *Knesset Ezra*, ed. Shulamit Elizur et al. (Jerusalem, 1994), 360.

[81]See Dinari, "Minhagei Tum᾽at Ha-Niddah Meqoram ve-Hishtalshelutam," 321–23; and Israel Ta-Shma, *Halakhah, Minhag u-Meẓi᾽ut be-Ashkenaz* (Jerusalem, 1996), 280–88. Ta-Shma argues that diminutions of the *harḥaqot* had already been advocated by Rashi. Among tosafists who accepted the diminished levels were R. Eliezer of Metz and Rabiah. Note that while Raban tried to explain away a problematic talmudic passage in order to justify the Ashkenazic custom that a *niddah* made the blessing following her immersion (rather than prior to the act, as is normally mandated for the recitation of a blessing), Rabbenu Tam (and his brother-in-law, R. Samson of Falaise) railed against this custom—which is found in the *Baraita de-Niddah*—in very strong terms. Ri, on the other hand, held that the custom was valid, without accepting Raban's exegesis. Interestingly, these developments form an excellent model or paradigm for the positions taken by twelfth-century tosafists regarding the efficacy of magic and *sod*; see the next chapter, and cf. Weinstock, *Be-Maᶜagalei ha-Nigleh*, 249–59.

[82]See *Sefer Or Zarua*ᶜ, pt. 1, sec. 360; Naḥmanides' commentary to Genesis 31:35; *Sefer Roqeaḥ*, sec. 318 (end); Dinari, "Minhagei Tum᾽at Ha-Niddah Meqoram ve-Hishtalshelutam," 303, 310, 322–23; and cf. Ta-Shma, *Halakhah Minhag u-Meẓi᾽ut*

As we shall see, R. Isaac *Or Zarua*ᶜ, like the German Pietists, was attuned not only to the existence of *shedim* and *maziqin*, but also to the magical nature of their powers.[83] His retention of the many stringencies associated with the *niddah* emerged, in all likelihood, from the nexus of *perishut* and magic. Moreover, within *Hekhalot* literature itself, menstrual impurity had to be assiduously avoided, lest it interfere with the mystical rituals and visions sought by the adepts. The slightest trace of impurity could lead to immediate recall from a mystical vision.[84] Similarly, accounts about *Ḥasidei Ashkenaz* and others who were aware of the mystical and magical powers of *Shemot* describe their attempts to keep menstruants far away from Holy Names and rituals that involved them, lest the *niddot* unwittingly wreak havoc with the Names by their very presence.[85] Although other tosafist halakhists were aware of the *Baraita de-Niddah* and were prepared to retain some of its stringencies as bona fide halakhic *ḥumrot*—if not demonstrations of piety—R. Isaac *Or Zarua*ᶜ

---

be-Ashkenaz, 287. (*Maḥzor Vitry* endorsed these prohibitions because of *hergel* ᶜ*averah*, a more neutral kind of reason.) Many of these *harḥaqot* were also adopted by the Zohar, despite their relative absence in the early medieval Spanish tradition. See Ta-Shma, *Ha-Nigleh shebe-Nistar*, 24. Ramban notes that the negative powers attributed to the *niddah* were also recognized by "the philosophers." Cf. C. T. Wood, "'The Doctors' Dilemma': Sin, Salvation and the Menstrual Cycle in Medieval Thought," *Speculum* 56 (1981):710–27; and H. J. Zimmels, *Magicians, Theologians and Doctors* (New York, 1952), 117.

83 See Dan, *Torat ha-Sod shel Ḥasidut Ashkenaz*, 188, n. 19, and below, ch. 4. Regarding *Sefer Or Zarua*ᶜ and the stringencies of *Ḥasidei Ashkenaz*, see above, n. 40; ch. 1, nn. 16–17; and below, n. 86; ch. 5, n. 8. *Tosafot Pesaḥim*, 111a, s.v. ʾ*im*, explains the talmudic passage at hand—that if a woman passes between two men at the beginning of her menstrual period she will kill one of them—to mean that if the woman had practiced sorcery (*kishuf*) on one of the men, the power of her impurity would make it effective. Cf. Swartz, *Scholastic Magic*, 165, n. 69. (Rashi, and Rashbam, ad loc., interpret simply that her passing between them damages them, without indicating the vehicle for the damage or its nature.)

84 See Swartz, *Scholastic Magic*, 154–72. The rituals include the cleansing of one's clothes and body, immersion, fasting and the avoidance of certain foods, and the avoidance of sexual and social contact. See also below, ch. 3, n. 8.

85 See the Qalonymide chain of tradition recorded in *She*ʾ*elot u-Teshuvot Maharshal*, #29 (end; on the origins and nature of this source, see above, introduction, n. 13), and Sharon Koren, "Mysticism and Menstruation: The Significance of Female Impurity in Jewish Spirituality" (Ph.D. diss., Yale, 1999), ch. 1. The concern of these adepts (which included figures found in *Megillat Aḥimza*ᶜ*aẓ* in addition to *Ḥasidei Ashkenaz*) was also based on their familiarity with the requirements and regulations for purity found in *Hekhalot* literature. For other efforts to protect books of *Shemot*, see *SHP*, secs. 213, 1819. On the danger associated with a *niddah*, cf. *SHB* 1126.

(following R. Eleazar of Worms) appears to have had additional considerations in arguing for their almost complete retention.[86]

With these kinds of correlations in mind, we are now prepared to trace the involvement of Ashkenazic rabbinic scholars with magic and mysticism, from the pre-Crusade period through the end of the tosafist period.

---

[86]Ta-Shma, "Miqdash Meʿat—Ha-Semel veha-Mashmaʿut," 351–64, and Zimmer, ʿ*Olam ke-Minhago Noheg*, 220–49, relate the Ashkenazic *ḥumrot* regarding the *harḥaqot* of a *niddah* to other stringencies—those regarding the duration of the *niddut* period and the status of *dam tohar* following the birth of a child. For Zimmer, these *ḥumrot* reflect, for the most part, the pietistic impact and influence of R. Judah *he-Ḥasid*, especially (as suggested almost explicitly by R. Meir of Rothenburg) on his followers in the "outlying" areas of central and eastern Europe, and thereby on *minhag Austreikh* in general. See above, n. 44. This pattern of influence is also evident with regard to the ability of a *baʿal qeri* to pray and lead the prayers in the synagogue, and to pronounce the priestly blessing; see Eric Zimmer, "Moʿadei Nesiʾat Kappayim," *Sinai* 100 (1987):455–57 [=ʿ*Olam ke-Minhago Noheg*, 135–40; cf. above, n. 51]; and cf. Sperber, *Minhagei Yisraʾel*, 4:39–40; Ta-Shma, 360, n. 29; and Yedidyah Dinari, "Ḥillul ha-Qodesh ʿal Yedei Niddah ve-Taqqanat Ezra," *Teʿudah* 3 (1983):17–38. [R. Isaac *Or Zaruaʿ* held virtually all these stringencies as well. See Zimmer, ʿ*Olam ke-Minhago Noheg*, 136; 229–30, nn. 37–38; 242, n. 14; 245–48.] Ta-Shma suggests that Ashkenazic rabbinic culture, following the Palestinian tradition, invested the holiness and sanctity of the synagogue with particular significance and stringency (note, e.g., *Sefer Yereʾim*, sec. 104). These overarching analyses accord quite well with the presence and place of *perishut* and pietism in medieval Ashkenazic rabbinic thought that have been demonstrated in this chapter. See now Avraham Grossman, "Mi-Morashatah shel Yahadut Sefarad: Ha-Yahas ʾel ha-Ishah ha-'Qatlanit' Bimei ha-Benayim," *Tarbiz* 67 (1998):551–58.

3

Mysticism and Magic: Pre-Crusade Traditions and the Reaction of Early Tosafists

I

There was substantial interest in *torat ha-sod* on the part of rabbinic scholars in pre-Crusade Germany, but it existed almost exclusively in Mainz and, within Mainz, among members of the Abun and Qalonymus families.[1] R. Simeon b.

[1]*Sodot* that circulated in Italy (and France) during the late ninth and early tenth centuries were brought to the Rhineland by migrating Qalonymides, members of the Abun family, and others. See, e.g., Joseph Dan, "The Beginnings of Jewish Mysticism in Europe," *The Dark Ages*, ed. Cecil Roth (Ramat Gan, 1966), 282–90; idem, *Torat ha-Sod shel Ḥasidut Ashkenaz* (Jerusalem, 1968), 13–20; idem, "Hithavvut Torat ha-Sod ha-ᶜIvrit," *Maḥanayim* 6 (1994):12; Avraham Grossman, *Ḥakhmei Ashkenaz ha-Rishonim* (Jerusalem, 1981), 29–35; and cf. Robert Bonfil, "Bein Ereẓ Yisraʾel le-Bavel," *Shalem* 5 (1987):1–30; idem, "ᶜEduto shel Agobard mi-Lyons ᶜal ᶜOlamam ha-Ruḥani shel Yehudei ᶜIro ba-Meʾah ha-Teshiᶜit," *Meḥqarim be-Qabbalah, be-Filosofyah Yehudit uve-Sifrut ha-Mussar vehe-Hagut* [*Muggashim li-Yeshayah Tishby*], ed. J. Dan and J. Hacker (Jerusalem, 1986), 327–48; Elliot Wolfson, "The Theosophy of Shabbetai Donnolo, with Special Emphasis on the Doctrine of *Sefirot* in his *Sefer Ḥakhmoni*," *The Frank Talmage Memorial Volume*, vol. 2 [=*Jewish History* 6 (1992)], ed. Barry Walfish (Haifa, 1993), 282–84; *Megillat Aḥimaᶜaẓ*, ed. Benjamin Klar (Jerusalem, 1974), 13–15, 21–23, 33–34, 50–51, and the editor's comments, 118–19; Ezra Fleischer, *Ha-Yoẓerot be-Hithavvutan uve-Hitpatḥutan* (Jerusalem, 1984), 660–772; and Stephen Benin, "Megillat Aḥimaᶜaẓ u-Meqomo be-Sifrut ha-Bizantit," *Meḥqerei Yerushalayim be-Maḥshevet Yisraʾel*, 4 (1980):237–50. *Piyyutim* from tenth-century Italy contain verbatim extracts as well as interpolations of *Hekhalot* material. See also *Piyyutei R. Shimᶜon b. Yiẓḥaq*, ed. A. M. Habermann (Jerusalem, 1938), 18–20; Zvi Malachi, "Ha-Mistiqah ve-Shirat ha-Qodesh ha-ᶜIvrit," *Maḥanayim* 6 (1994):79; and Elliot Ginsburg, "The Many Faces of Kabbalah," *Hebrew Studies* 36 (1995):118, n. 13.

Isaac *ha-Gadol*, whose pietism was noted at the beginning of the first chapter, included in his *piyyutim* such concepts as the ineffable Name of seventy letters (שם ה׳ המפורש בשבעים אותיות) and descriptions of the names and functions of angels in their devotional services to the Almighty, a well as references to *Hekhalot* literature.[2] A passage in a late thirteenth-century manuscript refers to an ᵓ*ofan* composed by R. Simeon *ha-Gadol* and set to a particular melody (*niggun*). The *niggun*, which was purported to be a tune of the angels, was transmitted to R. Simeon in a dream by the heavenly *ba*ᶜ*al ha-ḥalom*.[3] R. Simeon

---

[2]See Grossman, *Ḥakhmei Ashkenaz ha-Rishonim*, 100–101 [and cf. Peter Schäfer, *The Hidden and Manifest God* (Albany, 1992), 36]; *Perushei ha-Siddur la-Roqeaḥ*, ed. Moshe Hershler (Jerusalem, 1992), 1:255; *Piyyutei R. Shim*ᶜ*on b. Yiẓḥaq*, 58, 98, 160; and *Maḥzor le-Yamim ha-Nora*ᵓ*im*, ed. Daniel Goldschmidt (Jerusalem, 1970), vol. 1, 77–78, 109–11, for *piyyutim* of R. Simeon b. Isaac and R. Eleazar *ha-Qallir* that list and compare (favorably) the praises to God offered by human beings to those offered to God by the angels. A *piyyut* from the less mystically inclined French talmudist, R. Yosef *Tov* ᶜ*Elem*, however, lists only the human praises (*Maḥzor le-Yamim ha-Nora*ᵓ*im*, vol. 1, 201–2). Cf. Avraham Grossman, *Ḥakhmei Ẓarefat ha-Rishonim* (Jerusalem, 1995), 79–80. [The messianic predictions from R. Yosef *Tov Elem*'s son, R. Zekharyah/Zevadyah, are based on verses that were subjected to midrashic (and political) analysis; he did not say that he received a "prophetic" dream about a particular year, as others did. See Grossman, *Ḥakhmei Ẓarefat ha-Rishonim*, 51–52; and below, n. 41; ch. 4, nn. 8–9, 37; ch. 5, n. 67.] For additional examples of descriptions of angelic names and functions in pre-Crusade Italy and Germany (by authors such as R. Solomon *ha-Bavli*, R. Amittai, and R. Benjamin b. Zeraḥ), see *Maḥzor Sukkot*, ed. Daniel Goldschmidt (Jerusalem, 1981), 88, 258–62, 358, 362, 364, 366. [On the name Adiriron, found in some of these *piyyutim* and in *Hekhalot* literature, see *Synopse zur Hekhalot-Literatur*, ed. Peter Schäfer (Tübingen, 1981), secs. 204, 301, 411; and cf. Gershom Scholem, "Havdalah de-R. Aqivah: Maqor le-Massoret Mageyah ha-Yehudit bi-Tequfat ha-Geonim," *Tarbiz* 50 (198–81):253, note to line 10; ms. Bodl. 1812, fol. 91r; ms. Montefiore 6, fol. 15; ᶜ*Arugat ha-Bosem*, ed. E. E. Urbach, vol. 3 (Jerusalem, 1963), 537; Reuven Margoliot, *Mal*ᵓ*akhei* ᶜ*Elyon* (Jerusalem, 1988^{3}), 2–3; and Peter Schäfer and Shaul Shaked, *Magische Texte aus der Kairoer-Geniza*, vol. 2 (Tübingen, 1997), 115.]

[3]Ms. Bodl. 1153, fols. 167v–168r: אופן לרבינו שמעון הגדול בניגון. וקבלתי שהניגון מסר לו בעל החלום הוא כעין ניגון שיר של מלאכים. On the role of the *ba*ᶜ*al ha-ḥalom* in transmitting material to people, see, e.g., Rashi to *Yevamot* 24b, s.v. *gerei ḥalomot; Sanhedrin* 30a, s.v. *ba*ᶜ*al ha-ḥalom* (cf. Reuven Margoliot, *Margaliyyot ha-Yam* [Jerusalem, 1977], ad loc.); and cf. Rashi's biblical commentary to Esther 4:1. See also *SHP*, secs. 324, 382, 1550; R. Eleazar of Worms's *Ḥokhmat ha-Nefesh*, fols. 4a–b, 6a; the description of R. Eleazar's colleague, R. Menaḥem b. Jacob of Worms, cited in Henry Malter, "Dreams as a Cause of Literary Composition," *Studies in Jewish Literature in Honor of Kaufmann Kohler* (Berlin, 1913), 202; and see also Jacob Elbaum, "Shalosh Derashot Ashkenaziyyot Qedumot," *Qiryat Sefer* 48 (1973):342–43, and esp. n. 22; Michael Swartz, *Scholastic Magic* (Princeton, 1996), 49; and below, n. 44. Cf. the responsum of

R. Hai in which he acknowledges hearing about *she'elot ḥalom* but is somewhat skeptical about the possibility of achieving them in his day (*Oẓar ha-Geonim* [vol. 4] *le-Massekhet Ḥagigah*, ed. B. M. Lewin [Jerusalem, 1931], 17–18, 24–25; and see now *Teshuvot ha-Geonim ha-Ḥadashot*, ed. Simcha Emanuel [Jerusalem, 1996], 126, 137–38, and below, n. 10). Note the more positive reaction regarding *shirim u-ma'amarim* received via a dream in Moshe Ibn Ezra, *Sefer ha-ʿIyyunim veha-Diyyunim*, ed. A. S. Halkin (Jerusalem, 1975), 121–23 [=*Shirat Yisra'el*], ed. B. Z. Halper (Leipzig, 1924), 101–8. See also A. J. Heschel, "Al Ruaḥ ha-Qodesh Bimei ha-Benayim," *Sefer ha-Yovel li-Khevod Alexander Marx* (New York, 1950), 176–77. For a dream experience similar to that of R. Simeon—in which R. Uri, the martyred brother of Rabiah, transmitted a *seliḥah* (and the tune to which it should be chanted) to another scholar, who then presented it—see below, n. 80.

On the transmissions of songs or *piyyutim* in dreams, cf. Shraga Abramson, *ʿInyanut be-Sifrut ha-Geonim* (Jerusalem, 1974), 31–35; idem, "Navi, Ro'eh ve-Ḥozeh—R. Avraham ha-Ḥozeh," *Sefer ha-Yovel li-Khevod ha-Rav Mordekhai Kirshblum* (Jerusalem, 1983), ed. David Telsner, 121–22; below, ch. 5, n. 67; and *Sefer Or Zaruaʿ*, pt. 2, sec. 276, regarding *U-Netanneh Toqef*. (R. Qalonymus b. Meshullam, who is listed as having received this *piyyut* from R. Amnon of Mainz, was a contemporary of R. Simeon *ha-Gadol*. See Grossman, *Ḥakhmei Ashkenaz ha-Rishonim*, 35, 101–2.) Reports of other instances of liturgical poems and melodies being received from the heavenly realm at this time in Mainz and other locales contribute to the historicity of the story of R. Amnon, or at least to the plausibility of its Ashkenazic origin. Cf. Ivan Marcus, "Qiddush ha-Shem be-Ashkenaz ve-Sippur R. Amnon mi-Magenẓa," *Qedushat ha-Ḥayyim ve-Ḥeruf ha-Nefesh*, ed. I. Gafni and A. Ravitzky (Jerusalem, 1993), 140–45, and see now Eli Yassef, "Aggadah ve-Historiyyah," *Zion* 64 (1999):192-200. [A version of *U-Netanneh Toqef*, quite close to the one attributed to R. Amnon, appears in the Cairo Geniza. See ms. B. M. Or. 5557G, fols. 67v–68v; *Maḥzor le-Yamim ha-Nora'im*, ed. Goldschmidt, 2:404; Naftali Wieder, *Hitgabshut Nosaḥ ha-Tefillah ba-Mizraḥ uve-Maʿarav* (Jerusalem, 1998), 1:441–42. Prof. Yosef Yahalom informs me that a forthcoming study will argue that this prayer is part of the corpus of the early medieval Israeli *payyetan* Yannai.] See also the description of R. Samuel of Spires, father of R. Judah *he-Ḥasid*, in ms. JNUL 8° 1070, fol. 58v: **אלו החרוזים ששמע ר' שמואל משפירא בשעה שעלה לרקיע בשם הנורא הנכבד שבח יפה**. On this passage, see Daniel Abrams's review of *Shirat ha-Roqeaḥ*, ed. Isaac Meiseles, in *Kabbalah* 1 (1996):285–87.

Receiving songs of angels and *sodot* through dreams or heavenly ascents was also part of the *Hekhalot* mystical experience. See Dan, "Hithavvut Torat ha-Sod ha-ʿIvrit," 13–14. Dan holds that *Ḥasidei Ashkenaz* did not actually experience this as the *yordei ha-merkavah* did, but rather viewed these issues as keys to understanding God. Cf., however, Elliot Wolfson, *Through a Speculum That Shines* (Princeton, 1994), ch. 5, who offers extensive proofs in support of the experiential dimension of *ḥasidut Ashkenaz*. See also Peter Schäfer, "The Ideal of Piety of the Ashkenazi Ḥasidim and Its Roots in Jewish Tradition," *Jewish History* 4 (1990):9–23. Cf. Nicholas Watson, "John the Monk's *Book of Visions*," *Conjuring Spirits*, ed. Claire Fanger (Phoenix Mill, 1998), 163–81.

was also a proponent of directing prayer through angels, who could serve as intermediaries to the Divine realm and to the *kisse ha-Kavod*.[4]

In a *yozer* for *Shavu*ᶜ*ot*, R. Simeon describes the relationship between the female Torah and the male Deity and how the Torah rests on the knee of God, in addition to laying a foundation for a mystical motif involving the feet of God.[5] Several fifteenth- and sixteenth-century Italian manuscripts record brief

---

[4]See *Seder ha-Selihot ke-Minhag Lita*, ed. Goldschmidt (Jerusalem, 1965), 189–90, and cf. Goldschmidt's introduction, 11–12, for the origins of these notions in *Hekhalot* literature. On prayer to angelic intermediaries, see Rashi, *Sanhedrin* 44b, s.v. *le-*ᶜ*olam yevaqesh* ᵓ*adam raḥamim*. Rashi interprets a statement of R. Yohanan, לעולם יבקש אדם רחמים שיהו הכל מאמצין את כוחו ואל יהו לו צרים מלמעלה, as follows: שיסייעוהו מלאכי השרת לבקש רחמים ושלא יהו לו מסטינים מלמעלה. For additional approbation for the practice of directing prayers to angels, cf. *Shibbolei ha-Leqet*, ed. Solomon Buber (Vilna, 1887), sec. 282, in the name of R. Avigdor Katz (based on Rashi in *Sanhedrin* and a passage in *Shir ha-Shirim Rabbah*); Y. S. Zachter, "Teshuvah le-Ba*ᶜ*al ha-Roqeaḥ be-ᶜInyan Amirat Makhnisei Raḥamim," *Yeshurun* 3 (1997):41–46; Simcha Emanuel, "Al Amirat ha-Piyyut Makhnisei Raḥamim," *Ha-Ma*ᶜ*ayan* 38:1 (1997):5–11; Shlomo Sprecher, "Ha-Polmos ᶜal Amirat Makhnisei Raḥamim," *Yeshurun* 3, 706–18; *Sefer Gematri*ᵓ*ot le-R. Yehudah he-Ḥasid* (Los Angeles, 1998), Daniel Abram's introduction, 11, and Israel Ta-Shma's introduction, 16–18, and 61 (fol. 19r); *She*ᵓ*elot u-Teshuvot Mahari Bruna*, #274 (cited in *Seder ha-Seliḥot*, ed. Goldschmidt, 12, n. 12); below, n. 38, and ch. 5, nn. 15, 50. Note also the *piyyut* מכניסי דמעות העלוב, written by the eleventh-century *payyetan* Moses b. Shabbetai of Rome, that was recited on the High Holidays in northern France. See *Maḥzor le-Yamim ha-Nora*ᵓ*im*, ed. Goldschmidt, 1:125–26. (On R. Shabbetai, see Grossman, *Hakhmei Ashkenaz ha-Rishonim*, 350.) See also the *kinah* ציון צפירת פאר by R. Meir b. Eleazar *ha-Darshan* of Lombardy, listed in Israel Davidson, *Ozar ha-Shirah veha-Piyyut* (New York, 1970), 3:323 (#36); the *selihah* מלאכי רחמים by R. Samuel b. Judah *ha-Kohen* of Mainz, in *Seder ha-Seliḥot ke-Minhag Lita*, ed. Goldschmidt, 35–36 (and cf. Grossman, *Ḥakhmei Ashkenaz ha-Rishonim*, 325); תפלה תקח (end), by R. Meir שליח ציבור (in Goldschmidt, 135–36); and R. Simon b. Isaac's תורה הקדושה (Goldschmidt, 166–68); and below, n. 111. Cf. ms. Cambr. Add. 858 (Ashkenaz, fifteenth century), fols. 46v–47r, which maintains that R. Simeon b. Isaac had a son named Elḥanan who was kidnapped by Christians and eventually became the pope. He was reunited with his father under unusual circumstances, renounced Christianity, and followed in his father's footsteps, dying a martyr's death. This account (which has different versions) is, however, a later legend. Cf. Grossman, *Ḥakhmei Ashkenaz ha-Rishonim*, 89–90, and Eli Yassif, *Sippurei ha-*ᶜ*Am ha-*ᶜ*Ivri* (Jerusalem, 1994), 335–36. R. Simeon did have a descendant called פחד ר׳ יצחק הזקן (בן יוסף), who transmitted *sodot ha-tefillah*; see Grossman, 91, 118, and above, ch. 2, n. 14. For other descendants of R. Simeon involved with *sod*, see below, ch. 4, n. 5 (R. Elḥanan b. Yaqar), and ch. 5, n. 33 (R. Elijah Menaḥem of London).

[5]See Elliot Wolfson, "Images of God's Feet: Some Observations on the Divine Body in Judaism," *People of the Body*, ed. Howard Eilberg-Schwartz (Albany, 1990), 154. Cf. Wolfson, "Demut Ya*ᶜ*aqov Ḥaquqah be-Kisse ha-Kavod: ᶜIyyun Nosaf be-Torat ha-Sod

magical and mystical techniques (*kabbalah ma^casit*) in the name of R. Simeon, usually in conjunction with *sodot ha-tefillah* and other esoteric teachings of the German Pietists, and occasionally with kabbalistic works. These include a "*Shem ha-meforash* that R. Simeon brought down from the heavens" (having ascended to the heavens using a mystical technique), which had been used in Creation (and could produce a *golem*),[6] as well as *sod* interpretations of liturgical and esoteric texts,[7] and a means of receiving heavenly guidance or prognostication upon awakening from a sleep induced through the use of specially prescribed Divine Names (שאלה בהקיץ).[8] Rabbenu Tam, citing a

---

shel Ḥasidut Ashkenaz," *Massu^cot*, ed. Michal Oron and Amos Goldreich (Jerusalem, 1994), 174, n. 190, and 177, n. 209; and idem, *Along the Path* (Albany, 1995), 53, 150, n. 203. See also Wolfson, "The Mystical Significance of Torah-Study in German Pietism," *JQR* 84 (1993):58, n. 59, for a *yoẓer* of R. Simeon *ha-Gadol* asserting that when a precept is performed, the Divine *Kavod* is increased or enhanced. *Kavod* here may refer not only to honor for God, but to the esoteric conception of the *Kavod*, which was developed in the thought of the German Pietists. Cf. Wolfson, *Along the Path*, 171, n. 307.

[6]For R. Simeon's *Shem ha-Meforash*, see Bodl. 1960, fol. 102r, and ms. B. M. 752, fol. 96. Cf. Gershom Scholem, "Ha-Im Nitgalleh ^cIzzavon ha-Sodot shel Abu Aharon ha-Bavli?" *Tarbiz* 32 (1963):255–57.

[7]See ms. Parma 540/3, fol. 19 [and cf. *Perushei Siddur ha-Tefillah la-Roqeaḥ*, ed. Moshe Hershler (Jerusalem, 1992), 1:228–29; R. Simeon was part of the chain of *torat ha-sod* tradition of *Ḥasidei Ashkenaz*; cf. above, introduction, n. 13]; Cambr. Add. 647/9, fols. 30–39; B. M. 752, fol. 7r: ומה שכתוב בתורה כי יד על כס י-ה, פרש"י שכסא של הבורא יתברך שמו לא יהיה שלם עד שיקח נקמה בעמלק. ולא פירש מה כח יש בחסרונו. אבל פי' רבינו שמעון הגדול שם בכתיבתו בחציו... לאו תיבתו. וזה העיקר חצי השם פשוט י-ה; and see below, n. 23.

[8]Ms. Sassoon 290, fol. 612: שאלה בהקיץ אמתית ומנוסה בקבלה מפי הרב שמעון הגדול. In preparation for this experience, the petitioner had to purify and immerse himself, don white clothing, observe a three-day preparation period, and adjure a series of Divine Names. These techniques reflect the influence of *Hekhalot* literature. See, e.g., Michael Swartz, "'Like the Ministering Angels': Early Jewish Mysticism and Magic," *AJS Review* 19 (1994):135–67; Rebecca Lesses, "Speaking with Angels: Jewish and Greco-Roman Revelatory Adjurations," *Harvard Theological Review* 89 (1996):57; idem, "Ritual Practices and God's Power: Adjurations in the Hekhalot Literature, Jewish Amulets, and Greek Revelatory Adjurations" (Ph.D. diss., Harvard University, 1995), 153–97; and *Synopse zur Hekhalot-Literatur*, ed. Schäfer, secs. 501–7, 517, 623–39. See also ms. Sassoon 290, fol. 291 (sec. 777): "Wash and purify by nightfall, write in the evening on the left palm... and lie down; this [dream] question is *beduqah* from the *ḥakham* R. Shabbetai." Cf. *Ḥarba de-Mosheh*, ed. Yuval Harari (Jerusalem, 1997), editor's introduction, 89–99. For additional *she^celat ḥalom* material in ms. Sassoon 290, as well as *she^celat ḥalom* techniques (including *she^celah be-haqiẓ*) in kabbalistic literature, see Moshe Idel, "Iyyunim be-Shitat Ba^cal 'Sefer ha-Meshiv,'" *Sefunot* n.s. 2 [17] (1983):201–26. Cf. the *she^celat ḥalom* formula attributed to R. Judah *he-Ḥasid* in ms. Vienna 28 (Heb.

tradition of *Ḥakhmei Lothaire* that originated in the pre-Crusade period, characterized R. Simeon as a master of magical or esoteric techniques (מלומד בנסים).[9]

It should be noted that three of the prevailing elements in Jewish magical texts of late antiquity and the early middle ages—the magical and theurgic powers of Divine Names and their mystical meanings, the conjuring of angels as intermediaries to negotiate between Divine providence and earthly needs, and the magical application of Divine Names and ritual practices for the purposes of individuals[10]—are attributed to R. Simeon *ha-Gadol*. These same elements form the structure for the involvement of subsequent Ashkenazic rabbinic figures as well.

---

148), fol. 58r; Yosef Dan, "Le-Torat ha-Ḥalom shel Ḥasidei Ashkenaz," *Sinai* 68 (1971):288–93; and Monford Harris, *Studies in Jewish Dream Interpretation* (Northvale, 1994), 33–34. Harris (19–20) notes a distinction in *Sefer Ḥasidim* between visions, which one sees when awake, and dreams, which occur during sleep. For the general medieval context, see, e.g., Steven Kruger, *Dreaming in the Middle Ages* (Cambridge, 1992), 99–122; *Moreh Nevukhim*, 2:36; and Ronald Finucane, *Miracles and Pilgrims: Popular Beliefs in Medieval England* (New York, 1977), 83–85. On the notion of *she᾿elah be-haqiẓ*, cf. the commentaries of Radaq and Ralbag to 1 Samuel 28:6; P. Schäfer and S. Shaked, *Magische Texts aus der Kairoer-Geniza*, vol. 1 (Tübingen, 1994), 133–50; and see also Lesses, "Ritual Practices and God's Power," 274–98.

On *she᾿elat ḥalom* in medieval rabbinic literature, see Joshua Trachtenberg, *Jewish Magic and Superstition* (New York, 1939), 241–43; *She᾿elot u-Teshuvot min ha-Shamayim*, ed. Margoliot, editor's introduction, 15–20; Heschel, "Al Ruaḥ ha-Qodesh Bimei ha-Benayim," 198–201; Isaac Peḥah, "Divrei Ḥalomot ba-Halakhah," *Teḥumin* 5 (1984):422–26; and below, n. 115, and ch. 5, nn. 22, 49. Cf. Ibn Ezra's long commentary to Exodus 14:19, and 28:9; his short commentary to Exodus 3:15; and R. Baḥye b. Asher's commentary to Deuteronomy 29:28 (end). On the phrases בדוק [אמיתית / טובה] ומנוסה with regard to magical teachings and *segullot* (including general medieval parallels), see H. J. Zimmels, *Magicians, Theologians and Doctors* (London, 1952), 112, n. 1; and ms. Vat. 244, passim.

[9]See *Maḥzor Vitry*, ed. Simon Hurwitz (Nuremberg, 1923), 364; *Shibbolei ha-Leqet ha-Shalem*, ed. Buber, sec. 28 (p. 26) [=ed. S. K. Mirsky (New York, 1966), 216]. Cf. Avraham Grossman, "Zemiḥat Parshanut ha-Piyyut," *Sefer Yovel li-Shelomoh Simonsohn* (Tel Aviv, 1993), 69; Moshe Idel, *Kabblah: New Perspectives* (New Haven, 1988), 320, n. 119; *Teshuvot Ḥatam Sofer, OḤ*, #16; and below, ch. 5, n. 24. The Talmud refers to both R. Shimᶜon bar Yoḥai and R. Naḥum of Gimzo as *melummad be-nissim*, although the connotation may be somewhat different. See *Meᶜilah* 17b, and *Sanhedrin* 109a. R. Simeon is also characterized as בר סגולתו of R. Elijah *ha-Zaqen*; see above, ch.1, n. 24.

[10]See Schäfer, *The Hidden and Manifest God*, 49, 81, 89–92, 105–7, 109, 112, 143–45, 150–59, 161, 165; Swartz, *Scholastic Magic*, 18–20, 157–58; idem, "Scribal Magic and Its Rhetoric: Formal Patterns in Hebrew and Aramaic Incantation texts from the Cairo Genizah," *Harvard Theological Review* 83 (1990):179; idem, "Magical Piety in

R. Eliezer *ha-Gadol* (c.990–1060), a prominent ancestor of R. Judah *he-Ḥasid*, was the source of a number of liturgical and ritual interpretations and customs.[11] Among them is the practice at the Passover Seder, presented by R. Eleazar of Worms, of repeatedly dipping a finger in the cup of wine and releasing sixteen drops, as the various plague listings are recited during the Seder. According to R. Eleazar, this practice was transmitted by R. Eliezer *ha-Gadol* and his household to subsequent Qalonymides. Some who had not received this tradition were apparently unsure of its authenticity and purpose. It was understood by the Qalonymides, however, as a means of summoning or conjuring the sixteen-sided avenging sword of the Almighty. This Divine sword could diminish the powers of pestilence and other *maziqin* that were represented by the sixteen times the word *dever* is mentioned in the book of Jeremiah. In addition, the sword could grant meaningful life. This aspect of the sword's powers is symbolized by the sixteen scheduled weekly *ᶜaliyyot* to the Torah (characterized in the Bible as a source of life) and by the eight references to life in the special insertions during the *ᶜAmidah* of the High Holidays that

---

Ancient and Medieval Judaism," *Ancient Magic and Ritual Power*, ed. Marvin Meyer and Paul Mirecki (Leiden, 1995), 171; Norman Golb, "Aspects of the Historical Background of Jewish Life in Medieval Egypt," *Jewish Medieval and Renaissance Studies*, ed. Alexander Altmann (Cambridge, Mass., 1967), 12–16; L. H. Schiffman and M. D. Swartz, *Hebrew and Aramaic Incantation texts from the Cairo Genizah* (Sheffield, 1992), 12–22; Brigitte Kern-Ulner, "The Depiction of Magic in Rabbinic Texts: The Rabbinic and the Greek Concept of Magic," *Journal for the Study of Judaism* 27 (1996): 289–303; and *Magische Texte aus der Kairoer-Geniza*, ed. Schäfer and Shaked, vol. 2, 1–6, 35, 43, 71, 155, 171, 275. See also the responsum of R. Hai, possibly to R. Nissim Gaon, on various issues of magic and sorcery. (For the most complete version, see now *Teshuvot ha-Geonim ha-Ḥadashot*, ed. Emanuel, sec. 115, 124–46.) Among the magical techniques discussed by R. Hai are the use of Divine Names for a variety of purposes: knowledge and transmission of these names, *sheʾelat ḥalom*, and various forms of *kishuf*. On the use of Divine Names to be saved from robbers, to harm someone, or for *qefiẓat ha-derekh*, see, e.g., *Megillat Aḥimaᶜaẓ*, ed. Klar, above, n. 1; Sharon Koren, "Mysticism and Menstruation: The Significance of Female Impurity in Jewish Spirituality"; (Ph.D. diss., Yale, 1999), ch. 1; Mark Verman and Shulamit Adler, "Path Jumping in the Jewish Magical Tradition," *Jewish Studies Quarterly* 1 (1993–94):131–48; and Yuval Harari, "Im Biqqashta Laharog Ben Adam: Kishfei Hezeq ve-Hitgonenut Mipneihem ba-Mageyah ha-Yehudit ha-Qedumah," *Maddaᶜei ha-Yahadut* 37 (1997):111–42; and *Synopse zur Hekhalot-Literatur*, ed. Schäfer, sec. 830. See also Gershom Scholem, *Reshit ha-Qabbalah* (Tel Aviv, 1948), 203; Richard Kieckhefer, *Magic in the Middle Ages* (Cambridge,1989), 85–90; and below, ch. 4, sec. 2.

[11] Grossman, *Ḥakhmei Ashkenaz ha-Rishonim*, 230–31. See also below, n. 25. On R. Eliezer's piety, see Grossman, 221–23.

were recited twice during each prayer service (by the congregation and by the *ḥazzan*) for a total of sixteen times.[12]

R. Qalonymus b. Isaac, a grandson of R. Eliezer *ha-Gadol* (and the father of R. Samuel *he-Ḥasid*) lived in Mainz during the late eleventh century, and he was a link in the transmission of Qalonymide *sod* traditions. Indeed, R. Qalonymus, who is referred to as both *ha-zaqen* and *he-ḥasid*, was listed as one of those who followed the custom of spilling the drops of wine during the Passover Seder. Moreover, R. Qalonymus also wrote, in an unrelated context, of the sixteen-sided sword of the Almighty. According to R. Qalonymus, God would use this sword to slay the angel of death. R. Qalonymus gives the source of this teaching as *Sefer Hekhalot*.[13]

---

[12] In addition to being found in *Sefer Amarkal*, fol. 27a, and in ms. Bodl. 1103, fol. 34v [which are cited by Grossman, *Ḥakhmei Ashkenaz ha-Rishonim*, 230, n. 105; and see also the citations in Israel Yuval, "Ha-Naqam veha-Qelalah, ha-Dam veha-ᶜAlilah," *Zion* 58 (1993):38–39], this passage appears, with variants, in ms. B. M. 610 (Add. 14762), fol. 17r (in the margin), and in ms. Frankfurt 227, fol. 67r. Cf. *Tosafot ha-Shalem, Haggadah shel Pesaḥ*, ed. Jacob Gellis (Jerusalem, 1989), 94; *Sefer Roqeaḥ*, *Hilkhot Yom ha-Kippurim*, sec. 214 (p. 107); ms. Bodl. 2273 (a Torah commentary composed in the early thirteenth century by a R. Avigdor, who appears to have been associated with *Ḥasidei Ashkenaz*; see above, ch. 2, n. 9), fols 8r–9v; and see A. Y. Goldmintz, "Perush ha-Torah le-R. Avigdor," *Sefer Zikkaron le-R. Shemuʾel Barukh Werner*, ed. Yosef Buksboim (Jerusalem, 1996), 177–79. [At this point, ms. Bodl. 2273 also mentions that the priestly blessing was done each day; see Zimmer, *ᶜOlam ke-Minhago Noheg*, 135–40, and cf. above, ch. 2, n. 86.] Ms. Bodl. 945, a biblical commentary composed by Eleazar (or Eliezer) b. Moses *ha-Darshan*, a grandson of R. Samuel *he-Ḥasid* (cf. above, ch. 2, n. 52), suggests (fol. 72v) that the sword is alluded to by Exodus 15:3. This verse, which characterizes God as a warrior, begins with the letter *yod* (10) and ends with the letter *vav* (6). See *Tosafot ha-Shalem*, ed. Gellis, 7:221. [On the compiler of this commentary, see *Kitvei R. Avraham Epstein* 1 (Jerusalem, 1950):250, n. 11; Israel Ta-Shma in *Shalem* 6 (1992):315–16; and Adolf Neubauer, in the next note.] Cf. *Darkhei Moshe* to *O. Ḥ.* 473, sec. 18. For the sequencing of items that represent the number sixteen in texts associated with *Ḥasidei Ashkenaz*, see also ms. Vat. 324, fol. 4r, cited in Moshe Hallamish, "Beᶜayyot be-Ḥeqer Hashpaᶜat ha-Qabbalah ᶜal ha-Tefillah," *Massuʾot*, ed. Oron and Goldreich, 215; *Sefer Gematriʾot le-R. Yehudah he-Ḥasid*, 29 (fol. 3r); and cf. Bodl. 1575, fol 24r. [Note also *Shibbolei ha-Leqet*, sec. 218: ובזרוע נטויה זו החרב, פי׳ אחי ר׳ בנימין זהו שם המפורש שנקרא חרבו של משה והוא כתוב בספר הרזים ובו היה עושה משה רבינו כל האותות שעשה במצרים. On this passage, see below, ch. 5, n. 33; and cf. *Ḥarba de-Mosheh*, ed. Harari, editor's introduction, 54–58.]

[13] Parma 541, fol. 266v, sec. 78. For an example of this notion in *Hekhalot* literature, see *Synopse zur Hekhalot-Literatur*, ed. Schäfer, #49. See also B. Z. Luria, "'Ḥarbel' ve-Gilgulah be-Sifrut ha-Midrash," *Beit Miqra* 7:4 (1963):107–8; and the passage in *Midrash Avkir*, published by A. Marmorstein, *Meʾassef Devir* 1 (1923):138ff. [On the relationship between this midrash and *Hekhalot* literature, and the citation of

This passage appears as part of a larger section or treatise of *segullot* and *hashbaʿot* in an Ashkenazic manuscript (Parma 541) that was copied in the thirteenth or fourteenth century. Although some of the material is recorded anonymously and may represent the pre-Crusade period, as the R. Qalonymus passage does, names of twelfth- and thirteenth-century German Pietists and

---

this midrash in particular by Ashkenazic scholars and German Pietists (esp. R. Eleazar of Worms), see Adolf Neubauer, "Le Midrasch Tanḥuma," *REJ* 14 (1887):109–10 (cited in Bodl. 945, the Torah commentary attributed to a grandson of R. Samuel *he-Ḥasid*, see the previous note); Moshe Idel, "'Ha-Maḥshavah ha-Raʿah' shel ha-E-l," *Tarbiz* 49 (1980):358–59, nn. 7–8; *Perushei Siddur ha-Tefillah la-Roqeaḥ*, ed. Hershler, 1:294, 2:428, 467; Urbach, *Baʿalei ha-Tosafot*, 1:395; *ʿArugat ha-Bosem*, ed. Urbach, 4:173–74; ms. Paris 640, fol. 13d; R. Avigdor Katz in *Perushim u-Fesaqim le-R. Avigdor* (Jerusalem, 1996), 123–24 (see above, ch. 2, n. 28); and cf. Idel, *Kabbalah: New Perspectives* (New Haven, 1988), 117–22. See also Toviah b. Eliezer, *Leqaḥ Tov (Pesiqta Zutarti)*, ed. Solomon Buber (Vilna, 1880), editor's introduction, 40; Solomon Buber in *Ha-Shaḥar* 11 (1883):339; M. D. Herr in *Encyclopaedia Judaica*, 16:1516–17; Epstein, *Mi-Qadmoniyyot ha-Yehudim*, 301–4.]

This idea is found also in *Midrash Tehillim (Shoḥer Tov)*, ed. Solomon Buber (Vilna, 1891) [to Psalms 31, sec. 6 and 78, sec. 19, and cf. 36, sec. 8], but R. Qalonymus mentions only the *Hekhalot* source. Although the locale and date of the composition of *Midrash Tehillim* are far from certain (Israel or Byzantium during the geonic period?), it is likely that this material came to the midrash from the *Hekhalot* literature rather than vice versa. Cf. Moshe Idel, "Tefisat ha-Torah ba-Hekhalot uva-Kabbalah," *Meḥqerei Yerushalayim be-Maḥshevet Yisraʾel* 1 (1981):36–37, n. 39. (On the dating of the *Hekhalot* corpus, see, e.g., Wolfson, *Through a Speculum That Shines*, 74–81, and Swartz, *Scholastic Magic*, 9–13.) Indeed, *Midrash Tehillim*, and *Midrash Mishlei* as well, contain a number of allusions to rituals and mystical and magical materials of Ashkenazic provenance (although it should be noted that the passages about the sixteen-sided sword do not appear solely in the Ashkenazic manuscripts of the midrash). See *Midrash Tehillim*, ed. Buber, editor's introduction, sec. 12, and 128, n. 36 (at Psalms 17:5); Israel Ta-Shma, *Minhag Ashkenaz ha-Qadmon* (Jerusalem, 1992), 142–43, 202, 285; idem, *Ha-Nigleh shebe-Nistar* (Tel Aviv, 1995), 22. See also *The Midrash on Proverbs*, ed. Burton Visotsky (New Haven, 1992), editor's introduction, 3–4, 10; and see also 128, n. 28; 136, n. 9; 139–40, nn. 39, 45, 51; 142, n. 7; 146, n. 10. And cf. Gershom Scholem, "Reste neuplatonischer Spekulation in der Mystik der Deutschen Chassidim und ihre Vermittlung durch Abraham bar Chija," *MGWJ* 75 (1931):175, n. 3. Note also the citation from *Midrash Tehillim* in *Sefer Roqeaḥ*, in the final section of *hilkhot ḥasidut* (**שורש קדושת הייחוד ושמו ומרכבה וסודותיו**), and cf. *SḤP* 1044, and below, ch. 5, n. 43. My thanks to Mordechai Silverstein, who is writing a doctoral dissertation at Hebrew University on *Midrash Tehillim*, for checking the manuscripts of the midrash and for confirming a number of my impressions. On R. Qalonymus b. Isaac and the transmission of *sod* in early Ashkenaz, see also Grossman, *Ḥakhmei Ashkenaz ha-Rishonim*, 398, n. 175, 418, 423.

tosafists also appear (including R. Menaḥem of Joigny, a student of Rabbi Tam), in addition to Ashkenazic rabbinic figures whose identities are unclear.[14] Among the magical techniques and aims described, without attribution, are the transporting of a person from afar, the apprehension of a thief through the recitation of various Divine Names, and the achieving of *petiḥat ha-lev*.

In the Parma manuscript passage, *petiḥat ha-lev* connotes the ability to understand Torah teachings clearly and recall those teachings effortlessly.[15] According to this manuscript passage, the state of *petiḥat ha-lev* was to be accomplished through the writing of a request formula (and adjuration) on a well-boiled egg that was determined to have been the first ever laid by a hen, by the recitation of the adjuration that was directed to the *Sar ha-Torah* as well as the *Sar ha-Panim*, and by eating the egg. These procedures, and the angels to whom they are directed, reflect known concepts and figures within *Hekhalot* literature, although the precise application in the Ashkenazic text at hand constitutes a partial synthesis of different *Hekhalot* rituals.[16]

Similar procedures for achieving *petiḥat ha-lev* and for fending off forgetfulness were also part of an educational initiation ceremony, as well as other ritual practices that appear in rabbinic texts from both northern France

---

[14]See ms. Parma 541, fols. 262r–263v, 266v–267r, secs. 76–83. On this section of the ms., see also above, ch. 1, n. 163; ch. 2, n. 9; and below, ch. 4, nn. 31–32. Regarding R. Qalonymus *he-Ḥasid*, cf. Dan, *Torat ha-Sod shel Ḥasidut Ashkenaz*, 59, n. 36.

[15]Cf. Israel Ta-Shma, "'Sefer ha-Maskil'—Ḥibbur Yehudi-Ẓarefati Bilti-Yaduaᶜ mi-Sof ha-Meʾah ha-Yod Gimmel," *Meḥqerei Yerushalayim be-Maḥshevet Yisraʾel* 2:3 (1983):436–37; idem, *Minhag Ashkenaz ha-Qadmon*, 213–14; Ivan Marcus, *Rituals of Childhood* (New Haven, 1996), 49–50, 56–57, 115–16; Ta-Shma's review in *JQR* 87 (1996):237–38; and Scholem, *Reshit ha-Qabbalah*, 65, n. 1. [On the connotation of *lev satum*, see *SHP*, sec. 748, and Ralbag's commentary to Job 39:30.]

[16]See, e.g., Peter Schäfer, "Jewish Magic Literature in Late Antiquity and the Early Middle Ages," *JJS* 41 (1990):75–91; idem, *The Hidden and Manifest God*, 89–95, 106–7, 114–17, 142–45; and M. D. Swartz, "Magical Piety in Ancient and Medieval Judaism," *Ancient Magic and Ritual Power*, ed. Meyer and Mirecki, 167–83. For memory practices, see Swartz, *Scholastic Magic*, 33–50, and Rebecca Lesses, "The Adjuration of the Prince of the Presence: Performative Utterance in a Jewish Ritual," *Ancient Magic and Ritual Power*, 185–206. On *petiḥat ha-lev* and memory, see Gerrit Bos, "Jewish Tradition on Strengthening Memory and Leone Modena's Evaluation," *Jewish Studies Quarterly* 2 (1995):41–45. On the development of a culture of memory in thirteenth-century northern Europe, see Jacques Le Goff, *The Medieval Imagination* (Chicago, 1988), 78–80. On the heart as a seat of memory, see, e.g., Mary Carruthers, *The Book of Memory* (Cambridge, 1990), 48–49, and the sources cited in Eric Jager, "The Book of the Heart: Reading and Writing the Medieval Subject," *Speculum* 71 (1996):2, n. 4. Cf. Ioan Couliano, *Eros and Magic in the Renaissance* (Chicago, 1987), 132–35.

and Germany in the twelfth and thirteenth centuries.[17] In the educational initiation ceremony, a teacher cited biblical verses (and letters of the alphabet) that were written both on a cake whose dough had been kneaded with honey and on hard-boiled eggs. The young initiate then imitated what he heard; he ate these foods and the verses on them. One version of this ceremony contains a magical incantation against *Potah*, the prince of forgetfulness, which was intended to ensure that the child would succeed in his studies and remember what he learned. Divine Names were invoked to activate this adjuration.[18] In addition, all the German versions of this ceremony place it on the festival of *Shavu*ᶜ*ot*. According to *Sar ha-Torah* and other *Hekhalot* magical texts, *Shavu*ᶜ*ot* was the most propitious time to draw down Torah knowledge using magical techniques, for it was then that adepts would conjure the *Sar ha-Torah*.[19]

Ivan Marcus, in his analysis of the initiation ceremony, cites formulations from R. Eleazar *ha-Qallir*, R. Saᶜadyah Gaon, and *Sefer Razi*ʾ*el* (a work that often reflects geonic and other early medieval traditions) as models of magical techniques for "acquiring wisdom" or *petiḥat ha-lev* that involved the eating of cakes or eggs.[20] The procedure for achieving *petiḥat ha-lev* through the eating of the magical egg, as outlined in ms. Parma 541, suggests that the use of adjurations and *Shemot* for magical purposes was in vogue within Ashkenaz itself in the late eleventh or early twelfth century[21]—even before the first recorded description of the educational initiation ceremony.[22]

---

[17]See, e.g., Marcus, *Rituals of Childhood*, and Scholem, "Havdalah de-R. Aqivah: Maqor le-Massoret Mageyah ha-Yehudit bi-Tequfat ha-Geonim," 243–49, 256, 278–79.

[18]See Marcus, *Rituals of Childhood*, 29–31, 68. This version, found in *Sefer Assufot* (which was composed by a student of R. Eleazar of Worms and Rabiah; see above, ch. 1, nn. 37, 47, and below, ch. 4, n. 57), also includes several verses from Psalm 119 (a psalm that contains allusions to "expanding the heart"), among those to be inscribed on the cake and the egg. Cf. ms. JTS Mic. 8114 (end), fol. 17v.

[19]See Marcus, *Rituals of Childhood*, 45–46, 66–67, 151, n. 29. Marcus also notes the use of magical eggs (fresh, roasted, and eaten with incantations on them) in *Hekhalot* texts and in *Ḥarba de-Mosheh*. [See also R. Benjamin Beinish *ha-Kohen* of Krotoshin, *Amtaḥat Binyamin*, ed. Moshe Bakal (Jerusalem, 1970), 39, 76. On this work, which was written in 1716, see now Immanuel Etkes (above, introduction, n. 29).] Although the version of the initiation ceremony found in *Maḥzor Vitry* does not mention *Shavu*ᶜ*ot*, it links the ceremony to *mattan Torah*. See Marcus, 25–32, and cf. Swartz, *Scholastic Magic*, 43–67; and below, ch. 5, n. 63.

[20]See Marcus, *Rituals of Childhood*, 59–67, and Ezra Fleischer, "Inyanim Qiliriyim," *Tarbiz* 50 (1981):282–302. Note the association of R. Eleazar *ha-Qallir* with magical cakes by R. Nathan b. Yeḥiel of Rome, author of the *Sefer ha-*ᶜ*Arukh*. Cf. Schäfer, *The Hidden and Manifest God*, 92–95, and Joseph Naveh and Shaul Shaked, *Magical Spells and Formulae* (Jerusalem, 1993), 160–62, 177–78, 181–85.

R. Meshullam b. Moses (d.1094), a contemporary of R. Qalonymus b. Isaac in Mainz, describes the mystical completion of the name of God that is alluded to and achieved through the recitation of the Kaddish.[23] Together with

---

[21]Ms. Parma 1033 (Ashkenaz, 1310), fol. 25v, col. 2, records a recommendation that one who wishes to remember what he has studied should recite a magical formula over a cup of wine or beer. This formula includes an adjuration, בשם פתחיא רפיא יפתח לבי שלא אשכח מה שלמדתי ומה ששניתי לעולם. In addition, the person may take a small cake, knead it with honey, inscribe on it two verses from Ezekiel (3:2–3, in which Ezekiel envisions himself eating God's words) as well as the alphabet, and eat the cake. Cf. Marcus, *Rituals of Childhood*, 53–65; ms. Bodl. 1598, fols. 92v–93v; ms. Vat. 244, fol. 31r; and Swartz, *Scholastic Magic*, 161, n. 49. The section of ms. Parma 1033 in which this passage is found contains halakhic material from the Rhineland in the late eleventh century, various anonymous formulae to achieve happiness and success (including *petiḥat ha-lev*) or protection, a *shemirat ha-derekh* attributed to R. Eleazar of Worms (see above, ch. 2, n. 10), and several pietistic modes of conduct in the name of R. Judah *he-Ḥasid* (see above, ch. 1, n. 12).

Ms. Vat. 243, a sixteenth-century Italian manuscript that contains magical practices attributed to a number of tosafists (see below, ch. 5, nn. 16, 46, 78), records a technique for achieving *petiḥat ha-lev* (fol. 13r) that is also quite similar to aspects of the passage in Parma 541. It calls for taking the first egg from a hen that has never laid an egg before, boiling the egg, and writing a formula with *Shemot* on it. [Cf. Naveh and Shaked, *Magic Spells and Formulae*, 177, for a magical technique, using a new egg, to induce sleep.] For other similar *petiḥat ha-lev* techniques in medieval Ashkenaz rabbinic circles, see ms. Vat. 243, fols. 4v, 12r [a *petiḥat ha-lev* for every *Moẓa'ei Shabbat*, to insure that *Potah*, the angel of forgetfulness, should not rule, using the names אגף סגף נגף; see below, n. 59]; ms. Paris 716, fol. 23r; and ms. Vienna 28 (Hebrew 148), fol. 57r; mss. JNUL 8°476, fol. 23r, and 8°397, fol. 207r; and Gershom Scholem, *Kitvei Yad be-Qabbalah* (Jerusalem, 1930), 8, 110. Cf. *Sefer Gematri'ot le-R. Yehudah he-Ḥasid*, 95–96 (fol. 36): ט' פסוקים שבת' בהם ישרי לב טוב לאומרם ולנער המכניסין אותו לראשונה למקרא.

[22]The angelic figure גליצור, associated in the Parma 541 text with the adjuration on the egg (ומשביע אני עליכם זגזגאל שר התורה וגליצור המגלה טעם התורה ומשביע אני יפיפיה שר הפנים בשם א-היה א-שר א-היה), is found in ms. Sassoon 290, sec. 1024 (fol. 387) as part of a *segullah* from R. Judah *he-Ḥasid* to stop blood from the nostrils (דם נחריים). Cf. R. Benjamin Beinish, *Amtaḥat Binyamin*, ed. M. Bakal (Jerusalem, 1970), 75–76. On this angel's roles in *Hekhalot* literature, see David Halperin, *The Faces of the Chariot* (Tübingen, 1988), 416–17; and cf. Margoliot, *Mal'akhei Elyon*, 47, sec. 63. [On זגזגאל as the *Sar ha-Torah* in the Parma passage, see Margoliot, 54, sec. 93; and cf. Ta-Shma, *Ha-Nigleh shebe-Nistar*, 97, n. 59a, and Halperin, 408.] Ms. Sassoon 290, sec. 1019, fol. 385, also has a *petiḥat ha-lev* technique using a newly laid egg (ביצה בת יומא), which is characterized as טובה ומנוסה. The egg is boiled, various Divine *Shemot* are written on it, and it is eaten within one hour. Cf. *Synopse zur Hekhalot-Literatur*, ed. Schäfer, secs. 574–78.

[23]Ms. JNUL 8° 3037, fol. 37r, cited in Haviva Pedaya, "Mashber ba-E-lohut ve-Tiqquno ha-Te'urgi be-Qabbalat R. Yiẓḥak Sagi Nahor ve-Talmidav" (Ph.D. diss., Hebrew University, 1989), 261, n. 52: הכס ושם י-ה חסרין וכשימלאו שיהא שלמים...

R. Qalonymus b. Isaac, R. Meshullam is credited with maintaining interest in mysticism in Mainz in the last part of the eleventh century. Several texts and *piyyutim* link R. Meshullam to *sodot* that were later received by the German Pietists. Several of the *piyyutim* reflect the influence of *Hekhalot* literature, although some of these may have been composed by R. Meshullam b. Qalonymus of Lucca (d.c.1000), rather than by R. Meshullam b. Moses.[24] R. Meshullam's son, R. Eleazar (or Eliezer), *ḥazzan* of Spires, was known for prolonging the chanting of *Barekhu* at the conclusion of the Sabbath—a prayer practice commended later by the German Pietists as a means of prolonging the return of the souls to *gehinnom*. Indeed, R. Eliezer *Ḥazzan* was another direct link in the chain of *sodot ha-tefillah* (and esoteric or magical practices, including the spilling of sixteen drops of wine during the Seder described above) that were transmitted from the Qalonymides to R. Judah *he-Ḥasid*. R. Eliezer passed these secrets to R. Judah's father, R. Samuel *he-Ḥasid*.[25] R. Jacob b. Yaqar, Rashi's principal teacher, also displayed a distinct interest in *Sefer Yeẓirah*[26] and appears, on the basis of manuscript fragments, to have composed a commentary on it.[27]

Pedaya also cites a related formulation of R. Eliezer *ha-Gadol* from ms. JNUL 8° 4199, fol. 35. See also above, n. 7, regarding R. Simeon *ha-Gadol*, and below, n. 55. On R. Meshullam's ascetic practices, see *Maᶜaseh ha-Geonim*, 34; and see above, ch. 1, n. 21.

[24]See Grossman, *Ḥakhmei Ashkenaz ha-Rishonim* 76–78, and above, n. 9; also Abraham Epstein, *Mi-Qadmoniyyot ha-Yehudim*, ed. A. M. Habermann (Jerusalem, 1958), 232–34. Cf. Scholem, "Reste neuplatonischer Spekulation in der Mystik der Deutschen Chassidim," 173, n. 4.

[25]Grossman, *Ḥakhmei Ashkenaz ha-Rishonim*, 390–91. See also above, ch. 2, n. 7. [The manuscript text referred to by Grossman in 390, n. 136, can be found in *Perushei Siddur ha-Tefillah la-Roqeaḥ*, 2:588. The reference to *Sefer Or Zaruaᶜ* in this note should be to pt. 2, sec. 89 (end). See also ms. Paris 1408, fol. 143v.] R. Eliezer's student, R. Shemaryah b. Mordekhai of Spires—a contemporary (and neighbor) of R. Samuel *he-Ḥasid*—formally derived the practice of donating to charity in memory of departed souls from a passage in *Sifrei*. This derivation appears in *Sefer Ḥasidim*, which further encouraged the practice. See Ta-Shma, *Minhag Ashkenaz ha-Qadmon*, 301, n. 9; and above, ch. 1, n. 178. On the significance of prolonging the *Barekhu* prayer, see also below, n. 56.

[26]On the esoteric nature of *Sefer Yeẓirah* and its use as a magical text, see, e.g., Gershom Scholem, *Origins of the Kabbalah* (Princeton, 1987), 24–35; Moshe Idel, *Golem* (Albany, 1990), passim; Wolfson, "The Theosophy of Shabbetai Donnolo," 286–87; and idem, *Through a Speculum That Shines*, 70–72, 138–43. Cf. Yosef Dan, "Ha-Mashmaᶜut ha-Datit shel Sefer Yeẓirah," *Meḥqerei Yerushalayim be-Maḥshevet Yisraʾel* 11 (1993): 7–35.

[27]Ms. Rome Angelica Or. 45, fols. 118–19, noted in Grossman, *Ḥakhmei Ashkenaz ha-Rishonim*, 257; see also Idel, *Golem*, 58. [On R. Jacob b. Yaqar as a role model for

II

Rashi was himself familiar with mystical traditions on Divine Names and with a number of esoteric texts and magical and theurgic techniques. In his talmudic commentary to tractate *Sukkah*, Rashi reproduces a scriptural derivation for the Divine Name of seventy-two letters that is found in *Sefer ha-Bahir*.[28] He explains, as did an anonymous Ashkenazic contemporary, that the creation of various beings by rabbinic scholars described in talmudic literature was accomplished by means of letter combinations involving Divine

---

R. Judah *he-Ḥasid*, see *SḤP* 99; Grossman, 246; D. Berger's review of Grossman, "Rabbanut Ashkenaz ha-Qedumah," *Tarbiz* 53 (1984):486–87; Eli Yasif, "Rashi Legends and Medieval Popular Culture," *Rashi, 1040–1990: Hommage à Ephraim Urbach*, ed. Gabrielle Sed-Rajna (Paris, 1993), 486; and above, ch. 1, n. 12.] Rabbenu Gershom, who taught R. Jacob at Mainz, may have also composed a commentary to *Sefer Yeẓirah* or contributed to a so-called Mainz commentary. See Grossman, 149. Also see Israel Ta-Shma in *Qiryat Sefer* 53 (1978):361, n. 15*; *Qiryat Sefer* 57 (1982):705; and *Qiryat Sefer* 60 (1985):307, nn. 50–51.

[28]See Rashi's commentary to *Sukkah* 45a, s.v. *ʾani va-ho*, and *Sefer ha-Bahir*, ed. Reuven Margoliot (Jerusalem, 1978), secs. 106, 110 [=ed. Daniel Abrams (Los Angeles, 1994), secs. 76, 79]. Cf. *Leqaḥ Tov (Pesiqta Zutarti)* to Exodus 14:21, ed. Buber, 88; *Midrash Sekhel Tov*, loc. cit; Ibn Ezra's citation from *Sefer Raziʾel* in his long commentary to Exodus 14:19; and Ibn Ezra's short commentary to Exodus 3:15 (citing *Sefer ha-Razim*). See also the discussion of this derivation in R. Eleazar of Worms's commentary on the liturgy, analyzed in Wolfson, *Through a Speculum That Shines*, 235–36; the so-called *Perush ha-Roqeaḥ ʿal ha-Torah*, ed. Chaim Konyevsky, vol. 2 (Bnei Brak, 1980), 73; and *Sefer Gematriʾot le-R. Yehudah he-Ḥasid*, introduction, 9–10, n. 46. Cf. Mark Verman, *The Books of Contemplation* (Albany, 1992), 162; Jordan Penkower, *Nosaḥ ha-Torah be-Keter Aram Ẓovah* (Ramat Gan, 1992), 48, n. 116; and below, n. 89. The Rashi passage was cited, in turn, by Naḥmanides in the introduction to his Torah commentary, where he sets forth his kabbalistic schema that the Torah is composed entirely of Divine Names; see Moshe Idel, "Tefisat ha-Torah be-Sifrut ha-Hekhalot ve-Gilgulehah ba-Qabbalah," *Meḥqerei Yerushalayim be-Maḥshevet Yisraʾel* 1 (1981):52–53; and below, ch. 5, n. 30. Rashi indicates in other places those Divine Names about which he received no interpretation or tradition. See *Qiddushin* 71a: שם בן שתים עשרה ובן ארבעים ושתים לא פירשו לנו. Cf. *Sanhedrin* 101b, s.v. *uvi-leshon*, and *Sanhedrin* 60a, s.v. *Shem ben ʾarba ʾotiyyot*.

On the other hand, Rashi seems to have been better informed than certain Geonim with regard to the Name of seventy-two letters. Cf. the responsum of R. Hai in *Teshuvot ha-Geonim ha-Ḥadashot*, ed. Emanuel, 134–35, and Theodore Schrire, *Hebrew Magic Amulets* (London, 1966), 93–99. On R. Hai's attitude toward esoteric knowledge and techniques, especially the use of *Shemot* for magic and theurgic purposes, see Trachtenberg, *Jewish Magic and Superstition*, 88–89, 94; Baron, *A Social and Religious History of the Jews*, 6:125–29, and cf. 5:45–46 regarding R. Ḥananʾel; Idel, *Kabbalah: New Perspectives*, 90–91; idem, *The Mystical Experience in Abraham Abulafia* (Albany,

Names as contained in *Sefer Yeẓirah* or *Hilkhot Yeẓirah*.[29] While *Sefer Yeẓirah* is mentioned in one of the talmudic passages on which Rashi comments, Moshe Idel has shown that the specific methods advocated by Rashi—which adumbrate methods recorded by R. Eleazar of Worms—are not inherent in the talmudic passages themselves, nor can they be derived directly from extant versions of *Sefer Yeẓirah*.[30] This indicates that Rashi was familiar with, and possibly even involved in, the formulation of independent *torat ha-sod* and magical concepts, and was not merely reflecting talmudic or rabbinic material. Rashi refers to *Sefer Yeẓirah* on other occasions in his biblical and talmudic commentaries, in the contexts of letter combination and Creation. In one instance, the reference is to a nonextant version of *Sefer Yeẓirah* that circulated in northern France and Germany during the twelfth and thirteenth centuries.[31]

1988), 15–17; idem, "Al Kavvanat Shemoneh Esreh Ezel R. Yiẓḥaq Sagi-Nahor," *Massuʾot*, 32; Wolfson, *Through a Speculum That Shines*, 110–11, 144–48, 155–56, 157, 216–17 (for R. Ḥananʾel as well); idem, "The Theosophy of Shabbetai Donnolo," *The Frank Talmage Memorial Volume*, ed. Walfish, 2:284; Asi Farber-Ginat, "Iyyunim be-Sefer Shiʿur Qomah," *Massuʾot*, ed. Oron and Goldreich, 373–74; I. Gruenwald, "Ha-Ketav, ha-Mikhtav veha-Shem ha-Meforash," in *Massuʾot*, 87–88. Although R. Hai himself appears to have rejected a mystical approach, his formulations and ideas were developed further by the German Pietists. See, e.g., Wolfson, *Through a Speculum That Shines*, 193, 197, 215–17, and note also (218, 226, 228, 252) the Pietist commentary on the forty-two letter Name, attributed (incorrectly) to R. Hai. For R. Nissim Gaon, see also Simcha Emanuel, "Serid Ḥadash mi-Sefer Megillat Setarim le-R. Nissim Gaon, *Sefer ha-Yovel le-R. Mordekhai Breuer*, ed. Moshe Bar-Asher (Jerusalem, 1992), 2:535–51, and Shraga Abramson, *Rav Nissim Gaon—Ḥamishah Sefarim* (Jerusalem, 1965), 278. The fact that R. Nissim, R. Ḥananʾel, and R. Nathan *baʿal ha-ʿArukh* were involved in these discussions points to an interface between rabbinism and mysticism but, as in the case of R. Hai, this does not necessarily indicate a personal interest. On R. Ḥananʾel, cf. A. J. Heschel, "Al Ruaḥ ha-Qodesh Bimei ha-Benayim, *Sefer ha-Yovel li-Khevod Alexander Marx* (New York, 1950) [Hebrew section], 176, n. 6. [In Bodl. 2575, fol. 1a, the reference concerning Akatriel should be to ר״ח =ר׳ חננאל, rather than to ר״ת =רבינו תם. Cf. below, n. 120.]

[29]Rashi, *Sanhedrin* 65b, s.v. *bara gavra*, and 67b, s.v. *ʿasqei be-hilkhot yeẓirah*. The statement of Rashi's contemporary, found in Bodl. 1207, is cited by Idel, *Golem*, 40, n. 19. Cf. Meiri's rationalistic conception of this talmudic passage as presented in *Beit ha-Beḥirah le-Rabbenu Menaḥem ha-Meiri, Massekhet Avot*, ed. S. Z. Havlin (Jerusalem, 1994), editor's introduction, 49, n. 123.

[30]Idel, *Golem*, 30–31, 50, 58. See also Gershom Scholem, *On the Kabbalah and Its Symbolism* (New York, 1965), 169, n. 1.

[31]See *Shabbat* 104a, s.v. *ʾamar lei; Menaḥot* 29b, s.v. *ʾaḥat be-heh*; *Berakhot* 55a, s.v. *ʾotiyyot*; Epstein, *Mi-Qadmoniyyot ha-Yehudim*, 226–31; Nicholas Sed, "Rashi et le Pseudo-Sepher Yeẓirah," *Rashi, 1040–1990*, ed. Sed-Rajna, 237–50; *Sefer ha-Pardes*, ed. H. L. Ehrenreich (Budapest, 1924), 314–15 [=*Maḥzor Vitry*, 108, and cf. *Tos. Ḥagigah*

Rashi interprets the talmudic assertion that R. Ḥanina b. Tradyon was consigned to a harsh death because he pronounced or expressed each letter of the Divine Name (*she-hayah hogeh ʾet ha-Shem be-ʾotiyyotav*) publicly, as follows: R. Ḥanina explicated the Name (*doresho*) according to its forty-two letters and did with it (magically) that which he wished (*ve-ʿoseh bo mah she-hayah roẓeh*).[32] Moreover, Rashi writes that the Tannaim who entered *Pardes* ascended to the heavens through a technique involving the recitation of a Divine Name (*ʿalu la-raqiaʿ ʿal yedei Shem*).[33] Similarly, in his interpretation of a talmudic statement that R. Yishmaʾel received revelations from the angel Suriʾel, Rashi writes that "R. Yishmaʾel ascended to the heavens via a *Shem* [as is found] in the *Baraita* of *Maʿaseh Merkavah*."[34] He defines unidentified *sitrei Torah* referred to in another talmudic passage as those secrets contained in "*Maʿaseh Merkavah, Sefer Yeẓirah*, and *Maʿaseh Bereshit*, which is a *Baraita*."[35] In his commentary to Isaiah 6:3, Rashi cites a work entitled *Midrash Aggadah*

3b, s.v. *u-mi*, and *Shibbolei ha-Leqet*, sec. 126]; and see now Sarah Japhet, "Massoret ve-Ḥiddush be-Perush Rashbam le-Sefer Iyyov," *Tefillah le-Moshe* [Biblical and Judaic Studies in Honor of Moshe Greenberg], ed. Mordechai Cogan et al. (Winona Lake, 1997), 129*–132*.

[32]Rashi, *ʿAvodah Zarah* 17b, s.v. *ʿalav li-serefah*. See also *Tosafot Sukkah* 5a, s.v. *yod heh*; *Tosafot ʿA. Z.* 18a, s.v. *hogeh ha-Shem*; and *Tosafot ʿal Massekhet ʿAvodah Zarah le-R. Elḥanan b. Yiẓḥaq*, s.v. *ʾela mai taʿama*; and cf. Ithamar Gruenwald, "Ha-Ketav, ha-Mikhtav veha-Shem ha-Meforash—Mageyah, Ruḥaniyyut u-Mistiqah," *Massuʾot*, ed. Oron and Goldreich, 92. [Note also that both *Tosafot* and *Tosafot R. Elḥanan* suggest that at the time of R. Ḥanina's death as a martyr, it was expected he would see angels or some other unusual (heavenly) sight.]

[33]*Ḥagigah* 14b, s.v. *nikhnesu le-pardes*. See also Moshe Idel, *The Mystical Experience in Abraham Abulafia*, 14–17; idem, *Kabbalah: New Perspectives*, 92; Wolfson, *Through a Speculum That Shines*, 111; Heschel, "Al Ruaḥ ha-Qodesh Bimei ha-Benayim," 177, n. 7; Daniel Abrams, "From Germany to Spain: Numerology as a Mystical Technique," *Journal of Jewish Studies* 47 (1996):91–92; Yehuda Liebes, *Ḥetʾo Shel Elisha* (Jerusalem, 1990), 4–5; and cf. Baron, *A Social and Religious History of the Jews*, 5:50–51, and 346, n. 56; and Rashi's commentary to Ezekiel 40:2.

[34]*Berakhot* 51a, s.v. *ʾeimatai yavo ʾadam*. Cf. Margoliot, *Malʾakhei ʿElyon*, 146, sec. 189, and *Die Geschichte von der Zehn Martyren*, ed. Gottfried Reeg (Tübingen, 1985), 19*–32*. The *qefiẓat ha-derekh* proposed by Rava in *Yevamot* 116a was accomplished, according to Rashi, s.v. *bi-qefiẓah, ʿal yedei Shem*. Cf. Ritva, ad loc.; Verman and Adler, "Path-Jumping in the Jewish Magical Tradition," 134; and Rashi, *Shabbat* 81b, s.v. *ʾamrei ʾinhumitta*.

[35]*Ḥagigah* 13a, s.v. *sitrei Torah*. In a subsequent comment on the same folio, Rashi describes both *Maʿaseh Merkavah* and *Maʿaseh Bereshit* as "*Beraitot*" (formal collections). Cf. Rashi to Ecclesiastes 1:9. On the identity of these works, cf. Joseph Dan, "Rashi and the Merkavah," *Rashi, 1040–1990*, ed. Sed-Rajna, 262, n. 13.

Maᶜaseh Merkavah. Gershom Scholem maintained that these references to *Maᶜaseh Merkavah* are to a recension of *Hekhalot Rabbati* (or, as the research of Peter Schäfer has characterized more precisely, a *Hekhalot* macroform with parallels to *Hekhalot Rabbati*),[36] which was also cited by R. Eleazar of Worms and by the mid-thirteenth century halakhic compendium, *Shibbolei ha-Leqet*.[37] Rashi asserts that a person may ask angels to assist him in ensuring the efficacy of his prayers. This suggests the notion of directing prayer through angels by adjuration, a *Hekhalot* construct that, as we have noted, was advocated by R. Simeon *ha-Gadol*.[38] Rashi also displays familiarity with magical techniques for the thwarting of *maziqin*[39] and for divination.[40]

---

[36]See Schäfer, *The Hidden and Manifest God*, 77–78.

[37]Gershom Scholem, *Jewish Gnosticism, Merkabah Mysticism, and Talmudic Tradition* (New York, 1960), 101–2. (For Rashi's awareness of *Shiᶜur Qomah*, see p. 129, in a note to p. 40, line 2.) Scholem's reference to *Shibbolei ha-Leqet* is to sec. 20. Additional references in medieval Ashkenazic rabbinic literature to the *Hekhalot* text entitled מעשה מרכבה can be found in *Tosafot ᶜAvodah Zarah* 2b, s.v. *Romi ḥayyevet (Tosafot R. Elḥanan*, ad loc. [s.v. *zu Romi ḥayyevet*], attributes this citation to Ri); *ᶜArugat ha-Bosem*, ed. Urbach, 1:204, 206: *Shibbolei ha-Leqet*, sec. 17; R. Avigdor of Vienna, *Shaᶜarei Musar* (Jerusalem, 1993), 5 (and cf. *Arbaᶜah Turim*, *O. Ḥ.*, sec. 125); in *Sefer ha-Maḥkim*, ed. Jacob Freimann (Cracow, 1908), 8; and in ms. Paris 1408, fol. 75v (col. 2), by the scribe Elqanah, a student of R. Meir of Rothenburg: אני אלקנה ראיתיה במעשה מרכבה וכו'. See Colette Sirat, "Le Manuscrit Hébreu 1408 de la Bibliothèque Nationale," *REJ* 123 [1964]:348; and below, ch. 5, n. 55. Cf. Daniel Abrams, "Maᶜaseh Merkavah as a Literary Work: The Reception of Hekhalot Traditions by the German Pietists and Kabbalistic Reinterpretation," *Jewish Studies Quarterly* 5 (1998):329–45; and above, ch. 2, n. 34.

Rashi is cited by both R. Judah *he-Ḥasid* and R. Eleazar of Worms regarding insertions he added to the *E-lohai neẓor* prayer following the *ᶜAmidah*. R. Judah's formulation (ms. Paris l'Alliance H48A, fol. 10v) suggests that these addenda came from a text entitled *Maᶜaseh Merkavah*. See Grossman, *Ḥakhmei Ẓarefat ha-Rishonim*, 181. Nonetheless, the possibility raised by Grossman, that the Pietists derived their addenda from *Maᶜaseh Merkavah* and that Rashi's addenda, in this instance, were from an earlier geonic source, is valid. On R. Judah *he-Ḥasid* and addenda to *E-lohai neẓor*, see also ms. Paris 646 (Ashkenaz, fourteenth century), fol. 237r=ms. Cincinnati 436 (Ashkenaz, 1435), fols. 212v–213r. On the somewhat curious absence of Rashi in *Sefer Ḥasidim*, cf. Israel Ta-Shma, "Miẓvat Talmud Torah ki-Veᶜayah Datit ve-Ḥevratit be Sefer Ḥasidim," *Bar-Ilan* 14–15 (1977):113 [=Ta-Shma, *Halakhah, Minhag u-Meẓiʾut be-Ashkenaz* (Jerusalem, 1996), 128–29.]

[38]See Rashi, *Sanhedrin* 44b, s.v. *le-ᶜolam yevaqesh ʾadam raḥamim*, and *Ḥiddushei ha-Rashash*, ad loc. Cf. *Shibbolei ha-Leqet*, sec. 282 (citing R. Avigdor Katz, who based his formulation on Rashi in *Sanhedrin* 44b and on a passage in *Shir ha-Shirim Rabbah*); *Sheʾelot Mahari Bruna*, #274; Frank Talmage, "Angels, Anthems and Anathemas: Aspects of Popular Religion in Fourteenth-Century Bohemian Judaism," *The Frank Talmage*

There are instances, to be sure, in which Rashi interprets a concept or passage in a manner that is antithetical to mystical or kabbalistic teachings. He was, of course, a *peshat*-oriented biblical exegete and a straightforward talmudic commentator who studied at the academies of Mainz and Worms.[41]

Memorial Volume, ed. Walfish, 2:13–16; Heschel, "Al Ruaḥ ha-Qodesh Bimei ha-Benayim," 183, n. 42; Swartz, "Magical Piety in Ancient and Medieval Judaism," 171; and above, n. 4. [Note Meiri's (rationalistic) comment on this talmudic passage: one should ask his *friends* for help.]

[39]See Rashi, *Shabbat* 81b, s.v. *ʾamrei ʾinhu milta* (and the parallel Rashi passage on *Ḥullin* 105a), and *Sanhedrin* 95a, s.v. *ʾein ḥavush*. Cf. Rashi, *Shabbat* 90b, s.v. *reaḥ ra; Shabbat* 66b, s.v. *ʾeven tequmah*; *Sanhedrin* 101, s.v. *roqeq* (and *SḤP* 1397); Trachtenberg, *Jewish Magic and Superstition*, 184; Moshe Catane, "Le Monde Intellectual de Rashi," *Les Juifs au regard de l'histoire*, ed. G. Dahan (Paris, 1985), 83–84; Harari, "Kishfei Hezeq ve-Hitgonenut Mipneihem" (above, n. 10), 120–21; Bernard Septimus, *Hispano-Jewish Culture in Transition* (Cambridge, Mass., 1982), 87; and Güdemann, *Ha-Torah veha-Ḥayyim*, 1:173.

[40]*Sanhedrin* 101, s.v. *sarei shemen*, 67b, s.v. *de-qappid*; and *Megillah* 3b, s.v. *mazlaihu*. Cf. Wolfson, *Through a Speculum That Shines*, 208–9, nn. 75, 81, 266, n. 334; Joseph Dan, "Samael, Lilith and the Concept of Evil in Early Kabbalah," *AJS Review* 5 (1982):27–28, n. 54; idem, *Torat ha-Sod shel Ḥasidut Ashkenaz*, 190–91; Scholem, "Havdalah de-R. Aqivah" (above, n. 17), 251–52, n. 5, 259, n. 31.

Given Rashi's familiarity with *Hekhalot* and other early mystical texts, and especially with the magical powers associated with *Shemot*, it would not have been inconceivable for Rashi to author or transmit magical *segullot*. Nonetheless, Grossman (*Ḥakhmei Ẓarefat ha-Rishonim*, 142, 181) is correct in concluding that the *segullah* to thwart armed robbers through the use of *Shemot*, attributed to Rashi in a manuscript from the eighteenth century (ms. Warsaw 285), is not his, primarily because of the late date of this text. Note also ms. JTS Mic. 7928, which records *segullot* for fear, danger on the road, *sheʾelat ḥalom*, difficulty in childbirth, and appearing before a ruler—all attributed to R. Solomon *Ẓarefati* and transcribed by *ha-navon*, R. Ḥalafta *ha-kohen* b. Shelomoh. See A. Marmorstein in *Me-Assef Zion* 1 (1931):31. The identity of R. Solomon of *Ẓarefat* remains a question, but it is unlikely that he is Rashi. The manuscript is found in the Cairo Geniza, and similar aims and techniques are found in other Geniza texts. See Naveh and Shaked, *Magic Spells and Formulae*, 149, 162, 185–86, 215, 217.

[41]See, e.g., Elliot Ginsburg, *The Sabbath in the Classical Kabbalah* (Albany, 1989), 105, 122; Elliot Wolfson, "Metatron and *Shiʿur Qomah* and in the Writings of Ḥasidei Ashkenaz," *Magic, Mysticism, and Kabbalah in Ashkenazi Judaism*, ed. K. E. Grözinger and J. Dan (Berlin, 1995), 79, n. 96; Margoliot, *Malʾakhei ʿElyon*, 179, sec. 289, nn. 1–2; Ivan Marcus, "The 'Song of Songs' in German Hasidism and the School of Rashi: A Preliminary Comparison," *The Frank Talmage Memorial Volume*, ed. Walfish, 1:181–89; and cf. Joseph Davis, "R. Yom Tov Lipman Heller, Joseph b. Isaac ha-Levi, and Rationalism in Ashkenazic Jewish Culture, 1550–1650," (Ph.D. diss., Harvard, 1990), 72–75. [In *Shibbolei ha-Leqet*, sec. 20, Rashi is cited as offering an exoteric interpretation of why it is appropriate to sway in prayer. But the verse he cites as part of his

Moreover, Eleazar Touitou has argued recently that Rashi's Torah commentary reflects the view that the Torah's orientation was anthropocentric rather than theocentric. Thus, although Rashi was aware of the esoteric approach to the creation of the world, he interpreted the biblical Creation story and other sections of the Torah as being interested primarily in imparting a didactic message that would mold man's behavior, rather than in transmitting theological constructs.[42] Nonetheless, great care must be exercised when drawing conclusions from the fact that Rashi does not appear to utilize *Hekhalot* material in a particular context, as the following analysis serves to illustrate.

In a brief article entitled "Rashi and the Merkavah," Joseph Dan presents two examples which suggest to him, at least tentatively, that Rashi "either did not have, or chose not to use, Hekhalot traditions," and that he "did not integrate Hekhalot material into his literary structure."[43] The second example adduced by Dan emerges from Rashi's commentary to Ezekiel. Rashi declines to discuss the esoteric meaning of the term *ḥashmal* in his commentary to Ezekiel,

---

explanation is the same one referred to in both *Hekhalot* and Pietist materials; see above, ch. 1, nn. 58–60.] It was suggested early on that the commentary on Chronicles attributed to Rashi was not written by him, because it contains *torat ha-sod* material and pietistic concepts and techniques not usually found in Rashi. Indeed, Y. N. Epstein argued (*REJ* 58 [1909]:189–99) that it was authored by R. Samuel *he-Ḥasid*.

The dates for the coming of the Messiah found in Rashi's commentary to Daniel 8:14, (1352) and to *Sanhedrin* 97b (1478) were primarily the result of exegetical considerations (see Gershon Cohen, "Messianic Postures of Ashkenazim and Sephardim," *Studies of the Leo Baeck Institute*, ed. Max Kreutzberger [New York, 1967], 126–27), as was the prediction offered by Rashi's French student R. Shemaᶜayah (see Grossman, *Ḥakhmei Ẓarefat ha-Rishonim* [Jerusalem, 1995]), 357, and see now Simcha Emanuel, "*Ḥeshbon ha-Luaḥ ve-Ḥeshbon ha-Qez*," Zion 63 (1998):143–55. Cf. above, n. 2; below, ch. 4, nn. 8, 37; ch. 5, n. 67; and Israel Ta-Shma, "Ḥishuv Qiẓzin le-Or ha-Halakhah," *Maḥanayim* 59 (1961):57–59. The phrase כמו שהראוני מן השמים, found in a responsum attributed to Rashi (see *Teshuvot Rashi*, ed. Elfenbein, 282, and Grossman, *Ḥakhmei Ẓarefat ha-Rishonim*, 137), does not necessarily reflect an actual quasi-prophetic or mystical experience on Rashi's part. See Isadore Twersky, *Rabad of Posquières* (Philadelphia, 1980²), 291–94; *Teshuvot Rashi*, loc. cit., nn. 12–13; and below, ch. 4, n. 60; ch. 5, n. 23. The phrase כמו שהראוני מן השמים appended to Rashi's commentary to Ezekiel 42:3, s.v. *ba-shelishim*, is a later interpolation. See Abraham Levy, *Rashi's Commentary on Ezekiel 40–48* (Philadelphia, 1931), 85.

[42]E. Touitou, "Bein Parshanut le-Etiqah: Hashqafat ha-ᶜOlam shel ha-Torah lefi Perush Rashi," *Sefer Zikkaron le-Sarah Kamin*, ed. Sara Japhet, 312–34. Cf. idem, "Ha-Reqa ha-Histori shel Perush Rashi le-Sefer Bereshit," *Rashi—ᶜIyyunim be-Yeẓirato*, ed. Z. A. Steinfeld (Jerusalem, 1993), 102.

[43]Joseph Dan, "Rashi and the Merkavah," *Rashi, 1040–1990*, ed. Sed-Rajna, 259–64.

offering instead a rabbinic interpretation, as well as his own interpretation—which was based on the biblical context. There is nothing in Rashi's interpretations to suggest an awareness of *Hekhalot* texts or ideas. Moreover, Dan maintains that Rashi's refusal to disclose the so-called esoteric interpretation, which was predicated on one version of a talmudic dictum, does not prove that he was actually aware of *Hekhalot* material. Rather, Rashi's concern may have been a theological or anthropomorphic one, having to do with the danger of interpreting **חשמל** as relating to the figure of God. Despite Dan's best efforts, however, this example as an indication that Rashi did not use or have *Hekhalot* material remains an argument from silence.

Dan's first example comes from Rashi's commentary to *Ḥagigah* 14b. A somewhat mysterious formulation attributed to R. Aqiva, which was linked to his entrance and that of his colleagues into *Pardes*, states that "when you arrive at stones of pure marble, do not say 'water, water.'" The Talmud does not explain this prohibition. Only in *Hekhalot* texts of the *Merkavah* tradition do we find that the mistaking of marble for water is an indication that the mystic has failed a test and may not enter into the sixth palace.

According to Dan, Rashi's comment, **מים מים יש כאן איך נלך**, taken together with the prior portion of the talmudic passage, **אל תאמרו**, "do not say," is diametrically opposed to the *Hekhalot* approach. In Dan's view, Rashi's interpretation of R. Aqiva's warning is that one who sees water should *not* say, in defeat, that it cannot be crossed (literally, how can we go on?)—that his quest has ended. R. Aqiva is offering encouragement rather than a stern warning. The mystic should not hesitate, because these waters are an imaginary obstacle. Rather, he should proceed further in his quest, against the guidelines in the *Hekhalot* literature.

David Halperin, in his study of early Jewish responses to the vision of Ezekiel that appeared several years before Dan's article, understands the comment of Rashi very differently. He considers it evidence of Rashi's awareness of *Hekhalot* material. In Halperin's view, Rashi's comment, **מים מים יש כאן איך נלך**, is a paraphrase of R. Aqiva's warning: "There is water, water here; how can we go further?" According to Rashi, and parallel to the *Hekhalot* material, the sight of water *does* stop the mystic from proceeding further. Indeed, Halperin suggests that Rashi is intimating that the mystic in this case may feel like the children of Israel at the Red Sea, who found their way blocked by water and could not proceed.

Moreover, Rashi glosses the phrase "pure marble" (when you arrive at stones of pure marble) with the words **מבהיק כמים צלולין** (shining like clear water). Halperin notes that the word **צלולות** appears in a related *Hekhalot* text in conjunction with the marble stones, and he suggests that Rashi perhaps derived his interpretation of "pure marble" from a *Hekhalot* source. In short, not only is Rashi's interpretation of this passage fully consonant with *Hekhalot* literature, it may well have been drawn from it.[44]

In both his biblical and talmudic commentaries,[45] Rashi was influenced by the mystical midrash *Otiyyot de-R. Aqiva*. In one instance in his talmudic commentary to *Ḥullin*, which is parallel to a passage in his commentary to Ezekiel, he interprets that *demut* or *parẓuf Yaʿaqov* represents the male aspect within the Godhead.[46] As Elliot Wolfson has demonstrated, this mystical formulation was espoused later by both R. Eleazar of Worms and members of the *Ḥug ha-Keruv ha-Meyuḥad*.[47]

---

[44]David Halperin, *The Faces of the Chariot*, 210, 534, n. 1. See also 184, 219–20, 243, for other instances in which Rashi's interpretation is consistent with *Hekhalot* literture. Cf. Avraham Grossman, *Ḥakhmei Ẓarefat ha-Rishonim*, 205, n. 249. See also Rashi, *Sanhedrin* 103a, s.v. *shalosh mafteḥot lo nimseru le-shaliaḥ*, which accords precisely with a *Hekhalot* conception of the heavenly אוצר. See Schiffman and Swartz, *Hebrew and Aramaic Incantations from the Cairo Genizah*, 159. Rashi interprets the talmudic term *baʿal ha-ḥalom* as שר המראה חלומות בלילה; see above, n. 3; and cf. Heschel, "Al Ruaḥ ha-Qodesh Bimei ha-Benayim," 176–77, nn. 6–7; Trachtenberg, *Jewish Magic and Superstition*, 72; Harris, *Studies in Jewish Dream Interpretation*, 33.

[45]See Israel Ta-Shma, "Sifriyyatam shel Ḥakhmei Ashkenaz Benei ha-Meʾah ha-Yod Alef/ha-Yod Bet," *Qiryat Sefer* 60 (1985):307; and Abraham Berliner, *Rashi ʿal ha-Torah* (Frankfurt, 1905), 427 (*liqqutim*), to Numbers 14:4. See also above, n. 31.

[46]See Rashi, *Ḥullin* 91b, s.v. פרצוף אדם שבארבע חיות בדמות יעקב: בדיוקנו של מעלה, and Rashi's commentary to Ezekiel 1:5, s.v. דמות אדם להנה: והוא דמות פרצופו של יעקב אבינו.

[47]See Elliot Wolfson, "Demut Yaʿaqov Ḥaquqah be-Kisse ha-Kavod: ʿIyyun Nosaf be-Torat ha-Sod shel Ḥasidut Ashkenaz," *Massuʾot*, ed. Oron and Goldreich, 137–41; 154–56, nn. 116–17; 162, n. 138; 165, n. 151; 170, n. 173; and cf. 137. n. 35. Idem, "The Image of Jacob Engraved upon the Throne: Further Reflection on the Esoteric Doctrine of the German Pietists," in his *Along the Path*, 8–12; 117, n. 37; 119, n. 54; 148, n. 192; 156, n. 225; 160–61, n. 239. [Pseudo-Rashi to *Taʿanit* 5a anticipates an association made by *Ḥasidei Ashkenaz*, that ישראל סבא is equivalent to דמות יעקב (a Divine hypostasis); see *ʿArugat ha-Bosem*, ed. Urbach, 4:85, n. 77, and cf. 7a, s.v. *yafuẓu*. This commentary was composed by a student of Rashi, possibly Riban or Rashbam. See J. P. Guttel, "Remarques sur le 'Pseudo-Raschi' de Taʿanit," *REJ* 125 (1966):93–100, and the literature cited in nn. 3–4. See also Zeraḥ Warhaftig, "Devarim ki-Feshutam—ʿal Massekhet Taʿanit," *Ha-Maʿayan* 36:1 (1996):43. One passage (*Taʿanit* 15a, s.v. *uve-qabbalah*), cites a question raised by *Tosafot*, suggesting that the author of this commentary was one of the tosafists.] On the similarities between Rashi's mythic approach to the understanding of the sanctification of the new moon and the approaches taken by *Sefer Ḥasidim* and by kabbalists, see Yehuda Liebes, *Studies in Jewish Myth and Jewish Messianism* (Albany, 1993), 48–53 [="de Natura Dei—ʿal ha-Mitos ha-Yehudi ve-Gilgulo," *Massuʾot*, 284–88.]

Rashi's genuine interest in aspects of *torat ha-sod* helps to explain not only the citation and amplification of passages in his commentaries by the late thirteenth-century work *Sefer ha-Maskil* (written by R. Solomon Simḥah of Troyes, a descendant of Rashi),[48] and by kabbalistic works such as the Zohar and *Sefer Maᶜarekhet ha-E-lohut*,[49] but also the notion expressed by the fifteenth-century *Sefer ha-Meshiv*—and by R. Mordekhai Jaffe and Ḥida, among others—that Rashi was thoroughly conversant with *sitrei Torah* and was immersed in their study when he wrote his commentaries.[50] Attribution of esoteric teachings to Rashi was not simply a case in which deep ideas were associated with a great scholar, with no firm basis. At the same time, Rashi's awareness of the various *sod* dimensions that were studied in pre-Crusade Mainz should not be overstated. Rashi was certainly not a mystic, nor did he involve himself in theosophy. Indeed, this higher form of kabbalah or *sod* was largely absent in the pre-Crusade period as a whole. It is perhaps for this reason, in addition to other exegetical considerations mentioned above, that

---

[48]See Israel Ta-Shma, "Sefer ha-Maskil—Ḥibbur Yehudi-Ẓarefati Bilti Yaduaᶜ mi-Sof ha-Meʾah ha-Yod Gimmel," *Meḥqerei Yerushalayim be-Maḥshevet Yisraʾel* 2 (1983):418; and Gad Freudenthal, "Ha-Avir Barukh Hu u-Varukh Shemo be-Sefer ha-Maskil le-R. Shelomoh Simḥah mi-Troyes," *Daᶜat* 32–33 (1994):205, n. 46; 221, n. 120.

[49]See Ephraim Gottlieb, *Meḥqarim be-Sifrut ha-Qabbalah*, ed. Joseph Hacker (Jerusalem, 1976), 203, for a passage in Rashi's commentary to *Ḥagigah* which may have been the source of a Zoharic conception of *gilgul*, and 319, for a characterization of Creation that *Sefer Maʾarekhet E-lohut* derived from Rashi's commentary to the beginning of the Torah.

[50]See Abraham Gross, "Rashi u-Mesoret Limmud ha-Torah she-Bikhtav bi-Sefarad," *Rashi, ᶜIyyunim be-Yeẓirato*, ed. Steinfeld, 50–53; Baron, *A Social and Religious History of the Jews*, above, n. 33; Raphael Halpern, *Rashi—Ḥayyav u-Perushav* (Jerusalem, 1997), 1:256–58; below, n. 98; and the studies cited in Grossman, *Ḥakhmei Ẓarefat ha-Rishonim*, 205, n. 248. See also Idel, *Kabbalah: New Perspectives*, 237–39; idem, "Iyyunim be-Shitat Baᶜal 'Sefer ha-Meshiv,'" 239–41; and idem, *Golem*, 131, 226. Cf. Rashi to *Bava Batra* 12a (end). Although his description of the relationship between *ḥokhmah* and prophecy is not as openly suggestive in mystical terms as compared to the comment of Ramban ad loc., Rashi's comments may still hold some significance in this regard. See Heschel, "Al Ruaḥ ha-Qodesh Bimei ha-Benayim," 179, and Shraga Abramson, "Navi Roʾeh ve-Ḥozeh—R. Avraham ha-Ḥozeh," *Sefer Yovel Muggash li-Khevod Mordechai Kirschblum*, ed. David Telsner (Jerusalem, 1983), 118. See also Rashi, *Taᶜanit* 4a, s.v. *u-khetiv*, and Yohanan Silman, *Qol Gadol ve-Lo Yasaf* (Jerusalem, 1999), 108. A manuscript passage maintains that prior to R. Jacob of Marvège, author of *Sheʾelot u-Teshuvot min ha-Shamayim*, Rashi had the capacity to undertake heavenly ascents in order to receive halakhic guidance; see Alexander Marx, "A New Collection of Mss. in the Cambridge Library," *PAAJR* 4 (1933):153, n. 29. See also Heschel, 194; and below, ch. 5, n. 24.

Rashi's descriptions of the Divine do not usually reflect a mystical orientation and that Rashi extended the talmudic prohibition of delving into esoteric interpretations of the Godhead in Ezekiel by at least one verse.[51]

Nonetheless, the interest and familiarity displayed by Rashi with regard to magical and mystical concepts and techniques carried over into works that were associated with his school. Passages in *Maḥzor Vitry* and other volumes of the so-called *sifrut de-Vei Rashi* (found in sections that can be shown to reflect traditions of Rashi himself or of his circle)[52] describe the marital imagery of the Sabbath in a manner later expanded upon by devotées of kabbalah,[53] adopt *Bahir* imagery to explain the efficacy of the Sabbath against *maziqin*,[54] analyze the role of the kaddish in filling out the Divine Name[55] and protecting the

---

[51]See Dan, "Rashi and the Merkavah" (above, n. 43); Touitou, "Bein Parshanut le-Etiqah" (above, n. 42); and Yaᶜakov Spiegel, "Meqorot be-Perush Rashi le-Yirmiyahu ve-Yeḥezqel," *Rashi, ᶜIyyunim be-Yeẓirato*, ed. Steinfeld, 204.

[52]*Sefer ha-Pardes* in particular reflects the halakhic positions of late eleventh-century Ashkenaz and, quite often, those of Rashi himself. Thus, *Shibbolei ha-Leqet* cites material in *Sefer ha-Pardes* as *hilkhot Rabbenu Shelomoh*. See Ta-Shma, *Ha-Nigleh shebe-Nistar*, 55, and idem, *Minhag Ashkenaz ha-Qadmon* (Jerusalem, 1992), 149–50.

[53]See E. K. Ginsburg, *The Sabbath in the Classical Kabbalah*, 106, 168, n. 189, 175, n. 230, and cf. 168, n. 186. Ginsburg's study demonstrates that a number of themes which were central to the Zohar's conception of *sod ha-Shabbat* derived from *Sefer ha-Pardes*. Cf. Ta-Shma, *Ha-Nigleh shebe-Nistar*, 32, and the next note.

[54]See Israel Ta-Shma, *Minhag Ashkenaz ha-Qadmon*, 148–56. The custom of changing the final blessing of the *Shema* on Friday evening (from the *shomer ᶜammo Yisraʾel laᶜad* ending recited during the weekdays to *ha-pores sukkat shalom ᶜaleinu ve-ᶜal kol ᶜammo Yisrael*) is supported by Bahiric parables, which indicate that when the Jewish people are closer to God through the performance of positive precepts, as on the Sabbath, they require less protection through prayer. These parables and their application were retained in full by *Perush ha-Tefillot le-Rabbenu Shelomoh*, which was composed either by Rashi himself or by one of his students and was recorded in *Sefer ha-Pardes* and in *Maḥzor Vitry* in shorter form. The custom, together with its interpretation and imagery, were recorded by the Zohar as well, confirming the presence of a mystical approach. See also Penkower, *Nosaḥ ha-Torah be-Keter Aram Ẓovah*, 48, n. 116.

[55]See Haviva Pedaya, "Pegam ve-Tiqqun shel ha-E-lohut be-Qabbalat R. Yiẓḥaq Sagi Nahor," *Meḥqerei Yerushalayim be-Maḥshevet Yisraʾel* 6 [3–4] (1987):253–59; and see above, nn. 6, 17. Cf. Ta-Shma's source corrections in *Ha-Nigleh shebe-Nistar*, 95, nn. 48–49; and Aryeh Goldschmidt, "Perush ha-Qaddish le-Baᶜal Maḥzor Vitry," *Yeshurun* 3 (1997):5–14. Pedaya notes (258, n. 15) that certain tosafists attempted to blunt the mystical interpretation of the kaddish; see below, ch. 4, n. 2. See Yaakov Gartner, "Ha-Meᶜaneh be-Qaddish 'Yehe Shemeh Rabbah Mevorakh,'" *Sidra* 11 (1996):40–41, for affinities between *sifrut de-Vei Rashi* and *Ḥasidei Ashkenaz* regarding the structure and wording of *qaddish*. For a mystical conception of the *demut Yaᶜaqov* that appears in *sifrut de-Vei Rashi*, see Wolfson, "Demut Yaᶜaqov" (above, n. 47), 137, n. 35.

deceased,[56] and recommend that Divine and angelic names and markings be included in *mezuzot*.[57]

---

[56]*Maḥzor Vitry*, ed. Hurwitz, 112–13, sec. 144, recounts the story of a deceased person who was spared the travails of *gehinnom* because his son recited *Barekhu* and *kaddish* (*yehe shemeh rabbah*) on *moẓaʾei Shabbat*. This story is extant only in late midrashic sources. It is cited (and embellished) by a number of Ashkenazic sources, including texts of *Ḥasidei Ashkenaz*, and by the Zohar as well. See M. B. Lerner, "Maʿaseh ha-Tanna veha-Met," *Assufot* 2 (1988):60–67; Ta-Shma, *Minhag Ashkenaz ha-Qadmon*, 299–306; and idem, *Ha-Nigleh shebe-Nistar*, 93, n. 33; and ms. Bodl. 378 (Ashkenaz, c. 1300), fol. 45v. At the beginning of the *Maḥzor Vitry* passage, the phrase **נמצא בספרים הפנימי'[ים]. ת' [=תוספת]** appears. This addendum, which was probably from R. Abraham b. Nathan, author of *Sefer ha-Manhig* (see *Sefer ha-Manhig*, ed. Y. Raphael, editor's introduction, 35–37), suggests the story originated in some type of esoteric text. On the use of the term *sefarim penimiyyim* in *Sefer ha-Manhig* to connote *Hekhalot* texts, such as *Sefer Hekhalot* or *Maʿaseh Merkavah*, see Raphael, 29, and above, ch. 1, n. 61. [On the use of this term, cf. *Sefer ha-Pardes ha-Gadol*, sec. 191.] The passage in *Maḥzor Vitry* concludes with the observation that "the custom is, therefore, to designate someone who has no father or mother as the prayer leader on *moẓaʾei Shabbat*, to recite *barekhu* or *kaddish*." See also *Siddur R. Shelomoh mi-Germaiza ve-Siddur Ḥasidei Ashkenaz*, ed. Moshe Hershler (Jerusalem, 1972), 75; and Hershler, "Sefer Ḥasidim le-R. Yehudah he-Ḥasid, Mahadurah ve-Nosaḥ Ḥadashah mi-Tokh Ketav Yad," *Genuzot* 1 (1984):129. The next passage in *Maḥzor Vitry* (sec. 145) notes that the custom is to lengthen the prayers on *moẓaʾei Shabbat*, since this delays the return of the souls who normally reside in *gehinnom* but who are let out on Shabbat. This custom was endorsed in pre-Crusade Ashkenaz by R. Eleazar *Ḥazzan* of Spires (above, n. 25; and see also the interpretation by R. Jacob b. Yaqar in M. Hershler, "Minhagei Vermaiza u-Magenẓa, de-Vei Rashi ve-Rabbotav u-Minhagei Ashkenaz shel ha-Roqeaḥ," *Genuzot* 2 [1985]:23, sec. 53), and subsequently by R. Eleazar of Worms, by (his student) R. Isaac *Or Zaruaʿ*, and by liturgical texts of the German Pietists. See Ta-Shma, *Minhag Ashkenaz ha-Qadmon*, 307–10; ms. Paris 1408, fols. 143v–144r; below, ch. 5, n. 11; *Sefer ha-Manhig*, 1:191; *Shibbolei ha-Leqet*, sec. 129, regarding the slow and deliberate recitation of **ויהי נועם** at the conclusion of the Sabbath; and cf. *Sefer Tashbeẓ*, secs. 257–58; and I. Ta-Shma, "Vihi Noʿam u-Qedushah de-Sidra bi-Tefillat Moẓaʾei Shabbat," *Ḥazon Naḥum*, ed. Y. Elman and J. Gurock (New York, 1997), 58–62.

[57]See *Maḥzor Vitry*, 648–49; *Siddur Rashi*, ed. Solomon Buber (Berlin, 1911), sec. 455; *Sefer ha-Pardes ha-Gadol*, sec. 285 (citing also the views of R. Judah *ha-Ḥasid*). Cf. Victor Aptowitzer, "Le Nom de Dieu et des Anges dans la Mezouza," *REJ* 60 (1910):40–52; above, ch. 1, n. 45; and below, ch. 4, n. 16. On the use of material from *Maḥzor Vitry* by the Zohar, see Ta-Shma, *Ha-Nigleh shebe Nistar*, 21–22, and 92–93, n. 33. Ta-Shma's larger claim (21–31) is that numerous halakhic practices and customs in the Zohar derived from earlier Ashkenazic sources. Included also in this path of transmission is the "white magic" in the Zohar, which Ta-Shma believes is of Ashkenazic origin, having arrived there via *Hekhalot* texts. On counting the words in prayer, a practice usually associated with *Ḥasidei Ashkenaz*, see *Maḥzor Vitry*, 519, and cf. above, ch. 2, n. 26.

Fending off forgetfulness by means of magical adjurations—a practice that had its roots in *Hekhalot* mysticism—is a component of the *Havdalah* ceremony in *Maḥzor Vitry*.[58] The version of the educational initiation ceremony in *Maḥzor Vitry* does not contain the magical adjurations against *Potah* found in the thirteenth-century *Sefer Assufot*.[59] Nor were there any verses written on the

---

[58]See *Maḥzor Vitry*, 115–16. The basic formula, to neutralize *Potah*, and to remove an uncomprehending heart (לב טיפש) from the person reciting the formula, is also found in earlier geonic sources, such as *Seder R. Amram*, and in subsequent Spanish sources as well. Cf. Scholem, "Havdalah de-R. Aqiva," 23–49, 278–79, n. 138; and I. Marcus, *Rituals of Childhood*, 138, n. 34. In addition, the fuller *Havdalah de-R. Aqiva* contains a series of magical *hashbaᶜot*, which often reflect *Hekhalot* formulations, to be recited after the Sabbath to ensure that one's wishes will be granted, especially with regard to thwarting *kishuf* and other nefarious forces. See, e.g., Scholem, 256, line 18, which contains a section from *Hekhalot Zutarti* that includes the Divine Name אזבוגה, found in other *Hekhalot* texts. On this Name, cf. *Synopse zur Hekhalot-Literatur*, ed. Schäfer, secs. 415–19; Scholem, *Jewish Gnosticism, Merkavah Mysticism and Talmudic Tradition*, 66–71; Yosef Dan, "Shem shel Sheminiyyot," *Minḥah le-Sarah*, ed. Moshe Idel et al. (Jerusalem, 1994), 119–34; Theodore Schrire, *Hebrew Amulets* (London, 1966), 112–13; Verman and Adler, "Path Jumping in the Jewish Magical Tradition," 145; ms. Moscow-Guenzberg 1302, fol. 15v; and *ᶜArugat ha-Bosem*, ed. Urbach, 4:77. Invoking this Name guaranteed that תורתו ותלמודו מתקיימים ואינו ניזוק לעולם, even if one finds himself among *maziqin* and *shedim*. Virtually all the manuscripts of the *Havdalah de-R. Aqiva* are of German provenance and associated with members or students of *Ḥasidei Ashkenaz*, who also cite it in their works. Cf. Y. Dan, "Sefer ha-Navon le-Eḥad me-Ḥasidei Ashkenaz," *Qoveẓ ᶜal Yad* 6:1 (1966): 203, n. 12, 209–10; and *Perushei Siddur ha-Tefillah la-Roqeaḥ*, ed. Moshe Hershler (Jerusalem, 1992), 1:182, 247, 2:606. According to Scholem, the magical material may have originated in Babylonia during the geonic period, after which it was brought to southern Italy and from there to Germany.

[59]See above, n. 18. According to the *Assufot* text, the words נגף סגף אגף are recited ten times, followed by the incantation against *Potah*, which concludes with a series of Divine Names. These names are not actually written in the *Assufot* text but can be found in the almost identical formula against *Potah* used in the Havdalah ceremony (see the preceding note). On the significance of the words נגף סגף אגף, see Moshe Idel, "Tefisat ha-Torah be-Sifrut ha-Hekhalot ve-Gilgulehah ba-Qabbalah," *Meḥqerei Yerushalayim be-Maḥshevet Yisraʾel* 1 (1981):47, who notes a passage from ms. Berlin Tübingen Or. 942, that the *gematria* of חשמל (which refers to the anthropomorphic Glory) is equal to סגף, which means the latter term connotes a Divine Name. [Cf., however, *SḤB* 1154: since the final form of the letter *peh* appears in the names of many angels with the power to do damage (*malʾakhei habbalah*, including נגף and אגף, among others), no final *peh* is found in any prayer except the *musaf* service, in which the appropriate additional sacrifice for the day (ואת מוסף יום) must be mentioned in any case. See also *Sefer Roqeaḥ*, sec. 337, and *Sefer Assufot* itself (ms. Jews College 134/Montefiore 115, fol. 157v): "All letters are utilized in the grace after meals except final *peh*, so that none of these (bad)

foods which the young initiate should eat, as in *Sefer Roqeaḥ*,[60] although several magical elements are present in the *Maḥzor Vitry* version. As in the *Roqeaḥ* passage, the child licked honey off the letters of the alphabet written on a tablet, after reciting them. Also, the cakes that had been kneaded with honey and the hard-boiled eggs (both of which are more numerous in the *Maḥzor Vitry* version) were eaten specifically to achieve *petiḥat ha-lev.*[61] The additional recitation of the alphabet backward, which appears to have been part of the ceremony in the Reggio manuscript of *Maḥzor Vitry* (as it was in *Sefer Roqeaḥ* and *Sefer Assufot*), mystically represented a Divine Name, according to R. Eleazar of Worms in his *Sefer ha-Ḥokhmah.*[62] Even the swaying of the child

---

angels are indicated. These angels will not affect anyone who recites the grace. Similarly, no final *peh* appears in יוצא אור or in the *shemoneh ᶜesreh* either." See also ms. Moscow-Guenzberg 182, fol. 153v, and ms. Bodl. 784, fol. 98r; and cf. Moritz Güdemann, *Ha-Torah veha-Ḥayyim*, vol. 1 (Warsaw, 1897), 37, n. 3; Margoliot's *Meqor Ḥesed* to *SḤB*, loc. cit.; and above, ch. 1, n. 163. The so-called *Perush ha-Roqeaḥ ᶜal ha-Torah*, ed. Chaim Konyevsky, vol. 2, (Bnei Brak, 1980), 24, written by a member of *Ḥasidei Ashkenaz*, asserts that the recitation of a series of certain verses, none of which contains the letter *peh*, will ward off the various harmful angels whose names end with this letter. Cf. below, n. 110.]

[60]See Marcus, *Rituals of Childhood*, 32. *Horayot* 13b recommends five techniques to improve memory, including the eating of an unsalted, hard-boiled egg. This is recorded as normative by medieval rabbinic texts, such as *Pisqei R. Yeshayah di Trani* (*Rid*), ed. Abraham Wertheimer (Jerusalem, 1990), 66, although it should be noted that R. Isaiah di Trani himself had some proclivities for *sod*; see below, ch. 5, nn. 19–21. On the other hand, the rationalistic R. Menaḥem ha-Meiri, clearly wishing to downplay the notion of magical foods, maintains that all these practices point to the general notion of eating only well-cooked and properly checked foods, which will not be *metamtem et ha-lev.* Cf. Mary Carruthers, *The Book of Memory*, 50. Generally speaking, a good diet and the right foods are important for memory, although Carruthers is writing from the nonmystical standpoint. See also Swartz, *Scholastic Magic*, 150–62.

[61]Cf. above, n. 16.

[62]See Marcus, *Rituals of Childhood*, 39, 100, 145, n. 29. As Marcus notes, the recitation of the alphabet backward at the time a child begins to study is also described in the pietistic Torah commentary, *Teᶜamim shel Ḥumash*. The author of this commentary was an older contemporary of R. Eleazar of Worms, R. Solomon b. Samuel. R. Solomon studied with R. Samuel and R. Judah *he-Ḥasid* in Spires and Regensburg before returning to his native northern France. See above, ch. 2, n. 5. The *gematria* derivation of this practice given by R. Samuel, and its application, is found also in the so-called *Perush ha-Roqeaḥ ᶜal ha-Torah*, ed. Konyevsky, vol. 3 (Bnei Brak, 1981), 284–85 (*Devarim* 33:4). Cf. *Sefer ha-Pardes*, ed. Ehrenreich, 310. In the ancient world, the alphabet was learned and remembered by reciting it forward and backward. See Marcus, 36, and Carruthers, *The Book of Memory*, 111.

during his recitation of verses—found in the *Maḥzor Vitry* version and in a later German liturgical commentary (ms. Hamburg 152)—and the covering of the child with a cloak on the way to and from the ceremony—found also in the liturgical commentary (and partially in *Sefer Roqeaḥ*)—may have been derived from *Hekhalot* constructs.[63] Indeed, the four earliest and most complete versions of the Ashkenazic initiation ceremony—those found in *Maḥzor Vitry, Sefer Roqeaḥ, Sefer Assufot*, and ms. Hamburg, which include the magical uses of *Shemot* and the implementation of *Hekhalot* techniques and practices—suggest that these underlying concepts were known to those who performed and participated in the ceremony.[64]

---

[63]See Marcus, *Rituals of Childhood*, 149, n. 97, and above, ch. 1, nn. 58–59. [Marcus, 73, notes also the (practical) reason given for swaying during Torah reading and study by the *Sefer Kuzari*.] According to Marcus, 69–71, the wrapping of the child (so that he cannot see certain objects) reflects either considerations of purity based on the *Hekhalot*-related *Baraita de-Masskhet Niddah* (in which seeing impurities renders the observer impure) or the symbolic initiation of the child into wisdom. Cf. Swartz, *Scholastic Magic*, 163, and above, n. 8. See also Marcus, 98, for the relationship between the initiation ceremony as recorded in *Maḥzor Vitry*—which is the only version to include vicarious atonement—and the pietistic *Sefer Ḥuqqei ha-Torah*—which was the product of German Pietists or Provençal mystical circles. Cf. my *Jewish Education and Society in the High Middle Ages* (Detroit, 1992), 101–5.

[64]Marcus considers the version of the initiation ceremony found in *Sefer Roqeaḥ* (whose author, R. Eleazar of Worms, lived ca.1160–1230) to be the earliest one (having been written down in the late twelfth or early thirteenth century), while he suggests that the *Maḥzor Vitry* version appeared some time later. This dating schema supports Marcus's thesis that the reaffirmation of this ceremony was a significant step in a larger effort by the German Pietists and German Jews more generally to preserve earlier Ashkenazic culture—which was more custom-oriented and contained magical components—in the face of tosafist dialectical incursions that were causing these cultural aspects to fade. The ceremony was found initially in the work of a German Pietist, who claimed it was a venerable custom, while its first appearance in a northern French text (where it may not have been actually observed) was only later. See Marcus, *Rituals of Childhood*, 26, 32, 104, 112–14, 137, n. 27, 138–39, nn 35, 41.

Marcus's argument concerning the dating of the versions of the initiation ceremony is, however, somewhat problematic. According to Marcus, the earliest manuscript of *Maḥzor Vitry* that contains the ceremony is the Reggio Manuscript [=JTS Mic. 8092]. But this manuscript, as Marcus notes, is dated 1204; see *Rituals of Childhood*, 138, n. 41, and cf. Ta-Shma's review (above, n. 15), 238. As such, the *Maḥzor Vitry* version of the ceremony is not necessarily any later than the one found in *Sefer Roqeaḥ*. In addition, Marcus's suggestion (32, 114) that the ceremony was perhaps not in vogue in northern France has not been amply demonstrated.

Nonetheless, it is possible to preserve the overall thrust of Marcus's theory in light of the present study. The issue of retaining or eliminating mystical and magical practices

III

In addition to the magical and mystical material found in *sifrut de-Vei Rashi*, there is an astrological work with mystical overtones[65] produced by R. Jacob b. Samson, a student of Rashi. The disposition of pre-Crusade

---

was not simply a case of German Pietists or German Jews versus tosafists. As we shall see, a number of northern French tosafists also wished to retain these aspects of early Ashkenazic rabbinic culture. Indeed, as we have already seen, *Maḥzor Vitry* contains other magical practices and elements as well, even if its version of the initiation ceremony is not identical to the one found in *Sefer Roqeaḥ*. Thus, the presence of this ceremony in both Germany and northern France, although not universally held, testifies to the relative strength of the more traditional position in Ashkenazic rabbinic circles generally, despite the advance of the tosafist innovations and changes that Marcus describes. Cf. S. E. Stern, "Seder Ḥinnukh Yeladim le-Torah ule-Yirʾah mi-Beit Midrasham shel Ḥakhmei Ashkenaz," *Ẓefunot* 1:1 (1988):15–21, and A. N. Z. Roth, "Ḥinnukh Yeladim le-Torah be-Shavuᶜot," *Yeda ᶜAm* 11 (1966):9–12. On the availability and usage of *hashbaᶜot* and *Shemot* in northern France, in prayer liturgies and other public contexts, see below, esp. nn. 98–99, 110.

[65]Grossman, *Ḥakhmei Ẓarefat ha-Rishonim*, 418–23; Ronald Kiener, "Astrology in Jewish Mysticism from the *Sefer Yeṣira* to the Zohar," *Meḥqerei Yerushalayim be-Maḥshevet Yisraʾel* 6 [3–4] (1987): 1*–42*. Cf. Ta-Shma, *Ha-Nigleh shebe-Nistar*, 32, and Trachtenberg, *Jewish Magic and Superstition*, 249–59. See also Bodl. 2275 (Germany, 1329). This manuscript contains several amulets, *Sefer Miẓvot Qatan, Midrash va-Yosha*, and *minhagim de-Vei Maharam* (including also passages from *Sefer Ḥasidim*, and from R. Eleazar of Worms and Rabiah). Fols. 48r–50v consist of material on *qiddush ha-ḥodesh*, *ᶜibbur*, and the like. Fols. 49v–50r contain a lengthy passage from *Sefer ha-Alqoshi* on the deleterious effects (particularly with regard to the poisoning of water) that may result when the *tequfot* change (**טעם סכנת תקופה אשר הועתק מספר האלקושי שהיה בקי בחכמת המזלות**). These effects are caused because there is a period when the angelic figure (*memuneh*) responsible for the new *tequfah* has not yet assumed his role, allowing conflicts between various *mazzalot* to produce various *maziqim*. Amulet-writers may attempt to ward off these effects [See also ms. Bodl. 692 (Ashkenaz, 1305), fols. 88r–99v, which lists the *sod ha-ᶜibbur* of R. Jacob b. Samson, from ch. 23 of *Sefer ha-Alqoshi* (the calculations are for 1123).] For partial transcriptions and analyses of the material in *Sefer ha-Alqoshi* on the changing of *tequfot*, see Grossman, *Ḥakhmei Ẓarefat ha-Rishonim*, 420–22, and Israel Ta-Shma, "Issur Shetiyyat Mayim ba-Tequfah u-Meqoro," *Meḥqerei Yerushalayim be-Folqlor Yehudi* 17 (1995):27–28. Additionally, as Grossman notes, other material in *Sefer ha-Alqoshi* reads like a commentary to *Sefer Yeẓirah* (which R. Jacob b. Samson may also have composed). On the similarity between R. Jacob's view of the change of the *tequfah* and that of *Ḥasidei Ashkenaz*, see below, ch. 4, n. 9; and cf. *ᶜArugat ha-Bosem*, ed. Urbach, 4:79–80. For other *sod* material attributed to students of Rashi, see Grossman, *Ḥakhmei Ẓarefat ha-Rishonim*, 173 [ms. Vat. 422, fol. 51v, and ms. Lund 2, fol. 74r, record that a student of Rashi named R. Judah fixed a liturgical reading based on what was written in a *sefer sodot*], 368.

rabbinic scholarship toward mysticism and magic was not shared, however, by all of Rashi's immediate students and successors. Rashi's grandson, R. Samuel b. Meir (Rashbam), was aware of the mystical powers of *Shemot* and of the existence of esoteric texts, as a passage in his commentary to *ʿArvei Pesaḥim* indicates.[66] In at least two significant contexts, however, he distances himself from mystical interpretation and symbolism.

Sara Kamin has demonstrated that Rashbam's interpretation of the Creation story was intended to bypass any possibility of cosmogonic or theosophic speculation. In his commentary to *Qohelet* (2:3, 2:13), Rashbam asserts that only exoteric wisdom, which is absolutely necessary for mankind to master, be pursued. חכמה עמוקה ויתירה, which Rashbam (7:24) identifies as the wisdom contained in *Maʿaseh Merkavah* and *Sefer Yeẓirah*, is not needed by mankind and therefore should not be pursued.[67] In addition, Rashbam

[66]Rashbam, *Pesaḥim* 119a, s.v. *sitrei ha-Torah*: מעשה המרכבה ומעשה בראשית ופירושו של שם כדכתיב זה שמי לעולם. Unlike Rashi, who merely mentions *maʿaseh merkavah* and *maʿaseh bereshit* as examplars of *sitrei Torah*, Rashbam here connects, as *Ḥasidei Ashkenaz* did with even greater emphasis, speculation on the chariot with the mystical knowledge of the Divine Name. See, e.g., *Sefer Roqeaḥ*, [*Hilkhot Ḥasidut*] *Shoresh Qedushat ha-Yiḥud u-Shemo u-Merkavah ve-Sodotav* (end): וכל השמות יוצאין משם הנכבד ב"ה וב"ש ספר המרכבה וספר מעשה בראשית וס' יצירה וס' שמות וס' הכבוד אין לכתוב בס' הזה. Cf. Wolfson, *Through a Speculum That Shines*, 235; Haviva Pedaya, "Pegam ve-Tiqqun," 157, n. 2; and Koren, "Mysticism and Menstruation," above, n. 10. A formulation similar to Rashbam's is found in *Maḥzor Vitry*, 554–55 (commentary to *Avot*). See also Moshe Idel, "Tefisat ha-Torah be-Sifrut ha-Hekhalot ve-Gilgulehah ba-Qabbalah," 36, n. 38. Rashbam may have had a hand in the *Avot* commentary, along with other students of Rashi (including R. Jacob b. Samson). See Israel Ta-Shma, "Al Perush Avot shebe-Maḥzor Vitry," *Qiryat Sefer* 42 (1977):507–8. And cf. Grossman, *Ḥakhmei Ẓarefat ha-Rishonim*, 413–16; and below, ch. 4, n. 2. In one place in his Torah commentary (Exodus 3:15), Rashbam employs an אתב"ש technique to interpret the verse's usage of a Divine name. Cf. *Ḥizquni ʿal ha-Torah*, ad loc.

[67]Sara Kamin, "Rashbam's Conception of the Creation in the Light of the Intellectual Currents of His Time," *Scripta Hierosolymitana* 31 (1986):91–132. Cf. Rashbam's comment to *Pesaḥim* 119a in the preceding note; *Perush R. Shmuʾel b. Meir le-Qohelet*, ed. Sara Japhet and Robert Salters (Jerusalem, 1985), 52–53, and n. 187; Rashi's commentay to *Qohelet*, 7:24; Gila Rozen, "Perush Rashi le-Qohelet," (M.A. thesis, Bar Ilan University, 1996), 57, 111, 162; *Perush ha-Roqeaḥ ʿal ha-Megillot*, ed. Chaim Konyevsky, vol. 2 (Bnei Brak, 1984), 162; and above, n. 35. See also Eleazar Touitou, "Shitato ha-Parshanit shel Rashbam ʿal Reqa ha-Meẓiʾut ha-Historit shel Zemanno," *ʿIyyunim be-Sifrut Ḥazal, ba-Miqra, uve-Toledot Yisraʾel*, ed. Y. D. Gilat et al. (Jerusalem, 1982), 69; Moshe Greenberg, "Darkah shel Sarah Kamin ba-Meḥqar," *Ha-Miqra bi-Reʾi Mefarshav* [*Sefer Zikkaron le-Sarah Kamin*] (Jerusalem, 1994), 25 (who notes also the anti-cosmogonic tendency of R. Yosef *Bekhor Shor*, also known as the tosafist R. Joseph

attempted to explain away talmudic superstitions and folk magic.[68] Rashbam has been described and portrayed as a rationalist,[69] although it is highly doubtful that he was exposed to the study of philosophy in any form.[70]

---

of Orleans); Judah Galinsky, "Rabbenu Mosheh mi-Coucy ke-Ḥasid, Darshan u-Folmosan: Hebbetim me-ᶜOlamo ha-Maḥashavti u-Feᶜiluto ha-Ẓibburit" (M.A. thesis, Yeshiva University, 1993), 59–61; and see now Sarah Japhet, "Massoret ve-Ḥiddush be-Perush Rashbam le-Sefer Iyyov" (above, n. 31), 132*–33*. R. Ḥayyim Yosef David Azulai (Ḥida, d.1806) records a tradition in which Rashi appeared after his death to R. Samuel b. Meir in a dream and taught him the secret vocalization of the Tetragrammaton. The unusual nature of this transmission notwithstanding, a fifteenth-century manuscript source (Sassoon 290, fol. 218, sec. 299, which may have formed the basis of this tradition) contains a pasage in which this pronunciation is placed in the mouth of ר' שמואל בן קלונימוס החסיד (father of ר' יהודה החסיד), who argued with another figure associated with חסידי אשכנז, R. Meshullam of צרפת, about the proper reading of the Divine Name. It is possible that the names of the two R. Samuels became interchanged. This type of discussion would certainly have been appropriate for members of חסידי אשכנז. Cf. below, ch. 5, n. 66. It is also interesting to note once again, in this regard, that R. Samuel *he-Ḥasid* was suggested as the real author of the pietistic pseudo-Rashi commentary to Chronicles. See above, n. 41.

68 See Louis Rabinowitz, *The Social History of the Jews of Northern France in the 12th–14th Centuries* (New York, 1972), 197, 206–7; and E. E. Urbach, "Maddaᶜei ha-Yahadut—Reshamim ve-Hirhurim," *Meḥqarim be-Maddaᶜei ha-Yahadut* (Jerusalem, 1986), 17–18. Cf. Rashbam, *Bava Batra* 58, s.v. *ʾamar lehu kulhu nekhasei de-hai*; the commentary of R. Samuel Strashun of Vilna (Rashash), ad loc.; and *Bava Batra* 73b, s.v. *shamᶜin bei malka ve-qatluhu*.

69 Throughout his study cited above (n. 67), Touitou portrays Rashbam as a rationalist, very much in the spirit of the twelfth-century Renaissance. See also Touitou, "Darko shel Rashbam be-Ḥeleq ha-Halakhi shel ha-Torah," *Millet* 2 (1984):275–88; Joseph Davis, "R. Yom Tov Lipman Heller, Joseph b. Isaac ha-Levi, and Rationalism in Ashkenazic Jewish Culture, 1550–1650," 6–42; and Baron, *A Social and Religious History of the Jews*, 6:294–95. Regarding Rashbam and R. Joseph Qara as well, see Grossman, *Ḥakhmei Ẓarefat ha-Rishonim*, 261–66, 318–23, 467–80; idem, "Galut u-Geʾulah be-Mishnato shel R. Yosef Qara," *Tarbut ve-Ḥevrah be-Toledot Yisraʾel Bimei ha-Benayim*, ed. Reuven Bonfil et al. (Jerusalem, 1989), 269–301; and below, n. 86. See also Joseph Davis, "Philosophy, Dogma, and Exegesis in Medieval Ashkenazic Judaism: The Evidence of *Sefer Hadrat ha-Qodesh*," *AJS Review* 18 (1993): 213, n. 67, for the suggestion that Rashbam's insistence on *peshat* and his rejection of "metaphysics and esoteric doctrines" was perhaps at the root of some of R. Moses Taku's criticisms. [For Taku's negative attitude toward esoteric texts, see, e.g., J. Dan, "Ashkenazic Hasidism and the Maimonidean Controversy," *Maimonidean Studies* 3 (1992–93): 42–44; Y. N. Epstein, "R. Mosheh Taku ben Ḥisdai ve-Sifro Ketav Tamim," in his *Meḥqarim be-Sifrut ha-Talmud uvi-Leshonot Shemiyyot*, 1:294–302; *ᶜArugat ha-Bosem*, ed. Urbach, 4:81; Urbach, *Baᶜalei ha-Tosafot*, 1:423–24; and cf. above, ch. 1, n. 31.] An epistle from the Maimonidean controversy of the 1230s, which was written by an Ashkenazic rabbinic

Rashbam's German contemporary, R. Eliezer b. Nathan (Raban), also avoided recourse to *sod*. Raban's lack of involvement in the transmission of *sodot* and esoteric studies is evident in a number of instances. His introduction to his commentary on the prayers and *piyyutim* is strikingly similar in both style and content to that of R. Eleazar of Worms's prayer commentary. These two introductions have, in fact, been arrayed side by side and compared in contemporary scholarship.[71] This comparison serves, however, to highlight a glaring difference. While R. Eleazar of Worms expresses keen interest in elucidating *sodot ha-tefillah* and *sod ha-berakhah*, Raban makes no mention of

---

figure (who may have hailed from northern France), appears to maintain (in agreement with Rashbam) that the study of *sod*, as well as philosophy, is unnecessary. See Shatzmiller, above, ch. 2, n. 11. The polemical nature of this epistle must weigh most heavily, however, in any assessment of its intentions.

[70]On the relative absence of philosophical (and scientific) study in Ashkenaz during the high Middle Ages, see above, introduction, n. 1; David Berger, "Judaism and General Culture in Medieval and Early Modern Times," *Judaism's Encounters with Other Cultures*, ed. Jacob Schacter (Northvale, 1997), 117–22; Davis, "Philosophy, Dogma and Exegesis," 209–13; A. Grossman, *Ḥakhmei Ashkenaz ha-Rishonim*, 424; H. Soloveitchik, "Religious Law and Change: The Medieval Ashkenazic Example," *AJS Review* 12 (1987):213, n. 12; Daniel Lasker, "Jewish Philosophical Polemics in Ashkenaz," *Contra Judaeos*, ed. Ora Limor and Guy Stroumsa (Jerusalem, 1996), 195–200. Note that the Ashkenazic figures identified by Davis in 209, n. 57, as being aware of the Hebrew paraphrase of Saᶜadyah's *Emunot ve-Deᶜot* were either themselves *Ḥasidei Ashkenaz* (R. Judah *he-Ḥasid*, R. Eleazar of Worms, members of the *Ḥug ha-Keruv ha-Meyuḥad*) or tosafists who were closely associated with *ḥasidut Ashkenaz* (R. Moses of Coucy, R. Meir of Rothenburg). Cf. Moshe Idel, "Perush Mizmor Yod-Tet le R. Yosef Bekhor Shor," *Alei Sefer* 9 (1981):63–69, who suggests that Yosef Bekhor Shor was influenced, uniquely amongst the tosafists, by Baḥya Ibn Paquda's *Ḥovot ha-Levavot*; Sarah Kamin, "Ha-Polmos Neged ha-Allegoriyyah be-Divrei R. Yosef Bekhor Shor," *Meḥqerei Yerushalayim be-Maḥshevet Yisra'el* 3 (1984):367–92; Yosefa Raḥaman, "Melekhet ha-Sevarah be-Perush Bekhor Shor la-Torah," *Tarbiz* 53 (1980):615–18; and above, n. 67. Regarding science, see above in the introduction, n. 1, and below, ch. 4, n. 40.

Rashbam's approach regarding the playing down or discarding of the esoteric treatises and concepts of which he was aware (which holds true to an extent for Rabbenu Tam as well, as we shall see shortly) accords with a trend in twelfth-century Franco-German rabbinic scholarship noted by Israel Ta-Shma, "The Library of the French Sages," *Rashi, 1040–1990*, ed. Sed-Rajna, 535–40. Unlike the pre-Crusade period, in which leading scholars tried to acquire and adapt any earlier Jewish texts they could find, in an eclectic manner, tosafists restricted their libraries and were not nearly as interested in integrating earlier texts other than the Talmud and related rabbinic texts. Cf. below, n. 124.

[71]See Grossman, *Ḥakhmei Ashkenaz ha-Rishonim*, 348, and *Siddur Rabbenu Shelomoh mi-Germaiza ve-Siddur Ḥasidei Ashkenaz*, ed. Hershler, editor's introduction, 29.

these subjects at all.[72] In a methodological statement, Raban suggests that his omission of esoteric material was by design, even though he (like Rashbam) was aware of this kind of material: "I do not need to interpret and explain *ʾofannim* [liturgical poems on that portion of the *Shema* which mentions various angelic and heavenly beings], because *maʿaseh Bereshit* and *maʿaseh Merkavah* may not be explicated even in private. But I will explain the *peshat* in order that one can have a basic understanding of what he is saying."[73]

Raban records in his *siddur* the Ashkenazic custom of switching the final blessing of the Shema on Friday night from *ha-shomer ʿammo Yisraʾel la-ʿad* to *ha-pores sukkat shalom*, and he attributes this change to the protection against danger that the Sabbath affords its adherents. But only in a parallel passage from a *siddur* produced by *Ḥasidei Ashkenaz*, which appended material to the *siddur* of Raban, is a *Bahir*-like *exemplum* included, similar to those found in *Sefer ha-Pardes* and *Maḥzor Vitry.*[74]

---

[72]On the absence of *sod* in Raban's prayer and *piyyut* commentaries, see *ʿArugat ha-Bosem*, ed. E. E. Urbach, 4:24–39, 73–74. Urbach concludes his analysis of Raban's prayer and *piyyut* commentaries by stating unequivocally that הוא [ראב"ן] לא הכניס לתוכם ענייני סוד. See also Stefan Reif, "Rashi and Proto-Ashkenazi Liturgy," *Rashi, 1040–1990*, ed. Sed-Rajna, 450–52; idem, *Judaism and Hebrew Prayer* (Cambridge, 1993), 171–75; and cf. Simcha Emanuel, "Sifrei Halakhah Avudim shel Baʿalei ha-Tosafot" (Ph.D. diss., Hebrew University, 1993), 85–87. The so-called pseudo-Raban prayer commentary contains mystical material. See Chaim Levine, "Perush ʿal ha-Maḥzor ha-Meyuḥas le-Raban," *Tarbiz* 29 (1959–60):162–75; A. Y. Hershler, "Perush Siddur ha-Tefillah veha-Maḥzor Meyuḥas le-R. Eliezer b. Nathan mi-Magenẓa (ha-Raʾavan) Ketav Yad Frankfurt," *Genuzot* 3 (1991): 1–128; and cf. *ʿArugat ha-Bosem*, 4:38, n. 81.

[73]Cited in *ʿArugat ha-Bosem*, ed. Urbach, 4:29. Cf. Alexander Shapiro, "Polmos Anti-Noẓeri ba-Meʾah ha-Yod Bet," *Zion* 56 (1991):79–85, for further evidence of Raban's rationalism.

[74]See *Siddur Rabbenu Shelomoh mi-Germaiza ve-Siddur Ḥasidei Ashkenaz*, ed. Hershler, 139–40, and see esp. n. 28. On the identification of this *siddur*, which was published primarily from ms. Bodl. 794, see Grossman, *Ḥakhmei Ashkenaz ha-Rishonim*, 346–48. Various versions and pieces of Raban's commentary to the prayers, such as ms. Budapest/Kaufman A399 and Bodl. 1102, have marginal notes or even addenda attributed to, e.g., R. Judah *he-Ḥasid*, R. Eleazar of Worms, and R. Samuel Bamberg, which contain *sod* material. See *ʿArugat ha-Bosem*, ed. Urbach, above, n. 72; *Siddur Rabbenu Shelomoh mi-Germaiza*, editor's introduction, 15–30; and above, ch. 2, nn. 19–21. [Hershler, 23–24 and Urbach, 4:24, note that a piece of *perush ha-Raban* appears in ms. Parma 1033; on this manuscript, see above, n. 21.]

Moshe Hallamish ("Beʿayot be-Ḥeqer Hashpaʿat ha-Qabbalah ʿal ha-Tefillah," *Massuʾot*, ed. Oron and Goldreich, 212, n. 67), noting Grossman's identification of the main *siddur* published by Hershler as that of Raban, points to a conflict between a position of Raban in that *siddur* and a view attributed to Raban in another *siddur* in ms.

Moreover, Raban reports an interpretation by his brother Hezekiah that, according to Elliot Wolfson, was intended to vigorously deflect a mystical approach. Hezekiah writes that one bows before a Torah scroll not because of any inherent Godliness in the Torah itself, but rather because the *Shekhinah* dwells within the Holy Ark. A mystical tradition embraced and expanded upon by the German Pietists identified the Torah with the Divine glory, the *Kavod*. The Torah scroll is described as the Divine footstool. According to this tradition, one bows to the Torah because it is in fact a manifestation of the Divine. In their formulation, Hezekiah and Raban wished to offset this view.[75]

Hamburg 153. According to ms. Hamburg (cited by Urbach and reproduced by Hallamish, 214), Raban held that the word *barukh* was meant to appear thirteen times in the *Barukh she-ʾamar* prayer. (Interestingly, while R. Eleazar of Worms agreed with this number, his reasons are different and tend to be more theologically based than those offered by Raban, which are completely exoteric.) But Hallamish notes that on p. 21 of Hershler's *siddur*, the number given is ten; this casts some doubt on Grossman's identification. What Hallamish failed to notice, however, is that this material comes from a section of the *siddur* manuscript labeled by Hershler (on p. 19) as *siddur Ḥasidei Ashkenaz* (based, for the most part, on ms. Munich 393), not from the body of the larger *siddur* published by Hershler. [The number ten is primarily the view of kabbalists, including R. Judah b. Yaqar; see Hallamish, 212–13, and below, ch. 4, n. 25. On the affinity noted by Hallamish, 213, between R. Nathan b. Judah's *Sefer ha-Maḥkim* and *ḥasidut Ashkenaz*—despite R. Nathan's French origins—see my "Rabbinic Figures in Castilian Kabbalistic Pseudepigraphy," *Journal of Jewish Thought and Philosophy* 3 (1993):97, n. 73. R. Nathan cites a rite from *Maʿaseh Merkavah*; see above, n. 37.]

[75]See Elliot Wolfson, "The Mystical Significance of Torah-Study in German Pietism," *JQR* 84 (1993):71–73, and idem, *Through a Speculum That Shines*, 248–50. As Wolfson notes, R. Eleazar of Worms cites this formulation in the body of his halakhic work, *Sefer Roqeaḥ*, despite the fact that both he and R. Judah he-Ḥasid espoused the more mystical view in esoteric and pietistic texts. See also *Sefer Raban, massekhet Berakhot*, sec. 127. R. Ḥananʾel interpreted the talmudic passage (*Berakhot* 6a) that the Almighty dons *tefillin* to mean not that God has a visible body which can be seen, but that certain human beings may perceive Him through *reʾiyat ha-lev*—loosely translated as imagination. Cf. Wolfson, *Through a Speculum That Shines*, 147–48; *Sefer Gematriʾot le-R. Yehudah he-Ḥasid*, introduction, 10–11; and below, ch. 4, n. 2. Thus when the Torah states that Moses saw God's back, it refers to this process of *reʾiyat ha-lev*. Similarly, when R. Yishmael *Kohen Gadol* in the Holy of Holies saw Akatriʾel seated *ʿal kisse ram ve-nissa* (*Berakhot* 7a), it was through the powers of *reʾiyat ha-lev*. When R. Isaac b. Moses *Or Zaruaʿ*, a student of *Ḥasidei Ashkenaz*, cites R. Ḥananʾel (*Sefer Or Zaruaʿ, hilkhot qeriʾat shema*, secs. 7–8), he adds that R. Ḥananʾel, in offering the interpretation involving *reʾiyat ha-lev*, supports the interpretation that Akatriʾel was not merely an angel but a manifestation of the Divine *Kavod* (which could not be physically seen by man), a notion associated with *Ḥasidei Ashkenaz*. This is also included by R. Judah b. Qalonymus of Spires, an associate of R. Judah *he-Ḥasid* (see above, ch. 1,

Raban is referred to in a late medieval *Maʿaseh Bukh* as a *baʿal Shem*, capable of effecting miraculous acts such as *qefiẓat ha-derekh*.[76] This later perception may have been predicated on an incident in which Raban reversed one of his halakhic rulings. He initially permitted wine that had come into contact with a particular utensil that had been used for libation wine (*yayn nesekh*). After issuing this ruling, Raban went to sleep and dreamed that his teacher (and father-in-law) was reading a verse that Raban then interpreted, in the dream, as referring to those who drink *yayn nesekh* and eat pork. When Raban awoke, he understood from this dream that he had incorrectly permitted the wine. Raban then reviewed a key factor in his lenient ruling and discovered, after a time, that his main assumption had been incorrect. At that point, both he and those who drank the wine, at his instruction, fasted for two days.[77]

Two related experiences help to put Raban's dream in perspective. R. Ephraim of Regensburg, a contemporary of Raban, ate a fish called *barbuta*, believing it to be from a kosher species. That night an elderly man with flowing hair and a lengthy beard appeared to him in a dream with a plate full of insects (*sheraẓim*), bidding R. Ephraim to eat them. When R. Ephraim protested, the old man suggested that these *sheraẓim* "are as permitted as those that you ate today." When R. Ephraim awoke, he knew that Elijah (*Eliyyahu zakhur la-tov*) had appeared to him, and from then on he refrained from eating that fish.[78] As

---

n. 76) in his *Sefer Yiḥusei Tannaim va-Amoraim*, from which *Sefer Or Zaruaʿ* may have received its material; see Urbach, *Baʿalei ha-Tosafot*, 1:376–77; and below, ch. 4, n. 51, and ch. 5, n. 7. Raban, however, cites from R. Ḥananʾel only the concept of *reʾiyat ha-lev*, making no mention of the notion of the *Kavod*. [Cf. above, ch. 2, nn. 81–82. Raban offered a rationalistic approach to various *harḥaqot* for a menstruant that were proposed in the *Baraita de-Massekhet Niddah*, which contributed to a lessening of these stringencies, a goal shared by Rabbenu Tam. On the other hand, the thirteenth-century tosafist R. Isaac Or Zaruaʿ, following the lead of *Ḥasidei Ashkenaz*, continued to stress the more esoteric or magical nature of these stringencies, as a means of protection from danger.]

[76]See A. J. Heschel, "Al Ruaḥ ha-Qodesh Bimei ha-Beinayim," 196, and Sara Zfatman, *Bein Ashkenaz li-Sefarad: Le-Toledot ha-Sippur ha-Yehudi Bimei ha-Benayim* (Jerusalem, 1993), 82, n. 7, 105.

[77]See *Sefer Raban*, sec. 26. The event is described as having occurred in 1152. Cf. R. Hayyim David Joseph Azulai, *Shem ha-Gedolim* (Warsaw, 1876), Maʿarekhet ha-Gedolim, 26, sec. 199. Ḥida adduces talmudic examples of Tannaim and Amoraim who, like Raban and others, had dreams that had an impact on their halakhic decisions. See also *Shem ha-Gedolim*, 62–64, sec. 224.

[78]*Sefer Tashbeẓ*, sec. 252. According to this text, the story of R. Ephraim's dream was related by R. Barukh (of Worms, author of *Sefer ha-Terumah*?). But according to *Sefer Or Zaruaʿ*, pisqei *ʿAvodah Zarah*, sec. 200 (and see also *Semaq mi-Ẓurikh*, ed. Y. Y.

opposed to R. Ephraim, whose dream was, in any case, more pointed, Raban never claimed a *gillui Eliyyahu*. As we shall see, there were other tosafists who also rendered or changed halakhic decisions because they claimed to have seen Elijah in a dream. Moreover, upon awakening, Raban proceeded to "verify" the instruction in his dream by reviewing his ruling, while R. Ephraim (and the others) did not.[79]

R. Uri b. R. Joel *ha-Levi*, a grandson of Raban, was burned to death as a martyr in 1216. R. Mordekhai b. Eliezer composed a *seliḥah* to commemorate R. Uri. A manuscript that records the *seliḥah* indicates that R. Uri himself was its author. He transmitted the text of the *seliḥah* to R. Mordekhai in a dream, along with the liturgical tune (*niggun*) to which it should be chanted.[80] The nature of the communication during this dream, which is reminiscent of a dream that R. Simeon *ha-Gadol* had,[81] further suggests that Raban's dream was not primarily a mystical experience. Although Raban's dream testifies to his deep spirituality, it entails neither magical techniques nor mystical perspectives.[82]

Har-Shoshanim, vol. 2 [Jerusalem, 1977], 293, n. 135), it was R. Judah *he-Ḥasid* who initially recounted the dream of R. Ephraim of Regensburg, suggesting some relationship between R. Ephraim and *Ḥasidei Ashkenaz*. Cf. Urbach, *Ba*ʿ*alei ha-Tosafot*, 1:204; and Tamar Alexander, "Rabbi Judah the Pious as a Legendary Figure," *Mysticism, Magic and Kabbalah in Ashkenazi Hasidism*, 135–36. Similar regimens of *tiqqunei teshuvah* for a penitent murderer were prescribed by R. Judah *he-Ḥasid* and R. Ephraim of Regensburg. See ms. Parma 1237, fol. 36v. See also above, ch. 2, n. 40. In discusssing the reliability of dreams in halakhic contexts, R. Samuel, the son of R. Ezekiel Landau, raises the issue of verification; see *Noda Bi-Yehudah, Yoreh De*ʿ*ah (mahadura tinyana)*, #30. In R. Samuel's view, R. Ephraim's piety caused him to prohibit the *barbuta* because of his dream, despite the fact that Rabbenu Tam and other tosafists (who were not granted a dream by the "*ba*ʿ*al ha-ḥalom*") permitted this fish because they believed it had scales. See also R. Samuel's *Shivat Zion*, #52.

[79]See below, ch. 4, n. 59 (Rabiah), and ch. 5, n. 20 (R. Isaiah di Trani). Cf. *SḤP* 386, and below, ch. 4, n. 3, regarding *halakhah* and prophecy.

[80]See ms. Bodl. 1155 (Ashkenaz, fourteenth century), fol. 171v: סליחה זו עשאה בחזיון ליל אורי החסיד בן ר׳ יואל הלוי בניגון תוחלת ישראל; and the text cited by Aptowitzer, *Mavo la-Rabiah*, 67: סליחה יסד החסיד החבר ר׳ אורי בן רבינו יואל הלוי. אחר אשר נפגע בו ונהרג ונשרף... וצוה להעתיקה לר׳ מרדכי בן אליעזר בחלומו, כי רמז בה שמו, וצוה לו להתפלל אותה בניגון תוחלת ישראל. Cf. ms. Moscow 348, fol. 246v.

[81]See above, n. 3; and cf. *Sefer Yere*ʾ*im*, secs. 334–35 (below, ch. 4, n. 19).

[82]Cf. Urbach, *Ba*ʿ*alei ha-Tosafot*, 1:180; *She*ʾ*elot u-Teshuvot min ha-Shamayim*, editor's introduction, 6–7; R. J. Z. Werblowsky, *Joseph Karo: Lawyer and Mystic* (Philadelphia, 1977), 41–43; *Sefer Raban*, pt. 2, *Massekhet Yoma*, end; above, ch. 1, n. 126; and Judah Galinsky, "R. Moshe mi-Coucy veha-Polmos ha-Yehudi-Noẓeri ba-Me'ah ha-Yod Gimmel" (forthcoming), n. 64.

In light of the shifting attitudes toward *torat ha-sod* in medieval Ashkenaz during the first half of the twelfth century, it is helpful to consider briefly the changing status of magic in medieval Christian society. In the early part of the Middle Ages, magic was considered a practical science or skill. From the mid-eleventh century through the mid-thirteenth century, however, magic was denigrated generally, and associated with heretics and Jews. Secret knowledge was feared, and penances were prescribed for those who resorted to the use of magic.[83] But these penances were directed only at those who invoked demons or prescribed charms and amulets. According to John of Salisbury (d.1180) and other contemporary masters, the manipulation of demonic powers (black magic) was to be eschewed. Other magical arts, such as divination—which relied on natural objects or the initiation of quasi-prophetic or dream-like states—were still considered acceptable.[84] In Christian Europe also, the twelfth century witnessed a move away from the supernatural and toward the rational, which further limited the role that magic could play.[85]

IV

Rabbenu Tam, the greatest of the early tosafists, has been characterized as a rationalist.[86] Like Rashbam, Rabbenu Tam interpreted talmudic passages in ways that eliminated the roles of superstition and *shedim*, which had been left

---

[83]See Edward Peters, *The Magician, the Witch and the Law* (Philadelphia, 1978), 47, 56, 66–67, 70–80, 160–61.

[84]Benedicta Ward, *Miracles and the Medieval Mind* (Philadelphia, 1989^2), 10–13; Valerie Flint, *The Rise of Magic in Early Medieval Europe* (Princeton, 1991), 6–7, 29–35, 66–68, 87–92, 146–57; and Lynn Thorndike, *A History of Magic and Experimental Science*, 2:7–8 (Peter Abelard), 13–15 (Hugh of St. Victor), 137–54 (Hildegard of Bingen), 155–70 (John of Salisbury), 341–60 (William of Auvergne).

[85]See, e.g., Peter Brown, "Society and the Supernatural: A Medieval Change," *Daedalus* 104 (1975):133–51; John Baldwin, "The Intellectual Preparation for the Canon of 1215 Against Ordeals," *Speculum* 36 (1961):611–36; C. M. Radding, "Superstition to Science: Nature, Fortune, and the Passing of the Medieval Ordeal," *American Historical Review* 84 (1978):945–69; Gabor Klaniczay, *The Uses of Supernatural Power* (Princeton, 1990), 45–50; Richard Kieckhefer, *Magic in the Middle Ages*, 176–201; Jonathan Elukin, "The Ordeal of Scripture," *Exemplaria* 5.1 (1993):135–60. Note, however, that rationalism wanes, and is supplanted, once again, by more popular beliefs, from the mid-thirteenth century through the fifteenth-century. See, e.g., David Knowles, *The Evolution of Medieval Thought* (London, 1962), 311–17; Shulamit Shahar, *The Fourth Estate* (London, 1983), 268–80; and E. Peters, *The Magician*, 89, 110-37.

[86]See, e.g., Urbach, *Ba^calei ha-Tosafot*, 1:70–71, 88–93; Grossman, *Ḥakhmei Ashkenaz ha-Rishonim*, 94–95; idem, "Ẓemiḥat Parshanut ha-Piyyut," *Studies in Honor of Shlomo Simonshohn*, ed. Daniel Carpi et al. (Tel Aviv, 1993), 69; idem, "Shorashev shel

intact by Rashi and other predecessors.[87] Moreover, Rabbenu Tam was unswervingly talmudocentric. He was not even inclined, as Rashbam was, toward the study and interpretation of Scripture as a distinct discipline.[88]

Qiddush ha-Shem be-Ashkenaz ha-Qedumah," *Qedushat ha-Ḥayyim ve-Ḥeruf ha-Nefesh*, ed. I. Gafni and A. Ravitzky (Jerusalem, 1993), 108–9, n. 22; and cf. R. Jacob Ibn Ḥaviv, *ᶜEin Yaᶜaqov* to *Shabbat* 119a, s.v. *Katvu ba-Tosafot*: כוונת ר"ת לקרב אל השכל; and Rami Reiner, "Le-Ofi Tiᶜuneihem ve-Taᶜanoteihem shel Rabbenu Tam ve-Rabbenu Meshullam," *Shenaton ha-Mishpat ha-ᶜIvri* (forthcoming). On Rabbenu Tam's mathematical prowess, see ms. Paris BN 633, fol. 250v, and Colette Sirat, "Un Rituel Juif de France: Le Manuscrit Hébreu 633 de la Bibliothèque Nationale de Paris," *REJ* 119 (1961):22. [On applied mathematics by tosafists and possible contemporary Christian influence, see Martin Stern, "A Mathematical Tosafot—A Case of Cross-Cultural Contact," *Niv ha-Midrashia* 22–23 (1990):37–41. Cf. below, ch. 4, n. 2; and see my *Jewish Education and Society*, 69–73; Grossman, *Ḥakhmei Ẓarefat ha-Rishonim*, 21–24, 453–56; and Ta-Shma, *Halakhah, Minhag u-Meẓiᵓut be-Ashkenaz*, 28–35, regarding Christian dialectic and its possible influence on the tosafists.]

87See, e.g., Rashi, *Menaḥot* 32b, s.v. *sakkanah; Tosafot Menaḥot* 32b, s.v. *sakkanah*; and R. Yeroḥam b. Meshullam, *Toledot Adam ve-Ḥavvah* (Venice, 1553), sec. 21, pt. 7 (fol. 179c). As opposed to Rashi, who interpreted the talmudic dictum that a misplaced *mezuzah* was harmful because it could not serve to eliminate *shedim*, Rabbenu Tam saw the potential harm merely as the risk of injury if one bumped into the *mezuzah* because of its poor placement. Cf. *Teshuvot R. Meir mi-Rothenburg* (Cremona, 1557), #108, and Daniel Sperber, *Minhagei Yisraᵓel*, vol. 1 (Jerusalem, 1989), 46–56. As compared to Rashi (above, n. 45), Rabbenu Tam cites *Otiyyot de-R. Aqiva* in purely halakhic contexts (i.e., only as a source for the technical writing of *sifrei Torah*), as does Rabiah, with no concern for its mystical implications. See Israel Ta-Shma, "Qavvim le-Ofiyyah shel Sifrut ha-Halakhah be-Ashkenaz ba-Meᵓah ha-Yod Gimmel/ha-Yod Daled," *ᶜAlei Sefer* 4 (1977):26–27; Rabbenu Tam's *Hilkhot* [*Tiqqun*] *Sefer Torah* in *Ginzei Yerushalayim*, ed. S. A. Wertheimer, vol. 1 (Jerusalem, 1896), 97–99; *Sefer Rabiah*, ed. D. Deblitzky (Bnei Brak, 1976), 220 (sec. 1149); *Sefer ha-Manhig*, ed. Raphael, 2:587, 620; R. Samson b. Eliezer, *Barukh Sheᵓamar*, ed. M. M. Meshi-Zahav (Jerusalem, 1970), 74 (sec. 41), 101. Cf. *Tosafot R. Elḥanan* to *ᶜAvodah Zarah* 28b, s.v. *shoryeinei de-ᶜeina*, and above, ch. 2, n. 67. [Note also the differences between Rabbenu Tam and R. Judah *he-Ḥasid* in defining the thirteen Divine attributes. See, e.g., *Tosafot Rosh ha-Shanah* 17b, s.v. *ve-shalosh*, and *SHP*, secs. 414–15; *Sefer ha-Manhig*, 1:277–78; J. Gellis, *Tosafot ha-Shalem*, vol. 10 (1969):124–35; and S. E. Stern, "Perush Yod Gimmel Middot le-Rabbenu Tam," *Yeshurun* 3 (1997):3–4. Cf. Ibn Ezra to Exodus 34:6; Moses Zucker ed., *A Critique Against the Writings of R. Saᶜadya Gaon* by R. Mevaser b. Nissi *Ha-Levi* (New York, 1955),118; and my "Rabbinic Figures in Castilian Kabbalistic Pseudepigraphy," 93, n. 57, 95, n. 67, regarding R. Isaac of Corbeil.]

88See, e.g., my "On the Role of Bible Study in Medieval Ashkenaz," *The Frank Talmage Memorial Volume*, ed. Walfish, 1:151–66. Even Rabbenu Tam's interest in *piyyut* was partially motivated by his interest in *halakhah*. See Urbach, *Baᶜalei ha-Tosafot*, 1:107–10. Grossman, "Perush ha-Piyyutim le-R. Aharon b. R. Ḥayyim ha-Kohen,"

There are only a handful of passages in Rabbenu Tam's substantial corpus which, as far as I can determine, reflect mystical considerations, but their implications must be considered carefully. *Tosafot Ḥagigah* cites Rabbenu Tam as defining *Maᶜaseh Bereshit* as the Divine Name of forty-two letters that can be derived from the first two verses of the Torah and that played a role in Creation. As we have noted, however, there were extant Ashkenazic traditions about Divine Names (and mystical speculation) that Rashbam had mentioned. Moreover, this particular tradition (which had apparently not yet reached Ashkenaz by Rashi's day, but was later expanded upon by both R. Eleazar of Worms and the Zohar) was also cited in the name of R. Hai Gaon.[89] In two of the places where *sod* or magic is involved, Rabbenu Tam cites the material as having been transmitted by his father, R. Meir, in the name of *Ḥakhmei/Geonei Lothaire* of the pre-Crusade period. Rabbenu Tam makes no attempt to explain or analyse these instances; he simply accepts them as earlier traditions or perceptions to be upheld as a matter of custom or respect.

In the first instance, Rabbenu Tam endorses the notion that one should not eat after sunset on the Sabbath because of the danger from *shedim/maziqim* that had befallen those who did. As we shall see, this was not merely an issue of popular belief or superstition; it was related to mystical concepts.[90] Rabbenu Tam also reported an earlier tradition, in the context of a statement on the importance of reciting *piyyutim*, which described how R. Eleazar *ha-Qallir* appeared when he composed *piyyut(im)* that referred to the angels who surrounded the *kisse* or *merkavah*. According to this tradition, a fire lit up and burned around him (ליהטה אש סביביו). It was in this context as well

---

Be-Oraḥ Madda [*Sefer Yovel le-Aharon Mirsky*], ed. Zvi Malachi (Lod, 1986), 453, explains the sustained involvement of talmudocentric, rationalistic tosafists such as Rabbenu Tam in *piyyut* as a function of the sheer importance of this discipline in the hierarchy of the Ashkenazic tradition. Cf. Haym Soloveitchik, "Three Themes in the *Sefer Ḥasidim*," *AJS Review* 1 (1976):345, 352, n. 131, and Zvi Malachi, "Rashi and his Disciples in Relation to the Old Paytanim," *Rashi, 1040–1990*, ed. Sed-Rajna, 455–62. [On Rabbenu Tam and R. Eliezer *ha-Gadol* concerning the order of the Torah portions in the *tefillin shel rosh*, see Grossman, *Ḥakhmei Ashkenaz ha-Rishonim*, 227.]

[89] See *Tosafot Ḥagigah* 11b, s.v. *ᵓein dorshin*; Elliot Wolfson, "Letter Symbolism and Merkavah Imagery in the Zohar," *Alei Shefer: Studies in the Literature of Jewish Thought*, ed. Moshe Hallamish (Ramat Gan, 1990), 217*–218*; and cf. ms. Bodl. 2344, fol. 3r; and above, n. 28.

[90] See Ta-Shma, *Minhag Ashkenaz ha-Qadmon*, 102, 203–13. Cf. *Teshuvot Baᶜalei ha-Tosafot*, ed. I. A. Agus (New York, 1954), 56; *Shibbolei ha-Leqet*, sec. 130; ms. Bodl. 659, fol. 35; and below, ch. 4, n. 34, regarding R. Menaḥem of Joigny, who was much more active in analyzing and applying this precaution, and in arguing his own interpretations.

that Rabbenu Tam characterized R. Simeon b. Isaac *ha-Gadol* as *melummad be-nisim*.[91]

In another formulation, Rabbenu Tam offered a position on the name Metatron, usually associated with the highest angel (*Sar ha-Panim*). According to Rabbenu Tam, "the Holy One blessed be He is Himself called Metatron."[92] Some Pietist authors similarly identified Metatron with *Shekhinah*, the Divine Presence. Although R. Moses b. Eleazar *ha-Darshan*, a grandson of R. Judah *he-Ḥasid*, was against identifying the angelic Metatron with the Divine Presence, he allowed the name Metatron to be attributed to *Shekhinah*. "This [identification] is not a mistake. This is another secret that is explained in the name of Rabbenu Tam (*sod she-meforash be-shem Rabbenu Tam*)."[93]

Although R. Moses viewed this formulation of Rabbenu Tam as a *sod*, it is far from certain that Rabbenu Tam did. The last part of R. Moses b. Eleazar's statement may mean that this identification was a secret from the perspective of someone familiar with *sod*, which Rabbenu Tam expressed openly or unwittingly. Indeed, it was suggested by Rabbenu Tam to solve a problem of exoteric scriptural exegesis. Following an older rabbinic view, Rashi identified the angel in Exodus 23:20—sent by God to "guard the way" of the Jewish people following the sin of the golden calf—as Metatron. Rashi arrived at this interpretation by means of a *gematria* approach. Some had questioned this conclusion, since the *gematria* that Rashi used could be wielded differently.

---

[91]See above, n. 9, and cf. Rami Reiner, "Rabbenu Tam: Rabbotav (ha-Ẓarefatim) ve-Talmidav Benei Ashkenaz" (M.A. thesis, Hebrew University, 1997), 15–21, 45. See also R. Moses Taku's *Ketav Tamim* in *Oẓar Neḥmad* 4 [1863], 85 [=Joseph Dan's transcription of ms. Paris H711 (Mercaz Dinur, Jerusalem, 1984), fol. 34v], in which R. Eleazar *ha-Qallir* is described as a *malʾakh E-lohim*; Fleischer, above, n. 20; and cf. *Va-Yiqra Rabbah*, 16:4, and Ruth Langer, "Kalir Was a Tanna," *HUCA* 67 (1996):95–106.

[92]*Moshav Zeqenim ʿal ha-Torah*, ed. S. D. Sassoon (London, 1959), 198. See Daniel Abrams, "The Boundaries of Divine Ontology: The Inclusion and Exclusion of Metatron in the Godhead," *Harvard Theological Review* 87 (1994):299–300.

[93]The text is cited in Wolfson, *Through a Speculum That Shines*, 260, with manuscript references given in n. 306. (On this text and its milieu, see also ms. Berlin Or. Qu. 942, fol. 127r; Scholem, *Reshit ha-Qabbalah*, 195–205; and Dan, *Torat ha-Sod shel Ḥasidut Ashkenaz*, 255–58.) This text also intimates that the "secret" attributed to Rabbenu Tam is found, with other names of Metatron, in a book by R. Neḥemyah [b. Solomon], another follower of the German Pietists in the late thirteenth-century. E. E. Urbach, "Sefer ʿArugat ha-Bosem le-R. Avraham b. Azriel," *Tarbiz* 10 (1939):50–51, suggests that this R. Neḥemyah was the son of R. Solomon b. Samuel, himself a student of the German Pietists; see above, ch. 2, at n. 9. Cf. *ʿArugat ha-Bosem*, ed. Urbach, 4:119, and Wolfson, 231–32, n. 177. [A R. Neḥemyah describes *teʿamim* of *Gog* and *Magog* in ms. Parma 541, fol. 266v; see above, nn. 13–14, and below, ch. 4, n. 32; ch. 5, n. 67.]

At this point, Rabbenu Tam stepped in and confirmed the role of Metatron in this verse, citing a passage in *Pesiqta* in which the Almighty characterizes Himself as the guard (*manitor/shomer*) of the Jewish people. The net effect of Rabbenu Tama's interpretation is to identify Metatron with God (with the help of the *Pesiqta*), but this came about in the course of establishing a biblical interpretation. Indeed, a *Tosafot* passage cites R. Tam's resolution of contradictory talmudic and *piyyut* texts that seem to identify Metatron as both *Sar ha-ᶜOlam* and *Ḥanokh*, two different angels who cannot be the same. Rabbenu Tam did not question the angelic nature of Metatron and made no mention of God. Moreover, in this instance as well, R. Tam offered his resolution regarding the names of Metatron with a passage from the *Midrash Pesiqta*.[94] Rabbenu Tam was interested in clarifying the role of Metatron (and other heavenly figures) on the basis of rabbinic (rather than esoteric) texts. One of the positions he formulated in this endeavor may have been helpful to *baᶜalei sod*, but it cannot be demonstrated from this instance that he was a *baᶜal sod* himself.

Caution must also be exercised with regard to several other passages that mention Rabbenu Tam's name in connection with esoteric phenomena and techniques. In three such texts, Rabbenu Tam is paired with another contemporary scholar who had perceived affinities with secret lore—a detail that confirms the inherently pseudepigraphic nature of these passages. Moreover, the mystical techniques are done in Rabbenu Tam's presence or with respect to his teachings. They are never performed by Rabbenu Tam himself. In one passage, Rabbenu Tam is joined with R. Elijah of Paris, who was known for his deep piety and for his mystical traditions concerning the end of days.[95] In response to a request from a father who had been unable to

---

[94]See *Tosafot Yevamot* 16b, s.v. *pasuq zeh*; and see also the parallel *Tosafot Ḥullin* 60a, s.v. *pasuq zeh*, and the variant in *Tosafot Yeshanim ha-Shalem ᶜal Massekhet Yevamot*, ed. Abraham Shoshana (Jerusalem, 1994), ad loc. Cf. Margoliot, *Malʾakhei ᶜElyon*, 79–80, nn. 13–14; and *Tosafot ha-Shalem*, ed. Gellis, 8:343 (sec. 11), 346–47 (secs. 9, 11).

[95]These traditions, which lend credence to R. Elijah's reputation as a *baᶜal sod*, were recorded by his grandson, R. Jacob of Provins (a student of Rabbenu Tam), who was associated with other esoteric teachings. See *Teshuvot u-Fesaqim*, ed. Efraim Kupfer (Jerusalem, 1973), 309–12, and below, n. 98, and ch. 4, n. 37. On the piety of R. Elijah, see Urbach, *Baᶜalei ha-Tosafot*, 1:76, 79, 122; and see above, ch. 1, n. 66. R. Elijah (b. Judah) of Paris is sometimes confused with another northern French pietist from the first half of the eleventh century, R. Elijah b. Menaḥem of Le Mans; see above, ch. 1, n. 24. See also Avraham Grossman, "Ha-ᶜAliyyah la-Regel shel R. Eliyyahu b. Menaḥem," *Tarbiz* 56 (1987):273–278, and idem, *Ḥakhmei Ẓarefat ha-Rishonim*, 86–87, 98, 104–5.

attend the burial of his murdered son, Rabbenu Tam and R. Elijah supposedly permitted the use of a Divine Name in order to resurrect (the image of) the son.[96]

According to a text of the *Ḥug ha-Keruv ha-Meyuḥad*, a mystical circle that flourished in northern France and England and was associated with the German Pietists, Avraham Ibn Ezra created a *golem* in the presence of Rabbenu

---

[96]Vienna 152 [Hebr. 47] (Italy, fifteenth/sixteenth centuries), fols. 1v–2r (following a section entitled פירוש לשם המפורש):

> אמר ר׳ יצחק מעשה ונהרג אליהו בן הרב ר׳ תודרוס מעיר קרנות כבן עשרים שנה ונהרג בתוך העיר. ונקבר ואביו לא היה בעיר ובשובו לא רצה לאכול ולשתות עד שיתירו לו גדולי הדור רבינו יעקב ברמרו ורבינו אליהו בפריש להעלות לפניו בנו בשם המפורש. ויוציא לו כל הקהל... ויצתה ונשלח להם שיתירו לו וכן עשו והתירו לו. ורחץ וטבל ולבש לבנים והתענו כל הקהל ביום ה׳ והלכו כולם לבית הכנסת והכניסה ה׳ [השם] בין הספרים והשביע נפש ונראה בין הספרים ולקח בנו להורידו מן הארון לעיני כל הקהל ודבר לו כרצונו לעיניהם ואח״כ החזירו בארון. וזה ספר לנו הרב להורות סדר המעשה. [2א- והילך תפלת אליהו זכרונו לטובה בשם ה׳ אלקי ישראל... ובסוף: ואשמרה עדותיך נגד מלכים ולא אבוש. בא״ה שומע תפלה.]

This passage is part of a small treatise, several pages long, on the use of *Shemot* for *hashbaʿot*. See A. Z. Schwarz, *Die Hebräischen Handschriften der Nationalbibliothek in Wien* (Leipzig, 1925), 161–63. The Divine Names that appear prior to this text and were the ones used in this story represent, by implication, a tradition shared by *Sefer ha-Bahir* and the German Pietists. See Scholem, *Reshit ha-Qabbalah*, 38–39, n. 2, and idem, *Origins of the Kabbalah* (Princeton, 1987), 100–102. Urbach, *Baʿalei ha-Tosafot*, 1:123, considers this story "characteristic of the Jewish experience in northern France," although he includes it in his discussion of R. Elijah of Paris rather than Rabbenu Tam. [Once again, it should be noted that the preparations for using the *Shem* in this passage are very similar to what is prescribed in *Hekhalot* literature; cf. above, n. 8. For magical techniques attributed to a ר׳ טודרוס מאשכנז, see ms. Vat. 244 (Spain, fourteenth century), fols. 2v, 28r; and cf. Henri Gross in *MGWJ* 49 (1905): 695, n. 3.] On locating a corpse through magical means, see also *Sefer ha-Yashar le-Rabbenu Tam* (*ḥeleq ha-teshuvot*), ed. Shraga Rosenthal (Berlin, 1898), 191: אבל בטביעת עין מעשים בכל יום אפילו לאחר שנים עשר חדש מת ניכר. והרב הקדוש ר׳ שמשון כשהגיד בעל החלום לאחר חצי שנה ניכר כאלו הוא חי. Cf. *Sefer Or Zaruaʿ*, *Hilkhot ʿAgunah*, pt. 1, sec. 692 (fol. 97c). R. Samson of Falaise, brother-in-law of Rabbenu Tam and the grandfather of Riẓba and R. Samson of Sens, was martyred. As Urbach (1:119) interprets this passage, his body was found or handed over six months later, through the efforts of a *baʿal ha-ḥalom* (who initiated or interpreted a dream). See also Aptowitzer, *Mavo la-Rabiah*, 420. At that point, the body could still be identified through distinguishing signs or features (*teviʿat ʿayin*). Here, too, Rabbenu tam was not the initiator of any magical processes, nor was he necessarily involved in them. Cf. Heschel, "Al Ruaḥ ha-Qodesh Bimei ha-Benayim," 182, n. 37 (end).

Tam. The figure of Ibn Ezra was often co-opted by medieval Jewish mystics, including the German Pietists, just as Ibn Ezra was himself the subject of legends and tales involving *torat ha-sod* practices.[97] In the third instance—which appears in the sixteenth-century *Shalshelet ha-Qabbalah* and is characterized by Urbach as a popular legend—*Mosheh Rabbenu* was summoned by adjuration to decide if Rabbenu Tam or R. Elijah of Paris was correct in their argument about whether the *qesher shel tefillin (shel yad)* must be tied anew each day.[98]

The final case is perhaps the most instructive. Several non-Ashkenazic manuscripts contain a *tefillah* or *baqqashah* (which begins with a form of the phrase אנא ה׳ אלקי ישראל שליט בעליונים ובתחתונים) that is attributed at the outset to Rabbenu Tam. The earliest of these is an Italian manuscript dated 1286. The prayer begins with standard requests for salvation from various types of afflictions and other forces that may seek to harm a person. But it then moves to a series of adjurations (*hashbaᶜot*), which adjure both Divine and angelic names not only for purposes of protection, but also to acquire and retain Torah knowledge, to receive forgiveness from the Almighty, and to achieve long-lasting success in temporal and spiritual mattes. Two of the adjurations or requests involve Metatron. There are also statements—attributed

---

[97]See Idel, *Golem*, 81–82, 86–87, 92–93, nn. 4, 11, and see also the revised Hebrew edition of *Golem* (Jerusalem, 1996), 276–77. The *Ḥug ha-Keruv ha-Meyuḥad* produced a number of pseudepigraphic treatises in addition to the Pseudo-Saᶜadyah commentary in which this passage is found. See Yosef Dan, "Ḥug ha-Keruv ha-Meyuḥad bi-Tenuᶜat Ḥasidei Ashkenaz," *Tarbiz* 35 (1966):349–72. Note that Ibn Ezra praised Rabbenu Tam as a *malᵓakh ha-E-lohim* (See Heschel, "Al Ruaḥ ha-Qodesh Bimei ha-Benayim," 182, n. 34), and there was certainly literary contact between them (Urbach, 1:109–10). On Ibn Ezra in the thought of *ḥasidut Ashkenaz*, see, e.g., Yosef Dan, *Torat ha-Sod shel Ḥasidut Ashkenaz* (Jerusalem, 1968), 29–31, 113–16, 138–43, and Wolfson, *Through a Speculum That Shines*, 177, 193, 215, 222, 246–47. For legends about Ibn Ezra, see, e.g., Naftali ben Menaḥem, *Avraham Ibn Ezra—Siḥot va-Aggadot ᶜAm* (Jerusalem, 1943), and idem, *ᶜInyanei Ibn Ezra* (Jerusalem, 1978), 337–73.

[98]See Urbach, *Baᶜalei ha-Tosafot*, 1:88; Norman Golb, *Toledot ha-Yehudim be-ᶜIr Rouen Bimei ha-Benayim* (Jerusalem, 1976), 98–100; and cf. Eli Yasif, "Rashi Legends and Medieval Popular Culture," *Rashi, 1040–1990*, ed. Sed-Rajna, 483–92; ms. Moscow-Guenzberg 926 (Lisbon, 1474), fol. 174r (cited in Grossman, *Ḥakhmei Ẓarefat ha-Rishonim*, 142); and above, introduction, n. 21. According to this text, the request to summon Moses was made to R. Samuel *ha-navi/navi ᵓemet* (=R. Samuel *he-Ḥasid*?; cf., e.g., Heschel, "Al Ruaḥ ha-Qodesh Bimei ha-Benayim," 181, and Wolfson, *Through a Speculum That Shines*, 191) by R. Jacob of Provins. [Note also the late variant, ms. JTS Lutski 1062 (*Mizraḥ*, seventeenth/eighteenth century), fols. 26v–27r, which substitutes R. Yeḥiᵓel of Paris for R. Elijah of Paris.]

to R. Yishma'el and R. Aqiva on the salutary effects of studying (and utilizing) these esoteric procedures—that are paraphrases of material in *Hekhalot* literature.[99]

---

[99]Ms. Parma 1390, fols. 15r–16r. In this manuscript, the prayer is introduced by a note indicating that it is efficacious for someone who becomes suddenly mute, or perhaps unable to pray (תפלה למי שיאלם לשונו פתאום). It is also entitled (as in other manuscripts) *tefillah nora'ah le-R. Yishma'el*:

> אנא ה׳ אלקי ישראל מושל בעליונים ושולט בתחתונים... שמע נא את תפלת עבדך כי עני ואביון אני והשלך אימה ופחד... ועורון ושגעון וזיק ומזיק וכל שיקומו עלי לרעה... ידמו כאבן... ואני לא אבוש. בבקשה מכם מלאכי השרת מטטרון מיכאל וגבריאל מיכאל וסוריל שתעמידו בבקשה לפני הקב״ה לשמוע תפלתי ובקשתי... למחול ולסלוח לכל עוונותי... משביע אני עליכם בשם אכתריאל יושב תהלות ישראל בשם שבעים שמותיו הקדושים המפורשים בנקיות ובטהרה שתקחו המפתחות ותפתחו השערים ברשות מלך מלכי המלכים... לדעת בינה והשכל פרישות נקיות רוח והצלה והצלחה ארוכה כשמש בתקופה והלבנה בחצי החדש זו בדבר וזו בבקשה בכל מקום שאני הולך... ומאמריי יהיו מתוקים כדבש ונופת צופים אמן אמן סלה. משביע אני עליך אהבאל הממונה על האהבה ובכך חיבה לבקש לפני הקב״ה לחן ולחסד ולרחמים... ומחילה וסליחה לכפר... אמר ישמעאל מי ששונה הרז הגדול הזה פניו מצהיבות וקומתו נאה לו ואימתו עליו שאינו שוכח דברי תורה כל ימיו ויצר הרע אינו שולט בו וניצל מן הרוחות ומן השדים... ור׳ עקיבה כתב שלמדנו שיעור של יצרנו טוב לנו בעוה״ז ונוח לנו בעוה״ב ומי ששונה הרז הגדול הזה שונה המשנה כל יום אחר תפלתו מעלה לו לכל וזו היא... משביע אני עליך מטטרון... ושמי הטוב ילך בכל המקומות ויהיו חלומותי מיושבין [15ב] שמורה בגופי ואל אשכח דבר מפי ומלב ותיטב לי מטובך והעבר כל פיות דוברי שקר ורעות מעלי. בא״ה שומע תפלה.

[On the *Hekhalot* formulations in this text (in the names of R. Yishma'el and R. Aqiva), see Schäfer, *The Hidden and Manifest God*, 107, 115, 117. Cf. Swartz, *Scholastic Magic*, 221, n. 38; idem, "Jewish Magic in Late Antiquity and the Early Middle Ages," *JJS* 41 (1990):79–88; Lesses, "Speaking with Angels," 46–54; and Harari, "Kishfei Hezeq ve-Hitgonenut Mipneihem" (above, n. 10), 111–13.] The material following this prayer (fol. 16r; a series of verses about sacrifices and the service of the *kohanim*, and a collection of seventy verses from Psalms beginning with the phrase ואתה ה׳ מגן בעדי) suggests that it is part of a *seder maᶜamadot* (see below). The manuscript consists almost entirely of kabbalistic and philosophical works [including *Keter Shem Tov*, by R. Abraham of Cologne; a *tefillat yiḥud* attributed to R. Neḥunyah b. ha-Qanah and other kabbalistic *liqqutim*; a commentary on the ten *sefirot; Sefer Yiḥud* by R. Asher b. David b. Rabad; *Shaᶜar She'ol* by R. Azriel of Gerona; the prayer attributed to Rabbenu Tam; a *megillat setarim*; a philosophical analysis of the soul; a commentary on the *sefirot* by Jacob b. Jacob; Ramban's commentary to *Sefer Yeẓirah*; and R. Eleazar of Worms's *Ḥokhmat ha-Nefesh* and his *Ma'amar ᶜal ha-Nevu'ah*, which cites R. Saᶜadyah Gaon, R. Ḥanan'el, R. Nissim Gaon, Donnolo, R. Judah *he-Ḥasid*, and *Sefer ha-Ḥayyim*.] Cf. Moshe Idel, "Gazing at the Head in Ashkenazi Hasidism," *Journal of Jewish Thought and Philosophy* 6

This prayer is found, however, in a northern French manuscript dating from the mid-thirteenth century, with no mention of Rabbenu Tam. In this manuscript, which is a *maḥzor* or *siddur* and ritual compendium, the prayer is divided into two parts. The larger portion has the name of a little-known tosafist, R. Isaac b. Isaac of Chinon, inserted into the text as its author or client.[100] The smaller portion of the prayer (which is copied twice in this

---

(1997):277, nn. 31–33, and see now Idel, *R. Menaḥem Reqanati ha-Mequbbal*, vol. 1 (Tel Aviv, 1998), 42–45. JTS Mic. 2131 (Italy, c.1600), fols. 35v–36r, attributes the same prayer to Rabbenu Tam and describes it as **תפלה למי שיאלם לשנו פתאום**. The prayer is preceded by the same kabbalistic works as in ms. Parma 1390. Cfr. *Amtaḥat Binyamin* (above, n. 19), 10–11.

See also ms. B. M. Add. 26,883 (Italy, fourteenth century, unpaginated) [=#640 in *Catalogue of the Hebrew and Samaritan Manuscripts*, ed. G. Margoliouth (London, 1905), 2:255.] This manuscript consists of kabbalistic prayers, including a *teḥinnah* of R. Judah *he-Ḥasid* (**יוצרי ברוב רחמיך כבוש אפך וזעמך**, found also in ms. Parma 1138, fol. 139v [Hebrew pagination, fol. 96v], and in ms. Parma 1354, fol. 121v, with no name); an adjuration to send the angel Uriel, who is **הממונה על החכמה**; a prayer attributed to the prophet Elijah; the first prayer section attributed to Rabbenu Tam, **בבקשה מכם מלאכי השרת מטטרון וכו׳**; a *shemirat ha-derekh* of Ramban, which he derived from *Sefer Yeẓirah*; a second piece of *tefillat Rabbenu Tam*, **בבקשה מכם מטטרון וסוריאל**; another prayer of Elijah; and a *tefillat baʿal teshuvah* from *ha-qadosh ha-R. Yonah* beginning with the phrase, **אנא ה׳ חטאתי** (see above, ch. 1, n. 112). The prayer(s) attributed to Rabbenu Tam can also be found in ms. Vat. Rossiana 356 (Morocco, 1412), fol. 65v. This manuscript contains, among other things, a *viddui* of R. Judah *he-Ḥasid* (fol. 2v) [**תבוא לפניך תפלתנו... עברנו על מצוות עשה ועברנו על מצוות לא תעשה עברנו על תורה שבכתב ותורה שבעל פה... בוחן כליות ולב אין דבר נעלם ממך... תמחל ותסלח על כל עוונותינו**; regarding both the *teḥinnah* and *viddui* of R. Judah *he-Ḥasid*, cf. above, ch. 1, n. 112]; *Sefer ha-Maʿarakhah le-R. Eliyyahu* (fols. 7v–41v; cf. below, n. 107), including *shir ha-Yiḥud* (14r); *segullot* and *hashbaʿot* for daily blessings (43v–44r); a prayer by Ramban for the eve of *Rosh ha-Shanah* (fol. 65r); guidelines for repentance from R. Eleazar of Worms (fol. 74); as well as *segullot* and *hashbaʿot* (91–102) including **סגולה ע״י סנדלפון להצלה**; a means of escapaing detection by a ruler; and two *segullot* for *petiḥat ha-lev*, on fols. 96v–97v.

[100]See ms. Paris 633, fols. 196r–197v [transcribed in Colette Sirat, "Un Rituel Juif de France," 36–38]. There is no prior attribution of the prayer, and it is introduced by the instruction, "Say this after your prayers and it will help for everything. Say it in purity in your house or in the synagogue and here it is."

> **אנא ה׳ אלקי ישראל מושל בעליונים ושולט בתחתונים קרוב לקוראיו באמת מציל עני מחזק ממנו ואביון מגוזלו שמע נא על [196ב] תפלת עבדך ואל תחנוניו והסר ממני אימתה ופחד ורגש ושאג ותרדמה ושיגעון ועיורון וזיק ומזיק ולילין ושדין וכל בריאה רעה ויצר הרע שיקומו עלי להחטיא לי יצחק ב״ר יצחק. בגודל זרועך ידמו כאבן ובמוראך אם יראוני לא יזיקוני ואם יקדמוני לא יגיעוני... הם יפוצו ואני לא אפוץ... [197א]... בבקשה מכם אתם מלאכי השרת מטטרון**

manuscript) contains the second adjuration of Metatron and is unattributed.[101] Since this manuscript version of the prayer is the closest to Rabbenu Tam in terms of both geography and chronology, the absence of any reference to Rabbenu Tam is significant.[102]

> וסוריאל שר הפנים ועזריאל מיכאל וגבריאל שתעמדו בבקשה ובתחנונים לפני מלך מלכי המלכים ה׳ק׳ב׳ה׳ לשמוע תפלתי ותחנתי ובקשתי למחל ולסלוח על כל עונתי שעשיתי בין באונס בין ברצון בין בהרהור בין במחשבה בין בשוגג בין במזיד אני יצחק ב״ר יצחק בשם אכתריאל יושב תהלות ישראל ובעל שמות הקדושים המפורשים בנקיות ובטהרה שתקחו מפתחות של חן וחסד ורחמים ובינה והשכל להצליח לי בשמי [197ב] יצחק ב״ר יצחק בכל מקום שאלך ואשב ושמעי יצליחו מעשי ומאמרי ויהיו מתוקים כדבש ונופת צופים ומשביע אני עליך המלאך הגדול הממונה על האהבה ליתן אותי לחן ולחסד ולרחמים בעיניך ובעיני כל רואי בין ממעל בשמים בין מתחת לשמים ותהיה השעה הזאת והיום הזה יום רצון שעת רצון יום ישועה וגאולה מחילה וכפרה והצלה והצלחה וריוח ועושר וכבוד שלא אצטרך לידי מתנות בשר ודם ולא לידי הלוואתם ולא אבוש לעולם ועד אמן.

[101]See ms. Paris 633, fol. 74r. The formulation attributed to R. Yishmaʾel (in ms. Parma 1390 and others; see above, n. 99), מי ששונה הרז הגדול הזה, appears (preceded by a passage from *Shiʿur Qomah*) with the instruction that it is good to recite every night and day after prayers. See also fols. 6v–7r, in the name of R. Yishmaʾel: אשרי אדם שיגמור הרז הזה משחרית לשחרית וגו׳. On fol. 74v (and again on fol. 129; see Sirat, 39), the following is found:

> משביע אני עליך מטטרון עבדו של יצרינו ששמך כשם רבך שתיזקק לי לעשות חפצי ויהיו פני מצהיבות ושמי הטוב ילך בכל מקומות ישראל ויהיו חלומותי מיושבים לי ותהי תורתי שמורה בגופי ואל ישכח דבר מפי ומלבי מן היום הזה עד היום הבא ותטיב לי מטובך בעולם הזה וגם לעולם הבא ותבקש רחמים לפני כסא הכבוד ומחול לי כל עונותי שעשיתי ואל ישלוט בי יצר הרע לעולם ותצילני מכל חיות רעות [ומכל שדין ולילין ומגרים] ומפגעים רעים ולסטים [ומכל בני אדם הרעים] ותפלטני מכל נחש ועקרב ושרף [ומכל חיות ומכל בריות רעות שבעולם] ותסכיר פיות מכל דוברי רעות. ברוך אתה ה׳ שומע תפלה.

On the division of this prayer into different sections, cf. ms. B. M. Add. 26,883 (above, n. 99).

[102]Ms. Cambr. Add. 1176 (Ashkenaz, fifteenth century), fols. 115v–116r, has a version of the larger portion of the prayer (in the midst of a *seder maʿamadot*; see below) that is almost identical to the Paris 633 version (above, n. 100) for the first part and is very similar to Parma 1390 (above, n. 99) for the second part, beginning with the phrase בבקשה מכם מלאכי השרת מטטרון וכו׳. The name חיים ב״ר יחיאל הלוי appears in the first part and יחיאל ב״ר שמואל הלוי in the second, as those who recited the various *baqqashot*. On fol. 49r of ms. Cambr. Add. 1176, ר׳ חיים ב״ר יחיאל is identified as the *ḥatan Torah* who received the honor of completing the yearly cycle of the Torah reading. At the end of the version of the prayer found in ms. Vat. Rossiana 356 (above, n. 99), the words אני שלמה בן אליהו appear. [A later version of the prayer, with addenda but

At the same time, the attribution of these requests and *hashbaᶜot* to R. Isaac b. Isaac of Chinon is both reasonable and appropriate. Despite its decidedly French base, the *maḥzor* as a whole contains prayers and *nusḥaᵓot*

---

unattributed, is found in a Sefardic *siddur*, ms. Paris 592 (1444), fols. 56r–57v. The prayer follows a *baqqashah la-Ramban* (52r) and a *baqqashah le-aḥar ha-tefillah la-ḥakham he-ḥasid*, R. Isaac b. ha-Rav R. Avraham b. David. A version like the one in Parma 1390, but in a different order, is found, also unattributed, in ms. Parma 1124 (Italy, fifteenth century). The client is simply **פלוני בן פלוני**. In this case, the prayer is situated within a number of prayers and *segullot* attributed to R. Judah *he-Ḥasid* and Ramban. See below, n. 110, and ch. 5, n. 74.]

Another brief version of the prayer is found anonymously in ms. Paris 391 (Ashkenaz, fourteenth century), fol. 69r. This version contains an angelic *hashbaᶜah*, which begins like those found in Paris 633 (although the name of Metatron is omitted) but continues with standard requests for physical protection on the road, from robbers, from *shedim*, from [evil] men, women, the sword, pestilence, and so on:

> בבקשה מכם מיכאל וגבריאל ורפאל ואכתריאל שתעמדו תפלה בבקשה ובתחנונים לפני מלך מלכי המלכים הקב״ה שיצליח דרכי בכח מקום שאני הולך הן מליסטין שלא יזיקוני הן משדים הן מלילין הן מאדם ומאשה הן מכל פגע רע הן מחרב הן מרעב הן מכל מיני פורעניות הבאות ומתרגשות לעולם. מן הכל הצילני ה׳ א-להי ישראל ושלא ישלוט שליטה במעשה ידי ולא בגופי ולא בממוני. יה״ר מלפניך ה׳ א-להי וא-להי אבותי שתהא השעה הזאת שעות רצון מלפניך שתשמע תחינתי ובקשתי א׳ א׳ א׳ סלה. ה׳ צב-אות עמנו וכו׳ לישועתך קויתי ה׳. גד גדוד יגודנו והוא יגוד עקב (הרבה פעמים). [בסוף: כדי שיצליח בידינו כמו שעשה גד כשעבר את הירדן למלחמה על הכנענים וחזר לאבינו בשלום. עלינו לשבח]

Note the similar prayer in ms. Cambr. Or. 71 (see above, ch. 2, n. 10), and cf. *Derekh Ereẓ Rabbah*, ch. 11 (end).

[This prayer appears in ms. Paris 391 as part of a *siddur* that is interspersed with *piyyutim* and *seliḥot* from Ashkenazic figures such as R. Meir of Rothenburg and Rabiah (fols. 55–61, 76v, 80v) and R. Eleazar, the son of R. Judah *he-Ḥasid* (fol. 82r), whose *seliḥah* is based on the *Shem ha-Meforash* derived from the verses in Exodus 14:19–21, as well as the Name of 216 letters corresponding to **אריה**. There are also halakhic formulations from Maharam (93r) and R. Samson of Coucy and Riẓba (107v–108). See also below, n. 111.]

This version of the prayer is almost identical to one that R. Joseph Hahn of Frankfurt (d.1803) cites in his *Yosef Omeẓ* (102, sec. 484) as a prayer from Rabbenu Tam, to be recited daily, which would remove any *pega ra* and grant success in all of one's endeavors. R. Joseph writes that he copied this prayer from the treatise of R. Eliezer Treves of Frankfurt (i.e., the kabbalistic prayer commentary, *Diqduq Tefillah*, on the *siddur Malᵓah ha-Areẓ Deᶜah* [Thunegen, 1560], composed by R. Naftali Hertz [Drifzan] Treves and published by his sons Joseph and Eliezer [d.1566]). Cf. Heschel, "Al Ruaḥ ha-Qodesh Bimei ha-Benayim," 182–83.

associated with *Ḥasidei Ashkenaz*, as well as esoteric material.[103] R. Isaac of Chinon, who had connections to the academy at Evreux, was one of the copyists of this manuscript. Indeed, the largest share of mystical formulations is found in sections that he copied, including both parts of the esoteric and magical prayer under discussion.[104]

---

[103]See ms. Paris 633, e.g., fols. 6v–7r (above, n. 101); 18 (שיר הייחוד ושיר הכבוד לר׳ יהודה החסיד); 19 (יהי רצון מלפניך י-ה-ו-ה השם הגדול והקדוש והנורא שתצליח דרכי ותישר אורחותי ותמלא משאלותי ותעשה חפצי היום אמן; this section of the ms. is from the early thirteenth century); 30r (סליחה מר׳ יהודה החסיד; see above, ch. 1, n. 112); 48v, 76v, 81r, 104r (cf. Zimmer, *ᶜOlam ke-Minhago Noheg*, 115–18); 104v, 117–20, 125–27, 138, 183 (see below, n. 113); 188–89, 204, 205v (יהי רצון שתשמע קולי בשמותיך הקדושים היוצאים מראשי תיבות סליחה זו; cf. *She'elot u-Teshuvot min ha-Shamayim*, ed. Margoliot, #9, 53–54; below, n. 111; and *Amtaḥat Binyamin*, 14), 209, 211–12 (see below, n. 114), 215, 218v, 220, and 222 (the prayer of R. Yishma'el; cf. *Amtaḥat Binyamin*, 10). [Fol. 250v has a mathematics problem with the solution of Rabbenu Tam (see above, n. 86). This underscores the fact that Rabbenu Tam's name does not appear at any point in the manuscript in conjunction with the prayer under discussion.]

[104]R. Isaac b. Isaac's involvement as a scribe serves to confirm that this manuscript is earlier (c.1250) than ms. Parma 1390 (dated 1286). For R. Isaac's genealogy, which dates him with some precision, see Sirat, "Un Rituel Juif de France," 32; for the sections copied by Isaac, see Sirat, 11–23. The manuscript also contains a calendar for the years 1263–74. R. Isaac b. Isaac of Chinon also composed *piyyutim*; see ms. Bodl. 2550, sec. 57; Parma 855, fol. 161r; and Sirat, 33. He is mentioned in *Tosafot Nazir* and *Tosafot Meᶜilah*, two collections that emanated from the academy at Evreux. See Sirat, 30; Henri Gross, *Gallia Judaica* (Paris, 1897), 580; *Tosafot Rabbenu Pereẓ le-Massekhet Bava Meẓiᶜa*, ed. Hayyim Hershler (Jerusalem, 1970), editor's introduction, 12; ms. Vat. Urb. 27, fol. 27v (in the margin: כך שמעתי ממורי הר׳ יצחק בן הר׳ יצחק); Urbach, *Baᶜalei ha-Tosafot*, 2:636, 673; and cf. Adolf Neubauer, "Documents Inedits," *REJ* 12 (1886):81; Norman Golb, *The Jews in Medieval Normandy* (Cambridge, 1998), 514–23; and below, ch. 5, n. 37.

For additional linkages between the academies at Evreux and Chinon at this time, see the reference to R. Isaac's older contemporary, R. Netan'el of Chinon, in the Evreux-based *Sefer ᶜal ha-Kol*, sec. 1 (cf. above, ch. 2, n. 65). See also *Tosafot Maharam ve-Rabbenu Pereẓ ᶜal Massekhet Yevamot*, ed. Hillel Porush (Jerusalem, 1991), which cites *ha-qadosh* R. Nentan'el (157a) and cites him two other times as R. Netan'el of Chinon (see the index, 15–16); *Tosafot R. Meir mi-Rothenburg* in *Shitat ha-Qadmonim ᶜal Massekhet Yevamot*, ed. M. Y. Blau (New York, 1986); and cf. Samson of Chinon, *Sefer Keritut*, ed. S. B. Sofer (Jerusalem, 1965), editor's introduction, 26, and Israel Ta-Shma, "Netan'el of Chinon," *Encyclopaedia Judaica*, 12:972–73. R. Moses of Evreux is mentioned four times, as is *ha-qadosh* [R. Solomon] *mi-Dreux*; cf. ch. 2, n. 10, and ms. Cambr. Add. 561 (Ashkenaz, fourteenth century), fol. 66r. R. Samuel *he-Ḥasid* is also mentioned once. See also *Tosafot Yeshanim ha-Shalem ᶜal Massekhet Yevamot*, ed. Abraham Shoshana (Jerusalem, 1994), 616–17 (index), which includes, in addition to those scholars already noted, R. Samuel of Evreux and R. Moses *ha-Kohen* of Mainz

Additional excerpts of these prayers (or related variants) are found, without attribution, in several other medieval Ashkenazic *maḥzorim* or prayer collections. These prayers appear most often in a liturgical unit, toward the end of the prayer service, known as the *seder ha-maᶜamadot*. This unit, which has been described and analyzed by E. E. Urbach on the basis of northern French

---

(a teacher of R. Eleazar of Worms). Moreover, this *Tosafot* collection cites R. Netanᵓel of Chinon more than any other extant medieval rabbinic text; it also cites R. Moses of Evreux quite frequently. See the editor's introduction, 22–26, which lists a number of texts that note specific interactions between R. Netanᵓel and the brothers of Evreux. See also *Shitat ha-Qadmonim*, ed. M. Y. Blau (New York, 1992), "*Pisqei Rabbenu Yosef*," 377, and *Kol Bo*, sec. 114 (fol. 85a, and cf. fol. 88b: והקדוש רבינו נתנאל מקינון היה אבל וישב בתענית וסמך לדבר לא תאכלו על הדם ובלילה היה אוכל משלו). Cf. Solomon Schechter, "Notes on a Hebrew Commentary to the Pentateuch in a Parma Manuscript," *Semitic Studies in Memory of Alexander Kohut*, ed. George Kohut (Berlin, 1897), 487–94; Urbach, *Baᶜalei ha-Tosafot*, 1:457–58, 480–81; and Eric Zimmer, "Seder ha-Posqim le-R. Azriᵓel Trabot," *Sinai* 76 (1975):248. Note that ms. Parma 159 (late twelfth century) was copied by an Isaac b. Netanᵓel.

[A. R. Netanᵓel b. Joseph of Chinon composed a *shir ha-yiḥud* (י״ה מן הקר״ן) that was sometimes connected to Elijah's *seder ha-maᶜarakhah*. Like R. Elijah's work, R. Netanᵓel's composition ended each day with a *baqqashah* or *segullah*. See ms. Parma 363 (Italy, fourteenth century), fol. 5v, where R. Netanᵓel's work follows "seventy verses (of protection)" and the *seder ha-maᶜarakhah* of R. Elijah. See also ms. Parma 591, fol. 6v; Parma 654, fol. 258; A. M. Habermann, *Shirei ha-Yiḥud veha-Kavod* (Jerusalem, 1948), 73–85; and below, n. 110. R. Netanᵓel also composed a *seder ha-tamid* (קרוב לעמך ונדרש). See ms. Cambr. Add. 394 (Ashkenaz, fourteenth century), fols. 88–96, and Bodl. 2502 (Ashkenaz, thirteenth century), fols. 12v–13v. See also ms. Parma 963 (Italy, fifteenth century), fol. 431, and Cambr. 561, fol. 66. This R. Netanᵓel is probably the grandson of the earlier R. Netanᵓel. See Urbach, 1:458, n. 41*, and Avraham Grossman in *Meḥqarim be-Talmud* 3 (forthcoming).]

As a result of her study of ms. Paris 633, Sirat makes the passing but perceptive observation ("Un Rituel Juif," 15, 31, n. 1) that material in this manuscript—especially from portions copied by R. Isaac (such as an acrostic of the letters in Exodus 14:19 representing Divine Names [fol. 202] and his presentation of R. Neḥunyah b. ha-Qanah's prayer [see above, n. 99], as well as other mystical prayers and incantations to avoid danger and achieve other states discussed above, which found their way into the kabbalistic collection *Amtaḥat Binyamin*)—suggests that the religious thought of the (northern French) tosafists was affected by (German) mysticism, and that angels and demons played a great role in their world view. See also Sirat, "Le Livre hébreu en France au Moyen Age," *Michael* 12 (1991):306–7, and M. Banitt, "Une formule d'exorcisme en ancien français," *Studies in Honor of Mario Pei*, ed. John Fisher and Paul Gaeng (Chapel Hill, 1972), 37–48. The group of parallel and related manuscript passages (to be discussed in the following notes)—of which Sirat was unaware—and many other aspects of the present study confirm Sirat's intuition.

manuscripts from the thirteenth century[105]—and more recently by I. Ta-Shma, on the basis of an English manuscript dated 1189[106]—sought to represent the readings and activities of the so-called *ʾanshei mishmarot* who, during the days of the Temple, mirrored the sacrificial rites performed by the *kohanim* with readings and recitations.

The *seder ha-maʿamadot* consisted typically of verses for each day of the week: from the beginning of *Sefer Bereshit*, the psalm of the day (and other psalms), daily chapters from the books of the prophets, as well as a *seder maʿarakhah*—a description of the order of the altar service based on talmudic formulations (especially those of Abbaye found in *Yoma* 27b and 33a), often attributed to the eleventh-century scholar and pietist R. Elijah b. Menaḥem of Le Mans.[107] Several of the manuscripts add additional biblical sections, as well as lists of seventy (or seventy-two) verses, and eleven verses that begin and end with the letter *nun*. They also contain requests or supplications for personal protection and support, as well as the *ʿAleynu* prayer.[108]

The pietistic and mystical dimensions of the *maʿamadot* sections are substantial. In addition to the material from R. Elijah of Le Mans—which perhaps also masks *Hekhalot* passages attributed to Elijah the prophet—Ta-Shma has focused attention on the *Hekhalot* background of the *ʿAleynu* prayer, which was given great prominence by R. Judah *he-Ḥasid* and R. Eleazar of Worms as well, and also on the presence of additional *Hekhalot* passages in the earliest versions of these sections.[109] It should also be noted that the "eleven verses beginning and ending with *nun*" (as well as one version of the "seventy verses"), which were recited as magical forms of protection, are associated in various texts with R. Judah *he-Ḥasid* or other members of *Ḥasidei Ashkenaz*.[110]

---

105 E. E. Urbach, "Mishmarot u-Maʿamadot," *Tarbiz* 42 (1973): 313–27.

106 Israel Ta-Shma, "Meqorah u-Meqomah shel Tefillat ʿAleynu le-Shabeaḥ' be-Siddur ha-Tefillah: Seder ha-Maʿamadot u-Sheʾelat Siyyum ha-Tefillah," *The Frank Talmage Memorial Volume*, ed. Walfish, [Hebrew section] 1:85–98. Cf. Habermann, *Shirei ha-Yiḥud veha-Kavod*, 87–97, and ms. Paris 632, fols. 2v–3v.

107 See Grossman, *Ḥakhmei Ẓarefat ha-Rishonim*, 102–4, and above, n. 95.

108 See the manuscripts described by Urbach in "Mishmarot u-Maʿamadot," esp. ms. Cambr. Add. 667.1; ms. B. M. Add. 11.639; ms. Bodl. 1105; ms. Parma 591.

109 See Ta-Shma, above, n. 106, esp. 87–88, 95. See also Moshe Hallamish, "Nosaḥ Qadum shel ʿAleynu Leshabeaḥ,'" *Sinai* 110 (1992):262–65; Elliot Wolfson, "Hai Gaon's Letter and Commentary on ʿAleynu: Further Evidence of Moses De Leon's Pseudepigraphic Activity," *Jewish Quarterly Review* 81 (1990–91):365–409; and Naftali Wieder, "Be-ʿItyah shel Gematria anti-Noẓerit ve-anti-Islamit," *Sinai* 76 (1975):5–10.

110 See, e.g., *Sefer Gematriʾot le-R. Yehudah he-Ḥasid*, 16, 138 (fol. 57v); ms. B.M. 1056 [Add. 11, 639] (northern France, 1278; cf. *Catalogue*, ed. Margoliouth, 3:422),

In several instances, the supplications for personal protection found in *seder ha-ma*ᶜ*amadot* are enhanced by mystical prayers and magical *hashba*ᶜ*ot* of the type under discussion. An Ashkenazic manuscript, copied in the fourteenth

---

fols. 161r–167r, and fol. 528v; ms. Cambr. Add. 1176 (above, n. 102), which also concludes the *seder ha-ma*ᶜ*amadot* with a *shir ha-Yiḥud* by R. Judah *he-Ḥasid*, as does ms. Bodl. 1105 (Germany, 1326), fols. 384v–420v; cf. Urbach, "Mishmarot u-Maᶜamadot," 317, n. 54); ms. Paris 391, fol. 61r–64v (see the next note); ms. Paris 633, fol. 183 (below, n. 113); ms. Parma 1390 (above, n. 99); ms. Parma 1124, fol. 50v–51r, which lists the eleven verses just before a קבלה מר׳ יהודה החסיד; ms. Bodl. 659, fol. 112v (מטעמי ר׳ יהודה החסיד), and *Sefer Gematri*ʾ*ot le-R. Yehudah he-Ḥasid*, 48 (fol. 12v), which maintains that the first three of the eleven verses were cited by the prophet Elisha in formulating the purification process for the leper נַעמן (2 Samuel 5); and cf. above, n. 102. [Ms. Parma 363 has the seventy (-two) verses, whose recitation constitutes a kind of magic formula to assure protection, followed (fol. 5v) by R. Elijah's *seder ha-ma*ᶜ*arakhah* (whose various versions also contain exensive requests for different types of protection and salvation) and the *shir ha-yiḥud* entitled י״ה מן הקר״ן by R. Netanʾel of Chinon. After describing the greatness of the Almighty using *Hekhalot* passages, this *shir ha-yiḥud* ends with requests for atonement (*kapparah*) and for redemption. See Habermann, *Shirei ha-Yiḥud veha-Kavod*, 73–77, 88, 190. Ms. Parma 591 does not list the verses but does have a German *shir ha-Yiḥud* as well as the one by R. Netanʾel of Chinon.] See also ms. Macerata Biblioteca Comunale 310, described by B. Richler in *Me-Ginzei ha-Makhon le-Taẓlumei Kitvei ha-Yad ha-*ᶜ*Ivriyyim* (Jerusalem, 1996), 99. The manuscript is from Provence, c.1400. Fols. 136–41 contain the names of talmudic tractates and "seventy-two verses" from Psalms to be said each morning, followed by the mystical *seliḥah*, א-להים בישראל גדול יחודך, attributed to R. Judah *he-Ḥasid* (see above, ch. 1, n. 112). After this *seliḥah* there is a brief prayer *tefillah*, יהי רצון ... שתעשה למען שמותיך היקרים הסדורים בתפלה הזאת; cf. above, n. 103. In ms. Paris 646, fol. 237r, the seventy verses are followed immediately by R. Judah *he-Ḥasid*'s addenda to the א-לוהי נצור prayer (see above, n. 37). See also the listing of the seventy-two verses (beginning with ואתה ה׳ מגן בעדי) to be recited after several penitential poems, in R. Jacob *Ḥazzan mi-London, Eẓ Ḥayyim* [composed in 1287], ed. Israel Brody (Jerusalem, 1962), 132–34; and in ms. Sassoon 408 (Italy, fourteenth century)=ms. B. M. Or. 14055, fols. 3–19. [The seventy verses, which begin with this phrase, are occasionally attributed to Ramban. See, e.g., ms. Vat. Rossiana 356, fol. 41v; Parma 1124, fol. 36; and *Amtaḥat Binyamin*, fols. 21–23.]

On the power of the eleven verses according to Pietist sources, see *Perush ha-Roqeaḥ* ᶜ*al ha-Torah, Vayiqra (parashat Tazria*ᶜ), ed. Konyevsky, 239–40, for a list of these verses (which appear throughout the Bible), with the instruction that if one recites them without interruption, good tidings will occur. Moreover, they should be recited before going to sleep and in any dangerous situation, and it is good to read them with heartfelt intention. R. Judah *he-Ḥasid* (רי״ח בשם) is cited as organizing the first words of the verses in a particular order, perhaps to allow them to be remembered more easily. It is also noted that neither the letter *samekh* nor the letter *peh* appears in these verses. *Peh* is the last letter in the names of a number of negative angelic *memunnim*, such as נגף, זעף, (הת)אנף, קצף, שצף; cf. above, n. 59. Similarly, *samekh* stands for *satan*. One who

century, contains an unattributed variant of one of the so-called *tefillat Rabbenu Tam*.[111] The English manuscript described by Ta-Shma has an even more extensive adjuration, which invokes a lengthy string of Divine Names to provide protection for the individual reciting them.[112] One of the adjurations

---

knows how to recite these verses with proper inention will render these *mal'akhei ḥabbalah* unable to harm him (*le-satan lo*); see also *Sefer Gematri'ot le-R. Yehudah he-Ḥasid*, 138. In addition, the letter *nun* creates a *siman tov*. As the Talmud indicates (*Berakhot* 56b), one who sees the letter *nun* in a dream will be successful. Cf. *Perushei Siddur ha-Tefillah la-Roqeaḥ* [Jerusalem, 1992], 2:442; and *Sefer Gematri'ot le-R. Yehudah he-Ḥasid*, Ta-Shma's introduction, 16. [This material is also found in *Moshav Zeqenim* to *Va-Yiqra* 13:9; in ms. Bodl. 2344 (*Pa'aneaḥ Raza*), fol. 89v; and in different form in *Perush Rabbenu Baḥya b. Asher* to *Bamidbar* 32:32, where reciting these eleven verses is deemed important because the *Shem ha-Meforash* emanates from them. Thus, one who mentions these verses with the Name that emerges from each of them will be spared any fear.]

[111]See ms. Paris 391, fol. 69r (above, n. 102). The *ma'amadot* component in this manuscript is diminished, consonant with the trend over the course of time noted by Ta-Shma (above, n. 107). Nonetheless, the adjurations appear toward the end of the service and conform to the patterns of the *ma'amadot* texts described above. The prayer is followed (fol. 73v) by *taḥanun* and *seliḥot* prayers, including the invocation of angels to ask the Almighty for mercy (מכניסי רחמים). Prior to the prayer, there are two sets of seventy verses (the first set beginning with the phrase ואתה ה׳ מגן בעדי; fols. 61r–v). These are followed by the eleven verses beginning and ending with the letter *nun*, whose recitation will protect a person (fol. 64v). Next come two *piyyutim* (fol. 65r) often associated with *Ḥasidei Ashkenaz*, האוחז ביד משפט and אדרת והאמונה. [See the commentary on האוחז ביד משפט attributed to R. Eleazar of Worms in, e.g., ms. Parma 1138, fols. 120–21 (in the Hebrew foliation, =fols. 79r–81v in the standard foliation); Cambr. Add. 858, fols. 15r–16v; JTS Mic. 2367, fols. 177v–178r, and Rab. 689, fol. 194; Darmstadt 25, fol. 110; Budapest/Kaufman A174, fols. 194–95; Bodl. 1812, fol. 94; Munich 212, fol. 26v; Bologna 2914, fols. 220v–223r. האדרת והאמונה originated in *Hekhalot* literature and was also the focus of a commentary by *Ḥasidei Ashkenaz*. See Bar-Ilan, *Sitrei Tefillah ve-Hekhalot*, 16–18, and the study of Joseph Dan cited on 17, n. 10.] These *piyyutim* are followed by a series of supplications, including the suggestion that our prayers are like sacrifices; thus they should be accepted along with our repentance, and they should be viewed by the Almighty as the prayers of the *Avot* and other pious ancestors. After some requests and praises, fol. 68r contains Abbaye's *seder ha-ma'arakhah*, and fol. 68v lists the ten commandments (which are found in other samples of *sefer ha-ma'amadot*; cf. Urbach, "Mishmarot u-Ma'amadot," 319, and idem, "Ma'amadam shel 'Asseret ha-Dibberot ba-'Avodah uva-Tefillah," *'Asseret ha-Dibberot bi-Re'i ha-Dorot* [Jerusalem, 1986], 141–42), followed by *Adon 'Olam* and then the *hashba'ot* in the middle of fol. 69r. A similar order is found in the earlier ms. Paris 633; see below, n. 113, and cf. ms. Parma 3499, fol. 108.

[112]Ta-Shma, "Meqorah u-Meqomah shel Tefillat 'Aleynu le-Shabeaḥ'," 89–90 (ms. Corpus Christi, 133). At the end of the morning service, prior to the recitation of

of Metatron copied by R. Isaac of Chinon also appears in close proximity to a list of the "seventy verses" and among other supplications and requests similar to one of those found in the English manuscript.[113] Moreover, another adjuration is found toward the end of R. Isaac of Chinon's *mahzor*; this closely resembles the extensive adjuration found in the English manuscript.[114]

ʿ*Aleynu* and the verses representing the *maʿamadot*, the group of seventy verses beginning **ואתה ה׳ מגן בעדי** is listed (fol. 300r), followed by other verses "which, when recited after the seventy verses, will protect against military arms." This section opens with the eleven verses that begin and end with the letter *nun* (fol. 302v). The remaining verses are followed by a brief *yehi razon* to guard the individual from sin and grant him salvation and success, and then by a complex esoteric *hashbaʿah*, which invokes a lengthy series of angelic and Divine Names—including the *Shem E-hyeh Asher E-hyeh*; the *Shem* that is inscribed on the head-plate of Aaron the High Priest; the *Shem ha-Meforash* of forty-two letters; and the *Keter ha-Gadol ha-Gibbor veha-Nora*. The adjuration seeks protection from many forms of evil and suffering and asks for mercy, success, and fulfillment (fol. 303). It ends with the blessing of *shomeaʿ tefillah* (304r–v). Cf. ms. Paris 391, in the above note, and ms. Parma 1138, fols. 134r–141v. Close parallels can also be found in ms. 290, fol. 381r, sec. 1003, in the name of R. Elijah Menahem of London (see below, ch. 5, n. 40) and in *Sefer Raziʾel* (Amsterdam 1701, repr. 1985), 144: **קמיע טוב ובדוק ומנוסה לחן, לתפיסה, לחרב, לפתיחת הלב... מלאכים הממונים על ה׳ תמוז... הצליחני כתיבת זה הקמיע לפב״פ לשמרהו מחרב פיפיות ועזרוהו ופלטהו וימלטהו מאדם רע בין ברית בין שאינו ברית... ותצילהו מכל כישוף ומכל מיני פורעניות ועניות... משביע אני פב״פ בשם אורירון ואדיריון**. To be sure, the formula in *Sefer Raziʾel* is for an amulet, while ms. Corpus Christi's formula is purely liturgical. [On the angelic names invoked, cf. above, n. 2.] For other similar usages, see the *segullah* that appears in Bodl. 1107–8 (German prayer rite, 1341), fols. 306v–307r, and the *hashbaʿah* to implement a *herem* that appears in *Kol Bo*, sec. 139 (**בשם אכתריאל, בשם מיכאל השר הגדול, בשם מטטרון, סנדלפון, שם של מ״ב אותיות, בסוד שם המפורש, בשם הגלגלים וגו׳ בשם כל המלאכים הקדושים... ארור הוא לה׳ וכו׳**; see also above, ch. 1, n. 54); below, n. 115; and cf. *Kol Bo*, sec. 66 (*Moreh Hattaʾim le-R. Eleazar mi-Worms*), fol. 31b.

[113]See ms. Paris 633, fol. 183. The seventy verses, beginning with the phrase **ואתה ה׳ מגן בעדי**, appear in close proximity to one of the *hashbaʿot* of Metatron, followed by an expanded *tefillat ha-derekh* and other personal requests; see Sirat, "Un Rituel Juif de France," 20. The verses are part of a *seder ha-maʿamadot* (copied by someone other than R. Isaac of Chinon) that follows the ʿ*Aleynu* prayer (fol. 104v). It consists of Abbaye's *Seder ha-Maʿarakhah* (fols. 157–173r), verses to be recited each day, the eleven verses which begin and end with *nun*, the *Hekhalot* prayer *Ha-Adderet veha-Emmunah*, and the ten commandments, as well as two chapters of the Pentateuch (fols. 173v–182r). See Sirat, 12–13; and cf. above, nn. 111–12.

[114]Ms. Paris 633, fols. 211v–212r:

> כל צרה שיהיה לאדם יאמר זה וינצל: בשם א׳ אשר א׳ החקוק במצח אהרן ובזעקתא דשלמה ובזעקתא בהמדיאל (תטריאל) ובזעקתא דמטטרון קדישא רבא עבדא ה׳ (יקוק) הנקרא על שמו ובזעקתא דבריאל ובנו ר׳ ישמעאל ובזעקתא

In short, all these *maḥzorim* demonstrate that there was much interest in theurgic prayer and magical uses of *Shemot* in rabbinic circles in northern France, England, and Germany from the second half of the twelfth through the thirteenth centuries. Magical *hashbaʿot* and requests for protection and other aims may have been commonplace, and they undoubtedly carried a high degree of rabbinic approbation. Some of this material originated in *Hekhalot* literature or was found in texts of the German Pietists. In addition, several of the *maḥzorim* contain material on *sheʾelat ḥalom*, another *Hekhalot* technique that appears in rabbinic circles,[115] as well as procedures for dream

---

דשמשיאל ובזעקתא דנהריאל ובשם המפורש שהיא בן מ"ב אותיות [אבגת"ץ קרע
שטן]. משביע אני עליכם הקדושים האילו שתעזרוני ותסייעוני והצילוני ... לשוני
מלטוני והשמרוני ותהגוני ותתני לחן ולחסד ולרחמים בעיני כל רואי אותי ...
[212א] והסר את כעסך מעלינו יגדל רחמיך על מדותיך ... והתנחם על בניך במדת
רחמיך ותכנס להם לפנים משורת הדין ה' יברך את עמו ישראל בשלום. [כשאדם
יושב בתענית יאמר אחרי תפלה-יה"ר מלפניך ... (תענית שלי במקום קרבן)]

The introductory list of *Shemot* and angelic names is virtually identical to those found in ms. Corpus Christi 133 (published by Ta-Shma; see above, n. 112). See also *Teshuvot ha-Geonim ha-Ḥadashot*, ed. Emanuel, 125, 133. The requests are worded in somewhat different fashion, but they are essentially similar. The only significant stylistic difference is that the passage in ms. Corpus Christi is part of a prayer formulation that ends with a blessing, while the passage in Paris 633 is recited as a separate request. Note, however, the short mystical adjuration found in ms. Paris 633 (fols. 74 and 129; see above, n. 101), which also ends with the blessing of *shomeaʿ tefillah*. See also ms. Vat. Rossiana 356, above, n. 99. Although many personal *teḥinnot* from Ashkenaz ended with this blessing, and there was halakhic justification for this practice, some Ashkenazic authorities, including R. Judah he-Ḥasid, were against the inclusion of the blessing. See Ta-Shma, *Minhag Ashkenaz ha-Qadmon*, 140, n. 10, and the literature cited. [The passage cited from *Sefer ha-Yirʾah*, which allowed this blessing, constitutes a rare disagreement between this work and the teachings of R. Judah he-Ḥasid; see above, ch. 1, n. 84.]

[115]For *sheʾelat ḥalom*, see, e.g., ms. Paris 1408 (Ashkenaz, fourteenth century [1329]), fol. 146r. The tosafists mentioned in this manuscript are primarily German. The manuscript also contains customs, liturgical comments, ethical insights, and esoteric comments from R. Eleazar of Worms; a talmudic commentary and a series of penitentials from R. Judah he-Ḥasid; and a number of halakhic rulings, responsa, and brief treatises from R. Meir of Rothenburg. A significant role was played in the copying of this manuscript by the scribe Elqanah, a student of Maharam, who cites a passage from *Maʿaseh Merkavah*. See Colette Sirat, "Le Manuscrit Hébreu 1408 de la Bibliotèque Nationale," *REJ* 123 (1964): 335–58, esp. 348; see also the description by M. Schwab in *REJ* 64 (1912):280–81; and see above, n. 37. On fol. 146r, at the bottom of a section about a ruling in *ʾissur ve-heter* (in the same handwriting, but shifted on the folio page), there is a *sheʾelat ḥalom be-shem Sandalfon*:

שרא רבא השבעתי אותך סנדלפון שאתה ממונה על השאלה שתבוא לי בזה
הלילה ותפתר לי חלומי כשם שפתר גבריאל ליוסף חלום פרעה. ותבוא לי

interpretation. Specific attribution of any mystical or magical prayers to Rabbenu Tam, however, remains totally unsubstantiated.[116]

שאלתי ובקשתי ממה שאבקש ממך בזה הלילה. השבעתי אותך השר סנדלפון בשם המפורש היושב בעבי שחקים השמים העליונים היושב בערבה... השבעתי אותך סנדלפון בשם א׳ אשר א׳... ורעדו גדולי עליונים ותחתונים... תרעש הארץ... השבעתי אותך השר סנדלפון בשם הקב״ה שהוא מפורש בע׳ שמות והוא מפואר בעליונים ובתחתונים. השבעתי אותך השר סנדלפון בשם מיכאל תקופת ניסן בשם עניאל שהוא על זרעא בארעא. השבעתי אותך השר סנדלפון בשם תימניא תקופת תמוז שהוא על אילנו דעלמא. השבעתי בשם מטריאל תקופת תשרי שהוא על מיטרא גינזיא. השבעתי וכו׳ בשם סמטיאל תקופת טבת שהוא על חלומות. הראינו כי בזה הלילה מה שבלילה ותן לי שאלתי ובקשתי. תצום ג׳ ימים.

Another request is found on the other corner at the bottom of the page:

בדוק- ירחץ עצמו ויצום אותו יום... ויאמר... בשלשים שנה למפרע. בזה הענין... מראות ואראה השמים נפתחים כבר זוהר על הגולה בתוך ואני לחודש בחמשה ברביעי שנה בשלשים ויהי (= למפרע). ויאמר ז׳ פעמים ה׳ אלקי האמת הראיני חלום אמת. ה׳ אלקי ישראל הצדק הראיני חלום צדק... ה׳ טוב הראיני חלום טוב... ה׳ מפואר הראיני ח׳ מפואר וכו׳ ויחשוב בלבו ויאמר בלבו י׳ פעמים כל אחד ואחד ויבוא מה שבקש.

[The first *baqqashah* is to know something through *she*ʾ*elat ḥalom*, the second is more of a free request. On these forms of *she*ʾ*elat ḥalom*, cf. *Sefer Razi*ʾ*el*, 114, 137–38; above, n. 8; ms. Bodl. 2312, fol. 57v (below, ch. 4, n. 39); and below, ch. 5, n. 37. On Sandalfon in this literature, see, e.g. Schäfer, *The Hidden and Manifest God*, 92, 106; Margoliot, *Mal*ʾ*akhei Elyon*, 148–50; Wolfson, *Through a Speculum That Shines*, 264; idem, "Mystical-Theurgical Dimensions of Prayer in *Sefer ha-Rimmon*," *Approaches to Judaism in Medieval Times*, ed. David Blumenthal, vol. 3 (Atlanta, 1988), 77, n. 146; Daniel Abrams, "The Boundaries of Divine Onthology: The Inclusion and Exclusion of Metatron in the Godhead," *Harvard Theological Review* 87 (1994):301; and see now Arthur Green, *Keter* (Princeton, 1997), 23–32, 100–101. Sandalfon is also invoked in *Kol Bo*, sec. 139 (above n. 112). See also above, n. 99 (end), and cf. *Tosafot Ḥagigah* 13b, s.v. *ve-qosher*.]

[116]Regarding dream interpretation, see the section entitled *pittaron ḥalomot* in Paris 633, fols. 118–20. See also ms. Moscow-Guenzberg 13 (Ashkenaz, fourteenth century), fols. 25, 27–38; ms. Paris 187 (Italy, fifteenth/sixteenth centuries), fols. 61r–63v (following *seder ha-teshuvah* by R. Eleazar of Worms, a *viddui* attributed to Ramban and texts of *gittin* from *Semaq* and *Sefer ha-Terumah*); and ms. Paris 644 (Ashkenaz, thirteenth/fourteenth centuries), fols. 22r–25v (*pittaron ḥalomot*). Cf. Harris, *Studies in Dream Interpretation*, 29–30; Trachtenberg, *Jewish Magic and Interpretation*, 230–41; Thorndike, *A History of Magic and Experimental Science*, 2:290–302; and Kruger, *Dreaming in the Middle Ages*, 7–16. It should be noted that magical material in the *maḥzorim* is all formulaic. There is no evidence in these texts for magical amulets or symbols that might be applied in addition to the prayers. Cf. *Sefer Razi*ʾ*el*, above, n. 112. For an example of a northern French daily prayer rite that followed the rulings of Rabbenu Tam in particular and contains none of the mystical or magical elements discussed here, see ms. Cambr. 790 (thirteenth century), fols. 1–14.

It should be noted that there are a number of other texts and statements incorrectly attributed to Rabbenu Tam, especially in the realm of Jewish-Christian polemics.[117] These mistaken attributions may have occurred simply because Rabbenu Tam was the leading scholar of his day.[118] In addition, R. Jacob *ha-Levi* of Marvège, a younger Provençal contemporary of R. Jacob Tam and author of *She᾽elot u-Teshuvot min ha-Shamayim*, was also referred to as Rabbenu Tam. R. Jacob *ha-Levi*'s responsa utilize the mystical technique of *she᾽elat ḥalom* to resolve halakhic questions, heightening the difficulty in identifying "Rabbenu Tam" when this name appears in *sod* or magical contexts.[119] Indeed, the very way the name Rabbenu Tam is usually recorded,

---

[117]See David Berger, *The Jewish-Christian Debate in the High Middle Ages* (Philadelphia, 1979), 13, n. 22, 248–49; Frank Talmage, "Ha-Polmos ha-Anti-Noẓeri be-Ḥibbur Leqet Qaẓar," *Michael* 4 (1976):67–68; *Sefer Yosef ha-Meqanne*, ed. Judah Rosenthal (Jerusalem, 1970), 45, sec. 23, n. 1; *Tosafot ha-Shalem*, ed. Jacob Gellis, vol. 5 (Jerusalem, 1986), 57; Heschel, "Al Ruaḥ ha-Qodesh Bimei ha-Benayim," 182, n. 37; and my "On the Role of Bible Study in Medieval Ashkenaz," *The Frank Talmage Memorial Volume*, ed. Walfish, 1:163, n. 42. On the attribution of the mildly kabbalistic ethical work *Sefer ha-Yashar* (thirteenth century) to Rabbenu Tam (whose halakhic work and talmudic compendium bear the same title), see Urbach, *Baᶜalei ha-Tosafot*, 1:107–8, and Shimon Shokek, *Jewish Ethics and Jewish Mysticism in Sefer ha-Yashar* (Lewiston, 1991), 3–27.

[118]Cf., e.g., Gottlieb, *Meḥqarim be-Sifrut ha-Qabbalah*, 516–24; Tuvia Preschel, "Iggeret she-Yuḥasah be-Taᶜut la-Ramban," *Talpiyyot* 8 (1961):49–53; my *Jewish Education and Society*, 174–75, n. 69; Ta-Shma, "Quntresei 'Sodot ha-Tefillah' le-R. Yehudah he-Ḥasid," *Tarbiẓ* 65 (1996):74–77; above, n. 110, and ch. 1, n. 89; *Sefer Tagmulei ha-Nefesh le-Hillel ben Shemuᶜel mi-Verona*, ed. Yosef Sermonetta (Jerusalem, 1981), 154, n. 136; and cf. Avraham Epstein in *Daᶜat ve-Ḥevrah be-Mishnatam shel Ḥasidei Ashkenaz*, ed. Ivan Marcus (Jerusalem, 1987), 32–33, n. 21.

[119]See *She᾽elot u-Teshuvot min ha-Shamayim le-Rabbenu Yaᶜaqov mi-Marvège*, ed. Margoliot, editor's introduction, 21; Urbach, *Baᶜalei ha-Tosafot* 1:238, n. 45*; Israel Ta-Shma, "She᾽elot u-Teshuvot min ha-Shamayim: Ha-Qoveẓ ve-Tosafotav," *Tarbiẓ* 57 (1988):57; Sperber, *Minhagei Yisra᾽el*, 1:41, n. 5, 2:256, 4:313–14; the studies cited in my "Rabbinic Figures in Castilian Kabbalistic Pseudepigraphy," 82, n. 21, and 95, n. 66; above, ch. 1, n. 88; and below, ch. 4, n. 61. [For references to R. Jacob of Orléans, a student of Rabbenu Tam, as ר״ת מאורליינש, see, e.g., Urbach, 1:142; and *Tosafot ha-Shalem*, ed. Gellis, vol. 3, 200; vol. 4, 212, 241; vol. 5, 3, 38; vol. 9, 48, 196, 205, 208–9, 215; vol. 10, 15, 151. For R. Jacob of Chinon as ר״ת מקינון, see *Tosafot Rabbenu Pereẓ he-Shalem ᶜal Massekhet ᶜEruvin*, ed. Chaim Dickman (Jerusalem, 1991), passim; and H. Gross, *Gallia Judaica*, 579. For R. Jacob of Corbeil as ר״ת מקורביל, see *Tosafot ha-Shalem*, ed. Gellis, vol. 9, 133, and cf. below, ch. 4, n. 27.] The sources cited by Heschel, "Al Ruaḥ ha-Qodesh Bimei ha-Benayim," 182–84 (nn. 36, 37, 46), that associate ר״ת with *she᾽elat ḥalom* can be shown to refer to R. Jacob of Marvège. See also *She᾽elot u-Teshuvot min Ha-Shamayim*, ed. Margoliot, editor's introduction, 21–22; ms.

using only the *rashei tevot* ר״ת, lends itself to imprecise or confused reference.[120]

Beginning in the middle of the twelfth century, R. Samuel b. Qalonymus *he-Ḥasid* of Spires and his son, R. Judah *he-Ḥasid* (followed by the latter's student, R. Eleazar of Worms), rejuvenated and greatly expanded (to include a highly developed theosophy) the mystical teachings and expressions of *ḥasidut* they had received from their Pietist ancestors and teachers who studied almost exclusively in Mainz.[121] Perhaps the relative lack of interest in *torat ha-sod* shown by Rashbam, Raban, and Rabbenu Tam—despite their clear awareness of this material—was because the methodology of the academy at Worms in the last part of the eleventh century adumbrated and, through R. Meir b. Samuel (the father of Rashbam and Rabbenu Tam) and others, helped stimulate the development of tosafist dialectic. The influence of Worms, where mystical teachings were not in evidence, was dominant at the beginning of the tosafist period.[122]

Bodl. 2274, fol. 28; and cf. ms. Bodl. 781, fols. 91–95. Two other texts that make this association (cited by Heschel in nn. 42, 44), *Sefer Yosef Omeẓ* and *Shalshelet ha-Qabbalah*, are significantly later works, and the distortions in both cases in regard to Rabbenu Tam have already been noted (above, nn. 98, 102). The reference in *Sefer ha-Yashar* to Rabbenu Tam as a *navi* has been shown to have an exoteric connotation; see Shraga Abramson, "Navi, Roʾeh ve-Ḥozeh," *Sefer Yovel Muggash li-Khevod ha-Rav Mordekhai Kirschblum*, ed. David Telsner (Jerusalem, 1983), 118–23. Cf. R. Reiner, "Rabbenu Tam: Rabbotav (ha-Ẓarefatim) ve-Talmidav Benei Ashkenaz," 47–48, n. 169.

[120]See, e.g., ms. Sassoon 290 sec. 751, fols. 284–85: שאלה לר״ת אם יש כח בזה השם [ה׳ צ-באות] לעשות הדבר הגדול הזה. A second question, which is not directed to any particular scholar, concerns the use of other Divine Names. See also above, n. 28, and Daniel Abrams, "Sefer Shaqod le-R. Shemuʾel b. R. Qalonymus ve-Torat ha-Sod shel Talmid R. Eleazar mi-Worms," *Assufot* (forthcoming), nn. 58, 60. In an Eastern manuscript dated 1636, ms. Jerusalem/Menaḥem Feldman 3, the following appears in an addendum to the body of *Sefer Shoshan Sodot* (fol. 182r–183r): שאלה לר״ת דרך גמטריות... שאלה ששאל מאן לר״ת... סליק סוד.

[121]On Mainz traditions and *ḥasidei Ashkenaz*, see above, ch. 1, nn. 11–12, 22, and above, nn. 11–13. For the concentration of pietism in Mainz during the pre-Crusade period, see also above, ch. 1, n. 22. On the dating of *Sefer Ḥasidim*, cf. Haym Soloveitchik, "Le-Taʾarikh Ḥibburo shel 'Sefer Ḥasidim,'" *Tarbut ve-Ḥevrah be-Toledot Yisraʾel Bimei ha-Benayim*, ed. Reuven Bonfil et al. (Jerusalem, 1989), 383–88; and Ivan Marcus, *Piety and Society* (Leiden, 1981), 136–37, 153, n. 88.

[122]See my *Jewish Education and Society*, 69–74; Grossman *Ḥakhmei Ashkenaz ha-Rishonim*, 343, 412–15, 437–38; idem, "Reshitan shel ha-Tosafot," *Rashi: ʿIyyunim bi-Yeẓirato*, 57–68; and idem, *Ḥakhmei Ẓarefat ha-Rishonim*, 437–54. The only master associated exclusively with Worms who was involved in the transmission of *sodot ha-tefillah* and esoteric *taʿamim* and with the use of *Shemot*—in addition to his activity as

The influence of Mainz, on the other hand, was barely felt in the early twelfth century, although it did return at a later point. Even Raban, who studied in Mainz before the First Crusade, makes almost no reference to pre-Crusade rabbinic material from there, probably because of the disruptive impact of the First Crusade.[123] Israel Ta-Shma has argued that there was a conscious effort by twelfth-century tosafists (especially in northern France) to constrict their libraries, at least with respect to earlier halakhic writings, in order to focus without distraction on their independent approach to talmudic interpretation. For this reason, the rabbinic literature of eleventh-century Ashkenaz was largely ignored by the early tosafists.[124] Whether by design or by circumstance, these tosafists did not embrace the mystical, magical, and pietistic teachings and practices that had been prevalent in pre-Crusade Mainz.[125]

V

Although the dialectical method and approach to talmudic interpretation pioneered by Rabbenu Tam and his contemporaries dominated Ashkenaz through the end of the thirteenth century, there is much evidence to suggest that not all tosafists shared their attitude toward the disciplines of mysticism and magic, which had been a scholarly endeavor in the pre-Crusade period, as we have noted. Indeed, we shall see that several students of Rabbenu Tam—including Ri, R. Eleazar of Metz, and Ribam, among others—were involved in aspects of mystical studies and practices. All this activity stands in addition to the presence of related material that has been noted in *sifrut de-Vei Rashi*, and in prayer texts and interpretations from the late twelfth century and beyond.

Once again, the question should be raised as to whether the German Pietists, who were coming into their own at this very point in time, were particularly influential in disseminating mystical and magical materials in northern France (and Germany), or whether there was a broader stream within rabbinic culture throughout medieval Ashkenaz that valued these disciplines—just as there was a stratum represented by Rashbam and Raban that apparently

---

a *payyetan*—(all of which calls to mind R. Simeon *ha-Gadol*) was R. Meir b. Isaac חזן (*Shaliaḥ Ẓibbur*). See Grossman, *Ḥakhmei Ashkenaz ha-Rishonim*, 293–95; and above, ch. 1, n. 55; ch. 2, n. 65.

[123]Grossman, *Ḥakhmei Ashkenaz ha-Rishonim*, 439.

[124]See Ta-Shma, "The Library of the French Sages," *Rashi, 1040–1090*, ed. Sed-Rajna, 535–40, and cf. above, n. 70.

[125]For Rabbenu Tam's (negative) attitude toward *perishut*, see above, ch. 1, nn. 26–28, and see also ch. 2, n. 81 for Raban. Cf. Urbach, *Ba^calei ha-Tosafot*, 1:176, 2:742.

did not. Although Divine Names and their uses and powers were an area of great interest and significance in the esoteric thought of the German Pietists,[126] we shall see that the leaders of *Ḥasidei Ashkenaz* were not as supportive of the actual use of *Shemot* and *hashbaᶜot* for practical purposes as might have been expected. This suggests that Ashkenazic tosafists who discussed and advocated these techniques were motivated to do so because of their own spiritual heritage or religious commitment.

---

[126]See, e.g., Haviva Pedaya, "Pegam ve-Tiqqun," 157, n. 1, and the literature cited there, and Wolfson, *Through a Speculum That Shines*, ch. 5, passim.

4

Between Tosafists and German Pietists

I

The dialectical method pioneered by Rabbenu Tam and other early tosafists held sway in northern France and Germany throughout the twelfth and thirteenth centuries.[1] The influence of these scholars is perhaps also evident in those *Tosafot* texts that appear to downplay or modify mystical or magical interpretations proposed by Rashi and others.[2] At the same time, however,

---

[1]For a survey of the contours of tosafist dialectic, see my *Jewish Education and Society in the High Middle Ages* (Detroit, 1992), 69–79, and the literature cited in 168, nn. 21–26; 172, n. 53; 173, n. 57; 179–80, n. 88.

[2]See, e.g., *Tosafot Berakhot* 3a, s.v. *ve-ᶜonin* (=*Tosafot R. Yehudah Sir Leon, Tosafot Rabbenu Pereẓ*, ad loc.), and Haviva Pedaya, "Pegam ve-Tiqqun shel ha-E-lohut be-Qabbalat R. Yiẓḥaq Sagi Nahor," *Meḥqerei Yerushalayim be-Maḥshevet Yisraʾel* 6 [3–4] (1987):258; *Tosafot Ḥagigah* 14b, s.v. *nikhnesu la-pardes* (כגון על ידי שם ולא עלו למעלה ממש אלא היה להם כמו שעלו וכן פי' בערוך), and *Tosafot ha-Rosh*, ad loc. (ms. Moscow-Guenzberg 488, fol. 39r); *Tosafot ha-Rosh, Gittin* 84a, s.v. *ᶜal menat shetaᶜali*; *Tosafot Qiddushin* 73a, s.v. *maiʾikka lememar*; *Tosafot ha-Rosh* and *Tosafot Tukh*, ad loc. (ed. A. Z. Scheinfeld [Jerusalem, 1982], 130); *Tosafot Sukkah* 45a, s.v. *ʾani va-ho*; and see Rashi above, ch. 3, nn. 28, 33–34. The approach of the ספר הערוך, which was also espoused by R. Hai and R. Ḥananʾel, locates the experience of the *Merkavah* mystic in his own mind or imagination. See Elliot Wolfson, *Through a Speculum That Shines* (Princeton, 1994), 144–48. Despite the influence of this view on mystical doctrines of *Ḥasidei Ashkenaz* (Wolfson, 214–17, and see above, ch. 3, n. 75), it is apparent that *Tosafot Ḥagigah* is attempting to skirt the more explicit *sod* implications of Rashi's interpretation. See also Moshe Idel, *Kabbalah: New Perspectives* (New Haven, 1988), 90–91,

there are *Tosafot* texts whose interest in concepts such as the function of *ḥayyot* and *ʾofannim*, the use of *Shemot* to achieve revelation, and the possibility of

---

who stresses the rationalistic nature of R. Hai's approach; Joseph Dan, "The Beginnings of Jewish Mysticism in Europe," *The Dark Ages* [*The World History of the Jewish People*, vol. 11], ed. Cecil Roth (Ramat Gan, 1966), 284–85; idem, "Sefer Shaʿarei ha-Sod ha-Yiḥud veha-Emunah," *Temirin* 1 (1972):149–50; above, ch. 3, n. 28; and cf. *Tosafot ʿAvodah Zarah* 28b, s.v. *shoryeinei de-ʿeina*.

See also *Tosafot R. Yehudah Sir Leon ʿal Massekhet Berakhot*, ed. Nissan Zaks (Jerusalem, 1969–72), 2:599 (*Berakhot* 53b, s.v. *gadol ha-ʿoneh ʾamen*). The interpretation of the talmudic dictum—that one who answers *ʾamen* to a blessing is greater than the one who makes the blessing, since *ʾamen* is the *gematria* equivalent of the letters of the Tetragrammaton in both its written and vocalized forms (and the one who answers, therefore, has, in effect, invoked the name of the Almighty two times)—is rejected by R. Yehudah Sir Leon as לא נהירא. This interpretation originates in *Maḥzor Vitry*, 97 (sec. 126), and *Sefer Ḥasidim* (*SḤB* 18, in the "French" recension of the work; cf. above, ch. 1, n. 2); it is found almost exclusively in works that were part of the circle of the German Pietists or connected to it, such as *Sefer Roqeaḥ*, *Sefer ʿArugat ha-Bosem*, and *Sefer Or Zaruaʿ*. See also *Tosafot ha-Rid* (cf. below, ch. 5, n. 21) and *Perush Baʿal ha-Turim ʿal ha-Torah*, ed. Y. K. Reinitz (Jerusalem, 1993), 2:522 (to *Devarim* 27:26). See the sources cited in *Tosafot R. Yehudah Sir Leon*, ed. Zaks, nn. 316–17 (and note R. Menaḥem *ha-Meiri*'s rationalistic interpretation). Cf. Ruth Langer, *To Worship God Properly* (Cincinnati, 1998), 219, n. 111. *Sefer ha-Manhig*, ed. Y. Raphael, 1:31–32, cites this interpretation in the name of Rashbam, whose awareness of esoteric teachings related to Divine Names has been noted (above, ch. 3, n. 66), although this attribution has been questioned by David Rosin (in the introduction to his edition of Rashbam's *Perush ʿal ha-Torah* [Breslau, 1882], xvii), in light of Rashbam's rationalism; and see also Raphael's note, loc. cit. This Ashkenazic interpretation ultimately made its way into the Zohar [and should be added to the list of examples compiled by Israel Ta-Shma, *Ha-Nigleh shebe-Nistar* (Tel Aviv, 1995), 21–26] and into the biblical commentary of R. Baḥya b. Asher (*Shemot* 14:31). Rashba (*Responsa*, 5:53) refers to the esoteric interpretation of this talmudic passage (*ʿinyan neʿelam le-baʿalei ḥokhmah*). In his aggadic commentary to *Berakhot*, he links the esoteric interpretation of the passage to the *sefirot*. See also the formulation of Rabbenu Yonah cited in *Beit Yosef, O. Ḥ.*, sec. 124, and Maharsha to *Sotah* 40b, s.v. *minayin sheʾein ʾomrim*. [R. Judah Sir Leon's awareness and rejection of the suggested esoteric interpretation is consistent with the fact that he is cited as proposing a messianic date on the basis of a calculation, rather than through a dream or quasi-prophecy as a number of his contemporaries did. See E. E. Urbach, *Baʿalei ha-Tosafot* (Jerusalem, 1980²), 1:344; my "Rabbinic Figures in Castilian Kabbalistic Pseudepigraphy: R. Yehudah *he-Ḥasid* and R. Elḥanan of Corbeil," *Journal of Jewish Thought and Philosophy* 3 (1993):88, n. 41; above, ch. 3, n. 41; and below, n. 8.]

See *Tosafot Shabbat* 156b, s.v. *kaldaʾei*, regarding the prohibition of using *goralot* to predict the future, and cf. *Beit Yosef, Yoreh Deʿah*, sec. 179. See also *Semag, lo taʿaseh* 52; *Tosafot Niddah* 16b, s.v. *ha-kol bidei shamayim*; and Jacob Bazak, *Le-Maʿalah min ha-Ḥushim* (Tel Aviv, 1985²), 61–62.

solving halakhic dilemmas by quasi-prophetic means transcends the realm of pure *sugya* interpretation or the resolution of conflicting talmudic passages.[3]

Moreover, a number of Rabbenu Tam's leading students in both northern France and Germany exhibited familiarity with esoteric teachings, even though they do not appear to have had any formal connection to *Ḥasidei Ashkenaz*. An eschatological formulation by R. Isaac b. Samuel of Dampierre (Ri), R. Tam's nephew and most important student—which describes those who will merit their reward in *gan ʿeden* but will not continue to exist in *ʿolam ha-ba*, and also details the fates of complete *reshaʿim* and *ẓaddiqim*—is cited by R. Elḥanan b. Yaqar of London in his mystical commentary to *Sefer Yeẓirah* in the name of R. Isaac *ha-Zaqen* [=Ri].[4] R. Elḥanan, who spent time in northern France with

---

[3]See *Tosafot Ḥagigah* 13b, s.v. *katuv ʾeḥad ʾomer*; 13a, s.v. *ve-raglei ha-ḥayyot* (based on midrash and Yerushalmi), and *Tosafot ha-Rosh*, ad loc. (ms. Moscow 488, fols. 38v–39r); and *Ḥullin* 92a, s.v. *barukh ofannim* (and see ms. Vat. 159, fol. 91r). This *Tosafot* is interested in the difference between functions of various types of angels, but the discussion is couched in *ʾim tomar/yesh lomar* terms and proceeds on the basis of talmudic texts. Cf. *Synopse zur Hekhalot-Literatur*, ed. Peter Schäfer et al. (Tübingen, 1981), secs. 146, 197, 236, 723–24. See also *Tosafot Gittin* 84a, s.v. *ʿal menat she-taʿali*, and *Tosafot Sukkah* 45a, s.v. *ʾani va-ho*. Cf. Rashi, above, ch. 3, n. 28; *Tosafot Sanhedrin* 22a, s.v. *arbaʿim yom qodem yeẓirat ha-valad*, and *Pisqei ha-Tosafot*, ad loc. (and cf. *SḤB*, 794–95, and *Levush, O. Ḥ.*, 230:1); *Tosafot Eruvin* 60b, s.v. *ʾein ʾelu ʾela divrei neviʾut* (and cf. *Tosafot Bava Batra* 12a, s.v. *R. Yose*; *Tosafot Menaḥot* 109b, s.v. *ba-teḥillah*; *Tosafot Yevamot* 14, s.v. *R. Yehoshuaʿ*; Shraga Abramson, *R. Nissim Gaon: Ḥamishah Sefarim* [Jerusalem, 1965], 292, n. 237; and E. E. Urbach, "Halakhah u-Nevuʾah," *Tarbiẓ* 18 [1947]:10–22; 22, n. 188). *Tosafot ʿAvodah Zarah* 2b, s.v. *zu Romi*, cites the *Hekhalot* text, *Maʿaseh Merkavah*, which asserts that Rome merited large-scale destruction following the murder of R. Ḥananyah b. Traydon. In *Tosafot R. Elḥanan*, ad loc., this reference is attributed to Ri. See *Synopse zur Hekhalot-Literatur*, secs. 115–20; Gershom Scholem, *Jewish Gnosticism, Merkavah Mysticism, and Talmudic Tradition* (New York, 1960), 101–2; and above, ch. 3, n. 37. A passage attributed in *Sifrut de-vei Rashi* to *Sefer Yeẓirah* is cited by *Tosafot Ḥagigah* 3b, s.v. *u-mi*. Cf. above, ch. 3, n. 31.

[4]Ms. JTS Mic. 8118 (ENA 838), fol. 65v. Joseph Dan, who transcribed R. Elḥanan's commentary from this manuscript, inadvertently missed the passage. His transcription skips from the beginning of fol. 65r and resumes at the same point on fol. 66r. See his *Tekstim be-Torat ha-E-lohut shel Ḥasidut Ashkenaz* (Jerusalem, 1977), pt. 2, 34–35, and his "Sifrutam ha-ʿIyyunit shel Ḥasidut Ashkenaz" [Hebrew University, M. A. seminar] (Jerusalem, 1973), 34–35. This passage does not appear in the other version of R. Elḥanan's commentary published by Georges Vajda. See Vajda, "Perush R. Elḥanan b. Yaqar le-Sefer Yeẓirah," *Qoveẓ ʿal Yad* n.s. 6 [16] (1966):148–50 [and cf. lines 183–93]. The only other northern French rabbinic scholar mentioned by R. Elḥanan in his commentary [most of his sparse references are to Spanish or Provençal philosophers] is Rashi, who is cited in both versions regarding *mazzalot*. See JTS Mic. 8118, fol. 65v, and Vajda, line 250. [In another manuscript that contains the version published by Vajda—

fellow members of the *Ḥug ha-Keruv ha-Meyuḥad*,[5] indicated that he studied *Sefer Yeẓirah* with an unnamed scholar who himself had studied it with R. Isaac *ha-Zaqen*.[6] There is an additional instance in which a member of the *Ḥug ha-Keruv ha-Meyuḥad* associated Ri with the study of *Sefer Yeẓirah*. According to one variant of the *Ḥug's* Pseudo-Saʿadyah commentary to *Sefer Yeẓirah*, Ri [ר״י הזקן = ר״ז] and his disciples wished to create a *golem* in the course of their study of *Sefer Yeẓirah*, but the students became endangered in the process. Ri directed them to reverse the letters of the alphabet they had recited previously, and the students were spared.[7]

Ri is included among a list of Ashkenazic scholars who purportedly received and transmitted mystical prognostications: **ר״י עלה למרום וקבל דברים ממלאכי השרת**.[8] He is perhaps the only rabbinic figure in that group who has not been associated with the German Pietists, although it is likely that he was

---

Nuremberg (Municipal Library) Cent. V app. 5/1 (seventeenth century), of which Vajda was apparently unaware—the letters representing Rashi are fully written out in the margin (fol. 59v) as R. Shelomoh Yarḥi (of Lunel). See Ḥida, *Shem ha-Gedolim* (Warsaw, 1878), *Maʿarekhet ha-gedolim*, 116; and Maurice Liber, *Rashi* (Philadelphia, 1904), 34.]

[5]See above, ch. 1, n. 65. The precise connection and relationship between the *Ḥug ha-Keruv ha-Meyuḥad* and *Ḥasidei Ashkenaz* remain somewhat elusive. See also Vajda, "Perush R. Elḥanan b. Yaqar," 148; Dan, *Tekstim be-Torat ha-E-lohut*, 22; and the literature cited in my "Rabbinic Figures in Castilian Kabbalistic Pseudepigraphy," 84–85, nn. 27–31, 106, nn. 100–101. In his *Sod ha-Sodot*, R. Elḥanan writes that he is a descendant of R. Simeon *ha-Gadol* (**מגזע ר׳ שמעון הגדול**), who was a significant figure in esoteric studies in Mainz during the eleventh century and was originally from northern France. See above, ch. 3, n. 4. For *segullot* and *hashbaʿot* by R. Elḥanan, similar to those composed by *Ḥasidei Ashkenaz*, see below, n. 49.

[6]See Vajda, "Perush R. Elḥanan b. Yaqar," 148, 184; Gershom Scholem, *Origins of the Kabbalah*, ed. R. J. Z. Werblowsky (Princeton, 1987), 250–51, n. 103; Urbach, *Baʿalei ha-Tosafot*, 1:237; and below, n.9.

[7]See Moshe Idel, *Golem* (Albany, 1990), 81–82, 91–92, n. 4. As Idel indicates, the more common reading of the scholar who was teaching *Sefer Yeẓirah* is **ריב״א**. It is likely that this refers to R. Isaac b. Abraham of Dampierre, a student of Ri. Cf. my "Rabbinic Figures in Castilian Kabbalistic Pseudepigraphy," 105–6, n. 99; the revised Hebrew edition of *Golem* (Jerusalem, 1996), 309–10, n. 4; above, ch. 1, n. 156; and below, n. 37.

[8]See Alexander Marx, "Maʾamar ʿal Shenat Geʿulah," *Ha-Ẓofeh le-Ḥokhmat Yisraʾel* 5 (1921):194–202, and cf. above, ch. 3, n. 6. The text published by Marx from ms. Bodl. 388 (fourteenth century) includes similar heavenly prognostications from R. Samuel and R. Judah *he-Ḥasid*, R. Ezra *ha-Navi* of Moncontour, and R. Troestlin *ha-Navi*. Cf. Gershon Cohen, "Messianic Postures of Ashkenazim and Sephardim," *Studies of the Leo Baeck Institute*, ed. Max Kreutzberger (New York, 1967), 128–30. Urbach, *Baʿalei ha-Tosafot*, 1:238, suggests that this account of Ri should be dated (like the manuscript itself) from the fourteenth-century. Grossman, *Ḥakhmei Ẓarefat ha-Rishonim*, 51, has located a parallel manuscript, ms. JTS Rab. 1609. On fol. 32r,

visited in northern France by R. Judah *ha-Ḥasid* and that he met R. Samuel *he-Ḥasid* as well.[9] R. Abraham b. Nathan *ha-Yarḥi* (of Lunel) studied with Ri.

R. Hai Gaon and R. Zevadyah (Zekharyah), son of R. Yosef *Tov ᶜElem*, offer (political) signs that would signify the approach of the *geᶜulah* (cf. above, ch. 3, n. 2): "And my father told me in the name of R. Judah [Sir Leon] of Paris that Bilᶜam lived in the middle of (the duration of) the world." According to Grossman, this suggests that the writer or compiler of (part of) this text was from the mid-thirteenth century (a position held also by Adolf Neubauer; see his *Catalogue of the Hebrew Manuscripts in the Bodleian Library* [Oxford, 1886], 85). This is confirmed by the fact that most of the messianic dates listed in the text are in the 1230s. See also Scholem, *Origins of the Kabbalah*, 230, n. 5. The latest messianic date found in the text (1296) suggests that no part of it was composed later than 1280. Although this text is thus somewhat late in terms of authenticating the positions of R. Hai and R. Zevadyah b. Yosef *Tov ᶜElem*, the characterization of Ri is not in question. Cf. Urbach, 1:337, n. 21. On the reliability of this text, see also below, ch. 5, n. 67. [On the other hand, the formulation attributed to Ri in the introduction to the fourteenth-century Spanish compendium *Ẓedah la-Derekh*—that no one else could have composed a work comparable to R. Isaac Alfasi's *Halakhot* unless he communicated with the *Shekhinah* (Urbach, 1:251)—remains unsubstantiated. Cf. Jacob Katz, *Halakhah ve-Qabbalah* (Jerusalem, 1986), 348, and my *Jewish Education and Society*, 66–67. The description of Ri as משיח ה' in ms. Bodl. 847, fols. 36r–36v, is a reflection of Ri's position as the outstanding talmudist of his generation. See also below, n. 64.]

[9]See my "Rabbinic Figures in Castilian Kabbalistic Pseudepigraphy," 88, nn. 41–42. The similar messianic dates suggested by all the central figures in the so-called *maʾamar ᶜal shenat ha-geʾulah* discussed in the preceding note (R. Samuel *he-Ḥasid*, R. Judah *he-Ḥasid*, R. Ezra *ha-Navi*, R. Troestlin *ha-Navi*, and Ri) imply some relationship among these figures.

On Ri's deep piety and his tendencies toward fasting and self-denial, similar to those of R. Judah *he-Ḥasid*, see above, ch. 1, nn. 29–30. [*Ha-Qadosh mi-Danpira*, mentioned several times in *Pisqei Rabbenu Yeḥiel mi-Paris*, refers to Ri rather than to his martyred son R. Elhanan. See Urbach, *Baᶜalei ha-Tosafot*, 1:459, n. 45, and cf. my "Rabbinic Figures in Castilian Kabbalistic Pseudepigraphy," 84–85, n. 30.] For Ri's awareness of *Hekhalot* literature, see above, ch. 3, n. 37. R. Judah *he-Ḥasid* (d.1217) was a younger contemporary of Ri, who died between 1185 and 1190; see Urbach, 1:253. Ri and R. Judah *he-Hasid* (in *Sefer ha-Kavod*, and as cited by R. Eleazar of Worms) held the same view concerning the danger of drinking water at the *tequfah* and the permissibility of using water for *maẓẓah* from the day on which the *tequfah* changes, which includes both an awareness of the *sakkanah* involved (due to the absence of the angelic *memunim* who protect the water supply from *maziqim*) and the notion that religious devotion can supersede forms of *sakkanah*. Similar approaches to this issue are found only in *Sefer ha-Alqoshi* (written by a student of Rashi who was adept in astrology; see above, ch. 3, n. 65); *Sefer Assufot* (written by a student of R. Eleazar of Worms); *Sefer ha-Manhig* (by an author who studied with Ri; see the next note); the Zohar; and R. Menaḥem *Ẓiyyoni*, who followed closely the teachings of *Ḥasidei Ashkenaz*. See Israel Ta-Shma, "Issur Shetiyyat Mayim ba-Tequfah u-Meqoro," *Meḥqerei Yerushalayim be-Folklor Yehudi* 17 (1995):21–32. [On the generally more conservative posture of Ri as compared to

It was within Ri's circle that R. Abraham observed certain pietistic and mystical practices in prayer that he attributed to scholars and pietists in northern France.[10]

A talmudic passage that alludes to the tactics of *poterei ḥalomot* (dream interpreters) was understood by Ri as referring to those who arrived at their interpretation on the basis of the *mazal* under which a person was born, rather than through the application of any kind of *ḥokhmah*.[11] The Talmud prohibits the use, even for medicinal purposes, of trees worshipped by idolaters. Ri

---

Rabbenu Tam, in terms of both personality and their tendencies in legal reasoning, see, e.g., Jacob Katz, *Exclusiveness and Tolerance* (New York, 1961), 30–36, 46–47, and Haym Soloveitchik, "Three Themes in the *Sefer Ḥasidim*," *AJS Review* 1 (1977):341, n. 98.]

[10]See, e.g., *Sefer ha-Manhig*, ed. Y. Raphael (Jerusalem, 1978), 1:363, 2:475, 478, 519, 526. On R. Abraham of Lunel (and R. Judah b. Yaqar) as students of Ri, see also Israel Ta-Shma, "Ḥasidut Ashkenaz bi-Sefarad: Rabbenu Yonah Gerondi—ha-Ish u-Foᶜalo," *Galut Aḥar Golah*, ed. Aharon Mirsky et al. (Jerusalem, 1988), 171–73; my "Rabbinic Figures in Castilian Kabbalistic Pseudepigraphy," 97–98, n. 73; and below, n. 34. On the role of R. Abraham as a conduit during the Maimonidean controversy, see above, ch. 1, n. 50. On *sod* in *Sefer ha-Manhig*, see above, ch. 1, nn. 61–63.

Urbach, *Baᶜalei ha-Tosafot*, 1:237–38, suggests that R. Abraham of Lunel was Ri's contact with the mystics of southern France. The scholars of Lunel (who were both talmudists and mystics), including R. Asher b. Meshullam, asked halakhic questions of Ri. R. Asher was characterized by R. Benjamin of Tudela as renouncing worldly affairs, studying day and night, and fasting and not eating meat. See also Israel Ta-Shma, *R. Zeraḥyah ha-Levi Baᶜal ha-Maʾor u-Vnei Ḥugo* (Jerusalem, 1992), 162–66. (For Ri's ascetic tendencies, see the preceding note.) On awareness in southern France of the ascetic renunciations usually associated with German Pietism, cf. Marc Saperstein, "Christians and Christianity in the Sermons of Jacob Anatoli," *The Frank Talmage Memorial Volume*, ed. Barry Walfish (Haifa, 1992), 2:233. R. Jacob b. Saul *ha-Nazir* of Lunel, also had connections to *Ḥasidei Ashkenaz* and to rabbinic scholars in northern France. See Moshe Idel, "Ha-Kavvanah ba-Tefillah be-Reshit ha-Qabbalah: Bein Ashkenaz li-Provence," *Porat Yosef*, ed. Bezalel and Eliyahu Safran (New York, 1992) [Hebrew section], 5–14; idem, "Al Kavvanat Shemoneh ᶜEsreh ʾeẓel R. Yiẓḥaq Sagi Nahor," *Massuʾot*, ed. Oron and Goldreich, 31–36; *ᶜArugat ha-Bosem*, ed. Urbach, 4:117–19; Ta-Shma, *Minhag Ashkenaz ha-Qadmon* [Jerusalem, 1992], 127–28, and n. 10; Avraham Grossman, "Perush ha-Piyyutim le-R. Aharon b. Ḥayyim ha-Kohen," *Be-Oraḥ Madda* [*Sefer Yovel le-Aharon Mirsky*], ed. Zvi Malachi et al. (Lod, 1986), 462, n. 23; and above, ch. 2, n. 14. [Note that more than twenty manuscripts of Rashi's commentary to Job add exegetical material from R. Jacob *ha-Nazir*, following the last of Rashi's comments in ch. 40; see, e.g., ms. Parma 181 (Ashkenaz, twelfth/thirteenth centuries), fols. 263–64.]

[11]See *Tosafot Berakhot* 55b, s.v. *potrei ḥalomot; Tosafot R. Yehudah Sir Leon*, ad loc.; and cf. above, ch. 3, n. 116. Cf. the similar approach suggested in the response to the

suggested that the effectiveness of these trees, as opposed to others of the same kind, was unlocked because the idolators invoked *shedim*.[12] Moreover, Ri. approved the magical summoning of *shedim* in order to ascertain through divination the whereabouts of lost objects.[13] In light of Ri's familiarity with mystical teachings and magical techniques, it is likely that his support of the magical summoning of *shedim* to find lost objects reflects more than a simple acceptance of popular beliefs or superstitions.[14]

Another leading student of Rabbenu Tam, R. Eliezer of Metz (1115–98), has a lengthy discussion in his *Sefer Yere'im* about *hashbaat shedim* and *hashba'at malakhim*. He concludes that these techniques, which are akin to methodologies found in *Sefer Yezirah*, are not prohibited as *ma'aseh keshafim*. When a person, however, "creates an actual object or changes a person's mind through his own magical manipulations" (not through *hashba'at malakhim* or *hashba'at shedim*), that person is guilty of sorcery.[15]

---

she'elat halom of R. Jacob of Marvège in his *She'elot u-Teshuvot min ha-Shamayim*, ed. Margoliot, #22, 61–62. See also Heschel, "Al Ruah ha-Qodesh Bimei ha-Benayim," 179, n. 17, on Ri's use of the phrase *divrei nevi'ut* in a halakhic context; and cf. *Shitah Mequbbezet* to *Bava Mezi'a* 85b, in which Ri is cited by *Tosafot Shanz* (אומר ר' שבחלום הראהו).

[12]See *Tosafot Pesahim* 25, s.v. *huz*, and *Tosafot Rash mi-Shanz*, ad loc.

[13]See Abraham Halpern, "Sefer Mordekhai ha-Shalem le-Massekhet Bava Qamma" (Ph.D. diss., Hebrew University, 1978), vol. 2, 211–12 [to *Bava Qamma* 116a=idem, (Jerusalem, 1992), 2:213]: פסק ר"י לתת לו כל אשר התנה דבר זה רגילין לתת יותר מכדי טירחו. Ri expressed this view in an actual case, and it was recorded by R. Judah Sir Leon. See also *Semag, 'aseh* 74 (fol. 153), and cf. *Semag, lo ta'aseh* 55 (fol. 11a); R. Eliezer of Metz (below, n. 19); *Sefer Or Zarua', Bava Qamma*, sec. 457; and below, ch. 5, n. 13. For other medieval Ashkenazic halakhic texts that deal with the permissibility of consulting *shedim* to apprehend a thief and for other purposes, see below, ch. 5, nn. 21, 72; and cf. below, n. 49, and the next note.

[14]For magical techniques and *segullot* (from Ashkenazic scholars) that could be used to catch a thief, see, e.g., ms. Parma 541, fol. 267r (sec. 80), and ms. Vat. 243, fol. 12r. [Cf. ms. Milan Ambrosiana P12, sup. 53/10 (on this manuscript, cf. Gershom Scholem in *Qiryat Sefer* 11 [1934–35]:185–86), fol. 138v (end), in the name of Isaac b. Samuel, regarding the philosophical possibility of immersion in air as well as water. This figure is, however, R. Yizhaq *de-min Akko*, rather than Ri. Note that a R. Isaac (*ha-Navi*) *Zarefati* is referred to in writings of the German Pietists as well as Geronese kabbalists. See my "Rabbinic Figures in Castilian Kabbalistic Pseudepigraphy," 100, n. 80; below, ch. 5, n. 49; and cf. Chavel, *Kitvei ha-Ramban*, 2:346.]

[15]*Sefer Yere'im ha-Shalem*, ed. Avraham Abba Schiff (Vilna, 1892–1902), sec. 239. This position is attributed to R. Eliezer in R. Yeroham b. Meshullam, *Toledot Adam ve-Havvah*, sec. 17, pt. 5 (fol. 159d). See also *Semag, lo ta'aseh* 55; *Tosafot ha-Shalem*, ed. Jacob Gellis, vol. 6, 186–87; above, ch. 3, n. 29 (Rashi); above, n. 13 (Ri); and below, ch. 5, n. 13 (R. Avigdor Katz), and n. 21 (Rid).

R. Eliezer also suggests that mystical names and markings quite similar to those found in *Maḥzor Vitry* be included in *mezuzot*. Unlike *Maḥzor Vitry*, however, and perhaps in deference to Rabbenu Tam, R. Eliezer writes that these are not absolutely required by Jewish law (*ʾeino le-ʿikkuvah ve-lo le-miẓvah*) but should be included for added protection (*le-tosefet shemirah*).[16] R. Eliezer is cited by his student, R. Eleazar of Worms, as ruling that it is appropriate to stand during the recitation of the first portion of *Qeriʾat Shema*. This ruling, which has pietistic overtones, is based on (a passage in) *Hekhalot* literature. All subsequent proponents of this view in Europe during the thirteenth century were either German Pietists or among those associated with *ḥasidut Ashkenaz*.[17]

R. Eliezer of Metz cautioned against a person saying, even in jest, that God had told him something directly. This warning may be indicative of R. Eliezer's familiarity with quasi-prophetic experiences—of the kind experienced by Ri's student, R. Ezra *ha-Navi* of Moncontour, and others—that will be discussed more fully below.[18] On the other hand, R. Eliezer permitted the binding of a dying individual by oath to return after his death, to tell or answer whatever he is asked (*ha-mashbiaʿ ʾet ha-ḥoleh lashuv le-ʾaḥar mitah le-hagid lo ʾasher yishʾal lo*). In R. Eliezer's view, this is not a violation of the prohibition against communicating with the dead (*doresh ʾet ha-metim*), since the request was made to the individual while he was still alive. Although R. Eliezer cites two talmudic texts in support of this arrangement, he once

---

[16]*Sefer Yereʾim ha-Shalem*, sec. 400. See also *Haggahot Maimuniyyot, Hilkhot Tefillin* 4:4; *Maḥzor Vitry*, 648–49 (and above, ch. 3, n. 57); *Sefer Pardes ha-Gadol*, sec. 285 (which includes the practice of R. Judah *he-Ḥasid*; cf. Ta-Shma, *Halakhah, Minhag u-Meẓiʾut be-Ashkenaz*, 282–87); Urbach, *Baʿalei ha-Tosafot*, 1:161; and Victor Aptowitzer, "Le Nom de Dieu et des Anges dans la Mezouza," *REJ* 60 (1910):40. Cf. *Semag*, *ʿaseh* 22, *ʾasur le-hosif*. R. Abraham b. Azriel cites R. Judah *he-Ḥasid*, R. Eleazar of Worms, and R. Eliezer of Metz concerning the halakhic and mystical implications of erasing certain Divine Names; see *ʿArugat ha-Bosem*, ed. Urbach, 3:32. In general, *Sefer Yereʾim* is cited extensively by R. Abraham; see *ʿArugat ha-Bosem*, 4:164.

[17]See Erich Zimmer, "Tenuḥot u-Tenuʿot ha-Guf bi-Sheʿat Qeriʾat Shema," *Assufot* 8 (1995):346–48, esp. 348, n. 25. Among those who supported this practice (which originated in *Ereẓ Yisraʾel*) were the *Sefer Minhag Tov*, R. Meir of Rothenburg, and several Spanish kabbalists. Cf., e.g., above, n. 2, for a similar pattern of development.

[18]See *Sefer Yereʾim*, sec. 241 (fol. 110a); *Haggahot Maimuniyyot, Hilkhot ʿAvodah Zarah* 5:8 [1]; and Urbach, "Halakhah u-Nevuʾah," 22, n. 188. Urbach suggests that R. Eliezer's published warning in this matter demonstrates that it was a fairly frequent occurrence. R. Jacob of Marvège, author of *Sheʾelot u-Teshuvot min ha-Shamayim*, was a younger contemporary of R. Eliezer of Metz. Although R. Jacob flourished in Provence, his work had an impact in Ashkenaz and perhaps also raised the specter of baseless claims for Divine guidance. See below, ch. 5, nn. 22–24, 67.

again displays clear interest in occult practices.[19] Indeed, R. Eliezer's formulation adumbrates a lengthier passage in *Sefer Ḥasidim* concerning a commitment made between two people that the first of them to die would communicate with the other, either through a dream or in a more vivid form.[20]

In referring to the way that *kohanim* hold their hands during the priestly benediction (with their fingers separated), R. Eliezer writes that he does not know the origin of this custom, but he asserts that it was practiced *be-qabbalah*. He also heard that it was based on a midrashic interpretation of the biblical phrase, *meẓiẓ min ha-harakkim*. In light of the mystical formulations that relate to the placement of the hands of the *kohanim*, this term perhaps reflects the impact of esoteric teachings.[21]

A contemporary of R. Isaac of Dampierre and R. Eliezer of Metz, R. Jacob of Corbeil (d.1192)—who is referred to as both *ha-Qadosh* and *he-Ḥasid*

---

[19]See *Sefer Yere*ʾ*im*, secs. 334–35; *Haggahot Maimuniyyot, Hilkhot* ʿ*Avodah Zarah* 14:13 [8]; and *Beit Yosef, Yoreh De*ʿ*ah*, sec. 179, s.v. ʾ*ov*. According to R. Eliezer, the biblical prohibition called אוב involves the use of sorcery to raise the deceased from his grave. In the case at hand, however, the communication takes place while the deceased remains in his grave (which is further reason to permit it). This passage from *Sefer Yere*ʾ*im* is also included by Zedekiah b. Abraham *ha-Rofe* in his *Shibbolei ha-Leqet* (*ha-ḥeleq ha-sheni*), ed. Simcha Hasida (Jerusalem, 1988), 43, sec. 11). [Maimonides, *Hilkhot* ʿ*Avodah Zarah*, loc. cit., writes that any act by which a dead person can inform the living is punished by lashes.] Cf. *Shulḥan* ʿ*Arukh, Yoreh De*ʿ*ah*, 179:14; and *Shakh*, ad loc., sec. 16 (who notes the correlation between R. Eliezer's view and positions of the Zohar and *ḥakhmei ha-qabbalah*).

[20]See *SḤP* 324: אם שני בני אדם טובים בחייהם נשבעו או נתנו אמונתם יחד אם ימות אחד מהם שיודיע לחבירו היאך באותו עולם וכו'. Cf. Monford Harris, *Studies in Jewish Dream Interpretation* (Northvale, 1994), 20; and above, ch. 1, n. 105, and ch. 2, nn. 52, 70.

[21]*Sefer Yere*ʾ*im*, sec. 269 (end; fol. 127b). Cf. *Midrash Leqaḥ Tov* to Numbers 6:23; *Perushei ha-Torah le-R. Yehudah he-Ḥasid*, ed. Y. S. Lange (Jerusalem, 1975), 166; *Arba*ʿ*ah Turim, O. Ḥ.*, sec. 128; and the kabbalistic sources cited in *The Book of the Pomegranates*, ed. Elliot Wolfson (Atlanta, 1986), 254 (note to line 12). See also Elliot Horwitz, "Al Ketav-Yad Meẓuyar shel Sefer Mishneh Torah," *Qiryat Sefer* 61 (1986): 584–85; and Hananel Mack, "Midrash Askenazi le-Pereq Alef be-Sefer Yeshayahu," *Zion* 63 (1998):124. On the mystical implications of *meẓiẓ*, see Moshe Idel, "Tefisat ha-Torah be-Sifrut ha-Hekhalot ve-Gilgulehah ba-Qabbalah," *Meḥqeri Yerushalayim be-Maḥshevet Yisra*ʾ*el* 1 (1981):35, n. 36. [According to *Shibbolei ha-Leqet*, sec. 23, this positioning of the hands by the *kohanim* signifies that אימת שכינה עליהם.] In *Sefer Yere*ʾ*im*, sec. 322 (fol. 360), R. Eliezer ruled that a deceased non-Jew does not engender *tum*ʾ*at* ʾ*ohel*, based on the fact that the prophet Elijah conducted himself this way and entered a non-Jewish cemetery. Cf. Urbach, "Halakhah u-Nevu'ah," 12, n. 96. Other *rishonim* also ruled according to Elijah; cf. *Tosafot Yevamot* 61a, s.v. *mi-magga* citing Ri, found in *Haggahot Maimuniyyot, Hilkhot Avelut* 2:3, in the name of Rabbenu Tam.

[*mi-Corbeil*][22]—was cited concerning the number of words to be recited in *Shema* and the effects of their recitation, in a manner that modern scholarship has already noted reflects a mystical or pietistic bent.[23] R. Zedekiah b. Abraham Anav *ha-Rofe* offered a reason for the established Ashkenazic custom of maintaining the number of words that comprise the core of *Qeri*ʾ*at Shema* at 248. He found this reason, which was formulated on the basis of a *gematria*, among the "*Ta*ʿ*amei R. Yehudah he-Ḥasid.*" It is essentially an embellishment of a passage in *Midrash Tanḥuma*, that the words of the *Shema* correspond to the number of man's limbs. Reciting the *Shema* properly will save a person from both sin and demon (*shed*).[24] The only other contemporary rabbinic figures to

---

[22]See, e.g., *Tosafot Shabbat* 27a, s.v. *she-ken*; Shabbat 61a, s.v. *dilma*; *Sefer Or Zarua*ʿ, *pisqei* ʿ*avodah zarah*, pt. 4, sec. 270; and Henri Gross, *Gallia Judaica* (Paris, 1897), 562. R. Jacob of Corbeil was martyred. The epithet *ha-Qadosh* was also used, however, to connote saintliness, piety, or ascetic tendencies. See Isadore Twersky, *Rabad of Posquières* (Philadelphia, 1980²), 27–28, and above, n. 9. [Jacob was characterized by *Sefer Yuḥasin* as a mequbbal; see Urbach in the next note.]

[23]See Urbach, *Ba*ʿ*alei ha-Tosafot*, 1:150–51; Norman Golb, *Toledot ha-Yehudim be-Ir Rouen Bimei ha-Benayim* (Jerusalem, 1976), 239, n. 400; Avraham Grossman, "Perush ha-Piyyutim le-R. Aharon b. Ḥayyim ha-Kohen," 461–62. The formulation from R. Jacob cited in these studies was preserved in a *piyyut* commentary written by his nephew, R. Aaron *ha-Kohen* (ms. Bodl. 1206, fol. 148v). R. Jacob was quoted as advocating the recitation of the complete *Shema* at one's bedside, since, according to the *Tanḥuma*, the 248 words in it (including the phrase *E-l melekh ne*ʾ*eman*) would protect the 248 limbs of the human body. (A more complete reference, that the recitation of *Shema* would also protect specifically against *maziqin*, is found only in ms. Paris 167; see below, n. 26). As far as I can tell, the name of R. Jacob's father does not appear in any rabbinic texts of Ashkenazic origin (nor is there any indication of a father's name in texts that mention R. Jacob's brother, R. Judah of Corbeil). See my "Rabbinic Figures in Castilian Kabbalistic Pseudepigraphy," 88, n. 43. *Sefer ha-Manhig*, whose author R. Abraham b. Nathan of Lunel studied in northern France with Ri (see above, n. 10), does, however, give their father's name as R. Isaac. See *Sefer ha-Manhig*, ed. Raphael, 2:649. Scholem, *Origins of the Kabbalah*, 249–51, 324, suggested generally that Corbeil was a seat of mystical studies. In my "Rabbinic Figures in Castilian Kabbalistic Pseudepigraphy," I endeavored to document this assertion with regard to several tosafists and other known rabbinic figures associated with Corbeil, but there are still names that remain unidentified. A *gematria* interpretation of the phrase היתה תוהו, which hints at the destruction of both Temples, and *gematriya* and אתב"ש interpretations of the ensuing biblical phrases that yield references to Divine Names and eschatological dates, are cited in ms. Bodl. 2105 [the biblical commentary of R. Ephraim b. Samson] (fol. 101v), in the name of R. Eliezer of Corbeil. See *Tosafot ha-Shalem*, ed. Gellis, vol. 1 (Jerusalem, 1982), 19; and cf. my "Rabbinic Figures," 81, n. 16.

[24]See *Shibbolei ha-Leqet ha-Shalem*, sec. 15, ed. S. K. Mirsky (Jerusalem, 1976), 175; and ms. Bodl. 659 (*Shibbolei ha-Leqet ha-Qaẓar*), fol. 9. *Shibbolei ha-Leqet* records

cite both the midrash itself and the notion that the proper recitation of *Shema* will protect a person by warding off demonic forces (*maziqin*) were the talmudist and kabbalist R. Judah b. Yaqar (d.c.1215)—whose receipt of esoteric traditions from the German Pietists has been documented recently[25]—and R. Jacob of Corbeil. Indeed, R. Judah b. Yaqar's formulation corresponds precisely to the formulation of R. Jacob of Corbeil as it appears in a fuller version still in manuscript.[26] A biblical comment by R. Jacob anticipates almost

---

additional passages from the otherwise unknown treatise of *Taamei R. Yehudah he-Ḥasid*. See sec. 185 (ed. Solomon Buber, 144) and the end of sec. 236; ms. Bodl. 659, fols. 41r, 62, 112v, 113v, and cf. Jacob Freimann's introduction to *SHP*, 6; and ms. Paris 1408, fol. 40v. Cf. Elliot Wolfson, "Circumcision and the Divine Name: A Study in the Transmission of Esoteric Doctrine," *JQR* 78 (1987):110–11. In the pietistic introduction to his *Sefer Roqeaḥ* (*Hilkhot Ḥasidut, shoresh neqiyyut me-ḥet*) [Jerusalem, 1967], 15, R. Eleazar of Worms cites (anonymously) a *gematria* of the word *ᶜavon* in the context of the 248 words of *Shema* that is also found in the passage from *Taᶜamei R. Yehudah he-Ḥasid* cited in *Shibbolei ha-Leqet*, but he makes no reference to demons. In his discussion of the recitation of *Shema* in the body of *Sefer Roqeaḥ* (p. 211), R. Eleazar merely cites the *Tanḥuma* text to support the custom of 248 words, without any of the pietistic embellishment. See also *Perushei Siddur ha-Tefillah la-Roqeaḥ*, ed. Moshe Hershler (Jerusalem, 1992), 1:282. On *Shibbolei ha-Leqet* and *sod*, see below, ch. 5, nn. 28–30.

[25]See *Perush ha-Tefillot veha-Berakhot le-R. Yehudah b. Yaqar* (Jerusalem, 1979), 30. The uniqueness of R. Judah's interpretation of the protection offered by the recitation of *Shema* has been noted by Elliot Wolfson, "Dimmui Antropomorfi ve-Simboliqqah shel Otiyyot Sefer ha-Zohar," *Meḥqerei Yerushalayim be-Maḥshevet Yisraʾel* 8 (1989):161, n. 162. On R. Judah's receipt of mystical teachings from the German Pietists, see my "Rabbinic Figures in Castilian Kabbalistic Pseudepigraphy," 97–98, n. 73, and below, n. 35. Ta-Shma, *Ha-Nigleh shebe-Nistar*, 95, n. 42, notes that the hymn *E-l Adon* (recited as part of the Sabbath morning prayer service) was included in the *siddurim* of both R. Judah b. Yaqar and R. Eleazar of Worms. This custom reached both R. Yeḥiʾel of Paris and the Zohar. See below, ch. 5, n. 43.

[26]Ms. Paris 167/2, fols. 93r–93v: לשמירה מפני המזיקין. R. Judah b. Yaqar also studied with the tosafist Riẓba in northern France (see Urbach, *Baᶜalei ha-Tosafot*, 1:263–64, and below) and may have gained access there to R. Jacob's material. Whether R. Judah received his material from R. Jacob or from R. Judah *he-Ḥasid*, the fact that only he—a devotée of *Ḥasidei Ashkenaz*—R. Judah *he-Ḥasid*, and R. Jacob of Corbeil had this interpretation cements the relationship or at least the common approach of R. Jacob and German Pietism. [For the impact of the accepted Ashkenazic custom concerning the number of words in *Shema* on the Zohar, see the pioneering study of Israel Ta-Shma, "E-l Melekh Neʾeman—Gilgulo shel Minhag (Terumah le-Ḥeqer ha-Zohar)," *Tarbiz* 40 (1970):184–94; idem, *Minhag Ashkenaz ha-Qadmon*, 285–96; idem, *Ha-Nigleh shebe-Nistar*, 15; and my "Rabbinic Figures in Castilian Kabbalistic Pseudepigraphy," 108–9, n. 108.]

precisely a passage in the Pietist biblical commentary attributed to R. Eleazar of Worms, which was actually composed by another student of R. Judah *he-Ḥasid*.[27] The specific methods of interpretation utilized by R. Jacob were among those favored by R. Judah.[28]

R. Jacob's full comment appears in ms. Paris 167 among a collection of tosafist interpretations, especially those of Rabbenu Tam, that were grouped under the heading *Perush ha-Torah me'et Shelomoh ha-Kohen b. Yaᶜaqov ha-Kohen*. The manuscript was copied in Byzantium in 1443. In the version in ms. Bodl. 1206 (see above, n. 23), R. Aaron also notes that there was a controversy between his uncle R. Jacob, *ha-qadosh mi-Corbeil*, and Rabbenu Jacob [Tam] of Ramerupt. His uncle adduced proofs that the *Shema* recited at bedtime (after nightfall) was more important, while Rabbenu Tam argued that the *Shema* recited during the evening prayer in the synagogue (after sundown) was more crucial. Cf. Ta-Shma, *Minhag Ashkenaz ha-Qadmon*, 319, n. 17, and Grossman, above, n. 23. As Urbach notes (*Baᶜalei ha-Tosafot*, 1:151, n. 48), this controversy involved many more Ashkenazic (and Sefardic) rabbinic figures than the two R. Jacobs. Urbach indicates, however, that the only other known reference to the position of R. Jacob of Corbeil in this matter is found at the beginning of *Sefer Or Zarua'*, *Hilkhot Qeri'at Shema* (sec. 1), in which R. Jacob is quoted as responding to one of Rabbenu Tam's questions against the position of Rashi (who held that the later *Shema* was the more important). Ms. Paris 167 (fols. 92r–93v) records a lengthy version of the argument between Rabbenu Tam and R. Jacob of Corbeil, while commenting on the biblical locus of *Shema* in the portion of *Va-Etḥanan*. In this fuller version of R. Jacob of Corbeil's position, he suggests answers to all four of the questions Rabbenu Tam had posed against Rashi's position (as recorded in the *Or Zaruaᶜ*, the position with which R. Jacob of Corbeil concurred). The essential element of R. Jacob of Corbeil's resolution of the conflicting talmudic sources was that a scholar who recited the *Shema* at the preferred time (after nightfall) did not have to recite it again at his bedside upon retiring, but others (nonscholars) who had read the *Shema* earlier must recite it fully (i.e., not just the first paragraph) at their bedsides. In this regard, R. Jacob was advocating the earlier Ashkenazic position, which was also held by *Sefer Ḥasidim*. Cf. Jacob Katz, "Maᶜariv bi-Zemanno u-Shelo bi-Zemanno," *Zion* 35 (1972):39–48, and my *Jewish Education and Society*, 86–99.

[27]See *Daᶜat Zeqenim* to Deuteronomy 12:21; the so-called *Perush ha-Roqeaḥ ᶜal ha-Torah*, ed. Chaim Konyevsky, ad loc. (3:221); and cf. Victor Aptowitzer, "Le Commentarie du Pentateuque Attribué à R. Ascher ben Yeḥiel," *REJ* 51 (1906): 75–76; *Tosafot Ḥullin* 28a, s.v. *ve-ᶜal rov*, and *Tosafot ha-Rosh*, ad loc.; and *Tosafot ha-Rosh* to *Ḥullin* 122b, s.v. *ve-gam*. The striking correspondence between R. Jacob's comment and the material found in *Perush Roqeaḥ* blunts Aptowitzer's claim that the *gematria* interpretation(s) in the style of *Ḥasidei Ashkenaz* offered by R. Jacob do not link him directly to the teachings of the German Pietists. On the author of the *Perush Roqeaḥ*, see Joseph Dan, "The Ashkenazi Hasidic Gates of Wisdom," *Hommage à Georges Vajda*, ed. Gerard Nahon and Charles Toutati (Louvain, 1980), 183–89, and idem, "Perush ha-Torah le-R. Eleazar mi-Germaiza," *Qiryat Sefer* 59 (1984):644.

R. Isaac b. Mordekhai (Ribam) of Bohemia, another devoted student of Rabbenu Tam, was asked a question by R. Judah *he-Ḥasid* with regard to *torat ha-malʾakhim*. One biblical passage implies that many angels watch over a righteous person, while another suggests that only one angel is involved. The answer given by Ribam is that the single angel is the *Sar ha-Panim*, who commands other angels under his control to traverse the world and ensure that nothing will harm righteous people (*she-lo yaziq shum davar la-ẓaddiqim*). E. E. Urbach has suggested that, in the absence of any other evidence for R. Isaac's involvement in mystical studies, it was probably Ribam who asked the question of R. Judah *he-Ḥasid*, rather than the reverse. Urbach supports his claim by emending the text of the question to read "הריב״ם שאל מאת ר׳ יהודה חסיד," rather than "הריב״ם נשאל מר׳ יהודה חסיד."[29] Aside from the interest in

---

A passage in ms. Bodl. 682, fol. 37r (in a gloss), which cites a ruling of R. Jacob of Corbeil, *mi-pi baʿal ha-ḥalom*, refers apparently to R. Jacob of Marvège. See *Sheʾelot u-Teshuvot min ha-Shamayim*, ed. Margoliot, #5, 49–52; cf. Eric Zimmer, *ʿOlam ke-Minhago Noheg* (Jerusalem, 1996), 136–37; and above, ch. 3, n. 119, and below, ch. 5, n. 48.

[28]On the *gematria/hatḥalot tevot* methodologies of R. Judah *he-Ḥasid*, cf. Wolfson, "Circumcision and the Divine Name," 88; Urbach, *Baʿalei ha-Tosafot*, 1:399; *ʿArugat ha-Bosem*, ed. Urbach, 4:110, n. 32; Joseph Dan, "The Ashkenazi Concept of Langauge," *Hebrew in Ashkenaz*, ed. Lewis Glinert (New York, 1993), 11–25; and above, ch. 2, n. 1.

[29]See ms. Paris 772 (R. Eleazar of Worms's prayer commentary), fol. 23v (שאל ר׳ יהודה החסיד ממורי הר״י בר׳ מרדכי), cited in *ʿArugat ha-Bosem*, ed. Urbach, 4:99, n. 75; and cf. Urbach, *Baʿalei ha-Tosafot*, 1:199, n. 38; and *Perushei Siddur ha-Tefillah la-Roqeaḥ*, ed. Moshe Hershler, 1:87. [The Philadelphia ms. noted by Hershler is, in fact, ms. Moscow-Guenzberg 614. See below, and see also S. Emanuel, "Ha-Polmos ʿal Nosaḥ ha-Tefillah shel Ḥasidei Ashkenaz," *Meḥqerei Talmud* 3 (in press), n. 25.] Prior to making his emendation, Urbach pointed out that Ribam was purely a talmudist who was uninvolved in *sod*, except in this instance. (Note also that in *Baʿalei ha-Tosafot*, 1:389, Urbach does not list Ribam among R. Eleazar of Worms's teachers. In the first edition of that work [1955], Urbach notes Ribam's lack of involvement in *torat ha-sod* but suggests no emendation of the text.)

In ms. Moscow-Guenzberg 614 (fol. 21r) the question is asked by R. Judah of "R. Mordekhai." Aptowitzer, *Mavo la-Rabiah*, 317, n. 5a, suggests that this reading should be corrected on the basis of Paris 772. Israel Ta-Shma, on the other hand, argues that this is the correct reading. See his "Le-Toledot ha-Yehudim be-Polin ba-Meʾot ha-Yod Bet/ha-Yod Gimmel," *Zion* 53, (1988): 363–64. Ta-Shma points out that although Ribam was from Regensburg—which was also R. Judah *he-Ḥasid*'s residence during the latter part of his life, thus affording ample opportunity for contact between the two scholars—Ribam was much older than R. Judah. Because of this age difference, it is hard to imagine that R. Eleazar of Worms was Ribam's student. At the same time, there is a R. Mordekhai of Poland who was connected with R. Judah's circle in Regensburg (see *Perushei ha-Torah le-R. Yehudah he-Ḥasid*, 94); there is also an

mystical teachings to be found among other students of Rabbenu Tam, Ribam's pietistic and meta-halakhic tendencies with respect to fasting on *Rosh ha-Shanah* further support the fact that he was the source of the information rather than the questioner.[30]

---

unidentified R. Mordekhai whose name appears in a *sod* context in a text of the *Ḥug ha-Keruv ha-Meyuḥad*. (See the so-called *perush le-Sefer Yeẓirah meyuḥas le-R. Saᶜadyah Gaon* in ms. B. M. 754, fol. 124r). It is perhaps this R. Mordekhai (assuming that both these references are to the same person) of whom R. Judah asked his question.

In response to Ta-Shma's suggestion, several points should be made. First, R. Eleazar of Worms's reference to Ribam as his teacher may be purely honorific, as is the case in countless instances involving tosafists and other *rishonim*. Indeed, there is also no evidence that R. Eleazar was a student of "R. Mordekhai." R. Judah *he-Hasid*'s relative youth lends credence to the fact that he was asking the question and not the reverse, as Urbach suggests (although there is at least one other example from Ashkenaz of a teacher or senior scholar asking a student, or less venerable figure, a question concerning *sod*; see ms. B. M. 752, fol. 78r: שאל רבינו יב״ק ב״ר מאיר את תלמידו ר׳ אלעזר מגרמייזא היאך יש להמליכו בשמים ובארץ ובארבע רוחות. והשיב לו יש להמליכו בעשר ספירות ואלו הן עומק ראשית ועומק אחרית כו׳). Moreover, the solutions proposed by both Urbach and Ta-Shma were offered primarily because they had no other evidence linking Ribam to mystical teachings. Since we can now see that there was significant interest in this area among R. Tam's French students, not to mention his German ones, Ribam's association with this question is appropriate, especially in light of Ribam's own pietistic proclivities that bring him even closer to R. Judah *he-Ḥasid*. See the next note, and cf. Rami Reiner, "Rabbenu Tam: Rabbotav (Ha-Ẓarefatim) ve-Talmidav Benei Ashkenaz," (M.A. thesis, Hebrew University, 1997), 81.

[30]See above, ch. 2, nn. 38–40. Cf. *She'elot u-Teshuvot min ha-Shamayim*, #86. R. Judah *he-Ḥasid* did, of course, respond to pietistic and mystical questions. See, e.g., Ivan Marcus, "Ḥibburei ha-Teshuvah shel Ḥasidei Ashkenaz," *Studies in Jewish Mysticism, Philosophy and Ethical Literature Presented to R. Isaiah Tishby*, ed. Joseph Dan and Joseph Hacker (Jerusalem, 1986), 375, n. 30. See also *Orḥot Ḥayyim, Hilkhot ᶜErev Yom ha-Kippurim*, sec. 6 (fol. 103b), and ms. Bodl. 682, fols. 369r-370r.

The inclusion of Ri *ha-Lavan*, another student of Rabbenu Tam, together with R. Judah b. Yaqar and Ramban in a text regarding *sefirot* (produced by R. Moses of Burgos) is pseudepigraphic; see Urbach, *Baᶜalei ha-Tosafot*, 1:222. Ri *ha-Lavan* was not a contemporary of the other two; see Gershom Scholem in *Tarbiz* 3 (1924):276–77. Nonetheless, A. M. Habermann, in *Yediᶜot ha-Makhon le-Ḥeqer ha-Shirah ha-ᶜIvrit* 3 (1937):94, n. 3, suggested that the inclusion is accurate, based on the fact that R. Isaac received קצת טעמים מן המחזור from R. Judah b. Qalonymus, father of R. Eleazar of Worms, who was knowledgeable in *sod* teachings. See ms. Bodl. 970, fols. 126r–132r, and see also Neubauer's *Catalogue*, 209. In light of the actual involvement of a number of Rabbenu Tam's students in *sod*, the co-opting of Ri *ha-Lavan* is readily understood, even if his own involvement in this area is doubtful; see my "Rabbinic Figures in Castilian Kabbalistic Pseudepigraphy," passim, for Spanish distortions of Ashkenazic figures.

R. Menaḥem of Joigny, yet another student of Rabbenu Tam, is mentioned as transmitting a *siman* for the arrival of Elijah the Prophet.[31] This passage occurs in a manuscript section that, as noted above, is laden with references to German Pietists and their predecessors and to mystical techniques and *segullot*.[32] R. Menaḥem is cited in a *Tosafot* passage as suggesting that salt is put on bread to keep the *satan* away.[33] He also argues strongly against Rabbenu

---

[31]Ms. Parma 541, fol. 266v (sec. 76): אור זרוע לצדיק ולישרי לב שמחה סופי תיבות ר׳ עקיבה. וכן אביר יעקב בגימטריא ר׳ עקיבה. והוא היה בן גר י-ה-ו-ה. וסימן אליהו הנביא קבלתי בשם ר׳ מנחם מיואני. [Note the linkage between Elijah and R. Aqiva in *Midrash Mishlei*, ch. 9 (Elijah buried R. Aqiva), and in *Nedarim* 50a (Elijah supported R. Aqiva, *parnasat ẓaddiqim*). Maimonides writes, in the introduction to his *Mishneh Torah*, that R. Aqiva's father, Joseph, was himself a גר צדק. Cf. *Perush R. Nissim Gaon* to *Berakhot* 27b, s.v. *nuqei le-R. Aqiva de-let leh zekhut* ᵓ*avot*, which asserts that R. Aqiva was descended from non-Jews.]

[32]See above, ch. 3, nn. 14–15. R. Menaḥem's *siman* appears immediately before "*te*ᶜ*amim*" of R. Neḥemyah [b. Makhir (?); see Grossman, *Ḥakhmei Ashkenaz ha-Rishonim*, 361–86] regarding *Gog u-Magog*. See below, n. 37, and ch. 5, n. 67. The *gematria* and/or *sofei tevot* derivations of the name R. Aqiva that precede R. Menaḥem's *siman* also appear in a contemporary manuscript, ms. Parma 563 (Ashkenaz, thirteenth century), fol. 40v (without attribution); in R. Eleazar of Worms's *Rimzei Haftarot* (to Isaiah 61), published in *Perush ha-Roqeah* ᶜ*al ha-Torah*, ed. Konyevsky, vol. 3 (Bnei Brak, 1981), 330; and in R. Isaac b. Moses' *Alpha-Beta* introduction to his *Sefer Or Zarua*ᶜ (see below, ch. 5, at n. 3), sec. 1. See also *Pitḥei Teshuvah*, to *Even ha-*ᶜ*Ezer, shemot nashim* (following sec. 129), under the letter *reish*. For additional *gematria* derivations (with pietistic implications) in Ashkenazic sources that involved the name of ר׳ עקיבה, see above, ch. 1, n. 39. Cf. Moshe Idel, "Tefisat ha-Torah be-Sifrut ha-Hekhalot ve-Gilguleha ba-Qabbalah," *Meḥqerei Yerushalayim be-Maḥshevet Yisra*ᵓ*el* 1 (1981):36–37, n. 39.

In ms. Moscow-Guenzberg 734, fol. 92v, the *sofei tevot* of אור זרוע לצדיק are shown to yield the word קרע; the *sofei tevot* of the words ולישרי לב שמחה are equivalent in *gematria* to the word טוב. The implication drawn from these *sofei tevot* is that complete repentance, when achieved through *yissurim*, redounds to the benefit of the individual. This derivation follows a *segullah* attributed to R. Judah *he-Ḥasid* (fol. 92r, מקובל מר׳ יהודה החסיד), which prescribes certain hand motions (or signs made with the fingers) and formulae to prevent an אדם רע, such as someone who is armed with a sword, from doing harm. [Fols. 88r and 89v contain *qabbalot* from Nahmanides for *shemirat ha-derekh* and for turning an enemy into a friend (מיד יהפוך לב אויב לאוהב).] Fol. 94r contains a *goral* from R. Meir of Rothenburg for taking action in the future; see below, ch. 5, n. 49. Cf. *Ohel Ḥayim* [A Catalogue of the Manuscripts of the Manfred and Anne Lehmann Collection], vol. 1, ed. Moshe Hallamish and Eleazar Hurvitz (New York, 1988), 193–94. In the Lehmann ms., the "*qabbalah*" from R. Judah *he-Ḥasid* to stop an ᵓ*adam ra* is on fol. 21 (and an additional *qabbalah* follows); Maharam's *goral* is on fol. 44.

[33]See *Tosafot Berakhot* 40a, s.v. *have melaḥ*, and Ta-Shma, *Minhag Ashkenaz ha-Qadmon*, 257–59. Cf. Isaac b. Judah *ha-Levi, Pa*ᶜ*aneaḥ Raza* (repr. Jerusalem, 1965), *parashat Qedoshim*, 311: שכן דרך ניחוש ההורגין את הנפש אוכלין עליו פת במלח שלא ינקמו

Tam that the problem of eating on the Sabbath during twilight (*bein ha-shemashot*), because the souls in *gan ʿeden* and in *gehinnom* would be disturbed (*gozel ʾet ha-metim*), applies to Friday evening rather than to *Shabbat* afternoon.[34]

נקמתו ממנו. On *Paʿaneaḥ Raza's* affinities with *Ḥasidei Ashkenaz*, see below, ch. 5, n. 79. Although the use of salt to protect against demons and witchcraft reflects an aspect of popular belief or superstition, discussions of the use of salt in Pietist and kabbalistic sources suggest dimensions of magic or esoteric teachings. See, e.g., *SḤP* 1465–67, and *Sefer Roqeaḥ*, sec. 353 (p. 240; and cf. Aaron Katchen, "The Convenantal Salt of Friendship," *The Frank Talmage Memorial Volume*, ed. Walfish, 1:167); Güdemann, *Ha-Torah veha-Ḥayyim*, 1:162, n. 4; and Trachtenberg, *Jewish Magic and Superstition*, 160. As Ta-Shma notes, the protective powers of salt in this instance can be correlated with other, older Ashkenazic ritual practices that also took into account protection from *maziqin*.

R. Menaḥem's interest in *mesorah*, similar to that of *Ḥasidei Ashkenaz* and their followers, has been noted (above, ch. 2, n. 52). See also the references to R. Menaḥem of Joigny and *ha-Qadosh* R. Yom Tov b. Isaac of Joigny (*min ha-perushim*; cf. above, ch. 1, n. 36) in ms. Bodl. 1150 (Ashkenaz, fourteenth century), fol. 19v, in a collection of ritual law that includes halakhists from the circle of R. Judah *he-Ḥasid*, such as R. Moses Fuller, R. Eliezer of Bohemia, and R. Jacob b. Naḥman of Magdeburg (fols. 17v–18r, 20r). These rulings follow *shirei ha-yiḥud veha-kavod* that are also associated with *Ḥasidei Ashkenaz*. See also ms. JNUL 8°476, fol. 107r; Ta-Shma (above, ch. 2, n. 41), 368–69; and the *piyyut* by R. Menaḥem b. Pereẓ *ha-Zaqen* in *Leqet Piyyutim u-Seliḥot me-ʾet Payyetanei Ashkenaz ve-Ẓarefat*, ed. Daniel Goldschmidt and Jonah Frankel (Jerusalem, 1993), 2:433–44. R. Menaḥem of Joigny is identified in Norman Golb, *Toledot ha-Yehudim be-ʿIr Rouen Bimei ha-Benayim*, 92, as the teacher of R. Samuel of Falaise. R. Samuel refers to an unidentified teacher of his as R. Menaḥem *Ḥasid*; see above, ch. 2, n. 10.

[34]See *Moshav Zeqenim ʿal ha-Torah*, ed. Solomon Sassoon (London, 1959), 144 (on Exodus 16:5) [=*Perushim u-Fesaqim le-R. Avigdor* (*Ẓarefati*), ed. E. F. Hershkowitz (Jerusalem, 1996), *pesaq* 125, pp. 95–96]: והטעם נכון לפי שבאים מתים קרוביו תוך שנתן י״ב חדש מדין שלהם וטובלין בנהר היוצא מגן עדן ונכנסין שם, ולכן כששותה מים אז [בבין השמשות בערב שבת] גוזל את קרוביו. (The souls who spent the week undergoing the rigors of judgment were able to quench their thirst only as the Sabbath approached.) The position taken by R. Menaḥem was also held by R. Meshullam of Melun (and by R. Judah *he-Ḥasid*). Cf. *Sefer Or Zaruaʿ*, vol. 2, *hilkhot moẓaʾei Shabbat*, sec. 89; S. E. Stern, "Shetiyyat Mayim be-Shabbat Bein ha-Shemashot," *Yeshurun* 2 (1996):3–4; Ta-Shma, *Minhag Ashkenaz ha-Qadmon*, 203–5; and *Sefer Gematriʾot le-R. Yehudah he-Ḥasid*, ed. Daniel Abrams and Israel Ta-Shma (Los Angeles, 1998), 49 (fol. 13r). For the view of Rabbenu Tam, see his *Sefer ha-Yashar* (*ḥeleq ha-teshuvot*), ed. Rosenthal, secs. 45:6, 48:12, and above, ch. 3, n. 90. As Ta-Shma notes, R. Jacob of Marvège posed a *sheʾelat ḥalom* to ascertain whether one who ate on the Sabbath between afternoon and evening prayers "sinned," as R. Jacob [Tam] had ruled (*Sheʾelot u-Teshuvot min ha-Shamayim*, #39). The answer he received was clearly in the negative. Cf. *Shibbolei ha-Leqet*, *ʿinyan Shabbat*, sec. 127, who cites this dream of "the *ẓaddiq*," R. Jacob of

R. Isaac b. Abraham (Riẓba), the older brother of R. Samson of Sens and one of Ri's most important students, is referred to in a kabbalistic formulation. There remains some doubt, however, as to whether a kabbalistic compiler appended his interpretation to a remark originally made by Riẓba in the course of analyzing a ritual concept or whether Riẓba actually discussed the mystical material himself.[35] On the other hand, Moshe Idel has suggested that either

---

Marvège, to counter the claim of Rabbenu Tam. Yaakov Gartner, *Gilgulei Minhag be-ᶜOlam ha-Halakhah* (Jerusalem, 1995), 183–89, demonstrates the insistence of kabbalists that the third meal must take place following *minḥah* on the Sabbath afternoon.

[35]See Scholem, *Origins of the Kabbalah*, 251, n. 107. To his student Naḥmanides, R. Judah b. Yaqar passed along tosafist talmudic methodology and Ashkenazic halakhic material and customs he received from Riẓba. See, e.g., *Ḥiddushei ha-Ramban to Pesaḥim* 117b (=*Orḥot Ḥayyim le-R. Aharon ha-Kohen mi-Lunel, hilkhot leil Pesaḥ*, sec. 21), and cf. *Sefer Roqeaḥ*, sec. 283; Urbach, *Baᶜalei ha-Tosafot*, 1:396, n. 57; and Solomon Schechter, "Notes on Hebrew Mss. in the University Library of Cambridge," *JQR* 4 (1892):250. Indeed, it appears that Ramban's awareness of the importance of maintaining the 248 words of *Shema* by reciting *E-l melekh neʾeman* came from the north via R. Judah b. Yaqar. See Israel Ta-Shma, "E-l Melekh Neʾeman—Gilgulo shel Minhag," 288–89, n. 7. R. Judah b. Yaqar also probably passed along esoteric material that he received from unidentified German Pietists; see, e.g., Elliot Wolfson, "Demut Yaᶜakov Ḥaquqah be-Kisse ha-Kavod: ᶜIyyun Nosaf be-Torat ha-Sod shel Ḥasidei Ashkenaz," *Massuʾot*, ed. Oron and Goldreich, 154–56 (cf. idem, *Along the Path*, 27–29); M. Idel, *Kabbalah: New Perspectives*, 96; idem., "R. Moshe ben Naḥman—Qabbalah, Halakhah u-Manhigut Ruḥanit," *Tarbiẓ* 64 (1995):542–43, 576–78; Elliot Ginsburg, *The Sabbath in the Classical Kabbalah* (Albany, 1989), 108–9; 168–69, nn. 183, 189; 175–76, n. 231, above, nn. 25, 26; and below, ch. 5, n. 43. But there is no firm basis on which to suggest that Riẓba was a source of mystical teachings for R. Judah b. Yaqar.

Wolfson, "By Way of Truth: Aspects of Naḥmanides' Kabbalistic Hermeneutic," *AJS Review* 14 (1989):176–77, observes that Ramban, who cites R. Judah b. Yaqar in his halakhic writings, never actually mentions R. Judah with regard to any kabbalistic doctrines. Nonetheless, it is clear that Naḥmanides was influenced by R. Judah in mystical matters, and it is therefore likely that Ramban received mystical teachings directly from R. Judah. See also Ginsburg, *The Sabbath in the Classical Kabbalah*, 21; 42, n. 20; 147, n. 55; 151–52, n. 88; 168–69, n. 189; idem, "Sacred Marriage and Mystical Union: Some Thoughts on the Kabbalah of Judah b. Yaqar and the Problematics of its Interpretation," (unpublished paper, 1992); and Hananel Mack, "Zemanno, Meqomo u-Tefuẓato shel Midrash Bamidbar Rabbah," *Teᶜudah* 11 (1996):94–95. [Cf. Haviva Pedaya, "Ẓiyyur u-Temunah be-Parshanut ha-Qabbalit shel ha-Ramban," *Maḥanayim* 6 (1994):114–23, for certain techniques of mystical *parshanut* that Ramban may have derived from Hugo of St. Victor.] For other examples of possible Christian influences on Naḥmanides' exegesis, see the literature cited in my "On the Assessment of R. Moses b. Naḥman (Naḥmanides) and His Literary Oeuvre," *Jewish Book Annual* 51 (1993–94):165, n. 25.

Riẓba or Ri is the intended figure in a cryptic reference to the making of a *golem* that appears in a text produced by the *Ḥug ha-Keruv ha-Meyuḥad*.[36] Riẓba also issued formulations on the coming of the Messiah and prognostications on the end of days that have mystical overtones.[37] Similar material was presented by

---

[36]Idel, *Golem*, 91–92, n. 4. Cf. above, n. 7.

[37]See ms. Darmstadt Cod. Or. 25 (Ashkenaz, fourteenth century), fols. 13v–17v. Among R. Isaac b. Abraham's formulations is an interpretation of the talmudic passage (*Bava Batra* 74b–75a) that Gabriel will hunt the Leviathan. Cf. Gottlieb, *Meḥqarim be-Sifrut ha-Qabbalah*, 327–28. Riẓba also offered a blueprint that divides the messianic age into two portions and projects dates for each. The first part will begin at the end of the fifth millenium (before 1240). This part will occur before the resurrection. During the second part (which will occur within the sixth millenium), resurrection will take place, with the righteous living forever. Cf. Heinrich Breslau, "Juden und Mongolen, 1241," *Zeitschrift fuer die Geschichte der Juden in Deutschland* 1 (1887):99–102; Urbach, *Baᶜalei ha-Tosafot*, 1:270, n. 46*; and I. J. Yuval, "Liqrat 1240: Tiqvot Yehudiyyot, Paḥadim Noẓeriyyim," *Proceedings of the Eleventh World Congress of Jewish Studies*, Div. B. (Jerusalem, 1994), 113–20; and A. H. Silver, *A History of Messianic Speculation in Israel* (New York, 1927), 99 (citing the tosafist biblical commentary *Daᶜat Zeqenim*). For similar divisions and (miraculous) conceptions of the messianic age, see *ᶜArugat ha-Bosem*, ed. Urbach, 2:255–56 (citing R. Moses Taku); *Tosafot Shabbat* 63a, s.v. *ᵓein bein ha-ᶜolam ha-zeh li-yemot ha-mashiaḥ* (and cf. Rashi, *Sukkah* 41a, s.v. *ᵓi nami; Tosafot*, ad loc., and Rashi's commentary to Jeremiah 31:3); *Tosafot Shavuᶜot* 16b, s.v. *ᵓein bein*; and cf. Don Isaac Abravanel, *Yeshuᵓot Meshiḥo, ᶜiyyun shelishi*, ch. 7. The formulations of Riẓba are recorded as part of a larger treatise entitled *derashot shel ha-melekh ha-mashiaḥ, ve-gog u-magog* (fol. 13v) by one of Riẓba's students, ostensibly R. Moses of Coucy. Cf. Urbach, 1:270, n. 46, 1:468–69; and A. Grossman, "Ziqato shel Maharam mi-Rothenburg ᵓel Ereẓ Yisraᵓel," *Cathedra* 84 (1997):81–82.

The nature of this treatise, including Riẓba's material, is further elucidated by noting what follows in ms. Darmstadt. Fols. 26–28 contain *(pirqei) Gan Eden*, similar to *pirqei Hekhalot* and related also to the Zohar (see Ta-Shma, *Minhag Ashkenaz ha-Qadmon*, 202–3, n. 6.). Fols. 28–29 contain questions asked by R. Eliezer about resurrection and *yeẓirat ha-velad ve-ᶜinyano* from R. Eleazar of Worms. Fol. 50 describes the wars to be waged by the Messiah, and fols. 50–54 contain pietistic *sheᶜarim* of R. Eleazar of Worms (cf. Yosef Dan, *Torat ha-Sod shel Ḥasidut Ashkenaz* [Jerusalem, 1968], 68–71). See fols. 68 and 77 for other *sodot* and messianic prognostications. And note fols. 102 (citing R. Samuel *ha-Navi*=R. Samuel *he-Ḥasid*); 110r (R. Eleazar of Worms's commentary to the *piyyut, Ha-ᵓoḥez be-yad mishpat*; cf. above, ch. 3, n. 111); 110v (the Tetragrammaton, including the *teᶜamim* of R. Isaac of Bamberg); 121v (*mazzalot* for men and women).

Ms. Cambr. Add. 1022/1 (cf. above, ch. 2, n. 50) contains a lengthy *ḥishuv ha-qeẓ*, which cites written interpretations and interpolations of verses in the Book of Daniel by ריב"א / ר' יצחק בן אברהם (fols. 151r, 152r, 153v). According to this material, Ri(ẓ)ba stressed that the messianic era could commence after the year 1200. [Riẓba is sometimes referred to as Riba; see Urbach, *Baᶜalei ha-Tosafot*, 1:261, and Ḥida, *Shem ha-Gedolim* (Warsaw, 1878), *maᶜarekhet gedolim*, 70 (sec. 291). In this case, the identification is

R. Jacob b. Meir of Provins, a relative and younger contemporary of Riẓba and a grandson of R. Elijah of Paris.[38] Riẓba may have given instructions for the magical use of *Shemot*. The instructions that bear his name are patterned after guidelines found in *Hekhalot* literature for the use of Divine Names.[39]

---

made good by the text itself.] The different time frames for the messianic era outlined by Riẓba (d.1210; see Israel Ta-Shma in *Shalem* 3 [1981]:320) here (1403, 1468) and in ms. Darmstadt Or. 25 are perhaps a function of the different methods of prediction employed in these texts. Rashi also suggested two dates that were separated by more than a hundred years; see above, ch. 3, n. 41. The material in the Cambridge ms. is similar in a number of respects to calculations made by Naḥmanides. See Robert Chazan, *Barcelona and Beyond* (Berkeley, 1992), 176–85, and cf. above, n. 35. For messianic predictions and calculations by other Ashkenazic rabbinic figures and tosafists, see above, ch. 3, n. 2; above, nn. 8–9; and below, ch. 5, n. 67. On ms. Cambr. 1022, see Marc Saperstein and Ephraim Kanarfogel, "Ketav-Yad Byzanti shel Derashot," *Pe*ᶜ*amim* 78 (1999):164–84.

Cf. ms. Hamburg 293 (Ashkenaz, fifteenth/sixteenth centuries), fols. 22v–23r, for a *shir shel ge*ʾ*ulah* by Isaac b. Abraham. Each stanza ends with an acrostic of Elijah.

[38]See *Teshuvot u-Fesaqim*, ed. Kupfer, 308–12, and Golb, *Toledot ha-Yehudim be-*ᶜ*Ir Rouen*, 103. R. Jacob apparently received his tradition concerning the end of days from his grandfather. The tradition was also linked to a date for the advent of the Messiah given by R. Eleazar of Worms, which in turn followed material from R. Judah and R. Samuel *he-Ḥasid* concerning angelic powers and the neutralizing of *maziqin* and *shedim*. On R. Jacob of Provins and Riẓba, see ms. Bodl. 783, sec. 158, cited in Urbach, *Ba*ᶜ*alei ha-Tosafot*, 1:271, n. 48. R. Isaac b. Moses *Or Zarua*ᶜ, a student of both R. Jacob and R. Eleazar of Worms, may also have had a role in the transcription of R. Jacob's material. See Kupfer, 312, n. 25. See also above, ch. 3, n. 98.

[39]See ms. Bodl. 2312 (Germany, 1591), fol. 51r: כך קבלתי מהר׳ יצחק בן אברהם... שכל מי שרוצה לפעול משם מ״ב או ע״ב יתענה ויטבול... To be sure, this manuscript is relatively late, and we cannot be certain that the tosafist Riẓba is the intended reference. Note that *Hekhalot* forms can also be seen in the *segullot* on fol. 53r, and in the *she*ʾ*elat halom* on fol. 57v. On Riẓba and *Ḥasidei Ashkenaz*, with respect to the *teshuvah* required for an apostate who returns to Judaism, see *Semaq mi-Ẓurich*, sec. 156 (ed. Y. Har-Shoshanim [Jerusalem, 1973], 2:49); *Teshuvot ha-Rashba ha-Meyuḥasot la-Ramban* (Warsaw, 1883), #180; Urbach, *Ba*ᶜ*alei ha-Tosafot*, 1:407; and cf. J. Elbaum, *Teshuvat ha-Lev ve-Qabbalat Yissurim*, 225–26. On Riẓba, *Ḥasidei Ashkenaz*, and *Hekhalot*, see also Ginsburg, "Sacred Marriage and Mystical Union," nn. 48, 58–59, 77, 83.

R. Barukh of Worms (d.c.1211, in Israel) was a dedicated student of Ri, who also displayed some ideological and textual links with *Ḥasidei Ashkenaz*; see above, ch. 2, n. 61. See also ms. Sassoon 290, fol. 107 (sec. 207), which records a procedure for preparing an amulet to insure שלא תירא ממלך ושלטון (which was בדוק ומנוסה) by a R. Menaḥem, who received it from his father-in-law, R. Barukh. Three Divine Names were to be engraved on three lines on a band of silver (טס של כסף). The silver band was to be rolled into an amulet form and placed between the arms and chest of the bearer (בחיקו), who would then feel no fear of any ruler or government. [See also ms. Rome

II

R. Judah *he-Ḥasid*, the central figure among *Ḥasidei Ashkenaz*, was a contemporary of these students of Rabbenu Tam and Ri. An assessment of the attitude of late twelfth- and thirteenth-century tosafists to magic must take into account the nuanced views of the German Pietists concerning magic. The German Pietists invested commonly held beliefs in demonic and other forces with theological meaning. They also recognized the efficacy of *sodot* and the adjuration of *Shemot* for magical purposes, such as *she*ʾ*elat ḥalom*, or as part of *segullot* for protection (such as *shemirat ha-derekh*) and healing.[40] The Pietists

---

Casanatense 137 (Ashkenaz, thirteenth century), which contains *liqqutim* from *Sefer ha-Terumah* followed by a *ḥazaqah*, **רעמים ורעשים קולות וברקים** (45r), **ספר רפפות** (45v), **פתרון חלומות** (46v), **תענית, דינים וסגולות**. Cf. above, ch. 3, n. 116.] R. Barukh traveled to Israel via Candia, where he and his son-in-law, R. Menaḥem, were signatories on the so-called *Taqqanot Qandi*ʾ*ah*. Urbach, *Ba*ʿ *alei ha-Tosafot*, 1:352; Israel Ta-Shma, "Keroniqah Ḥadashah li-Tequfat Baʿalei ha-Tosafot me-Ḥugo shel Ri ha-Zaqen," *Shalem* 3 (1981):321–22; and Elhanan Reiner, "ʿAliyyah ve-ʿAliyyah la-Regel le-Ereẓ Yisraʾel, 1099–1517" (Ph.D. diss., Hebrew University, 1988), 69–73. [Two other signatories on the *Taqqanaot Qandi*ʾ*ah*—R. Matatyah (*Ḥasid*) and his son, R. Eleazar (*Ḥasid*)—also came to Candia from northern France. R. Eleazar authored a commentary on Ibn Ezra, as well as a collection entitled *Sodot Derekh Derash* (which includes such themes as *sod yedi*ʿ*at ha-Shem ve-*ʿ*ahavato ve-*ʿ*avodato, ve-sod* ʾ*avot u-gevurotav u-qeddushot ha-Shem . . . ve-sod tefillin, ve-sod mezuzah, ve-sod ẓizit*). See Avraham David, "Le-Toledotav shel R. Eleazar b. he-Ḥasid R. Matatyah me-Ḥakhmei Ereẓ Yisraʾel (?) ba-Meʾah ha-Yod Gimmel," *Qiryat Sefer* 63 (1991):996–98. Cf. above, ch. 2, nn. 6, 8.]

[40]See Dan, *Torat ha-Sod shel Ḥasidut Ashkenaz* 19–20, 28, 37–39, 58–59, 88–94, 184–202; idem, "Sarei Kos ve-Sarei Bohen," *Tarbiz* 32 (1963):359–69; and above, ch. 3, n. 8. Cf. Israel Ta-Shma, "Quntres *Zekher* ʿ*Asah le-Nifle*ʾ*otav* le-R. Yehudah he-Ḥasid," *Qoveẓ* ʿ*al Yad* n.s. 12[22] (1994):123–46; Wolfson, *Through a Speculum That Shines*, 208–14; Michael Swartz, *Scholastic Magic* (Princeton, 1996), 179–80; and below, ch. 5, n. 10.

See also above, introduction, n. 1. Against the view of Gad Freudenthal, that Ashkenazic Jewry was completely opposed to the study of philosophy and science, David Ruderman notes that *Ḥasidei Ashkenaz* were aware of some of the philosophical trends of their day and were even more strongly aware of certain scientific and natural phenomena, despite the absence of a sustained philosophical tradition. This interest, however, was not directed toward a rationalistic investigation of science or nature per se. Rather, it was designed to marshal empirical evidence for compelling or unusual natural phenomena in order to support a theological point concerning the powers of the Almighty (*zekher* ʿ*asah le-nifle*ʾ*otav*). Magic as well was viewed as a function of godliness. There was no involvement in the study of science in Ashkenaz until the late Middle Ages, following significant exposure to philosophy. See also David Berger, "Judaism and General Culture in Medieval and Early Modern Times," *Judaism's Encounters with Other Cultures*, ed. Jacob Schachter (Northvale, 1997), 117–22.

preferred the higher-level *hashbaʿat malʾakhim* for accomplishing magical acts, rather than *hashbaʿat shedim*,[41] although passages in *Sefer Ḥasidim* suggest that even the use of *Shemot* in this way should be avoided in practice, except in cases of particular need. Indeed, *Sefer Ḥasidim* asserts that a number of prophets were killed, rather than resort to the adjuration of Divine Names to save themselves. They were prepared to rely only on their prayers.[42]

---

[41]See Dan, *Torat ha-Sod shel Ḥasidut Ashkenaz*, 218–22. Indeed, the Almighty Himself adjures angels through his own *Shemot*. *Hashbaʿat malʾakhim* is an important theological construct that demonstrates the cosmic power of adjuration when coupled with Divine Names. Cf. *ʿArugat ha-Bosem*, ed. Urbach, 4:84 (angels make use of the ineffable Name of forty-two and seventy-two letters), and below, n. 47. See also *Sefer Ḥasidim [Parma]*, ed. J. Wistinetski (Frankfurt, 1924), sec. 80, 327, 367, (371), 1453, 1818, 1983. [On *SḤP* 80, in which a *ḥasid* undertook a *sheʾelat ḥalom* to ascertain who would sit next to him in *gan ʿeden*, see also Ivan Marcus in *Jewish History* 1 (1986):19; idem, in *Rabbinic Fantasies*, ed. D. Stern and M. Mirsky (Philadelphia, 1990), 227–28; Tamar Alexander, "Folktales in *Sefer Ḥasidim*," *Prooftexts* 5 (1985):22–25, and the literature cited in nn. 8–9; and Monford Harris, *Studies in Jewish Dream Interpretation*, 33. Cf. *SḤP* 1556. On the use and significance of *sheʾelat ḥalom* in *Sefer Ḥasidim*, see also Monford Harris, "Dreams in Sefer Ḥasidim," *PAAJR* 31 (1963):51–80; idem, *Studies in Jewish Dream Interpretation*, 33–34; and Yosef Dan, "Le-Torat ha-Ḥalom shel Ḥasidei Ashkenaz," *Sinai* 68 (1971):288–93.] The Pietist work *Sefer ha-Ḥesheq* contains a number of examples of *hashbaʿat malʾakhim*. See, e.g., *Sefer ha-Ḥesheq ʿal Shemot Metatron Sar ha-Panim she-Masar le-R. Yishmaʾel Kohen Gadol keshe-ʿAlah la-Marom*, ed. I. M. Epstein (Lemberg, 1865), 1b–7a (secs. 3, 4, 12, 14, 24, 39, 54); ms. Moscow-Guenzberg 90, fols. 127v, 134v, 135v; ms. Florence Plut.II.5/12, fols. 241–43; and Yehuda Liebes, "Malʾakhei Qol Shofar," *Meḥqerei Yerushalayim be-Maḥshevet Yisraʾel* 6:1–2 (1987):177–95. Cf. *Perushei ha-Torah le-R. Yehudah he-Ḥasid*, ed. Y. S. Lange (Jerusalem, 1975), 106 [=Yosef Dan, "Sippurim Dimonologiyyim mi-Kitvei R. Yehudah he-Ḥasid," *Tarbiz* 30 (1961):288–89]; Trachtenberg, *Jewish Magic and Superstition*, 83; Ta-Shma, *Ha-Nigleh shebe-Nistar*, 31–32 (on the Ashkenazic base of the magic in the Zohar); idem, "Quntres *Zekher ʿAsah le-Nifleʾotav*," 138–39, 142; Claire Fanger, "Medieval Ritual Magic," *Conjuring the Spirits*, ed. Fanger (Phoenix Mill, 1998), vii–ix; and below, n. 48.

[42]See *SḤP*, sec. 211: **כל שעוסק בהשבעות מלאכים או בהשבעות שדים או בלחישת כשפים לא יהיה סופר טוב ויראה רעות בגופו ובבניו כל ימיו. לכך יתרחק אדם מעשות כל אלה ולא בשאילת חלום ולא יעסוק שאחרים יעשו לו... ואם יצא בדרך אל יאמר אשביע מלאכים שישמרוני אלא יתפלל לפני הקב״ה. וכמה נביאים נהרגו ולא השביעו בשם הקדש אלא בתפלה עמדו**. A similar formulation to the first part of the passage is found in ms. Moscow-Guenzberg 182 (Ashkenaz, 1391; a manuscript version of R. Judah's ethical will), fol. 150v. See also the anecdote about R. Judah *he-Ḥasid* and his students in *Sefer Mizvot Qatan, mizvah* 3 (above, ch. 1, nn. 156–58); and R. Eleazar of Worms in *Sefer ha-Shem* (ms. B.M. 737, fol. 18v): **כי היה [דניאל] אוהב השם ולא רצה אלא בתפלה... ואוהבי השם לא ישביעו בשמו**. See also, e.g., *SḤP*, secs. 210, 212, 379, 1055–56, 1137–39, 1444, 1448–1457. [The last sections are part of a unit entitled **עניני השבעות ומזיקים**.

Nonetheless, Ramban and Rashba point to unnamed *Ḥasidei Ashkenaz* as those who were involved consistently in the manipulation of *shedim* for divination and other purposes.[43] R. Isaac *de-min ʿAkko* writes that R. Judah

---

In this unit, *Sefer Ḥasidim* advises inter alia that Divine Names may not be employed even to cause people to fear the Almighty, nor can their use influence the ultimate fate of a soul in either direction.] *SḤP* 213 recommends that one who has young sons should not leave a book of *Shemot* in his house, lest they use it without his knowledge; cf. Sharon Koren, "Mysticism and Menstruation: The Significance of Female Impurity in Jewish Spirituality" (Ph.D. diss., Yale, 1999), ch. 1. *SḤP* 1458 instructs that Divine Names should be taught only to a *ḥakham*, כדי שלא יעסוק בהם ואם סבור לטובה לעשות. See also secs. 1459–60, 797, and Dan, *Torat ha-Sod shel Ḥasidut Ashkenaz*, 74–76. Cf. *Sefer Ḥasidim* [Bologna], ed. Reuven Margoliot (Jerusalem, 1957), secs. 204–6, 1153, 1172, and the appendix by the editor (entitled *Ḥasidei ʿOlam*), pp. 586–89; the *Ẓavvaʾah* published in *SḤB*, p. 16, sec. 20, and the sources cited in *Meqor Ḥesed*, ad loc.; Dan, "Sippurim Dimonologiyyim," 288–89 (=*Perushei R. Yehudah he-Ḥasid la-Torah*, ed. Lange, 106); Mark Verman and Shulamit Adler, "Path-Jumping in the Jewish Magical Tradition," *JSQ* 1 (1993/94): 138; and Güdemann, *Ha-Torah veha-Ḥayyim*, 165–66. In his *Sodei Razaya*, R. Eleazar of Worms cites extensively from *Sefer ha-Razim* with regard to its descriptions of the levels of heaven and the angels who dwell at each level. He does not, however, record any of the practical magical material, which included angelic adjurations as well as symbolic acts. See *Sefer ha-Razim*, ed. Mordechai Margoliot (Jerusalem, 1967), editor's introduction, xiv. Cf. *Ḥarba de-Moshe*, ed. Yuval Harari (Jerusalem, 1997), editor's introduction, 149–52. *Sefer Ḥasidim* is also decidedly anti-amulet; see *SḤP* 379, 1455, 1457, and *SḤB* 1114, although cf. *SḤP* 367.

[43]Ramban's formulation, found in his name in *Sheʾelot ha-Rashba ha-Meyuḥasot leha-Ramban*, 283, is also cited in *Sheʾelot u-Teshuvot ha-Rashba*, 1:413 (fol. 149a): כי אני שמעתי שמנהג חסידי אלמנייא לעסוק בדברי שדים ומשביעין אותן ומשלחין אותן ומשתמשים בהם לכמה ענינים. Therefore, Ramban concludes, מעשה שדים לחוד ומעשה כשפים לחוד. Some of these texts (or their variants) omit the word חסידי, perhaps suggesting a somewhat wider Ashkenazic phenomenon. See also *Kitvei ha-Ramban*, ed. C. Chavel (Jerusalem, 1968[3]), 1:381; *Teshuvot ha-Rashba*, ed. H. Z. Dimitrovsky (Jerusalem, 1990), 1:307, and cf. 2:473, 478; Ramban's commentary to Leviticus 17:7; Marc Saperstein, "Christians and Christianity in the Sermons of Jacob Anatoli," *The Frank Talmage Memorial Volume*, ed. Walfish, 2:238, n. 10; David Horwitz, "Rashba's Attitude Towards Science and Its Limits," *Torah u-Madda* 3 (1991–92):52–81; José Faur, "Two Models of Jewish Spirituality," *Shofar* 10:3 (1992):30–34; Bazak, *Le-Maʿalah min ha-Ḥushim*, 99–102; Haviva Pedaya, "Ẓiyyur u-Temunah be-Parshanut Magit," *Maḥanayim* 6 (1994):123; and Josef Stern, "The Fall and Rise of Myth in Ritual," *Journal of Jewish Thought and Philosophy* 6 (1997):240–45. Cf. *Tosafot ha-Shalem*, ed. Gellis, vol. 6, 186–87 (to Exodus 7:11, ויקרא פרעה לחכמים ולמכשפים ויעשו גם חרטומי מצרים בלטיהם כן); *Margaliyyot ha-Yam* to *Sanhedrin* 67b; Lynn Thorndike, *A History of Magic and Experimental Science*, vol. 2 (New York, 1923), 7–8; above, n. 13; and Septimus, *Hispano-Jewish Culture in Transition*, 86–87. On the term חסידי אלמניא in Ramban's writings, see also his *derashah* entitled *Torat ha-Shem Temimah*, in *Kitvei ha-Ramban*,

he-Ḥasid was adept in the use of *Shemot* for both white and black magic.[44] Even more striking is the formulation of R. Moses Taku, in which he censures the Pietists for "making themselves like prophets" through the pronunciation of Holy Names with theurgic intentions, thereby producing results similar to those achieved by magicians or exorcists.[45] According to an account transmitted by his son (R. Zal[t]man) and grandson, R. Judah *he-Ḥasid*, while living in Spires, conjured the spirit of a dead person. The person proceeded to describe how, following his death, *shedim* in the form of cows walked on his face, just as R. Judah had predicted, because he had been guilty of shaving off his beard (and *pe*ʾ*ot*) with sharp scissors during his lifetime.[46] According to a

---

1:162. Cf. above, ch. 1, n. 36, and *She*ʾ*elot u-Teshuvot ha-Rashba*, 1:548, fol. 72a. For the impact of the *torat ha-sod* of *Ḥasidei Ashkenaz* on Ramban, see, e.g., my "On the Assessment of R. Moses b. Naḥman (Naḥmanides) and His Literary Oeuvre," 170–71; Moshe Idel, "Defining Kabbalah: The Kabbalah of the Divine Names," *Mystics of the Book*, ed. R. A. Herrera (New York, 1993), 99–104; above, n. 35; and below, ch. 5, n. 30.

[44] *Sefer Me*ʾ*irat* ʿ*Enayim*, ed. Amos Goldreich (Jerusalem, 1981), 409, n. 11: **ר' יהודה חסיד היה יודע לעשות טוב ורע; יודע להשתמש בשם של טהרה ובשם של היפך טהרה**. Cf. Wolfson, *Through a Speculum That Shines*, 268, n. 341; Moshe Idel, "Al Kavvanat Shemoneh ʿEsreh ʾEẓel R. Yiẓḥaq Sagi-Nahor," *Massu*ʾ*ot*, ed. Oron and Goldreich, 40–41; idem, "Shelomoh Molkho ke-Magiqqon," *Sefunot* 18 (1985):199–200 (with reference also to R. Eleazar of Worms; see below, n. 48); and Zimmer, ʿ*Olam ke-Minhago Noheg*, 22–23.

[45] See R. Moses Taku, *Ketav Tamim*, ed. Raphael Kirchheim, in *Oẓar Neḥmad* 4 (1860):84 [=Fascimile of ms. Paris H711, ed. Joseph Dan (Jerusalem, 1984), fol. 33r; cf. the editor's introduction, 13, n. 29]: **לעשות עצמם נביאים מרגילים עצמם בהזכרת שמות ופעמים מכוונים בקריאתן והנשמה מתבהלת**. Cf. above, ch. 3, n. 69. On the connotations of this passage in terms of prophecy, theurgy, and theosophy, cf. Scholem, *Major Trends in Jewish Mysticism*, 100–103; Idel, *Kabbalah: New Perspectives*, 98–99; idem, *The Mystical Experience in Abraham Abulafia* (Albany, 1988), 18; idem, "Al Kavvanat Shemoneh ʿEsreh," 32; idem, "Le-Gilgulehah shel Tekhniqah Qedumah shel Ḥazon Nevuʾi Bimei ha-Benayim," *Sinai* 86 (1980):1–7; Wolfson, *Through a Speculum That Shines*, 267–68; and below, ch. 5, n. 67.

[46] See the passage in *Sefer ha-Gan* 6b–7a, cited in Zimmer, ʿ*Olam ke-Minhago Noheg*, 49, n. 37; ms. Bodl. 973 [*Sefer Hadrat Qodesh le-R. Zeligmann Bing*] (Ashkenaz, 1465–69), fols. 16r–16v; ms. London (*Beit Midrash*) 73 (1518), fol. 14r; ms. Bodl. 1589 [*Adam Sikhli* ʿ*im Perush Hadrat Qodesh le-R. Shim*ʿ*on b. Shemu*ʾ*el*] (Ashkenaz, 1537); I. J. Yuval, *Ḥakhamim be-Doram* (Jerusalem, 1989), 296–97, n. 54; H. H. Ben-Sasson, "Ḥasidei Ashkenaz ʿal Ḥaluqat Qinyanim Ḥomriyyim u-Nekhasim Ruḥaniyyim Bein Benei Adam," *Zion* 35 (1970), 66, n. 36; and Yassif, *Sippur ha-*ʿ*Am ha-*ʿ*Ivri*, 364–65, 396. [*Sefer ha-Gan*, not to be confused with a tosafist biblical commentary of the same name, is an early fourteenth-century work composed by R. Isaac b. Eliezer, a student of R. Yedidyah of Spires and Nuremberg. R. Yedidyah was a colleague of R. Meir of Rothenburg and a student of R. Samuel of Evreux; see above, ch. 1, n. 80. On this work,

passage in *Paʿaneaḥ Raza*, R. Judah related the situation of an adept (*tahor*) with whom an angel regularly conversed (שהיה רגיל המלאך לדבר אליו).[47]

R. Solomon Simḥah of Troyes (c.1235–1300), author of *Sefer ha-Maskil*, named R. Judah as a leading authority on the use of *Shemot* and the adjuration of angels and demons, even though R. Solomon held that these techniques should be studied but not actually used.[48] There are a number of *hashbaʿot* and *segullot* in manuscript attributed to R. Judah *he-Ḥasid* and R. Eleazar of Worms, although some of the manuscripts are from the sixteenth century and beyond, raising questions about the reliability of the attributions in them.[49]

---

see Israel Ta-Shma, "Ḥasidut Ashkenaz asher bi-Sefarad: Rabbenu Yonah Gerondi—Ha-Ish u-Foʿalo," *Galut Aḥar Golah*, ed. Aharon Mirsky et al. (Jerusalem, 1988), 171.] Cf. my "Rabbinic Attitudes Toward Nonobservance in the Medieval Period," 26, n. 66, on the prohibition against shaving in Pietist penitentials, and above, ch. 1, n. 12. On communication with departed souls, see also *Arbaʿah Turim, O. Ḥ.*, sec. 268, citing *Sefer Ḥasidim* (1073); *SḤP* 555, 1556; Yassif, *Sippur ha-ʿAm ha-ʿIvri*, 314–15; Tamar Alexander-Frizer, *The Pious Sinner* (Tübingen, 1991), 22; above, nn. 19–20; and below, ch. 5, nn. 11, 43.

[47]See ms. Bodl. 2344, fol. 133r. One day, the angel did not appear. The adept fasted for three days, after which the angel reappeared. The adept asked him why he had not appeared earlier, and the angel explained that when the *tahor* ate from a fowl that had been fattened by ingesting portions of a pig's intestines, he had unwittingly eaten pig.

[48]See below, ch. 5, n. 54. According to R. Moses Cordovero (cited in Idel, "Shelomoh Molkho ke-Magiqqon," above, n. 44): ומעולם לא ראינו מי שנכנס בזה [עיסוק בשמות] שלא יפול בזה זולת הקדושים הטהורים כגון ר׳ יהודה החסיד ור׳ יוסף גיקטליא ור׳ אלעזר מגרמייזא ורמב״ן וכיוצא רבים שהיו יודעים כח השם ולא נשתמשו בו ולא בפעולות ולא הטריחו קונם. [For the notion that one who pronounces adjurations "bothers" the Almighty or the angels (מטריחים את המלאכים), cf., e.g., *SḤP* 212.]

[49]Examples from manuscripts of the fourteenth century or earlier include: ms. Bodl. 1098, fol. 77r (a magical *tefillat ha-derekh*, including various permutations of Divine Names, which would ward off all armed robbers and non-Jews); Vienna 28 (Heb. 148), 58r (a *sheʾelat ḥalom* formula; cf. above, ch. 3, n. 8); Bodl. 1038, fol. 17v; Parma 1033, fol. 26; and Paris 716, fols. 294v–295v (a *shemirat ha-derekh* that mandated the placement and retrieval of stones, together with the recitation of biblical verses); cf. Vat. 243, fols. 10r, 14r, 15r; Warsaw 374, fol. 270r; Cambr. Or. 71, 166r; Livorno Talmud Tora 138, fol. 38r; above, ch. 2, n. 10, and ch. 3, n. 21; Paris 646, fols. 237v–238r [in the margin] (=mss. Cincinnati 436, fols. 212v–213r: *segullot* followed by prayers for individual needs, to be recited after the completion of the *ʿAmidah*); and ms. Paris 632, fol. 41r. See also Mark Verman and Shulamit Adler, "Path Jumping in the Jewish Magical Tradition," 136–39; Wolfson, *Through a Speculum That Shines*, 268, n. 341; above, n. 32; and below, ch. 5, nn. 16–17, 63–65, 74, 78. A number of these (practical) magical techniques are characterized by the term *qabbalah* (as in *qabbalah mi-R. Eleazar mi-Germaiza*). Cf. D. Abrams, "The Literary Emergence of Esotericism in German Pietism," *Shofar* 12:2 (1994):75, n. 24; and D. Sperber, *Minhagei Yisraʾel*, vol. 3

The Pietists' complex posture regarding the use of magical *Shemot* and incantations appears to be similar to their view regarding messianic speculation. While insisting that messianic speculation should not take place openly, *Ḥasidei Ashkenaz* nonetheless engaged in such speculation on their own, through various mystical or magical means. The dangers inherent in messianic speculation could only be mitigated by those few who were capable of applying the proper (mystical) techniques and safeguards.[50]

German tosafists such as R. Judah b. Qalonymus (Ribaq, d. c. 1199), who lived in Spires while R. Judah *he-Ḥasid* was there, refer to pieces of *torat ha-sod* they received from R. Judah. Ribaq's *Sefer Yiḥusei Tanna'im va-Amora'im* contains a lengthy passage, citing *Hekhalot* literature, which interprets the activities of R. Yishma'el *Kohen Gadol* based on the *torat ha-Kavod* of the German Pietists. Ribaq's passage also deals with the role of Akatri'el as a representation of the Divine (*Shem*) or as an angel, another issue dealt with extensively by the Pietists.[51]

(Jerusalem, 1994), 199. For similar types of *hashba^cot* attributed to R. Elḥanan b. Yaqar, see JTS Mic. 1878, fol. 128r, and ms. HUC Acc. 14, fol. 86v. For a magical means of injuring (and apprehending) a thief, see *SḤB* 1162, and R. Eleazar of Worms, *Ḥokhmat ha-Nefesh*, fol. 17b. [Note also the formula for *petiḥat ha-lev* and other *segullot* (*le-happil 'eimah 'al benei 'adam, le-qiyyum banim*, and for overall personal security—*'eino nizoq le-'olam*) found in ms. B.M. 737 (Add. 27, 199; Italy, 1515), fols. 470v–471v, and ms. Munich 81, fols. 201–2, interspersed among writings of R. Eleazar of Worms.] Cf. Paris 776, fol. 174v; Prague 45, fol. 145v; Parma 997, fol. 321r; Parma 1354, fol. 147r. (prophylactic techniques attributed to R. Judah *he-Ḥasid*), and below, ch. 5, nn. 46–47, 74.

[50]See, e.g., Dan, *Torat ha-Sod shel Ḥasidut Ashkenaz*, 241–45; Baron, *A Social and Religious History of the Jews*, 6:47; Avraham David, "Sibbuv R. Petaḥyah me-Regensburg be-Nosaḥ Ḥadash," *Qoveẓ 'al Yad* n.s. 13 [23] (1996):240–43, 252–53; *Sefer Gematri'ot le-R. Yehudah he-Ḥasid*, introduction, 14, 66 (fol. 21v); below, ch. 5, n. 67; and cf. Peter Schäfer, "The Ideal of Piety of the Ashkenazi Ḥasidim and Its Roots in Jewish Tradition," *Jewish History* 4 (1990):15–16; Israel Ta-Shma, "Ḥishuv Qiẓẓin le-Or ha-Halakhah," *Maḥanayim* 59 (1961):57–59; Shlomo Eidelberg, "Gilgulav shel ha-Ra'ayon ha-Meshiḥi Bein Yehudei Ashkenaz," *Bein Historiyyah le-Sifrut*, ed. Stanley Nash (Tel Aviv, 1997), 25–26; and Moshe Idel, *Messianic Mystics* (New Haven, 1998), 47–51.

[51]See Urbach, *Ba'alei ha-Tosafot*, 1:379; and below, ch. 5, n. 7. Cf. Yaacov Sussmann, "Massoret Limmud u-Massoret Nosaḥ shel Talmud ha-Yerushalmi," *Meḥqarim be-Sifrut Talmudit* [*Yom 'Iyyun le-Regel Melot Shemonim Shanah le-Sha'ul Lieberman*] (Jerusalem, 1983), 14, n. 11, 34–35; and below, ch. 5, n. 12. (Ribaq also cites a R. Menaḥem *Ḥasid*; see Urbach, 1:369–70, and above, ch. 2, n. 10.) *Ḥasidei Ashkenaz* were heavily involved in the preservation and transmission of *Hekhalot* literature. As has been noted throughout this study, familiarity with this literature on the part of certain tosafists suggests that it was available more widely in Ashkenaz, in non-Pietist circles as well. Cf., e.g., Michael Swartz, *Scholastic Magic*, 218–19; Robert

R. Ephraim b. Jacob (b. Qalonymus) of Bonn (b.1132) was a slightly older contemporary of R. Judah *he-Ḥasid*, and succeeded his teacher R. Joel *ha-Levi* as *ʾav bet din* in Bonn. R. Ephraim was in contact with R. Judah and with Ribaq, and he may even have received material from R. Samuel *he-Ḥasid*.[52] In addition to counting words and letters in prayers and interpreting the prayers based on these sequences, as R. Judah *he-Ḥasid* and other *Ḥasidei Ashkenaz* did,[53] R. Ephraim offered a description of the ***kisse*** *ha-Kavod* in a liturgical commentary that is quite similar to esoteric formulations of R. Eleazar of Worms and versions of *Sod ha-Egoz*.[54]

As we noted in the first chapter, *Ḥasidei Ashkenaz* influenced a number of northern French tosafists in the areas of educational curriculum, liturgy, ethics, and repentance. Given the presence of mysticism and magic in pre-Crusade Ashkenaz, evidence for these disciplines in northern France from the early thirteenth century may reflect the influence of the German Pietists, in addition to any existing northern French traditions. Interestingly, a Provençal broadside issued during the Maimonidean controversy censures "*Ẓarefatim* and their scholars, their heads and men of understanding" for "hearken[ing] to soothsayers and dreamers of false dreams... with the vanities of [magical] names, appelations of angels and demons and to practice conjuration and to write amulets.... For they fancy themselves masters of the Name, like the true prophets of renown. But they are fools and madmen, full of delusions."[55]

The influence of *Ḥasidei Ashkenaz* in these matters should not be overstated, however, even with regard to Germany. We have already confirmed the assessment of Victor Aptowitzer that R. Eliezer b. Joel *ha-Levi* (Rabiah)—the leading German tosafist of his day and a contemporary of Riẓba and R. Judah *he-Ḥasid*—was not involved significantly with *sod*, despite several

---

Bonfil, "Eduto shel Agobard mi-Lyons ʿal ʿOlamam ha-Ruḥani shel Yehudei ʿIro be-Meʾah ha-Teshiʿit," *Studies in Jewish Mysticism, Philosophy and Ethical Literature Presented to Isaiah Tishby*, ed. J. Dan and J. Hacker, 327–48; and above, introduction, nn. 25–26.

[52]See *ʿArugat ha-Bosem*, ed. Urbach, 4:40.

[53]See *Siddur Rabbenu Shelomoh mi-Germaiza ve-Siddur Ḥasidei Ashkenaz*, ed. Hershler, 60, 109, n. 38, 114; Simcha Emanuel, "Ha-Polmos ʿal Nosaḥ ha-Tefillah shel Ḥasidei Ashkenaz," n. 2; and above, ch. 2, n. 26.

[54]See *Siddur Rabbenu Shelomoh mi-Germaiza*, 70–71, and Elliot Wolfson, "Iyyun Nosaf be-Torat ha-Sod shel Ḥasidut Ashkenaz," *Massuʾot*, ed. Oron and Goldreich, 140, n. 44 [=idem, *Along the Path* (Albany, 1995), 121, n. 65].

[55]**... בהבלי שמות כנויי מלאכים ושדים ולעשות השבעות ולכתוב קמיעות... כי עשו עצמם בעלי שם כנביאי האמת הידועים**. See Septimus, *Hispano-Jewish Culture in Transition*, 86–87.

manifestations of *ḥasidut*.[56] In addition to the sources noted and analyzed by Aptowitzer, Rabiah suggested a substitute letter representation for the Tetragrammaton, that was the same as one suggested by R. Eleazar of Worms in his *Sodei Razayya*. But practical *halakhah* was at issue in this case, and a mystical approach is not necessarily reflected.[57] There is also a reference to Rabiah having compiled a *seliḥah* based on a Name combination used by *Ḥasidei Ashkenaz*. The manuscript that records this information is quite late, however, and there is even a gloss at the end attributing this piece to **אבי עזרא** (Abraham Ibn Ezra) rather than to Rabiah.[58]

A quasi-mystical experience is attributed to Rabiah. This episode was not connected in any direct way to *Ḥasidei Ashkenaz*, however, and, indeed, the nature of the experience itself requires clarification. According to a passage in an Ashkenazic manuscript from the fourteenth century, Rabiah (*Avi ha-ʿEzri*)

---

[56]See Aptowitzer, *Mavo la-Rabiah*, 19–20, 481–82; and cf. *Sefer Rabiah Ḥullin*, ed. David Deblitsky (Bnei Brak, 1976), 22 (sec. 1081); Ta-Shma, *Ha-Nigleh shebe-Nistar*, 94, n. 33; and above, ch. 1, n. 45.

[57]See Rabiah in *Sefer Assufot*, cited in Jacob Lauterbach, "Substitutes for the Tetragrammaton," *PAAJR* 2 (1930–31):60–61, and cf. Wolfson, *Through a Speculum That Shines*, 253, n. 269. The author of *Sefer Assufot*, a collection that contains magic and *sod* material (see above, ch. 3, n. 18), was a student of both Rabiah and R. Eleazar of Worms. See above, ch. 1, n. 37; and cf. Wolfson, 253, nn. 269, 271; Simcha Emanuel, "Sifrei Halakhah Avudim shel Baʿalei ha-Tosafot" (Ph.D. diss., Hebrew University, 1993), 196; and ms. Parma 563, fols. 120–21.

R. Samson b. Eliezer, *Barukh She-ʾamar* (Jerusalem, 1970), 74, cites Rabiah about the importance of consulting *Alfa Beta de-R. Aqiva* regarding the written formulation of the letters in a *Sefer Torah* or *tefillin*: **וכל מי שאומנתו מלאכת שמים יבין ויראה בא"ב דר' עקיבא לעשות כמאמרה**. This is a matter of technical usage, however, and does not imply any affinity to the mystical materials found in the *Alfa Beta*. Indeed, R. Tam is also cited as espousing a similar view in his *Tiqqun Sefer Torah*; see also *Barukh She-ʾamar*, 101, and cf. above, ch. 3, n. 87. Rabiah wished to ignore completely the problem of *gozel ʾet ha-metim* (**כתב להיתר שאין לחוש בדבר**) associated with drinking and eating on the Sabbath afternoon (*bein ha-shemashot*), a prohibition that Rabbenu Tam received from his father and retained (see above, ch. 3, n. 90). Rabiah's father, R. Joel, had also observed the prohibition. See *Haggahot Maimuniyyot, Hilkhot Shabbat*, 30:10:[20]; and cf. above, ch. 3, n. 80.

[58]See Gershom Scholem, *Kitvei Yad be-Kabbalah* (Jerusalem, 1930), 113; above, ch. 3, nn. 8, 28, 97; and see now Dov Schwartz, "Ha-Mashmaʿut ha-Magit shel ha-Shem ha-E-lohi bi-Yeẓarato shel R. Avraham Ibn Ezra," *Biqqoret u-Parshanut* 32 (1998):39–51. R. Jacob *ha-Nazir* (in ms. Vat. 274, fol. 206r; see above, ch. 2, n. 14) cites an analysis of the angelic figure in the *E-l Adon* hymn from **מהר"י העזרי**. Urbach, in his edition of *ʿArugat ha-Bosem*, 4:119, raises the possibility that the reference is to R. Joel, son of Rabiah, but then he goes on to suggest that this identification is improbable.

maintained that Elijah the Prophet instructed him to side with the view of those authorities who prohibited a particular malformation of the lung as a *terefah* (ואליהו הנביא זכור לטוב הורה לנו לאסור אונא באומא). The passage also notes that the case at hand was one of considerable controversy between major rabbinic decisors in northern France and Germany throughout the eleventh and twelfth centuries. By Rabiah's day, all of the communities in northern France followed the stringent view, while most of the leading German communities favored the lenient view.[59]

To be sure, a claim of heavenly or angelic instruction does not automatically signify that the decisor in question underwent a mystical experience. It may mean that after studying the point of controversy, he was able to reach a firm and unimpeachable conclusion.[60] This possibility is strengthened when the decisor claims that the guidance came from Elijah, whose role in deciding unsolved controversies of Jewish law is commonplace in rabbinic thought.

Moreover, Rabiah presented both sides of the controversy in his *Sefer Rabiah*, along with the names of various important scholars who supported each position, without reaching an unequivocal decision himself. His students and successors in Germany, however, decided ultimately in favor of the stringent view. Rabiah also did not state in his own work that Elijah aided him. At the same time, R. Jacob of Marvège posed this very issue (of how to decide the controversy) as one of the questions that he addressed to Heaven. The response that he received was to be stringent.[61] These factors suggest the possibility that a later Ashkenazic figure embellished Rabiah's view in the manuscript passage.

But even if the experience attributed to Rabiah actually occurred, it must be compared with those of his family members who were involved in

---

[59]See ms. Paris 1408, fols. 2r–2v. This passage appears as part of a brief treatise entitled הל' טריפות מאבי העזרי in a section of the manuscript copied by Elqanah *ha-Sofer*, a student of R. Meir of Rothenburg who was familiar with *Hekhalot* literature and other mystical texts. See above, ch. 3, nn. 37, 115.

[60]See Isadore Twersky, *Rabad of Posquières* (Philadelphia, 1980²), 291–97, and above, ch. 1, n. 130.

[61]See *Sefer Rabiah, Ḥullin*, ed. Deblitsky, 49 (sec. 1089), and n. 23 (for the parallel passages in *Sefer Or Zarua*ᶜ, *Sefer Mordekhai*, and *Haggahot Maimuniyyot*). See also ms. Bodl. 659 (*Shibbolei ha-Leqet ha-Qaẓar*), fol. 102v; Parma 1237, fol. 140v; *Shibbolei ha-Leqet*, ed. Buber, *hilkhot terefot*, sec. 8; and R. Jacob of Marvège, *She*ʾ*elot u-Teshuvot min ha-Shamayim*, #62–64, and esp. #68: ועוד שאלתי על אומא דסריך לאונא אם הלכה כדברי המתירין או כדברי האוסרין... והשיבו זה כלל גדול בטריפות דמוסיף יוסיף... ונראה מזה שכל המחמיר מתברך. Cf. above, ch. 3, n. 119, and below, n. 63.

establishing or confirming ritual or liturgical practices on the basis of dreams. A comparison indicates that Rabiah's experience was somewhere between the relatively superficial dream of his grandfather, Raban—through which Raban realized, upon awakening from his Sabbath nap, that he had ruled incorrectly in a matter that had presented itself just prior to his going to sleep[62]—and the more intensely mystical dream in which Raban's martyred brother, R. Uri, dictated a liturgical poem to a R. Mordekhai b. Eliezer.[63] Thus, Rabiah's interest in mysticism generally remains unsubstantiated, and there is no evidence, in any case, for *Ḥasidei Ashkenaz* playing a role in this matter.

R. Samson of Sens, who was a major figure in the composition, redaction, and dissemination of *Tosafot* texts in northern France, showed no interest in magic or in mystical ideas. Indeed, the confluence of Rabbenu Tam, Raban, Rash *mi-Shanẓ*, R. Judah Sir Leon, and perhaps Rabiah my be partially

---

[62]See above, ch. 3, nn. 77–79.

[63]See above, ch. 3, nn. 80–82. R. Isaiah of Trani supported a ruling of his in another aspect of *hilkhot terefot* on the basis of a *gillui Eliyyahu*. In this case, however, R. Isaiah reported a more involved exchange between himself and Elijah; in addition, R. Isaiah's formulation is similar to those of R. Jacob of Marvège in his *Sheʾelot u-Teshuvot min ha-Shamayim*; see below, ch. 5, nn. 19–20. Rabiah's reported dream is more of a *gillui* than Raban's, but far less explicit than that of Rid. On the distinction between dreams and visions in a medieval context, see R. C. Finucane, *Miracles and Pilgrims* (New York, 1977), 83–85. See also above, ch. 1, n. 128, and ch. 3, n. 8. On prophecy and *halakhah*, cf. above, n. 3.

Yosef Kafaḥ, "Teshuvot Rabbenu Yaʿaqov me-Ramerug," *Qoveẓ ʿal Yad*, n.s. 7 (1968), 95–96, records a passage in which *Sefer ha-Ezer (Sefer Rabiah?)* came across some kind of heavenly indicator (מצא מציאה כנבואה או כבת קול מן השמים), which held that הלכה כרי"ף בכל מקום. R. Jacob of Marvège received this principle—that the law is always in accordance with R. Isaac Alfasi—in response to one of his heavenly שאלת חלום. See his *Sheʾelot u-Teshuvot min ha-Shamayim*, #2, and cf. above, n. 61. Since *Sheʾelot u-Teshuvot min ha-Shamayim* was composed at the end of the twelfth century, perhaps Rabiah (assuming that *Sefer ha-ʿEzer* does in fact refer to one of his compositions)—whose work was written a bit later—is citing this principle from that work. This citation does not appear, however, in extant versions of *Sefer Rabiah*, nor are there any other citations from *Sheʾelot u-Teshuvot min ha-Shamayim* in Rabiah's writings. *Shibbolei ha-Leqet*, a mid-thirteenth-century compendium that refers to *Sheʾelot u-Teshuvot min ha-Shamayim* on a number of occasions, openly cites this responsum, in *ʿInyan Tefillin* (ed. Buber, 383) [=ed. Mirsky, 90]. Cf. Israel Ta-Shma, "Sheʾelot u-Teshuvot min ha-Shamayim, ha-Qoveẓ ve-Tosefotav," *Tarbiz* 57 (1988):56–63, and below, ch. 5, n. 23. The great weight given to Alfasi in halakhic matters can be characterized, according to *Shibbolei ha-Leqet*, by the biblical phrase ואת בריתי אקים את יצחק. [The *gematria* Torah commentary attributed to R. Eleazar of Worms at the end of ms. Bodl. 1812 cites a scholar called *Avi ha-ʿEzri*; cf. Urbach, *Baʿalei ha-Tosafot*, 1:401, 405–6.]

responsible for the current perception of minimal tosafist involvement in mysticism and magic.[64] This perception is also supported by the fact that the standard *Tosafot* texts published together with the various talmudic tractates devote relatively little space to consideration of these issues, although as we noted at the beginning of this chapter, they do appear in *Tosafot* from time to time. The relative absence of this material in *Tosafot* texts may be, however, as much an issue of genre as an indication of lack of involvement. Indeed, Naḥmanides' talmudic commentaries are almost completely devoid of references to esoteric or kabbalistic material, despite Naḥmanides' obvious commitment to the study of *torat ha-sod*. We should expect that tosafists who were interested in *sod* and magic, no less than Naḥmanides, would wish to separate these disciplines from their talmudic commentaries and halakhic analyses.[65]

The material presented in this chapter suggests that interest in magic and mysticism that can be detected among a number of tosafists and rabbinic scholars in northern France and Germany during the second half of the twelfth century and into the first part of the thirteenth century may have developed independently of the German Pietists. As we have seen, the Pietists expressed a reticence in connection with the magical use of *Shemot* (despite their obvious familiarity with the magical techniques and their willingness to employ them under certain circumstances) that contemporary tosafists did not express.[66]

Several considerations, not shared by tosafists, may have motivated the Pietists. As we have noted, the Pietists were highly aware of the theoretical underpinnings and practical manifestations of demonology and magic commonly available in the world around them. They sought to utilize these disciplines as a means of achieving a deeper understanding of the Creator, who, they believed, operates not only within natural spheres, but in supernatural ways as well. Indeed, even prophecy could be better appreciated through an

---

[64]Cf. Ḥida, *Shem ha-Gedolim, ma*ᶜ*arekhet gedolim*, s.v. *R. Shimshon b. Avraham mi-Shanẓ*; Joseph Davis, "R. Yom Tov Lipman Heller, Joseph b. Isaac ha-Levi and Rationalism in Ashkenazic Culture, 1550–1650" (Ph.D. diss., Harvard, 1990), 48–49; Moshe Halbertal, *People of the Book* (Cambridge, Mass., 1997), 161–62, n. 40; and above, n. 11. See also above, nn. 2, 8, regarding R. Judah Sir Leon of Paris. The characterization of R. Samson of Sens in ms. Bodl. 847, fol. 36r, as an *ʾish* ᶜ*iyyun* refers, in context, to his analytical prowess with regard to talmudic studies. Cf. *Sheʾelot u-Teshuvot Maharshal*, #29; *Teshuvot u-Fesaqim*, ed. Kupfer, 115 (sec. 70); above, n. 8; introduction, n. 13; and below, ch. 5, n. 72.

[65] See above, preface, nn. 4–5.

[66]Occasionally, however, tosafists raise objections, both theoretical and practical, regarding the manipulation of *shedim* that bordered on sorcery (*kishuf*). See, e.g., above, n. 19; below, ch. 5, n. 21; and Bazak, *Le-Ma*ᶜ*alah min ha-Ḥushim*, 77–90.

analysis of certain magical techniques.[67] At the same time, their intimate involvement with magic and demonology made the Pietists uniquely aware of the dangers inherent in these disciplines. The only tosafist who analyzed the properties of *shedim* and their destructive powers in a manner close to that of the *Ḥasidei Ashkenaz* was R. Isaac b. Moses of Vienna. R. Isaac's theories will be reviewed in the next chapter.

In addition, the Pietists were involved in the study of two areas that do not appear to have evinced much interest among tosafists, but which may further explain the Pietists' hesitations regarding magic and demonology. The Pietists were influenced by systems of philosophical thought, especially forms of Neoplatonism and material found in the Hebrew paraphrase of R. Saᶜadyah Gaon's *Emunot ve-Deᶜot*.[68] It was their philosophical orientation, for example, that caused *Ḥasidei Ashkenaz* to deny the possibility, in simple terms, of Divine

[67]See above, nn. 40, 45.

[68]See, e.g., Ronald Kiener, "The Hebrew Paraphrase of Saᶜadiah Gaon's *Kitab ᶜal Amanat Waʾl-Iᶜtiqadat*," *AJS Review* 11 (1986):1–25; Gershom Scholem, "Reste neuplatonischer Spekulation in der Mystik der deutschen Chassidim und ihre Vermittlung durch Abraham bar Chija," *MGWJ* 75 (1931):172–92; E. E. Urbach, "Ḥelqam shel Ḥakhmei Ashkenaz ve-Ẓarefat ba-Polmos ᶜal ha-Rambam," *Zion* 12 (1946):150–54; Dan, *Torat ha-Sod shel Ḥasidut Ashkenaz*, 18, 22–24, 28–30, 99–100, 111–13, 129–43 (and in the next note); Wolfson, *Through a Speculum That Shines*, 192–205; and cf. idem, "The Mystical Significance of Torah-Study in German Pietism," *JQR* 84 (1993):65–67, regarding Judah of Barcelona. See also *Sefer Gematriʾot le-R. Yehudah he-Ḥasid*, 70 (fol. 23v): פילוסופים בגימ' מחוכמים נבונים.

Interestingly, it appears that the Hebrew paraphrase of Saᶜadyah's *Emunot Deᶜut* was actually cited in thirteenth-century Ashkenaz only by figures and works with a palpable connection to *Ḥasidei Ashkenaz*. These include *Sefer Ḥasidim* and various esoteric texts of *ḥasidut Ashkenaz*; R. Eleazar of Worms; his student, R. Abraham b. ᶜAzriel; R. Elḥanan b. Yaqar (of the *Ḥug ha-Keruv ha-Meyuḥad*) and *Sefer ha-Navon*; and tosafists who had a close association with German Pietism, such as R. Moses of Coucy and R. Meir of Rothenburg. (R. Moses Taku, the sharp critic of *Ḥasidei Ashkenaz*, was also keenly aware of the paraphrase, citing it in order to attack it.) The lone exceptions occur (not surprisingly) in two instances of polemic. R. Samson of Sens cites the paraphrase in one of his responsa to R. Meir *ha-Levi* Abulafia (who had himself cited it during the earliest phase of the Maimonidean controversy), as does the handbook of Jewish-Christian polemics, *Sefer Yosef ha-Meqanne*, ed. Judah Rosenthal (Jerusalem,1970), 3–6. See Kiener, 16–17, 22–23, nn. 84, 86; Y. Dan, *Ḥasidut Ashkenaz be-Toledot ha-Maḥshavah ha-Yehudit* (Tel Aviv, 1990), 1:150; Joseph Davis, "Philosophy, Dogma, and Exegesis in Medieval Ashkenazic Judaism," *AJS Review* 18 (1993):209, n. 57; Dov Schwartz, *Ha-Raᶜayon ha-Meshiḥi be-Hagut ha-Yehudit Bimei ha-Benayim* (Ramat Gan, 1997), and above, ch. 2, n. 11. Cf. Berger, "Judaism and General Culture in Medieval and Early Modern Times," 118, and Daniel Lasker, "Jewish Philosophical Polemics in Ashkenaz," *Contra Iudaeos*, ed. Ora Limor and Guy Stroumsa (Tübingen, 1996), 198–99.

corporeality, even as a number of other Ashkenazic rabbinic scholars embraced such a view.[69] With regard to practical magic and demonology as well, the Pietists' philosophical background may have caused them to pull back a bit, just as the "rationalists" among the tosafists—such as Rabbenu Tam and Rashbam—also wanted to downplay these notions.

Moreover, Moshe Idel has argued that among Spanish kabbalists who viewed the magical arts favorably, those who were engaged in theosophy were inclined to consider magic from a less practical, more theoretical standpoint.[70] The powers and properties of the Divine Names were considered in Pietist thought to be areas of esoteric study, a means of comprehending the Godhead. Indeed, the most comprehensive esoteric work composed by R. Eleazar of Worms, *Sefer ha-Shem*—in which R. Eleazar interprets the Name in accordance with *torat ha-sod* and describes the functions and implications of the Name in both the higher and lower worlds—contains a ceremony in which the Name is passed to adepts. Formal transmission of the Name was not intended so that adepts could make use of it for magical purposes, but so they could receive the theosophical secrets connected with it,[71] or the mystical practices and revelatory experiences related to its pronunciation.[72] Because tosafists were involved neither in the study of philosophy nor in the study of theosophy, the issues that confronted *Ḥasidei Ashkenaz* regarding magic and demonology need not have troubled them.

When we look at the thirteenth century, we shall see that the influence of German Pietists appears to grow in matters of magic and *sod*, as has been demonstrated with regard to asceticism and *perishut*. At the same time, the overall interest and involvement of tosafists in mystical studies and magical techniques continued to take root and became even more widespread. It is not always possible to discern, however, whether a particular development reflects the influence of *ḥasidut Ashkenaz* or whether it is a result of the broader influence of Ashkenazic rabbinic culture as a whole.

---

[69]See, e.g., Septimus, *Hispano-Jewish Culture in Transition*, 78–81; Berger, "Judaism and General Culture," 95–100; Dan, *Torat ha-Sod shel Ḥasidut Ashkenaz*, 71–73; idem, "Ashkenazi Hasidism and the Maimonidean Controversy," *Maimonidean Studies* 3 (1992–93):29–47; Davis, "Philosophy, Dogma and Exegesis," 213–14, n. 69; and *ᶜArugat ha-Bosem*, ed. Urbach, 4:74–83. Cf. Wolfson, *Through a Speculum That Shines*, 195–234, and Moshe Idel, "Gazing at the Head in Ashkenazi Hasidism," *Journal of Jewish Thought and Philosophy* 6 (1997):280–94.

[70]See Moshe Idel, "Yahadut, Mistiqah Yehudit u-Mageyah," *Maddaᶜei ha-Yahadut* 36 (1996):25–40.

[71]See Dan, *Torat ha-Sod shel Ḥasidut Ashkenaz*, 74–76.

[72]See Moshe Idel, "Defining Kabbalah: The Kabbalah of the Divine Names,", 97–122; Wolfson, *Through a Speculum That Shines*, 234–47; and above, ch. 3, n. 126.

5

Integration and Expansion during the Thirteenth Century

Two of the most important thirteenth-century tosafist halakhists, R. Isaac b. Moses *Or Zarua*^{c} of Vienna (d.c.1250) and R. Meir of Rothenburg (d.1293, who studied in his youth with R. Isaac), represent German rabbinic traditions. Nonetheless, they also spent considerable time studying with leading rabbinic scholars in northern France and should be considered, on balance, as the heirs of the tosafist enterprise there.[1] At the same time, R. Isaac and R. Meir not only embraced aspects of the pietism of *Ḥasidei Ashkenaz*, as we saw in the second chapter, but also expressed significant interest in mysticism and magic, quite possibly under Pietist influence as well. These dimensions in the writings of R. Isaac and R. Meir will be considered together with those of R. Avigdor b. Elijah *Kohen Ẓedeq* (d.c.1275, often referred to as R. Avigdor Katz)—a lesser-known tosafist who was both the successor of R. Isaac b. Moses in Vienna and a teacher of R. Meir of Rothenburg[2]—and those of several other contemporaries.

R. Isaac begins his *Sefer Or Zarua*^{c} with an analysis of the Hebrew alphabet (*le-falpel be-ʾotiyyot shel ʾalfa beta*). In addition to citing mystical and esoteric texts such as *Otiyyot de-R. Aqiva*, *Alfa Beta de-R. Aqiva*, and *Sefer Yeẓirah*,[3] this treatise refers to letter combinations, *gematriyyot*, and *sofei tevot*

---

[1]See E. E. Urbach, *Ba*^{c}*alei ha-Tosafot* (Jerusalem, 1980^{4}), 1:436–39; 2:527–28; Haym Soloveitchik, *Halakhah, Kalkalah ve-Dimmui* ^{c}*Aẓmi* (Jerusalem, 1985), 82–83; and idem, "Three Themes in the *Sefer Ḥasidim*," *AJS Review* 1 (1976):349.

[2]See above, ch. 2, n. 28.

[3]R. Isaac cites the *Alfa Beta de-R. Aqiva* twice in the first section of his treatise (and in sections 21, 28, 33) and suggests he is modeling his treatise after that type of work.

utilized in other Ashkenazic *sod* literature[4]; to pietistic prayer practices based on *Hekhalot* texts[5]; and to other mystical teachings, including *torat ha-mal'akhim.*[6] R. Isaac *Or Zarua*ᶜ interprets the talmudic account of

---

The introductory mnemonic alphabets reflect *Shabbat* 104a, which itself has clear affinities with *Sefer Yeẓirah*. See Israel Ta-Shma, "Sifriyyatam shel Ḥakhmei Ashkenaz Bnei ha-Me'ah ha-Yod Alef/ha-Yod Bet," *Qiryat Sefer* 60 (1985):307; Ivan Marcus, *Rituals of Childhood* (New Haven, 1996), 138–39, n. 41; and cf. Yosef Dan, *Torat ha-Sod shel Ḥasidut Ashkenaz* (Jerusalem, 1968), 69–70. The passage in sec. 28 mentions both the *Alfa Beta* and *Sefer Yeẓirah* for a letter derivation of שם המפורש שבו נברא העולם. [Cf. the *Alfa Beta be-Yihud ha-Bore* in R. Elḥanan b. Yaqar's *Sod ha-Sodot* (ms. JTS Mic. 8118), cited in Yosef Dan, *Tekstim be-Torat ha-E-lohut shel Ḥasidut Ashkenaz* (Jerusalem, 1977), 22. R. Elḥanan asserts that "I saw it written and intended to copy it to the best of my ability, in order to transmit it to Israel."]

[4]R. Isaac begins the treatise by expressing his joy at being able to identify the correct formal spelling of the Hebrew name Aqivah (עקיבה rather than עקיבא) on the basis of a *sofei tevot* analysis of the verse אור זרוע לצדיק ולישרי לב שמחה. [According to *Seder ha-Dorot*, R. Isaac was unsure of how to spell this name for a bill of divorce, and this solution came to him in a dream. His gratefulness for the Heavenly edification caused him to name his book *Sefer Or Zarua*ᶜ; see *She'elot u-Teshuvot min ha-Shamayim*, ed. Reuven Margoliot (Jerusalem, 1957), editor's introduction, 8.] This *sofei tevot* analysis is similar to a *gematria* analysis that R. Isaac himself (among others) attributes to R. Samuel *he-Ḥasid* (*Sefer Or Zarua*ᶜ, pt. 2, sec. 281): ור' שמואל החסיד היה אומר אבי"נו מלכ"נו חטא"נו לפני"ך עולה בגי' רב"י עקיב"ה (הו"א) יס"דו (וחד חסר הקריאה). Cf. above, ch. 1, n. 39, and ch. 2, n. 30. Note Urbach's observation (*Ba*ᶜ*alei ha-Tosafot*, 1:439), that R. Isaac's דרוש על האלפא-ביתא, with which he begins his work, testifies that he is a disciple of R. Judah *he-Ḥasid* and R. Eleazar *Roqeaḥ* (who also began his halakhic work, *Sefer Roqeaḥ*, with a pietistic introduction; cf. above, ch. 2, n. 86, and below, n. 8.) In the first section of his introduction and in secs. 11–13, and 21, R. Isaac utilizes the *gematria* technique of *millui*, a technique associated especially with the German Pietists. See Ivan Marcus, "Exegesis for the Few and for the Many: Judah he-Ḥasid's Biblical Studies," *Meḥqerei Yerushalayim be-Maḥshevet Yisra'el* 8 (1989):1*–24*, and Joseph Dan, "The Ashkenazi Concept of Language," *Hebrew in Ashkenaz*, ed. Lewis Glinert (New York, 1993), 17. For the possible esoteric connotation of the phrase found in sec. 12, that circumcision constitutes a seal of the Divine Name, see below, n. 29.

[5]See sec. 2 for the raising of the eyes during *qedushah* (a practice based on *Hekhalot* texts that became fairly widespread in Ashkenaz; see above, ch. 1, nn. 42, 60). Note also *Sefer Or Zarua*ᶜ, pt. 2, sec. 281, in which R. Isaac bases the practice of prostrating oneself at the recitation of the *Shem ha-Meforash* as described in the Yom Kippur ᶜ*avodah* on a teaching of R. Neḥunyah b. *ha-Qanah* found in *Sefer shel Qedushot* (=*Hekhalot Rabbati*, cited also in *Sefer Rabiah*, 2:196–97, in the name of *Sifrei Ḥizoniyyim*). See above, ch. 1, n. 43.

[6]According to sec. 3, the letter *'alef* (which is פלא spelled backward) teaches a person to pay attention to the wonders of the Torah, לידע סוד הדבר ולעמוד על עיקרו. Torah study is referred to several times in this treatise as a means of acquiring special or

R. Yishmaʾel and Akatriʾel in terms of the *torat ha-Kavod* of *Ḥasidei Ashkenaz*, perhaps influenced also by a passage in *Sefer Yiḥusei Tannaʾim va-Amoraʾim*.[7]

---

secret knowledge. See, e.g., the theme repeated in sec. 6: Torah study leads to the revelation of *taʿamei Torah*; cf. sec. 24. Note the reference to the *malʾakh Sar ha-Torah* in sec. 29 (cf. secs. 35, 41), and see also the last section (sec. 50), which discusses the proper manipulation of angels so that *malʾakhei ḥabbalah* will not be granted control over a person. An annotated version of this treatise has recently been published by Yosef Movshowitz in *Sefer Zikkaron le-R. Shiloh Raphael*, ed. Movshowitz (Jerusalem, 1998), 95–144. For two passages in this text found also in the pietistic introduction to *Sefer Roqeaḥ*, see the notes to 134–35.

On the power of dreams to influence halakhic decisions in *Sefer Or Zaruaʿ*, note (in addition to the suggestion that R. Isaac himself had a dream about the spelling of Aqivah, above, n. 4), pt. 1, sec. 692, in which R. Isaac records the incident of the *baʿal ha-ḥalom* who located the corpse of R. Simeon *ha-Qadosh* (the brother-in-law of Rabbenu Tam) so that it could then be identified; see above, ch. 3, n. 96, and *Sheʾelot u-Teshuvot min ha-Shamayim*, editor's introduction, 9, n. 6. See also *Sefer Or Zaruaʿ*, pt. 4, *pisqei ʿAvodah Zarah*, sec. 200: ואני המחבר שמעתי מפי הקדוש רבינו יהודה חסיד שאמר בלשון הזה שכל מי שיאכל בלבוטא לא יזכה לאכול לויתן. The text then continues with an account of R. Ephraim of Regensburg, who permitted this kind of fish and experienced a dream that demonstrated to him the error of his decision. See above, ch. 3, n. 78. R. Isaac's son, R. Ḥayyim, dreamed that he saw R. Meir of Rothenburg, whom he had never seen when R. Meir was alive. The unanticipated appearance of R. Meir communicated a message to R. Ḥayyim about retaining a particular talmudic *girsa*; see *Sheʾelot u-Teshuvot Maharaḥ Or Zaruaʿ*, #164, and cf. below, nn. 69, 72.

[7]See *Sefer Or Zaruaʿ hilkhot qeriʾat Shema*, secs. 7–8; and above, ch. 4, n. 51. R. Isaac rejects the view of R. Ḥananʾel that R. Yishmaʾel saw Akatriʾel only in his mind (imagination), as well as the view that Akatriʾel is only an angel (who could therefore be perceived). He accepts the notion (in accordance with *ḥasidut Ashkenaz*) that Akatriʾel is the *Kavod* which is Divine, but is nonetheless revealed. Cf. Gershom Scholem, *Major Trends in Jewish Mysticism* (Jerusalem, 1941), 110–16; Reuven Margoliot, *Torat ha-Malʾakhim* (Jerusalem, 1988[3]), 12; Elliot Wolfson, *Through a Speculum That Shines* (Princeton, 1994), 127, 147, 262, nn. 314–15; Arthur Green, *Keter* (Princeton, 1997), 62–65, 99; Daniel Abrams, "Sefer Shaqod le-R. Shemuʾel b. R. Qalonymus ve-Torat ha-Kavod shel Talmid R. Eleazar mi-Vorms," *Assufot* (forthcoming), nn. 65–66; and above, ch. 3, n.75.

Yehuda Liebes notes that the approach of R. Isaac *Or Zaruaʿ* (whom he characterizes as "one of the leading Ashkenazic halakhists in the twelfth and thirteenth centuries who knew nothing about Kabbala") in highlighting the connections between women and the (new) moon was one step removed from the (fully mystical) approach found in *Sefer Ḥasidim*, which was itself quite close to the view of kabbalists. In light of the material assembled here, R. Isaac's affinity for these teachings is hardly surprising. See Liebes, *Studies in Jewish Myth and Jewish Messianism* (Albany, 1993), 50–51 [="de Natura Dei—Al ha-Mitos ha-Yehudi ve-Gigulo," *Massuʾot*, ed. Amos Goldreich and Michal Oron (Jerusalem, 1994), 285–86; and see also *Darkhei Mosheh* to *O. Ḥ.* 426, end.]

R. Isaac cites R. Eleazar of Worms, that the *sheliaḥ ẓibbur* sustains the chanting of *barekhu* at the conclusion of the Sabbath, because the souls return to *gehinnom* after this point. As long as the chanting continues, they cannot return.[8]

In his discussion of a talmudic passage implying that *shedim* do not observe Jewish law—and interpreted in this way by Rashi—R. Isaac *Or Zarua*ᶜ cites R. Judah *he-Ḥasid*, who maintained that *shedim* "believe in the Torah and [also] do whatever the *ḥakhamim* decreed." Thus, they would not violate even a rabbinic prohibition (of *teḥum*). In a case where it appears that they traveled on the Sabbath, they were merely communicating through long tubes. In reality, however, *shedim* observe even the [rabbinic] requirements of the Oral Law.[9] When R. Judah was asked how, in light of this principle, *shedim* could engage

---

[8]*Sefer Or Zarua*ᶜ, *hilkhot moẓa*ʾ*ei Shabbat*, pt. 2, sec. 89 (fol. 24a). R. Eleazar noted that this was also done by R. Eliezer b. Meshullam *Ḥazzan* (of Spires). R. Eliezer *Ḥazzan* was a direct link in the esoteric chain of tradition of the German Pietists. Cf. Ta-Shma, *Minhag Ashkenaz ha-Qadmon* (Jerusalem, 1992), 307; and above, ch. 3, n. 25.

Sec. 44 of R. Isaac's introductory *Alfa Beta* treatise contains a lengthy discussion about the importance of achieving *ḥasidut*, and it includes one formulation by R. Isaac's teacher, R. Simḥah of Spires (whose own affinities with *ḥasidut Ashkenaz* will be reviewed below)—that one cannot receive a more important blessing than *yir*ʾ*at shamayim*—and another formulation on ʾ*ahavat ha-Shem* that is quite similar to a passage in an introductory section (*Hilkhot Ḥasidut—Shoresh Ahavat ha-Shem*) of *Sefer Roqeaḥ* (see Urbach, *Ba*ᶜ*alei ha-Tosafot*, 1:420, n. 56). A biblical interpretation of R. Judah *he-Ḥasid* is cited by R. Isaac in sec. 25. It should also be noted that the first halakhic topic that *Sefer Or Zarua*ᶜ addresses is *hilkhot ẓedaqah*, which contains a number of pietistic themes (although doctrines of *ẓedaqah* unique to *Sefer Ḥasidim* are not necessarily espoused; see, e.g., Haym Soloveitchik, "Three Themes," 344, n. 104). Indeed, the entire *Alfa Beta* treatise is a kind of *hilkhot ḥasidut* introduction, similar in a number of respects to the beginning sections of *Sefer Roqeaḥ* (which took its cue from Rambam's *Mishneh Torah*; see, e.g., Dan, *Torat ha-Sod shel Ḥasidut Ashkenaz*, and Ivan Marcus, *Piety and Society* [Leiden, 1981], 131–32); and cf. above, ch. 2, nn. 40, 83, 86. Note the *Sefer Ḥasidim*-like critique of unbridled dialectic in sec. 23. One is allowed to be *mefalpel* but must be careful not to permit what is prohibited, to declare pure that which is impure, or the reverse. Cf. *Sefer Or Zarua*ᶜ, *hilkhot* ᶜ*erev Shabbat*, pt. 2, sec. 33. R. Isaac did not wish to rely on a ruling of Rabbenu Tam in practice because he believed it was the product of Rabbenu Tam's powerful intellect, which could prove, in theory, that a reptile was pure (והדבר ידוע גודל לבו של ר"ת שהיה בידו לטהר שרץ). Cf. Urbach, 1:69–70, n. 62*.

[9]*Sefer Or Zarua*ᶜ, *hilkhot* ᶜ*Eruvin*, sec. 147. Cf. Y. L. Zlotnick, *Ma*ᶜ*aseh Yerushalmi* (Jerusalem, 1947), 29–30, and above, ch. 4, n. 15. *Sefer Or Zarua*ᶜ cites (*ha-Qadosh*) Rabbenu Yehudah *he-Ḥasid* in other meta-halakhic as well as halakhic contexts. See, e.g., *hilkhot Shabbat*, sec. 42 (cf. the material in the gloss to *SHP*, sec. 427, and *hilkhot moẓa*ʾ*ei Shabbat* in the preceding note); *she*ʾ*elot u-teshuvot*, sec. 114; *hilkhot Tefillin*, secs.

in illicit sexual relations with certain women,[10] he responded that *shedim* have an arrangement whereby their observance of the Torah is contingent on being treated properly by human beings. If someone harms (or bothers) them, however, they can, in turn, harm that person. The discussions in *Sefer Or Zarua*ᶜ concerning *shedim* correspond closely to material found in *Sefer Ḥasidim* and in an esoteric text of *Ḥasidei Ashkenaz, Sefer ha-Kavod*.[11]

R. Avigdor b. Elijah Katz was born in Italy and studied under R. Simḥah of Spires.[12] R. Simḥah permitted R. Avigdor to perform *leḥishah* over

---

555, 561–63; *pisqei* ᶜ*Avodah Zarah*, sec. 200; Simcha Emanuel, "Ha-Polmos ᶜal Nosaḥ ha-Tefillah shel Ḥasidei Ashkenaz," *Meḥqerei Talmud* 3 (in press), nn. 130–32; and see above, n. 6. Cf. *hilkhot moẓa*ʾ*ei Shabbat*, sec. 95; *hilkhot qeri*ʾ*at Shema*, sec. 17; *pisqei Bava Mezi*ᶜ*a*, sec. 3; and Ta-Shma, *Ha-Nigleh shebe-Nistar*, 96, n. 56. [For R. Isaac as a student of R. Abraham b. ᶜAzriel, see also ᶜ*Arugat ha-Bosem*, ed. Urbach, 4:112–13, 119, 126–27, 165. On the association of R. Jonathan b. Isaac of Würzburg, another of R. Isaac's teachers, with *sod* material, see Gershom Scholem, *Reshit ha-Qabbalah* (Tel Aviv, 1948), 197–98, and Urbach, *Ba*ᶜ*alei ha-Tosafot*, 1:222, 438.]

[10]This is apparently a reference to *Niddah* 13b, which R. Isaac *Or Zarua*ᶜ addresses independently at the end of *hilkhot ba*ᶜ*al qeri* (pt. 1, sec. 124). In that section, he also recounts the story of a *ḥasid* who was seduced by a female demon on Yom Kippur. Cf. Yosef Dan, "Sippurim Dimonologiyyim mi-Kitvei R. Yehudah he-Ḥasid," *Tarbiz* 30 (1961):278–89; idem, *Torat ha-Sod shel Ḥasidut Ashkenaz*, 194–200; and above, ch. 4, n. 42. Dan notes that not all the stories or anecdotes about demons preserved by *Ḥasidei Ashkenaz* necessarily reflect Pietist beliefs. These were often popular stories, preserved in their original form in order to make particular points of theology.

[11]See Dan, *Torat ha-Sod shel Ḥasidut Ashkenaz*, 186–88. The notion that *shedim* observe *miẓvot* is part of the larger view of the German Pietists (which conflicts with the views of both philosophers and kabbalists) that demonic powers emerge from the positive aspect of the Divine realm. Cf. *Sefer Ḥasidim Parma*, secs. 733, 1763, 379 Barbara Newman, "Possessed by the Spirit: Devout Women, Demoniacs, and the Apostolic Life in the Thirteenth Century," *Speculum* 73 (1998): 749–57; and Dorit Alloro-Cohen, "Ha-Mageyah veha-Kishuf be-Sefer ha-Zohar" (Ph.D. diss., Hebrew University, 1989). See also *Sefer Or Zarua*ᶜ, pt. 2, sec. 50 (end), which records the story of R. Aqivah (ר׳ עקיבה) and his meeting with a dead person who had to gather trees every day in order to be burned with them. He had been a tax collector who had hurt (or killed) the poor. He would be released from this plight only if he had a son who could say ברכו and קדיש, to which the community would answer יהא שמיה רבה וכו׳. Although this story is present in a number of midrashim, the only other medieval Ashkenazic sources in which it is found are mystical texts or texts associated with *Ḥasidei Ashkenaz* and their followers. See Ta-Shma, *Minhag Ashkenaz ha-Qadmon*, 299–308; M. B. Lerner, "Maᶜaseh ha-Tanna veha-Met, Gilgulav ha-Sifrutiyyim veha-Hilkhatiyyim," *Assufot* 2 (1988):29–68; *Sippurei Gilgulim ve-Ruḥot*, ed. M. Y. Blau (New York, 1995), 40–41; and above, ch. 3, n. 56.

[12]R. Simḥah studied with R. Eleazar of Metz and with R. Abraham b. Samuel *he-Ḥasid*, among others. See Urbach, *Ba*ᶜ*alei ha-Tosafot*, 1:411–20, who also notes that

R. Simḥah's eyes on the Sabbath, when R. Simḥah experienced severe discomfort. R. Avigdor learned the *leḥishah* technique from a woman and performed it twice a day.[13] R. Avigdor authored a commentary to the *Avinu Malkenu* prayer that was copied after R. Eleazar of Worms's esoteric treatise, *Ḥokhmat ha-Nefesh*. The commentary refers to *sod* dimensions of *Avinu Malkenu*, in addition to describing exoteric concepts of repentance and redemption. It also identifies parts of the prayer that are related to *Hekhalot* literature.[14]

R. Avigdor espoused the notion of directing prayer through angels who could serve as intermediaries (ותהיו מליצי יושר לפניו).[15] Moreover, several manuscripts attribute a magical *shemirat ha-derekh* to him. After a person has departed his city, and he is at the distance of an arrow's flight, he should turn his back toward the city. According to one version, he should then recite the verse that records Jacob's recognition of the angels who met him (and protected him) following his departure from Lavan, and then state: "Just as Jacob was not harmed by his brother Esau, I should certainly not be harmed."[16] In a second

---

R. Judah *he-Ḥasid* asked a halakhic question of R. Simḥah. R. Simḥah, in turn, authored a commentary to *Sifra*, and he is included in the "Spires circle" that was influenced by *Ḥasidei Ashkenaz*. For these and additional affinities with *Ḥasidei Ashkenaz*, see above, ch. 1, n. 145–46, and ch. 2, n. 16. For R. Avigdor Katz's pietism, see above, ch. 2, sec. 1 (end).

[13]See ms. Bodl. 666 (*Mordekhai Gittin*, at the end of *pereq ha-zoreq*); *Teshuvot Maharam* (Prague), #55; *Mordekhai Shabbat*, sec. 385; Urbach, *Baᶜalei ha-Tosafot*, 1:411, n. 20; Yuval, *Ḥakhamim be-Doram*, 260–61; and Joshua Trachtenberg, *Jewish Magic and Superstition* (New York, 1939), 199–200. In response to a question from R. Zedekiah b. Abraham *ha-Rofe*, R. Avigdor prohibited *leḥishot* that invoked *shedim*, whether for personal needs or to divine the future. See *Shibbolei ha-Leqet—Ha-heleq ha-Sheni*, ed. Simcha Hasida (Jerusalem, 1988), 41–43 (sec. 10). Cf. above, ch. 4, n. 15, and below, nn. 23, 54. Cf. the position of Ri, cited in *Arbaᶜah Turim, Yoreh Deᶜah*, sec. 179; *Beit Yosef*, ad loc.; *Arbaᶜah Turim, Oraḥ Ḥayyim*, sec. 306; and *Sefer Gematriʾot le-R. Yehudah he-Ḥasid*, ed. Daniel Abrams and Israel Ta-Shma (Los Angeles, 1998), introduction, 16, and 59 (fol. 18r).

[14]See ms. Cambr. Add. 858 (Ashkenaz, fifteenth century), fols. 34r (העתקתי מספר חכמת הנפש סוד הר' אלעזר) and 45r–45v (פירוש אבינו מלכנו דקדוק מהרא"ך); and see above, ch. 2, n. 30. Cf. *Synopse zur Hekhalot-Literatur*, ed. Peter Schäfer et al. (Tübingen, 1981), sec. 334. On R. Avigdor's ethical treatise, *Shaᶜarei Musar*, which has parallels to *Sefer Ḥasidim* and cites *Hekhalot* literature, see above, ch. 2, nn. 32–34.

[15]See *Shibbolei ha-Leqet*, sec. 282, and above, ch. 3, nn. 4, 38. R. Avigdor bases his reading primarily on an interpretation of Rashi. Cf. below, n. 50.

[16]See ms. Sassoon 408=B.M. Or. 14055 (Italy, fourteenth century), fols. 192–93: כתב הר' אביגדור כהן צדק, and ms. Vat. 243, fol. 12r (שמירת הדרך משום הר' אביגדור). Vat. 243 also contains magical formulae from R. Meir of Rothenburg (fol. 4v), his student R. Dan [Ashkenazi] (fols. 6v, 10r; see below, n. 46), and a number of other

version, the person recites a specific Divine Name that will protect him from all kinds of *maziqin* (*u-mikol maziq u-maziq yishamer*).[17] An Italian manuscript contains a brief commentary on Ezekiel's vision of the chariot according to both *peshat* and *sod* ascribed to R. Avigdor of Rome.[18]

Ashkenazic rabbinic figures (and to solve a number of different problems). See also ms. Livorno Talmud Torah 138, fols. 28r, 29v, 36r, 38r. [Both ms. Sassoon 408 (fol. 70) and ms. Vat. 243 (fol. 17r) contain a *shemirah la-derekh* that Ramban purportedly sent from Akko. See also ms. Sassoon 408, fols. 76–77, 85–89; ms. Vat. 243, fol. 8v; ms. Moscow-Guenzberg 1302; and below, n. 74. R. Avigdor's *shemirat ha-derekh* was based on *Sefer Yeẓirah*, and it includes the verse(s) that describe Jacob meeting the angels; cf. below, n. 78. See also ms. Cambr. Or. 71 (Ashkenaz,1398), fol. 166r, for a similar *shemirat ha-derekh* involving the brother of the tosafist R. Solomon (*ha-qadosh*) of Dreux (cited above, ch. 2, n. 10).] Just prior to R. Avigdor's *segullah* in Vat. 243, a series of amulets and *kelaf* pieces are described. These contain Metatron and other angelic names, linked with various *avot*, to be used for revenge (*neqamah*). Also described is a properly prepared *kelaf* text that, if attached to the neck of a chicken, will lead to the identification of a thief. R. Avigdor's formulation is followed by a *petiḥat ha-lev* for after the Sabbath, which is meant to conjure and neutralize *Potah*, the angel of forgetfulness, and ensure that certain nefarious angelic figures (מלאכי חבלה) should not dominate, such as אגף, נגף, סגף. Cf. *Sefer Assufot*, ms. Mont. 134, 67r (published by S. A. Stern in *Ẓefunot* 1 [1989]:20–21); Marcus, *Piety and Society*, 113; and above, ch. 3, n. 59. Fol. 14r contains a *kabbalah me-R. Yehudah he-Ḥasid* to aid in childbearing. It includes the instruction that after a three-day period, the Names that Moses gave to Joshua should be written on the bark of a fruit-bearing tree. Fol. 14v contains a *qefiẓat ha-derekh* procedure attributed to R. Eleazar of Worms. It involves immersion and anointing of the body and the writing of *Shemot* on snakeskin, which should be worn as an amulet suspended from the left arm. See Mark Verman and Shulamit Adler, "Path-Jumping in the Jewish Magical Tradition," *Jewish Studies Quarterly* 1 (1996):139. Fol. 15r has another *qabbalah me-R. Yehudah he-Ḥasid*: whoever recites the following three verses will be saved from all troubles (אתה סתר לי ... בטחו בה' עדי עד וכו'). This is followed by other means of protection against robbers, aids to travel, aids for difficult births, and the like, which also appear throughout ms. JNUL 8°476—partially described in Gershom Scholem, *Kitvei Yad be-Qabbalah* (Jerusalem, 1930), 8–12—and cf. above, ch. 4, n. 49.

[17]See ms. B.M. Or. 10619 (sixteenth century), fol. 23r, and ms. Parma 671 (fifteenth century), fol. 93. [Fol. 95 has a *shemirat ha-derekh la-Ramban*; see the preceding note.] Cf. Parma 112 (46–50), 997 (297), 3499 (112). The biblical commentary associated with R. Avigdor and his circle, Hamburg 45, describes an unusual situation in which the noses of a Jew and a non-Jew were cut off and transplanted to the other person. This event and its results also appear in a collection of tales attributed to R. Judah *he-Ḥasid*. See H. J. Zimmels, "Ketav Yad Hamburg Cod. hebr. 45 ve-Yiḥuso le-R. Avigdor Katz," *Maʾamarim le-Zikhron R. Ẓevi Pereẓ Chajes*, ed. A. Aptowitzer and Z. Schwarz (Vienna, 1933), 260, and Dan, "Sippurim Dimonologiyyim mi-Kitvei R. Yehudah he-Ḥasid," 289.

[18]See ms. Cambr. Add. 3111 (fifteenth century), fols. 63v–65r.

R. Isaiah di Trani, another Italian tosafist and student-colleague of R. Simḥah of Spires who cites northern French and German rabbinic figures and works, ruled in a responsum that a particular adhesion of the lungs rendered an animal a *terefah* on halakhic grounds. But in addition, R. Isaiah writes, Elijah appeared to him in a dream and confirmed his ruling.[19] To be sure, R. Isaiah stresses that dreams are not authoritative in and of themselves, and that his ruling is well-based in talmudic law. Nonetheless, R. Isaiah's experience is suggestive. R. Isaiah writes that when Elijah appeared in his dream, he asked for Elijah's guidance (אליהו זכור לטוב נדמה לי בחלום ושאלתי את פיו). Moreover, R. Isaiah provided an indicator (*siman*) for the lenient and strict positions using a biblical phrase, a technique commonly used by R. Jacob of Marvège in his *Sheʾelot u-Teshuvot min ha-Shamayim*.[20] In another instance, R. Isaiah is cited as permitting divination that is done using holy Divine Names (*Shemotav ha-qedoshim*), since "this is the greatness and might of the Almighty." Only the conjuring of *shedim* for this purpose is prohibited (because the manipulation of *shedim* is a form of sorcery).[21]

The Italian halakhist R. Zedekiah b. Abraham *ha-Rofe min ha-Anavim*, who studied in Germany and cites both R. Isaiah di Trani and R. Avigdor Katz frequently, among other tosafists and Ashkenazic authorities, reports in his

---

[19]See *Teshuvot R. Isaiah di Trani* [Rid], ed. Wertheimer, #112, 510–11; and cf. Israel Ta-Shma, "Ha-Rav Yeshayah di-Trani ha-Zaqen u-Qesharav ʿim Bzyantiyyon ve-Ereẓ Yisraʾel," *Shalem* 4 (1984):409–16, and idem, "Sefer Shibbolei ha-Leqet u-Khfelav," *Italia* 11 (1996): 46–47. On Rid's place within the tosafist enterprise, cf. Urbach, *Baʿalei ha-Tosafot*, 1:413; Isadore Twersky, "The Contribution of Italian Sages to Rabbinic Literature," *Italia Judaica* (Rome, 1983), 390–400; and my "Progress and Tradition in Medieval Ashkenaz," *Jewish History* 14 (2000; in press).

[20]See Ta-Shma, "Ha-Rav Yeshayah di-Trani," 415, n. 28. Cf. above, ch. 3, n. 79, and ch. 4, n. 59. See also *Tosafot Rid* to *Ḥagigah* 16a.

[21]See R. Jacob b. Asher, *Arbaʿah Turim, Yoreh Deʿah* 179, and *Beit Yosef*, ad loc., s.v. *katav ha-Ramah*. Cf. *Tosafot Rid* to *Qiddushin* 71a, and above, ch. 4, n. 15. (For the view of R. Jacob and his father, R. Asher, see below, n. 72.) Rid records a mystical interpretation found in *Sefer Ḥasidim* and other Pietist sources concerning the response of *ʾamen* to a blessing. See *Pisqei R. Yeshayah di-Trani le-Massekhet Berakhot*, ed. A. Y. Wertheimer (Jerusalem, 1964), 164–65, and above, ch. 4, n. 2. On Rid and interpretations of *Ḥasidei Ashkenaz*, see above, ch. 1, nn. 88, 123. Rid's grandson Riʾaz composed formulations against the study of philosophy, although he did not necessarily advocate the study of *sod*. See Simcha Assaf, *Meqorot le-Toledot ha-Ḥinnukh be-Yisraʾel*, vol. 2 (Tel Aviv, 1931), 96–98. Abraham Abulafia had apparently taught (pieces of) *Moreh Nevukhim* to Riʾaz (and to R. Zedekiah b. Abraham *ha-Rofe*; cf. the next note). See Ta-Shma, "Ha-Rav Yeshayah di-Trani ha-Zagen," 411, and Moshe Idel, *R. Menaḥem Reqanati ha-Mequbbal*, vol. 1 (Tel Aviv, 1998), 36.

Shibbolei ha-Leqet that unnamed *rabbanim* performed a *she᾿elat ḥalom* to know if the burning of the Talmud in *Ẓarefat* in 1244 (1242?) was ordained by the Creator in Heaven. The response they received was that, indeed, this tragic event was a Divine decree (*gezerah de-Oraita*).[22] R. Ḥayyim Yosef David Azulai (Ḥida, d.1806) noted that *Shibbolei ha-Leqet* was influenced by R. Jacob of Marvège's *She᾿elot u-Teshuvot min ha-Shamayim* (Provence, c.1200), which *Shibbolei ha-Leqet* cites a number of times, referring to R. Jacob as *ha-Ẓaddiq*.[23] It should also be noted that R. Mikha᾿el *ha-Mal᾿akh*, an otherwise unknown thirteenth-century rabbinic figure from northern France, is described as having "ascended to the heavens" to resolve doubts or questions through trances and other methods similar to those ascribed to R. Jacob of Marvège.[24]

---

[22]See *Shibbolei ha-Leqet*, sec. 263 (*hilkhot taᶜanit*), and the parallel citation in Yeḥiel b. Yequti᾿el, *Tanya Rabbati* (Warsaw, 1879), sec. 58 (end), fol. 63. Cf. *She᾿elot u-Teshuvot min ha-Shamayim*, ed. Margoliot, editor's introduction, 18–19, and the description in *Midrash ᶜAsarah Harugei Malkhut* (above, ch. 3, n. 34) of R. Yishma᾿el's heavenly ascent to ascertain whether the decree against the martyrs had emanated from the Almighty. See also above, n. 13, ch. 3, n. 9; and ch. 4, n. 19. On the relationship between *Shibbolei ha-Leqet* and Ashkenazic rabbinic literature, see now Yaᶜakov Spiegel, *Seder Ḥovat Leil Shimmurim* (Lod, 1998), editor's introduction, 7–8, 12, 26; and above, ch. 3, n. 52.

[23]See, e.g., *Shibbolei ha-Leqet*, secs. 9, 31, 127, 157 (typically cited as בשאלות חלום ששאל הצדיק ר׳ יעקב); *Shibbolei ha-Leqet* (*Ha-ḥeleq ha-Sheni*), ed. S. Hasida, 4 (sec. 1, end), 75 (sec. 17); and ms. Bodl. 659 (*Shibbolei ha-Leqet ha-Qaẓar*), fols. 10v, 17v, 34, 40r, 49v, 100v; and above, ch. 4, n. 61. Cf. Ḥida, *Shem ha-Gedolim, maᶜarekhet ha-gedolim*, s.v. *R. Yaᶜaqov he-Ḥasid*; *She᾿elot u-Teshuvot min ha-Shamayim*, ed. R. Margoliot, 19–21; Israel Ta-Shma, "She᾿elot u-Teshuvot min ha-Shamayim, Ha-Qoveẓ ve-Tosfotav," *Tarbiz* 57 (1988):56–63; idem, *Minhag Ashkenaz ha-Qadmon*, 205; Yosef Dan, "Shut min ha-Shamayim Meyuḥasot le-R. Eleazar mi-Vermaiza," *Sinai* 69 (1971):195; and my "Rabbinic Figures in Castilian Kabbalistic Pseudepigraphy: R. Yehudah *he-Ḥasid* and R. Elḥanan of Corbeil," *Journal of Jewish Thought and Philosophy* 3 (1993):95, n. 66. The phrases *kefi mah she-yoruni min ha-shamayim* and *kol mah she-yar᾿uhu min ha-shamayim* appear in a document that binds the litigants to the decisions of the judges, found in *Shibbolei ha-Leqet*, vol. 2, ed. M. Z. Hasida (Jerusalem, 1969), *hilkhot dayanim*, 202. Cf., however, Twersky, *Rabad of Posquières*, 291–97, and above, ch. 1, n. 130.

[24]See Alexander Marx, "A New Collection of Mss. in the Cambridge Library," *PAAJR* 4 (1933):153, n. 29; R. Abraham Torrutiel's supplement to Ibn Daud's *Sefer ha-Qabbalah* in *Sefer ha-Ḥakhamim ve-Qorot ha-Yamim*, ed. Adolf Neubauer (Oxford, 1887) [*Sefer ha-Qabbalah le-R. Avraham b. Shelomoh*], 105, and in Avraham David, *Shetei Keroniqot Ivriyyot mi-Dor Gerush Sefarad* (Jerusalem, 1979), 28; and Moshe Idel, *Kabbalah: New Perspectives* (New Haven, 1988), 91; and cf. ms. Bodl. 2423 (Ashkenaz, fourteenth century), 4v. Interestingly, in this description, Rashi is considered to be a predecessor of R. Jacob of Marvège in these matters; see above, ch. 3, n. 50. The name R. Mikha᾿el is found in proximity to Ashkenazic pietistic material in ms. Parma 541, fol. 264r, and in ms. Bodl. 271, fol. 107r. Cf. Chaim Levine, "Al Perush ha-Maḥzor ha-Meyuḥas

Shibbolei ha-Leqet's inclusion of passages and practices from *Hekhalot* literature has already been noted, as has its use of pietistic material from R. Judah *he-Ḥasid* (including the little-known quasi-mystical *teᶜamim shel R. Yehudah he-Ḥasid*[25]) and other teachings and stringencies of *ḥasidut Ashkenaz*.[26] Indeed, precisely because of its pietistic bent, *Shibbolei ha-Leqet* has also been shown to be an important source of Ashkenazic customs for the Zohar.[27]

Moreover, *Shibbolei ha-Leqet* refers to esoteric concepts held by *Ḥasidei Ashkenaz* and the members of the *Ḥug ha-Keruv ha-Meyuḥad*. Among these are the notion of the feminine aspect of the Godhead,[28] the mystical correlation between the performance of *berit milah* and the Tetragrammaton (through circumcision, one cleaves to the Divine Name,)[29] as well as the concept—found in *Shiᶜur Qomah* and other earlier mystical works—that the Torah is comprised of a series of Divine Names (the Torah in its entirety can be transmuted through a new division of letters into names of God). This concept was also espoused by R. Eleazar of Worms (and other Pietist writers) and by Ramban, raising the possibility that both Ramban and *Shibbolei ha-Leqet* received it from *Ḥasidei Ashkenaz*.[30]

---

le-Raban," *Tarbiz* 29 (1960):167, for a R. Mikhaʾel *mi-Yavan*, and Zohar Amar, "Ẓiyyunei Qevarim be-Ereẓ Yisraʾel," *Qoveẓ ᶜal Yad* n.s. 14 (1998):289, for a R. Meir *Ẓarefati Baᶜal ha-Nes* who lived in the early thirteenth century.

[25]See above, ch. 4, n. 24, and cf. Elliot Wolfson, "The Mystical Significance of Torah-Study in German Pietism," *JQR* 84 (1993):44–46. Note also the citation of *Sefer Gematriʾot* in *Shibbolei ha-Leqet*, sec. 137, and cf. Sefer Gematriʾot le-R. *Yehudah he-Ḥasid*, ed. Abrams and Ta-Shma, 4.

[26]See above, ch. 1, n. 60, and ch. 2, n. 34. Regarding *Sefer Yeẓirah*, see *Shibbolei ha-Leqet*, sec. 126, and above, ch. 3, n. 31.

[27]See, e.g., Ta-Shma, *Ha-Nigleh shebe-Nistar*, 21, n. 36, 22, 27–28; my *Jewish Education and Society*, 177–78, n. 81; and cf. above, ch. 3, n. 57.

[28]See Wolfson, *Along the Path*, 25–29, 142–43, n. 184; and above, ch. 2, n. 34.

[29]See Elliot Wolfson, "Circumcision and the Divine Name: A Study in the Transmission of Esoteric Doctrine," *JQR* 78 (1987): 85–112, esp. 110–11.

[30]See *Shibbolei ha-Leqet*, sec. 8, citing unnamed earlier authorities (מצאתי הטעם לגאונים); *Sefer Roqeaḥ*, sec. 311; Trachtenberg, *Jewish Magic and Superstition*, 314, n. 4; Wolfson, "The Mystical Significance of Torah-Study in German Pietism," 47–50; Moshe Idel, "Tefisat ha-Torah be-Sifrut ha-Hekhalot ve-Gilgulehah ba-Qabbalah," *Meḥqerei Yerushalayim be-Maḥshevet Yisraʾel* 1 (1981):27–30, 53–54 (esp. n. 102); idem, "We Have No Kabbalistic Tradition on This," *Rabbi Moses Naḥmanides (Ramban): Explorations in His Religious and Literary Virtuosity*, ed. Isadore Twersky (Cambridge, Mass., 1983), 54, n. 10; Israel Ta-Shma, "Be-Koaḥ ha-Shem—Le-Toledotav shel Minhag Nishkaḥ," *Sefer Bar Ilan* 26–27 (1995):389–99; and above, ch. 3, nn. 4, 28. Cf. Ruth Langer, *To Worship God Properly* (Cincinnati, 1998), 217–19.

In light of R. Zedekiah's affinities with *ḥasidut* and *sod*, the question of whether the *payyetan* R. Benjamin b. Abraham *ha-Navi* (ostensibly R. Zedekiah's brother Benjamin, who is mentioned constantly in *Shibbolei ha-Leqet*)[31] had *sod* leanings, as his title *navi* suggests, must also be reevaluated. Shraga Abramson has argued that this title refers to R. Benjamin's superior Torah knowledge on an exoteric level, rather than to an inclination toward esoteric studies, and notes that *Shibbolei ha-Leqet* never refers to his brother by his title in any event.[32] But if the author of *Shibbolei ha-Leqet* was himself sensitive to *sod*, as we have seen, it was perhaps not necessary to single out his brother in this manner. R. Benjamin is cited by *Shibbolei ha-Leqet* as interpreting the biblical phrase *zeroa*ᶜ *netuyah* (the Almighty's might)—which was active in securing the release of the Jews from Egypt—as "the *Shem ha-Meforash* which is called *Ḥarba de-Moshe*." This magical formula is found in a version of *Sefer ha-Razim*, and it was alleged that Moses used it to perform all the signs he did in Egypt.[33]

---

[31]A הלכות שחיטה לר׳ בנימין בן אברהם הרופא is found in ms. Paris 620, fols. 247–58, 294–97; and see also fols. 240v–249 (הלכות שחיטה לר׳ יהודה בן בנימין ענו). Cf. Ta-Shma, *Ha-Nigleh shebe-Nistar*, 27; idem, in *Zion* 54 (1989):205; and Simcha Emanuel, "Sifrei Halakhah Avudim shel Baᶜalei ha-Tosafot" (Ph.D. diss., Hebrew University, 1993), 253–59. Benjamin authored a brief, rhymed ethical treatise (*Shaᶜarei/ Darkhei Eẓ [ha-] Ḥayyim*), that was mildly ascetic (פרוש מן המותר לך כדי להתרחק מן האיסור). It was published in *Qoveẓ ᶜal Yad* 1 (1885):71–74, and see also, e.g., ms. Parma 918, fols. 8v–11v; and above, ch. 2, n. 35.

[32]Shraga Abramson, "Navi, Roʾeh ve-Ḥozeh—R. Avraham ha-Ḥozeh," *Sefer Yovel Muggash li-Khvod ha-Rav Mordechai Kirschblum*, ed. David Telsner (Jerusalem, 1993), 119–20, 125, 132. On the esoteric implications of the title *navi* and its usage in Ashkenaz, see below, n. 67.

[33]See *Shibbolei ha-Leqet*, sec. 218 (fol. 97a); Y. Spiegel, *Seder Ḥovat Leil Shimmurim*, 90–91; above, ch. 3, n. 12, and cf. *Sefer ha-Razim*, ed. Mordekhai Margoliot (Jerusalem, 1967), editor's introduction, 61–62 (which notes that *Shibbolei ha-Leqet* is citing a different version of *Sefer ha-Razim* than the one that is extant). On *Ḥarba de-Moshe* in this context, cf. Simcha Emanuel, *Teshuvot ha-Geonim ha-Ḥadashot* (Jerusalem, 1995), 131. On the use by Moses of *Shem ha-Meforash* to perform the signs in Egypt (see Rashi to Exodus 2:4), cf. *Tosafot ha-Shalem*, ed. Jacob Gellis, vol. 6, 186–87, and above, ch. 4, n. 42. For a mystical formulation in one of R. Benjamin *Anav's piyyutim*, see Wolfson, *Along the Path*, 119, n. 54. See also *Shibbolei ha-Leqet—Ha-ḥeleq ha-Sheni*, ed. Hasida, editor's introduction, 37–41, and esp. 40, n. 119.

For another reference to a nonextant version of *Sefer ha-Razim*, see Daniel Abrams, "Sefer Shaqod le-R. Shemuʾel b. R. Qalonymus ve-Torat ha-Kavod shel Talmid R. Eleazar mi-Vorms," *Assufot* (forthcoming), n. 87. R. Eleazar of Worms cites the extant version of *Sefer ha-Razim* frequently, especially in his *Sodei Razzaya*, but almost exclusively with regard to descriptions of the heavens rather than for its magical material; see Margoliot, xiv, 59, and above, ch. 4, n. 42. Generally speaking, however, *Sefer ha-Razim* is not cited

R. Elijah Menaḥem b. Moses of London (1220–84), a contemporary of R. Meir of Rothenburg who studied also in northern France and was a descendant of R. Simeon *ha-Gadol*,[34] inserted formulae involving Divine Names in *mezuzot* (literally, he carved Names on the doorpost) that protected the home from fire.[35] He referred to the *sod* interpretations implicit in the Targum to the verses of *qedushah de-sidra*.[36] R. Elijah is also credited with transmitting two magical adjurations that included both Divine and angelic names. One of them was designed to bring on a dream that would answer particular questions (similar to a *she᾿elat ḥalom*). This procedure involved the release of a Divine Name that could be found by pronouncing formulae over certain grasses or herbs (*Shem ha-katuv be-yereq*) and was described as *seder ha-she᾿elah*.[37] R. Eliyahu also reports a prophetic dream he had (**והנה אקיץ משנתי והנה חלום נבואה ולא אחת משׁשים ולא אחד משׁשים**) in which he offered, in response to a question, an interpretation of a problematic passage in the

---

extensively by Ashkenazic rabbinic sources, despite its relationship to *Hekhalot* literature (see, e.g., Margoliot, 41). This is perhaps because much of the magic in *Sefer ha-Razim* is associated with amulets and substances, in addition to any magical formulae. Ashkenazic rabbinic magic is, almost exclusively, formulaic or literary. See above, introduction, at n. 28.

[34]See Cecil Roth, "Toledot Rabbenu Eliyyahu Menaḥem mi-Londrish," in *Perushei Rabbenu Eliyyahu mi-Londrish u-Fesaqav*, ed. M. Y. Zaks (Jerusalem, 1956), 20–22, 29, 41. Cf. Grossman, *Ḥakhmei Ashkenaz ha-Rishonim*, 87–88, and above, ch. 4, n. 5. On R. Elijah's ascetic tendencies, see Roth, *The Intellectual Activities of Medieval English Jewry*, 62–64.

[35]See A. Marmorstein, "Some Hitherto Unknown Jewish Scholars of Angevin England," *JQR* 19 (1928–29):32—**להציל בית ר׳ מנחם חזן מלונדון [ר׳ מנחם מל׳= ר׳ אליהו מנחם] חקק על משקוף הבית בסכין את השמות וניצל כל הבית**. On the *mezuzah* as a means of protection, cf. Victor Aptowitzer, "Les Noms de Dieu et des Anges dan la Mezouza," *REJ* 60 (1910):39–52, and *REJ* 65 (1913):54–60 (and see above, ch. 3, n. 57, and ch. 4, n. 16); and Wolfson, "Circumcision and the Divine Name," 81–82.

[36]See *Perushei Rabbenu Eliyahu* (*Pesaqim mi-Sefer Zeraᶜim*), 34–35, and cf. Langer, *To Worship God Properly*, 211, 219, n. 11.

[37]See ms. Sassoon 290, fol. 381r, sec. 1003:

> זה מה שיסד הר׳ אליהו מלונדריש כשתרצה לעשות שאלתך תפנה לבבך משאר עסקים ותיחד כוונתך ומחשבתך בהכנסת הפרדס. ישב בדד באימה מתעטף בטליתו ותפלין בראשו וכך יתחיל מכתם לדוד כל מזמור בכוונת הלב... ויקראם בניגונים ואח״כ יכרע על ברכיו ופניו למזרח וכה ידבר... י״ר מלפניך כל יחשוב ויחשוב בשם שכתוב לפניו ולא״ב יבטאהו בשפתיו. ועוד אני מתחנן לפניך כשמך הגדול ויחשוב בששה קצות השם הגדול החקוק במצח אהרן הנחלק לשלשה בתים... אותיות ע״פ צירוף הנקודות. ועוד אני מתחיל לפניך בשם ה׳ המפורש י-ה-ו-ה... עולה למנין שבעים ושתים... וכל אלו הדברים בשאלה הראשונה. אמנם בכל שאר פעמים די כשזכר השם הנכתב... שיכתוב בעמדו במים חיים עד

grace after meals.[38] There appears to have been a strong connection between R. Elijah's father, R. Moses of London, and R. Moses of Evreux.[39]

צווארו ויהיו בידיו למשמרת עד עת צורך ואח״כ יאמר... השר הגדול כמו שכתוב למעלה בסוד הראשון [בגליון — שאלת חלום בערב — קלף קשור במצחו ובנקיות וכו׳]. ואם ירצה להשתמש בשם המפורש בעשבים לבד יאמר יר״מ כל יכול מוטל על כל יודע כל... שתקבל תפלתי אני פ׳ עבדך בן אמתך וצוה למשרתך השר הגדול שנקרא מטטרון שתשלח לי את יבתביאל ואת יתתביאל ואת קפקפיאל אשר הם מתחת רשותו שיודיעוני בכתביתך מפורשת בזה הנייר ששמתי במקום פ׳ תשובת שאלתי שהיא כך וכך בשם ה׳... שכתובים למעלה בראשון. 381ב- גם לבת קול למעלה מהש׳ הנכבד ב״ה בשם הכתוב בעשבים ולעשות קודם הבקשה על דרך הכתובים ולחשוב בו ככתבו. ובהלוך האחרון לשני ושני לראשון גם הוא מנוע עדין מכם עד יאבה הצור ב״ה ליתן לנו פנאי. השתדל בו למען תדע כל. 382א- (סי׳ 1004) שולח עשבים ואומר שמות... ועוד כתב ר׳ אליהו כתב ששלח השם הכתוב בעשבים וכן אמר זה השם עם העשב... ואח״כ תזכיר את השמות הכתובים למטה בכוונת הלב ואלו הן השמות... משביע י-ה-ו-ה. נ״א קבלה מגדולי אשכנז יכתוב בעשבין שלוטין... יר״מ מדת הדין והוא א-להים ויכוין ה׳ ו׳ וכו׳.

[The end of sec. 1002 discusses the Name of fourteen letters (see below, n. 63) in a kabbalistic context. See also ms. JNUL 8° 397, fol. 364r.]

Cf. Roth, "Toledot Rabbenu Eliyyahu," 39–40. Once again, the preparations involved in this procedure are reminiscent of material found in *Hekhalot* literature. The *hashbaᶜot* themselves are similar to those found in earlier Ashkenazic manuscripts; cf. above, ch. 3, n. 112. [On the angel קפקפיאל, see Theodore Schrire, *Hebrew Magic Amulets* (New York, 1966), 130.] In addition, R. Isaac of Chinon, whose familiarity with *hashbaᶜot* and interest in mystical prayers and supplications has been documented (above, ch. 3, n. 104), was a northern French contemporary of R. Elijah. [R. Isaac's son, R. Samson b. Isaac of Chinon (author of *Sefer Keritot*, d.c.1330) is reported, by R. Pereẓ b. Isaac *ha-Kohen*, to have prayed with simple *kavvanah* (אני מתפלל לדעת זה התינוק). This description was meant by R. Samson to show his disagreement with the approach of the kabbalists, who prayed to one *sefirah* or another, depending on the particular prayer. See *Sheʾelot u-Teshuvot min ha-Rivash*, 157.]

38 See Urbach, *Baᶜalei ha-Tosafot*, 2:505–6. Urbach makes no note of the prophetic experience in this passage, citing it with regard to a different issue entirely. (Interestingly, R. Elijah—like R. Zedekiah b. Abraham, author of *Shibbolei ha-Leqet*—was a medical doctor).

39 See Y. N. Epstein, "Perishat R. Eliyyahu Menaḥem b. Mosheh mi-Londrish," *Maddaᶜei ha-Yahadut* 1 (1926):64–65; E. E. Urbach, "Mi-Toratam shel Ḥakhmei Angliyyah mi-Lifnei ha-Gerush," *Sefer ha-Yovel li-Khevod Yisraʾel Brody* (London, 1967), 7; and Israel Ta-Shma, "Ketav Yad Parma 933 ('Tosafot Ḥakhmei Angliyyah') ve-ᶜErko," *ᶜAlei Sefer* 5 (1978):92–96. See also Y. S. Lange, "Le-ᶜInyan ha-Semaq mi-Ẓurich," *ᶜAlei Sefer* 4 (1978):178–79, who suggests, like Urbach, that R. Moses of London may have studied in Evreux. Regarding R. Jacob *Ḥazzan* of London and *sod*, see, e.g., his *Eẓ Ḥayyim*, ed. Israel Brody (Jerusalem, 1962), 1:198–205; 2:334–39, 378–79; *Siddur Rabbenu Shelomoh mi-Germaiza ve-Siddur Ḥasidei Ashkenaz*, ed. Moshe Hershler (Jerusalem, 1972), 82, n. 86; and above, ch. 3, n. 110.

Another son of R. Moses of London, R. Yom Tov, whose pietistic tendencies were characterized by the phrase חסיד היה וירא שמים, took his own life as a means of achieving expiation. The text that reports this incident refers also to R. Moses as a *ḥasid* and suggests that R. Yom Tov was troubled by demonic forces within him that caused him to consider conversion to Christianity. To atone for these thoughts, he committed suicide. The writer of this text recommended, in the spirit of *ḥasidut Ashkenaz*, various forms of ascetic and physical penances (including עינויים, סיגופים, מלקות) that would allow the sinner to repent without having to lose his life.[40] It should be noted, however, that included in a series of questions concerning penances to which R. Judah *he-Ḥasid* responded is the following: if a person kills himself because of his sins (as a means of expiation), does he transgress the prohibition of committing suicide (as derived from the biblical phrase, אך את דמכם לנפשותיכם אדרוש)? In his response, R. Judah *he-Ḥasid* allowed or even prescribed suicide (טוב הוא לאדם) to atone for sins.[41]

R. Meir of Rothenburg was a student of R. Isaac *Or Zarua*ᶜ and R. Avigdor of Vienna, and of other rabbinic figures linked to magic and *sod*, including R. Ezra *ha-Navi* of Moncontour[42] and R. Yeḥiel of Paris.[43] R. Meir exhibited

---

[40]Ms. Paris 1408, fol. 31. The text was published by Efraim Kupfer in *Tarbiz* 40 (1971):385–87. See also Urbach, *Ba*ᶜ*alei ha-Tosafot*, 2:498–99; Avraham Grossman, "Shorashav shel Qiddush ha-Shem be-Ashkenaz ha-Qedumah," *Qedushat ha-Ḥayyim ve-Ḥeruf ha-Nefesh*, ed. I. Gafni and A. Ravitzky (Jerusalem, 1992), 126–27; idem, *Ḥakhmei Ẓarefat ha-Rishonim*, 503–4; and cf. Alexander Murray, *Suicide in the Middle Ages*, vol. 1 (Oxford, 1998), 339–47.

[41]See ms. Bodl. 682 (Ashkenaz, after 1452), fol. 370r (published now in Shlomo Spitzer, "*She*ʾ*elot u-Teshuvot Rabbenu Yehuda he-Ḥasid be-Inyanei Teshuvah*," *Sefer ha-Zikkaron le-R. Shemu*ʾ*el Barukh Werner*, ed. Yosef Buksboim [Jerusalem, 1996], 202). For a description of the manuscript (which consists primarily of an annotated קיצור פסקי הרא"ש), cf. S. Emanuel in *Me-Ginzei ha-Makhon le-Taẓlumei Kitvei ha-Yad ha-*ᶜ*Ivriyyim*, ed. Avraham David (Jerusalem, 1995), 105. [For other examples of R. Judah *he-Ḥasid*'s penitential responsa, see Ivan Marcus, "Ḥibburei ha-Teshuvah shel Ḥasidei Ashkenaz," *Studies in Jewish Mysticism, Philosophy and Ethical Literature Presented to Isaiah Tishby*, ed. J. Dan and J. Hacker (Jerusalem, 1986), 375, n. 30. And cf. my "Rabbinic Figures in Castilian Kabbalistic Pseudepigraphy," 94, n. 63, and above, ch. 4, n. 30.] In this fascinating (and troubling) responsum, R. Judah *he-Ḥasid* cites several incidents and texts as proofs—including the death of R. Eliezer b. Haradia, who killed himself for his sins and was praised by a heavenly voice; a passage in *Bereshit Rabbah* asserting that the nephew of R. Yose b. Yoᶜezer killed himself in a torturous manner and was considered meritorious; and the case of an apostate who said he sinned through water (the baptismal font) and therefore threw himself into water (and drowned) as a means of expiation.

[42]On R. Ezra *ha-Navi* of Moncontour, see below, n. 67.

affinities with the German Pietists, and with R. Judah *he-Ḥasid* in particular, on a wide range of issues. These include conservatism in halakhic decision-making, the conception of *qiddush ha-Shem*, biblical interpretations characterized as *taᶜamei massoret*, liturgical practices and *nosaḥ ha-tefillah* (for which R. Meir adduced passages in *Hekhalot* literature in support of readings favored by R. Judah), procedures for repentance and *tiqqunei teshuvah*, and even protection of women from spousal abuse and attitudes toward *Ereẓ Yisraʾel*.[44]

---

[43]R. Yeḥiel (d.c.1265) wrote a commentary on the *Hekhalot*-based *E-l Adon* prayer. See ms. Paris l'Alliance 133, cited in Colette Sirat, "Un nouveau manuscrit du Maḥzor Vitry," *REJ* 125 (1966):262; Israel Ta-Shma, "Li-Meqorotav ha-Sifrutiyyim shel Sefer ha-Zohar," *Tarbiz* 60 (1991):663–65; and idem, *Ha-Nigleh shebe-Nistar*, 49, 95, n. 42. Although the recitation of *E-l Adon* was included in the *siddur* of R. Eleazar of Worms and in the *siddur* of R. Judah b. Yaqar (which means, as Ta-Shma notes, that it was known within the circle of Ri's students even before R. Yeḥiel of Paris), R. Yeḥiel's interest in this particular hymn is nonetheless significant. On the *Hekhalot* aspects of *E-l Adon* (which can be discerned from the prayer commentaries of *Ḥasidei Ashkenaz* and R. Judah b. Yaqar), see Meir Bar-Ilan, *Sitrei Tefillah ve-Hekhalot* (Jerusalem, 1987), 115–20.

Underscoring the need to recite the *berakhah ʾaḥat meᶜen sheva* in the *maᶜariv* service on Friday night carefully and without interruption, R. Yeḥiel is said to have been in contact with a *neshamah* who described how the angels throw him up and let him descend on his own because he used to talk during the *ḥazzan*'s recitation of this prayer. See S. Shaʾanan, "Pisqei R. Pereẓ va-Aḥerim be-ᶜInyanei Oraḥ Ḥayyim," *Moriah* 17:9–10 (1991):14, sec. 26, and above, ch. 2, n. 70. For a similar phenomenon in *Sefer Ḥasidim* (recorded also in *Arbaᶜah Turim*), see above, ch. 2, n. 52. The notion that there are forty-nine distinct approaches to every halakhic issue, associated by Ritva (*ᶜEruvin* 13b) and Maharshal (*Yam shel Shelomoh*, introduction to *Bava Qamma*), with esoteric teachings, is cited by R. Pereẓ of Corbeil from *Tosafot R. Yeḥiel* (on the basis of a passage in *Midrash Tehillim*). See Tosafot *R. Pereẓ ha-Shalem ᶜal Massekhet ᶜEruvin*, ed. Chaim Dickman (Jerusalem, 1991), 48. On R. Yeḥiel's interest in Avraham Ibn Ezra (and his contacts with R. Solomon b. Samuel), see above, ch. 2, n. 8. Cf. ms. Vat. 324, fol. 278 (questions concerning resurrection in which R. Yeḥiel of Paris's name appears), and *ᶜArugat ha-Bosem*, ed. Urbach, 4:39, n. 82.

[44][Although many of the following references are mentioned above, in a series of notes at the end of ch. 2 (in the section on Maharam's pietism and affinities with *ḥasidut Ashkenaz*), it is worthwhile listing them again here, with some additional sources, in a single comprehensive note.] See, e.g., ms. Cambr. Add. 1022, fol. 100v; *Sefer Tashbeẓ*, sec. 553; Urbach, *Baᶜalei ha-Tosafot*, 2:522, 536, 547, 564; *Taᶜamei Mesoret ha-Miqra lel-R. Yehudah he-Ḥasid*, ed. Y. S. Lange (Jerusalem, 1981), 11; idem, "Perush Baᶜalei ha-Tosafot ᶜal ha-Torah-Ketav Yad Paris 48," *ᶜAlei Sefer* 5 (1978):73; *Teshuvot u-Fesaqim le-R. Meir mi-Rothenburg*, ed. I. Z. Kahana, vol. 1 (Jerusalem, 1957), 14–15; my "Preservation, Creativity and Courage: The Life and Works of R. Meir of Rothenburg," *Jewish Book Annual* 50 (1992–93):249–59; Israel Ta-Shma, "Al Odot Yaḥasam shel Qadmonei Ashkenaz le-ᶜErekh ha-ᶜAliyah le Ereẓ Yisraʾel," *Shalem* 6 (1992):315–17, but

It should also be noted that R. Meir studied for a time with R. Samuel of Evreux.[45]

As reflected in a number of manuscript passages, R. Meir was involved in aspects of both magic and practical esoteric applications, through the recitation of *Shemot* and mystical formulae, and the writing of amulets involving letter combinations and the use of Divine Names. In some instances, his formulae are recorded in manuscripts in close proximity to those of R. Judah *he-Ḥasid*, R. Eleazar of Worms, and other Ashkenazic figures, including his own student, R. Dan. The purpose of these formulae was to achieve certain aims and states of being, such as *petiḥat ha-lev*,[46] and protection from physical harm and danger, whether caused by rulers and *maziqin*, or through incarceration.[47] Maharam

---

cf. my "The *ʿAliyah* of 'Three Hundred Rabbis' in 1211: Tosafist Attitudes Toward Settling in the Land of Israel," *JQR* 76 (1986): 205–9; Avraham Grossman, "Ziqato shel Maharam mi-Rothenburg ʾel Ereẓ Yisraʾel," *Cathedra* 84 (1997):63–84; idem, "Yaḥasam shel Ḥakhmei Yemei ha-Benayim ʿal Hakaʾat Nashim," *Proceedings of the Tenth World Congress of Jewish Studies*, Div. B, vol. 1 (Jerusalem, 1990), 121–23 [="Medieval Rabbinic Views on Wife-Beating," *Jewish History* 5 (1991):57–61]; idem, "Haggahot R. Shemayah be-Nosaḥ Perush Rashi," *Tarbiz* 60 (1991):91–92; Naftali Wieder, "Beʿityah shel Gematria Anti-Noẓerit ve-Anti-Islamit," *Sinai* 76 (1975):5–10; idem, "Tiqqunim be-Nosaḥ ha-Tefillah be-Hashpaʿat Leshonot Loʿaziyyot," *Sinai* 81 (1977): 27–29; *Sefer Berakhot le-Maharam*, ed. Shlomo Spitzer (Jerusalem, 1988), 133; R. Meir of Rothenburg, *Responsa* (Prague), 517; *ʿArugat ha-Bosem*, ed. Urbach, 4:59–60; and cf. R. Langer, *To Worship God Properly*, 215–24, 233.

[45]See Urbach, *Baʿalei ha-Tosafot*, 2:528 [For R. Meir's impact on Ashkenaz throughout the fourteenth century and beyond, especially with regard to *tiqqunei teshuvah* and conservationism in halakhic decision-making, see above, ch. 1, n. 148; ch. 2, n. 48; and my entry in *The Yale Companion to Jewish Writing and Thought in German Culture, 1096–1996*, ed. S. Gilman and J. Zipes (New Haven, 1997), 27–34.

[46]See ms. Vat. 243, fol. 4v [and cf. Israel Ta-Shma, "Rabbenu Dan be-Ashkenaz uvi-Sefarad," *Studies... Presented to Isaiah Tishby*, ed. Dan and Hacker, 390–91, and ms. Livorno Talmud Tora 138, fol. 36r. A *qabbalah* (for salvation) from R. Dan is on fol. 6v; see also fol. 10r, and below, n. 78.] See also ms. JNUL 8°476, fol. 50v, and above, n. 16. For a Sabbath practice that Maharam mi-Rothenburg endorsed as a means of achieving *petihat ha-lev*, see the passage in ms. Montefiore 130, fols. 54v–55r, cited by Israel Ta-Shma, "Beʾerah shel Miryam," *Meḥqerei Yerushalayim be-Maḥshevet Yisraʾel* 4 (1985): 263 [=*Minhag Ashkenaz ha-Qadmon*, 213–14]; and cf. ms. Moscow-Guenzberg 182, fol. 156r, in the name of מהרמנ"ע (=מהר"ם נשמתו עדן).

[47]See Gershom Scholem's transcription of ms. Cambr. Add. 664, fol. 72r, in *Qiryat Sefer* 4 (1927–29):317—"When the king wished to detain R. Meir in prison, R. Meir uttered a verse and was willingly released." See also *Shitat ha-Qadmonim ʿal Massekhet Yevamot*, ed. Moshe Blau (Jerusalem, 1986), editor's introduction, 8. Scholem writes that R. Meir is mentioned as a "*baʿal Shem* and *baʿal nissim* in numerous old manuscripts of practical kabbalah." See also ms. Moscow-Guenzberg 717, fol. 185, and ms. Bodl. 1936,

fols. 72r–72v, for *hashba*ᶜ*ot* and amulets from R. Meir of Rothenburg and Ramban that could be employed to ease childbirth, to thwart enemies, to make a person beloved by all, and to secure the Almighty's assistance. Cf. David Berger, *The Jewish-Christian Debate in the High Middle Ages* (Philadelphia, 1979); 253; *Sefer Tashbeẓ*, secs. 257–58 (and *Matteh Mosheh*, sec. 370); Elliot Wolfson, "Sacred Space and Mental Iconography," *Ki Barukh Hu*, ed. Robert Chazan et al. (Winona Lake, 1999), 624, n. 110; and above, ch. 3, n. 56. [Mystical and magical material from Ramban is frequently linked to and interchanged with material from Ashkenazic figures, hardly surprising in light of Ramban's genuine affinities with Ashkenazic teachings in these areas. See, e.g., the literature cited in my "Rabbinic Figures in Castilian Kabbalistic Pseudepigraphy," 108–9, n. 108; Ta-Shma, *Ha-Nigleh shebe-Nistar*, 31–40, 50–52; A. Grossman, "Ziqato shel Maharam mi-Rothenburg ʾel Ereẓ Yisraʾel," 66, n. 8; and above, ch. 4, n. 35. Regarding liturgical texts attributed to R. Judah *he-Ḥasid* and to Ramban, cf. above, ch. 1, nn. 89, 112; ch. 3, n. 110; and below, n. 74. See also ms. Parma 540, fol. 19 (above, ch. 3, n. 7).]

R. Meir's perception of the *mezuzah* as a protection from *shedim* and other forces emerges quite clearly from his well-known responsum on the need for *mezuzot* throughout one's residence (Cremona, #108): **מובטחים שכל בית שמתוקן במזוזה כהלכתא, אין שום מזיק יכול לשלוט בו**. Cf. Baron, *A Social and Religious History of the Jews*, 5:317–18, n. 72. Note also a related formulation in *Arba*ᶜ*ah Turim, Yoreh De*ᶜ*ah*, sec. 286 (and in R. Asher b. Yehiʾel, *Halakhot Qetanot, Hilkhot Mezuzah*, sec. 10): **וכן עשה הר"מ מרוטנבורג מזוזה לפתח בית מדרשו ואומר כשהיה ישן בו שינת הצהרים היה רוח רעה מבעתו קודם שתקן בו מזוזה**. [See also Maharam's responsum (Lemberg, #140=Samson b. Ẓadoq, *Sefer Tashbeẓ*, sec. 60) concerning the wearing of coral as a means of avoiding ᶜ*ayin ha-ra*. Cf. *Teshuvot ha-Rashba*, 4:245, and H. J. Zimmels, *Magicians, Theologians and Doctors* (London, 1952), 136.]

In a responsum concerning the educational initiation ceremony that was in vogue in Ashkenaz throughout the high Middle Ages (see above, ch. 3, n. 17), R. Meir permitted eating the peeled eggs as part of the ceremony, despite talmudic concerns about the presence of *ruaḥ ra*ᶜ*ah*, either because *ruaḥ ra*ᶜ*ah* was perhaps no longer a common phenomenon in his day or because the (holy) writing on the eggs repelled the spirits. R. Meir was also not concerned that when children ate the cakes on the festival (*Shavu*ᶜ*ot*, when the ceremony normally took place), they would be liable for erasing the letters written on the cakes when they ate them. At the same time, R. Meir asserted that the writing on the cakes given to the children for *petiḥat ha-lev* should not include Divine Names (as was apparently the practice) but only angelic ones. See Marcus, *Rituals of Childhood*, 115–16. R. Meir's concern was not, however, a legalistic one designed to curtail or undercut the ceremony per se. As we have seen (above, n. 46), Maharam himself fully understood and supported the religio-magical conception of *petiḥat ha-lev.* Rather, R. Meir's concern was similar to the one expressed by R. Judah *he-Ḥasid* (Marcus, 114, with which R. Eleazar of Worms disagreed)—that biblical verses should not be written on the cakes (or that the cakes should not be given to the children to eat) because it was improper to excrete these verses. R. Meir was concerned about the improper treatment of *Shemot* themselves, while R. Judah extended this concern to the biblical verses in general (which contained and also represented *Shemot* in Ashkenazic thought; see above, n. 30). Both R. Meir and R. Judah had higher pietistic concerns that

decided a matter of monetary law that he had not studied or discussed with his teachers based on what he learned from the angelic *baʿal ha-ḥalom* (הוכחתי מפי בעל חלום) in a dream he had while being held captive in the tower of Ensisheim.[48] Moreover, R. Meir issued a *sheʾelat ḥalom* and a *goral* for predicting or knowing the future.[49]

---

caused them to seek to modify this ceremony for *petiḥat ha-lev*. Cf. above, ch. 3, n. 21. It is also possible that R. Meir was seeking to create a kind of compromise between the views of R. Judah and R. Eleazar of Worms. The author of *Sefer Assufot*, whose interest in this ceremony was also centered on its *petihat ha-lev* aspect, followed the view of his teacher, R. Eleazar of Worms. See above, ch. 3, n. 18; S. E. Stern, "Seder Ḥinnukh ha-Yeladim le-Torah ule-Yirʾah mi-Beit Midrasham shel Ḥakhmei Ashkenaz," *Ẓefunot* 1:1 (1988):20–21; and cf. R. Yeḥezkel Landau's commentary, *Dagul me-Revavah*, to *O. Ḥ.* 340:3.

[48]See *Teshuvot Maimuniyyot le-Sefer Qinyan* (*hilkhot sekhirut*, ch. 5), #31; and cf. *Sheʾelot u-Teshuvot min ha-Shamayim*, ed. Margoliot, editor's introduction, 9; *Teshuvot Maharam b. Barukh*, ed. M. A. Bloch (Berlin, 1891), 201 [ms. Amsterdam II], #108 (end). See also *Tifʾeret Shemuʾel* to *Perush R. Asher b. Yeḥiʾel, Bava Meẓiʿa*, ch. 6, n. 2. For additional examples of R. Meir's reliance on *ḥalomot*, see *Sefer Mordekhai, Bava Qamma*, sec. 1, and *Sefer ha-Parnas le-R. Mosheh Parnas Rothenburg* (Vilna, 1891), sec. 415.

[49]See ms. Parma 1221 (Spain, fifteenth century), fol. 189r–290v, for a *sheʾelat ḥalom* to ascertain the end of days attributed to Maharam (שאלת הר׳ מאיר מרוטנבורק על קץ גאולתינו מה שהראו לו בחלום). Cf. Adolf Neubauer, "Documents Inedits," *REJ* 12 (1886):92; Scholem, above, n. 47; idem, *Qiryat Sefer* 7 (1930–31):162. For the *goral*, see the manuscript described in *Ohel Ḥayim* [A Catalogue of the Manuscripts of the Manfred and Anne Lehmann Family], ed. Moshe Hallamish and Elazar Hurvitz, vol. 1 [Kabbalistic Manuscripts], (New York, 1988), 193–94. Fol. 21 contains a *qabbalah* from R. Judah *he-Ḥasid* on what to do if one sees an *ʾadam ra* and is afraid of him. [Also in this passage, *he-Ḥakham vehe-Ḥasid R. Yiẓḥaq Ẓarefati* (cf. my "Rabbinic Figures in Castilian Kabbalistic Pseudepigraphy," 100, n. 80) is linked to the recitation of a Divine Name by an unnamed Jew, which caused an attacker hoisting a sword to fall.] Fol. 44r records the *goral* of Maharam ("to know what will be"). Cf. ms. Moscow-Guenzberg 734, fols. 92r (*mequbbal me-R. Yehudah he-Ḥasid*, for protection from an evil person) and 94r (*shʾelat goral Maharam*, which required washing one's body and waiting three days before writing a formula to be used in connection with a *ḥumash*; certain verses would suggest themselves, ואח״כ יהיה לו תשובה נכונה לאלתר). See above, ch. 4, n. 32. In ms. Paris 776 (Sefarad, fifteenth/sixteenth centuries), fol. 175r, a similar oracular technique (opening a codex of the Pentateuch according to a prescribed pattern in order to predict the future) attributed to R. Meir is found just after an adjuration for protection (*shelo yukhlu le-haziq lo*) by R. Judah *he-Ḥasid* (fol. 174v). Cf. Verman, *The Books of Contemplation*, 201, n. 32; ms. Parma 563, fols. 95r–96r; and Jonathan Elukin, "The Ordeal of Scripture," *Exemplaria* 5.1 (1993):142–60. See also the references to *goral* in *Sefer Ḥasidim Parma*, 169, 255, 371.

Although some of the manuscripts in which this material appears are relatively late, or are of non-Ashkenazic provenance, R. Meir's involvement in *torat ha-sod* can be confirmed[50] from the writings of a number of his students and followers.[51] R. Solomon Simḥah b. Eliezer of Troyes, author of a work entitled *Sefer ha-Maskil*, studied rabbinic literature with Maharam and with Rabbenu Pereẓ of Corbeil. He displayed a clear familiarity with the *torat ha-Kavod* of *ḥasidut Ashkenaz* and with a form of the doctrine of the ether (referred to by R. Solomon as *ʾavir mufla barukh Hu u-varkukh Shemo*) that was akin to the *ʾavir* recognized by the German Pietists. R. Solomon was also interested in the use of Divine Names to achieve certain effects and in the manipulation of demonic and angelic forces. He mentions as the greatest

---

[50]A passage that appears in a collection of Maharam's responsa—[*Sefer Shaʿarei*] *Teshuvot Maharam b. Barukh,* ed. Bloch, 325–26 [ms. Munich], #5—decries the use of *hashbaʿot* composed of Divine or angelic names. This passage was not written, however, by Maharam. As the conclusion of the passage indicates, it comes from *Sefer Malmad ha-Talmidim* (Lyck, 1866, fol. 68a), by the Provençal rationalist R. Jacob Anatoli (who later settled in Italy). Cf. Trachtenberg, *Jewish Magic and Superstition*, 243, 311, n. 23, who was unaware of R. Jacob's authorship of this passage; Marc Saperstein, *Decoding the Rabbis* (Cambridge, Mass., 1980), 192; and idem, "Christians and Christianity in the Sermons of Jacob Anatoli," *The Frank Talmage Memorial Volume*, ed. Barry Walfish (Haifa, 1993), 2:236, 238, n. 10, and 241, n. 34. In this passage, R. Jacob also decries the role of angels as mediators between man and God during prayer (and he specifically rejects the liturgical phrase that refers to angels as *makhnisei raḥamim*), as did R. Meir of Narbonne and R. Isaac b. Yedayah in Provence. See Saperstein, 191–93. A number of Ashkenazic rabbinic scholars we have encountered approved of the notion of angels as mediators. See above, ch. 3, n. 4.

[51]R. Ḥayyim b. Makhir characterizes the greatness of R. Meir in terms of his ability to seek out and uncover hidden *sitrei Torah*. See *Teshuvot Maharam*, ed. Bloch, 57 [ms. Parma], #476: וזה אשר כתבתי למורי רבי׳ מאיר מעיין החכמה ומקור המזימה מסלותיו רומה ויורדים תהומה עברו הימה מחפשים מפשפשים סתרי תורה בחדרי חדרים מפענחים צפונותיה ונבעו מצפוניה מתייפים ומסלסלים ונבחנים ונצרפים זכים חפים ויפים ונמתקים מדבש לכל שומעיהם ישוקו עצמותיהם ויעלזו כליותיהם כמוני הצעיר הבא בשיטה אחרונה כורע ומשתחוה לעומת כבוד מורי שיאיר עיני על מה ששמעתי מכבודך. In the context of the halakhic issue raised by R. Ḥayyim, however, this description may refer solely to R. Meir's achievements in the realm of exoteric Torah knowledge. For the use of similar descriptive phrases in liturgical poems by R. Eleazar *ha-Qallir*, R. Joseph *Tov Elem*, and Raban, see Y. Oppenheimer, "Ha-Shem Ẓafnat Paʿaneaḥ-Perusho ve-Gilgulav," *Sinai* 115 (1995):79–80. On Maharam's spirituality, see also Michael Fishbane, *The Kiss of God* (Seattle, 1994), 51–55, and idem, "The Imagination of Death in Jewish Spirituality," *Death, Ecstasy and Other Worldly Journeys*, ed. John Collin and Michael Fishbane (Albany, 1995), 191. On R. Ḥayyim b. Makhir, cf. I. A. Agus, *Rabbi Meir of Rothenburg* (Philadelphia, 1947), xxvii–xxviii, and Simcha Emanuel, "Teshuvot Maharam Defus Prague," *Tarbiz* 57 (1988):572–73, n. 54.

authorities in these areas R. Yehudah *he-Ḥasid* and Rabbenu Meir *ha-Gadol* (*ha-me'orot ha-gedolim, Rabbenu Yehudah he-Ḥasid ve-Rabbenu Meir ha-Gadol*), indicating his own direct teacher, R. Meir of Rothenburg. Indeed, R. Solomon's consistent application of the addendum *barukh Hu u-varukh Shemo* to the *'avir ha-mufla*, which he considered to be an aspect of the Divine Being, also reflects a convention associated with *Ḥasidei Ashkenaz*. In addition, R. Solomon provides a physiological description of the state of *petiḥat ha-lev* and suggests the ways that this phenomenon facilitates the understanding and retention of Torah knowledge and other wisdom.[52]

According to R. Solomon, the Almighty gave man the ability to control *shedim* through the aegis of two fallen angels (Shemḥaza'el and Azza)[53] and also by invoking Divine Names that were known to some. Indeed, the correct recitation of a sequence of *Shemot* has the capacity to bring the Messiah. At the same time, however, use of these powers might cause men to lose sight of their Divine origins and experience a diminution of *yir'at shamayim*. Moreover, the power of Divine Names over demons is effective even when activated *be-tum'ah*, by sorcerers or those who err in their ways, because all is derived from the Almighty and from the power of His six names. Therefore, Divine Names should not be utilized in practice, although teaching (or learning) about their powers is permitted.[54]

---

[52]See Israel Ta-Shma, "Sefer ha-Maskil—Ḥibbur Yehudi-Ẓarefati Bilti Yaduʿa mi-Sof ha-Me'ah ha-Yod Gimmel," *Meḥqerei Yerushalayim be-Maḥshevet Yisra'el* 2 (1983): 416–38. [Note that the attitude toward astrology and the way it affects man as expressed in *Sefer ha-Maskil* is quite close to what is found in *Perush le-Sefer Yeẓirah le-R. Elḥanan b. Yaqar.*] For further discussion of *'avir* and related concepts in *Sefer ha-Maskil*, see Gad Freudenthal, "Ha-Avir Barukh Hu u-Varukh Shemo be-Sefer ha-Maskil le-R. Shelomoh Simhah mi-Troyes," *Daʿat* 32–33 (1994):187–234. Freudenthal also published and annotated selected illustrative passages from Moscow-Guenzberg 508 (the lone extant ms. of this work) in *Daʿat* 34 (1995):87–129. See now his "Stoic Physics in the Writings of R. Saʿadia Gaon al-Fayyumi and Its Aftermath in Medieval Jewish Mysticism," *Arabic Sciences and Philosophy* 6 (1996): 133–36. See also J. Davis, "R. Yom Tov Lipman Heller, Joseph b. Isaac *ha-Levi*, and Rationalism in Ashkenazic Culture, 1550–1650" (Ph.D. diss., Harvard, 1990), 67; and cf. Scholem, *Origins of the Kabbalah* (Princeton, 1987), 251.

[53]For earlier versions of this motif, and for its presence in the Zohar, see Margoliot, *Mal'akhei ʿElyon*, 274–75, 292; Moshe Idel, "Ha-Maḥshavah ha-Raʿah shel ha-E-l," *Tarbiz* 49 (1980):359, n. 8; Rashi to Numbers 13:33; and B. J. Bamberger, *Fallen Angels* (Philadelphia, 1952), 129–33, 177–81.

[54]See ms. Moscow 508, fol. 47v (transcribed by Freudenthal in *Daʿat* 34, 118, and see also n. 3): כי הכל נעשה ע״י שדים או מכח אבנים או עשבים כי הכל בא מכח הקב״ה ומכח שמותיו. ולא צוה הקב״ה שלא ישאל אדם באוב וידעוני וכו׳ אלא מפני שהם ממעטים את יראת שמים מלב בני האדם... ולא יתלו הכח והממשלה בהקב״ה... ומפני שלא ירגילו בהם צוה

Mark Verman identified a *Ḥug ha-ᶜIyyun* text, in a fourteenth-century Spanish manuscript, in which R. Meir of Germany (*me-Allemagne*) and R. Pereẓ of France (*mi-Ẓarefat*) offered definitions and explanations of an unusual celestial name, *Araᵓaryeta*—an appellation for the Primal Ether (*ᵓavir ha-qadmon*). R. Meir identified this Divine representation as *ᵓor qadmon*: "It is from the pure and holy name and it corresponds to One, His unity, First, His unicity, His transformation, One." R. Pereẓ called its name "Tenth level. ... There is in this the secret of the Cherubs." Verman cites this text (and another related one) as proof of the impact of *Ḥasidei Ashkenaz* upon the *Ḥug ha-ᶜIyyun* (in addition to other evidence that R. Eleazar of Worms directly influenced the *Ḥug*). Verman writes that "the individuals referred to in this text such as R. Meir or R. Pereẓ of France are not known to us from other sources."[55] At the same time, he notes two mystical techniques attributed to an "unidentified" R. Meir, one in ms. Vat. 243 and the other in Paris 776, in close proximity to a prophylactic technique attributed to R. Judah *he-Ḥasid*.[56]

In light of the array of evidence presented above, there can be little doubt that the R. Meir of Germany mentioned in this text is R. Meir of Rothenburg, just as the R. Pereẓ of France is probably the tosafist R. Pereẓ b. Elijah of Corbeil.[57] R. Pereẓ studied with R. Samuel of Evreux, R. Isaac of Corbeil, and Maharam. He is best known for his editing of *Tosafot* texts and for his glosses on R. Isaac's *Sefer Miẓvot Qatan* and on *Sefer Tashbeẓ*, a compilation of customs and practices of R. Meir.[58] Although there is less evidence, as compared with

הקב"ה שלא לעשותם אבל ללמדם מותר. See also fol. 46v (transcribed by Ta-Shma, "Sefer ha-Maskil," 438): ומה שיש כח למכשפים ולשמות... כי הכל בא מכח הקב"ה ומכח ו' שמותיו... ומפני שלא ירגילו בהם רבים צוה הקב"ה שלא לעשותם, אבל ללמדם מותר; fols. 32r–33v; and cf. R. Moses Cordovero, above, ch. 4, n. 48.

[55]See Verman, *The Books of Contemplation*, 101, n. 201, and 200–204.

[56]Verman, *The Books of Contemplation*, 201, n. 32. Cf. above, nn. 16, 49. Magical techniques attributed to R. Judah and R. Meshullam are found in close proximity in ms. Bodl. 123/4; see below, n. 63.

[57]The identification of R. Meir and R. Pereẓ in the *ᶜIyyun* text with the tosafists R. Meir of Rothenburg and R. Pereẓ of Corbeil offers further support for Verman's dating of the *ᶜIyyun* circle texts (between 1230 and 1270 in Castile) contra Gershom Scholem (who argued for the first quarter of the thirteenth century in Provence). Cf. my "Rabbinic Figures in Castilian Kabbalistic Pseudepigraphy," 83, n. 24, and Wolfson, *Along the Path*, 179, n. 351. The one easily identified contemporary name mentioned in *Ḥug ha-Iyyun* texts is that of R. Eleazar of Worms. For the influence of *Ḥasidei Ashkenaz* on the *Ḥug ha-ᶜIyyun*, see the literature cited in my "Rabbinic Figures," 80, n. 13, and 104, n. 96.

[58]See Urbach, *Baᶜalei ha-Tosafot*, 2:575–81. On R. Pereẓ and R. Isaac of Corbeil, see also Getzel Ellinson, "Le-Ḥeqer Qavvei ha-Pesiqah shel ha-Rosh," *Sinai* 93 (1983):236.

Maharam *mi-Rothenburg*, to connect Rabbenu Pereẓ directly with the German Pietists or with magical techniques, the asceticism and pietism manifested in his glosses to *Semaq* and in his *pesaqim*[59] make him a good choice for the role that he plays in the *ᶜIyyun* texts.

Ḥug ha-ᶜIyyun texts intimate that members of the circle learned about the teachings of R. Meir and R. Pereẓ, as well as the teachings of R. Eleazar of Worms, from a R. Meshullam who came from Brittany or elsewhere within northern France or *malkhut Ashkenaz*.[60] Although R. Meshullam is unknown to us in any non-kabbalistic contexts, it is likely that he was the direct link between the tosafists, the Pietists, and the *Ḥug ha-ᶜIyyun*. Virtually all extant manuscript references to R. Meshullam link him with teachings of the German Pietists.

In the *Ḥug ha-ᶜIyyun* text described above, which includes the teachings of R. Meir and R. Pereẓ, R. Meshullam's own *qabbalah* for the Divine Name associated with the Primal Ether is also mentioned.[61] In another manuscript, which contains large blocks of material from the German Pietists, R. Meshullam has a homiletical discussion on the angelic hosts who participated in revelation at Mount Sinai.[62] In still another, a *qabbalah* from R. Meshullam on the magical use of Divine Names in amulets, derived from *Sefer Raziʾel*, is preceded by a magical *shemirat ha-derekh* attributed to R. Judah *he-Ḥasid* on the use of a magical egg to induce feelings of love.[63] An additional *qabbalah* from R. Meshullam is found in a manuscript containing a similar technique from

---

[59]See above, ch. 2, nn. 69–71. For R. Pereẓ's use of *Hekhalot* literature, see *Tosafot Rabbenu Pereẓ ᶜal Massekhet ᶜEruvin*, ed. S. Wilman (Bnei Brak, 1980), 43b, s.v. *ha lo ʾata Eliyyahu be-Shabbata*, and cf. *Hekhalot Rabbati*, ch. 39, in *Battei Midrashot*, ed. S. A. Wertheimer (Jerusalem, 1950^2), 1:30–31. See also R. Langer, *To Worship God Properly*, 215. On the mistaken attribution of *Sefer Maᶜarekhet ha-E-lohut* to R. Pereẓ of Corbeil, see Ephraim Gottlieb, "Maᶜarekhet ha-E-lohut," *Encyclopaedia Judaica* 11:637–39 (=Gottlieb, *Meḥqarim be-Sifrut ha-Qabbalah*, ed. J. Hacker [Jerusalem, 1976], 775–78).

[60]The broad (and occasionally diverse) geographic references with regard to R. Meshullam are typical of the way Spanish kabbalists refer to Ashkenazic figures. See my "Rabbinic Figures," 107, n. 105.

[61]See above, n. 58. R. Meshullam's *qabbalah* represents the view of *ʾanshei ha-dat ha-penimit* (devotées of esotericism) and is followed by Naḥmanides characterization of the Primal Ether that was received (and adopted) by kabbalist-sages (*ḥakhmei ha-qabbalah*).

[62]See ms. Bodl. 2282 (Ashkenaz, fourteenth century), fol. 13r. Cf. Verman, *The Books of Contemplation*, 204, n. 39.

[63]See ms. Bodl. 123/4 (Mizraḥ, fifteenth/sixteenth centuries), fols. 70v–71r: **מקבלת רבינו משולם צרפתי- מה שקבלנו מן הספר הנקרא רזיאל כשתכתוב ג׳ פסוקים הללו על דרך זה... יעלו ע״ב שמות והם מועילים לענינים גדולים. זהו שם המפורש של אורים ותומים. על קלף צבי וימצא חן ושכל טוב וכו׳ ומכל מרעין בישין ושדים ויתרפא מחולי ויפול אויבים...**

Nahmanides, together with a formula for *qefiẓat ha-derekh* from R. Eleazar of Worms.[64] A *qabbalah* from R. Meshullam on the use of the *Shem ha-Meforash*, which was based on *Sefer Hekhalot*, indicates that R. Eleazar of Worms used this Name to transport himself on a cloud.[65] Finally, a manuscript passage discusses an argument between R. Samuel *he-Ḥasid* and R. Meshullam about how to vocalize the Tetragrammaton (*Shem ha-Meforash*).[66]

משביעני אני שתצילנו היום ובכל יום... יהי בשם זה שישלוט על כל בנ״א גוים ישמעאלים וכו׳. Cf. Verman, *The Books of Contemplation*, 205. Prior to this *qabbalah* are a number of *segullot*, using a variety of *Shemot*. On fol. 68r, the fourteen-letter and twenty-two-letter Names (ה׳ אלקינו ה׳=כוזו במוכסז כוזו / אנקתם פסתם פספסים דיונסם) are recorded. Cf. *Sefer Razi᾽el*, 145; Trachtenberg, *Jewish Magic and Superstition*, 92; Schrire, *Hebrew Magic Amulets*, 97; ms. Bodl. 1812, fol. 96v; Peter Schäfer and Shaul Shaked, *Magische Texte aus der Kairoer Geniza*, vol 2 (Tübingen, 1997), 127, 130, 288; and above, ch. 1, n. 156. Fol. 68v has a *shemirat ha-derekh* attributed to R. Judah *he-Hasid*: שמירת הדרך מר׳ יהודה החסיד וצריך לאומרה ביציאתו מן העיר... שר לויה ששמו יוהך משביע אני בשם י-ה-ו-ה שתוליכנו לשלום עד מקום פלוני בלי שום פגע וכו׳ ובלי היזק בשקט והצילנו. The *segullot* on fols. 69r–70v are to achieve success and the approbation of others, to instill fear in or weaken one's enemies, to prevent forgetfulness, to assist a woman who cannot produce milk, and to cause feelings of love. In one instance, the formula was to be written on a magical egg; see above, ch. 3, nn. 18–19.

64 See ms. Ancona 23/3 (Italy, 1717), fols. 51v (קבלה מר׳ משולם לצער כגון לרפואה), 53v (Ramban), 73v (קפיצת הדרך לר׳ אלעזר). Cf. Verman and Adler, "Path-Jumping in the Jewish Magical Tradition," 139.

65 Ms. Milan Ambrosiana 62, fol. 109v (Meshullam the Zadokite from Brittany [Treport] transcribed a Name from the *Sefer Hekhalot* found by R. Neḥunyah b. Ha-Qanah: "R. Eleazar conjured this Name, that he had received, when he rode on a cloud as he did frequently.") On this passage, cf. Verman, *The Books of Contemplation*, 204–10; Wolfson, "Demut Yaᶜaqov Ḥaquqah be-Kisse ha-Kavod: ᶜIyyun Nosaf be-Torat ha-Sod shel Ḥasidut Ashkenaz," *Massu᾽ot*, ed. Oron and Goldreich, 184–85, n. 236; and Moshe Idel, *The Mystical Experience in Abraham Abulafia* (Albany, 1988), 159, n. 146. Various theosophical teachings are also found in this passage (and in another from R. Meshullam). The presence of theosophical material in R. Meshullam's case is readily understood, just as it is for R. Meir of Rothenburg and *Sefer ha-Maskil*, given their connection to the mystical teachings of *Ḥasidei Ashkenaz* that were being disseminated in the second half of the thirteenth century. These developments serve, however, to highlight once again the fact that theosophy was largely absent from Ashkenazic *sod* in general, and that Ashkenazic *sod, pace Ḥasidei Ashkenaz*, was limited for the most part to the magical and mystical properties of Divine Names. [In the one extant instance in which R. Meshullam discusses halakhic material (ms. Cambr. Or. 786, fol. 174v; noted by Verman, 205, n. 41), he cites a ruling of R. Abraham Ḥaldiq, a rabbinic decisor associated with *Ḥasidei Ashkenaz*; see above, ch. 2, nn. 18, 37.]

66 Ms. Sassoon 290, fol. 218, sec. 299. Cf. above, ch. 3, n. 67, for the tradition of Ḥida regarding Rashi and Rashbam. See also *Siddur Rabbenu Shelomoh mi-Germaiza ve-Siddur Ḥasidei Ashkenaz*, ed. Hershler, 157.

In his *Sefer ha-Maskil*, R. Solomon Simḥah of Troyes offers an almost immediate date for the beginning of the redemption and refers to the prophetic *ḥishuv ha-qeẓ* activities of R. Ezra *ha-Navi* of Moncontour. R. Ezra, "*ᶜalah la-shamayim*," ascended to heaven using *Hekhalot* magical or mystical techniques and inquired about the *qeẓ* from the prophets Ḥaggai, Zekharyah, and Malakhi. In the course of his heavenly experience, R. Ezra received certain verses or songs which he was then able to transmit.[67] R. Ezra studied in his youth with Ri, whose similar experience with prophetic messianism has been noted.[68] In his later years, R. Ezra taught R. Meir of Rothenburg during

---

[67]See Ta-Shma, "Sefer ha-Maskil," 432–33; and cf. above, ch. 3, nn. 3, 8, 80. On R. Ezra's heavenly and prophetic activities, see also Scholem, *Origins of the Kabbalah*, 239–40; Idel, *Kabbalah: New Perspectives*, 91–92; A. Marx, "Maʾamar ᶜal Shenat Geʾulah," *Ha-Ẓofeh le-Ḥokhmat Yisraʾel* 5 (1921):194–99; Joseph Shatzmiller's addenda to *Gallia Judaica* in *Qiryat Sefer* 45 (1970):609–10; Heschel, "Al Ruaḥ ha-Qodesh Bimei ha-Benayim," *Sefer ha-Yovel* li-Khevod Alexander Marx (New York, 1950) [Hebrew section], 184; Shraga Abramson, "Navi, Roʾeh ve-Ḥozeh," *Sefer ha-Yovel Muggash li-Khevod ha-Rav Mordekhai Kirschblum*, ed. David Telsner (Jerusalem, 1983), 121–23; and Urbach, *Baᶜalei ha-Tosafot*, 1:336–37. [R. Ezra is also called *malʾakh ha-Shem* in other texts.] R. Troestlin (=Menaḥem or perhaps Neḥemyah) *ha-Navi* is mentioned as having had experiences related to those of R. Ezra. Cf. ms. JTS Mic. 8114 (end), fol. 17v. Scholem, *Origins of the Kabbalah*, 239, n. 86, notes references to a R. Neḥemyah (*Ḥasid*) in texts associated with the German Pietists. See also ms. Parma 541, fol. 266v (sec. 77, and cf. above, ch. 4, n. 31), where a R. Neḥemyah records "*teᶜamim of milḥemet gog u-magog*." See also fols. 264v–265v for other eschatological events, and cf. above, ch. 4, n. 32. See above, ch. 4, n. 14, for a R. Isaac *Navi* mentioned in Pietist writings.

Messianic dates achieved through prophetic dreams, similar to the experiences of R. Ezra and R. Troestlin, are also attributed to R. Samuel and R. Judah *he-Ḥasid*. See Marx, "Maʾamar ᶜal Shenat Geʾulah," op. cit., and Gerson Cohen, "Messianic Postures of Ashkenazim and Sephardim," *Studies of the Leo Baeck Institute*, ed. Max Kreutzberger (New York, 1967), 128–30. See also Simcha Assaf, "Teᶜudot Ḥadashot ᶜal Gerim ve-ᶜal Tenuᶜah Meshiḥit," *Zion* 5 (1939–40):116–17, 123–24 [=idem, *Meqorot u-Meḥqarim* (Jerusalem, 1946), 146–48, 153–54] for R. Eleazar of Worms's validation of the date generated by R. Ezra's prophetic messianism. And cf. *Teshuvot u-Fesaqim*, ed. Efraim Kupfer (Jerusalem, 1973), 310; Dan, "Sippurim Dimonologiyyim," 280–81; Moshe Idel, "Le-Gilgulehah shel Tekhniqah Qedumah shel Ḥazon Nevuʾi Bimei ha-Benayim," *Sinai* 86 (1979):1–7; *Teshuvot ha-Rashba*, 1:548; and below, n. 79. At the same time, *Sefer Ḥasidim* (*SḤP* 212) denounces those engaged in messianic prognostication because this activity involves the inappropriate summoning of angels or *shedim* and the use of Divine Names. The tension inherent in Pietistic writings in this respect is similar to what has been observed in their writings concerning the use of magic generally. See Dan, *Torat ha-Sod shel Ḥasidut Ashkenaz,* 241–45; Israel Ta-Shma, "Le-Toledot ha-Yehudim be-Polin ba-Meʾot ha-Yod Bet/ha-Yod Gimmel," *Zion* 53 (1988):352, n. 16; and above, ch. 4, n. 50.

[68]See above, ch. 4, nn. 8–9.

R. Meir's student days in northern France. It is therefore possible that Maharam received esoteric and magical material from R. Ezra as well.[69]

Additional manuscript evidence suggests that several other students or associates of Maharam may have been involved with *sod* or magic. R. Yeḥiel—the father of Maharam's most famous student, R. Asher (Rosh)—adopted the practice of reciting *barukh Hu u-varukh Shemo* each time a Divine Name was mentioned, a practice that originated with the German Pietists (and was also followed by R. Solomon Simḥah of Troyes).[70] Magical *segullot* as well as *sodot* are also attributed to R. Asher b. Yeḥiel himself, although the presence of this material only in relatively late manuscript passages and the specific contents in certain cases weaken some of the attributions. According to one text, Rosh transmitted a formula that would protect an individual and his money from thieves or demonic forces.[71] The authenticity of this passage is perhaps heightened by the fact that R. Asher is cited by his son, R. Jacob *Baᶜal ha-Turim* (who also studied with R. Meir of Rothenburg), as having allowed divination utilizing *shedim* (as Ri did) in order to locate a stolen object.[72] Also likely to be

---

[69]See above, n. 49, for a *she'elat ha-qeẓ* attributed to R. Meir of Rothenburg. One of the three references in *Tosafot* texts to R. Ezra as *ha-Navi* is found in *Tosafot R. Pereẓ* (to *Bava Qamma* 23b). Cf. Urbach, *Baᶜalei ha-Tosafot*, 336, nn. 14*, 16: Abramson, "Navi, Ro'eh ve-Ḥozeh"; and above, n. 6.

[70]See Naftali Wieder, "Barukh Hu (u-)Varukh Shemo—Meqoro, Zemanno ve-Nosaḥo," *Sefer ha-Yovel le-Ezra Zion Melammed* (Ramat Gan, 1982), 277–90; above, n. 52; and cf. Y. S. Zachter, "Kavvanat Shema," *Yeshurun* 2 (1996):29, n. 9. Note also R. Asher's *Responsa*, 4:20: **כי יש לי קונטריס מעשה ישן וכתוב בו כל הברכות של כל השנה וסכום כמה תיבות יש בכל ברכה וברכה וכנגד מה נתקנה**; and see above, ch. 2, n. 52, and below, n. 75.

[71]Ms. Warsaw 9 (Ashkenaz, sixteenth century), fols. 152r–153r. Rosh also ruled that one who drinks *yayn nesekh*, even unwittingly, must fast for five days. This penance was also prescribed by R. Judah *he-Ḥasid* on the basis of the number of times that wine or products of the vine are referred to in Deuteronomy 32:32 (which begins **כי מגפן סדום גפנם**). See ms. Bodl. 784, fol. 99v; my "Rabbinic Attitudes Toward Nonobservance in the Medieval Period," *Jewish Tradition and the Nontraditional Jew*, ed. J. J. Schacter (Northvale, 1992), 25–26, nn. 64–66; above, ch. 1, nn. 148–49, and ch. 3, n. 77. For other dimensions of R. Asher b. Yeḥiel's piety, see A. H. Freimann, *Ha-Rosh ve-Ẓe'eẓa'av* (Jerusalem, 1986), 82–84, and Zimmels, *Ashkenazim and Sefardim*, 22, 32–33. The anti-philosophy stance taken by Rosh during the early fourteenth-century phase of the Maimonidean controversy is certainly compatible with his involvement with magic and *sod*.

[72]See *Arbaᶜah Turim, Yoreh Deᶜah*, sec. 179 (end), and *Beit Yosef*, ad loc. For Ri (and others), see above, ch. 4, nn. 13–14. See also the responsum by R. Isaac b. Elijah (a contemporary of Maharam) [in *Teshuvot Baᶜalei ha-Tosafot*, ed. I. A. Agus (New York, 1954), 223–24], in which R. Isaac approves the use of *hashbaᶜat shedim* for finding

authentic is a *sod* that R. Jacob b. Asher received from his father. R. Asher is described in this passage as *mequbbal ve-ḥakham.*[73] A *shemirat ha-derekh* attributed to R. Asher is found together with magical techniques of Ramban and others associated with *Ḥasidei Ashkenaz.*[74]

---

stolen property and for predicting the future (עתידות). This responsum tends to support Jacob Katz's contention (see his *Halakhah ve-Qabbalah* [Jerusalem, 1986], 349), that R. Isaac b. Elijah's criticism of students who engaged in עיון ולא גמרא (found in *She*ʾ*elot u-Teshuvot Maharaḥ Or Zarua*ᶜ, #163) refers to those who generated excessive *pilpul* without concern for the halakhic ramifications of the talmudic text, rather than the suggestion of Urbach (*Ba*ᶜ*alei ha-Tosafot*, 2:586, n. 2) that עיון connotes the study of philosophy and/or *sod*.

[73]Ms. JTS Mic. 1851 (Sefarad, fifteenth/sixteenth centuries), fols. 1r–1v. The Spanish kabbalist David b. Yehudah *Ḥasid*, who spent time in Germany and acquainted himself with Ashkenazic esoteric teachings (see, e.g., Idel, *Kabbalah: New Perspectives*, 98, and my "Rabbinic Figures in Castilian Kabbalistic Pseudepigraphy," 97, n. 73), records a *qabbalah* from Rosh that the *ge*ʾ*ulah* would occur in 1328, as well as a question from Rosh's son, R. Judah, regarding *gilgul ha-nefesh*. See also *Ta*ᶜ*am Zeqenim le-R. Eliezer Ashkenazi* (Frankfurt, 1855), 64–66; and Iris Felix, "Peraqim be-Haguto ha-Qabbalit shel ha-Rav Yosef Angelet," (M.A. Thesis, Hebrew University, 1991), 5. [The question on *gilgul ha-nefesh* from R. Yehudah ben *ha-Rosh* may have been due to the influence of Spanish Kabbalah. It is found also in ms. Paris 738 (Spain, fifteenth/sixteenth centuries), fol. 367–69.] At the same time, R. Judah b. *ha-Rosh* rejected the validity of astral magic. See Dov Schwartz, "Astrologiyyah u-Mageyah Astralit bi-*Megalleh Ammuqot* le-R. Shelomoh Alqonstantin," *Meḥqerei Yerushalayim be-Folqlor Yehudi*, 15 (1993):59, and idem, *Astrologiyyah u-Mageyah be-Hagut ha-Yehudit Bimei ha-Benayim* (Ramat Gan, 1999), 266–67. For the possible impact of *Ḥasidei Ashkenaz* on R. Judah with regard to curricular matters, see S. Assaf, *Meqorot le-Toledot ha-Ḥinnukh be-Yisra*ʾ*el*, vol. 1, 26–27; and cf. my *Jewish Education and Society in the High Middle Ages*, 79–80, 88–90.

[74]See ms. Moscow-Guenzberg 1302 (Mizrah, 1431), fol. 14r: שמירת הדרך לרא"ש. כשתראה לסטים או [אדם] שאתה ירא ממנו תאמר ששה פעמים על סדר אצבעות . . . ותזקוף ידך נגד פניך ותתחיל מן הזרת וכו׳. A *shemirah* attributed to Ramban, designed to protect against thieves while traveling on the road, involves taking two stones and reciting various Divine Names (fol. 10r). A second *shemirah*, which Ramban sent from Barcelona, also included various finger movements (fol. 12r). An anonymous *shemirah la-derekh* (fol. 11r) cites verses that describe the angels who protected Jacob during his flight from Esau and verses depicting the ᶜ*ananei ha-kavod*. Several prayers for protection during an ocean-going voyage, including one that Ramban purportedly recited during his journey to Israel, are also recorded (fols. 10v, 12v–13r, 13v; on the *shemirot* and prayers attributed to Ramban, cf. ms. Vat. 243 [above, n. 16], and Israel Ta-Shma, "Qoveẓ Hilkhot Tefillah u-Moᶜadot le-Eḥad mi-Talmidei Rabbenu Yonah," *Qoveẓ* ᶜ*al Yad* n.s. 13 [1996]: 274, n. 2). Fol. 15r lists a שמירה בדוקה ומנוסה that entailed hand movements and the phrase to be recited, אזבוגה ישמרני. For similarities between these magical formulae and techniques within Ashkenaz, see above, n. 16; ch. 3, nn. 58, 99; and ch. 4, nn. 32, 49. See also the parallel material in ms. Parma 1124 (Italy,

R. Jacob b. Asher's own connections to *Ḥasidei Ashkenaz* are readily evident. In his *Arbaᶜah Turim* there are frequent references to (and general approbation of) pietistic and ascetic practices of *Ḥasidei Ashkenaz* and to Pietist approaches to *tefillah*. These include the cultivation of proper *kavvanah* and the establishment or retention of proper liturgical texts, often through the application of *sodot ha-tefillah*.[75] Indeed, biblical interpretations of the *Baᶜal ha-Turim* often include masoretic and other kinds of comments from the Pietists themselves, or in their style, including notions that can be characterized as *sod*.[76]

R. Asher b. Yeḥiel and his family fled Germany for Toledo, Spain, in the face of persecutions during the early years of the fourteenth century. R. Dan, another student of R. Meir of Rothenburg, followed the same path, ultimately earning, as Rosh did, the approbation of leading Spanish talmudists.[77] Two

---

fifteenth century), fols. 48r–54r, which includes a *qabbalah* from R. Judah *he-Ḥasid* to ensure security each day through the recitation of certain verses in a particular order, as well as the eleven verses for protection that begin and end with the letter *nun*, attributed to German Pietists (fols. 50v–51r). Cf. above, ch. 3, nn. 102, 110; ch. 4, n. 49.

[75]See, e.g., *O. Ḥ.*, secs. 51, 113 (דורשי רשומות הם חסידי אשכנז אשר היו שוקלין וסופרין מספר מנין תיבות התפילות והברכות וכנגד מה נתקנו), 114, 118, 125, 241, 551; Moshe Hallamish, "Siḥat Ḥullin be-Veit ha-Knesset—Meẓiᵓut u-Maᵓavaq," *Milet* 2 (1985):243; and above, ch. 1, n. 35. For the overall impact of the German Pietists and their literature (as well as Rabbenu Yonah's *Sefer ha-Yirᵓah*) on the structure and content of *Arbaᶜah Turim* (esp. in *Oraḥ Ḥayyim*), see Yehudah Galinsky, "Sefer Arbaᶜah Turim veha-Sifrut ha-Hilkhatit bi-Sefarad ba-Meᵓah ha-Yod Daled" (Ph.D. diss., Bar Ilan, 1999). Cf. R. Langer, *To Worship God Properly*, 213, 233. On the connotation of *dorshei reshumot* in sec. 113, as a representation of *Ḥasidei Ashkenaz*, cf. Y. K. Reinitz in *Shemaᶜatin* 109 [1991]:110, and *Shemaᶜatin* 111–12 [1993]:141; Daniel Abrams, "From Germany to Spain: Numerology as a Mystical Technique," *JJS* 47 (1996):92–93; ms. B.M. Or. 2853, fols. 3r, 47v; *Perushim u-Fesaqim ᶜal ha-Torah le-R. Avigdor Ẓarefati* (above, ch. 4, n. 2), 32, 37, 57–58, 120, 263, 386, 420, and the editor's introduction, 15–16. Cf. Trachtenberg, *Jewish Magic and Superstition*, 18, n. 8, 322; Zimmels, *Ashkenazim and Sephardim*, 112, 189–190, 232; Jacob Lauterbach, "The Ancient Jewish Allegorists in Talmud and Midrash," *JQR* 1 (1910–11):332–33, n. 36; and above, ch. 1, n. 93.

[76]For examples of affinities between the biblical interpretations of the German Pietists (and Zohar) and those of the *Baᶜal ha-Turim* (with particular reference to counting words or letters), see, e.g., *Baᶜal ha-Turim ᶜal ha-Torah*, ed. Y. K. Reinitz (Jerusalem, 1993), 1:2, 105, 157–58, 251; 2:272, 282–83, 299, 332, 347, 540–41, 549, 555; cf. the editor's introduction, 16. See also Aharon Arend, "Ha-Perush ha-Qaẓar shel Baᶜal ha-Turim ᶜal ha-Torah," *Maḥanayim* 3 (1993):180–87, and above, ch. 2, n. 52.

[77]See Israel Ta-Shma, "Ashkenazi, Dan," *Encyclopaedia Judaica*, 3:725, and *Perush R. Baḥya ᶜal ha-Torah*, ed. C. D. Chavel (Jerusalem, 1977), 2:19, and the editor's introduction, 1:10; and S. Z. Havlin, "Teshuvot Ḥadashot leha-Rashba," *Sefer Zikkaron le-R. Yaᶜaqov B. Zolty*, ed. Yosef Buksboim (Jerusalem, 1987), 220–21, n. 5.

magical *segullot* and formulae are found in manuscripts in R. Dan's name, in close proximity to those of R. Judah *he-Ḥasid* and other Ashkenazic figures. In addition, R. Dan transmitted a *sod* formulation concerning resurrection and the miracles of the messianic era—although, to be sure, these passages may have been composed in Spain, under the influence of Spanish Kabbalah, rather than in Germany.[78] R. Yaqar of Cologne, a contemporary of R. Meir of Rothenburg, is mentioned in two parallel manuscript passages (from *Sefer Sodot/Raza Rabba*, a work associated with *ḥasidut Ashkenaz*) regarding esoteric derivations and uses of *Shemot*.[79]

---

[78]See ms. Sassoon 290, fol. 254, sec. 565: שמירה מופלאה בשם הר׳ דן אם אתה הולך ברגלים עמוד בדרך ורגלך ישרה ואם הולך ברכב בשעת הרכיבה שים רגל אחד על ברזל האוכף. Various biblical verses and *Shemot* are recited. [Sec. 566 contains a שמירה מעולה from R. Judah *he-Ḥasid* that involves carrying a piece of wood from the gate of one's city and exchanging it along the way for wood that comes from bridges that are crossed or villages that are visited; cf. above, ch. 4, n. 49.] See also ms. Vat. 243, fols. 6r (*kabbalah be-shem ha-R. Dan*), and 10r (a *segullah* from R. Dan, in close proximity to a שמירה ממלך from R. Judah *he-Ḥasid*); ms. Bodl. 916, fol. 40; and above, nn. 16, 46, esp. Ta-Shma, "Rabbenu Dan be-Ashkenaz uvi-Sefarad." See also Scholem, *Kitvei Yad be-Qabbalah*, 78 (ms. JNUL. 8°151, Italy/Ashkenaz, sixteenth century) for a ... שם מקובל מפי ר׳ דן; ms. Bodl. 1618, fol. 109v, and note the formulations of R. Judah *he-Ḥasid* on fols. 55v, 59v, 77v.

[79]See ms. JTS Mic. 1885 (Italy, fifteenth century), fols. 71–73; ms. Paris 843 (fifteenth century), fols 69–70; and Scholem, *Reshit ha-Qabbalah*, 197–98. On R. Yaqar, see Israel Ta-Shma, "R. Yeshayah mi-Veil: Ḥakham Bilti Noda mi-Zeman Maharam mi-Rothenburg," *Sinai* 66 (1970):140–46; Urbach, *Baᶜalei ha-Tosafot*, 1:222, 413, 438, 2:538; Y. M. Pelles, "Teshuvah le-Rabbenu Yaqar b. Samuel ha-Levi," *Moriah* 16:11–12 (1989):5–7; and Simcha Emanuel, "Sifrei Halakhah Avudim shel Baᶜalei ha-Tosafot," 280–81.

R. Isaac b. Judah *ha-Levi's Paᶜaneaḥ Raza* is a tosafist Torah commentary from the late thirteenth century that includes much exegetical and pietistic material from the German Pietists as well. See, e.g., Güdemann, *Ha-Torah veha-Ḥayyim*, 1:121, 129–30, n. 8, 138, 164, n. 5, 218; Y. S. Lange, "Le-Zehuto shel R. Ḥayyim Paltiᵓel," *ᶜAlei Sefer* 8 (1980):142–43; Abba Zions, "Al ha-Mehabber shel *Paᶜaneaḥ Raza*," *Or ha-Mizraḥ* 29 (1981):210–14; Ta-Shma, "Le-Toledot ha-Yehudim be-Polin ba-Meᵓot ha-Yod Bet ha-Yod Gimmel," *Zion* 53 (1988): 357–58; Joseph Davis, "Philosophy, Dogma and Exegesis in Medieval Ashkenazic Judaism: The Evidence of *Sefer Hadrat Qodesh*," *AJS Review* 18 (1992):218; Eric Zimmer, *ᶜOlam ke-Minhago Noheg* (Jerusalem, 1996), 233–34; A. J. Heschel, "Al Ruaḥ ha-Qodesh Bimei ha-Benayim," 181–82, n. 31; Norman Golb, *The Jews of Medieval Normandy* (Cambridge, 1998), 187, n. 30; and above, ch. 3, n. 110; ch. 4, nn. 33, 47. Just as Eleazar of Worms named his halakhic work *Sefer Roqeaḥ*, since רקח is the *gematria* equivalent of אלעזר, Isaac notes in his introduction that both פענח and רזא are the equivalent of יצחק. There are *remazim* to a date for the advent of the Messiah in the portions of *Va-Yishlaḥ* (*Paᶜaneaḥ Raza* [Jerusalem, 1965],

With these students of R. Meir of Rothenburg, the tosafist period comes to a close. The second half of this study has demonstrated that during the twelfth and thirteenth centuries in Ashkenaz, there was sustained interest in esoteric studies and magical theory and practice among tosafists. Moreover, many of the tosafists who expressed interest in these disciplines also exhibited a tendency toward *perishut* and pietism. While the talmudic methodologies of Rabbenu Tam and Raban dominated the entire period, their downplaying of other pre-Crusade disciplines, such as *torat ha-sod*, was not fully accepted. Indeed, later tosafists expanded their *sod* interests, perhaps under the influence of the German Pietists. Although the Pietists also developed a unique theosophical system in which tosafists were not involved, the common level of mystical and magical discourse among Ashkenazic talmudists was significantly higher than has heretofore been thought.

---

137), *Balaq* (376–77), *Ki-Tavo* (432) and *Va-Yelekh* (437–38); cf. above, n. 67; ch. 4, n. 37; *Perush R. Yosef Bekhor Shor ʿal ha-Torah*, ed. Yehoshafat Nevo (Jerusalem, 1994), 373–75; and A. H. Silver, *A History of Messianic Speculation in Israel*, (New York, 1927), 85–87. Moreover, *Paʿaneaḥ Raza* also contains pieces of magical and mystical material. See, e.g., *parashat Shemini*, 297, for a description of charms made from the tongue and the eye of a peacock that could guarantee victory in any litigation and induce other salutary states. These charms were tested by *Ḥakmei Yavan* and by others, and they were found to be genuine. Cf. ms. Munich 50, fol. 191v. See also *parashat Shemot*, 193; *Ẓav*, 287; *Qedoshim*, 312. *Baʿalei ha-sod* are cited in *parashut Toledot*, 110, and *Ki Tissa*, 255. In addition, the author himself suggests, in the colophon, that he had an interest in esoteric studies. See *Paʿaneaḥ Raza*, introductory section, 2, and see also ms. Bodl. 2344, fol. 144r. Cf. Güdemann, 168, n. 3; Abba Zions, "Paʿaneaḥ Raza le-R. Yiẓḥaq b. Yehudah ha-Levi" (D.H.L. diss., Yeshiva University, 1974), 1–10, 44–51; Wolfson, *Through a Speculum That Shines*, 211, 251–52, 254, n. 275; and idem, "The Mystical Significance of Torah-Study in German Pietism," *JQR* 84 (1993): 55, n. 45. For *sod* in the biblical commentary of R. Ḥayyim Paltiʾel (composed by a younger contemporary of R. Meir of Rothenburg, and similar in several respects to *Paʿaneaḥ Raza*), see Lange, op. cit. Cf. above, ch. 2, n. 43, and Hananel Mack, "Midrash Askenazi le-Pereq Alef be-Sefer Yeshayahu," *Zion* 63 (1998):124. On the level of awareness of kabbalistic and magical material in late thirteenth-century Ashkenaz, see also Moshe Idel, "Notes in the Wake of the Medieval Jewish-Christian Polemic," *Immanuel* 18 (1984):54–63; Naomi Feuchtwanger, "The Coronation of the Virgin and of the Bride," *Jewish Art* 12–13 (1987):213–24; and Wolfson, *Through a Speculum That Shines*, 264, n. 322. Cf. Y. Dan, *Torat ha-Sod shel Ḥasidut Ashkenaz*, 252.

6

Conclusions and Implications

The data assembled and presented in this study suggest that ascetic practices and mystical and magical teachings were a recognizable part of the spiritual lives of a number of twelfth- and thirteenth-century tosafists. Although the *ba^{c}alei ha-Tosafot* were known primarily for their achievements and advancements in the realm of talmudic studies, many of them were familiar with both the techniques and the theories of these other disciplines as well.

We have seen that considerations of *perishut* and *ḥasidut* did have an impact, at times, on the talmudic interpretations and legal rulings of these tosafists. Additional examples can undoubtedly be discovered through further research. Mystical and magical dimensions remain, however, mostly behind the scenes. They do not occupy a prominent place in tosafist writings, although they become more easily recognizable by the middle of the thirteenth century. Given the esoteric nature of these disciplines, however, this pattern of development is not unexpected. Indeed, the firm correlation that has been documented—between those tosafists who displayed ascetic tendencies and those who were most familiar with esoteric teachings—is a reflection of the more general characteristics of *torat ha-sod* and its adherents as well.

This revision of the dominant perception of tosafist spirituality constitutes a significant shift in the perceived balance of intellectual proclivities displayed by medieval rabbinic figures. According to the prevailing view, tosafists were uniformly halakhocentric.[1] They occupied a kind of middle

[1] On the full connotation of this term, see Isadore Twersky, "Religion and Law," *Religion in a Religious Age*, ed. S. D. Goitein (Cambridge, Mass., 1973), 69–82.

ground between the outstanding *rishonim*, led by Maimonides, who supplemented their talmudic and rabbinic studies with philosophical studies and investigation, and those, led by Naḥmanides, who were devotees of mysticism and Kabbalah.[2] Although a significant group of tosafists, led by Rabbenu Tam, did occupy the middle position in which talmudic studies alone dominated, the present study offers evidence which places many Ashkenazic rabbinic figures—including R. Isaac of Dampierre, R. Eliezer of Metz, R. Jacob and R. Isaac of Corbeil, R. Isaac and R. Avigdor of Vienna, R. Zedekiah *Anav*, and R. Meir of Rothenburg, among others—on the mysticism/asceticism side of the ledger. Further research must be undertaken to ascertain whether the anti-philosophical (anti-Maimonidean) approach taken by a number of tosafists and other Ashkenazic rabbinic figures during various phases of the Maimonidean controversy, which was linked also to a literal reading of aggadic literature, resulted at least partially from mystical leanings—in addition to the lack of philosophical awareness and training in medieval Ashkenaz.[3]

To be sure, no tosafists can be classified as kabbalists, since none of them formulated anything that could be construed or labeled as Kabbalah. Nonetheless, we have seen that tosafists were involved with a number of distinctly mystical and magical dimensions. These include analyses of Divine and angelic names and functions, various kinds of protective or prophylactic adjurations and *she'elot ḥalom* (that utilized both angelic and Divine Names),

---

[2]Naḥmanides was also quite familiar with philosophical literature and concepts, and he made extensive use of them. Nonetheless, Ramban should certainly be considered a kabbalist, first and foremost. See my "On the Assessment of R. Moses b. Naḥman (Naḥmanides) and His Literary Oeuvre," *Jewish Book Annual* 51 (1993–94):158–72.

[3]See E. E. Urbach, "Ḥelqam shel Ḥakhmei Ashkenaz ve-Ẓarefat be-Folmos ʿal ha-Rambam u-Sefarav," *Zion* 12 (1947):149–59; Joseph Dan, "Ashkenazi Hasidim and the Maimonidean Controversy," *Maimonidean Studies* 3 (1992–93):29–47; Joseph Davis, "Philosophy, Dogma, and Exegesis in Medieval Ashkenazic Judaism: The Evidence of *Sefer Hadrat Qodesh*," *AJS Review* 18 (1993):208–19; Israel Ta-Shma, "Sefer Nimmuqei Ḥumash le-R. Yeshayah di Trani," *Qiryat Sefer* 64 (1993):752; Joseph Shatzmiller, "Les Tossafists et la Premiére Controversie Maïmonidienne," *Rashi et la culture juive en France du Nord au moyen âge* (Paris, 1997), 55–82; David Berger, "Judaism and General Culture in Medieval and Early Modern Times," *Judaism's Encounter with Other Cultures*, ed. J. J. Schacter (Northvale, 1997), 95–125; Moshe Halbertal, *People of the Book* (Cambridge, Mass., 1997), 109–19; and above, ch. 2, n. 4. To be sure, an anti-philosophical stance taken by a rabbinic scholar should not cause us to automatically presume that he is pro-mysticism. See, e.g., Bernard Septimus, *Hispano-Jewish Culture in Transition* (Cambridge, Mass., 1982), 104–15.

theurgic prayer, and quasi-prophetic experiences through which messianic dates and other kinds of guidance were received.

The mystical dimensions that have been identified within rabbinic scholarship in medieval Ashkenaz would support the larger view that mystical teachings and practices were highly compatible with this scholarship. Indeed, the claim that rabbinic culture in the talmudic period, and by extension the writings of its adherents in the medieval period, were virtually devoid of a mythic substrate and of any theurgic or mystical impetus would appear to be severely undercut by the results of this study. It should be possible, however, to define more narrowly the parameters of mystical activity within rabbinic circles and arrive at a more nuanced assessment of the relationship between these disciplines or fields.[4]

The involvement of tosafists with mysticism and magic, and with asceticism and *perishut*, represents the continuation of a pattern established during the pre-Crusade period in Mainz. Indeed, it was the strict talmudocentric approach, favored by Rabbenu Tam and other early tosafists in twelfth-century Germany and northern France, that marks a change within Ashkenaz. While these twelfth-century tosafists may have taken their cue from the academy at Worms, their talmudocentricity did not dominate all subsequent tosafist creativity, even as their dialectical method did. Interest in the study of Talmud and *halakhah* alone was not necessarily the rule.

Although the tosafists saw themselves as direct successors or later models of the Tannaim and Amoraim,[5] it is important to consider how mystical and magical material reached the tosafists (and their predecessors in the pre-Crusade period). Clearly, *Hekhalot* literature played a major role in this process. Irrespective of the scholarly debate about whether *Hekhalot* literature was produced for and by rabbinic scholars or for less learned individuals who

---

[4]For a brief overview of these issues and the positions taken by contemporary scholars, see Elliot Ginsburg, "The Many Faces of Kabbalah," *Hebrew Studies* 36 (1995):116–20. Cf. Hava Tirosh-Rothschild, "Continuity and Revision in the Study of Kabbalah," *AJS Review* 16 (1991):161–92; Michael Swartz, *Scholastic Magic* (Princeton, 1996), 11, n. 28; Moshe Idel, "Kabbalah and Elites in Thirteenth-Century Spain," *Mediterranean Historical Review* 9 (1994):6–13; idem, "R. Mosheh b. Naḥman—Qabbalah, Halakhah u-Manhigut Ruḥanit," *Tarbiz* 64 (1995):535–78; and Israel Ta-Shma, "R. Yosef Karo Bein Ashkenaz li-Sefarad—Le-Ḥeqer Hitpashtut Sefer ha-Zohar," *Tarbiz* 59 (1990):153–70. The nature of the *Hekhalot* literature is also related to this discussion. See below, n. 6.

[5]See my "On the Right to Open an Academy in Medieval Ashkenaz," *Michael* 12 (1991):233–50, and my "Progress and Tradition in Medieval Ashkenaz," *Jewish History* 14 (2000).

wished to use the magical *Sar ha-Torah* techniques to acquire Torah knowledge—an approach which, to date, can be fairly characterized as the minority position—magical techniques and mystical conceptions from *Hekhalot* texts penetrated into medieval Ashkenaz in both exoteric and esoteric form.[6] Although *Ḥasidei Ashkenaz* have been assigned a large role in the editing and redaction of the *Hekhalot*, there is no reason to assume that only they were aware of this corpus. Indeed, we have encountered a number of citations of *Hekhalot* literature in medieval Ashkenazic rabbinic texts, including passages from a little-known work entitled *Maᶜaseh Merkavah*. *Hekhalot* texts and practices were the sources of several widespread liturgical and ritual customs as well. *Hekhalot* literature is also replete with magical techniques and incantations that, as we have seen, influenced tosafist formulations both directly and indirectly.[7]

Moreover, there is an ascetic aspect to this literature as well. Ascetic practices are designed primarily to prepare an individual to use Divine and angelic names in various adjurations, after which a number of tosafist formulae are modeled. Nonetheless, the asceticism favored by the *Hekhalot* texts may have also been a source of the more general tendencies toward pietism and *perishut* that we have detected in the pre-Crusade and tosafist periods.[8]

Peter Schäfer has made a similar argument with regard to *Ḥasidei Ashkenaz*. He suggests that the rise of *ḥasidut Ashkenaz* ought not be explained mainly as a response to twelfth-century stimuli (such as persecution, Christian asceticism, or the rise of tosafist dialectic). There are, in fact, roots in *Hekhalot* literature for many of the ascetic and self-effacing behaviors affected by *Ḥasidei Ashkenaz*. Self-perfection, especially through physical restraint, was considered by *Hekhalot* writers to be a significant means of achieving a closer relationship

---

[6]See the summary and analysis in Elliot Wolfson, *Through a Speculum That Shines* (Princeton, 1994), 74–80, 111–17. Cf. David Halpern's review of Peter Schäfer's *The Hidden and Manifest God*, in *AJS Review* 19 (1994):254–57; Swartz, *Scholastic Magic*, 7–18; and Reuven Bonfil, "Eduto shel Agobard me-Lyons ᶜal ᶜOlamam ha-Ruḥani shel Yehudei ᶜIro ba-Meᵓah ha-Teshiᶜit," *Meḥqarim be-Qabbalah, be-Filosofyah Yehudit uve-Sifrut ha-Musar vehe-Hagut*, ed. J. Dan and J. Hacker (Jerusalem, 1986), 333–38, 347–48.

[7]For the impact of *Hekhalot* literature on exoteric magical practices, cf. Shaul Shaked, "On Hekhalot, Liturgy and Incantation Bowls," *Jewish Studies Quarterly* 2 (1995):203–7. See also Michael Swartz, "'Like the Ministering Angels': Ritual and Purity in Early Jewish Mysticism and Magic," *AJS Review* 19 (1994):135–67.

[8]Cf. S. D. Fraade, "Ascetical Aspects of Ancient Judaism," *Jewish Spirituality from the Bible Through the Middle Ages* (New York, 1987), 253–88, and Yitzḥak Baer, *Yisraᵓel ba-ᶜAmmim* (Jerusalem, 1955), 99–117.

with the Almighty, even without undertaking magical adjurations or heavenly journeys.[9] To be sure, the asceticism and *ḥasidut* espoused in *Sefer Ḥasidim* is more pronounced and more extensive than the ascetic and pietistic patterns we have found among certain tosafists. Nonetheless, this tendency among tosafists as well (which includes not only regular fasting and a diminution in the pleasures of food and drink, but also strictures against gazing at women and their clothing, looking into the face of a wicked person, and taking walks for pleasure) may have been inspired, in part, by *Hekhalot* literature and related texts, such as the *Baraita de-Massekhet Niddah*.

At the same time, the fact that certain tosafists recognized the legitimacy of the full program of *tiqqunei teshuvah* associated with the German Pietists, the appropriateness of confessing one's sins to a *rav* (which some Pietists advocated), and the value of reciting lengthy and sometimes physically demanding confessionals (*vidduyim*) helps to explain why these aspects of the Pietists' program were accepted by a significant number of Ashkenazic rabbinic authorities in the late Middle Ages and beyond.[10] Indeed, the interest displayed in magical and mystical concepts by Ashkenazic talmudists and halakhists in the late medieval and early modern periods and beyond also needs to be reevaluated in light of the tosafist period—although, to be sure, the number of non-Ashkenazic influences grows as the centuries unfold.[11] The serious interest in these concepts during the tosafist period also helps to explain why

---

[9]See Peter Schäfer, "The Ideal of Piety and Ashkenazi Ḥasidim and Its Roots in Jewish Tradition," *Jewish History* 4 (1990):9–23. See also Robert Chazan, "The Early Development of *Ḥasidut Ashkenaz*," *JQR* 75 (1985):199–211.

[10]See, e.g., Jacob Elbaum, *Teshuvat ha-Lev ve-Qabbalat Yissurim* (Jerusalem, 1993); Yedidyah Dinari, *Ḥakhmei Ashkenaz be-Shilhei Yemei ha-Benayim* (Jerusalem, 1984), 85–106; and Shlomo Eidelberg, *Jewish Life in Austria in the XVth Century* (Philadelphia, 1962), 43–44, 85, n. 19, 90–91.

[11]See Israel Yuval, *Ḥakhamim be-Doram* (Jerusalem, 1989), 87–90, 285–310; Dinari, *Ḥakhmei Ashkenaz*, 285–86. Cf. David Knowles, *The Evolution of Medieval Thought* (New York, 1962), 311–17; Immanuel Etkes, "Meqomam shel ha-Mageyah u-Vaᶜalei Shem ba-Ḥevrah ha-Ashkenazit be-Mifneh ha-Meᵓot ha-Yod Zayin/ha-Yod Ḥet," *Zion* 60 (1985):69–104; Moshe Rosman, *Founder of Hasidism: A Quest for the Historical Baᵓal Shem Tov* (Berkeley, 1996), 13–48; Meir Raffeld, "Al Meᶜat Sheqiᶜin Qabbaliyyim be-Mishnato ha-Hilkhatit shel ha-Maharshal," *Daᶜat* 36 (1996):15–33; and the ascetic practice attributed to the *Beit ha-Levi* in *Mesorah* 12 (1996):35–36. References to *Ḥasidei Ashkenaz* in later Ashkenazic literature may be to medieval Ashkenazic rabbinic scholars/tosafists as a whole. See my *Jewish Education and Society in the High Middle Ages* (Detroit, 1992), 191, n. 24 (regarding R. Ḥayyim b. Bezalᵓel), and R. Jacob of Karlin, *Mishkenot Yaᶜaqov* (repr. Jerusalem, 1960), 121.

tosafists are cited and mentioned in various kabbalistic works[12] and why the Zohar chose to adopt Ashkenazic *minhagim* in a large number of instances.[13]

This study suggests that within medieval Ashkenaz itself the German Pietists were not as unique as heretofore thought. Indeed, I have wrestled throughout this work with the question of whether the Pietists were the source of a particular phenomenon espoused by certain tosafists, or whether these tosafists received this material from pre-Crusade Ashkenazic rabbinic culture or from tosafist predecessors. This question is particularly acute with regard to developments in northern France through the first quarter of the thirteenth century. For the remainder of the thirteenth century, it is possible to conclude that while northern French rabbinic creativity was dominant with respect to talmudic commentary and study, in the realms of prayer and *piyyut* and their interpretation—including their mystical components—German rabbinic scholars led the way.[14]

To be sure, significant differences between Pietists and tosafists remain. *Sefer Ḥasidim* contains passages that frame, at least in theory, an elite pietist movement or community that wished to separate itself from the mainstream in Ashkenaz in order to pursue a life of *ḥasidut* to the fullest extent. These passages are in addition to the peculiar forms of necromancy and the systematic interest in *shedim* found throughout *Sefer Ḥasidim*, the more pronounced pietistic and ascetic tendencies that have been noted (including the search for the hidden Divine Will), and the strong concerns expressed with regard to the use of dialectic and contentious talmudic study. With regard to *torat ha-sod*, only the German Pietists (and their associates, such as the *Ḥug ha-Keruv ha-Meyuḥad* in northern France) were significantly engaged in the study of theosophy, developing a system of *sefirot*-like hypostases and other theosophical concepts—especially the *Kavod*—that had an impact on subsequent developments in Spanish Kabbalah.[15] The sustained interest in

---

[12]See my "Rabbinic Figures in Castilian Kabbalistic Pseudepigraphy: The Case of R. Judah *he-Ḥasid* and R. Elḥanan of Corbeil," *Journal of Jewish Thought and Philosophy* 3 (1993):77–109.

[13]See Israel Ta-Shma, *Ha-Nigleh shebe-Nistar* (Jerusalem, 1995).

[14]See Yaacov Sussmann, "Mifʿalo ha-Maddaʿi shel Ephraim Elimelekh Urbach," *Mussaf Maddaʿei ha-Yahadut* 1 (1993):61; and cf. Ta-Shma, *Halakhah, Minhag u-Meẓiʾut be-Ashkenaz, 1000–1350* (Jerusalem, 1996), 17–19, and Haym Soloveitchik, "Catastrophe and Halakhic Creativity in Ashkenaz—1096, 1242, 1306, and 1298," *Jewish History* 12 (1998):71–85.

[15]See, e.g., Gershom Scholem, *Major Trends in Jewish Mysticism* (New York, 1956), 111–18; Yosef Dan, *Torat ha-Sod shel Ḥasidut Ashkenaz* (Jerusalem, 1968), 104–70; Wolfson, *Through a Speculum That Shines*, 195–269.

these areas by the German Pietists alone within medieval Ashkenaz[16] is directly related to the fact that only *Ḥasidei Ashkenaz* expressed familiarity with the philosophical teachings of several Jewish Neoplatonists. Even the Hebrew paraphrase of R. Saᶜadayah Gaon's *Emunot ve-Deᶜot* is cited almost exclusively in Pietist texts. The philosophical leanings of the Pietists account, in part, for their preference in studying the esoteric properties and characteristics of the Divine Names, rather than adjuring them for personal needs or other more mundane purposes.

Recently, there has been much discussion about whether *Hekhalot* texts and procedures reflect an approach that was fundamentally esoteric or exoteric.[17] This issue can also be raised concerning certain geonic and other early medieval formulations (such as those of R. Hai and R. Ḥananʾel on visionary experiences).[18] Even the mystical study and manipulation of Divine Names within the kabbalistic framework can be divided into theosophical and more experiential components.[19]

With these kinds of distinctions in mind, it is clear that the tosafists highlighted in this study were not mystics who approached Judaism from the perspective of esotericism, just as they were not trying to form a separate pietistic movement. They were rabbinic scholars who received, as part of the intellectual culture of medieval Ashkenaz, an awareness of and interest in pietistic and mystical teachings and practices.[20] Although some tosafists ignored or downplayed these impulses, others acknowledged and adopted them in a moderate or partial way, and still others cultivated them more fully and developed them further.

---

[16]Overall, references by tosafists to Pietist conceptions of *torat ha-Kavod* are few and far between. At least one of the tosafists who refers to this material, R. Isaac b. Moses *Or Zaruaᶜ*, was part of the Pietists' circle in thirteenth-century Ashkenaz and was directly influenced by them—as were R. Meir of Rothenburg and the author of *Sefer ha-Maskil*, who discuss theosophical concepts and issues. See above, ch. 5, nn. 7, 65.

[17]See above, n. 6, and see now Rachel Elior, "From Earthly Temple to Heavenly Shrine," *JSQ* 4 (1997):217–23, and Moshe Idel, "Al ha-Qedushah veha-Zefiyyah ba-Merkavah," *Me-Qumran ᶜad Qahir*, ed. Joseph Tabory (Jerusalem, 1999), 7–15.

[18]See, e.g., Wolfson, *Through a Speculum That Shines*, 144–48, 155–56; Moshe Idel, *Kabbalah: New Perspectives* (New Haven, 1988), 90–91; and cf. idem, *Golem* (Albany, 1990), 48–49; and Yehuda Liebes, *Ḥetʾo* shel Elisha (Jerusalem, 1990), 1–10, 105–10.

[19]See Moshe Idel, "Defining Kabbalah: The Kabbalah of the Divine Names," *Mystics of the Book*, ed. R. A. Herrera (New York, 1993), 97–122, and cf. idem, "Yahadut, Mistiqah Yehudit u-Mageyah," *Maddaᶜei ha-Yahadut* 36 (1996):25–40.

[20]Cf. M. Idel's preface to A. J. Heschel, *Prophetic Inspiration After the Prophets*, ed. M. M. Faierstein (Hoboken, 1996), 8–9.

In any case, the inner spiritual lives of the *ba^calei ha-Tosafot* cannot be characterized as monolithic. Rather, we have encountered among the tosafists a range and richness of religious virtuosity and expression that suggests a more balanced or nuanced view of their composite personality. This degree of intellectual and spiritual breadth surely befits rabbinic scholars of their stature and rank.

Appendix: Ashkenazic Rabbinic Scholars

The chart on the following page provides an overview of many of the Ashkenazic rabbinic figures referred to in this study. Only the most basic chronological and geographic details are given. It may be assumed that those scholars for whom no specific dates have been supplied are roughly contemporaneous with the other names on their line in the chart, although differences in life span may mean that the transitions from line to line are not as neat as they appear to be. Familial and teacher-student relationships, which are noted throughout the body of the book, have generally not been included here. The column(s) on the left contain(s) the names of rabbinic scholars from northern and central France (and England). The middle columns consist of scholars from Germany, Austria, and Italy. The column furthest to the right lists several key figures among the German Pietists.

APPENDIX: ASHKENAZIC RABBINIC SCHOLARS

Menaḥem of Le Mans and his son, Elijah *ha-Zaqen* (c.980–1060)

Simeon b. Isaac *ha-Gadol* (c.950–1030, Mainz)

Joseph b. Samuel *Tov Elem* (c.980–1050, Anjou and Limoges)

Eliezer b. Isaac *ha-Gadol* (c.990–1060, Mainz)

Jacob b. Yaqar (c.990–1064, Mainz)

Isaac b. Eliezer *ha-Levi* (c.1000–1075, Worms)

Isaac b. Judah (c.1010–1085, Mainz)

Solomon b. Isaac רש"י (1040–1105, Troyes)

Meshullam b. Moses (d.c.1095, Mainz) and his son, R. Eleazar *Ḥazzan*

Solomon b. Samson (c.1030–1096, Worms)

Meir b. Samuel (c.1060–1135, Ramerupt)

Elijah b. Judah (Paris)

Isaac b. Asher *ha-Levi* (d.c.1130, Spires)

Qalonymus b. Isaac (d.1126, Mainz/Spires) and his son,

Samuel b. Meir רשב"ם (c.1080–1160)

Jacob b. Meir ר' תם (c.1100–1171, Ramerupt)

Eliezer b. Nathan ראב"ן (1090–1170, Mainz)

Isaac b. Mordekhai ריב"ם and Ephraim b. Isaac (1110–1175) (Regensburg)

Samuel b. Qalonymus *he-Ḥasid* (b.1115, Spires)

Isaac b. Samuel (ר"י (הזקן (d.1189, Dampierre)
Yom Tov b. Isaac (d.1190) and Menaḥem b. Pereẓ (Joigny)
Jacob of Corbeil (d.1192)
Eliezer b. Samuel (d.1198, Metz)

Judah b. Qalonymus b. Meir (d.1199, Spires)

and his son,

Isaac b. Abraham ריצב"א (d.1210), and his brother, Samson b. Abraham (d.1214, Sens)

Barukh b. Isaac (d.1211, Worms)

Judah b. Samuel *he-Ḥasid* (d.1217, Spires/Regensburg)

Judah b. Isaac Sir Leon (1166–1224, Paris)

Eliezer b. Joel *ha-levi* ראבי"ה (c.1140–1225, Bonn)

Barukh b. Samuel (c.1150–1221, Mainz), and his son, Samuel Bamberg

Solomon b. Judah (Dreux)

Ezra *ha-Navi* (Moncontour)

Jacob b. Meir (Provins)

Simḥah b. Samuel (Spires)

Moses b. Ḥisdai Taku

Eleazar b. Judah (d.c.1230, Worms)

Moses b. Jacob (Coucy)

Yeḥiel b. Joseph (d.c.1265, Paris)

Netan'el and Isaac b. Isaac of Chinon
Moses and Samuel of Evreux

Isaiah b. Mali di Trani (d.c.1250)

Isaac b. Moses *Or Zarua*ʿ (d.c.1250, Vienna)

Abraham b. Azriel (d.c. 1240, Bohemia)

Abraham Ḥaldiq

Avigdor b. Elijah *Kohen Ẓedeq* כ"ץ (c.1200–1275, Vienna)

Isaac b. Joseph (d.1280, Corbeil)

Elijah Menaḥem b. Moses (c.1220–1284, London)

Zedekiah b. Abraham *ha-Rofe* Anav (Rome)

Pereẓ b. Elijah (Corbeil, d.1298)

Meir b. Barukh of Rothenburg (c.1220–1293)

Asher b. Yeḥiel רא"ש and his son, Jacob *Baʿal ha-Turim*

Index of Manuscript References

Ancona
23 ... 243

Berlin
Or. Qu. 942 ... 169

Bologna (University Library)
2914 ... 181

Breslau
255 ... 65

British Museum
Cat. Margoliouth–
243 (Or. 2853) ... 94, 247
534 (Harley 5529) ... 102
610 (Add. 14762) ... 138
640 (Add. 26883) ... 73, 174
737 (Add. 27199) ... 209, 213
752 (Add. 15299) ... 98, 202
754 (Harley 5510) ... 202
756 (Or. 1055) ... 98
1056 (Add. 11639) ... 179–80

Or. 5557G ... 133
Or. 9931 (Gaster 730) ... 105
Or. 10619 ... 227
Or. 14055 ... 46, 180

Budapest (Kaufmann)
A174 ... 181
A266 ... 123
A399 ... 88, 100, 104, 122, 162

Budapest (National Museum)
2° 1 ... 111

Cambridge (University Library)
Add. 377 ... 65
Add. 394 ... 81, 100–102, 178
Add. 491 ... 100
Add. 561 ... 101–2, 178
Add. 664 ... 236
Add. 667.1 ... 179
Add. 858 ... 48, 109, 134, 181, 226
Add. 1022.1 ... 116, 206, 235
Add. 1176 ... 175, 180
Add. 2580 ... 65
Add. 3127 ... 62, 65, 91
Add. 3111 ... 227

Or. 71 ... 98, 100, 176, 227
Or. 786 ... 39, 44, 91, 103, 115, 243
Or. 790 ... 184

Cincinnati (HUC)
436 ... 72, 147
Acc. 14 ... 213

Darmstadt
Cod. Or. 25 ... 78, 206–7

Florence (Laurenziana)
Plut. II.5/12 ... 209

Frankfurt
Hebr. 8° 227 ... 138

Hamburg
45 ... 94–95, 227
152 ... 48, 157
153 ... 163
293 ... 207

Jerusalem (Feldman)
3 ... 186

Jerusalem (JNUL)
4° 621 (Livorno 2) ... 70
8° 151 ... 248
8° 397 ... 142, 233
8° 476 ... 142, 204, 227, 236
8° 1070 ... 133
8° 3037 ... 142
8° 4199 ... 143

Leipzig
1 ... 117

Livorno (Talmud Tora):
2 ... 70
138 ... 212, 227, 236

London (Jews' College)
Beth Hamidrash
73 ... 211
Montefiore
6 ... 73
130 ... 236
134 ... 48, 155, 227

Mantua
36 ... 94

Macerata (Biblioteca Comunale)
310 ... 73, 180

Milan-Ambrosiana
53/10 (P 12, sup.) ... 98, 195
62 (S 13, sup.) ... 243

Moscow-Guenzberg
13 ... 184
82 ... 117
90 ... 209
182 ... 156, 209
303 ... 77
348 ... 104, 124, 165
488 ... 189, 191
508 ... 240–41
614 ... 201
717 ... 236
734 ... 203, 238
1302 ... 155, 246

Munich
5 ... 96
50 ... 249
92 ... 98
212 ... 181
393 ... 100, 163
423 ... 104

New York (JTS)
Lutski 1062 ... 172
Rab. 689 ... 181
Rab. 1077 ... 124
Rab. 1609 ... 192-93
Mic. 1640 ... 73
Mic. 1851 ... 246
Mic. 1878 ... 213
Mic. 1885 ... 248
Mic. 2131 ... 174
Mic. 2367 ... 181
Mic. 7928 ... 148
Mic. 8092 ... 157
Mic. 8114 ... 141, 244
Mic. 8118 ... 191, 222
Mic. 8122 ... 101

Nuremberg (Municipal Library)
Cent. V. app. 5/1 ... 192

Oxford (Bodleian)
Cat. Neubauer–
123 ... 242
271 ... 117, 229
378 ... 123, 154
388 ... 192
554 ... 72
659 ... 103, 180, 198–99, 216, 229
682 ... 111, 201–2, 234
692 ... 158, 171
696 ... 113
781 ... 90, 186
783 ... 207
784 ... 156, 245
794 ... 162
847 ... 24, 193, 218
875 ... 59, 65, 90

884 65
900 52
913 110
916 248
945 138–39
970 202
973 211
1038 212
1098 .... 65, 212
1102 .... 100, 104, 162
1103 .... 102, 138
1105 .... 72, 74, 179–180
1106 123
1108 182
1114 .... 65, 72, 74
1118 .... 72, 74
1150 204
1153 132
1204 101
1205 102
1206 .... 198, 200
1207 145
1209 73
1575 138
1589 211
1598 142
1618 248
1812 .... 73, 181, 217, 243
1936 236
2105 198
2273 .... 97, 138
2274 .... 65, 102, 186
2275 158
2282 242
2287 110
2312 .... 184, 207
2343 .... 65, 90
2344 .... 181, 249
2423 229
2502 178
2550 177
2575 145
2858 110

Corpus Christi

133 181–83

Paris (Biblioteque Nationale, héb.)

167 198–200
187 184
353 95–96
390 90
391 .... 176, 180–82
407 .... 62, 91, 124
592 176
620 231
632 .... 179, 212
633 .... 73, 94, 167, 174–78, 180–184
640 139
644 184
646 .... 72, 102, 147, 180, 212
711 .... 169, 211
716 .... 142, 212
738 246
772 201
776 .... 213, 238
835 73
839 109
843 248
1408 .... 108, 147, 154, 183, 216, 234

Paris (l'Alliance)

H 48A (153) 147
H 133A (187) 235
H 482 73

Parma

Cat. De Rossi–
112 227
147 110
159 178
166 .... 65, 90
181 194
363 .... 178, 180
425 108
540 135
541 .... 88, 97, 138–42, 169, 195, 203, 229, 244
563 .... 203, 238
591 178–79
654 178
655 98
671 227
855 177
918 108
929 108
963 178
997 .... 213, 227
1033 .... 99, 116, 142, 212
1124 .... 176, 180, 246–47
1138 .... 46, 73, 174, 182
1220 72

1221 .... 73, 238
1237 .... 108, 165, 216
1274 107
1354 .... 73, 174, 213
1390 .... 173–77, 180

Prague (Jewish Museum)
45 213

Rome (Angelica)
Or. 45 143

Rome (Casanatense)
117 65
137 208
159 109

Sassoon
290 .... 121, 135, 142, 160, 182, 186, 207, 232, 243, 248
405 109
408 .... 46, 180, 226

Sweden
Lund L.O.2 158
Uppsala 21 94

Vatican
Ebr.
159 191
243 .... 142, 195, 226–27, 236
244 .... 142, 171
251 109
274 .... 100-2, 215
324 .... 138, 235
331 73
422 158
Rossiana–
356 .... 46, 73, 174–75, 183
Urb. Ebr.–
22 110

Verona (Municipal Library)
101 (85.2) 100

Vienna (National Library)
28 (Hebr. 148) 142, 212
152 (Hebr. 47) 171

Warsaw
9 245
285 148
374 212

Index of Names and Subjects

Abbaye, 179, 182n. 113

Abraham b. Azriel, R., 20, 21n. 3, 81–82, 87, 102n. 14, 112, 260

Abraham b. Nathan *ha-Yarḥi*, R., 51–53, 56–58, 193–94

Abraham b. Samuel *he-Ḥasid*, R., 103n. 16

Abraham Ḥaldiq, R., 95, 113, 260

Abun family, 41, 131

academies: at Evreux, 26, 59–63, 71, 89, 90–92, 124, 177; at Mainz, 148; at Worms, 148, 186

adjurations, 141, 155, 181–82, 209, 212, 252. *See also* prayers; supplications

ʾ*aggadah,* 60n. 76, 100n. 11

Agobard of Lyons, 27–28

Aharon *ha-Kohen* of Lunel, R., 89

Akatriʾel (angel), 223

ʿ*Aleynu* prayer, 87, 179, 182n. 112

Alfasi, R. Isaac, 193n. 8

ʿ*aliyyah*/ʿ*aliyyot,* 53, 137

alphabet, Hebrew, 28, 86n. 156, 95n. 5, 97n. 9, 156, 221. *See also* numerical analyses

ʿ*Amidah* prayer, 43, 53, 54, 80, 91n. 175, 137–38

ʿ*Ammudei Golah. See Sefer Miẓvot Qatan*

Amnon, R., story of, 107n. 26, 133n. 3

Amoraim, 253

Amtaḥat Binyamin, 178n. 104

amulets, 98n. 10, 227n. 16, 236

angelic names, 29, 53n. 54, 86, 97n. 9, 132, 154, 172, 182n. 112, 252

angels, 41n. 24, 112, 114, 168; adjuration of, 140, 212; of death, 138; Divine Names and, 244n. 67; in heaven, 210n. 42; as intermediaries, 13, 134, 226, 239n. 50; prayers and, 124n. 70, 147, 235n. 43; righteous people and, 201; in worldview of tosafists, 178n. 104. *See also names of specific angels*

approbations, 89n. 169

Aqiva, R., 48, 150, 173, 225n. 11

*Arba*ʿ*ah Turim,* 46, 247

ʿ*Arugat ha-Bosem,* 20n. 3

asceticism, 33–37, 119, 124, 127, 242; antecedents in pre-Crusade period, 37–42; atonement and, 234; Christian, 126, 254; Evreux academy and, 62; German Pietists and, 220; R. Isaac of Corbeil and, 91; Rabbenu Yonah and, 66–67; of tosafists, 251, 253; in twelfth-century tosafist literature, 42–58

Asher b. Jacob *ha-Levi* of Osnabruck, R., 103

Asher b. Meshullam of Lunel, R., 43, 194n. 10

Ashkenaz, medieval, 30, 65, 79, 93, 107, 125, 256; adjuration of Divine Names in, 168; conception of piety in, 20; education initiation ceremony in, 237n. 47; esotericism in, 249; magic in, 141; mysticism in, 214; Passover customs in, 99n. 11; philosophical awareness in, 252; practice of fasting in, 111; rabbinic culture/literature of, 33–34, 187, 257; *torat ha-sod* in, 166. *See also* France, northern; Germany

astrology, 158, 193n. 9, 240n. 52

atonement, 25, 180n. 110, 234

Austria, 113, 260

Av, 39, 40, 42, 51, 62, 122

Avigdor b. Elijah *Kohen Ẓedeq* (Katz) of Vienna, R., 95n. 5, 97–98n. 9, 107, 108–9, 115, 221, 225–27, 234, 252, 260

Avigdor b. Isaac, R., 98n. 9
Avinu Malkenu prayer, 48, 108–9, 226
ᶜ*Avodah* prayer, 49
Azulai, R. Ḥayyim Yosef David, 229

Baraita de-Massekhet Niddah, 49, 127–30, 157n. 63, 164n. 75, 255
Barekhu prayer, 96n. 7, 101n. 14, 143, 154n. 56, 224
Barukh b. Isaac of Worms, R., 68, 119, 120, 260
Barukh b. Samuel of Mainz, R., 68, 103, 105–6, 260
Benjamin b. Abraham *ha-Navi,* R., 231
Benjamin of Tudela, R., 194n. 10
Bereshit Rabbah, 53–54, 234n. 41
Bible, 108n. 110, 137
biblical commentaries/interpretations, 77, 95, 104, 145, 148, 235
black magic, 166, 211
Bohemia, 20, 113
Bonn, Germany, 214
burials, 119

charity, 91, 105, 108n. 28, 143n. 25
children, 42, 92n. 178, 109, 141, 156
Christianity, 69, 83, 123; Christian-Jewish polemics, 185; conversion to, 234; legend of Jewish pope, 134n. 4; magic and, 166
circumcision, 86n. 157, 230
commentaries, 26, 61, 95, 100, 101, 103–4, 145, 159
confession, 47, 91, 255
cosmogony, 159
Creation story, 149, 159
Crusades, 23, 40n. 20, 44, 126, 187
customs, 99n. 11, 107, 114, 128n. 81, 137, 138, 254, 256

dam niddah, 38
dam tohar, 38, 113, 130n. 86
Dan, R., 236, 247–48
death, 109, 123, 211; angel of, 138; communicating with the dead, 196–97
demons (*shedim*), 114, 178n. 104, 195, 198, 212, 219, 224–25, 239, 245; Divine Names and, 240; protection against, 204n. 33
derashot, 70
Devarim ha-Meviʾim Lidei Yirʾat ha-Het, 64
dialectic, 23, 59, 69, 92, 256; Christian, 167n. 86; Rabbenu Tam and, 189; tosafist, 26, 68, 69, 89, 186, 254
Diaspora, 44
divination, 147, 166, 210, 228, 245
Divine Being, 240, 241
Divine Names, 29, 53n. 54, 135, 155n. 59, 239, 252; alphabet and, 95n. 5; amulets and, 236; angels and, 101n. 14; biblical commentaries and, 95; catching thieves with, 140; children and, 92n. 178; circumcision and, 230; commentaries on, 106n. 26; divination and, 228; esotericism and, 190n. 2, 220, 257; German Pietists and, 188; *Hekhalot* guidelines for use, 207; kabbalism and, 242–43; kaddish and, 153; magic and, 30, 182n. 112; *mezuzot* and, 154, 232; Primal Ether and, 242; Rashi and, 144–45, 146; reasons for adjuring, 172; ritual practices and, 141; theurgic powers of, 136; Torah and, 230; used for protection, 85–87, 137n. 10, 181, 209, 227. *See also Shemot*
Divine Will, 36, 75, 104, 256
Donnolo, R. Shabbetai, 75
dreams, 78, 107n. 26, 132, 133n. 3, 160n. 67, 232; contrasted with visions, 136n. 8; halakhic rulings and, 164, 165, 217, 238; interpretation of, 184n. 116, 194
dress, modes of, 127
drink, abstention from, 51

eastern Europe, 30, 113, 130n. 86
education, 214, 237n. 47
eggs, magical, 140–41, 142n. 21, 156, 242
Eleazar b. Judah of Worms, R., 19–20, 24, 45, 48, 81, 128, 202n. 30, 260; ᶜ*Aleynu* prayer and, 179; *Baraita de-Massekhet Niddah* and, 130; biblical commentaries of, 97n. 9, 108n. 28, 156, 200; on Divine Names, 95n. 5, 156, 220, 230, 243; esotericism and, 183n. 115, 226, 236; Evreux academy and, 67–68; on fasting, 111; halakhic works and, 147; *hilkhot ḥasidut* of, 84; influence of, 20; *kavvanah* and, 61n. 79; magic and, 142n. 21, 212; messianism and, 207n. 38; mysticism and, 151, 186; Passover customs and, 137; penitential prayers of, 72, 73n. 112; personal pietism of, 25, 126; prayer commentaries of, 101; Rashi and, 145; on Sabbath practices, 224; *sodot ha-tefillah* and, 161; students of, 81–82, 112; *ta*ᶜ*amei ha-mesorah* and, 117; teachers of, 115, 196; Tetragrammaton and, 215; on Torah, 230; treatise by, 62. *See also Sefer Roqeaḥ*

Eleazar b. Meshullam, R., 96n. 7
Eleazar *ha-Qallir,* R., 106, 141, 168
Eleazar *Ḥazzan* of Spires, R., 143, 154n. 56, 260
Eleazar of Forcheim, R., 100, 107n. 26
Elḥanan b. Yaqar of London, R., 191–92
Eliezer b. Elijah *ha-Kohen,* 109
Eliezer b. Haradia, R., 234n. 41
Eliezer b. Isaac *ha-Gadol* of Mainz, R., 39n. 17, 137, 138, 260
Eliezer b. Joel *ha-Levi,* R., 39, 260
Eliezer of Metz, R., 21n. 7, 68, 69, 71n. 110, 102, 103n. 16, 187, 195–97, 252, 260
Elijah b. Judah of Paris, R., 57, 170–71, 207, 260
Elijah b. Menaḥem of Le Mans, 179, 260
Elijah Menaḥem b. Moses of London, R., 232–33, 260
Elijah the Prophet, 203, 216, 228
Emunot ve-Deᶜot, 219, 257
England, 46, 171, 183, 260
Ephraim b. Isaac of Regensburg, R., 164–65, 260
Ephraim b. Jacob of Bonn, R., 106, 214
Ereẓ Yisraʾel, 128, 235
esotericism, 78, 79n. 134, 116n. 50, 159, 161, 218; German Pietists and, 67n. 94, 127, 135, 188, 199; *Hekhalot* literature and, 173, 254; kabbalism and, 125; Rashi and, 144, 149–50, 152
ethics, 109, 214
Evreux (France), academy at, 26, 59–63, 71, 89, 90, 177; asceticism and, 62; on *kavvanah* in prayer, 124; *Tosafot* and, 91–92
exegesis/exegetes, 95–96, 169, 205n. 35
exempla, 89
exotericism, 19, 93, 95, 159, 226, 231, 254
Ezra *ha-Navi* of Moncontour, R., 115, 196, 234, 244, 260

fasting, 41–42, 47, 115–16, 124; excessive, 66; inspired by *Hekhalot* literature, 255; penance and, 38, 91; personal declaration of, 43; on *Rosh ha-Shanah,* 108, 111–12, 114, 202; *Sefer Ḥasidim* on, 34, 35n. 3; on Yom Kippur, 44, 48
Ferrara, Italy, 107
festivals, 114
fires, 46–47
folk religion, 29
food, 35n. 3, 66, 91, 124, 255
France, northern, 20, 28, 41, 51, 53, 56, 95, 242; biblical exegetes in, 95–96; dialectic in, 189; esotericism in, 191; influence of *Ḥasidei Ashkenaz* in, 214; magic in, 183; prayer interpretation in, 107; predominance in talmudism, 67, 253, 256; rabbinic culture in, 81; rabbinic scholars from, 23, 260; ritual practices in, 140–41; *Sefer Yeẓirah* in, 145; Spanish Jews in, 71; tosafists in, 59, 68, 79, 187; *Tosafot* texts in, 217. *See also* Ashkenaz, medieval
France, southern. *See* Provence
frivolous behavior, 83, 91

gematria, 48, 93, 95, 96, 97n. 9, 169, 200n. 27; prayers and, 87, 116; *Qeriʾat Shema* and, 198–99; Tetragrammaton and, 190n. 2. *See also* numerical analyses
Gentiles, 70, 84n. 151, 98n. 10, 119, 227n. 17
geonic period, 50, 111, 122n. 65, 128, 141, 155n. 58
Germany, 20, 46, 81, 125; dialectic in, 189; esotericism in, 191; magic in, 183; prayer interpretation in, 107; predominance in mysticism, 256; rabbinic scholars from, 260; ritual practices in, 140–41; *Sefer Yeẓirah* in, 145; talmudocentrism in, 253; tosafists in, 214–15. *See also* Ashkenaz, medieval; Rhineland
Gerona, kabbalism in, 125
Gershom, Rabbenu, 37
Godhead, feminine aspect of, 230
golem, 135, 171, 206

Hai Gaon, R., 168
hair-cutting, 44n. 30
halakhic rulings, 20, 38, 82, 92, 105, 113, 164, 183n. 115
halakhic works, 19–20, 54–55, 77, 89, 99, 185n. 117; asceticism and, 34n. 1; codes, 76, 81; compendiums, 110n. 34, 147; monographs, 103; mysticism and, 215; Sefardic, 84; Torah and, 68–69
halakhists, 27, 39n. 16, 82, 105, 129, 221, 228–29, 255
Ḥananʾel, Rabbenu, 84, 163n. 75
Ḥanina b. Tradyon, R., 146
Ḥannukah, 122n. 64
Ḥanokh (angel), 170
ha-Qadosh title, 57
hashbaᶜot, 176, 180, 182n. 113, 183, 188, 212

ḥasid title, 90, 97n. 9, 125, 234
Ḥasidei Ashkenaz, 22, 75, 103–4, 115, 162, 191; asceticism and, 247; biblical exegesis and, 96; esotericism and, 33–37, 188, 225, 230; Evreux academy and, 67; *Hekhalot* literature and, 254–55; *Ḥug ha-Keruv ha-Meyuḥad* and, 192n. 4; on lineage and marriage, 23; magic and, 220, 246; messianism and, 213; numerical analyses of, 102; *nusḥa*ʾ*ot* associated with, 176–77; *perushim* and, 45–46; philosophy and, 208n. 40, 257; pietism of, 221; prayer and, 80, 93, 107, 116; Rabiah and, 47–51; *Semaq* and, 88–89; tosafists and, 24–25, 111, 120–21, 214. *See also* Pietists, German
Ḥasidei Provence, 58
Ḥasidei Ẓarefat, 56, 57
Hasidism, 30, 125
ḥasidut, 21, 99, 125, 215, 224, 231; in *Sefer Ḥasidim,* 255, 256; talmudic interpretations and, 251
ḥasidut Ashkenaz, 47, 52, 77, 79, 123, 230, 248; Evreux academy and, 62, 68; experiential dimension of, 133n. 3; *Hekhalot* literature and, 127; magic and, 220; meaning of, 58; mysticism and, 31, 126, 196; in northern France, 59n. 71; penances and, 234; Rabbenu Yonah and, 70–71; rise of, 254; *Sefer Ḥasidim* and, 24, 104; talmudism and, 22; *torat ha-Kavod* of, 239
Havdalah ceremony, 155
Ḥayyim *ha-Kohen,* R., 57n. 67
ḥazaq custom, 54n. 57
Hekhalot literature, 27–28, 29, 49, 55, 101, 110n. 34, 123, 125, 132, 196; *ʿAleynu* prayer and, 179; *Ḥasidei Ashkenaz* and, 56; *ḥasidut Ashkenaz* and, 127; *Baraita de-Massekhet Niddah* and, 127–28; Divine Names in, 207; esotericism and, 173; magic/mysticism and, 30–31, 213, 244; menstrual impurity in, 129; *nosaḥ ha-tefillah* and, 235; prayers and, 226; rabbinic scholars and, 253–54; Rashi and, 149–51; ritual and, 140; synagogue practices and, 50
Hekhalot Rabbati, 49, 109, 147. *See also* *Maʿaseh Merkavah; Sefer Hekhalot*
High Holidays, 137
hilkhot ḥasidut, 84, 126
hilkhot teshuvah, 82
Hilkhot Yeẓirah, 145
Ḥokhmat ha-Nefesh, 226
Holy Ark, 37, 163
ḥovat ha-ʾevarim, 75
Ḥug ha-ʿIyyun, 241, 242
Ḥug ha-Keruv ha-Meyuḥad, 67n. 94, 151, 171, 192, 206, 230, 256
humility, 33, 64, 87

Ibn Ezra, R. Avraham, 95, 171–72, 215
idolatry, 194–95
Isaac b. Eliezer *ha-Levi,* R., 38–40, 260
Isaac b. Isaac of Chinon, R., 174, 176–77, 260
Isaac b. Joseph of Corbeil, R., 62, 63n. 84, 81–92, 119, 241, 252, 260
Isaac b. Judah of Mainz (Mayence), R., 39n. 17, 40, 42, 260
Isaac b. Moses of Mainz, R., 39–40
Isaac b. Moses *Or Zaruaʿ* of Vienna, R., 21, 39, 107, 112, 219, 221–24, 234; on burial customs, 119; *Ḥasidei Ashkenaz* and, 51n. 47; magic and, 128–30, 164n. 75; *Sefer Or Zaruaʿ* of, 69; as teacher, 115
Isaac b. Shneʾur of Evreux, R., 26
Isaac *de-min ʿAkko,* R., 210–11
Isaac *ha-Lavan,* R., 52
Isaac *ha-Navi* Ẓarefati, R., 195n. 14
Isaac *ha-Zaqen,* R. *See* Ri (R. Isaac b. Samuel of Dampierre)
Isaac *Sagi Nahor,* R., 56
Isaiah b. Mali di Trani, R., 77n. 123, 228, 260
Israel, ancient, 115
Italy, 28, 107, 120n. 60, 131n. 1, 155n. 58; pre-Crusade, 132n. 2; rabbinic scholars from, 260; tosafists in, 228

Jacob b. Asher *Baʿal ha-Turim,* R., 46, 117, 245, 246–47, 247, 260
Jacob b. Meir of Provins, R., 98, 207, 260
Jacob b. Samson, R., 158
Jacob b. Yaqar, R., 37–38, 143, 260
Jacob *ha-Levi* of Marvège, R., 185, 195n. 11, 216, 228, 229
Jacob of Corbeil, R., 57, 197–200, 252, 260
Jacob of Orleans, R., 47
Jaffe, R. Mordekhai, 152
Jewish law, 107, 118–20, 119, 128, 196, 216
Jewish Magic and Superstition: A Study in Folk Religion (Trachtenberg), 27
Jewish pope, legend of, 134n. 4
Jews, 27–28, 69, 166, 231
John of Salisbury, 166
Joseph b. Samuel *Tov Elem,* R., 96, 260

Joseph *Bekhor Shor,* R., 77

Judah b. Isaac Sir Leon, R., 39n. 16, 68, 217, 260

Judah b. Moses *ha-Kohen* of Mainz, R., 115

Judah b. Samuel *he-Ḥasid,* R., 20–21, 24, 25–26, 39, 45, 81, 82, 95, 116, 169; ancestors of, 23, 137; on angels, 201, 202n. 29; *Bereshit Rabbah* and, 54; biblical commentaries of, 104, 108n. 28; as central figure of *Ḥasidei Ashkenaz,* 208; cited in *Sefer Miẓvot Qatan,* 85–87; esotericism and, 236; Evreux academy and, 67–68; on fasting, 34, 36, 48, 115; influence of, 130n. 86; liturgical interpretations of, 101; magic and, 142n. 21, 143, 179, 180n. 110, 183n. 114, 210–14; messianism and, 78; *minhagim* and, 114; mysticism and, 186; on penances, 47; pietistic works of, 230; prayers and, 72, 106; responsa of, 185; Ri and, 193; on *shedim,* 224–25; Spires circle and, 117n. 52; students of, 111, 156n. 62, 200; on suicide, 234; *taʿamei ha-mesorah* and, 117; testament of, 65n. 88

Judah b. Yaqar, R., 199–200, 235n. 43

kabbalah/kabbalism, 21n. 6, 125, 135, 178n. 104, 199, 205, 218; Divine Names and, 242–43; magic and, 21n. 8; new moon and, 223n. 7; in Provence, 20, 55n. 61; *rishonim* and, 252; in Spain, 27, 55n. 61, 248, 256; talmudic scholars and, 30; Torah and, 144n. 28; tosafists and, 256; use of salt in, 204n. 33; works of, 152

Kaddish prayer, 142, 153, 154n. 56

kavvanah, 61, 67n. 93, 84–85, 106, 124; in *Arbaʿah Turim,* 247; Provençal mysticism and, 55–56; sin and, 109

Keter ha-Gadol ha-Gibbor veha-Nora, 182n. 112

kisse ha-Kavod, 28, 106n. 26, 134

Kohen Zedeq. See R. Avigdor b. Elijah of Vienna

lashes, 47, 115, 116

Le Mans, France, 41

legal practices. *See* Jewish law

leḥishah technique, 225–26

liturgical texts, 93, 96, 100–101, 104, 106, 135, 154n. 56, 157, 247. See also *piyyutim;* prayers

Luria, R. Solomon, 23–24n. 13, 235n. 43

Maʿaseh Bereshit, 146, 162, 168

Maʿaseh ha-Geonim, 128

Maʿaseh Merkavah, 22, 55, 109, 146, 147, 159, 162, 254. *See also Hekhalot Rabbati*

Magdeburg, Germany, 113

magic, 21, 27, 29, 54, 78, 86, 125, 168, 221, 236; amulets, 98n. 10; ascent to Heaven with, 244; in Christian society, 166; Divine Names and, 86–87; eggs and, 140–41, 142n. 21, 156; *perishut* and, 129; protection from danger, 99n. 10, 179–81; rabbinic scholars and, 30, 159, 234; secrecy and, 30n. 30; in the Zohar, 154n. 56

Maharam (R. Meir b. Barukh) of Rothenburg, 21n. 7, 47, 61n. 80, 103, 232, 252, 260; approbation of *Semaq,* 89n. 169; esotericism and, 234–39; German Pietists and, 115–24; *Ḥasidei Ashkenaz* and, 92; on penance, 82; pietistic practices of, 105n. 24; rabbinic traditions and, 221; students of, 245, 247, 249; teachers of, 107

Maḥzor Vitry, 153, 154n. 56, 155–57, 162, 190n. 2, 196

Maimonidean controversy, 20, 99–100n. 11, 214, 252

Maimonides (R. Moses b. Maimon), 71n. 110, 72n. 112, 78, 252; magic and, 246; *Mishneh Torah* of, 76, 203n. 31; on Torah and Divine Names, 230

Mainz, Germany, 38, 40, 41, 44, 60, 138, 152; academy at, 148, 186–87; mysticism in, 143, 186; R. Amnon and bishop of, 107n. 26; rabbinical court in, 106; *torat ha-sod* in, 131

martyrdom, 40, 123–24, 133n. 3, 134n. 4, 165, 217

masoretic text, 93, 117, 123, 204n. 33

maziqin (demonic forces), 147, 153, 155n. 58, 158n. 65, 168; Divine Names and, 227; protection from, 198n. 23, 199, 236

mazzot, 58, 99n. 11

meat, abstention from eating, 51

Megillot, 107

Meir b. Qalonymus of Spires, R., 117n. 52

Meir b. Samuel, R., 186, 260

Meir *ha-Gadol,* Rabbenu, 240

Menahem b. Perez, R., 260

Menahem ha-Meiri, R., 156n. 60

Menahem *Ḥasid,* R., 98

Menaḥem of Joigny, R., 117n. 52, 140, 168n. 90, 203–4
Menaḥem of Le Mans, R., 41, 260
Menaḥot (tractate of Talmud), 59, 64n. 85
menstruation, 38, 49, 127, 128–30
Meshullam b. Moses, R., 142–43, 260
Meshullam b. Qalonymus of Lucca, R., 143
Meshullam of Brittany, R., 242–43
Meshullam of Melun, R., 46
Messiah/messianism, 72n. 112, 78, 206, 207n. 38, 213, 240, 244, 248
Metatron (angel), 169, 170, 172, 175, 182, 227n. 16
mezuzah, 121n. 62, 125n. 71, 154, 196, 237n. 47
middat ḥasidut, 85
*Midrash Aggadah Ma*ᶜ*aseh Merkavah,* 146–47
Midrash Mishlei, 126n. 76, 139n. 13
Midrash Pesiqta, 170
Midrash Tanḥuma, 104, 198
Midrash Tehillim, 55n. 60, 74n. 113, 139n. 13
Mikhaᵓel *ha-Malᵓakh,* R., 229
minhag Österreich, 113, 114n. 44, 130n. 86
miraculous acts, 164
Mishneh Torah, 76, 203n. 31
miẓvot, 77n. 124
modesty, 64
Mordekhai b. Eliezer, R., 165
Mordekhai b. Hillel, R., 119
Moses b. Eleazar *ha-Darshan,* R., 169
Moses b. Jacob of Coucy, R., 26, 68–72, 71n. 108, 75–80, 81, 82, 119, 260
Moses b. Meir of Ferrara, R., 45n. 34
Moses b. Shneᵓur of Evreux, R., 59–63, 76, 178n. 104, 233, 260
Moses *ha-Kohen* of Mainz, R., 26n. 21, 103n. 16
Moses of London, R., 233, 234
mourning, 38n. 15, 66n. 91
mysticism, 27, 125, 221, 252; magic and, 29; *Merkavah,* 22; messianism and, 78; pietism and, 127; rabbinic scholarship and, 159; wine and, 96n. 7

Naḥmanides, 20, 65n. 88, 128; Christian influence on, 205n. 35; on divination, 210; *kabbalah* and, 252; talmudic commentaries of, 218
Name, ineffable, 132, 209n. 41
nazir title, 36, 125
necromancy, 256
Neḥunyah b. *ha-Qanah,* R., 49–50, 178n. 104
new moon, 44, 151n. 47, 223n. 7
Nissim Gaon of Kairwan, R., 111
non-Jews. *See* Gentiles
nosaḥ ha-tefillah, 235
notariqon, 93, 97
numerical analyses, 48, 52, 101n. 14, 102, 106n. 26, 198n. 23, 205n. 35. *See also* alphabet, Hebrew; *gematria*
nusḥaᵓot, 104, 109, 176–77

Otiyyot de-R. Aqiva, 151

*Pa*ᶜ*aneaḥ Raza,* 248–49
Paltiᵓel, R. Ḥayyim, 113
parush title, 38, 125
Passover, 47n. 36, 99n. 11, 137, 138, 143
payyetan, 105, 106, 231
penance, 33n. 1, 73–74, 81–82, 123, 166, 214, 226. See also *teshuvah; tiqqunei teshuvah*
Pentateuch, 52, 77, 96n. 6
Pereẓ b. Elijah of Corbeil, R., 62, 124, 239, 241, 260
perishut, 37, 47, 99, 125; fasting and, 42; German Pietists and, 33, 81, 220; magic and, 127, 129; R. Isaac of Corbeil and, 91; talmudic interpretations and, 251; tosafists and, 249, 253
persecutions, 123, 126, 247
perushim, 36, 39, 41–42, 45–46, 57
pesaqim, 103, 108n. 28
peshat, 160n. 69, 162
petiḥat ha-lev, 140–41, 142n. 21, 156, 227n. 16, 236; education initiation ceremony and, 238n. 47; Torah knowledge and, 240
philosophy, 208n. 40, 219, 220, 257; formulations against study of, 228n. 21; Maimonides and, 252
Pietists, German, 25, 61–62, 79, 115; anti-French animus of, 104n. 21; biblical interpretations of, 93; chart of, 259–60; Divine Names and, 245; esotericism of, 127, 135, 188, 199; Evreux academy and, 64; exegetical methods of, 97n. 9, 107; *Hekhalot* literature and, 27; liturgical interpretations of, 104; magic and, 29, 218; mystical circles associated with, 171; northern French pietists and, 56, 58; penance and, 255; *perushim* and, 51; preservation of Ashkenazic culture and, 157n. 64; social status of, 23; *torat ha-sod* and, 19; tosafists and, 22–23, 59, 158n.

64, 249. *See also Sefer Ḥasidim; Ḥasidei Ashkenaz*
Pirqei de-R. Eliezer, 51
Pisqei ha-Tosafot, 44
Pisqei Reqanati, 44
piyyutim, 20n. 3, 26, 37, 106–7, 116, 161–62, 168, 217, 256; esotericism and, 21n. 6; German Pietists and, 65; *Hekhalot* literature and, 143; ineffable Name and, 132; supplications and, 181n. 111
Poland, 125
polemic, 219n. 68
posqim, 20
Potah (angel), 155, 227n. 16
poterei ḥalomot, 194
Prague, 112
prayers, 23, 29, 45, 48, 60n. 76, 64, 74, 80n. 140, 92, 94n. 2, 247, 256; angels and, 147; commentaries to, 100, 101, 103–4; comportment in synagogue and, 83; directed to angels, 134; esotericism and, 174–84; High Holidays and, 137–38; *kavvanah* and, 61, 67n. 93, 84–85, 124; magic and, 187; penitential, 72; proper intention in, 26; protection and, 209; quorum and, 58n. 69; swaying during, 54, 148n. 40; theurgic, 144, 211, 253. *See also* adjurations; *sodot ha-tefillah;* supplications; *specific prayers*
pre-Crusade period, 23, 58, 79, 95n. 5, 139, 253; antecedents of pietism in, 37–42; curriculum of, 61; disciplines of, 249; eclecticism in, 161n. 70; France in, 113; *Ḥakhmei/Geonei Lothaire,* 136, 168; *kabbalah* and, 152; magic/mysticism in, 130, 131, 158–59, 214; *perishut* in, 254; pietistic practices in, 115; rabbinic culture in, 81, 187, 256; *tefillin* in, 120n. 60
Primal Ether, 241, 242
prophecy/prophets, 152n. 50, 209, 244
Provence, 20, 29, 36, 51, 53, 56, 196n. 18
pseudepigraphic literature, 170, 172n. 97
Purim, 41n. 22
purity, 119

qabbalah. See kabbalah/kabbalism
Qalonymides, 23, 24n. 13, 102, 131, 137, 143
Qalonymus b. Isaac, R., 96n. 7, 97n. 9, 138–39, 142, 143, 259
Qalonymus b. Meshullam, R., 107n. 26
Qara, R. Yosef, 96n. 7
Qedushah prayer, 49, 55n. 60, 101n. 14
Qeriʾat Shema prayer, 106, 196, 198
Qiddushin, 59
Qohelet, 159
quorum, 108n. 28

Raban (R. Eliezer b. Nathan of Mainz), 70, 100, 128, 161–65, 187, 217, 249, 259
rabbanei Ẓarefat, 20
rabbinic literature, 25, 42, 60n. 76, 103n. 16, 187, 239
rabbinic scholars, 96n. 6, 144, 220; chart of, 259–60; esotericism and, 257–58; *Hekhalot* literature and, 253–54; kabbalism and, 125; legalists, 23; in northern France, 23, 218, 221; R. Judah *he-Ḥasid* and, 113, 115; *torat ha-sod* and, 131; tosafists and, 100
Rabiah (R. Eliezer b. Joel *ha-Levi),* 21n. 7, 44n. 30, 45, 57, 78, 111, 119; German Pietists and, 47–51; magic and, 214–17; on majority rule, 122n. 65
Rambam. *See* Maimonides
Ramban. *See* Naḥmanides
Rashba (R. Solomon Ibn Adret), 210
Rashbam (R. Samuel b. Meir), 77, 102n. 14, 187, 259; Divine Names and, 168; rationalism of, 159–60, 190n. 2; study of Scripture and, 167; *torat ha-sod* and, 186
Rashi (R. Solomon b. Isaac), 38, 59, 79, 120, 167, 168, 259; appearance in dream, 160n. 67; *gematria* and, 169; magic and, 189; mystical traditions and, 144–53; students of, 158–59; Talmud and, 60n. 75; teachers of, 143
rationalism, 160, 166, 220
redemption, 108n. 110, 226, 244
Regensburg, Germany, 26, 95, 112, 113, 201n. 29
repentance. *See* penance
responsa, 48, 103, 106n. 26, 123, 183n. 115, 185, 234n. 41
resurrection, 206n. 37, 248
Rhineland, 28, 41, 113. *See also* Germany
Ri (R. Isaac b. Samuel of Dampierre), 43, 44n. 30, 45, 51, 57, 68, 69, 84, 187, 252, 260; dream interpreters and, 194; esotericism and, 191; mysticism/magic and, 194–95; *Sefer Yeẓirah* and, 192; students of, 205, 208; as teacher, 244
Riba (R. Isaac b. Asher *ha-Levi),* 44, 260
Ribam (R. Isaac b. Mordekhai of Bohemia/Regensburg), 21n. 7, 187, 201–2, 260

Ribaq (R. Judah b. Qalonymus b. Meir of Spires), 60n. 76, 103n. 16, 106n. 26, 120n. 60, 202n. 30, 213, 214, 260
Rif (R. Isaac al-Fasi), 84
rishonim, 252
rituals, 111, 119, 129
Rizba (R. Isaac b. Abraham), 78, 111, 205–7, 260
Rosh (R. Asher b. Yeḥiel), 117, 119, 245, 247, 260
Rosh ha-Shanah, 44n. 30, 108, 111–12, 114, 119, 202
Rosh Ḥodesh, 40

Saᶜadyah Gaon, R., 141, 219, 257
Sabbath, 36, 153, 162; *Barekhu* prayer and, 143, 224; eating on, 204, 215n. 57; fasting on, 111–12, 114; fires on, 46–47
Safed, mysticism in, 125
Samson b. Abraham of Sens, R., 205, 217, 260
Samson of Falaise, R., 128n. 81
Samuel b. Barukh of Bamberg, R., 102–5, 260
Samuel b. Judah, R., 26n. 21, 67n. 94
Samuel b. Qalonymus *he-Ḥasid* of Spires, R., 24, 48, 53, 95, 96n. 7, 109, 143, 186, 260; father of, 138; liturgical interpretations of, 101; Ri and, 193; students of, 156n. 62; on Tetragrammaton, 243
Samuel b. Shneᵓur of Evreux, R., 59–63, 82, 90, 115, 119, 260; on Passover stringencies, 99n. 11; as teacher, 236, 241
Samuel b. Solomon of Falaise, R., 96, 99, 115
Sar ha-ᶜOlam (angel), 170
Sar ha-Panim (angel), 201
science, 208n. 40
sectarianism, 25
seder ha-maᶜamadot, 178–80
Seder Qodashim, 60–61
Sefardic influence, 69, 111
Sefer Assufot, 155, 156, 157, 238n. 47
Sefer ha-Bahir, 144, 171n. 95
Sefer ha-Hokhmah, 68, 105, 156
Sefer ha-Kavod, 225
Sefer ha-Manhig, 51–56, 58, 79
Sefer ha-Maskil, 152, 212, 239, 244
Sefer ha-Pardes, 120n. 60, 153n. 54, 162
Sefer ha-Razim, 231, 232n. 33
Sefer ha-Shem, 220
Sefer Ḥasidim, 22, 24, 25, 74, 75, 89, 225; on asceticism, 34, 35n. 3, 255; on charity, 105; on children's moral responsibility, 92n. 178, 104; on communicating with the dead, 197; on comportment in synagogue, 83; on Divine Names, 86, 209, 210n. 42; on fasting, 66; halakhic works and, 69; *ḥasidut* and, 256; legal methodology and, 118, 119; magic in, 27; parallels to, 61, 63; pietism in, 37; on prohibition, 44n. 30; Tetragrammaton in, 190n. 2; Torah study in, 109. *See also* Pietists, German
Sefer ha-Terumah, 68
Sefer ha-Yashar, 185n. 117
Sefer ha-Yirᵓah, 54n. 59, 62–63, 63–66, 72, 80, 90
Sefer Ḥayyei ᶜOlam. See Sefer ha-Yirᵓah
Sefer Hekhalot, 123, 138, 243
Sefer Kol Bo, 61, 62
Sefer Maᶜaseh ha-Geonim, 39–40
Sefer Minhag Tov, 45
Sefer Miẓvot Gadol, 68, 69, 71n. 108, 73, 74–75, 77, 80
Sefer Miẓvot Qatan, 81, 84, 85, 88, 89–90, 158n. 65, 241
Sefer Moreh Ḥattaᵓim/Sefer ha-Kapparot, 62
Sefer Or Zaruaᶜ, 69, 80, 112, 120n. 60, 190n. 2, 221, 225
Sefer Orḥot Ḥayyim, 61, 63n. 84, 80n. 138, 87–89
Sefer Raban, 70
Sefer Rabiah, 68, 216
Sefer Raziᵓel, 141, 242
Sefer Roqeaḥ, 19–20, 25, 68, 89; food in, 156; *hilkhot ḥasidut* preamble, 126; initiation ceremony in, 157; penances in, 82; Tetragrammaton in, 190n. 2
Sefer Sodot/Raza Rabba, 248
Sefer Takhkemoni, 75
Sefer Tanya Rabbati, 45, 110n. 34
Sefer Tashbeẓ, 241
Sefer Yereᵓim, 68, 69n. 105, 195, 197n. 19
Sefer Yeẓirah, 143, 145, 159, 191–92, 195, 221
Sefer Yiḥusei Tannaᵓim va-Amoraᵓim, 213, 223
Sefer Yosef ha-Meqanne, 98n. 9
segullot, 203, 208, 212, 245, 248
self-denial. *See* asceticism
Semag. See Sefer Miẓvot Gadol
Semaq. See Sefer Miẓvot Qatan
Shaᶜarei ᶜAvodah, 65
Shaᶜarei Teshuvah, 66–67
Shabbat ha-Gadol, 96
Shalshelet ha-Qabbalah, 172
shaving, 44n. 30

*She*ʾ*elot u-Teshuvot min ha-Shamayim,* 185, 228, 229
Shem ha-Meforash, 182n. 112, 243
Shema prayer, 53, 90
Shemaryah b. Mordekhai of Spires, R., 143n. 25
Shemini ᶜ*Azeret,* 112
Shemoneh ᶜ*Esreh* prayer, 83, 84–85
Shemot, 141, 157, 207, 208, 236, 248; care required for use of, 86, 87; German Pietists and, 188, 218; menstruant women and, 129; Messiah and, 240; mystical powers of, 159; revelation and, 190; used for protection, 148n. 40
Sheqalim (tractate of Talmud), 60, 105
Shibbolei ha-Leqet, 54–55, 107, 110n. 34, 111, 147, 197n. 19, 229, 230–31
Shir ha-Yiḥud, 45
*Shi*ᶜ*ur Qomah,* 28, 230
*shiv*ᶜ*ah neqiyyim,* 113
Sifra, 103n. 16
sifrut de-Vei Rashi, 20, 38, 113, 114, 153, 158, 187
Simeon b. Isaac *ha-Gadol,* R., 37, 41, 106, 131–36, 165, 169, 232, 260
Simḥah b. Samuel of Spires, R., 21n. 5, 82, 102, 103, 107, 108, 111, 120n. 60, 225–26, 228, 260
sins, 35n. 3, 42, 61, 66n. 91, 74, 109, 198; avoidance of, 34; confession of, 80, 91; of golden calf, 169; suicide and, 123, 234
sod, 161, 201n. 29, 214, 222, 231; German Pietists and, 220; prayers and, 226; Qalonymide, 138; Rabbenu Tam and, 185; rabbinic figures linked to, 234; Rashi and, 152; of resurrection, 248; students of Maharam and, 245–46
sod ha-berakhah, 161
sod ha-yiḥud, 20
Sodei Razayya, 215
sodot ha-tefillah, 94, 100, 104n. 21, 135, 161; chain of, 143; liturgical texts and, 247; transmission of, 186n. 122
Solomon b. Judah of Dreux, R., 97–98, 260
Solomon b. Samson, R., 38, 40, 260
Solomon b. Samuel *ha-Ẓarefati,* R., 94–103, 98n. 9, 100, 102–3, 103, 115
Solomon Simḥah b. Eliezer of Troyes, R., 152, 212, 239, 240, 244, 245
Solomon Ẓarefati, R., 148n. 40
songs, 132, 244
sorcery, 195, 197n. 19
Sotah, 59
Spain, 20, 29, 63, 68, 220, 247, 248
Spires, Germany, 26, 95, 107, 213
spirituality, 23
suicide, 123, 234
Sukkah (tractate of Talmud), 144
summation, 69
superstition, 29, 160, 166, 168
supplications, 72–74, 172, 179, 180, 181n. 111. *See also* adjurations; prayers
Suriʾel (angel), 146
synagogue, 45, 50, 127; charity and, 105; decorum in, 46n. 34, 83; holiness of, 130n. 86; menstruant women barred from, 49

*ta*ᶜ*anit ḥalom,* 111–12
Taku, R. Moses, 160n. 69, 211, 260
tallit, 122
Talmud, 47n. 36, 50, 114, 150, 253; Babylonian, 42, 64n. 85, 111; burning of, 229; Jerusalem (Palestinian), 60, 111; talmudic interpretation, 187; tractates of, 103n. 16; on trees, 194; Trial of the, 60n. 75, 96
talmudic literature, 127, 144
talmudic period, 21
talmudism/talmudists, 22, 59, 70, 117n. 52, 247
Tam, Rabbenu (R. Jacob b. Meir of Ramerupt), 44, 68, 84, 120, 217, 259; on *Baraita de-Massekhet Niddah,* 128n. 81; dialectical method of, 69, 189; magic and, 135–36, 184, 185–86; on majority rule, 122n. 65; on *perishut,* 42, 43; as rationalist, 166–75; Sabbath customs and, 203–4, 215n. 57; students of, 46, 52n. 52, 115n. 46, 140, 187, 191, 195, 202, 203, 208; talmudism of, 249, 252, 253; *torat ha-sod* and, 186; tosafist interpretations of, 200n. 26
Tammuz, 39, 40
Tannaim, 146, 253
Taqqanot Shum, 25
*Te*ᶜ*amim shel Ḥumash,* 95
*Te*ᶜ*amim shel R. Yehudah he-Ḥasid,* 230
tefillin, 35n. 3, 52, 120, 122, 172
teshuvah, 81–82, 109, 115, 125, 207n. 39
Tetragrammaton, 50, 86n. 156, 124, 230; *gematria* and, 190n. 2; letter representation for, 215; Rashi and, 160n. 67; vocalization of, 243
theosophy, 27, 152, 159, 220, 249, 256
theurgic prayers, 144, 211, 253

thieves, protection against, 245, 246n. 74
tiqqunei teshuvah, 76, 124, 235, 255
Tishʿah be-Av, fast of, 38
tokheḥah, 71n. 110
Toledo, Spain, 51, 247
Torah, 20, 51, 53, 62, 71n. 108, 76, 109, 125; commentaries on, 77n. 123, 107, 149, 156n. 62; Divine glory and, 163; Divine Names and, 144n. 28, 168, 172, 230; goal of study, 89; Hebrew alphabet and, 222n. 6; magic and, 141; *petiḥat ha-lev* and, 140, 240; on post-partum bleeding, 38; relationship with God, 134; scholars of, 105; *shedim* and, 225; *sod* and, 126n. 76; sword of Almighty and, 137; women and, 88; *yom tov* and, 111
torat ha-Kavod, 239, 257n. 16
torat ha-malʾakhim, 222
torat ha-sod, 19, 21, 79, 213, 249; Divine Names and, 220; legends and tales about, 172; Maharam and, 239; in Mainz, 131; Naḥmanides' devotion to, 218; Rashi and, 145, 149n. 41, 152; Ribam and, 201n. 29; shifting attitudes toward, 166; theosophy and, 256; tosafists and, 22, 251; traditions of, 30
tosafists, 22n. 8, 36, 51, 125, 258; asceticism of, 42–58, 251; biblical interpretations of, 77, 93, 104; German Pietists and, 24–25, 58, 59, 111, 120–21, 158n. 64, 214; halakhic works of, 68–69; *Hekhalot* literature and, 127, 255; kabbalism and, 256; legal methodology and, 118; libraries of, 161n. 70, 187; liturgical commentaries and, 96–97; magic/mysticism and, 27, 31, 78–79, 93–94, 128n. 81, 178n. 104, 218, 220, 251; masoretic studies and, 117n. 52; in northern France, 57, 68; *perishut* and, 249; philosophical tradition and, 19
Tosafot, 43, 59–60, 68, 91–92, 103, 107, 170, 189–91, 203, 208
Tosafot Ḥagigah, 168, 189n. 2
Tosafot R. Samson of Sens, 59
trances, 229
Troestlein, R., 244n. 67
Troyes, France, 44

Uri b. R. Joel *ha-Levi,* R., 165
Uriel (angel), 174n. 99

Verona, Italy, 107

wandering, 115
water, 150, 158n. 65, 193n. 9
weddings, 48n. 39
white magic, 154n. 56, 211
women: conversation with, 124n. 70; gazing at, 63n. 84, 91, 92n. 178, 255; illicit sexual relations with, 225; menstruating, 49, 127, 128–30; new moon and, 223n. 7; spousal abuse and, 235; Torah and, 88
Worms, Germany, 38, 40, 148, 186

Yaḥya, Gedalyah ibn, 26n. 21
Yaqar of Cologne, R., 248
Yedidyah b. Israel, R., 105n. 23
Yeḥiʾel b. Yequtiʾel *Anav,* R., 110n. 34
Yeḥiʾel of Paris, R., 90, 91n. 175, 96, 115, 124, 234, 260
Yerushalmi Peʾah, 105
Ye-Sod ha-Teshuvah, 72
yiḥud ha-Shem, 126
yirʾat ha-Shem, 35n. 3
Yishmaʾel, R., 146, 173, 223
Yishmaʾel *Kohen Gadol,* R., 213
Yom Kippur, 38, 41n. 22, 42, 44–45, 48, 49; standing during, 51, 57, 58n. 68; Tetragrammaton and, 50
Yom Tov b. Isaac of Joigny, R., 46, 47n. 36, 57n. 67, 95n. 5, 105, 260
Yom Tov b. Moses of London, R., 234
Yonah of Gerona, Rabbenu, 27, 54n. 59, 63–64, 70–72, 76, 80, 90, 190n. 2

Zaltman, R. Moses, 104
Ẓedah la-Derekh, 193n. 8
Zedekiah b. Abraham *ha-Rofe* Anav, R., 110n. 34, 198, 252, 260; on burning of Talmud, 228–29; *Shibbolei ha-Leqet* and, 54–55, 107, 197n. 19, 231
ẓiẓit, 122
Zohar, 9, 152, 153n. 54, 168, 256